PENGUIN BOOKS

A WILDERNESS OF ERROR

Errol Morris is a world-renowned filmmaker—the Academy Award–winning director of *The Fog of War* and the recipient of a MacArthur "genius award." His other films include *Standard Operating Procedure*; *Mr. Death*; *Fast, Cheap & Out of Control*; *A Brief History of Time*; *The Thin Blue Line*; *Tabloid*; and most recently, *The Unknown Known.* He is the author of *Believing Is Seeing: Observations on the Mysteries of Photography.*

Praise for *A Wilderness of Error*

"The literary equivalent of one of [Morris's] movies. It's a rough-hewed documentary master class. . . . *A Wilderness of Error* upends nearly everything you think you know about these killings and their aftermath. Watching Mr. Morris wade into this thicket of material is like watching an aggrieved parent walk into a teenager's fetid, clothes- and Doritos-strewn bedroom and neatly sort and disinfect until the place shines. He will leave you 85 percent certain that Mr. MacDonald is innocent. He will leave you 100 percent certain he did not get a fair trial. . . . If this headstrong book doesn't change your sense of the Jeffrey MacDonald case, I'll eat my Chuck Taylors."
—Dwight Garner, *The New York Times*

"Critics sometimes confuse great books with important books—exceptionally written literature isn't always the same as literature that can powerfully affect society. But *A Wilderness of Error* is both great and important—it's a beautifully written book, and it has the potential to change the way the country thinks about a justice system that has obviously lost its way."
—Michael Shaub, NPR

"Mr. Morris has produced a brilliant book about the vulnerability of justice to the preconceptions of prosecutors and the power of certain narratives to crowd out all others, even highly plausible ones. I strongly recommend this book."
—*The Wall Street Journal*

"*A Wilderness of Error* is a beautifully produced book, with chapters set off by line drawings of crucial objects in the case: a toppled coffee table, a flowerpot, a rocking horse. It's reminiscent of the recurring images in *The Thin Blue Line*, iconic and mysterious, always on the verge of revealing the secrets they stand for but never quite yielding them. Morris may geek out on minutiae and hypotheticals, but he is enough of an artist to convey that every crime scene is a dialogue between time, as it sweeps away the irrecoverable past, and the material world."   —*Salon*

"The character studies are magnificent, the attention to detail extraordinary, and the effect on the audience is dizzying, disorienting, and thought-provoking."
—*The Boston Globe*

"Have I simply fallen under the spell of Errol Morris's book? I don't know the answer. It's a question that goes to the heart of what makes *A Wilderness of Error* so fascinating. Like criminal investigation more generally, the book serves as a high-stakes testing ground for the ability to keep absorbing facts and holding off the onrush of opinion, the ability to fend off the psychological weaknesses and creeping biases that beset us all."   —*The Awl*

"Morris has become one of America's most idiosyncratic, prolific, and provocative public intellectuals."   —*Smithsonian*

"Compared to McGinniss, Errol Morris has done a far more ethical job of rounding up the facts in this case. . . . And yet Morris is careful, in recounting all the evidence, to include facts that contradict his own view. After reading his book, it's difficult not to think it at least possible that MacDonald is innocent. And if his innocence is possible, he shouldn't be in jail."   —*Fortune*

"Morris has been researching the [MacDonald] case for over two decades, and the result of his inquiries is a thorough and compelling argument for the incarcerated doctor's innocence, a sobering look at the labyrinthine justice system, and a feat of investigative perseverance."   —*Publishers Weekly* (starred review)

A WILDERNESS OF ERROR

THE TRIALS OF JEFFREY MACDONALD

ERROL MORRIS

Penguin Books

PENGUIN BOOKS
Published by the Penguin Group
Penguin Group (USA) LLC
375 Hudson Street
New York, New York 10014

USA | Canada | UK | Ireland | Australia | New Zealand | India | South Africa | China
penguin.com
A Penguin Random House Company

First published in the United States of America by The Penguin Press,
a member of Penguin Group (USA) Inc., 2012
Published with a new postscript in Penguin Books 2013

Design and illustration by Pentagram

THE LIBRARY OF CONGRESS HAS CATALOGED THE HARDCOVER EDITION AS FOLLOWS:

Morris, Errol.
A wilderness of error : the trials of Jeffrey MacDonald / Errol Morris ; illustrations by Niko Skourtis.
p. cm.
Includes bibliographical references and index.
ISBN 978-1-59420-343-5 (hc.)
ISBN 978-0-14-312369-9 (pbk.)
1. MacDonald, Jeffrey R., 1943- 2. Murderers—United States—Case studies. 3. Murder—
North Carolina—Case studies. I. Title.
HV6248.M178M67 2012
364.152'3092—dc23
2012017906

Printed in the United States of America
10 9 8 7 6 5 4 3 2 1

Set in Minion Pro designed by Robert Slimbach and
Din Next Pro designed by Akira Kobayashi and Sandra Winter.

To my mother and stepfather, Cinnabelle and Benjamin Esterman, who always encouraged me to write. And to my mother-in-law, Julia Sheehan, and aunt, Elizabeth McColl, who first introduced me to Fayetteville.

Contents

I would wish them to seek out for me, in the
details I am about to give, some little oasis of fatality
amid a wilderness of error.
—Edgar Allan Poe, "William Wilson"

THE MACDONALD FAMILY

Jeffrey Robert MacDonald (1943–)
Born in Jamaica, New York. The husband of Colette Stevenson and the father of Kimberley and Kristen MacDonald. Attended Princeton University as an undergraduate, but left after three years for Northwestern University Medical School. After entering the army in 1969, he was assigned to the Special Forces as a group surgeon. Accused of the murder of his family in April 1970. All charges were dismissed by December 1970.

† **Colette Stevenson MacDonald (1943–1970)**
The wife of Jeffrey MacDonald and the mother of Kimberley and Kristen. Left Skidmore to marry Jeffrey MacDonald and start a family.

† **Kimberley Kathryn MacDonald (1964–1970)**
The older daughter of Jeffrey and Colette MacDonald.

† **Kristen Jean MacDonald (1967–1970)**
The younger daughter of the MacDonalds.

† **Dorothy "Perry" MacDonald (1919–1991)**
Jeffrey MacDonald's mother.

† **Mildred Stevenson Kassab (1916–1994)**
Colette MacDonald's mother. After the suicide of her first husband, married Alfred Kassab.

† **Alfred G. "Freddy" Kassab (1921–1991)**
Colette MacDonald's stepfather. The protagonist of the book *Fatal Vision* and the TV movie adaptation.

Robert "Bob" Stevenson (1939–)
Colette's older brother. Now a pastor's assistant.

Helen Fell (1938–)
A close friend of Dorothy MacDonald.

HELENA STOECKLEY (FAMILY, ASSOCIATES, AND WITNESSES)

† **Helena Werle Stoeckley Davis (1952–1983)**
Graduated from Terry Sanford High School. Confessed to witnessing the MacDonald murders. Found dead of acute bronchopneumonia, complicated by cirrhosis, on January 31, 1983.

† **Clarence F. Stoeckley (1920–2002)**
Helena Stoeckley's father, retired a lieutenant colonel.

† = deceased

† Helena Werle Stoeckley (1920–2009)
Helena Stoeckley's mother.

Eugene "Gene" Stoeckley (1959–)
Helena Stoeckley's younger brother. Obtained an affidavit from his mother detailing Helena's deathbed confession.

Ernest Leroy Davis (1957–)
Helena Stoeckley's husband. Now serving an eighty-year prison sentence for criminal sexual conduct in the Tyger River Correctional Institution in Enoree, South Carolina.

† Gregory "Greg" Mitchell (1950–1982)
Helena Stoeckley's boyfriend and an Army private at the time of the murders. Named in her confessions. A Vietnam veteran.

† Shelby Don Harris (1948–2008)
An acquaintance of Helena Stoeckley. Named in her confessions. An Army sergeant and a Vietnam veteran.

Dwight E. Smith (1946–)
An acquaintance of Helena Stoeckley. Named in her confessions. A veteran and drug counselor in Fayetteville, North Carolina.

† Cathy Perry Williams (1950–2006)
An acquaintance of Helena Stoeckley. Accused of multiple stabbings around Fayetteville in 1970. Diagnosed with schizophrenia. Confessed to the murders to the FBI in 1984.

William "Ed" Posey (1949–)
A laundry deliveryman. Lived at 1106 Clark Street, Fayetteville, next door to Helena Stoeckley, in 1970, and gave the first report of her existence to the defense in 1970. Testified at the 1979 trial, in the absence of the jury. Recently suffered a stroke.

Jane McCampbell Zillioux Graham-Bailey (1935–)
An artist who worked with Helena Stoeckley in Nashville in 1970. Witness to one of her confessions. Testified at the 1979 trial.

Charles "Red" Underhill (1938–)
A music promoter and an amateur expert on crime and American history. A neighbor of Helena Stoeckley in Nashville in 1970. Witness to one of her confessions. Testified at the 1979 trial. A Tea Party candidate for the Florida House of Representatives in 2010.

THE CRIMINAL INVESTIGATIVE DIVISION

† Franz "Joe" Grebner (1925–1986)
The investigator for the CID at Fort Bragg and a chief warrant officer, three, at the time of the murders.

Robert B. "Bob" Shaw
Criminal investigator for the CID at Fort Bragg and a chief warrant officer, one, at the time of the murders.

William F. "Bill" Ivory (1939–)
Investigator on duty and a specialist seven at the time of the murders, and the first CID agent on the scene. Inducted into the CID Hall of Fame in 2007.

† Hilyard O. Medlin (1923–1986)
A master sergeant and a latent fingerprint examiner at the CID laboratory in Fort Gordon, Georgia, from 1963 to 1971.

† Peter Edmund Kearns (1934–2007)
A USACIDA (United States Army Criminal Investigation Division Agency) investigator who conducted the posthearing investigation and prepared the investigative report regarding Freddy Kassab's allegations of CID misconduct and the CID reinvestigation of the case at large.

Jack G. Pruett (1925–)
The USACIDA investigator who conducted the posthearing investigation into Freddy Kassab's allegations of CID misconduct and the CID reinvestigation of the case.

† Richard J. Mahon (1936–2004)
The USACIDA investigator who conducted the posthearing investigation into Helena Stoeckley's involvement in the crimes.

Robert A. Brisentine, Jr. (1927–)
A polygraph expert with the USACIDA who examined the key figures in the MacDonald case. Winner of the American Polygraph Association's Leonarde Keeler Award in 1989 for long and distinguished service to the polygraph profession.

THE MILITARY POLICE

Kenneth Mica (1947–)
A specialist four in the 503rd Military Police Battalion at Fort Bragg at the time of the murders. Lives in Aquebogue, New York.

Joseph L. Paulk (1944–)
A lieutenant in Company C, 503rd Military Police Battalion, who was present at the scene of the crime.

THE FBI

Robert M. Murphy (1916–)
The special agent in charge of the FBI's Charlotte office at the time of the murders.

† Raymond "Butch" Madden, Jr. (1942–2012)
A special agent assigned to the Raleigh office of the FBI. First involved in the MacDonald case in August 1980, reinvestigating the case during the appeals process.

THE DEFENSE ATTORNEYS

† Bernard "Bernie" L. Segal (1930–2011)
A civil rights attorney from Philadelphia, and later a professor of law at Golden Gate University in San Franscisco. Represented Jeffrey MacDonald at his Article 32 hearing.

Wade Smith (1937–)
A prominent defense attorney based in Raleigh, North Carolina. Attended University of North Carolina Law School with James Blackburn. Represented MacDonald during the 1979 trial as co-counsel and Blackburn when he was indicted in 1993.

Michael Malley (1943–)

An attorney from San Antonio. Jeffrey MacDonald's freshman roommate at Princeton University, and later a member of his defense team.

† Dennis Eisman (1940–1991)

An attorney and Segal's assistant during the Article 32 hearing in 1970.

Wendy Rouder (1942–)

An aide to Bernie Segal in charge of taking care of Helena Stoeckley during the MacDonald trial in 1979.

Harvey A. Silverglate (1942–)

An attorney, writer, and civil rights advocate based in Boston. MacDonald's appellate attorney beginning in 1989. Argued MacDonald's case before the Fourth Circuit Court of Appeals in 1991. Formerly a partner at the firm Silverglate & Good, now a consultant.

Andrew "Andy" Good (1946–)

An appellate attorney based in Boston. Represented MacDonald beginning in 1989. A partner at the firm Good & Cormier.

Philip G. Cormier (1961–)

An appellate attorney based in Boston. MacDonald's appellate attorney beginning in 1989. Argued MacDonald's case before the Fourth Circuit Court of Appeals in 1991. A partner at the firm Good & Cormier.

Gordon Widenhouse (1954–)

A North Carolina appellate attorney specializing in post-conviction. In 2011, he took over MacDonald's appeal process and represented him at the 2012 evidentiary hearing.

THE PROSECUTORS

Clifford L. Somers (1940–)

A captain in the office of the Staff Judge Advocate, and chief government counsel at the Article 32 investigation.

† Victor Woerheide (1909–1977)

The chief Justice Department prosecutor at the grand jury that indicted Jeffrey MacDonald in 1975.

George M. Anderson (1921–)

The U.S. attorney for the Eastern District of North Carolina from 1977 to 1980. Replaced by James Blackburn in 1980.

Brian M. Murtagh (1946–)

A former CID Command JAG officer and later assistant U.S. attorney. One of the prosecutors at Jeffrey MacDonald's 1979 trial.

James L. Blackburn (1938–)

An assistant U.S. attorney and one of the prosecutors at Jeffrey MacDonald's 1979 trial. Disbarred in 1993 for ethical violations.

Jack B. Crawley, Jr. (1944–)

An assistant U.S. attorney and a supporting member of the prosecution team in 1979.

John Bruce (1954–)
An assistant U.S. attorney who joined the prosecution team and led the questioning at the 2012 evidentiary hearing.

OTHER ATTORNEYS

Hammond A. Beale (1942–)
Colonel Rock's legal advisor at the Article 32 hearing. Now a lawyer in private practice.

Richard C. Cahn (1932–)
An attorney based in Huntington, New York, who was hired by the Kassabs to pursue an indictment of MacDonald.

Gary Bostwick (1941–)
An attorney based in California who represented MacDonald in his 1987 civil suit of Joe McGinniss. Appears in Janet Malcolm's *The Journalist and the Murderer*.

Daniel Kornstein (1947–)
An attorney based in New York who represented Joe McGinniss in the 1987 civil trial. Appears in Janet Malcolm's *The Journalist and the Murderer*.

Jerry Leonard (1945–)
An attorney based in Raleigh, North Carolina, who was asked by Judge Dupree to represent Stoeckley from August 20 to August 23, 1979.

THE JUDGES

Warren V. Rock (1919–)
The colonel assigned as the investigating officer at the 1970 Article 32 investigation.

† Algernon Butler (1905–1978)
The U.S. district court judge who convened the grand jury that indicted MacDonald.

† Franklin T. Dupree (1913–1995)
The district court judge who oversaw MacDonald's 1979 trial and subsequent appeals.

† Francis D. Murnaghan, Jr. (1920–2000)
A federal judge who served on the Fourth Circuit Court of Appeals between 1979 and 2000. Wrote a concurring opinion on the MacDonald case in 1982.

James C. Fox (1928–)
A senior federal judge serving at the District Court for the Eastern District of North Carolina.

THE EXPERTS

Janice S. Glisson (1924–)
A forensic chemist and later chief of the serology section at the CID laboratory at Fort Gordon, Georgia. Conducted preliminary analysis of blood and fiber evidence from the MacDonald crime scene.

Dillard O. Browning IV (1924–)
A forensic chemist at the CID laboratory at Fort Gordon, Georgia, and later at the laboratory at Camp Zama, Japan. Conducted preliminary examination of hairs, fibers, paints, beeswax, and wood from the MacDonald crime scene.

Martin Lonky (1944–)

A forensic expert based in Southern California who was brought in to review physical evidence in the CID reinvestigation of the case.

† Paul Stombaugh (1926–2002)

An examiner in the Microscopic Analysis Unit of the FBI laboratory in Washington from 1960 to 1976. Conducted reexamination of evidence from the MacDonald crime, beginning in 1971. Thereafter the director of the Police Service Bureau in Greenville, South Carolina.

Dr. John I. Thornton (1941–)

An emeritus professor of forensic science at the University of California at Berkeley. A defense expert for the MacDonald case at the 1979 trial and a consultant through 1982.

Dr. Rex J. Beaber (1950–)

A psychologist, attorney, and assistant professor of medicine at the Medical School of the University of California at Los Angeles. Conducted psychological examination of Helena Stoeckley in 1980 at the behest of Ted Gunderson.

Kimberly "Kim" Murga (1972–)

A forensic investigator and an expert on DNA analysis. Worked at the Armed Forces Institute of Pathology in Rockville, Maryland. Identified the remains of Uday and Qusay Hussein. Conducted the first round of DNA testing of evidence from the MacDonald house in 2008.

THE PSYCHIATRISTS AND PSYCHOLOGISTS

Dr. Robert L. "Bob" Sadoff (1936–)

A forensic psychiatrist and a professor of psychiatry at the University of Pennsylvania. Former president of the American Academy of Psychiatry and the Law and director of the University of Pennsylvania's Center for Studies in Social-Legal Psychiatry. Examined Jeffrey MacDonald in 1970. Testified at the Article 32 hearing and at the grand jury.

Dr. James L. Mack (1936–)

A forensic psychologist and a partner of Dr. Robert Sadoff. Conducted an examination of Jeffrey MacDonald with Dr. Sadoff in 1970, and a reexamination in the summer of 1979.

† Dr. James A. Brussel (1905–1982)

A psychiatrist and criminologist. Interviewed George Metesky, the "mad bomber." Author of *Casebook of a Crime Psychiatrist*. Examined Jeffrey MacDonald on August 13, 1979.

Dr. Seymour L. Halleck (1929–)

A psychiatrist and professor at the University of North Carolina. Examined Jeffrey MacDonald in July 1979.

Dr. Hirsch Lazaar Silverman (1915–)

A clinical and forensic psychologist and psychotherapist. Poet and veteran of World War II. Emeritus professor at Seton Hall University. Examined Jeffrey MacDonald with James Brussel on August 13, 1979.

THE POLICE AND DETECTIVES

† Prince Everette Beasley (1925–1996)

A detective in the Fayetteville Police Department and the Interagency Narcotics Squad. Testified at the 1979 trial.

James T. "Jim" Gaddis (1943–)
A patrolman with the Nashville Police Department. On special assignment in 1971. Worked with Helena Stoeckley, an informant during that time. Testified at the 1979 trial.

† Theodore L. "Ted" Gunderson (1948–2011)
Once the special agent in charge of the Los Angeles office of the FBI, then a private investigator. Obtained confessions from Helena Stoeckley.

† Raymond "Ray" Shedlick (1930–1989)
The father of Ellen Dannelly. Detective in the New York City Police Department and deputy chief investigator for Nassau County District Attorney's office. From 1983 on, a private investigator based in Durham, North Carolina. Retained by the MacDonald defense team in 1984.

Ellen Dannelly (1958–)
The daughter of Ray Shedlick and a private investigator.

† Jimmy B. Britt (1938–2008)
A U.S. marshal who escorted Helena Stoeckley during the 1979 trial. Gave an affidavit in 2005 declaring that Stoeckley had confessed in his presence twice during the trial, and that on the second occasion she had been threatened by James Blackburn.

† John Dolan Myers (1944–1995)
A private investigator hired by Wade Smith.

THE JOURNALISTS

Joe McGinniss (1942–)
A journalist who first covered Jeffrey MacDonald in his column for the *Los Angeles Herald-Examiner* and worked with his defense team during the 1979 trial. Author of *The Selling of the President 1968, The Rogue,* and, in 1984, *Fatal Vision,* the first book on the MacDonald case.

† Jeffrey Elliot (1947–2008)
A professor of African American studies at North Carolina Central University and a journalist. Interviewed Jeffrey MacDonald for *Playboy* magazine and began a manuscript on the case.

Janet Malcolm (1934–)
A journalist and writer. Author of *In the Freud Archives, The Crime of Sheila McGough, Iphigenia in Forest Hills,* and *The Journalist and the Murderer,* a book based on the relationship between Joe McGinniss and Jeffrey MacDonald.

Ted Landreth
A documentary producer and investigator based in California. Producer of *False Witness,* a 1989 BBC documentary on the MacDonald case.

† Fred Bost (1926–2013)
A journalist based in Fayetteville, North Carolina. A veteran. One of the two authors of *Fatal Justice: Reinvestigating the MacDonald Murders.*

† Jerry Allen Potter, Jr. (d. 2004)
A writer and a journalist based in California. One of the two authors of *Fatal Justice: Reinvestigating the MacDonald Murders.*

A WILDERNESS
OF ERROR

544 CASTLE DRIVE

I first saw 544 Castle Drive on a cold Christmas morning in 1991.

My wife, my son, and I had flown from Boston to Raleigh-Durham to join my mother-in-law and aunt Elizabeth, her older sister, in St. Pauls, North Carolina, a small town about twenty miles south of Fayetteville. There were hardly any grandchildren; our son, Hamilton, who was four years old, was the adored new addition to the family. I can't remember whether it was the year of the train set or the year of the tricycle, but it was a perfect day.

Often on Christmas we would pick pecans at a nearby farm. You open them by holding two pecans in your hand so you can crack one against the other. It was a wonderful small-town world—the redbrick house with the glassed-in porch and rockers, the breakfast room that looked out on the garden. The green Spode china. The ribbons in the living room from unwrapped presents. We were a young and loving family.

My wife and I decided on a small excursion before Christmas dinner. She had wanted to get out of the house. The destination was more or less my idea. A short drive north on the old U.S. highway past Hope Mills (where my mother-in-law and aunt had been born) to Fayetteville, past a pygmy replica of the Eiffel Tower at the Bordeaux Shopping Center, and then on to Fort Bragg. In those days, Fort Bragg was an open base, easily accessible. It wasn't hard to get around, and after consulting various road maps, we found it.

There we were, standing in the cold, looking at the attached home where Jeffrey MacDonald, a physician and Green Beret, had lived with his family until February 17, 1970. Early that morning MacDonald's wife, Colette, and his two daughters—Kimberley, aged five, and Kristen, aged two—were brutally murdered there.

The MacDonald case has produced vast quantities of material. Some of this can be found on Web sites exclusively devoted to the case, some is in various law offices around the country—those of a dozen or so defense and appellate attorneys who have represented MacDonald over the years.

Somewhere in this material, I found a photograph of Jeffrey MacDonald, Colette, and Kimberley. I'm not sure when it was taken. It might have been before Kristen was born. It is Christmas. On the left, a tree covered in tinsel and surrounded by presents. On the right, a fireplace and mantel covered with decorations. Jeffrey is peeking in to the picture, just at the edge of frame, as if he's trying to decide which present to open next. Kimberley, in a party dress with a white collar, is being handed a big blond doll by her mother. She looks thrilled. It's a universal picture.

I had seen photographs of the house. The house the day after the story of the murders broke; the house in subsequent years, the windows covered by plywood. The house had been kept sealed from 1970 until 1984 in the event that it and its contents might be needed as evidence. But on the night of June 7, 1984, the contents were burned and then buried at the Fort Bragg landfill.

The government made a list of the property that had been destroyed:

Refrigerator
Stove
Broiler Pan
Occasional dining room table w/4 chairs
Government knee hole desk
Dresser
Army chair
Push Lawn Mower
Yard Rake
Sprinkler[1]

Everything that wasn't already locked up in a lab was incinerated, including the ceilings, interior walls, doors, windowsills, ledges, and hardwood floors. Was some piece of evidence that could have unraveled the entire mystery lost in that bonfire? Could the house itself have been interrogated? Could it have been forced to give up an answer?

I have asked myself many times since that Christmas Day, why didn't I plunge into the case then? It was shortly after I had finished *The Thin Blue Line,* the film based on my investigation of the Randall Dale Adams case—an investigation that had freed an innocent man from prison and had gotten a confession from the killer. I had struggled with that story for four years, only to be sued by the man I got out of prison. I told myself I didn't want to become involved in another miscarriage-of-justice story. They're difficult, perhaps too difficult. I didn't want to go through the agony, the risk, a second time.

And yet this was a different kind of miscarriage of justice, different from what we normally envision as a miscarriage of justice. The MacDonald story does have familiar themes: suppressed evidence, prosecutorial misconduct, bumbling investigators, forensic mix-ups, and so on. But there are new and different themes as well, many involving the media. Books, late-night talk shows, and a TV miniseries.

———

There is something disturbing about the MacDonald case, something that has made me return to it again and again over the years. It wasn't the brutality of the murders. I've interviewed my share of mass murderers, including Ed Gein and Edmund Kemper.[2] I was afraid of something even more chilling—that MacDonald was innocent. That he had been made to witness the savage deaths of his family and then was wrongfully convicted for their murders. I wondered if people needed him to be guilty because the alternative was too horrible to contemplate.

It has been so long since I first became interested. I recently looked at my notes on what I had imagined doing with it, beginning in 1991. I am a filmmaker, so I first imagined it as a movie. I went to a variety of studio meetings. But the movie I wanted to make was nonstandard.

The pitch: there are two opposed theories of what happened at 544 Castle Drive on the morning of February 17, 1970. Neither had been proven beyond a reasonable doubt. Yet most Americans had only ever been presented with half a story, the half that held that MacDonald was definitely the killer, the half that was the basis for Joe McGinniss's *Fatal Vision*, a bestselling book that was adapted into a TV miniseries.

So let me describe the movie that I imagined. I wanted to cast Gary Cole, who played MacDonald in the TV miniseries, and to use him for my own reenactments of the case. I would juxtapose these reenactments with scenes from the original TV movie. It would be a version of *Rashomon,* the film by Akira Kurosawa, with competing narrators and different points of view. Here, it would be by the same actor.

Such a movie, I thought, could open the case back up and show how critical evidence was ignored or suppressed, how the evidence that *was* introduced does not confirm MacDonald's guilt. It could help people think and decide for themselves.

I stopped. The studio executive across the table clearly wanted to say no. She paused for a moment and said, "We can't make that." I asked why. "Because he's guilty," she said. "The man killed his family." And I said, "But he might be innocent." And she said, "No. He killed his family."

It became a recurring theme. People thought they knew the story, but it was because they had read the book, or had seen the TV miniseries, or both. And the important question was lost under the heap: Had anyone proved that Jeffrey MacDonald was guilty of the murder of his family? Millions of words have been spoken, written, read—affidavits, court transcripts, lab reports, videotaped interviews, newspaper articles, and now even blogs—but what do they really tell us?

BOOK ONE

1841 ■ Edgar Allan Poe publishes "The Murders in the Rue Morgue," widely considered to be the first detective story.

1844– ■ Alexandre Dumas's *The Count of Monte Cristo* is serialized in the *Journal des Débats*.
1845 It becomes the most popular book in Europe.

1941 ■ *The Mask of Sanity* by Dr. Hervey Cleckley is published.

1943 ■ **May 10**
Colette Stevenson is born in New York, New York.

October 12
Jeffrey MacDonald is born in Jamaica, New York.

1963 ■ **September 14**
Colette and Jeffrey MacDonald are married. Both are sophomores in college: he at Princeton, she at Skidmore.

1964 ■ **April 18**
Kimberley MacDonald is born.

September 28
Jeffrey MacDonald's first day at Northwestern University Medical School in Chicago.

1965 ■ **March 8**
First American ground forces land in Vietnam.

1967 ■ **May 8**
Kristen MacDonald is born.

June 6
Gregory Mitchell enlists in the army.

1968 ■ Helena Stoeckley, a student at Terry Sanford High School, is arrested by Lieutenant Rudy Studer of the Fayetteville Police Department on a drug charge. She begins to work as a narcotics informant for Studer and Prince Beasley, also a detective in the Fayetteville Police Department.

June 15
Jeffrey MacDonald graduates from medical school.

July 1
Jeffrey MacDonald begins his internship at Columbia Presbyterian Hospital in New York.

1969 ■ **June**
Helena Stoeckley graduates from high school.

1969 ■ **June 20**
cont. Jeffrey MacDonald enlists in the army.

Early morning, August 9
The Manson family breaks into the home of Sharon Tate and Roman Polanski, killing Tate, Steven Parent, Wojciech Frykowski, Abigail Folger, and Jay Sebring.

Early morning, August 10
The Manson family breaks into the LaBianca residence, killing Leno LaBianca and his wife, Rosemary.

August 29
MacDonald reports to the 3rd Special Forces Group Airborne at Fort Bragg, North Carolina, as group surgeon.

October 10
Gregory Mitchell returns to the United States from his tour in Vietnam.

October 12
Charles Manson and his followers are arrested at Barker Ranch in Death Valley. The charge is grand theft auto.

December 24–25
Colette MacDonald's mother and stepfather, Mildred and Freddy Kassab, spend Christmas at the MacDonalds' Fort Bragg residence.

1970 ■ **February 15**
Jeffrey MacDonald works an uneventful twenty-four-hour shift at Hamlet Hospital in Hamlet, North Carolina.

February 16

6:00 a.m.
Jeffrey MacDonald ends his shift at Hamlet Hospital.

6:20 p.m.
Colette MacDonald leaves for an evening class in child psychology at Fort Bragg's North Carolina State University extension campus.

7:00 p.m.
Jeffrey MacDonald puts his two-year-old daughter, Kristen, to bed.

9:00 p.m.
After watching the TV show *Laugh-In,* Jeffrey MacDonald puts his five-year-old daughter, Kimberley, to bed.

Night
Helena Stoeckley asks to borrow her friend Margaret Mauney's blue 1968 Chevrolet Corvair. She does not return it by 11:30 p.m., as promised.

12:00 a.m.–1:00 a.m.
Sometime in the middle of *The Johnny Carson Show*, Colette goes to bed, leaving Jeffrey alone. Shortly afterward, Kristen begins crying. Jeffrey goes to the kitchen, fixes a bottle of chocolate milk for her, and carries her and the bottle to her bedroom.

3:33 a.m.
Jeffrey MacDonald telephones for help. The operator tells him he must phone the military police personally. He leaves the bedroom phone off the hook. The operator, now alarmed, calls the military police on another line.

3:42 a.m.
Military police dispatcher puts out a "domestic disturbance in progress" call.

Circa 3:45 a.m.
En route to the "domestic disturbance" call, military policeman Kenneth Mica, from the passenger side of his jeep, sees a woman standing in the rain on the corner of Honeycutt Road and North Lucas, not far from the MacDonald residence.

Circa 3:50 a.m.
The first military policemen begin arriving at the scene. MPs Tevere, Mica, Williams, Duffy, Morris, Dickerson, and Paulk enter the apartment through the utility room after finding the front door locked and getting no response to their knocking. They find Colette MacDonald dead and Jeffrey MacDonald beside her, wounded. CID agents and MPs will continue arriving for the next few hours.

Circa 4:30 a.m.
Jeffrey MacDonald arrives by ambulance at Womack Army Hospital. He will receive treatment for a punctured lung, a head bruise, and multiple stab wounds.

Circa 4:35 a.m.
MPs begin a search of the MacDonald yard and find an ice pick and a club.

▃ **February 18**

Morning
Helena Stoeckley is stopped by Detective Beasley because she matches the description of one of the assailants. Provost Marshal Robert Kriwanek tells UPI that Jeffrey MacDonald "enjoys the highest reputation in his unit and his neighborhood. He is not a suspect."

April 6
Jeffrey MacDonald is interviewed by Franz Grebner, William Ivory, and Robert Shaw of the Fort Bragg CID office. The army announces that Jeffrey MacDonald is the chief suspect in the murders of his family.

April 13
Helena Stoeckley is hospitalized at Womack Army Hospital for drug addiction.

May 12
Colonel Warren V. Rock is assigned to be the investigating officer of the Article 32 hearing.

July 6
The first day of testimony at the Article 32 hearing.

September 29
Gregory Mitchell is discharged from Tampa General Hospital after eight days of methadone treatments for heroin withdrawal. He returns to North Carolina, now discharged from the army.

October 13
Colonel Rock releases his final report on the Article 32 hearing.

October 19
Helena Stoeckley is first mentioned publicly as a suspect in an article in the *Fayetteville Observer*.

A CONVINCING STORY

*If God were suddenly condemned to live the life He
has inflicted on men, He would kill Himself.*
—Alexandre Dumas, "Pensées d'album"

It's a nineteenth-century image. An island fortress, forbidding, dark, isolated, surrounded on all sides by cliffs and the sea. In Alexandre Dumas's 1844 novel *The Count of Monte Cristo,* that fortress is the Château d'If.

Dantès (who will become the Count of Monte Cristo) has been taken prisoner. In a rowboat, he is pleading with his captors. He demands to know where he is being taken.

> "Unless you are blind, or have never been outside the harbor, you must know."
>
> "I do not."
>
> "Look round you then."
>
> Dantès rose and looked forward, when he saw rise within a hundred yards of him the black and frowning rock on which stands the Château d'If. This gloomy fortress, which has for more than three hundred years furnished food for so many wild legends, seemed to Dantès like a scaffold to a man condemned to death.
>
> "The Château d'If," he cried, "what are we going there for?"
>
> The gendarme smiled.

> "Surely, I am not going there to be imprisoned," said Dantès; "it is a prison for high crimes of state and is used only for political prisoners. I have committed *no* crime."[1]

Dantès, a fictional character, has been framed for a crime he did not commit.[2] He has been convicted and condemned by Dumas, his creator, to a prison from which there is no possibility of escape.

And yet Dantès *does* escape. Under an improbable set of circumstances that have been told and retold and that have inspired countless other stories. Dumas's tale is a variant of the theme "never say never." There is no fortress, no prison from which there is no escape. We marvel at Dantès's daring—the fake burial at sea, the swim to a nearby island, the construction of a new, fabulous identity. But we know that he has escaped only because Dumas wants it so. There can be no denying his innocence, just as there can be no thwarting his inexorable climb to a position of wealth, power, and influence. Dumas has *written* it that way.

In a fictional narrative all of the pieces can be engineered to fit perfectly together. But reality is different. We have to discover what is out there—what is real and what is merely a product of our imagination. A real Dantès could turn out to be a schemer, a rat, a traitor. There is in principle no limit to what we might find out about him, to what we might uncover. A real Dantès, like all real characters, is bottomless.[3] Bertrand Russell, the philosopher, captured this in his *Introduction to Mathematical Philosophy,* written while he was in prison as a conscientious objector to World War I. Prisoners often have the time to reflect on the difference between artificially constructed stories and reality.

> When you have taken account of all the feelings roused by Napoleon in writers and readers of history, you have not touched the actual man; but in the case of Hamlet you have come to the end of him. If no one thought about Hamlet, there would be nothing left of him; if no one had thought about Napoleon, he would have soon seen to it that some one did.[4]

It's now the twenty-first century. And we have a model of a prison that makes the Château d'If pale in comparison. Not an imagined prison of stone and steel, but a real prison built out of newsprint and media. A prison of beliefs. You can escape from prison, but how do you escape from a convincing story? After enough repetitions, the facts come to serve the story and not the other way around. Like kudzu, suddenly the story is everywhere and impenetrable.

Take the case of Jeffrey MacDonald. Throughout the 1970s and 1980s, the story was endlessly retold in the media. It was enshrined in a bestselling book (*Fatal Vision* by Joe McGinniss), in TV journalism (*60 Minutes* with Mike Wallace), and ultimately in an incredibly popular TV miniseries with the same title as the book, starring Karl Malden, Gary Cole, and Eva Marie Saint. The *60 Minutes* segment on September 18, 1983, was the season premiere of the show. It was watched by thirty million people. The book appeared a couple of months later and in the following years sold five million copies. The two-part miniseries on NBC was the most popular miniseries of the year.

Eventually, the media frenzy ran its course, and the public was sated with the version of events it had been fed. The case was cracked. Punishment was administered. Justice had been done. And Jeffrey MacDonald was condemned to the story that had been created around him.

The MacDonald case was once well-known but is quickly lapsing into obscurity. MacDonald was on the fast track: Princeton for three years, medical school at Northwestern, a Green Beret captain at Fort Bragg in North Carolina. He had been accepted for a residency in orthopedics at Yale to follow his service in the military. He was young, handsome, and married to his childhood sweetheart, Colette Stevenson. They had two young daughters—Kimberley, aged five, and Kristen, aged two. They dreamed of owning a farm in Connecticut; they had a bright and promising future.

That ended early in the morning on February 17, 1970. The MPs who had responded to a call for help had found Colette, who was four months pregnant with a son, lying on the floor of the master bedroom. She had been brutally beaten and stabbed. Both her arms had been broken, her skull had been fractured, and there were numerous knife stabs in her chest and neck as well as twenty-four of what appeared to be ice-pick stabs to her chest and arm. Kimberley and Kristen had been found dead in their beds. Kimberley had been stabbed and the right side of her head had been crushed in with a club. Kristen had been stabbed but there were no fractures. There was blood everywhere.

MacDonald told Ken Mica, one of the first MPs at the scene, "Check my kids. I can't breathe."[5] Mica began to give him mouth-to-mouth resuscitation. MacDonald was lapsing in and out of consciousness, but he described to Mica how he had been sleeping on the couch in the living room, then was awakened by screams. He saw people at the foot of the couch. Mica asked whom he had seen, and Mac-Donald described the assailants: "There were four of them. One blonde Caucasian female. She had a floppy hat on. Two male Caucasians, and one male Negro. Why did they do this?"

Mica told Lieutenant Joseph Paulk, one of his superiors, that he had seen a woman matching the description on his way to the MacDonald home. But no effort was made to pick her up.

Within minutes, MacDonald was loaded into an ambulance and taken to Womack Army Hospital, where he was treated for multiple bruises, an abrasion, small punctures, two stab wounds (one in his stomach and one on the right side of his chest), and a collapsed lung—a serious injury, but not a mortal one. Specialist Seventh Class William Ivory was the investigator on duty for the Fort Bragg office of the CID, the Criminal Investigation Division of the army. He arrived about fifteen minutes after the first MPs and took detailed notes on what he saw:

A woman, apparently dead, is lying on her back next to a green armchair. The upper portion of her body was extremely bloody. She was clad in what looks like pink pajama pants. Across her abdomen a towel or bath mat is laying. Across her chest was some blue cloth with a part of it trailing across the floor to her left side. This was later identified as a blue pajama [top].[6]

Ivory observed that Colette MacDonald had multiple head injuries and stab wounds in her chest and throat. And a large pool of blood was found under her head and shoulders. Nearby there was a pajama pocket, apparently torn from the pajama top. And then he found what appeared to be a murder weapon. "Between the green armchair & the dresser on the north wall there is observed a small wooden-handled knife. A close inspection revealed a blood stain near the point of the blade."

Ivory went on to note that the living room was relatively tidy:

The furnishings on the west side of the living room did not appear to have been disturbed. A coffee table in the east side of the living room in front of a brown divan was tipped on its edge & under the edge there were numerous magazines the titles of which were not noted at that time. There is a plant with the roots in dirt a few feet east of the overturned table & a white plant pot sitting upright just north of the edge of the table.

Complaint # _____	Value of GP/PP Stolen _____
ROI # _____	Value of GP/PP Recovered _____
Offense _____	Manhours _____
_____	CID Funds Expended _____

Time, Date and Investigator	SUMMARY OF INVESTIGATIVE ACTIVITY
0350 17 Feb. 70 IVORY	Monitored Radio call At Carolina that an incident was taking place at 544 Castle Drive involving a stabbing. Upon inquiring on Radio if any Deaths were involved it was learned that there was, but at that point the number of deaths had not been determined.

Call placed to SSG Alexander the Duty Photographer, collected equipment necessary to process # at crime scene & Proceeded with PMI Duty Inves. Hagan Rossi to the scene arriving about 0400 hrs.

Upon arrival it was noted that it was raining lightly & the ground was wet. The exterior of the building was appeared to be a two story brick dwelling with a wing on each end. The apartment in question, 544 Castle Drive is on the east end of this building about 50-60 meters west of the intersection of castle Drive & North Dougherty st.

Upon entering the front door of the APT, was met by MPDO 1LT, Paulk. Also in the house were medics from WAH & about 6 MPs in in uniform . The MPs were standing in the living room by the door & just in front of the desk by the door. In observing the furniture in the living room. The furnishings on the west side of the Living room did not appear to have been disturbed. A coffee table in the east side of the living room in front of a brown diven was tipped on its edge & under the edge there were numerous magazines the titles of which were not noted at that time. There is a plant with the roots in dirt a few feet east of the oven turned table & a white plant pot sitting up right just north of the edge of the table. Other furniture in the room included a black leather chair & a fabric covered rocker & a black leather foot stool. The chairs & stool being to the west of the table & appear undisturbed. On the couch there is a multicolored afgan & some small pillows. An octagonal table sits to the south of the divaon & on it are some candles, books, table lamp & a glass.

While the room is being observed, the MPDO relates that down a hallway which runs east to west there is a body of a woman laying on the floor on a white rug in what liiks to be a bed room. About this time two medics roll an ambulance stretcher into the living

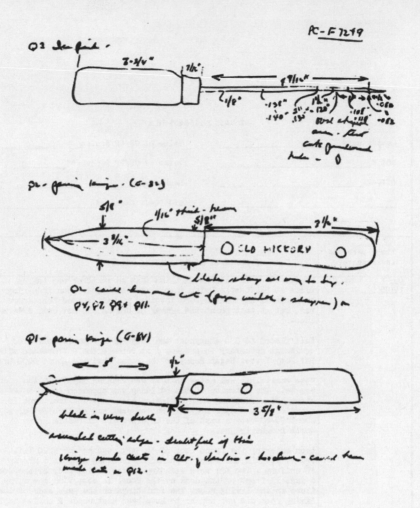

About a half hour later, Robert Shaw, another CID investigator, arrived. His case file continues the story of the investigation. Three weapons were discovered just outside the back door of the house:

> At 0642 hrs, a search of the outside of the quarters was conducted by this investigator. Found, located near the NE entrance to the quarters, a wooden club which appeared to bear blood stains and a paring knife with a brown handle; and an ice pick with a tan wood handle. The location of these items was sketched and the weapons were collected as evidence . . . The decision was made to collect this evidence . . . because the photographer on the scene had run out of film or bulbs

or had some other tech problem and there would be an appreciable delay before he could take a picture.[7]

Ivory, a young and relatively inexperienced agent, quickly came to the conclusion that there was something wrong with the crime scene.[8] There were signs of a struggle, but perhaps not enough to suggest the presence of four intruders. It wasn't long before Ivory and Shaw devised their own theory of the crime.

Narratives are ubiquitous. They are part of the way people see the world, part of the way people think. All of us. Myself included. Without them we would be overwhelmed with undigested, raw facts. But that doesn't mean that all narratives are created equal. There is fiction, and there is nonfiction. And one of the differences between fiction and fact is that a fictional character is controlled by its creator. It has no reality off the page. There is no physical evidence that can *prove* that Edmond Dantès is guilty or innocent of a crime. Only what the writer—the author—ultimately decides.

But what happens when the narrative of a real-life crime *overwhelms* the evidence? When evidence is rejected, suppressed, misinterpreted—or is left uncollected at the crime scene—simply because it does not support the chosen narrative? It is easy to confuse a search for revealing plot details with a search for evidence. But there is a difference. In one case, we are wandering through a landscape of words. In the other, we are in the physical world.

By all accounts, the crime scene was horrific. Three bloody and battered bodies. But one detail stood out. On the headboard in the master bedroom, the word "PIG" was written in blood, recalling—perhaps reenacting—the Manson family murders committed only months before. In a real sense, the story of the MacDonald murders begins in the summer of 1969 with Charles Manson and his drug-crazed followers.

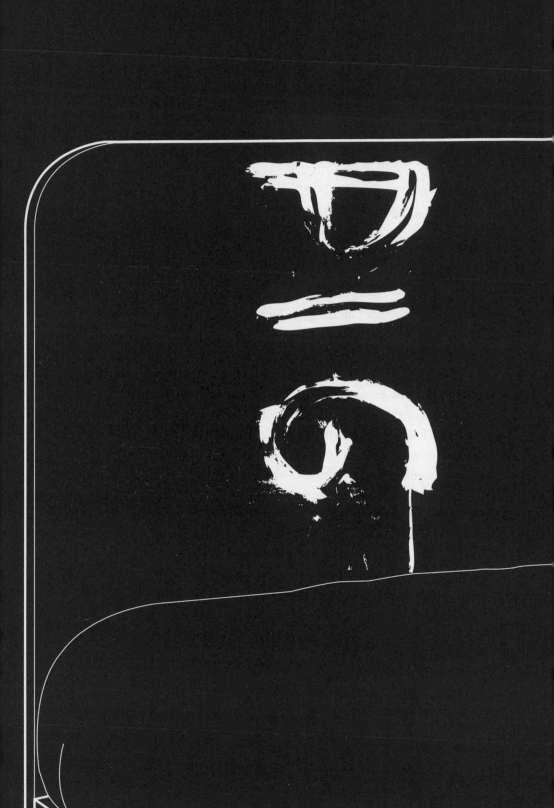

LEE MARVIN
IS AFRAID

On August 9, 1969, Sharon Tate (the wife of Roman Polanski and eight and a half months pregnant), Jay Sebring, Wojciech Frykowski, Steven Parent, and Abigail Folger were shot and stabbed to death in Polanski's Los Angeles home. Polanski was in Europe; otherwise he might have been a suspect in the case. The murders of Leno and Rosemary LaBianca followed the next day. At 10050 Cielo Drive, the Polanski home, the word "PIG" was written on the wall, as it later turned out, in Sharon Tate's blood; at the LaBianca home, two phrases, "death to pigs" and "healter skelter."[1]

At first the police believed the Tate and LaBianca murders were unrelated. They also were convinced that the murders were connected with a drug transaction gone awry. When evidence began to accumulate, the idea of "hippie killers" was explicitly rejected. One police sergeant simply said, "We know what's behind these murders. They're part of a big dope transaction."[2] Similarly, army investigators rejected the idea that "hippie killers" had broken into the house at 544 Castle Drive, had killed MacDonald's family, and had written "PIG" on the headboard of the bed.

On February 17, the day of the murders, the headline in the *Fayetteville Observer* took the form of a question: "Victims of Hippie Cult? Officer's Wife, Children Found Slain at Ft. Bragg." Apparently, there was already skepticism about MacDonald's account of what had happened the previous night.

The victims were identified as MacDonald's wife Colette, 26, and the couple's two daughters, Kimberloy, 5, and Kristen Jean, 2. Military authorities said MacDonald told them four people—three men and a woman—burst through the rear door of the home at approximately 4 a.m. chanting "LSD is great, LSD is great" while the family slept. One of the suspects, a blonde woman wearing a floppy hat and muddy white boots, was carrying a candle, according to a report from the investigating officers. Officers said another suspect was a Negro man wearing a jacket with sergeant stripes on the sleeves. The two other suspects were reportedly white men, they said.[3]

Just three days later, another question was raised about MacDonald's account of what happened. A February 20 article in the *New York Times* reported that Mac-Donald had made a comment to a friend, Lieutenant Ronald Harrison, who was reading an *Esquire* magazine article about the Manson murders: "Isn't that wild?"[4]

The cover story of the March 1970 issue of *Esquire* was "Evil Lurks in California. Lee Marvin Is Afraid." Amid the ads for Pierre Cardin slacks and Canoe aftershave, there was page after page of various kinds of malefaction—an "acid goddess" who copulates with a swan, a chair that spouts blood, Black Masses, drugs and more drugs, and, of course, Manson and his family. From Harrison's various comments to army investigators that were released to the press, it might be imagined that MacDonald was interested in some form of satanism or ritual abuse: "Isn't that wild?" But a signed statement from Harrison, dated July 13, 1970, paints a more ambiguous picture. Although various prosecutors eventually portrayed MacDonald's comment in a sinister light, Harrison was describing a happy home environment. *The Brady Bunch*, with a little witchcraft thrown in:

Since I was quoted in the newspapers as saying Jeff and I discussed the Sharon Tate murder case, I feel that I should explain the conversation in its entirety. On Saturday the 14th of February, I stopped by Jeff's about 7:30 or 8:00 in the evening. Working clockwise, Colette was seated on the couch, Jeff in his chair, I in mine, Kim on the floor with her PJs on, watching TV from a bear-shaped sleeping bag. We were watching TV and discussing the programs, and I was playing with Kim on the floor. I noticed an *Esquire* magazine among others on the coffee table. On the cover it said "Evil Lurks in California. Lee Marvin Is Afraid." I called attention to the magazine and picked it up, and Jeff said "Go ahead and read that—it's wild!" So I opened the magazine and the first article I saw was one with illustrations of necklaces in the form of devil signs and people participating in a witchcraft ceremony. The next page had an article about a girl called Leda, and her black swan, which we discussed. I turned the page and saw an article on the

U.S. OPENS CLINIC FOR LEPROSY HERE

Center Is 4th for Treatment of Disease in the City

By NANCY HICKS

The United States Public Health Service opened a new outpatient clinic for leprosy here yesterday. The new facility, in a building at 245 Houston Street, is the fourth in the city to treat the estimated total of 100 New Yorkers who have the disease.

The new clinic is a branch of the department of dermatology of the Public Health Service's hospital on Staten Island, which also has a clinic. The others are in Washington Heights and in the Morrisania section of the Bronx.

Leprosy, an ancient disease, affects about 12 million people throughout the world, usually those in the underdeveloped countries of Asia, Africa or Latin America. An estimated 2,000 Americans have the disease and all are presumed to have contracted it outside the country.

Most of the victims of leprosy here come from Puerto Rico and other areas in the Caribbean, Dr. James P. Fields, chief of dermatology at the Staten Island hospital said.

The new Manhattan facility was not established because of any epidemic in New York, said Dr. N. J. Galuzzi, director of the Staten Island hospital. Instead, he said, it is just a "more convenient location" for Manhattan residents to go for treatment.

More Patients Wanted

Doctors there, however, hope their caseload will increase as more people who have the disease "stop hiding it" and come in for treatment.

Officials of the Staten Island hospital said 342 outpatients from the tri-state area had been treated there last year, as compared with 28 ten years ago. There were 37 in-patients at the hospital last year, compared with five 10 years ago. The officials said the increased numbers were a result of better detection of the disease rather than an increase in its incidence.

The opening of the clinic was coordinated with the observance of World Leprosy Week, which began last Sunday. The

blood on the headboard of a bed in the MacDonald home on the base at Fort Bragg.

Lieutenant Harrison described Captain MacDonald as a very kind and considerate man who sympathized with drug addicts. He said that the doctor showed him the magazine articles last Saturday while he was visiting at the MacDonald home, and that his friend said, "Isn't that wild?"

Military and civilian investigators continued today to question hundreds of people in various parts of the United States. Photographs of scores of "hippie type" were taken to the Fort Bragg Hospital for viewing by Captain MacDonald.

The captain is reported to be recovering from a knife wound in the chest and a blow on the left side of his head.

The proprietor of a hippie hangout in Fayetteville posted a sign in the window today urging hippies to pass along to the police information they might have about the man.

An unnamed man was quoted in The Observer this morning as saying that the man who continued the Fayette ...

Friend Says Captain Discussed Tate Killing Before Family Died

By MARTIN WALDRON
Special to The New York Times

FAYETTEVILLE, N. C., Feb. 19—A Green Beret team commander said today that he and Dr. Jeffrey MacDonald of Pat chogue, L. I., discussed the ritualistic murders of the actress Sharon Tate and three of her friends only a couple of days before the doctor's family was found dead at Fort Bragg.

The doctor's wife and two children were knifed to death as were the victims in the Tate case.

Lieut. Ronald Harrison, 28 years old, of Columbus, Ohio, said that Dr. MacDonald, an Army captain, had called his attention to the current issue of Esquire magazine, which carries articles reviewing the Tate murders, the satanic religions and drug subcultures of the West Coast and what Esquire called "the banality of evil in California."

Lieutenant Harrison, who made his remarks at a news conference, said that he was Captain MacDonald's best friend in the Army.

Captain MacDonald told military investigators that two white men, a Negro man and a blonde woman carrying a candle attacked him and stabbed and clubbed his wife and daughters to death in the predawn hours Tuesday. The word "pig" was written in ...

center is a monthly treatment facility that will primarily dispense the drug Dapsone, a sulfone compound. The center will also serve as a referral agency for the Staten Island hospital.

Because of the stigma that is usually attached to the word leprosy, the clinic will be called a Hansen's Disease clinic. The disease is named for the Norwegian scientist who first identified the leprosy bacillus in 1874.

Although it is a contagious bacterial infection, leprosy is one of the least contagious of all the communicable diseases. It may appear as red lesions on the skin, but the bacillus may live in the body for years before the sores appear. The bacillus defies detection by laboratory tests before it becomes visible.

The disease cannot be cured.

New Books

FICTION

A Few Enquiries, by Howard Sackler, introduction by Martin Scorfied (Dial, $5.95). Book collection of four plays—"Sarah," "The Nine O'Clock Mail," "Mr. Welk," and Jersey Jim" and "Skippy."

The Amazing Mrs. Pollifax, by Dorothy Gilman (Doubleday, $4.95). Suspense-intrigue story.

The Temptation of Angelique: Suzanne-Union (Putnam, $6.95). Further adventures of Angelique on the New World's frontier.

White Horse to Banbury Cross, by Richard Llewellyn (Doubleday, $5.95). More adventures of agent Edmund Trothe, M.I.5.

GENERAL

A Reader's Guide to W. H. Auden, by John Fuller (Farrar, Straus & Giroux, $6.95 paperbound, $2.25). Response to the poetry. W. B. Gideon Cragg (Paul S. Eriksson, $6.95). On corporate support of the arts in the United States.

The Black, the White, by Ely Green, edited by Elizabeth R. and Arthur Ben Chitty (University of Massachusetts, $10). The journal of the son of a white father and a black mother.

God Creates Speaks, edited by Martin Kessler and James Pritard (Grove, $3.50).

Bridge: Holiday Tournament Here Begins With Full Schedule

By ALAN TRUSCOTT

THE George Washington Birthday Tournament of the Greater New York Bridge Association begins today at the New York Hilton Hotel with a full roster of events spread over four days in the following schedule:

Men's Pairs and Women's Pairs	P.M. today.
Mixed Pairs and Novice Pairs	P.M. today.
Open Pairs and Limited Pairs	
Masters Pairs in Three Flights	

(life masters, more than 100 master points and less than 100 points)—Sunday.

Open Teams (two sessions) and Novice Pairs—P.M. Monday. Novice Pairs—P.M. Monday.

Two special events are scheduled tonight. At 7:30 P.M. Alvin Roth will give a lecture for novice players, and at about 11:30 P.M. he will team with Barbara Rapaport in an exhibition Vu-Graph match against David Carlberg and Pedro Cabral.

The play in four stages begins simply: West takes three club tricks. The obvious lead at the fourth trick is a heart or a diamond, knowing that this can do no harm. South reaches his hand by way of the heart ace, and has to make the correct technical play of the spade nine. When this wins he can continue with the queen and remains in his hand to lead the ace a third time. West's spots are trapped and the spades are made.

South makes his game by the defense is unable not only of clubs with a heart. South must have the dummy's diamond, or the spade finesse if not, the declarer hopeless lead in any playing a ruff and discard to help the declarer, who is out to be the hold-

NORTH
♠ A J 10 4
♡ K Q J 10
♢ A 2
♣ 9 7 2

WEST   EAST (D)
♠ K 8 7 6   ♠ 5
♡ 8 8   ♡ 7 6 4 3 2
♢ Q 8 3   ♢ J 10 9 5
♣ A K Q 8   ♣ 2 6 4

SOUTH
♠ Q 9 3 2
♡ A 5
♢ 7 6 4 2
♣ 10 8 3

Neither side was vulnerable. The bidding:
East	South	West	North
Pass	1 ♣	Dbl.	
Pass	1 ♠	Pass	3 ♠
Pass	Pass	Pass	Pass

West led the club king.

alertly ruff the king of clubs with a five, an uppercut South to win with queen or nine, a certain trick.

THE TIMES ACQUIRES 2D GOLF MAGAZINE

The New York Times Company has purchased Golf World, a British golf magazine with a circulation of almost 60,000, described as the largest in its field in Britain.

The announcement was made jointly in London yesterday by R. Charles Brett, founder and owner of the magazine, and Ivan V. H. Veit, vice president of the New York Times Company.

Mr. Brett will continue as managing director, as will Keith Mackie as editor and Kenneth Clamp as advertising director. The editorial office will remain in Brighton and the advertising office in London.

Golf World's average circulation for the six months ended last December was 60,832. The previous month, Golf World purchased Golfing, a British monthly with 29,500 circulation. from Haymarket Press, Ltd. In January, Golfing was incorporated into Golf World and a new circulation base of 69,000 was announced.

The New York Times Company also owns Golf Digest, an American golf magazine. Its current circulation base is 430,000.

Sharon Tate murders—we said it was terrible and that drug abusers were sick, disturbed people. I closed the magazine and placed it back on the table, and we continued watching TV. Altogether, the conversation about the entire series of articles lasted about 10 minutes out of a 2½–3 hour visit, and most of that ten minutes we discussed Leda and her black swan.[5]

What was the *New York Times* headline really saying? "Friend Says Captain Discussed Tate Killing"? Was there a suggestion that the articles in *Esquire* might have been the trigger for MacDonald's homicidal rage? Was the reader being asked to wonder whether MacDonald had decided to *create* a Manson-like crime scene in order to deflect attention from himself? Harrison's statement, taken five months after the murders, was never publicized in the newspapers.

I spoke with another friend of the MacDonalds, Carol Butner. Her husband was a surgeon with the Special Forces at Fort Bragg.

CAROL BUTNER: They were the first people we met in Fort Bragg. Kimmy was the older one and Kristy was the younger one. And Kimmy was very articulate. You could tell her mind was really quick. They loved their daddy. Man, he would come in and they'd go hang on him and grab his boots. They just adored him.

I don't mean to say that I was over there all the time, but I would see the girls with him. And I remember I overheard a conversation Colette had at Thanksgiving on the phone. I was in the kitchen doing dishes with her or something. And she said, "Well, maybe you could tell by hearing my side of the conversation that I'm pregnant." And I hadn't known that until then. And I said, "Congratulations." And she had had some problems with pregnancies and she said, "I've just got to watch some things." And then sometime between Thanksgiving and Christmas, I remember I was over there after lunch, and Jeff was going back to the office. And I remember he said to Kimmy and Kristy, "Now, you make Mommy put her feet up on the coffee table and don't let her get up and do things because she needs to rest and she needs to keep her feet up." And so he said, "Now, I'm counting on you to do that." And they said, "Yes, Daddy."

ERROL MORRIS: What a horribly sad story.

CAROL BUTNER: Oh, I know. It was such a horrible, horrible thing, and it happened not so long after the Sharon Tate murders. And people who hear about the case now want to think that there's CSI and all this incredibly sophisticated evidentiary testing. And it just wasn't the case then. And the times were so turbulent. America was completely divided. It's hard for people to remember the '70s.

These guys, my husband and Jeff and others, being in Special Forces—they were real gung-ho America and military. And then there were all the antimilitary people, and it was a very contradictory and violent time.

Only ten weeks had elapsed between the first Manson arrests and the death of MacDonald's family. News reports of the Manson murders were everywhere—in national and local newspapers, on the evening news, and in countless magazine articles. It was the crime of the century. It was something people read about and talked about. Wouldn't it have been more remarkable if MacDonald had *not* read or talked about it? Given the notoriety of the Manson family, couldn't a local group of drug-crazed hippies have been just as easily (or more easily) inspired by any of the countless news stories about the Manson murders?

Was MacDonald imitating Manson in order to implicate some imagined group of hippies? Or were there real hippie intruders in the house, also possibly imitating Manson?[6] Can any piece of evidence flip back and forth? One moment it provides proof of one thing; the next moment, proof of its exact opposite?

BREAKING THE SOUND BARRIER

I was twelve years old, watching and rewatching on television David Lean's *Breaking the Sound Barrier*.[1] The film was part of a program called *Million Dollar Movie* that played on Channel 9 (WWOR-TV) in the New York metropolitan area. Each program started with various shots of New York City at night set to Max Steiner's theme music for *Gone with the Wind* and was repeated through the week. I saw *Breaking the Sound Barrier* many, many times. Maybe six or seven. It tells the story of how British pilots were the first to fly faster than the speed of sound—an apocryphal claim that did not particularly delight Chuck Yeager, the American pilot who actually *did* break the sound barrier. (It is a terrific film, despite its historical inaccuracies.)

The detail that still haunts me involves the movie's central plot point—that the controls of an airplane are *reversed* as it passes through Mach 1, the speed of sound. Normally, a pilot pulls back on the stick to pull out of a dive. In David Lean's film, we are told that at Mach 1, he has to do the exact opposite. We see shot after shot of a pilot approaching the sound barrier. The needle on the Machmeter twitching back and forth. Horrible buffeting and shaking. The forces are too great. The plane will be ripped apart. And then the pilot pulls back on the stick. His assumption is that the plane will pull out of its dive and soar into the air. But it doesn't. It goes into a steeper dive and plunges into a field, leaving a huge, smoking crater.

In the movie, Philip Peel, a test pilot, and Will Sparks, an aeronautical engineer, debate what this means. Could the controls of an airplane be reversed at Mach 1?

PHILIP PEEL: Is it possible that at the speed of sound, the controls are reversed?

WILL SPARKS: At the speed of sound, Philip, anything is possible. Why?

PHILIP PEEL: During the war once I put a Spitfire into a flat-out dive. No very good reason, just youthful high spirits. I think now that I hit the sound barrier. I remember that the more I pulled on the stick, the harder the nose went down. The same thing happened this morning.

WILL SPARKS: You're not supposed to do a high-mark number!

PHILIP PEEL: I know, but I did. Both times, I had the feeling that if I'd had the guts to put the stick forward, instead of pulling it back, I could have pulled out without having to lose speed. What do you think?

WILL SPARKS: There's nothing in the books to suggest, for one second, anything so Edgar Allan Poe–ish.

PHILIP PEEL: Well, it depends on the books, now, doesn't it, Will? There were books once that said the world was flat.

I have often thought that this idea—this breaking-the-sound-barrier idea, this Edgar Allan Poe–ish idea—captures a deep fear.[2] What if our expectations trick us into a false sense of security? What if everything is the *opposite* of what it seems? That plus becomes minus, left becomes right, up becomes down, pull forward becomes push back? Like the turkey that fails to realize that today is different from all previous days. It's Thanksgiving. The farmer is coming, but he isn't bringing food. This time he is bringing an ax.

––––––

Twenty-five years later, I traveled to Dallas (on my birthday) to interview a psychiatrist, James Grigson, who had earned the nickname "Dr. Death" because of the unusual role he played in death penalty cases in Texas. The Dallas district attorneys encouraged psychiatrists to testify in capital murder trials. But not just any psychiatrists. They had *two* psychiatrists in mind, psychiatrists who had been prosecution stooges in the past, Dr. James Grigson and Dr. John Holbrook. The DA's technique used to secure death sentences was crude but effective. Have the psychiatrists make predictions of future dangerousness based on a diagnosis of psychopathy. It was mumbo jumbo, but it worked. The psychiatrists and the diagnosis gave prosecutors the imprimatur of medical respectability and gave the jury the confidence to impose a death sentence.

Dr. Grigson was an affable presence. I rather liked him. In our first meeting, I had asked him about his private practice, and he ruefully admitted that it had suffered because of his newly minted notoriety. As he explained it, "Patients are a little reluctant to bare their souls to someone named 'Dr. Death.'" But about sociopaths and psychopaths, Grigson was unequivocal. His mantra was, "They're different from you and me." At his instigation I started interviewing Texas inmates who had been sentenced to death. And so my initial meeting with Dr. Grigson eventually led to Randall Dale Adams, an inmate who had been convicted of killing a Dallas police officer, labeled a sociopath, and sentenced to death. It also led me into a two-year investigation of a terrible miscarriage of justice—an innocent man (Adams) was almost executed—and to my movie *The Thin Blue Line*, which helped overturn his conviction and led to his release from prison in 1989.

The case against Randall Dale Adams involved the cold-blooded murder of a Dallas police officer, Robert Wood. He was shot and killed during a routine traffic stop early in the morning of November 28, 1976. When a police officer is gunned down in cold blood, there is enormous pressure to solve the case and punish the perpetrator. This crime remained unsolved for nearly a month. No clues. Nothing.

And then information was presented to the police that David Harris, a sixteen-year-old kid from Vidor, Texas, a small town three hundred miles away, had boasted to his friends that he had "offed a pig in Dallas." In custody, he blamed a hitchhiker, Randall Dale Adams, with whom he had spent the day prior to the killing. Adams was arrested and within a short amount of time was charged with the murder.

Harris told the police that he had been a passenger in the car and had witnessed the murder, but the crime had been committed by the driver. The alleged driver, Adams, had a bad excuse—although it happened to be the truth: He was home in bed at the time of the murder. At Adams's 1977 trial Grigson testified as expected: that Adams was a sociopath who had killed and would "kill and kill again." He was wrong on both counts. He also made an assessment that Harris had never killed and would never kill in the future. He was again wrong on both counts. I am fond of pointing out that on that occasion Dr. Grigson was 400 percent wrong. It's difficult to do, but he did it. And he did it with the aid of the diagnosis of *psychopathy*.

Dr. Grigson provided answers to the questions: Why didn't Randall Dale Adams change his physical appearance after the murder of the Dallas police officer? Why didn't he leave town? Why did he go to work every day? Normally, these pieces of evidence would be mildly exculpatory, but certainly they wouldn't count toward his guilt and against his innocence. Why didn't he run? Dr. Grigson had a simple explanation. Because he is *different* from you or me, because he doesn't have feelings like you or me. I also have a simple explanation. Because he hadn't done anything. He saw no reason to run. He was innocent. But the minute Grigson described him as a psychopath, evidence that would count for Adams's innocence suddenly counted for his guilt. Nothing has changed, except a diagnostic label—and suddenly, evidence that would normally be considered mildly *exculpatory* becomes strongly *inculpatory*.

———

To me, psychopathy is like the controls of the jet in *Breaking the Sound Barrier*. Everything is reversed.[3] Why didn't Adams change his appearance? Because he's a stone-cold killer. Why didn't he run? Because he doesn't have feelings like you and me. A normal person would have run, but a psychopath was able to make decisions based on reason, not emotion. Doug Mulder, Adams's prosecutor, summed it up in his elaborate notes taken in preparation for the trial. Mulder argued that Adams made a *calculation*—to run would be "the worst thing that he could do."

Adams found himself heading inexorably toward "Old Sparky," the Texas electric chair. I remember the first time I met him. This was long before I came to believe in his innocence. His voice at times had a singsong quality, as if he himself didn't believe what he was saying. At other times, he was clearly angry. Contemplating the colossal run of misconceptions and lying that led to his conviction, who wouldn't be angry? Later, I came to believe that so many people had questioned his veracity and his motives that he almost gave up pleading for his innocence. He assumed—correctly—that everybody thought he was lying and there was little point in claiming his innocence anymore. Is there a point where, if everyone thinks you're lying, you come to believe that you're lying, even when you're telling the truth? People have an idea about how innocent prisoners should conduct themselves, but they probably have never had the experience of being sentenced to death (or life imprisonment) for a crime they did not commit.[4]

A SUBTLY CONSTRUCTED REFLEX MACHINE

I will wear my heart upon my sleeve
For daws to peck at: I am not what I am.
—William Shakespeare, *Othello*

Very few people have heard of him, but Hervey Cleckley, a Georgia psychiatrist and Rhodes Scholar, wrote two of the most influential books of the twentieth century: *The Three Faces of Eve* and *The Mask of Sanity*. These books single-handedly created the myth of the multiple personality disorder and the myth of the psychopath—myths arguably as powerful as those created by Mary Shelley (*Frankenstein*) and Robert Louis Stevenson (*The Strange Case of Dr. Jekyll and Mr. Hyde*).[1] Psychopathy had been on my mind for years. It became an important theme in *The Thin Blue Line*, since the diagnosis had been instrumental in sending Randall Adams to death row. I wanted to talk to Cleckley, and I eventually called his home in Athens, Georgia, hoping for an interview. It was in early February 1984. He had died the week before.

The Mask of Sanity first appeared in 1941 and went through many subsequent editions.[2] The fourth edition appeared in 1964. Joseph J. Michaels, in his review, captured the strange quality of the work—something between fantasy and reality. "The book is well written, with many references to the literature. The style suggests that of a novelist although portraying real characters in a dramatic, fictional manner."[3]

Cleckley, indeed, provides his own bizarre case studies of psychopathic behavior. They consist of a series of absurd cautionary tales. He comes off as an eccentric, sex-obsessed uncle, like a family member who insists on bringing up unsavory and somewhat lascivious details at the dinner table. I might characterize the genre as the "pornuncular." He goes from one lurid case history to another. One of my favorites involves a young man accused of the wanton murder of forty-four people. Cleckley quotes a *Newsweek* report on the trial:

> At times he watched the proceedings with wide, staring eyes that showed no emotion; at other times, he read a book, *The Mask of Sanity*, by Dr. Hervey Cleckley. When the verdict was announced he bit his lower lip, but otherwise remained impassive. His wife, Gloria, 22, the mother of his two small children, broke down and sobbed hysterically.[4]

I couldn't help myself. I had to find out something more about the actual case. It concerned John Gilbert Graham, whose mother was going to visit his sister in Alaska. He placed a bomb in her luggage, and then bought six life insurance policies from a vending machine at the airport. Total cost: $1.50. Total payout: $37,500. Forty-four people died when the plane exploded over a sugar-beet field in Colorado. And no, Graham didn't collect. Not just because he had been caught. He had neglected to have his mother sign the policies.

Eventually Cleckley returns to his theme: the difference between disease and the feigning of disease. And the flip side, the difference between normalcy and the feigning of normalcy. It is this distinction that becomes central to Cleckley's idea of the psychopath. He writes:

> We are dealing here not with a complete man at all but with something that suggests a subtly constructed reflex machine which can mimic the human personality perfectly. This smoothly operating psychic apparatus reproduces consistently not only specimens of good human reasoning but also appropriate simulations of normal human emotion in response to nearly all the varied stimuli of life. So perfect is this reproduction of a whole and normal man that no one who examines him in a clinical setting can point out in scientific or objective terms why, or how, he is not real. And yet we eventually come to know or feel we know that reality, in the sense of full, healthy experiencing of life, is not here.[5]

Here it is. The psychopath as modern monster—the Terminator, the robot without feeling, the mechanical man devoid of a soul. And for Cleckley, this simulacrum, this golem, is indistinguishable from a *real* person. Even though "no one . . . can point out in scientific or objective terms why he is not real," something is missing.

What could any defendant do to defeat the diagnosis of psychopathy, if the diagnosis is based not on disease but on the feigning of normalcy?

The answer: nothing.

There is a fundamental problem. Since phenomenologically a psychopath is no different from a normal person, how can we prove that a seemingly normal person is a psychopath? The problem gets much worse when the diagnosis is used to establish guilt. How do we know he did it? Because he's a psychopath, and psychopaths do that sort of thing. He's guilty because he's a psychopath, and he's a psychopath because he's guilty. The underlying theory determines the interpretation of the evidence.

Cleckley's idea, unlike reversing the controls in *Breaking the Sound Barrier,* can't be tested.[6] At the sound barrier, a pilot can find out whether the controls are reversed. When you pull forward on the stick, does the jet pull out of its dive, or does it pitch headfirst into the ground? Regardless of whether the story is false in the real world, in the *narrative* it can be tested. It is an empirical principle. Cleckley's idea, on the other hand, cannot be tested.

> The psychopath's inner deviation from the normal impresses me as one subtly masked and abstruse. So, too, it has often seemed that interpersonal and environmental factors, if they contribute to the development of his disorder, are likely to be ones so disguised superficially as to appear of an opposite nature.

In the years since the publication of *The Mask of Sanity,* the concept of psychopathy has been changed along with its name. Psychopathy is now diagnosed alongside "sociopathy" or "antisocial personality disorder," with few experts able to agree on whether they are naming the same thing, or two or three things that are slightly different.[7] But the biggest change involves the idea that psychopathy involves predation, along with camouflage. The *Handbook of Psychopathy,* a recent compendium of articles on the subject, compares the psychopath to a spider:

> Like *Amyciaea lineatipes,* a species of arachnid that mimics the physical appearance of ants on which it preys, psychopathic individuals readily gain the trust of others because they come across on initial contact as likable, adjusted, and

well meaning. It is only through continued interaction and observation that the psychopath's true, "darker" nature is revealed.[8]

The key word is "interaction." It is not what a psychopath thinks so much as what a psychopath *does*. The mask of sanity—the false appearance of sanity—makes us think that we are being set up, lured, tricked by someone getting us to do his or her bidding. The smile masks a frown. The handshake conceals a weapon.

It is the psychopath as trickster, as confidence man.

This concept of psychopathy would eventually seal Jeffrey MacDonald's fate.[9] It explains the inexplicable: how someone who was so accomplished, so respected, could commit such a heinous crime. Psychopathy suggests that MacDonald was in disguise, hidden behind a mask of sanity, and that he was in reality "of an opposite nature."

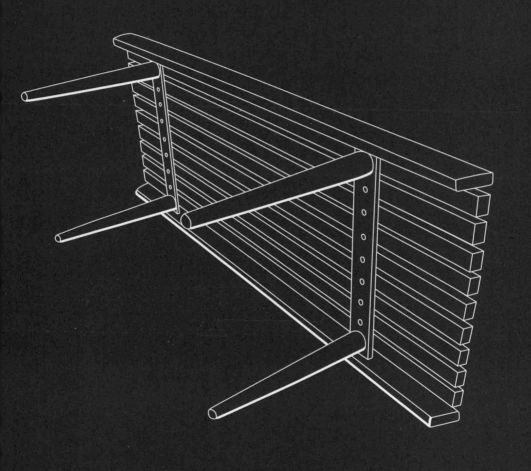

5

THE IMPOSSIBLE COFFEE TABLE

You'd better think less about us and what's going to happen
to you, and think a bit more about yourself. And stop making
all this fuss about your sense of innocence; you don't make
such a bad impression, but with all this fuss you're damaging it.
—Franz Kafka, *The Trial*

When Jeffrey MacDonald was brought in for questioning on April 6, 1970, less than two months after the murders, he was read his rights, declined to have an attorney present, and a tape recorder was turned on. The interview was conducted by CID chief investigator Franz Grebner, Agent William Ivory, and Agent Robert Shaw. Grebner first asked for MacDonald's account of the events of February 17.

> And I went to bed about—somewheres around two o'clock. I really don't know; I was reading on the couch, and my little girl Kristy had gone into bed with my wife.
>
> And I went in to go to bed, and the bed was wet. She had wet the bed on my side, so I brought her in her own room. And I don't remember if I changed her or not, gave her a bottle and went out to the couch 'cause my bed was wet. And I went to sleep on the couch.
>
> And then the next thing I know I heard some screaming, at least my wife; but I thought I heard Kimmie, my older daughter, screaming also. And I sat up. The kitchen light was on, and I saw some people at the foot of the bed.

So, I don't know if I really said anything or I was getting ready to say something. This happened real fast. You know, when you talk about it, it sounds like it took forever; but it didn't take forever.

And so, I sat up; and at first I thought it was—I just could see three people, and I don't know if I—if I heard the girl first—or I think I saw her first. I think two of the men separated sort of at the end of my couch, and I keep—all I saw was some people really.

And this guy started walking down between the coffee table and the couch, and he raised something over his head and just sort of then—sort of all together—I just got a glance of this girl with kind of a light on her face. I don't know if it was a flashlight or a candle, but it looked to me like she was holding something. And I just remember that my instinctive thought was that "she's holding a candle. What the hell is she holding a candle for?"

But she said, before I was hit the first time, "Kill the pigs. Acid's groovy."

Now, that's all—that's all I think I heard before I was hit the first time, and the guy hit me in the head. So I was knocked back on the couch, and then I started struggling to get up, and I could hear it all then—Now I could—Maybe it's really, you know—I don't know if I was repeating to myself what she just said or if I kept hearing it, but I kept—I heard, you know, "Acid is groovy. Kill the pigs."

And I started to struggle up; and I noticed three men now; and I think the girl was kind of behind them, either on the stairs or at the foot of the couch behind them. And the guy on my left was a colored man, and he hit me again; but at the same time, you know, I was kind of struggling. And these two men, I thought, were punching me at the same time. Then I—I remember thinking to myself that—see, I work out with the boxing gloves sometimes. I was then—and I kept— "Geeze, that guy throws a hell of a punch," because he punched me in the chest, and I got this terrible pain in my chest.

And so, I was struggling, and I got hit on the shoulder or the side of the head again, and so I turned and I—and I grabbed this guy's whatever it was. I thought it was a baseball bat at the time. And I had—I was holding it. I was kind of working up it to hold onto it.

Meanwhile, both these guys were kind of hitting me, and all this time I was hearing screams. That's what I can't figure out, so—let's see, I was holding— so, I saw the—and all I got a glimpse was, was some stripes. I told you, I think, they were E6 stripes. There was one bottom rocker and it was an army jacket, and that man was a colored man, and the two men, other men, were white.

And I didn't really notice too much about them. And so I kind of struggled, and I was kind of off-balance, 'cause I was still halfway on the couch and half off, and I was holding onto this thing. And I kept getting this pain, either in—you know, like sort of in my stomach, and he kept hitting me in the chest.

And so, I let go of the club; and I was grappling with him and I was holding his hand in my hand. And I saw, you know, a blade. I didn't know what it was; I just saw something that looked like a blade at the time.

And so, then I concentrated on him. We were kind of struggling in the hallway right there at the end of the couch; and then really the next distinctive thing, I thought that—I thought that I noticed that—I saw some legs, you know, that—not covered—like I'd saw the top of some boots. And I thought that I saw knees as I was falling.

But it wasn't what was in the papers that I saw white boots. I never saw white, muddy boots. I saw—saw some knees on the top of boots, and I told, I think, the investigators, I thought they were brown, as a matter of fact.

And the next thing I remember, though, was lying on the hallway floor, and I was freezing cold and it was very quiet. And my teeth were chattering, and I went down and—to the bedroom.[1]

The fact that MacDonald was *alive,* and his family dead, started the ball rolling. There was something funny about the living room, the scene of MacDonald's fight with the hippie intruders. It was too tidy, too neat. When the CID detectives tried to reconcile what they had seen in the house with MacDonald's account of what had happened, they became convinced that MacDonald was the murderer *and* that he had staged the crime scene to make it look like there had been intruders.

MacDonald was presented with a coffee table, a flowerpot, and a stack of magazines—as though they were smoking guns.

FRANZ GREBNER: I have been sitting here most of the morning not saying very much and just listening to your story, and I have been an investigator for a long time. And, if you were a PFC [private first class], an uneducated person, I might try to bring you in here and bluff you. But you are a very well educated man— doctor, Captain—and I'm going to be fair with you. But your story just doesn't ring true. There's too many discrepancies. For instance, take a look at this picture. Do you see anything odd about that scene?

JEFFREY MACDONALD: No.

FRANZ GREBNER: It is the first thing I saw when I came to the house that morning. Notice the flowerpot?

JEFFREY MACDONALD: It's standing up.

FRANZ GREBNER: Uh-huh. Notice the magazines?

JEFFREY MACDONALD: Yeah.

FRANZ GREBNER: Notice the edge of the table right there?

JEFFREY MACDONALD: I don't understand the significance of it.

FRANZ GREBNER: Okay. The lab technicians, myself, Mr. Ivory and Mr. Shaw and any number of other people have tipped that table over. It never lands like that. It is top-heavy and it goes all the way, even pushes the chair out of the way. The magazines don't land under the leaning edge of the table. They land on the floor.

JEFFREY MACDONALD: Couldn't this table have been pushed around in the struggle?

FRANZ GREBNER: It could have been, but it would have been upside down when it stopped. The plant and the pot always go straight out and they stay together in all instances.

JEFFREY MACDONALD: Well, what are you trying to say?

FRANZ GREBNER: That it is a staged scene.

JEFFREY MACDONALD: You mean that I staged the scene?

FRANZ GREBNER: That's what I think.

JEFFREY MACDONALD: Do you think that I would stand the pot up if I staged the scene?

FRANZ GREBNER: Somebody stood it up like that.

JEFFREY MACDONALD: Well, I don't see the reasoning behind that. You just told me I was college-educated and very intelligent.

FRANZ GREBNER: I believe you are.

JEFFREY MACDONALD: Well, why do you think I would—I don't understand why you think that I would stage it that way if I was going to stage it.[2]

Grebner keeps returning to this argument: that MacDonald had tried to fake evidence of a struggle in his living room, but he had bungled the job. As far as the CID was concerned, the coffee table was fated to land supine—its legs in the air— and if it landed on its edge, MacDonald had to be responsible. The flowerpot was standing up, the plant and root-ball some distance away. If someone had knocked it over, why was it standing up? The inanimate objects in the room seemed collectively to point an accusatory finger at MacDonald.

Grebner and Ivory believed they could reconstruct MacDonald's intentions simply by observing the configuration of the furniture in his living room. They believed they were offering proof of something. The living room scene frozen in time that morning was like an impossible figure in an optical illusion. It could not exist in the *real* world—unless MacDonald himself had created it.

Couldn't there be a multitude of other explanations for the position of the coffee table, or any other seemingly sinister detail for that matter? Even if it couldn't have possibly landed that way in a struggle, even if it had to be *placed* in that position, what did it ultimately show about MacDonald's guilt or innocence?

The orderliness of the living room was taken as proof by the CID of MacDonald's guilt—the flowerpot, the coffee table, the Valentine's Day cards standing up on the china cabinet in the dining room. But if MacDonald had indeed staged the scene, wouldn't he have done a better job? As MacDonald had said to the CID agents: "Do you think that I would stand the pot up if I staged the scene?"

The CID officers were suggesting that there were two MacDonalds. A MacDonald cunning enough to manufacture a crime scene, and a MacDonald too stupid to do it effectively.

MacDonald responded near the end of the interrogation:

JEFFREY MACDONALD: Jesus Christ, this is a nightmare. [*Pause.*] This is like Edgar Allan Poe. Wow! Apparently you don't know much about my family and myself, I'll tell you that, to come up with this conclusion.

ROBERT SHAW: What kind of man are you, Captain? You say we don't know much about you. What kind of man are you?

JEFFREY MACDONALD: Well, I'm bright, aggressive, I work hard, and I had a terrific family, and I loved my wife very much, and this is the most asinine thing I've ever heard in my whole life.

Shaw asked, "What kind of man are you?" But it was a rhetorical question. Mac-Donald's protests meant nothing; they were expected. The CID detectives had already decided that MacDonald *was* the kind of man who could brutally murder his family and stage the scene, because they already believed—for whatever reason—that he was guilty. He had to be the kind of man who *could* do it, because they had already determined that he *had* done it.

On April 7, 1970, the announcement went out from Fort Bragg: Jeffrey Mac-Donald was the army's prime suspect in the murder of his wife and two daughters.

6

TEN-HOUR DRIVE

*The test of a first-rate intelligence is the ability to hold two opposed
ideas in the mind at the same time, and still retain the ability
to function. One should, for example, be able to see that things are
hopeless and yet be determined to make them otherwise.*
—F. Scott Fitzgerald, *The Crack-Up*

Michael Malley and Jeffrey MacDonald had been roommates at Princeton in the
early 1960s. MacDonald was from Long Island; Malley, from San Antonio. They
were not particularly friendly in college, and they parted ways early. MacDonald
had been accepted at an accelerated program at Northwestern University Medical
School and had left Princeton at the end of his junior year. Malley had graduated
and gone on to Harvard Law School. He had joined ROTC there (this was unusual
in the years of the Vietnam War) and had become a lawyer in the military and
eventually one of MacDonald's defense attorneys at Fort Bragg.

I called Malley.

MICHAEL MALLEY: I really was unprepared for how emotional it became. I had
been in the army, I'd been a law clerk for a year for an appellate judge, and you
don't get any sense of personal involvement in the law that way. And then when
I was at Fort Bliss, I worked lots of basically low-level criminal cases. I did a lot
of AWOLs, but I did other things, too. So I kind of had a pretty good feeling for the

military justice system, and that's why I originally wrote to Jeff, to say, "Don't talk to the CID, because you can't trust them." But it turned out he had already talked to them, and he babbled on and on and on, and he kind of hung his own noose that way. I was totally surprised when he wrote back, but we started corresponding. I told him I wanted to drive to Washington to check out job opportunities since I was going to have three or four weeks' leave before I had to go to Vietnam, so I said, "I'll stop in and see you."

ERROL MORRIS: But you didn't want to become part of the defense team.

MICHAEL MALLEY: I didn't have much experience. I wasn't a very experienced trial lawyer. Jeff said, "Well, if I were to request you as part of the defense team, would you agree?" And I said, "It wouldn't be my job to say yes or no. It's the army. They either send you off a little order, or they don't." The next thing I knew I had orders. So I was there, and I kind of didn't really want to be there, because I felt— what could I contribute?

ERROL MORRIS: And Jeff's civilian attorneys had already been hired.

MICHAEL MALLEY: Yes, one of Jeff's mother's friends had hired Bernie Segal and Denny Eisman. Bernie said to me, "Can you imagine Jeff doing this?" And I said, "No, absolutely not." And he said, "Well, we're going to have to convince the Article 32 officer of that. Go find all these people who know Jeff and can tell you what kind of person Jeff is." So that was my job all summer. I went and found witnesses; I kind of convinced them to come down there, mostly at their own expense, because we couldn't pay for much of that. And the two witnesses I found that truly terrified me were Freddy and Mildred Kassab [Colette MacDonald's mother and stepfather]. I went to their house on Long Island, and it was a very nice house. Mildred was, even then, kind of spectral. She had heavy makeup, she was very . . . almost emaciated. But Freddy was voluble, because he drank a lot. I mean, he drank during the middle of the day as far as I could tell. And he talked all the time. They said, "Oh, we love Jeff. We'd do anything." I said, "Fine." I said, "Here's what's going to happen"—and I could not have been more prescient—I said, "We"—we being the lawyers—"are going to do everything we can to make sure that the government cannot prove its case. We are not going to try to prove that Jeff is innocent. We are going to try to prove that the government's wrong. There's a difference between not guilty and innocent."

And I explained it in a very lawyerlike, academic way. And they listened to me. And after I finished this long discussion, they said, "He's innocent." Again, I said, "Whether he's innocent or not is not the issue. The issue is, can the government prove he's guilty? And we"—we being the lawyers—"think they cannot."

Mildred was furious that I did not say, "He's innocent." And Freddy just bab-bled. And he started yelling, and he said, "He's innocent." And I said, "Okay, that's how you feel and that's how I feel. But that's not what we're going to do, because we may never, ever be able to prove he's innocent. What we can do is prove he's not guilty, or force the government to prove he's guilty by putting them to the test." It went right by them. And it's gone by almost everybody I've ever talked to since, including Jeff, that there's a difference between not guilty, which is a legal concept, and innocent, which is a fact. There's only one person in the whole world who knows whether he's truly innocent. That's Jeff.

ERROL MORRIS: Is the issue the lack of physical evidence?

MICHAEL MALLEY: Yes. Whatever the physical evidence is, it's all over the lot. And I even told Freddy and Mildred, "From a lawyer's point of view, from what little we know, the crime scene was disturbed, the evidence gathering was done in a bad way." The government's case really is, as we were starting to believe, based solely on physical evidence. They had sent these CID goons all over Long Island, and they had talked to all sorts of other people, and they couldn't find a motive. They said, "Oh, Jeff's queer. Oh, Jeff's fooling around. Oh, Jeff's doing this." But, you know, when you ran it down, you realized if they ever tried to put that into evidence, it would be ludicrous, because they couldn't substantiate it. So we're coming down to a physical evidence case with no motive, and, as I told Freddy and Mildred then and I've repeated over the years, I said, "You know, it's the gov-ernment's problem. If they can't prove beyond a reasonable doubt, by their own evidence, that he did it, he's not guilty." Now, as to whether or not he's innocent, that takes a little bit more. And I said then, and forty years later I still say, I said, "The little bit more is you have to believe him. You have to know him." And that's why we put all of these character witnesses on the stand.

ERROL MORRIS: Did *you* believe him?

MICHAEL MALLEY: You know, I personally believed him. That's why I am willing to say, "I believe he's innocent." But I cannot say, "He's innocent." Now, maybe to you that sounds like sophistry, but to me there is a big difference. There is a big difference in saying, "I believe he's innocent" and "He is innocent." When I say, "I believe he's innocent," I'm saying, "I'm adding that little bit of extra proof, if you want, to the physical evidence and whatever else there is, and what Jeff says."

I'm not God. I do not have any film, I do not have a recording, I do not have an absolute physical demonstration that Jeff is innocent. I do not have that. And so, what I'm going on is my own belief and knowledge of him over the years, plus a lot of what he says supports his story. But some of what he says does not. And he has no explanation for that.

ERROL MORRIS: Why do you think that the CID became so absolutely convinced that MacDonald was guilty?

MICHAEL MALLEY: Fort Bragg was locked down. People were buying guns. There were some gun shops that ran out of guns. People were really afraid, because it made sense to them. There were hippies everywhere with drugs, and they were all ex-army. I mean, it was like Harvard in the days when I was there, where people would drop out but hang around Harvard Square and they would sell these underground papers. At Fort Bragg, there were hundreds and hundreds and hundreds of soldier dropouts, of kind of hangers-on, and it was violent. There were violent crimes all over the place, and they were drug related.

And so this was a big deal. And when it happened, everybody believed Jeff right away, at least for a day or two, anyway. And so people bought guns, people were barring their doors. And there was enormous pressure from the command, from the three-star general on down, to do something about this, find the killers. Because it was 1970, there was a war on, there were drugs, America was—that's why I said this is the Vietnam War story in a lot of ways.

And so we have an enormous amount of pressure to solve this case, and we have this arrogant kind of doctor guy who's coming here and saying, "Hey, it isn't me, don't worry." And Jeff really did not cover himself in glory in those interviews, either. I mean, he was kind of dismissive and sort of casual about the whole thing. As far as the CID was concerned, they had solved the case. It was right there and then. And once they solved the case, once they said to somebody— and probably to the staff judge advocate and to the provost marshal—that it's MacDonald, then there's no turning back.

———————

Malley had produced a memoir written over four rainy days in San Antonio in July 1971—a 102-page typewritten journal of his early involvement with the case. Reading it, I felt that I was being introduced to the case at the same time as Malley. That I was there. That I had the same confusions, doubts, uncertainties. Malley, in those first few weeks, was trying to understand the possible motives for the crime. He goes through them one by one and then discards them— possible drug use, psychosis, psychopathy, or infidelity. Every investigator, every lawyer who has become involved with this case goes through a similar laundry

list of possibilities. And set off against all of this—the bungling and bullying of the army.

Michael Malley's Account

I'm writing this account of my impressions of the Jeff MacDonald case over a year after I got involved, without notes, having become in turn confused, saddened, angry, and again sad by time and the changing of me and the people I knew in the case . . .

I'll write about what I saw, did, felt firsthand. Someone else can write about the "facts" of the case, the crime, and the hearings; to me the fascination is not so much the crime or even the courtroom battle, but how Jeff's world flew apart and how people, including me, got caught in the debris. Fate I now believe in, inexorable, unswerving. I'll put down my little part, but the whole story belongs to Jeff, and it is to him alone that final judgments—if there can be such things—belong.

On my drive across the desert from El Paso to San Antonio, I kept coming back to Jeff, and wondering what had happened to him to lead him to where he was—suspected of murder. It is a long drive—ten hours—and I thought of little else after a while. Perhaps that was a defense mechanism to avoid thinking about going to Vietnam, which I didn't want to do. But it was a curiously troubling experience, to wonder and worry about a man I had not seen in years, and to imagine what strange and terrible turn his life had taken.

I wondered why Jeff would kill Colette and his children. I knew that Colette was pregnant when they were married, and my petty little mind discussed with itself the possibility that Jeff, who I remembered (accurately, I think) to be a handsome and somewhat egotistical jock, had finally gotten fed up with being trapped by a girl when he was a twenty-year-old boy who now was a twenty-seven-year-old man with enormous potential but with the impedimenta of a wife and family . . . But why kill—why not divorce? Jeff certainly was not that cocky that he would play for total elimination of the problem at such a potentially high cost, rather than suffer the more pedestrian heartache and dry bitterness of divorce. That made no sense.

Drugs? That seemed a better explanation. I had started to see in my clients the strange lives drugs built. It certainly seemed plausible that Jeff did the killing under drugs, perhaps acting out fantasies toward Colette and his children that sane, sober people would reduce to the formalized bitterness of family law . . .

As the drive wore on, as Texas wore on, my curiosity about the crime and how it had happened (to be more exact, how and why Jeff did it—I must confess I assumed he did it, though that didn't make too much sense to me) gave way to thoughts of what the whole thing was doing to Jeff.

I assumed that Jeff was not a monster, even if he were a drug freak, or mentally diseased, or both, and it seemed cruel to me that he should be caged up. I did not know whether he was in the stockade or not, but I pictured him there, pacing. I remember him at Princeton, walking fast and purposefully wherever he went, and it seemed strange to think of him standing in a sally port being handcuffed and frisked before he is led to an interview room to see his lawyer, and then walking back to his cell, not briskly, with no purpose. (I have an active imagination, but when you drive across Texas, you need something to occupy your mind.)

I spent hours on the road sympathizing with a man I assumed (without much conviction, still) to be a murderer. How terrible it must be to be made to suffer for your sins, not by God, but by some bunch of army bureaucrats who could have no earthly interest in Colette or her children, or Jeff . . . I do not believe much in criminal law as a righter of the tragic and inescapable violence of the world.

But what if you assume Jeff was innocent? What if he were being subjected to the organized cruelty of blind police investigation while his family still haunted him, while he was as alone as he would ever be? That was a painful thought I tried to avoid, because as stupid as criminal justice often seems to me when the accused is guilty, you can ultimately accept it with at least indifference, on the theory that, after all, people are at least responsible for what they do, and all of us have to pay our dues some way for something, including criminals unlucky enough to get caught. But what if he really were innocent? It was a painful thought.

But once it dawned on me that he might be innocent, and be feeling the terrible injustice of his position, I started thinking of Jeff as human . . . It doesn't make sense to me now, but in that ten-hour drive across Texas, Jeff became real to me again, though I had no knowledge of the facts of the case, and probably still believed he was somehow guilty of murder. I kept wondering, what if he's not?

The army formally charged MacDonald on May 1, 1970. That same day, MacDonald and his military lawyer, Jim Douthat, asked Malley to join the defense team.

Jim and I talked a while that first day about pretrial discovery, particularly of the CID reading file, a process which I knew a little bit about from Fort Bliss. It was apparent that Jim knew absolutely nothing about the government's "theory" (or theories) of the crime or the evidence . . . All that we hoped would be in the reading file, as well as reports on physical evidence, which apparently would play a great role in the case. Jim knew that all this stuff, and more, was floating around and didn't know how to grab hold. We talked about all sorts of pretrial motions for discovery.

That first day with Jim I read an account of the crime Jeff had written for Jim, and a long list of drugs Jeff had in his house, as well as a long list of potential character witnesses Jeff had prepared. After I read Jeff's account of the attack on him and his family, and after I had been duly warned by Jeff and Jim that I couldn't talk freely anywhere, I talked to Jeff in the rent-a-car I got at the airport, with the air conditioner going and the radio too. I think that was the only time I was embarrassed by my doing what I was doing . . .

Still, that was the first time I asked him about his use of drugs (he didn't use them except an occasional reducing pill), his marital and extramarital sex life, his children, his marriage in general. It was hard to start, and hard to keep going. But, from my viewpoint, it was worth it because the answers were straight, sincere, and all pointed to a conclusion that Jeff, despite his occasional extramarital affairs, was a loving and loved father and husband with a warmth about his family that could not be feigned. I really didn't care much whether Jeff was guilty or not, but it was better to know that he was innocent, not just of murder, but of guile . . . When Jeff gets a little embarrassed or confused, he smiles weakly. When he gets angry, he shows it. I do not think he can lie with a straight face.

He talked about his extramarital affairs without guilt though with a little embarrassment that it's him you're talking about. He did not really feel unfaithful to Colette, though he presumes she would have been hurt had she known, and the thought of hurting her was what made Jeff self-conscious, I think. But after talking with Jeff for a while, you take Jeff on his own terms, and you see that his wife and family were very special to him, and the rest was just froth, which Jeff enjoyed, but never at the expense of his life with his wife and children . . . After that, sex and/or an unhappy family life were a dead issue. So no matter what the CID uncovered (which wasn't much) or what Jeff might admit to on the stand regarding his marital irregularities, his basic joy at being a husband and father with a great future ahead for him and his family simply overwhelmed these irregularities.

It was inconceivable to me after our conversation that, absent some sort of mental illness or drug usage (which also seemed to be a dead issue), Jeff could or would harm his family unless there was such monstrous provocation—

totally unknown to me and skillfully concealed by Jeff—that all normal rules of human behavior were broken. Because Jeff did not appear to be lying or concealing anything, I could not see how there could be a case against him—there was no motive . . .

I never could bring myself to ask Jeff to narrate the whole thing [the night of the murders], because it was soon obvious he could not do so without crying and partially reliving the night of the killings. I did frequently—too frequently, I'm sure he thought—ask him for specific details, episodes which he related well, although often with emotional difficulty. He knew that sometimes I went back over details, and he knew that sometimes (though extremely rarely) I would sharpshoot him, particularly in reference to his actions after he regained consciousness and went to discover his murdered family. But the good thing about Jeff was, he soon came to realize that he couldn't remember some things well, and that efforts on his part at consistency were counterproductive if he really had changes or lapses of memory . . . Jeff knew more about what happened than anyone else, and I felt that the defense really should be able to know more about the crime and about Jeff himself than the government ever could, just by talking to Jeff as well as to the witnesses who were available . . .

I was at Patchogue [the town on Long Island where MacDonald grew up] for two and a half days, and I talked to a lot of Jeff's and Colette's high-school acquaintances, Jeff's brother, and the Kassabs. Mostly, I found out that people who knew Jeff in high school liked him, envied him a little for making it out of Patchogue to Princeton and med school, and were unsure what to believe after they talked to the CID . . . I don't think the CID ever evaluated evidence they thought was not adverse to Jeff, which under the circumstances was almost criminally negligent.

It was at this time I first met Jeff's in-laws, the Kassabs . . . Freddy launched into a tirade about the army, Colonel Kane, and almost everyone else he could think of. He showed me the press release he had prepared for when Jeff was released—he was single-mindedly obsessed with not only vindicating Jeff, but with catching the killers and embarrassing the army; Mildred, while not as voluble, shared his views more intensely than even he did, I think. I was surprised at how their sorrow had turned into hatred, so that only the hatred showed, though I knew and respected its genesis. It was militant grief, and it scared me.

I naively believed that all the legalism I knew or knew about would be helpful in getting quickly prepared for a hearing. Jim knew better: he warned me that the Fort Bragg SJA [Staff Judge Advocate] and Provost Marshal's Office authorities were totally prosecution-oriented and noncooperative with the defense;

extracting evidence pretrial would be virtually a worthless exertion. We would have to wait for the Article 32 itself. Jim said we would play the silliest sort of games for the most trivial stakes. As things turned out, Jim was right about the noncooperation we could expect, though I believe he was willing to give up too easily . . . We flooded the hearing officer and the prosecutor with requests for evidence, almost all of which requests were initially refused.

Most mornings I spent on basically nonlegal business. This usually involved frustrating telephoning of the CID or the prosecutors regarding some of Jeff's personal property locked in his house. Jeff wanted phonograph records, a new stereo system, some books, some jewelry of Colette's, and some photographs. It was a small matter, but it was illustrative of the overpowering obstructionism of the government in this case, and provided (at least as best an outsider like me could tell) a good idea of the mutual mistrust and lack of direction, intelligence, and basic humanity on the part of the prosecutors and the CID agents.

The easiest request for the government to refuse was the request for the stereo. It was, they said, part of the crime scene, since it was standing in the living room with a record of the sound track of *Hair* on it—very meaningful, we were told.

Jeff's photographs were even more frustrating. Jeff wanted them because they were mostly of Colette and his children. Again, they were not really part of a crime scene—they were in boxes in the master bedroom closet, and not considered relevant for fingerprint or other reasons . . . Late in summer, we heard that the CID wanted the photographs to look for people resembling Jeff's description of the assailants . . .

We did get a few things, early in June: a dictionary, a large "Pink Panther" coin bank filled with coins, and one of Colette's bracelets, after Jeff's father-in-law, Freddy Kassab, decided to come down to Fayetteville to visit Jeff. Freddy caused some concern to me and Jim and Jeff because of his drinking and his proclaimed aim of "getting" the army for what it was doing to Jeff and for its failure to catch the real killers. We did not want Freddy out of control yet, and we wanted to keep him happy so that Jim and I could concentrate on preparing the case, and not on helping Freddy with his schemes to embarrass the army. (I do not want to disparage Freddy. His loyalty to Jeff was invaluable, his grief genuine; but he was, and is, often trying.) So Jim and I made a concerted effort at least to get some of Colette's jewelry for Freddy, which Jeff had promised him and Mildred.

My days passed like that: phoning the prosecution, talking to Jim, talking to witnesses, looking at the pictures, just sitting and brooding sometimes, calling (or trying to call) Bernie and Denny, trying to figure out what to do next. Sometimes in the afternoon I'd meet Jeff to run a couple of miles (running for me was one of the things that kept me sane; whether Jeff was along or not, after a while you just don't think about much but how tired you are, how far to go, and forget most of what's bothering you), or run alone along the MAAD mile, a cross-country course about two miles long.

There weren't many people I knew at Bragg except those connected with the case. My world was quite small at Bragg; it was the loneliest period of my life. For that reason, I spent most of my evenings with Jeff, because he really was the only person I knew. My BOQ [Bachelor Officers' Quarters] room was bleak, and his was (he does not believe this) considerably more comfortable. He had a two-room suite with air conditioners he bought, a refrigerator, a color TV, a fish tank that offered him something to do in taking care of it, and me something to do in watching it. It was, all in all, a livable prison.

I would go there fairly early in the evening, read or talk, drink Jeff's booze, watch TV (the first, and last, serious TV watching I've done in ten years). At first I talked about the case. I was still learning, and Jeff was still curious about what his lawyers were or were not doing, the progress of acquiring the records, etc. But after a while it became clear that Jeff didn't want to talk about the case in the evening. It made sleep for him, I suppose, more difficult than usual, even with the sleeping pills he took. So we talked about other things, or watched TV, and I found that even I relaxed (with a little help from my friend Librax) after a while. I am grateful to Jeff for those evenings when I had nothing else to do. Sometimes Jeff didn't really want me, or anybody else around, and yet I stayed . . . After several drinks (mine—Jeff drank surprisingly little) I'd leave Jeff to his sleeping pills, his letters, his memories, and his nightmares.

7

THE FLOWERPOT

An Article 32 hearing is not a court-martial. Rather, it is a preliminary investigation to decide whether to proceed to a court-martial.[1] It is often compared to a civilian grand jury hearing. There are defense lawyers, prosecutors, witnesses. But there is no jury, just an "investigating" officer. Colonel Warren V. Rock, an infantry officer with thirty years of service, presided and was assisted by a legal advisor, Hammond A. Beale. The case against MacDonald was presented by a young captain, Clifford Somers.

Colonel Rock called MacDonald's Article 32 hearing to order on May 15, 1970.[2] The defense team—the civilian lawyers Bernard Segal and Denny Eisman and the military lawyers Jim Douthat and Michael Malley—immediately complained that they had not received critical evidence: crime scene photographs, lab reports, and autopsy records. The case was postponed until July. It became one of the ongoing themes of all the successive legal proceedings—the difficulty in getting the prosecution to disclose evidence to the defense. But in this instance, the defense finally did receive the requested documents. They were even allowed to interview the CID investigators—Ivory, Grebner, and Shaw.

When the hearing was reconvened on July 5, 1970, it was closed to the public. Freddy Kassab, MacDonald's father-in-law, felt strongly that it should be open to the public and sent a telegram on July 20, 1970, to President Nixon complaining that "AS COMMANDER IN CHIEF—you must order General Edward Flanagan to rescind his illegal order to hold secret pretrial hearings of Capt. Jeffrey

MacDonald at Ft. Bragg—who is charged with the murders of our daughter and her two children . . . The Press, senators and congressmen who have attempted to open these hearings to the public have gotten nothing but double talk from the Army's Judge Advocate General."[3]

The hearings remained closed.

Specialist Fourth Class Kenneth Mica was called as a witness by the government. Mica was one of the first MPs to testify. Mica provides a description of the crime scene, notable because he was shown photographs taken later that morning that were different from what he had seen. The first photographer got sick and ran out of flashbulbs. He was sent home, and another photographer had to be brought in from Fort Gordon in Georgia.[4] There was a third delay before the second set of photographs was taken. Bernie Segal asked Mica about a photograph from that second set:

> **BERNARD SEGAL:** I ask you to look at the photograph, A-6; do you observe any difference in the clothing or the fabric that appears on the body of Mrs. MacDonald . . . ?
> **KENNETH MICA:** Yes, sir.
> **BERNARD SEGAL:** And would you describe to the investigating officer what those changes are?
> **KENNETH MICA:** I saw her—Mrs. MacDonald's—midriff exposed.

A towel and a blue cloth—it turned out to be Jeffrey MacDonald's pajama top—had been moved.

> **KENNETH MICA:** I don't remember this blue piece of cloth here . . .
> **BERNARD SEGAL:** Would you be good enough to also examine A-5 at this time and describe for the court if there is any differences in terms of the covering of the body of Mrs. MacDonald?
> **KENNETH MICA:** Just the white towel which I don't remember seeing, and also this blue cloth. I don't remember seeing that.[5]

Things had been moved. The photographs served to record the crime scene, but only after it had *changed.* It gets worse.

> **BERNARD SEGAL:** What did you observe about physical things in the living room, dining room area? Did you see anything on the floor that struck you as unusual?
> **KENNETH MICA:** Yes, sir . . . The coffee table was overturned. Also there was a wallet laying on the floor.

BERNARD SEGAL: Now this wallet, where was it in reference to the sofa and coffee table which we already have photographs here of?

KENNETH MICA: Right, sir. As you are standing in the hallway, you have a sofa here and table on the left. The wallet would be out, more or less directly out from the hallway, approximately ten or twelve feet.

MacDonald's wallet was missing. An ambulance driver, James Paulsen, later confessed to taking the wallet. He threw it out of his ambulence window after pocketing the money.[6] Things were taken; stuff was moved, including the upright flowerpot, which Grebner had seen as yet another example of a failed attempt to stage the crime scene.

BERNARD SEGAL: I would ask you please to look further at the photograph marked as A-8 and tell us whether there is anything else there in that photograph that appears different than the living room scene appeared to you as you came in?

KENNETH MICA: Yes, sir.

BERNARD SEGAL: What is that?

KENNETH MICA: It appears to be the white flowerpot.

BERNARD SEGAL: Now what is different about that white flowerpot in the photograph than as you recall seeing?

KENNETH MICA: Well, in this photograph it is standing on what appears to be on its base. I remember it as being on its side.

BERNARD SEGAL: Do you have any doubt in your mind now when you first came into the living room, after Captain MacDonald was carried out that that white flowerpot was lying on its side, rather than standing on its base as it appears in the photograph?

KENNETH MICA: No, sir . . .

BERNARD SEGAL: Now, while you were in the living room, did you observe any person or persons touch any of the objects in the living room?

KENNETH MICA: Yes, sir.

BERNARD SEGAL: Who was [that person]?

KENNETH MICA: I don't recall who he was, sir. I remember vaguely what he was wearing.

Mica described a white man in his early twenties. His hair was longer than military regulation; he was wearing blue jeans and an army field jacket. He was one unidentified man among many in a crime scene filled with unidentified onlookers, interlopers.

> **BERNARD SEGAL:** And what did you observe this person, whom you have described, do?
>
> **KENNETH MICA:** Well, sir, he was standing there, and everybody was sort of just standing around waiting to see what was going to happen next. He walked across—across the rug there and as he walked past the coffee table he bent down as if to pick up something. Someone said—and again I don't know who it was that said it—but someone said, "Don't touch anything," and he said, "Oh." At that time he proceeded to walk across and sit down on the couch.
>
> **BERNARD SEGAL:** Did he actually touch the flowerpot?
>
> **KENNETH MICA:** Yes, sir, I believe he did . . .
>
> **BERNARD SEGAL:** . . . When you left the MacDonald house, the wallet was still on the rug where you described it?
>
> **KENNETH MICA:** Yes, sir.
>
> **BERNARD SEGAL:** The white flowerpot was still lying on its side as you had observed it?
>
> **KENNETH MICA:** No, sir.
>
> **BERNARD SEGAL:** What position was it in? Was it on its base?
>
> **KENNETH MICA:** It was on its base.
>
> **BERNARD SEGAL:** And how had it gotten from its position of lying on its side to standing on the base?
>
> **KENNETH MICA:** I don't know for certain, sir, but I believe it was that man who sat on the couch. I believe he sat it upright.

———

It is a comedy of errors. MacDonald was accused of having staged the crime scene, but could anyone be sure of the position of anything? Someone had repositioned the flowerpot. What about the coffee table? Had someone repositioned it, too? Was it really in an impossible position? William Ivory, one of the principal CID investigators, took the stand and was questioned by Somers:

> **CLIFFORD SOMERS:** Mr. Ivory, I'll back up a question so it will be clear in your mind what we were getting at. Have you ever had an occasion to tip that coffee table over?
>
> **WILLIAM IVORY:** Yes, sir, I have.

CLIFFORD SOMERS: And how many times was this done?

WILLIAM IVORY: I'd say thirty times, at a minimum.

CLIFFORD SOMERS: And with what degree of force was it done?

WILLIAM IVORY: The degree of force was anything from being violently over thrown, kicked in varying degrees on down to balancing the table on its legs and let it fall.

CLIFFORD SOMERS: Would you describe for us what the effect of these experiments was?

WILLIAM IVORY: The effect was that each time the table was kicked or whatever, instead of landing on its edge, as it was found by myself that morning, it would—it was a very top-heavy table—in other words, it would just keep right on rolling until it landed on its top with four legs straight in the air. Now, as I say, this was done with varying forces and so many times that I know of—thirty times that I have done it—other people have done it and observed the same end results. It would just roll over by itself or there is a rocking chair that was sitting by the over turned or the upturned coffee table, and if the table were to hit that chair, rather than stop it is so top-heavy that it would keep right on going, and slip right on the chair. When it was tipped, of course the magazines were placed on top of the table. The plant pot with the plant and root ball inserted in the plant pot were put on the table, and again, each time it was overthrown, overturned, however you want to term it, the magazines, instead of just falling under that table would just slide right across the rug, and the plant with its pot, if a lot of force was exerted upon the table to turn it over, it would fly—root ball and pot would stay together each time, and it stayed together regardless.[7]

Ivory was arguing that the coffee table could never just land that way. It had to be *placed* in that position. The adjacent rocking chair played a supporting role. Perhaps *it* could have been responsible for the impossible position of the coffee table. But Ivory was careful to exclude that possibility. In his thirty iterations of knocking over the table—think of them as reenactments—even when the coffee table hit the rocking chair, it still ended up completely overturned.

Colonel Rock became impatient with these seemingly endless discussions and decided to go to the crime scene and perform the "experiment" himself. He announced the results later in the hearing:

WARREN ROCK: Next, at this time I would like to read a statement concerning my visit to 544 Castle Drive. Let the record reflect that during our recess, on 19 August 1970 between the hours of 2100 and 2200 Captain Beale and I were escorted by

Mr. Grebner, Chief, CID Fort Bragg, to revisit 544 Castle Drive. Captain Beale made all arrangements with Mr. Grebner. I specifically instructed him to inform Mr. Grebner that at no time would I discuss the facts of the case with Mr. Grebner or ask any questions. These instructions were obeyed completely during my visit and Mr. Grebner's sole function was to secure the premises. During my visit I made certain observations as a result of entering all rooms. I now wish to inform counsel for both sides of the relevant observations as follows:

(1) In the utility room I generally noted the titles of the many pocket type books located therein.

(2) I noted the presence of feathers in several rooms.

(3) I read the messages on the several Valentine cards in the dining room.

(4) I measured and noted that the height of the ceiling in the living room was the same as the height of the master bedroom ceiling.

(5) I observed that [there] were no nicks on either the living room ceiling or the ceiling in Kimberley's room.

(6) I saw a few pair of rubber surgical gloves under the kitchen sink, apparently in their original packaging.

(7) I simulated the lighting conditions as per the accused's testimony. From a prone position on the couch, the length of which I noted, I was able to discern the facial features of Captain Beale at the end of the couch. The visibility increased considerably when I substituted as my source of light the lamp on the small dining room buffet.[8]

(8) And finally, I kicked over the coffee table. It struck the side of the rocking chair and came to a rest on its edge.

And so many days and several thousands of pages of testimony later, Colonel Rock and Grebner finally stood in the MacDonald living room next to the coffee table. Rock gave it a kick and subsequently testified about the result: "I kicked over the coffee table. It struck the side of the rocking chair and came to rest on its edge." In other words, it landed in a way that had been proven impossible by Grebner and Ivory in their various attempts to knock it over.[9]

Colonel Rock's proof was similar to Samuel Johnson's refutation of the philosophy of George Berkeley. Berkeley had claimed that the physical world does not exist. Johnson kicked a rock and said, "I refute it thus."

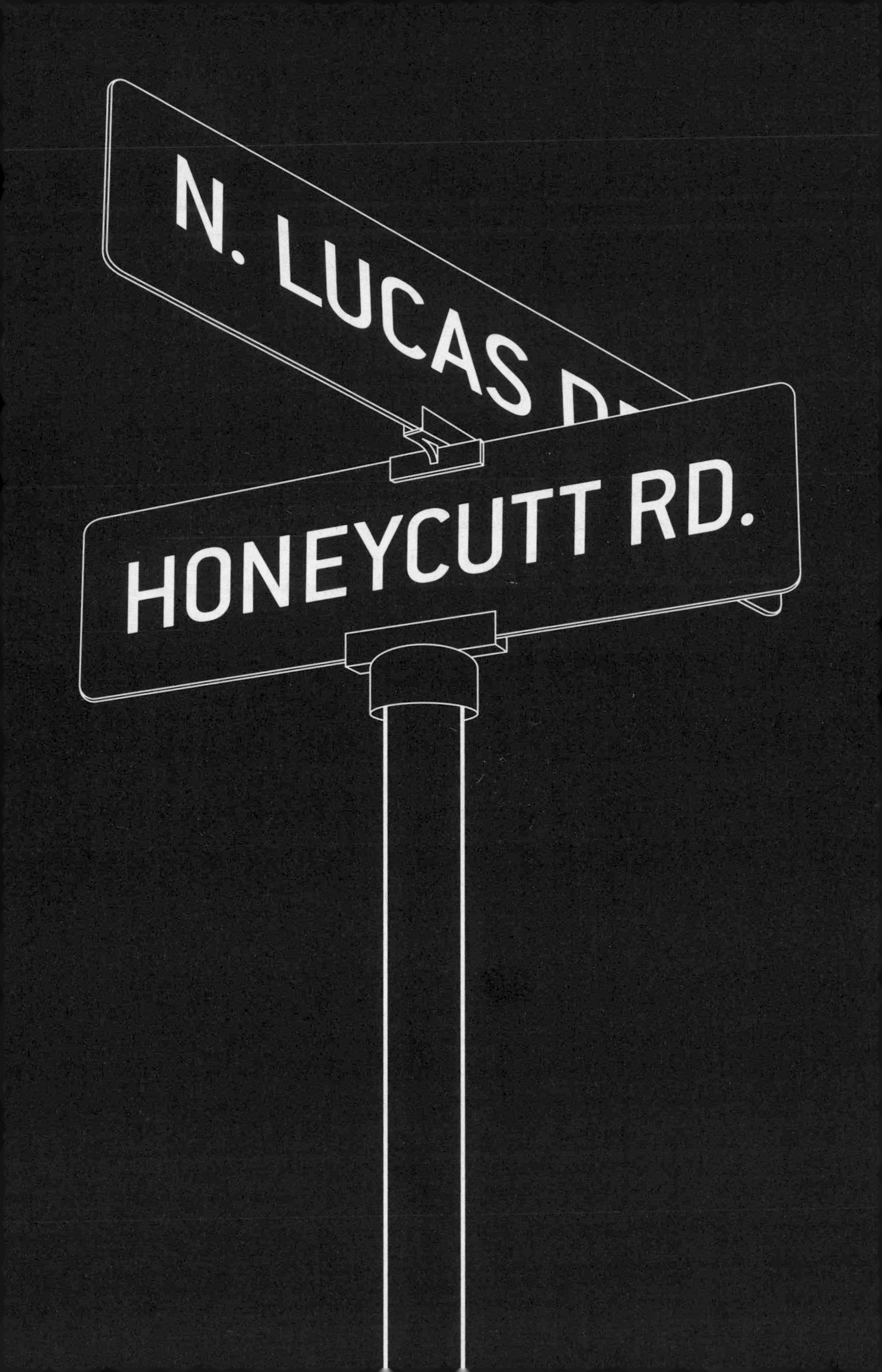
N. LUCAS
HONEYCUTT RD.

THE GIRL WITH THE FLOPPY HAT

In the middle of the Article 32 hearing, Ken Mica, who had already testified, bumped into MacDonald's mother, Dorothy, at the PX (post exchange). They were shopping. His conscience had been bothering him. He told her he had seen something—arguably an important piece of evidence—but as far as his superiors were concerned, he had seen nothing.

Mica took the stand again. This time for the defense. He revealed that he had seen a woman who matched the description he had heard MacDonald give—a blond woman wearing a floppy hat—a couple of blocks from the MacDonald house, on the night of the murders.

> **BERNARD SEGAL:** Would you tell the investigating officer approximately what location you observed a person?
>
> **KENNETH MICA:** Sir, I observed a person on the corner of Honeycutt Road and North Lucas.
>
> **BERNARD SEGAL:** And when did you observe that person in regard to the radio message that you received?
>
> **KENNETH MICA:** We observed this person as we were responding to the message. It was after we received the message.
>
> **BERNARD SEGAL:** And you were on your way to 544 Castle Drive?
>
> **KENNETH MICA:** Yes, sir.
>
> **BERNARD SEGAL:** What sex was this person that you observed?
>
> **KENNETH MICA:** Female.

BERNARD SEGAL: Can you describe to the investigating officer the appearance of that female, including any clothing that she may have had on that you recall?

KENNETH MICA: Yes, sir. She appeared to be wearing a type of a raincoat, dark color, which came to just above her knees. Also she was wearing a wide-brimmed hat.

BERNARD SEGAL: Was she a member of the Caucasian race?

KENNETH MICA: Yes.

BERNARD SEGAL: Did you have occasion to note anything about her hair?

KENNETH MICA: What I could see—I really didn't pay that much attention to it at the time—but it appeared to be approximately shoulder length.[1]

Segal asked for additional details—particularly, how *unusual* was this? Were there lots of women standing on street corners in the rain at 4:00 a.m. in this residential area?

BERNARD SEGAL: Specialist Mica, have you had occasion to patrol this particular area prior to February 17, 1970?

KENNETH MICA: Yes, sir.

BERNARD SEGAL: How often have you been through there on patrol?

KENNETH MICA: I'd say at least fifteen or twenty times.

BERNARD SEGAL: And have you had occasion to be in this area on patrol in the early morning hours?

KENNETH MICA: Yes, sir.

BERNARD SEGAL: Do you often observe females standing on the corner of the street at that time of the night in that particular area? . . .

KENNETH MICA: No, sir, it is not usual.

Minutes after seeing the woman, Mica arrived at 544 Castle Drive and heard Mac-Donald describe the assailants. Segal specifically asked Mica if he had made "any connection between his [MacDonald's] statement and the female you observed on the highway."

KENNETH MICA: Yes, sir.

BERNARD SEGAL: And what, if anything, did you do as the result of fitting those two pieces of information together?

KENNETH MICA: Well, sir, I turned around and Lieutenant Paulk and a few other MPs were behind me. I told Lieutenant Paulk at that time that I'd seen a female standing on the corner, and for them to send a patrol down to see if he could find her.

BERNARD SEGAL: Did Lieutenant Paulk indicate any response to the statement you made to him about the female you had seen?

KENNETH MICA: Well, sir, I didn't pay too much attention to what he did, but he was looking right at me when I told him. I know he heard it.

As Segal continued his questioning, it emerged that Mica had told his superiors—including the head of the investigation, Fort Bragg's provost marshal, Colonel Robert Kriwanek—about the woman on the corner.

BERNARD SEGAL: Can you tell us when you told Colonel Kriwanek about this young woman that you saw?

KENNETH MICA: Yes, sir, it was early that morning. I believe it was somewhere around five a.m.

BERNARD SEGAL: You are talking about the morning of February 17?

KENNETH MICA: Yes, sir . . .

BERNARD SEGAL: Did you have occasion to mention the description or the observation of this young woman to any other persons concerned with this investigation and the prosecution of this case?

KENNETH MICA: Yes, sir.

BERNARD SEGAL: To whom did you mention it?

KENNETH MICA: I remember mentioning it to an FBI agent that questioned me that night.

BERNARD SEGAL: You say that night. You mean the evening of February 17?

KENNETH MICA: Yes, sir.

———

And there was another surprise. William Posey, a laundry deliveryman, living in Haymount, the hippie area of Fayetteville, had also seen something the morning of February 17. He had read about the murders in the *Fayetteville Observer* and learned that MacDonald's lawyers were staying in town at the Heart of Fayetteville Motel. The motel was on his delivery route, and so he stopped in and told his story to Bernie Segal.

On August 13, 1970, Segal had him retell his story on the stand:

BERNARD SEGAL: Did you have any occasion to become awakened or to awake on February 17th? . . .

WILLIAM POSEY: I was fixing to get up to go to the restroom, and all of a sudden I heard a car whip in. There was a lot of laughing and carrying on, so I walked around to my front door to see what was going on . . .

BERNARD SEGAL: Now what happened when you heard this sound of the car pulling into the driveway and the voices? By the way, can you describe what the voices were saying or how they sounded?

WILLIAM POSEY: No, they were just, you know, laughing, you know. I didn't pay any attention to what they were saying. I don't believe they were saying too much, really. Just laughing, cutting up, giggling a lot. This type of thing . . .

BERNARD SEGAL: Could you indicate as to approximately how many voices there appeared to be?

WILLIAM POSEY: Well, there was more than two, and there was more than two people in the car. It was—it was a crowd.

BERNARD SEGAL: Now as a result of hearing that particular noise or those sounds, what did you do?

WILLIAM POSEY: Well, I walked around to my front door to see what was going on, and I noticed that the lights were on in the apartment—in their apartment and I looked over there and two of the girls were in there painting . . . I looked up and I saw the car that was pulled in. It was a Mustang, and the one girl got out . . . the girl I know . . .[2]

Posey went on to tell how "the girl he knows" often wore a blond wig, a floppy hat, and white boots, matching the description of the female assailant.

BERNARD SEGAL: And on the various occasions that you had seen this young lady before the morning of the 17th of February, would you describe, you know, what her normal wearing apparel was?

WILLIAM POSEY: Well, she had this purple outfit, you know, with the vest-type thing that she wore all the time. It was kind of silky, and she had a big old white floppy hat that she wore, and she had a pair of white boots that she wore a lot, and she use [sic] to—I mean the hat was part of her because you very seldom, you know, when she went out she always had the hat with her. I mean very seldom did you see her without the hat, and once or twice she had worn a blonde wig, you know, she had a blonde wig too, and she had worn it once or twice, but she didn't wear it too often, not real regular.

BERNARD SEGAL: Now did you have any occasion to mention the episode at the time it happened to any other person, your observance of the girl coming into the driveway at that time of morning?

WILLIAM POSEY: Well, you know, they've done a lot of crazy things over there, but that was about the craziest thing I'd seen them, painting away at that time in the morning, so, I, you know, I got my wife up and I—I brought her over to the front door to show her what was going on.

Posey then related a conversation he had about the woman with the floppy hat needing an alibi for the night of February 17.

BERNARD SEGAL: Now did you have any conversations with this young woman?

WILLIAM POSEY: Well, about a week or two after, a friend of hers who was a friend of mine, Paul Bowman, he was getting out of the Army, and I owed him some money for a telephone bill, and so he was, you know, over there with them, and so he was by the fence and I saw him. My wife and I were in the house and I went out to talk to him and my wife was standing on the porch. I started talking to him, and then we got on the subject about—she said that the police had questioned her several times about it, and so he said that she needed an alibi, and then she walked up, you know, in the meantime, with the three of us standing there, and they were both on the other side of the fence, and so I said, "Well, I could be your alibi, because I saw your girlfriends painting in their apartment, and I saw you when you got out of the car that morning." . . .

BERNARD SEGAL: Did she ever use the word "alibi," or [did] the word "alibi" come up in her presence?

WILLIAM POSEY: Paul, you know, brought up the word "alibi." He said that she needed an alibi.

BERNARD SEGAL: And what, if anything, did you say or do in response to his statement, that he thought she needed an alibi?

WILLIAM POSEY: Well, I made the remark, I said, "Well, I can be her alibi because I saw her that morning. I saw her two girlfriends painting the apartment, then I saw her when she come up and joined them, you know." And then when I said that, she kind of backed off and they had to go, they left, they left—they just dropped the subject then.

BERNARD SEGAL: What was your relationship with this young lady after the morning, after the day that you told her that you had seen her on the morning of 17 February?

WILLIAM POSEY: Well, I mean, she kind of shied away from me then, and then she left shortly after that.

BERNARD SEGAL: How long after that particular conversation did she leave?

WILLIAM POSEY: It was within a few days.

BERNARD SEGAL: You say she left. She moved away from there?

WILLIAM POSEY: She left completely.

Near the end of the Article 32 hearing, MacDonald's attorney, Bernard Segal, recalled William Ivory. It was revealed that the CID had known about the young woman—now identified as Helena Stoeckley—early on but had failed to investigate her thoroughly.

BERNARD SEGAL: Did you make notes of your interview with Miss Stoeckley?

WILLIAM IVORY: No, I did not . . .

BERNARD SEGAL: Is there any reason why you didn't make any notes of your interview with this lady?

WILLIAM IVORY: No particular reason, no.

BERNARD SEGAL: Isn't it standard operating procedure when you are conducting an interview that's related to an Article 32 inquiry [into] a triple homicide to make notes of interviews taken?

CLIFFORD SOMERS: I object. That's irrelevant.

BERNARD SEGAL: No, sir, it's not irrelevant. I suggest it's very relevant . . . It would be very helpful to know why an investigator would not write down all she has said so that he might even be able to refresh his own recollection, that he might be able to share with us all of her words as he was taking them down contemporaneously. It seems to me to be so elementary in procedure in criminal investigation as to defy even arguing its relevance. It seems to me we are entitled to know why a report was not made of this interview. Was it simply that the investigator treated it so lightly, as a matter of so little importance to him, that he did not trouble to take notes, or is there some other reason? . . .

HAMMOND BEALE: Your objection is overruled, Captain Somers. You may proceed, answer the question, if you can.

BERNARD SEGAL: Mr. Ivory, why were no notes taken of the interview with Miss Stoeckley?

WILLIAM IVORY: I did have a notebook with me, and I started to take notes, and she got very nervous and shied away, and I put my pen and notebook away.

THE WOMAN ON THE CORNER (1970)

	JEFFREY MACDONALD describing the female intruder (April 6, 1970)	KEN MICA describing the woman he saw (August 10, 1970)	WILLIAM "ED" POSEY describing Helena Stoeckley (August 13, 1970)
HAT	A floppy hat . . . A big hat . . .	A wide-brimmed hat . . .	This big old white floppy hat . . .
HAIR	Long, stringy blond hair . . .	It appeared to be approximately shoulder length . . .	She had a blond wig . . . [that] was long and stringy . . .
DRESS	I thought I saw knees as I was falling . . .	A raincoat, dark color, which came to just above her knees . . .	She had this purple outfit . . . She started wearing black . . .
BOOTS	I thought they were brown . . .	I don't remember . . .	When it was wet . . . she would wear her boots . . .

BERNARD SEGAL: Did you make any notes at all in your notebook?

WILLIAM IVORY: I just started—I believe I wrote her name down at the top of the page.

BERNARD SEGAL: And what did she do or say to indicate that she was objecting to your making notes of what she was saying?

WILLIAM IVORY: She said something to the effect of, "What are you doing? What are you writing?"

BERNARD SEGAL: And what did you say?

WILLIAM IVORY: I said, "Nothing. I'm not writing anything," and I just put it down.[3]

The questions then addressed the various items of clothing. The boots, the large floppy hat, the blond wig.

BERNARD SEGAL: Did you ask her about a blond wig?

WILLIAM IVORY: Yes, I did.

BERNARD SEGAL: And did she admit to having owned a blond wig up until about February 17th?

WILLIAM IVORY: I asked her specifically about the blond wig, and she said that she had worn one occasionally, but that it was not hers, that it belonged to a girlfriend and she did not have it.

BERNARD SEGAL: And did she say when she returned or disposed of that blond wig?

WILLIAM IVORY: No, she did not . . .

BERNARD SEGAL: Now, did you ask Miss Stoeckley whether she would be willing to come here to this inquiry and tell us what she knew about her whereabouts of February 17th, 1970?

WILLIAM IVORY: Yes, I did.

BERNARD SEGAL: And what, if anything, did she say?

WILLIAM IVORY: She said no, she would not.

BERNARD SEGAL: Did you ask her why she would not come?

WILLIAM IVORY: She indicated she didn't want to become involved.

At this point, Colonel Rock becomes clearly incredulous and interrupts the proceedings.

WARREN ROCK: I'm sorry. She didn't want what?

WILLIAM IVORY: To become involved.

9

NO EVIDENCE

Shortly after MacDonald was interviewed by the CID on April 6, Bernie Segal hired a number of psychiatrists to examine MacDonald. Dr. Robert Sadoff was the first. This is a report from Dr. Sadoff's three-hour examination on April 21, 1970.

Mental Status Examination: Reveals Captain MacDonald to be an average size, good-looking male who is neatly dressed in tasteful clothing. He presents his difficulties in a clear and pleasant manner, without evidence of psychotic thought disorder, hallucinations or delusions . . .

Summary and Recommendations: In summary, I see no evidence for serious psychopathology in Captain MacDonald . . . I see no evidence for psychotic thought progresses either present or underlying, no evidence for hallucinations or delusions. He does not reveal evidence for serious psycho-neurotic disorder with poor self control. He does not show evidence for a long-standing characterological disorder or a sociopathic personality disorder with acting out processes. He denies the use of drugs of any type, which could have stimulated an acute toxic psychotic state, resulting in loss of control and explosive violence.

In sum, I see no evidence in Captain MacDonald's personality, emotional and psychological make-up that could account either for the loss of control or calculated homicide that occurred in his home on February 17, 1970. I do see in him a depressed man who is trying to handle a very difficult situation, not only because of the loss of his wife and daughters, but also because of his loss of faith in himself, resultant shame, and feeling of helplessness and impotency.

There is nothing to suggest in my evaluation of Captain MacDonald that he is capable of committing the type of atrocious crime to his family, of which he is suspected.[1]

Unambiguous. "I see no evidence for serious psychopathology," and "there is nothing to suggest . . . he is capable of committing the type of atrocious crime." In his report, Dr. Sadoff had said that MacDonald "cries when he openly discusses the shame he feels at not being able to save his wife and children at a time when he was needed most." At the Article 32 hearing, Dr. Sadoff repeated this:

BERNARD SEGAL: Did you find as a result of your examination that Captain MacDonald was suffering from any mental illness?

DR. ROBERT SADOFF: Except for the reaction to what happened to him and his family, I would say that there was no serious mental illness that would be classifiable . . . I did not see any evidence for sociopathic personality disorder or psychopathy, or character and behavior disorders in Captain MacDonald.

Sadoff was asked by Segal about MacDonald's "normal grief reaction." According to Sadoff there was "sadness, more than sadness . . . what I would consider a normal reactive depression." Segal asked for a clarification:

BERNARD SEGAL: Now is the grief, or reactive depression you've described in Captain MacDonald, was it indicative of remorse at the loss of his wife and children, or might it have been indicative that he felt guilt for having actually committed those crimes . . . ?

CLIFFORD SOMERS: I object. The defense counsel is again leading the witness to a great extent.

HAMMOND BEALE: The objection is overruled. You may answer the question.

DR. ROBERT SADOFF: I feel that the depression he felt had a guilt element with it, but I don't think it was guilt for having participated in the killings of his wife and children. I think Captain MacDonald felt guilty that he was not able to save them. I think he felt that his whole life was geared toward a strong element of survival, that he has shown evidence in his past, football co-captain, playing baseball, that he was athletic, that he was strong; he would express his needs in a healthy masculine fashion; took boxing, ran track, had [become a] parachutist, and a Green Beret, but he was the epitome of the one who could take care of himself and protect his family when it came down to it. I think he felt guilty because he was not able to do it, and such a tragedy did occur.[2]

Sadoff was later asked by Captain Somers whether it was "mathematically impossible" for MacDonald to have committed these crimes.

DR. ROBERT SADOFF: There is the slightest possibility, but in my opinion it is extremely unlikely, and I'll tell you why. I think it's more likely that if he had a fight with his wife, I don't think this would have happened, but it is more than just— an infinitesimal amount that he might have lost control and harmed her; or if one of the children might have nagged him and bugged him on a hard day, it's possible, but remotely so, that he might have lost control with one child. But to take all three together and lose control against the world, against all three of those who were around him at that time, would have to be either that complete loss of control, which I think is most unlikely and near impossible for him, as I know him, or it has to be a cold calculated homicide, which, again, I don't feel he is capable of doing and reacting the way he is today . . .

CLIFFORD SOMERS: Is it possible—again I want to talk in a context of a person such as Captain MacDonald—for a person, assuming for the moment that he did commit such a crime, to have such complete self-control as to be able to present the picture that he presented to you?

DR. ROBERT SADOFF: Of course, I asked myself that also, and my answer is no. That if he were capable, which I don't think he is, of doing this, I don't think he would have been able to control himself and regain the composure that he has. One can see that in a person with great sociopathic tendencies—that is a person who doesn't have a conscience, doesn't have remorse—that one could commit destructive acts and still not feel guilt, not feel remorse, and compose himself. I don't see evidence for this in Captain MacDonald.

No sociopathy, no psychopathy, no character or behavior disorders. Nothing. This was the sentiment echoed by the other psychiatrists who interviewed MacDonald: James Mack, a psychologist who worked with Sadoff, for the defense; and three for the prosecution from Walter Reed Army Medical Center in Washington,

D.C.—Dr. Bruce Bailey, Dr. Henry E. Edwards, and Dr. Donald W. Morgan. Bailey, who testified, was less willing to make predictions about what MacDonald could or could not have done, but found no evidence of any kind of mental pathology. In contrast to the usual state of affairs, where defense and prosecution psychiatrists battle it out along predictable lines—here, there was unanimity.

10

NOT TRUE

The ostensible purpose of the Article 32 hearing was to determine whether there was sufficient evidence to charge the defendant in a formal court-martial. Normally, all the presiding officer has to determine is whether there is probable cause to take the case to a court-martial. But Colonel Rock went further.

Colonel Rock's findings were issued on October 13, 1970:

> (1) All charges and specifications against Captain Jeffrey R. MacDonald be
> dismissed because the matters set forth in all charges and specifications are
> not true. There are no lesser charges and/or specifications which are
> appropriate.
> (2) That appropriate civilian authorities be requested to investigate the alibi
> of Helen Stockley [sic], Fayetteville, North Carolina, reference her activities and
> whereabouts during the early morning hours of 17 February 1970, based on evi-
> dence presented during the hearing.[1]

Major General Edward Flanagan, the commanding officer at Fort Bragg, received Colonel Rock's recommendations—the charges are "not true." On October 23, 1970, he dismissed the charges because of "insufficient evidence." The distinction between Flanagan's statement—insufficient evidence—and Rock's findings—not true—became a recurring theme in all that followed.

I have considered the attached charges against Captain Jeffrey R. MacDonald . . . In my opinion there is insufficient evidence available to justify reference of the charges for trial by court-martial. Consequently, I have dismissed the charges.[2]

––––––––

MacDonald's friend and military lawyer, Mike Malley, summed up his feeling about the case in his journal:

I don't know where all of it leads. The Army officially dropped charges on October 28, and Col. Rock said the charges were untrue. That is right, and Jeff is free to go on wherever he wants. But the police involved, the CID, and probably the U.S. Attorney have not, to my knowledge, admitted their mistakes, have not come to grips with the confusion that engulfed everyone—and that is dangerous.

They have, I suppose, no poetry in them, no belief in tragedy, only in color photographs of blood and bodies lying dead, with no interest in the people who used to be the bodies, or in the people who remember the people whose bodies are lying dead in the color photographs. The government will not admit that human beings once figured in this case, still do, still remember, are sad, afraid, confused . . .

I am glad I was there, had some part in restoring to a good friend his freedom and some sense of self-respect. I still am confused and upset by a lot of my own emotional feelings of affection and dislike which grew out of the case—my image of myself before was of a rather detached and "professional" person, and that image suffered considerably. Getting to know Jeff made it worthwhile, though. He is the most courageous, decent person I know, whose friendship I value over most other things in my life—an emotional investment in the fate of a good man who I hope disproves by his future good luck my general pessimism about mankind. I like myself a little more than I used to, though I am harder for me to live with, knowing I am capable of some compassion. I suppose all that's left to do is go on from there, and see what happens.[3]

––––––––

Even though Colonel Rock had requested that civilian authorities investigate Stoeckley, the FBI refused to take on the case. FBI director J. Edgar Hoover sent a telex to Robert M. Murphy, the special agent in charge of the Charlotte office:

UNDER NO CIRCUMSTANCES SHOULD WE BECOME INVOLVED IN THIS
MATTER SINCE THE ARMY HANDLED THIS CASE POORLY FROM ITS
INCEPTION. IF THERE IS ANY INDICATION THAT THE USA ANTICIPATES
AUTHORIZING PROSECUTION, SUCH A MOVE WILL BE OPPOSED BY THE
BUREAU AND TAKEN UP WITH THE DEPARTMENT. CHARLOTTE KEEP
THE BUREAU CURRENTLY ADVISED OF ALL DEVELOPMENTS.[4]

———

Hoover had declined to become involved, but James C. Proctor, an assistant
United States attorney (AUSA) for the Fayetteville area, and the son-in-law of
newly appointed federal judge Franklin Dupree, wrote a letter to SAC Murphy. He
was once again asking for it to be reopened.

The wording of the letter lays out for us what was to happen in the next forty
years. Stoeckley was to be investigated not as a possible suspect; she was to "be
investigated so as to eliminate any possibility" of her being a suspect.

Dear Mr. Murphy:
. . . On Friday, October 30, 1970, Mr. Warren H. Coolidge, United States Attorney
for the Eastern District of North Carolina, made a request to your office, said
request also being communicated to the Department of Justice that this case
may be reopened for a complete investigation. It is very important that the
request made by Captain Somers' letter of 5 August 1970 be complied with as
soon as possible. There is a possibility that this matter will be presented to
a Grand Jury during the week of 9 November 1970 and we will desperately
need the information requested in Captain Somers' letter of 5 August 1970. We
also request an immediate follow-up of the request made by Colonel Rock that
Helena Stokely [sic] and William Posey, 505 Pearl Street, Fayetteville, North
Carolina, be investigated so as to eliminate any possibility of these people being
possible suspects.[5]

The grand jury was not convened, and on December 1, 1970, MacDonald was
given an honorable discharge from the army and left Fayetteville for New York
City. Kassab prepared a document accusing the army of mishandling the case. "I
put in everything I could think of. I had it printed. Rather than mail it, I decided
to personally deliver a copy to every Congressman and Senator, which I did, as
well as the Vice President and all standing committees. It worked."[6]

The "everything I could think of" document is addressed to the "Gentlemen of the Senate & Congress."[7]

THIS ARTICLE IS WRITTEN AS AN APPEAL FOR A CONGRESSIONAL INVES-
TIGATION INTO THE ARMY'S HANDLING OF THIS CASE AND EVERYTHING
SURROUNDING THE MURDERS AND THE INVESTIGATION. AN EFFORT MUST
BE MADE BY SOME INVESTIGATIVE BODY, OTHER THAN THE ARMY'S CRIMINAL
INVESTIGATION DEPARTMENT, TO FIND THE MURDERERS. THEY ARE STILL
AT LARGE, MAYBE TO KILL AGAIN. WHOSE FAMILY WILL BE NEXT?

What follows is a nine-page summation of all the errors made by the CID. It is titled:

THE MacDONALD CASE
PROSECUTION OR PERSECUTION?
EVIDENCE OR THEORY?

It is a blistering attack on the army—the CID in particular. A list of grievances. Thousands of interviews had been conducted, but the CID admitted "that all of those interviews produced only words of praise about Colette and Jeff Mac-Donald." Colonel Robert Kriwanek, the provost marshal, had been grossly incompetent. So incompetent that he was replaced and dispatched to Korea. But Kassab places the blame for the prosecution of his son-in-law squarely in his lap. It was Kriwanek who had called a press conference and placed MacDonald under house arrest. Kassab went on:

A C.I.D. agent Robert Shaw, when questioned as to what was done with the many sets of fingerprints, that could not be identified with any persons ever known to have been in the house, and were they sent to the F.B.I. lab in Washington for comparison with their files? replied "I didn't know the F.B.I. performed that service."
It was apparent from footprints found in the master bedroom that Kimberly, my eldest granddaughter, was there when her mother was attacked, yet she was found in her own bedroom. In regard to this, the following fantastic statement was made by a C.I.D. agent. "When hippies kill someone they let the body stay where it falls, they don't move it."
The Army's so-called fingerprint expert admitted that many photographs he had taken of fingerprints did not come out, so he went back to photograph them

a second time, however when he removed the tape that was covering them, he inadvertently destroyed them. When questioned as to his qualification as an expert, he admitted that his formal education in fingerprinting consisted of a six weeks correspondence course.

After much prodding by the defense, the Army finally admitted that my daughter's jewelry box had blood on it and unidentified fingerprints. They also admit that they didn't think to ascertain whether any jewelry was missing. Two rings my wife had given Colette which were family heirlooms were gone. It was established at the hearing that no one had taken an inventory of the contents of the house, and as of the end of the hearings it still had not been done.

The girl Capt. MacDonald described was carrying a lit candle during the murders. Only after insistence by the defense did the C.I.D. admit that candle drippings had been found in various rooms, further arguments ensued before the prosecution would produce the lab reports on the drippings. It turned out that the chemical analysis showed that the drippings did not come from any candle in the MacDonald house.

I could go on and on about shameful testimony and suppression of evidence by the C.I.D. and the prosecution that has brought disgrace to the United States Army, testimony that was so obviously perjured. For this reason the Army has consistently refused to make public the transcript of the hearings. They have absolutely refused to give me a copy to aid me in the investigation to find my daughter's and granddaughters' murderers, nor will they release Col. Warren Rock's report of this shameful episode.

BOOK TWO

1970 ■ **November 17**
Jeffrey MacDonald calls Freddy Kassab and tells him that he has killed one of the perpetrators.

December 5
Jeffrey MacDonald is honorably discharged from the army. He moves to New York City.

December 5
Freddy Kassab sends a nine-page letter detailing the CID's mismanagement of the case to every member of Congress.

December 15
Jeffrey MacDonald appears on *The Dick Cavett Show.*

1971 ■ **January 1**
An investigation begins into Kassab's claims of CID misconduct. It is led by Jack Pruett and Peter Kearns, two agents from the CID's national headquarters in Washington, D.C.

January 5
The Fort Bragg office of the CID is cleared of all charges.

January 15
The CID formally assumes responsibility for the reinvestigation of the MacDonald murders. Kearns and Pruett are put in charge of the reinvestigation.

February 1–2
The CID interviews former neighbors of the MacDonalds at Fort Bragg.

February 7
Kearns and William Ivory consult with forensic psychiatrist Dr. James Brussel.

February 11
Kearns and Pruett visit the Kassabs at their home. The Kassabs indicate they will cooperate with the reinvestigation.

February 19
Kearns and Pruett interview MacDonald at Bernie Segal's office in Philadelphia.

April 23
Helena Stoeckley, during an interview prior to her polygraph examination, confesses to being present at the homicides.

April 24
Helena Stoeckley is questioned further. CID polygrapher Robert Brisentine concludes that Stoeckley is convinced she was present at the murders.

June 27
The Kassabs host a "parting dinner" for Jeffrey MacDonald, who is moving to California. Helen Fell is one of the guests.

1971
cont.

October 30

Freddy Kassab calls Kearns to tell him that MacDonald lied about killing one of the assailants.

November 1

Freddy Kassab, upset that MacDonald returned to Long Island without telling him, writes a letter to him.

1974 **April 30**

The Kassabs and attorney Richard Cahn file a citizen's criminal complaint with the chief federal judge of the Eastern District of North Carolina, requesting a grand jury to indict MacDonald for murder.

August 12

A grand jury is convened to hear the complaint against MacDonald.

1975 **January 24**

The grand jury indicts MacDonald on three counts of murder. He is arrested at his home in Huntington Beach, California.

TOTALLY WRONG

There is no trap so deadly as the trap you set for yourself.
—Raymond Chandler, *The Long Goodbye*

On December 11, 1970, Walter Cronkite began a report on the "Green Beret murders" with the line, "Jeffrey MacDonald is a man under a cloud." It cuts to an interview with MacDonald and Congressman Allard Lowenstein, who had agreed to help with the case. They are seated on a couch in Lowenstein's Washington office, under a map of Southeast Asia.

Another blistering attack on the CID. Less than three months had passed since the conclusion of the Article 32 hearing and Colonel Rock's report that the charges against MacDonald were "not true." But the case remained unresolved. MacDonald remained a possible suspect, if only because no one else had been arrested or accused.

Days later, MacDonald appeared on *The Dick Cavett Show*. Lowenstein organized the *Cavett* appearance as part of a campaign to have the investigation into the murders reopened.

The show *did* draw attention to the case, but not as MacDonald had imagined. Some thirty-seven years later Cavett was interviewed by Bill Lagattuta for the CBS News show *48 Hours,* in an episode on the Jeffrey MacDonald case called "Time for Truth." It was a reminder of just how consequential MacDonald's interview had been.

DICK CAVETT: He knew how to do it, as they say in the talk-show trade. He knew how to handle himself.

BILL LAGATTUTA: Dick Cavett remembers well the night he was face-to-face with MacDonald.

DICK CAVETT: His affect is wrong, totally wrong. My affect was, "Gee, to find your wife and kids murdered." And even his answer to that was something like, "Hey, yeah, isn't that something?" Almost sounded like Bob Hope. Very like Bob Hope.[1]

————

A battle of affects. Mine was okay; his was wrong, totally wrong. Was the problem a problem of affects?

When he appeared on the show, MacDonald was focused not on the murderers of his family—the four "hippie killers"—but on the wrongs committed against him by the military investigators.

DICK CAVETT: My next guest is the central figure in this matter: Dr., now, Jeffrey MacDonald.

[*Applause.*]

DICK CAVETT: I call you Dr. MacDonald now, right?

JEFFREY MACDONALD: That's right. It's ex-captain and doctor.

DICK CAVETT: Yeah. I hope this isn't too painful for you. I feel like the journalist who asks the gory question. Could you talk about what happened, on that night in February?

JEFFREY MACDONALD: Well, I could skim through it briefly. To get deep into it does produce a lot of emotion on my part. But, very briefly, my wife went to an evening course at North Carolina, on post at Fort Bragg. And I took care of the children and put away the dishes. My wife came home, and we had a before-bedtime drink, really. We watched a late-night talk show.[2]

MacDonald smiles sheepishly as the audience laughs. Cavett asks him about the hippies.

DICK CAVETT: I guess we all read—most of us either read about it or heard about it on the radio, or something. And the story came out the one way, the first way: that the murder was committed by some people who were described as "hippie" in appearance. And then later, suddenly, that you had been charged. What evidence suddenly appeared that made you be charged?

JEFFREY MACDONALD: Well, at the risk of saying unbelievable things—but they're true—there was no evidence, which is the really fascinating thing about the whole case. What they did was, apparently, made some really gross, incompetent errors of judgment as they arrived at the house that night, approximately 4:30 to 5:00 a.m. And proceeded for the next six weeks along the wrong lines—looking at me, basically—all the while saying they were investigating this group of four people. And six weeks after the crime was committed they called me over for a conference. They had never really even questioned me, if you can believe that.

DICK CAVETT: Six weeks, now, has gone by?

JEFFREY MACDONALD: Right. They called me in and questioned me. It was really an interrogation. They turn the light up in front of your face, you know, and have all these little tricks. And they told me to go back to work. So I left the room and went back to work. And the next thing I knew it was on the radio that I was considered the prime suspect. And my commanding officer called me and told me he was putting me in confinement. So I had five armed guards outside my room with loaded .45s. And I couldn't make a phone call for three days. And friends of the family from Newville, Pennsylvania—Bob and Marian Stern—retained a civilian lawyer for me. And he got a hold of me, finally, after much trial and tribulation. Eventually, I was charged on May 1, and we underwent this charade of a hearing.

DICK CAVETT: Yeah, I'd love to get into some of the details of that, because they're most interesting. But had, had you been guilty, then you presumably would have inflicted sixteen wounds on yourself—

JEFFREY MACDONALD: Twenty-three.

DICK CAVETT: Twenty-three wounds on yourself. What was the theory about that?

JEFFREY MACDONALD: Well, apparently, they didn't think enough. I'm not being snide in any manner. I mean, apparently they really didn't think about any of these little things, like a motive for the crime, or how I could inflict twenty-three wounds on myself—some of which were potentially fatal . . .

DICK CAVETT: What's the motive for this? I still want to get some more of those details. Did it seem like a nightmare at that time? It's always easy to say, "He went through a nightmarish experience." Did you know that it was real and that it was happening, or did it actually seem like a dream?

JEFFREY MACDONALD: Yes. It still at times seems like a dream. "Nightmare" is a very mild term, really, for that night. What happened since has gotten so unbelievable—I mean, just getting worse and worse and worse—that you run out of words. "Unbelievable" kind of says it, but then you keep saying it, and it doesn't mean anything after a while.

DICK CAVETT: Yeah.

JEFFREY MACDONALD: There were no facts against me, as Colonel Rock's very beautiful report illustrates. He spent three months in the hearing, and then he spent five weeks writing his report. And the report says, and I think I'm saying it verbatim, that he recommends in the interest of military justice and discipline that all charges be dropped because they *aren't true* . . .

DICK CAVETT: Tell who Colonel Rock is, as opposed to the army investigators.

JEFFREY MACDONALD: Colonel Warren Rock was appointed as an investigating officer to look into the evidence to see if I should be court-martialed for the murders. And he actually acted as judge and jury for this three-month hearing. And fortunately—I was fortunate in getting a very intelligent, strong man, who could withstand some of the pressures that the army was bringing to bear. There were people in the army who wanted a court-martial, regardless of any evidence.

DICK CAVETT: Could that just be because they have to find somebody?

JEFFREY MACDONALD: Yes, that was a large part of it, I think. Absolutely. I think that's where I came up, at six weeks. They had done really nothing, performed very incompetently, and they realized that they had to do something. And they, uh, charged me.

DICK CAVETT: Well, let's talk about some of those things they did or failed to do when we come back. We have a message, and we'll be right—right back.

[*Commercial break.*]

I have watched the Cavett interview alone and with others—some disposed to believe that MacDonald is guilty, others that he's innocent. There is no argument. There *is* something weird about his affect. But appearing on a network talk show can be a deer-in-the-headlights kind of thing. Just how is one *supposed* to act? Break down in tears? Demand vengeance?

After the break, MacDonald talked briefly about Stoeckley. And about the girl who had been seen by Ken Mica near the crime scene that night. But mostly he talked about the botched investigation, the incompetence of the army investigators, and their claims that the crime scene had been staged. And clearly, the question that was still on everybody's mind: Did he do it?

DICK CAVETT: Do people look at you and say, "How do we know he didn't do it?"

JEFFREY MACDONALD: Most people, in face-to-face meetings, have been nice. I must say that. But I don't think I'm being paranoid when I say that there is certainly a flavor of suspicion in a lot of people's minds. And it comes out in various ways. Some people pat you on the back, as if to say, "Well, we know you did it, but it's okay, anyway." And other people say, "Well, it's going to be very hard to have patients come visit you in the future, isn't it?"

———

Freddy Kassab was watching the show at home. He did not like what he saw. Years later Kassab testified to his feelings about that night. He was still angry. He recalled that the minute the show went off the air, his phone started ringing. "People couldn't understand how the man could go on television and almost say nothing about his family and what was done to them, just complained about what the army did to him and how much money it had cost him."[3]

Later that month, the army finally acceded to Kassab's requests for a transcript of the Article 32 hearing.[4] It was over two thousand pages, but Kassab said he read "the entire thing at least twenty times and MacDonald's testimony over a hundred times."

12

TERRIBLE, TERRIBLE, TERRIBLE IDEA

Kassab and others would point to the *Cavett* appearance as a turning point in the case.[1] But it was one among many. MacDonald found several ways to make more trouble for himself.

A month before the *Cavett* appearance, on November 17, 1970, MacDonald placed a call to Freddy Kassab. Years later Kassab wrote about it. According to him, MacDonald said he had something "very important" to say. When MacDonald expressed concern that the phone was bugged, Kassab suggested that MacDonald phone his office the next day. Kassab, who taped the conversation, says that MacDonald told him "that he had gone on the town in Fayetteville looking for the murderers and found one; that after questioning him, beating him, the fellow admitted that he had participated in the murders so Jeff killed him."[2] I asked Mike Malley about this.

MICHAEL MALLEY: I left right at the end of the Article 32 to go to Vietnam, and I would get letters from Jeff. And I would read the *Stars and Stripes.* And actually I remember reading the *Stars and Stripes* and there was a picture, I think on the front page, of Jeff. And I think it was on *The Dick Cavett Show.* And I read the article—or maybe it was in *Time* magazine—and he said he was in favor of the death penalty because these people killed his family. And I read that and I thought, "You know, that's really kind of stupid." Well, shortly thereafter, I got a letter from Jeff, I think—I'm not sure—saying that Freddy had wanted Jeff to go down to North Carolina and hunt for the killers, and Jeff said he told Freddy that that didn't need to be done. And that's all I knew. After that, I didn't get much more information until I got out.

ERROL MORRIS: Did you see MacDonald after you got back?

MICHAEL MALLEY: When I got out of the army, I spent some time in San Antonio with my parents, and then I drove back east to see some friends, and I stopped in New York, where Jeff was working at the World Trade Center. They were still building the thing. And he was one of the doctors there, on the construction site.

And I stayed at his apartment somewhere, in Manhattan someplace. I remember I asked him what his plans were, and he said he was thinking about doing a residency at Columbia in orthopedics, but these friends of his from Fort Bragg, these doctors, had said, "Well, why don't you come out to California and work in emergency medicine?" Which he wanted to do, kind of. And I think he mentioned he'd had offers for books and things.

ERROL MORRIS: But when you stayed with MacDonald, you must have talked about developments in the case?

MICHAEL MALLEY: He said that Freddy had become difficult or something like that. And I said, "What does that mean?" And he said, well, Freddy was pushing him to do stuff and go to North Carolina and hunt for the killers, and Jeff didn't want to do that, he wanted to put it all behind him and move on. And I kind of remember saying, "Maybe you ought to just kind of distance yourself from Freddy." And Jeff said, "I can't do that. Freddy is now kind of a one-man investigator of the whole thing." I didn't know at the time, but I've subsequently learned that Freddy was the loudest complainer of all at the Article 32 when they closed the hearings, because Freddy wanted to be in there every day, listening. And he couldn't, because they closed the hearings to the public. Anyway, Freddy wanted the transcript of the Article 32. At some point, somebody gave Freddy a transcript, and Jeff mentioned that, that he'd been reading the transcript of the Article 32 and he'd been quizzing Jeff about stuff. And that's when I said, "You know, I really think you kind of ought to distance yourself."

Later that year I drove out west, and by that time Jeff had just moved out west, so I saw him there. He said Freddy was becoming a nuisance. And I said, "Why is that?" And he said, "Well, Freddy wants to keep going down to North Carolina and looking for the killers." Jeff told me at the time, I mean, I was just horrified, he said, "Well, I told Freddy, 'You don't have to do that. Me and my Special Forces buddies have taken care of them.'" And I said to Jeff, I said, "What do you mean by that?" And he said, "That's all I told him."

And I said, "Big mistake. Real big mistake. Because I don't know what you mean by that, either. I mean, it's one of these Special Forces fantasies that you folks seem to have when you're at Fort Bragg, wearing your green beret. But it's not the right thing to do." Well, apparently, right around that time is when Freddy really, really, really started reading the Article 32. I mean, he nitpicked it, from what I can gather. And he found out that Jeff had lied to him about killing the people who were involved in this.

And my guess is, right around that time, which would have been the summer or fall of 1971, is when Freddy really started turning.

ERROL MORRIS: Why do you think MacDonald would lie to Freddy like that?

MICHAEL MALLEY: What he told me is that he wanted to move on and Freddy wouldn't let him. And the only way he could get Freddy off his back was to say, "We've taken care of it. Don't worry about it. Don't do it anymore." I didn't know Freddy anywhere near as well as Jeff did, but what little I knew about Freddy was he's not the kind of guy to trifle with. He was a fanatic. He was a fanatic in Jeff's favor, and if he was going to turn, he was going to be a fanatic against Jeff. And I think that's around the time that happened, because, at some point, Freddy started agitating with the Justice Department and everybody else to reopen the case. But I think it all started when Jeff lied to him and said he'd taken care of it. And as I said, I remember saying, "Terrible, terrible, terrible idea."

13

COLONEL ROCK

Two CID documents are dated January 5, 1971. They could come from two separate universes.

In one document, Jack Pruett and Peter Kearns are in the process of absolving the three major investigators—Grebner, Shaw, and Ivory—of any wrongdoing. It is a twenty-nine-page document, signed by Colonel Henry Tufts, the CID commander. Here's one page. It is a series of claims and refutations. They did nothing wrong.

(17) CID agents recklessly conducted interviews into MacDonald's background using character assassination techniques and never evaluated the results of such investigation.

UNFOUNDED

Refutation: A principal reason for the extensive inquiry into the backgrounds of CPT and Mrs. MacDonald was to determine any possible motive anyone might have for murdering Colette and the children while leaving the strongest member of the household alive. The background investigation was necessary in order to determine the character, reputation, and way of life of the MacDonalds. The purpose of this investigation was to discover favorable as well as adverse information. Evaluation of the information received from these background inquiries led the CID to the conclusion that CPT MacDonald possessed a good reputation. No evidence has been found indicating CID agents used character assassination techniques, were reckless in their interviews, or failed to evaluate results of their inquiries.

(18) CID agents never developed a motive and assumed that this was not significant to the investigation.

UNFOUNDED

Comment: To date no motive has been found for the murders of Colette, Kimberley
and Kristen MacDonald. The absence of a clearly discernible motive supports
one of the leading theories of how the crime occurred, namely that it was a crime
of passion. However, CID agents have continued to search for a motive.

(19) CID agents recklessly placed CPT MacDonald in the position of having to
explain facts for which the CID could find no explanation, and because MacDonald
was unable to provide such an explanation, he was assumed to be guilty.

UNFOUNDED

Refutation: Although CPT MacDonald did not give adequate answers to questions
concerning certain aspects of events in his story, this alone was not the basis for
the suspicion that he murdered his family.[1]

The second document is an eight-page interview with Colonel Rock, by CID investigator Peter Kearns. It is as if the first document didn't exist. Had the CID been
cleared of mismanaging the case? Or was there still an ongoing investigation? It's
easy to think that this is just an exercise in cosmetics—that Colonel Rock was being
interviewed to no real end. In essence, Rock is being asked to comment on the
same charges that the CID has just cleared itself of. And Rock, although reserved,
finds fault with just about everything.

PETER KEARNS: Did CID agents give possible perjured testimony?

WARREN ROCK: At one point in the proceedings I was under the impression this
was a possibility, regarding certain testimony of Chief Warrant Officer Grebner
concerning the delay in submission of CID laboratory reports as evidence before
the Article 32 Investigation. When pressed on the point, Mr. Grebner changed his
testimony and admitted to error in prior testimony. Since the Government and
the accused were represented by legal counsel, the hearings were generally
conducted in an adversarial manner. The CID agents, in most instances, did not
volunteer information but answered questions. It was sometimes difficult and
a lengthy process to obtain the necessary facts.

PETER KEARNS: Were the CID agents grossly negligent?

WARREN ROCK: . . . I was impressed by the magnitude of the job facing a relatively
small number of agents and am of the impression that perhaps as a result they

were literally swamped with information. Perhaps "biased" would be a better descriptive word to use . . .

PETER KEARNS: Did CID agents take ordinary investigative steps to determine if and how the crime scene had been changed prior to their arrival?

WARREN ROCK: By the time the first of the CID agents arrived there had been, in my estimation, an unusually large number of military police in the apartment. The first effort of the agent was to try to determine what had happened and to call for assistance in a most unusual crime scene. He apparently did attempt to get excess military police out of the way and to preserve the crime scene, but to some extent it may have been too late. It is unfortunate that a relatively inexperienced military police officer (so far as capital crimes are concerned) was the duty officer . . .

PETER KEARNS: Did CID agents fail to inventory the crime scene?

WARREN ROCK: Yes. It would seem to be a logical procedure to inventory items of value, and then check with Captain MacDONALD to determine if the list was complete to cover a potential theory of theft.

PETER KEARNS: Did the CID make an erroneous conclusion that nothing was missing from the house and that no unidentified persons could have been in the house?

WARREN ROCK: Obviously something could have been missing from the house. From testimony it appears that perhaps one or more rings are missing. Unquestionably some unidentified individuals could have been in the apartment that morning. I am referring to [the period] prior to the arrival of the military police . . .

PETER KEARNS: Did CID agents assume positive identification of some of the weapons thought to have been used in the assault upon Captain MacDONALD and his family?

WARREN ROCK: I have no information relative to the CID agents' assumptions. Ownership and source of probable weapons were not established during the hearing, with the exception of the club, which was probably from the MacDONALD household . . .

PETER KEARNS: Lt. MALLEY alleges that the CID agents never developed a motive and assumed that this was not significant to the investigation. Can you comment on this?

WARREN ROCK: If a reasonably believable motive was ever developed by the CID, it was certainly never presented during the course of the Article 32 Investigation.

PETER KEARNS: Did CID agents recklessly place MacDONALD in the position of having to explain facts for which the CID could find no explanation, and because MacDONALD was unable to provide such an explanation, he was assumed to be guilty?

WARREN ROCK: This basically seems to be true; however, I would not use the word "recklessly" . . .

PETER KEARNS: Did the prosecutors, in conjunction with the CID agents, fail to produce laboratory reports concerning the wax samples found in the MacDONALD house?

WARREN ROCK: The first CID laboratory reports did not indicate a source of the wax drippings found in Kimberley's bedroom and on the coffee table in the living room. Subsequently a CID agent testified that additional candles from the MacDONALD apartment were sent to the laboratory for analysis. Toward the end of the investigation it was verbally reported by the Government that this second group of candles could not be matched with the wax drippings . . .

PETER KEARNS: Did the prosecutors and CID withhold the identity of a female resident of Fayetteville who may have been involved in the crime; further, did they not pursue the investigation of this obvious lead and withhold the information from the defense?

WARREN ROCK: I am under the impression that the CID did not know this female could have been connected with the crime until after the witness, Mr. POSEY, testified for the defense. Upon my instructions to the prosecution, CID Agent IVORY, through the Fayetteville Police Department, contacted her on two occasions. I do not think, however, that the questioning was too well-done . . .

PETER KEARNS: Mr. KASSAB alleges it was apparent from footprints in the master bedroom that Kimberley MacDONALD was there when her mother was being attacked, yet she was found in her own bedroom. In regard to this, the following fantastic statement was made by a CID agent: "When hippies kill someone they let the body stay where it falls. They don't move it." Can you comment on this allegation?

WARREN ROCK: In reference to the first question, I would only say this is Mr. KASSAB's assumption, not mine. Regarding the second question, this statement, as well as many other "fantastic" statements, was made during the course of the hearing, but I was seeking only evidence, and not assumptions or hypotheses.[2]

I called Colonel Rock, who is now in his nineties. But he hasn't been willing to talk about this case for the last forty years. Nothing much has changed. He didn't want to talk about it. And so I called Hammond Beale, the captain and lawyer who had been his advisor.

HAMMOND BEALE: It's hard to believe. MacDonald lost his wife, both kids, and then ends up losing his license and freedom forever. Pretty bad for something you didn't do.

ERROL MORRIS: You believe that he is innocent?

HAMMOND BEALE: Oh, I *know* he's innocent. I sat through the Article 32 for part of a year, and was Colonel Rock's legal advisor to rule on all the legal issues that came up. I saw every piece of evidence the government had, and hell, anytime they're arguing that the motive behind killing everybody was because the youngest kid wet the bed? Give me a break.

I went to Walter Reed when they shrunk him all up. The government was determined they wanted to get him all psychoanalyzed and all that stuff, and all that backfired on them. Even the government psychiatrist said there was no way in hell he could have done it, because he couldn't have kept it inside. He couldn't have hidden it.

ERROL MORRIS: Well, I would have certainly liked to have talked to Colonel Rock, but Colonel Rock evidently—

HAMMOND BEALE: Won't talk.

ERROL MORRIS: He is in his nineties now.

HAMMOND BEALE: Has got to be, because I'm seventy, and I know he was twenty years older than I was. He was a full colonel and I was just a captain. But what a delightful fellow—all business, of course—but just a delightful guy.

ERROL MORRIS: What was Colonel Rock's opinion of the CID investigation?

HAMMOND BEALE: He didn't think much of it, I can tell you that. They just bumbled it something terrible. But you've got to remember, most of them were young kids that had never worked a murder case in their life, particularly the MPs. And they tracked through that house and tracked blood, and picked stuff up. I remember just what a nightmare it was. But they were kids. They had never seen a murder scene with three dead bodies. I'm sure it was upsetting.

ERROL MORRIS: What was your role as legal advisor?

HAMMOND BEALE: We were there to seek out the truth, and wherever the chips fell is where they fell. And I can tell you right now, when all the evidence was in, he was not guilty of a damn thing. That's why the three-star general cut him loose and let him out of the army. And then to, what, ten years later get prosecuted in a civilian court? Really bad.

ERROL MORRIS: One of the strangest aspects of this whole story is this woman Helena Stoeckley.

HAMMOND BEALE: She was a jewel.

ERROL MORRIS: Did you ever meet her?

HAMMOND BEALE: No, never met her. Knew her address, phone number, her description, a picture of her. The CID claimed she was messed up on drugs.

Fort Bragg back at that time was an open base, or fort, or whatever you call it. Anybody could come on the fort anytime they wanted to, and by the time the cops got through screwing up the scene, it was too late. They had waited too long. So that's how Helena and her buddies got out.

But she was right there in Fayetteville. And if I remember correctly the FBI wouldn't touch it, because the CID and the MPs had screwed it up so bad they didn't want anything to do with it. And of course, we didn't have any authority to prosecute Stoeckley, because the government had no jurisdiction over civilians. That's why we turned it over to the FBI and said, "Go get 'em." But they wouldn't do it. And instead, because of the father-in-law, Freddy Kassab—wasn't that his name?

ERROL MORRIS: Yes.

HAMMOND BEALE: He was the biggest supporter MacDonald had throughout the whole Article 32 investigation, turned on him afterwards and was just determined to go and have him prosecuted. And of course, he was successful. I think it was the biggest miscarriage of justice that has ever been perpetrated.

ERROL MORRIS: As this case developed, did Colonel Rock get upset?

HAMMOND BEALE: He was upset because of the way the cops had bumbled it, and the silliness of the government's prosecutors arguing that he killed them because of the bedwetting business. What a silly bunch of bullshit.

Everything that the government would put forth was just such baloney. And the way it looked was that they had just gotten lazy. If they had only focused on trying to find the murderers instead of trying to find the most convenient person to charge. MacDonald was the only one that they had available to them—whatever.

ERROL MORRIS: But didn't MacDonald do himself a lot of damage by agreeing to an interview with those three detectives, Grebner, Shaw, and Ivory?

HAMMOND BEALE: I don't think so. I don't think that really had a whole lot to do with it, because they didn't get anything out of him. I mean, he told the truth, as best I remember what he said to them. And I think the reason why he was willing to allow them to interview him was because he hadn't done anything.

When you're young and dumb, you think that the cops really are trying to find the truth, and if you know you didn't do anything, then why not talk to them? That was kind of MacDonald's thinking on it.

A GREAT FEAR

On January 15, 1971, the CID formally assumed responsibility for the reinvestigation of the MacDonald murders.[1] Peter Kearns and Jack Pruett, the two CID agents in charge of investigating the CID since January 1, now refocused their efforts on MacDonald.

Pruett kept a diary, which provides a snapshot of their investigative interests during the first months of 1971. His first notes concerned the Kalins, MacDonald's next-door neighbors at the time of the killings. Donald Kalin, a chief warrant officer, had since been transferred to Heidelberg, Germany. From Pruett's diary:

1 February: Interview [of] Vicki Kalin at Auburn University by Agent Bennett. She admits to receiving driving lessons from MacDonald, but no involvement. Interviewed CW3 Kalin in Germany, who indicates that the family dog did not bark during the night of the murders and could provide no further information.[2]

Vicki Kalin, the "very attractive" (her mother's description) older daughter, had been a babysitter for the MacDonalds, along with Pamela, her younger sister. MacDonald had given Vicki driving lessons. And the CID remained interested in the possibility that there was something more to their relationship. She was asked a number of leading questions: Did you ever give your mother, or any other member of your family, reason to believe that there was something intimate between you and Jeff? Did Jeff ever make a pass at you during your association with him?

Do you think something might have developed out of your relationship with Jeff if your vacation had been longer?

In the investigators' report Vicki Kalin is quoted:

I like to think I was attractive to him, and I did like him, but I'm not naive enough to think that he would have had an affair with me in front of his family.[3]

The journal continues:

2 February: Interviewed Mrs. Kalin and daughter [Pamela], in Germany. Mrs. Kalin was uncooperative and would not provide hair samples or submit to fingerprinting. Neither could identify any of the knives. Mrs. Kalin did relate that during the middle of the night she heard the voice of Colette raised in anger.

According to the investigator's report, the Kalins felt they had been abused by the CID during the initial investigation. Mrs. Kalin said that "in some instances, the treatment of her family had been harsh and unprofessional. She cited, in particular, the incident, in which her daughter had been pushed, in Mrs. Kalin's mind, into identifying one paring knife as being part of the MacDONALD kitchen inventory."

The investigator in Heidelberg tried it again. He presented photographs of the alleged murder weapons—the two knives, the ice pick, and the piece of wood—to Pamela and her mother. Pamela stated that she couldn't recognize any of them.

I then asked her about the bent paring knife she allegedly identified as MacDONALD property on February 19, 1970. She stated to me that what she had said was that that particular knife could have been MacDONALD property. I asked her how familiar she was with the items in the MacDONALD kitchen, and she replied that she occasionally washed their dishes while babysitting at the MacDONALD home.[4]

The four weapons—whether they were in the house or brought in from outside—were of great interest to the CID. Where did they come from? Did they provide evidence of intruders? Or evidence that there were *no* intruders? The investigators didn't get the answer they wanted, and so they turned to another item of interest, unsourced hairs. Pamela Kalin had dyed her hair blond: "She recalls she occasionally used a white hair brush belonging to the MacDONALDs to brush her hair while babysitting." This, too, would become a relevant detail. And she was asked about the night of February 16. Just before she fell asleep, around 11:00 p.m., she was conscious of the voice of Jeffrey MacDonald in conversation with someone. She couldn't hear the words, but she was certain it was MacDonald's voice. (It was coming from the MacDonald living room, directly beneath her bedroom.) "She could not state any definite facts about the second voice, other than she felt it was a man's voice."

The Kalins had a dog, Sam, a beagle mix. A good watchdog. Supposedly. But on that morning, "they could not recall the dog barking until after the MPs began assembling."

And then there was Mrs. Kalin's vision, her Lady Macbeth moment. It appears at the very end of the CID statement. One of her daughters, presumably Pamela, was babysitting for the MacDonalds during Christmas vacation. She called home and asked to be relieved for a short period.

[Mrs. Kalin] agreed and took a *Ladies Home Journal* with her to the [MacDonald] house. She was engrossed in some article and wanted to finish it . . . Her daughter left and the house was quiet . . . She sat on the couch reading, when suddenly she was overcome with a great fear. She looked up and saw Captain MacDonald standing before her, dressed in a white shirt with rolled-up cuffs and dark slacks. He was bleeding and holding some sort of knife in his hand. The vision disappeared and a few minutes later her daughter came back.

And then there were the other neighbors, the Pendlyshoks, who lived in a detached house adjacent to the MacDonalds. Janice Pendlyshok's bedroom was about fifty feet from the MacDonald master bedroom. One more statement, one more dog:

Her dog, Sambo, was in the bedroom with her. At an undetermined time during the night of 16–17 February, Sambo woke her up with his barking . . . After shushing the dog, she heard the sounds of children crying and a woman screaming. She emphasized that she had heard these sounds concurrently.

Mrs. Pendlyshok had met Colette MacDonald at "an officers' wives coffee" just before the murders, and Colette told her that she felt so safe at Fort Bragg that she left her doors unlocked. Evidently, Mrs. Pendlyshok felt somewhat differently. About a month before, her house had been broken into. Someone had scrawled obscenities on the bathroom mirror using Mrs. Pendlyshok's lipstick. Nothing was stolen, but some of her underwear had been scattered about. Also, on the mirror was the command, "LOOK IN THE CLOSET." The intruder (or intruders) had misspelled both "look" and "closet." (Unfortunately, the report does not indicate how the words were misspelled.) Mrs. Pendlyshok looked in the closet but found nothing out of the ordinary.[5]

After the CID had finished its investigation of MacDonald's neighbors, it turned to psychiatry. Pruett's investigative journal continues:

5 February: Conducted background check on Dr. Brussels [*sic*].

7 February: Consultation with Doctor Brussels in New York City by Agent Kearns and Agent Ivory. Doctor Brussels discounted MacDonald's story of "hippie" intruders and suggests that we look for a strong motive as might be known by "Pep" Stevenson and other members of the family. Doctor Brussels suspects that the murders are a means to cover what initially started as a family fight.

The experts hired by the defense and prosecution had failed to find any significant pathology. The CID investigators felt they could do better and started shopping for a psychiatrist more congenial to their point of view.

Enter Dr. James Brussel.

William Ivory and Peter Kearns traveled to New York City on February 7, 1971. They furnished Dr. Brussel with "a briefing on the crime scene, statements of Jeffrey MacDonald, and other background and investigative data," and he provided a number of "salient" remarks that reiterated the conclusions that the CID investigators had already reached.

Dr. Brussel cut to the greatest infirmity in the prosecution's case—the need for a motive. Ivory writes in his summary of the meeting:

A clean cut motive must be established.

The bedwetting of Kristen may have been a contributing factor to an argument between the MacDONALDS but it in itself could not be considered the prime factor.

In regards to the hippie-type individuals described by MacDONALD, BRUSSEL stated that taking into consideration the fact that Kimberley had been injured in the master bedroom and carried back to her bedroom where she died. In his opinion this is not consistent with hippie types. According to BRUSSEL they would not pick up the child's body and place it in the bed and tuck the bed covers around her. He further stated that the female assailant's statement about "acid" rings false. Persons under the influence of LSD would not partake in such continued, deliberate strenuous activity such as attacking a family. He also stated that LSD is a group doing, and if one of the assailants took it, most likely all would have.

For use of this form, see AR 195-10 - TB PMG 3; the proponent agency is Office of the Provost Marshal General.

PLACE	DATE	TIME	FILE NUMBER
Fort Bragg, North Carolina	7 Feb 71		71-CID011-00015

LAST NAME, FIRST NAME, MIDDLE NAME	SOCIAL SECURITY ACCOUNT NO.	GRADE
IVORY, William F.		Crim Inves

ORGANIZATION OR ADDRESS

Det B, 3d MP Gp (CI), Fort Bragg, North Carolina

SWORN STATEMENT

I, _____William F. IVORY_____, WANT TO MAKE THE FOLLOWING STATEMENT UNDER OATH:

On 7 February 1971, Crim Inves Peter E. KEARNS and the writer interviewed Dr. James A. BRUSSEL, forensic psychiatrist, at his home, 175 W 12th St., Manhattan, New York City. Dr. BRUSSEL received a briefing on the crime scene, statements of Jeffrey MacDONALD, and other background and investigative data to include autopsy reports.

In essence, BRUSSEL advised that the following were the most salient remarks he could make regarding the conduct of the investigation at this stage:

A clean cut motive must be established.

The bedwetting of Kristen may have been a contributing factor to an argument between the MacDONALDs but it in itself could not be considered the prime factor.

In regards to the hippie type individuals described by MacDONALD, BRUSSEL stated that taking into consideration the fact that Kimberly had been injured in the master bedroom and carried back to her bedroom where she died. In his opinion this is not consistent with hippie types. According to BRUSSEL they would not pick up the child's body and place it in the bed and tuck the bed covers around her. He further stated that the female assailant's statement about "acid" rings false. Persons under the influence of LSD would not partake in such continued, deliberate strenuous activity such as attacking a family. He also stated that LSD is a group doing, and if one of the assailants took it, most likely all would have. Therefore there would have been at least four to six fairly lethargic persons in the house.

BRUSSEL stated that if hippies committed the murders, which he states he personally does not believe, it would be the first case he has heard of where they would be carrying and using an ice pick and paring knives. He pointed out that they would be involved in ritualistic killings and would use daggers or similar ceremonial type weapons. Also, if hippies had wielded the piece of wood as a club, all of the blows would be hard and vicious, and the attackers would not have struck so many blows. Dr. BRUSSEL also stated that of the information he reviewed, there is nothing to verify that any intruders were in the house. Hippies under the influence of LSD would not have entered the house by walking only on the side walk. They would "stroll" and not care where they walked. They would have left evidence of their presence, particularly if they were under the influence of LSD. Of all the drugs in use by the hippie or drug communities, Dr. BRUSSEL is of the opinion that "speed" (methamphetamine) is the drug which would make the persons act as described by MacDONALD. "Acid" (LSD) would make them lethargic, and they would not have been able to perform such continuing strenuous activities.

Dr. BRUSSEL also stated that in reference to MacDONALD's statements of how Colette used surgical rubber gloves for washing dishes, lab tests should be made to show that due to the fact that they would not protect the hands from hot water,

EXHIBIT	INITIALS OF PERSON MAKING STATEMENT	
O		PAGE 1 OF 2 PAGES

ADDITIONAL PAGES MUST CONTAIN THE HEADING "STATEMENT OF___ TAKEN AT___DATED___CONTINUED." THE BOTTOM OF EACH ADDITIONAL PAGE MUST BEAR THE INITIALS OF THE PERSON MAKING THE STATEMENT AND INITIALED AS "PAGE___OF___PAGES." WHEN ADDITIONAL PAGES ARE UTILIZED, THE BACK OF PAGE 1 WILL BE LINED OUT. AND THE STATEMENT WILL BE CONCLUDED ON THE REVERSE SIDE OF ANOTHER COPY OF THIS FORM.

Therefore there would have been at least four to six fairly lethargic persons in the house . . .

BRUSSEL stated that if the hippies committed the murders, which he states he personally does not believe, it would be the first case he has heard of where they would be carrying and using an ice pick and paring knives . . . BRUSSEL also stated that of the information he reviewed, there is nothing to verify that any intruders were in the house . . .

It was his opinion that the children were killed simply because they were witnesses to the attack on Mrs. MacDONALD or each other. He was also of the opinion that since the house was not vandalized and no food, drugs, narcotic paraphernalia or alcoholic drinks consumed or stolen, young adults or hippies most probably did not commit the murders ...

BRUSSEL related the physical and negative evidence at the crime scene refutes Dr. MacDONALD's version of the attack. In BRUSSEL's opinion, MacDON-ALD is not telling the truth but this fact alone does not mean he is the murderer.

BRUSSEL requested that he be furnished the psychological test results on MacDONALD and also the results of the Rorschach Test (ink blot) taken by MacDONALD.[6]

Brussel wondered whether the murder weapons all came from the house. He said, "[I]t would be the first case he has heard of where [hippies] would be carrying and using an ice pick and paring knives." Clearly, Brussel had not read about the LaBianca murders—one of the Manson homicides of 1969. The LaBiancas were killed with forks and knives from their own kitchen. Where drug-crazed hippies were involved, kitchen utensils were, at least in this one instance, the weapons of choice. Brussel also seemed convinced by the fact that nothing was stolen from the Mac-Donald home. A claim made by the investigators. (MacDonald had long claimed that jewelry was stolen.) But what does this really prove? Look no further than the LaBiancas. Items of jewelry and cash, clearly visible, were left undisturbed, and in a detail strangely reminiscent of the reports from the Kalins and Pendlyshoks, the neighbors did not hear barking from the three LaBianca dogs.

Brussel was lost in a world of hypotheticals. He had never examined MacDonald. He had seen nothing of the case but the CID's own reports—reports carefully selected to make a case for MacDonald's guilt. "There is nothing to verify that any intruders were in the house." Essentially, he became a psychiatric Xerox machine for the opinions of the investigators who retained him.

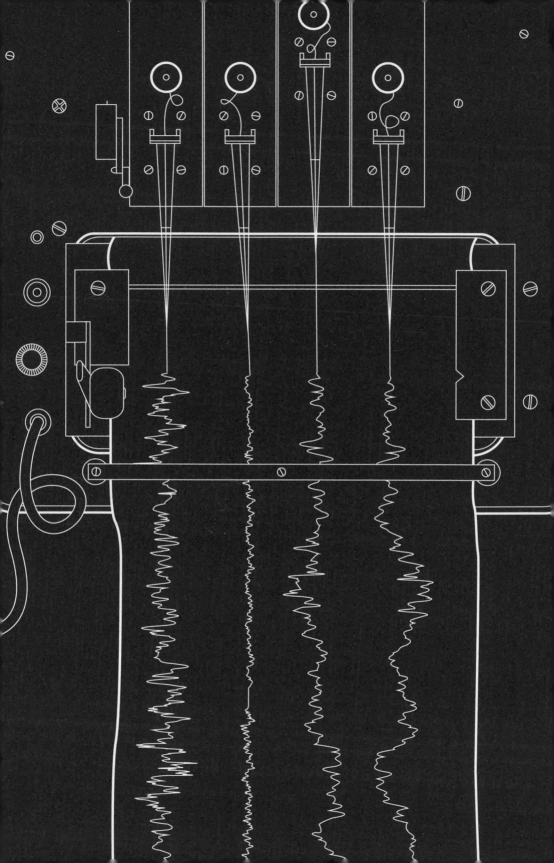

CONVINCED IN HER MIND

Richard Mahon was the member of the CID reinvestigation team assigned to investigate Helena Stoeckley. And so, from the end of 1970 through the first months of 1971 he tried to get Stoeckley to submit to a polygraph examination. He also tried to convince her to provide hair samples and fingerprints. She refused all requests.

Mahon turned to Prince Everette Beasley, a narcotics detective with the Fayetteville Police Department, who had first used Stoeckley as an informant in 1969, the year leading up to the murders. Beasley and Stoeckley had grown close. By all accounts, they were an effective team, making a number of significant drug busts. He told Mahon that "Stoeckley confide[d] in him . . . as a daughter confides in her father." And that he could convince Stoeckley to cooperate with the CID.[1] Stoeckley had moved to Nashville, and had written Beasley a letter on January 20, 1971.

I'm really sorry I didn't get to see you when I was home this time—I wanted to so badly because it looks like that may have been my last visit home. All I ever do in Fayetteville is get in trouble.

Beasley, what does the CID want of me? I didn't murder anyone?!! Are they going to keep hassling me? Is there any way I can take a polygraph to find out whether I was at MacDonald's house or not the night of the murders, without the CID finding out the results? . . . Are they still suspicious of me or can I come out of hiding now? . . . Right now I'm living in constant paranoia and need to know if that's even necessary.[2]

Dear Detective Beasley,

Hello, how are you? How are things going with the Interagency?

I'm really sorry I didn't get to see you when I was home this time – I wanted to so badly because it looks like that may have been my last visit home. All I ever do in Fayetteville is get in trouble.

Beasley, what does the CID want of me? I didn't murder anyone?!! Are they going to keep hassling me? Is there any way I can take a polygraph to find out whether I was at Mr. Dodd's house or not the night of the murders, without the CID finding out the results? That really _____ they still suspicious of me or _____ doing now. One of the agents _____ me to be fingerprinted _____ I sound like an inter- _____ I'm living in _____ need to know if thats _____ let me know anything.

Here, she wasn't refusing to take a polygraph; she wanted to take one. And there was a sentence in the letter with odd punctuation: "I didn't murder anyone?!!" A question mark followed by two exclamation marks. Was it a forceful denial, or was she asking Beasley's help in figuring out what had happened?

Mahon and Beasley traveled to Nashville and interviewed Stoeckley on March 1, 1971. Beasley took notes on the interview:

> Helena stated to me that she has been having dreams for the past few months that may indicate that she knows something about this case. I asked her then what type of dreams she had been having. She stated to me that she has dreamed of seeing people struggling and that she noticed violence being administered and that she dreamed of seeing a lot of blood . . .
>
> She again told me she had no knowledge of this night after 12:30 AM and that she does not know for sure what happened.[3]

And then an odd detail:

> After the night of the MacDONALD incident, I picked Helena STOECKLEY up for questioning in reference to this . . . She was in a joyful mood and joked about her ice pick. I then told her that this was a serious situation and to act that way . . .
>
> I have known Helena for some three (3) years. I know her to be a drug user and a drug pusher. She has furnished me with information that has resulted in the arrest and conviction of several drug dealers in the Fayetteville area.

When Helena moved to Nashville she became an informant again, this time for Jim Gaddis, a Nashville police officer. On March 25, 1971, he ran into Stoeckley during a drug bust at a house that (according to Gaddis) had been identified "as a hangout for hippies." Stoeckley asked if she could speak to him in private. It is a peculiar conversation to have with a police officer. It is both an admission that she is under suspicion for murder and an interview for a job.

> She asked me if I was familiar with the MacDonald murder case in North Carolina. I told her that I didn't know much about it. She told me that she was a suspect in the case and she asked me if I could find out if she was still "wanted" by the authorities investigating the case. I told her that I would check on it. Then she told me that she had been a police informant in North Carolina on narcotics cases and she told me that she wanted to inform for the Nashville police.

The job interview was evidently successful. Stoeckley became not just an informant, she set up a number of successful sting operations involving hidden microphones. This was the era of Watergate. People were eavesdropping on other people, even in the Oval Office of the White House.

> With her permission, we "bugged" her apartment. Through working with her, we identified about 30 drug users and/or drug dealers . . . We've also developed some other good police information. Our surveillance continues at this time.
>
> During this period, I've established a real good relationship with Stoeckley. I feel that she trusts me. On several occasions I've talked to her about the MacDonald case. She has told me a lot of things about the case. She has also contradicted herself several times about the things she previously told me . . .
>
> On April 23rd, 1971, Helena again told me that she wasn't involved in the murders but that she knew who the killers were. She wouldn't tell me who they were. When I asked her why she wouldn't tell me, she said, "those people are suffering enough as it is" . . . Whenever Helena talks about the murders, she gets real depressed. As of right now, she has me convinced that she really knows something about the murders. In fact, on the 23rd of April, she said that she wasn't involved in the actual killings but that she had been there and had witnessed the murders. But she wouldn't give me any details about it.[4]

Stoeckley was asked to take a polygraph examination. Three cops—Gaddis, Robert Brisentine (a CID polygrapher), and Richard Mahon—were present. Here are Brisentine's notes from the pre-test interview:

> During pre-test interview on 23 and 24 April 1971, Miss STOECKLEY made statements substantially as follows:
>
> A. That due to a "mental block" she does not remember her activities or whereabouts between 0030 and 0400 hours, 17 February 1970.
> B. That during a period of three or four months subsequent to the homicides in the MacDONALD residence she was convinced that she participated in the murder of Mrs. MacDONALD, and her two children.
> C. That she presently is of the opinion that she personally did not actively participate in these homicides but may have been physically present at the time of the murders.
> D. That prior to the homicides she had heard that the "hippie" element

was angry with CPT MacDONALD as he would not treat them by prescribing methadone for their addiction to drugs. Miss STOECKLEY later retracted this statement and said that she [only] thinks she heard of CPT MacDONALD before the murders.

E. That she had never been to CPT MacDONALD's residence prior to the homicides.

F. That prior to the homicides she had visited Castle Drive, Fort Bragg, North Carolina for the purpose of delivering illicit drugs to an officer she knows only as "Bob".

G. That approximately 2400 hours, 16 February 1970, she and a man named Greg Mitchell consumed LSD and Mescaline.

H. That she was using all types of drugs (Opiates-Heroin, Marijuana, depressants, stimulants, and hallucinogenics) prior to and immediately following the homicides.

I. That during April 1970, she was admitted to the University of North Carolina hospital for hepatitis and drug addiction.

J. That as a result of excessive drug use during the time of the homicides she was not always oriented as regards time, dates and surrounding.

K. That since the deaths of Mrs. MacDONALD and her children, she (STOECKLEY) has suffered nightmares whenever she sleeps.

L. That due to these frightening dreams, she is afraid to sleep, causing insomnia.

M. That her original dreams portrayed the word "Pig" in blood on the headboard of Mrs. MacDONALD's bed. Miss STOECKLEY described her dream by printing the word "Pig" horizontally on the left side of a drawn picture of a bed headboard. She asserted that in her dreams the word "Pig" is always on the left side of the headboard.

N. That during the past three or four months her dream places her on the couch in CPT MacDONALD's living room, and that CPT MacDONALD is pointing at her with one hand while holding an ice pick that is dripping blood with the other hand.

O. That during February 1970, she possessed and occasionally wore a pair of white boots, a "floppy" type white hat and a blonde wig.

P. That following the homicides she discarded the boots, wig and hat.

Q. That about the same time as the homicides she stole some floral wreathes from a florist in Fayetteville, North Carolina and displayed them in the front of her residence.

R. That one of the wreathes had the word "Mother" written on its ribbon while one or more of the other wreathes had the word "SISTER" written on them.

S. That immediately following the homicides she wore black clothing and on the day of the funeral of Mrs. MacDONALD and her children, she (Miss STOECKLEY) meditated and wore black clothing.

T. That she desired to attend the MacDONALD funerals but did not attend as none of her friends would accompany her.

U. That she went into hiding to evade police arrest subsequent to the homicides and considered fleeing from Fayetteville, North Carolina.

V. That she knew the identity of the persons who killed Mrs. MacDONALD and her children.

W. That if the Army would give her immunity from prosecution, she would furnish the identity of those offenders who committed the murder and explain the circumstances surrounding the homicides.[5]

On the morning of the twenty-fourth, the day after the pre-test interview, Stoeckley started to equivocate. Perhaps it was because she had not been given immunity from prosecution, and she thought better of continuing in the same vein. Anyway, her story became vague. She had been "incorrect in her statements," and "she only suspected some people of committing the homicides." But when Brisentine mentioned that it had been raining that night, Stoeckley corrected him: "It had been drizzling rain during the night but . . . it did not begin to rain hard until after the homicide." And when asked how she knew this, "Miss Stoeckley exclaimed, 'I have already said too much.'"

At this point, the three cops tried to convince Stoeckley to take a polygraph test. At first she refused, and then, after lunch, relented.

Gaddis was in the room; Mahon was hidden behind a one-way mirror. And Brisentine hooked Stoeckley up to the machine.

———

The notes are extensive. There is a preliminary report—something that was to be typed over for a more professional presentation—and the final report that was submitted to the CID. The draft contains edits, to be made before it became *official*.

Based on a polygraph examination conducted on 24 April 1971, it is concluded that Miss STOECKLEY is convinced in her mind that she knows the identity of those

During the interview on 23 April 1971, Miss STOECKLEY
repeatedly acknowledged knowing the identity of the persons who committed
the murders in question. However; on 24 April 1971, Miss STOECKLEY
related that she had been incorrect in her statements, had "talked too
much", and that she only suspected some people of committing the
homicides. At this time Miss STOECKLEY stated that she suspected Don
Harris, a caucasian male who told her after the homicide that he must
leave Fayetteville, North Carolina as he could not find an alibi
for the time of the murder; Bruce FOWLER, the owner of a blue Mustang
automobile in which she (Miss STOECKLEY) was a passenger or driver on
the night of the homicide; Janett FOWLER, the wife of Bruce FOWLER and
who was employed as a "Go-Go" dancer in Fayetteville, North Carolina at
the time of the homicides; Joe Kelly, a negro soldier who was assigned
to a Medical Holding Detachment at Womack Army Hospital, Fort Bragg,
North Carolina at the time of the homicides; and a negro male she knew
only as "Eddie", who introduced her (Miss STOECKLEY) to heroin. At one
time during the pre-test interview on 24 April 1971
asserted that she had been lying when she additi
the homicides and stated that Cpt LacDONALD h
Further, that her rationale was based on the
could not have entered Cpt LacDONALD's ho
neighbors or causing dogs to bark. The
homicide was alleged to have occurred at
morning and it was supposedly raining.
exclaimed that it had been drizzling ra
that it did not start to rain hard unti
the examiner inquired as to how she ac
STOECKLEY exclaimed "I have already sa
the interview Miss STOECKLEY repeated
she suspected "hippie type" individual

Based on a polygraph examination c
concluded that Miss STOECKLEY is convi
the identity of those person(s) who kill
Christine LacDONALD. It is further condl

　　　　　　　　　in her mind
is convinced/that she was physically prese
members of the LacDONALD family were killed.

No admissions were made by Miss STOECKLEY in post test interrogation.

No abnormal physiological responses were noted in the polygraph
tracings; however due to Miss STOECKLEY's admitted state of mind and
excessive drug use during and immediately following the homicides in
question, a conclusion can not be reached as to whether she, in fact,
knows who perpetrated the homicides or whether she, in fact, was present
at the scene of the murders.

Miss STOECKLEY cooperated during the entire examination.

All part of the examination were completed.

(Note: Linda, read this carefully and check typing errors before
you final type. Ask Mr Presson to take a look at it - a good hard look.)

　　　　　Thanks,

　　　　　　　　　Mr B.

person(s) who killed Colette, Kimberley and Kristen MacDONALD. It is further concluded that Miss STOECKLEY is convinced in her mind that she was physically present when the three members of the MacDONALD family were killed . . .

Miss STOECKLEY cooperated during the entire examination.

All part[s] of the examination were completed.

(Note: Linda, read this carefully and check typing errors before you final type. Ask Mr. Presson to take a look at it—a good hard look.)[6]

Thanks,

Mr. B.

Let's step back one moment. Over the course of two days, Stoeckley had told contradictory stories. Presumably, the lie-detector test was then administered to determine what she really believed. And guess what? The lie-detector test confirmed that Helena Stoeckley truly believed that she knew the identity of the killers. That she believed she had been in the house during the killings. Isn't that in Brisentine's report?

The fact that Brisentine had to add the phrase "in her mind" is evidence that he felt the need to qualify the result. The phrase occurs twice. The second time, Brisentine added it to his notes as an afterthought—a correction—before they were sent off to be retyped.

All polygraphs are about things in the mind. They measure whether you, the subject, believe you are telling the truth. As such, they are belief detectors, not truth detectors. How are we to know what knowledge she actually had of the crime scene, as opposed to the knowledge she convinced herself that she had? How do we know what anybody knows about anything? Because we investigate further.

16

THE IMPOSSIBLE COFFEE TABLE, PART II

*We expect regularities everywhere and attempt to find them even
where there are none; events which do not yield to these attempts we are
inclined to treat as a kind of "background noise"; and we stick to our
expectations even when they are inadequate and we ought to accept defeat.*
—Karl Popper, *Conjectures and Refutations:
The Growth of Scientific Knowledge*

The naive reader will assume that the coffee table issue had been laid to rest. Hadn't Colonel Rock shown, with one swing of his boot, that the coffee table could have landed on its side? Hadn't he provided the perfect counterexample?

And yet Martin Lonky, a crime scene research analyst, was contracted by the CID to file a report discussing in detail the weight, height, width, and center of gravity of the coffee table. The report was released on July 27, 1973—two years into the reinvestigation of MacDonald's crime—in the hopes of making a case.

It reads like postmodern fiction, an excursion not so much into the absurd as *past* it—and into the void. Section 3 repeats claims familiar from the Article 32 hearing with some scientific terminology:

The measured value of ΔE is 3.24 ft-lb. Hence, the total energy is more than three times that necessary to take the table past PSEUDO-STABLE POSITION 2. Under these conditions, it is reasonable to imply that the "coffee table" could not wind up on its side.[1]

But Lonky goes on to clarify that "if the 'rocking chair' had been parallel to and up against the 'coffee table' (as in one of the reenactments you have), the table *could be* prevented from completely falling over." Or a person could have somehow prevented the coffee table from landing facedown:

> Even if the fight took place between the couch and the table, someone could have blocked or otherwise prevented the table from completing its motion. Certainly, if the Captain's defense is pursued properly, it will be claimed that he was unconscious and hence could not account for the final position of the items.

Section 7 brings up a number of additional points. The rueful admission that "whereas the probability of finding the table in the position shown in the photographs is small, it is possible in some circumstances. There is no law of physics which will conclusively prove that the table should have turned completely over." And then in section 8, Lonky raises the "lack of evidence of any large-scale scuffle . . ."

But what does "lack of evidence" mean? Did the lack of evidence mean that there had been *no* intruders? Hadn't MacDonald already addressed this during the Article 32?

BERNARD SEGAL: Go ahead and describe the struggle that took place there.
JEFFREY MACDONALD: I thought I was being punched . . . I could feel like a rain of blows on my chest, shoulders, neck, you know, forehead or whatnot. I was just getting punched by what seemed like a lot of, what I thought was fists. While I was holding onto the club I suddenly got a very sharp pain in my chest, my right chest.
BERNARD SEGAL: Do you know the source of that pain?
JEFFREY MACDONALD: No, I do not. My instantaneous impression was, was that, I thought to myself, that he really threw a helluva punch, because it like took the breath out of me.
BERNARD SEGAL: You were of the impression that it was a punch that had caused that pain at that time?
JEFFREY MACDONALD: Well, yeah, but let's not make it black and white. I was being punched and I felt the pain in my chest, and I just instantaneously thought that was a—that was a good blow. I didn't stop and think, gee it could have been a stab or gunshot or a punch, or—and so, when I felt this pain, I let go of the

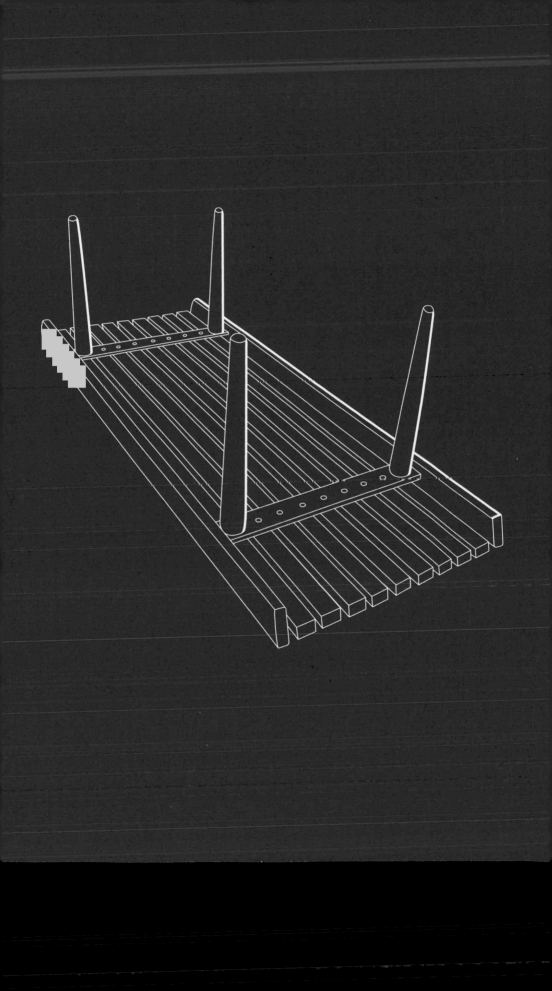

club and sort of, you know, just directed my attention more to the other two people. that—

BERNARD SEGAL: The two white males?

JEFFREY MACDONALD: Right. Now basically you'd have to get the picture. I'd already been hit in the head and it wasn't any titanic struggle, much to my chagrin. I was just trying to push up and I was being punched. This wasn't a matter of, you know, me picking up chairs and hitting people over the head in defense of myself at all. I had been hit on the head and I was struggling up, and more or less I had been holding onto this club trying to pull myself up, and when I felt the sharp pain in the right side of my chest I just let go of this and struggled with the other two people.[2]

Could this be why there was little evidence of a struggle? That Jeffrey MacDonald didn't fight back? Or if he did fight back, he failed to fight back *effectively*? He failed to save his family.

At the end of his report, Lonky rhetorically throws up his hands:

Based on the pictures and my visit to the residence . . . it appears that it cannot be said that the table *should have turned over completely,* due to the number of inter-actions that may have taken place (between the table, people, and the furniture). Therefore, based on the original statement of this problem, it is probably not worth-while to pursue this avenue in an attempt to negate CPT MacDonald's testimony.

—————

These renewed efforts to prove that MacDonald rigged the crime scene—the graphs, the measured value of ΔE—what were they *really* about? Absence of *enough* evidence of a struggle—the Valentine's Day cards standing upright and seemingly undisturbed in the dining room. The coffee table, the flowerpot, the *Esquire* magazine, in positions that suggested to the CID that MacDonald had placed them there in an effort to fool the detectives into thinking there were intruders in the home.

I tracked down Martin Lonky. His job had been to work with the *physical* evidence, but when we spoke he was more interested in the question of MacDonald's character.

ERROL MORRIS: What's so puzzling about the case is that on one hand you have all of this forensic evidence and on the other hand someone who doesn't seem to be the kind of person who could have committed the crime.

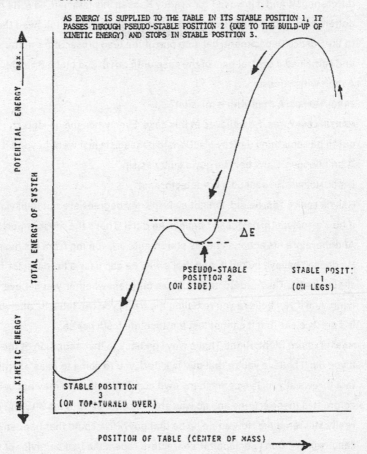

ENERGY DIAGRAM OF THE "COFFEE TABLE" IN A CONSERVATIVE SYSTEM.

AS ENERGY IS SUPPLIED TO THE TABLE IN ITS STABLE POSITION 1, IT PASSES THROUGH PSEUDO-STABLE POSITION 2 (DUE TO THE BUILD-UP OF KINETIC ENERGY) AND STOPS IN STABLE POSITION 3.

POTENTIAL ENERGY max.

TOTAL ENERGY OF SYSTEM

max. KINETIC ENERGY

ΔE

PSEUDO-STABLE POSITION 2 (ON SIDE)

STABLE POSIT: 1 (ON LEGS)

STABLE POSITION 3 (ON TOP-TURNED OVER)

POSITION OF TABLE (CENTER OF MASS)

MARTIN LONKY: Right. I think you may be looking at—what do they call those people?—sociopaths. They actually drink their own bathwater. They believe their own stories. I always thought that he was sociopathic in some sense. I live in Southern California, and even when the district attorney of North Carolina contacted me—I had just moved here—I had learned that at Memorial Hospital here, down in Long Beach, these people loved him. He was a gifted surgeon. He was a gifted doc. They loved him. His patients loved him; the hospital loved him.

ERROL MORRIS: You seem to be describing two different people.

MARTIN LONKY: I once sat down with a lawyer and said, "How do people do this? How does this happen?" Because he clearly did it. I mean, I didn't have any doubt.

How could he be this good guy and be the masked man [*laugh*] earlier in his life? Nobody could believe he was that guy. He was living the good life out there. A different guy. And if it wasn't for Freddy Kassab, his father-in-law, he might have gotten away with it. And Brian Murtagh [a JAG lawyer who followed the case to the Justice Department, became one of the lead prosecutors at the 1979 trial, and remained a central part of the case until 2011]. God bless Brian Murtagh. A man with a mission.

ERROL MORRIS: A man with a mission?

MARTIN LONKY: Yes. He believed in this case. Even when the lie-detector test turned out to be something Jeffrey MacDonald passed, he just went beyond it and said, "Can't happen. Can't be. The guy's guilty as sin."

ERROL MORRIS: He passed a lie-detector test?

MARTIN LONKY: Yes, he did. I'm not a shrink. My degrees are not in psychology. But if he's a sociopath, *he* doesn't believe he did it. That's the most important thing. And therefore his actions and his statements are coming from his heart of hearts. He doesn't believe he did it. And that's why he can pass a lie-detector test.

ERROL MORRIS: The lie-detector tests can only test whether you believe you're lying. And if you believe you're telling the truth, you can tell a lie and still pass. It's pretty clear that it cannot test for absolute truth per se.

MARTIN LONKY: Right. Right. That's why I go back to that definition of the sociopath. If you don't believe you're that guy [a killer], you're going to pass anything the test throws at you. I've come to my own conclusion that he may not believe he committed these crimes and so was able to continue with his life. The question really still remains: How could he be that guy? How could that happen?

ERROL MORRIS: Don't sociopathic characters repeat the bad behavior of their past? Take someone like O. J. Simpson.

MARTIN LONKY: Oh, don't go there. Don't go there. [*Laughs.*] I'm one of those few guys who believes O. J. actually didn't do the Nicole Simpson murder.

ERROL MORRIS: Really?!

MARTIN LONKY: Sure. I'm convinced he didn't do it. The only thing he's guilty of is being as dumb as a rock. And you know what? He didn't have to do what he did in Vegas to show you that. He's got a life history of showing he is not the brightest tool in the shed. And that's why Christopher Darden and Marcia Clark [Simpson's prosecutors] blew the case. They had him on both ends of it. They had him smart enough to plan it and dumb enough to be emotional. And you can't be both. You can't be both personalities at the same time. Try that one out for size. But I can go through the evidence. The evidence actually shows that he didn't do it.

ERROL MORRIS: But MacDonald is a different story.

MARTIN LONKY: Yes. MacDonald's unique. I sat down with a trial attorney, and I said, "How do people do this?" Same question you're asking. "How could he be that guy?" And I remember he just looked at me and said, "I wish I could tell you it doesn't happen. But these guys just get to a crisis point once in their life, they do something horrible, and then they get into a place where they believe they didn't do it." You got kids wetting their beds; you got a wife you don't want to be married to; she's pregnant again. Other guys have better things. You live on Fort Bragg, North Carolina. I'm making all this stuff up. I don't know if this went through Captain MacDonald's mind or not. You look around and you say, "Shit on this." You just have a breakdown. You do something, then you dismiss it from your mind. You believe you didn't do it. Because it's such a *bad* thing. How can you live with yourself? Right?

ERROL MORRIS: Right.

MARTIN LONKY: And he never does it again, because he isn't that kind of a guy.

———

Martin Lonky told me repeatedly that he is not a psychiatric expert. Still, he had presented a *new* theory of the psychopath, in an effort to explain Jeffrey MacDonald. Namely, that the psychopath sees himself as completely normal—is oblivious to his terrible misdeeds or crimes. "You do something, then you dismiss it from your mind. You believe you didn't do it." The monster with amnesia. The monster who forgets he's a monster. Not only are we unable to explain MacDonald's motivation, MacDonald is in the same position. He doesn't remember what he has done. He simply denies that he has done anything.

17

A LOSING PROPOSITION

The Kassabs were frustrated. Their attempts to secure an indictment and a conviction for the murders continued unabated—letters to newspapers, to Congress, to the attorney general, to the general counsel of the army, even a paid advertisement asking the public for support. At first they refused to cooperate with the CID reinvestigation, and then, following a visit from Pruett and Kearns on February 11, 1971, they relented. And on April 27, 1971, Pruett and Kearns visited the Kassabs again.

> Mrs. KASSAB opined that certain inconsistencies in Dr. MacDONALD's version of the incident as he recalls them may be possibly attributed to his confusion and sleepiness at the time he woke. [Pruett continues with a parenthetical remark:] (This comment by Mrs. KASSAB apparently was made because she has received information from her husband about the crime scene which apparently makes it obvious that the conditions which existed in the crime scene were not compatible with Dr. MacDONALD's tale and she wanted to offer an explanation.)[1]

Kearns adds:

> Both Kassabs still exhibit a strong feeling that Dr. MacDONALD did not participate in the murders [but] Mr. KASSAB stated he asked Dr. MacDONALD on his visit of

18 April 1971 how he could have seen all the details regarding the injuries to his wife and children with no lights on in the room.

If at the end of April Kassab still believed that MacDonald was not the killer, things were beginning to change. Later, Freddy Kassab cited several turning points: MacDonald's phone call in November, his appearance on *Dick Cavett* in December, his own visit to the crime scene with Pruett and Kearns in March 1971. Kassab later wrote, "On my return from this trip, there was not a shred of doubt in my mind as to MacDonald's guilt."[2] Letters and documents suggest that the final break came after MacDonald left for California to take a job as the director of emergency medicine at St. Mary's Hospital. On November 1, 1971, Kassab wrote an angry letter to MacDonald after he visited Long Island without visiting, or even calling. Freddy was indignant: "For one solid year we called you almost daily and did everything a human being can do to help you . . . Perhaps you would like to push the whole thing behind you, we can't and won't until whoever did this is punished."[3]

———

There was still no indictment. By 1974, Kassab had taken a threatening tone. On February 25, 1974, he wrote a letter to the U.S. attorney general, William Saxbe: "Any attempt to stop me, overt or covert, will have to be explained to the media." He then wrote a letter on March 4, 1974, to Colonel Henry Tufts, claiming that he was going to file his own criminal complaint and demanding a letter of support from the CID.

The turning point came when Freddy Kassab was referred to Richard Cahn, a Long Island lawyer, to file a federal complaint.

Cahn is the second generation of three generations of Cahns. The law firm is Cahn & Cahn, but it could be Cahn, Cahn & Cahn. His father started the law firm, and his son—who was born on February 17, 1970, the day of the MacDonald murders—is now a partner.

ERROL MORRIS: Can you tell me how you got involved in the MacDonald case?
RICHARD CAHN: It's a fairly simple story. The Kassabs were not my clients. They were clients of a friend of mine, Dick Scheyer, who was and still is a practicing lawyer in Suffolk County, Long Island. We owned a Cherokee Six together, and we flew it out of Islip Airport. We took some trips to Niagara Falls and upper

Maine and Key West, Florida, with our families. There were seven seats on the plane. And we became very friendly. He had the Kassabs as real estate clients. And they had this situation, and they were complaining about it: they couldn't get anybody's attention; they couldn't get any official response. Dick knew that I did federal court work, so Dick referred the Kassabs to me. This was probably around late 1972 or early '73.

ERROL MORRIS: They thought you could move the case forward.

RICHARD CAHN: Yes. I discovered there is no restriction as to who may file a criminal complaint in federal court.

ERROL MORRIS: Anyone?

RICHARD CAHN: Yes. I also talked to Pete Kearns, who was in charge of the reinvestigation, so he knew everything about it. I drafted a very long affidavit for him, and an affidavit for Fred and Mildred. And the law provided that such documents could be presented to a federal magistrate judge. It's the lowest level of federal judge. But they handle criminal complaints, they can issue warrants for people's arrests, they can fix bail, they can hold somebody over if there's probable cause for prosecution and see to it that they appear when needed.

So I thought I would use that procedure, except I wouldn't present these documents to a lowly magistrate judge, because federal district judges have all the powers of magistrates. So I said, "I'm going to go to a federal district judge. And I'm not going to go to any federal district judge. I'm going to go to the chief judge of the district." Just so there's no waffling, no uncertainty about what somebody ought to do. So I called Judge Butler's chambers. He came on the line, and we had a very interesting discussion. He told me that if I could come down on April 30, 1974, that would be a convenient time for him.

Judge Butler had already been involved with the case. He figured in Michael Malley's journal and had been involved in arguments over MacDonald's hair samples during the Article 32 hearings.[4] Malley wrote, "Judge Butler is an old, slow man who was most courteous and most skeptical about the case—he seems like some old corporate lawyer whose southern Republicanism paid off during the sleepwalk of the Eisenhower years by appointment to the federal bench." My interview with Richard Cahn continued:

RICHARD CAHN: Well, the Kassabs and I flew into Raleigh, and we had to drive quite a few miles to Clinton, North Carolina, where Judge Butler, the chief judge of

the district, had his chambers in the basement of a post office building. [*Laughs.*] So that's where we ended up, on that day.

ERROL MORRIS: Yes.

RICHARD CAHN: And he was very gracious. He had with him Tom McNamara, the U.S. attorney. I knew from other research that we had done that he was in favor of prosecuting MacDonald, but his superiors in Washington weren't having any of it. So he was there, and it was a very interesting dynamic between the judge and McNamara. I made a presentation, Tom McNamara said a few words, and the judge said he would take it under advisement. A few things happened behind the scenes, both before and after I arrived. Eventually, the government prosecuted him. And one of the key things—I thought I had it here on my wall, but I guess I don't. I had a copy of a letter that Judge Butler wrote, a letter to the attorney general—who was William Saxbe, of Ohio—and put it right to him: "If I convene a grand jury, will you allow the U.S. Attorney to present the case? If the grand jury indicts, will the government prosecute? If not, why not? Tell me why. I want you to be specific." This is 1974.

ERROL MORRIS: Right. So you come into this after the Kassabs were already absolutely convinced that Jeffrey was the culprit.

RICHARD CAHN: Oh yes. They never wavered.

ERROL MORRIS: Why do you think that the government was dragging its feet about it?

RICHARD CAHN: Well, I'm not sure. I think the army, having gone to the trouble and the expense of a lengthy Article 32 proceeding in an explosive and very public case—a horrifying case—and the hearing officer having gone out of his way to exonerate MacDonald, I think that the army didn't want to upset that. They just wanted to let it be. And the Justice Department had plenty to do, even before Watergate. And after Watergate, it was just out of the question. It was just too low of a priority. I don't think anybody was trying to protect MacDonald; I think it was just bureaucratic inertia.

ERROL MORRIS: But weren't there doubts about the evidence?

RICHARD CAHN: Yes. There were people in the chain of command and the Justice Department who made very public statements that they didn't think there was evidence sufficient to prosecute MacDonald. They were very vocal about it. But Freddy [Kassab] was more vocal, blasting them in public. And for whatever reasons—obviously because of the dramatic nature of the case and the terrible loss that he and his wife suffered—he got a lot of press, and he knew how to interest reporters in what was an injustice, not to have the thing properly tried.

That was his quest, and I felt it was a very worthwhile quest. Whether the guy was guilty or innocent almost didn't matter—it was a question of having a proper testing of the evidence, whatever it was. And of course, once I got into it, I formed this opinion that the guy was almost certainly guilty.

Generally, that's the story. Once the judge sent the letter to the attorney general, the Justice Department resistance to reopening the case melted away. And they sent one of their old warhorse trial lawyers, Victor Woerheide, to North Carolina to meet with the judge and to meet with Tom McNamara, the U.S. attorney. And next thing you know, a grand jury was convened.

The Kassabs and Richard Cahn filed their complaint on April 30, 1974. It states that there was "probable cause to believe [MacDonald] committed the murders," and their reasons to believe that that was the case:

A. Defendant was physically on the premises at the time the murders were committed.

B. There was no objective evidence whatsoever of any intruders having been present on the premises at the time the murders were committed.
  (1) There was no foreign material, grass, mud, or wet spots, although it was raining, on any of the floors, carpets, or rugs and the defendant testified that he observed 4 intruders in the living room of the apartment . . .
  (2) The military regularly patrolled the area in which the MacDonald apartment was situated and saw no sign of other vehicles or pedestrians or civilians at any time between midnight and 4 A.M. on February 16–17, 1970.

Page after page through the alphabet—C, D, E, F, G—to claim AA, which repeats the first two claims:

AA. MacDonald is the only person who is known to have been in the house at the time of the murders and there is no evidence whatsoever of intruders.

These claims would appear again and again in the various investigations, trials, and court proceedings over the next forty years. No intruders. No one in the vicinity of the house. But you can't have it both ways. You can't have more than twenty MPs, investigators, commanding officers, photographers, neighbors, and unidentified gawkers at the crime scene on a rainy morning with no evidence of intruders. Something was awry.

The Kassabs had become absolutely convinced of MacDonald's guilt. So was Thomas McNamara, the new U.S. attorney. Still, McNamara was not sure that he could get a conviction with the evidence in hand:

> I am convinced that Jeffrey MacDonald brutally murdered his wife and two children during the late evening and early morning hours of February 16–17, 1970. But I am afraid that we will not be able to convict him. In my opinion we can get to the jury with this case but there is no more than a 20 to 30 percent chance of actually obtaining a conviction. The Government lacks a solid motive on the part of MacDonald for the commission of these acts. The Government, therefore, must present a totally hypothetical motive and then substantiate this motive with an enormous amount of circumstantial evidence of a negative character in an effort to prove a positive premise . . .
>
> The Government investigators' failure to preserve the crime scene may be the most damning aspect of our case. The living room area of the MacDonald apartment appears to be clearly staged, but we lose the effect of this evidence when the defendant points to 4 or 5 admitted instances of the Government agents disturbing the crime scene upon their entry . . .
>
> It might seem unusual to devote so much time to what I classify as a losing proposition, but when one undertakes an extensive review of this case, as I have done over the past several months, and becomes convinced that a murderer will escape punishment, it is hard to stop working.[5]

The grand jury was convened on August 12, 1974.

MEDIA FREAK

MacDonald was sworn in before the grand jury on August 12, 1974. U.S. Attorney Victor Woerheide asked for his name and his address and explained the nature of the proceedings. "With respect to the murders, the finger has been pointed at various individuals; and one of the persons who has been a suspect in the past and who must be considered a suspect for the purpose of this grand jury proceeding is you, yourself, since you are the only survivor of the incident that occurred on the night of February 16–17, 1970."[1] He suggested that there were a number of suspects, but everyone, including MacDonald, knew that the government was interested in only one suspect—MacDonald himself.

Colonel Rock was now long gone. Hammond Beale described the proceeding as a "witch hunt."[2] There was a new presiding judge, Franklin T. Dupree, a Nixon appointee from 1970, who had asked Judge Butler—the judge visited by Richard Cahn and Freddy Kassab—to be assigned to the case. (He took the job even though there was a conflict of interest. James Proctor, the assistant U.S. attorney who had pressed for an indictment of MacDonald soon after the conclusion of the Article 32 hearing, had been his son-in-law before a divorce.) Brian Murtagh, a young lawyer, had also joined the prosecution team. MacDonald later described him as "that little viper . . . The little guy who doesn't have enough politeness to introduce himself. Or doesn't know any of the social amenities."[3]

MacDonald was questioned about the night of the murders, but eventually the questions turned to his relationship with Freddy Kassab.

VICTOR WOERHEIDE: What was your relationship with Mr. Kassab?

JEFFREY MACDONALD: He was my father-in-law. Colette's stepfather.

VICTOR WOERHEIDE: Apart from the legal aspects of the relationship, what was your personal relationship with him?

JEFFREY MACDONALD: It was very good. It's not so good now.

VICTOR WOERHEIDE: Did he visit you from time to time prior to the time that you were discharged from the army?

JEFFREY MACDONALD: During the Article 32 but not after the Article 32 was ended.

VICTOR WOERHEIDE: Would you call him up and talk to him from time to time?

JEFFREY MACDONALD: Surely.

VICTOR WOERHEIDE: Would he call you up and talk to you?

JEFFREY MACDONALD: Sure would.

VICTOR WOERHEIDE: How frequently did you have these communications?

JEFFREY MACDONALD: It seemed to me fairly frequently.

VICTOR WOERHEIDE: And were you holding anything back from him?

JEFFREY MACDONALD: No. Unfortunately I made some things up.

VICTOR WOERHEIDE: What did you make up?

JEFFREY MACDONALD: The extent of my investigation, my own investigation.

VICTOR WOERHEIDE: All right, tell the grand jury now what it was you made up.

JEFFREY MACDONALD: Let me just say that I was trying to rebuild my life and I was doing—I was trying to get out of the army and our communication at the time was relatively good. We—I say, my attorneys, my mother and myself—had begun to feel a little uneasy about Freddy, Mr. Kassab. Mr. Kassab kind of took over the Article 32 hearing and a lot [of] the publicity surrounding it. He would hold news conferences up at LaGuardia Airport. He was writing letters and firing off telegrams to anyone that would listen. It was all—

VICTOR WOERHEIDE: Was this [to] public officials, congressmen, senators, things like that?

JEFFREY MACDONALD: Anyone who would listen. *New York Times, Newsweek,* magazines, radios, whoever he could talk to . . . I was the greatest guy that had ever lived, the army was absolutely hosing me, giving me a bad deal.

VICTOR WOERHEIDE: You didn't disagree with that, did you?

JEFFREY MACDONALD: No. That in fact is what happened.

VICTOR WOERHEIDE: All right. Go ahead.

JEFFREY MACDONALD: He was aware of the Article 32 investigation . . . Except for little things, he knew the substance of all the testimony, he knew all the witnesses who were there, he came and testified. But what I was leading up to was there was . . . a sense of uneasiness. Freddy became a media freak, if you want me to be honest. Freddy became a true media freak. He would call us up and he'd say, "What do you want me to do now?" And Bernie would say, "We'd like for you to—" I don't know. Just, you know, "Has the CID been up there questioning any of Jeff's friends or Colette's friends? Could you ask them? Fine." Now, Bernie would— Mr. Segal would say, "Now Freddy, that's all I want you to do right now."

That night we'd be looking at TV and he'd be holding a nationally covered news conference.

And Bernie said many times, as did a lot of people, you know, he's really kind of a fanatic. So, I said, "Well, look, it's his stepdaughter and grandchildren."

Okay . . . I'm being sort of discharged out of the army. I say "sort of" because it was sort of a battle. It was a lot of letter writing, phone calling, congressmen calling down trying to speed up the discharge-type thing.

I was in a funny situation. I [was] still in the army. I had not been court-martialed. I had an Article 32, which is nonjudicial. So I wasn't subject to double jeopardy. And I was being counseled just to get out of the army. "Just do your job, show up for work if your commanding officer wants you to, and apply for your discharge." And Freddy's communications were to the effect, "Don't do anything dangerous. You don't know what they'll do. Your room's bugged." This whole thing. And "I'll take care of all the public statements now." Fine. And he started talking to me frequently and writing me frequently. It was always in reference to when we get our private investigation going.

So then . . . I told him, "Well, I've been in some bars and, you know, I've got some leads."

Critical mistake in my life, tell him that I got some leads. And that started it. And then it was incessant. "What do you have?" "Who have you found?"

And I'd lost my family and I'd been through the hearing. I'd been wrongfully accused. Colonel Rock's statement at the end of a five-month grand jury [sic] is: the charges are not true. He didn't say there was lack of evidence. He said the charges are not true. Right? So I'm trying to get out of the army. I'm trying to figure out what's going to happen. And what do I do? Do I drift? Do I go into my residency? Do I spend the rest of my life prowling around looking for these people? And Freddy's hammering away, you know, about this investigation that we're going to . . . John Cummings [a reporter with *Newsday,* a Long Island news-paper with a circulation in the millions] was driving me absolutely nuts. Day and night phone calls. Not day and night literally, but frequent communications. "When are we going to get together for the book?" Then the authors started calling.

"When are we going to do a book on this?" "I can hook you up with William Morrow in New York." Lawyers from Long Island say, "I have a good friend who is a writer." And it became this unbelievable public thing.

So I sat down and talked to my military lawyers; I talked to my civilian lawyers. I said, "What do I do?" And they said, "Do formal things. Do what you can do. You're a physician. Go to Washington."

So when I got out of the army I went to Washington. Allard Lowenstein takes me around and introduce[s] me to Sam Ervin. Can you imagine going to a cocktail party and talking about a homicide? So I go to the Justice Department, try to do things like that. Congressmen and lawyers advised me to go on TV talk shows. So I go on the TV talk show. I got sick to my stomach. After that I said I wasn't going to do it anymore. They didn't have a right. Meanwhile, Freddy's driving me crazy. "What have you found out?" So I told him I'd found other people. To make a long story short, I implied that I killed the person.

Absolute insanity. So [Mildred] wants to know the details. "Did they scream? Were they in agony?"

VICTOR WOERHEIDE: What did you say?

JEFFREY MACDONALD: I told him, "I can't talk about it."

My mother is over for dinner at their house, just to give you an example. My mother-in-law has another son. They have two kids. We were eating dinner. She says, "I wish Bobby's [Colette's brother] kids were killed, not yours." I said, "Mildred, how can you say that?" I said, "That's really perverse." She says, "I want revenge." I said, "I want revenge, too." So I left for California. What the hell was I supposed to do?

So I played along with this stupid game with Freddy. Freddy was an ex-intelligence officer in the Canadian secret service, or so he says, and he lives this day and night. He was in bars all through World War II listening to secret conversations. He was in D-Day. He was on a battleship on V-E Day. He was everywhere at all times. So I played this game. And finally I gave it up, and I wrote him a ten-page, fifteen-page letter. And I said, "Freddy, I didn't do it. I didn't do this."

VICTOR WOERHEIDE: When did you write that final letter saying I didn't do it?

JEFFREY MACDONALD: I don't know.

VICTOR WOERHEIDE: Dr. MacDonald?

JEFFREY MACDONALD: When I got to California. It was crazy.

VICTOR WOERHEIDE: How long did you play the game?

JEFFREY MACDONALD: I don't know. Months, verbally, with him. It was always the one incident. It was always the one thing. Mildred wanted to hear the details, "did they scream? Were they in agony?"

VICTOR WOERHEIDE: Mildred is Colette's mother?

JEFFREY MACDONALD: So-so mother. She's been bizarre for a long time. How can you sit at dinner and say that you wished your other grandkids were killed? So I made this tremendous mistake, this fantastic error. I tried to be a doctor. I tried to rebuild my life. And I moved away. And that's my three crimes.[4]

19

A CONCLUSION COULD NOT BE REACHED

Helena Stoeckley never appeared before the grand jury. She wasn't called as a witness. And as far as the prosecution was concerned, she was no longer a suspect. But as part of the reinvestigation of the murders in 1971, CID agent Richard Mahon had looked into the story of William Posey, Stoeckley's next-door neighbor, and he was asked to testify in front of the grand jury. Suddenly, Stoeckley or no Stoeckley, we are back in the story of "that morning."

VICTOR WOERHEIDE: Now, in the course of performing your official duties, were you assigned to conduct an investigation with respect to the certain allegations made by former Captain Jeffrey R. MacDonald?

RICHARD MAHON: Yes, sir, I was.

VICTOR WOERHEIDE: And was this investigation predicated on allegations made on the part of former Captain MacDonald with respect to the Article 32 proceedings and the investigation in connection with the Article 32 that had been had against him previously?

RICHARD MAHON: Yes, sir.

VICTOR WOERHEIDE: And these allegations were allegations of perjury and destruction of evidence and general incompetence, and this, that and the other thing?

RICHARD MAHON: I believe that was the nature of the allegations, yes, sir.

VICTOR WOERHEIDE: Now, in connection with the investigation, were you assigned to conduct, let's say, interviews with certain persons such as a man named Posey who had testified as a witness at the Article 32 hearing?

RICHARD MAHON: Yes, sir, I did.[1]

Posey was Stoeckley's neighbor, the man who saw Stoeckley arrive in a blue automobile early on the morning of February 17, 1970.

RICHARD MAHON: Well, [Posey] told me that . . . he had awakened from sleep to go to the bathroom. He didn't know what time it was as he hadn't looked at a clock, but he believed that it was sometime between three o'clock and 4:30 a.m. that morning.

He heard a car pull into the driveway at the residence where Miss Stoeckley lived and he said he saw Miss Stoeckley get out of that automobile and into the residence.

He said that he heard some giggling, although he didn't see people, he believed that there were at least two individuals in the car beside Miss Stoeckley, one of Miss Stoeckley's girlfriends—at that time she was residing with two young ladies—was up and painting in the apartment, and he could see her painting, he said.

He didn't recall specifically what she was wearing.

In any case, he talked to Helena a few days later and she told him that she didn't know where she had been on the night of 16 and 17 February, because she told him that, quote, she had been stoned that night; meaning she had used drugs.

She mentioned in a conversation with Posey that someone had seen a hobbyhorse inside the residence—child's hobbyhorse.

I don't specifically recall, but I believe there is a photograph of a hobby horse in the newspaper, or somewhere.

So this made Mr. Posey very suspicious. In another conversation with Miss Stoeckley she told him to tell his wife to keep her doors locked, which he said made him very apprehensive. And she had obtained a number of funeral wreaths, put them on the lawn in front of her house . . .

The testimony turned to Robert Brisentine's polygraph examinations of Posey.

VICTOR WOERHEIDE: Now, you say [Posey] was asked to submit to a polygraph examination . . . Did Mr. Brisentine arrive at any conclusion with respect to his truthfulness or lack of truthfulness with respect to the statements that he made?
RICHARD MAHON: He did.
VICTOR WOERHEIDE: What were his conclusions?

RICHARD MAHON: He concluded that Mr. Posey had not been truthful when he denied giving false information at the Article 32 hearing, and to CID investigators, CID agents, meaning myself . . . That Mr. Posey had not been certain of the actual date that he had seen the car arrive at Miss Stoeckley's and had seen Miss Stoeckley get out of the car and enter her house. Nor was he certain of the type of automobile.

Mahon's testimony suggested that Posey was lying about *everything*. When further questioned after the polygraph, however, Posey explained that he saw Stoeckley walking from the car, which is technically not getting out of the car. And that he was not certain that the car was a Mustang. In reviewing the evidence, I believe the essence of Posey's testimony is true. Part of his account is corroborated in a statement given by Kathy Smith, Stoeckley's roommate, on May 6, 1971.

On the night of the murders of the MacDONALD family, I was out with Bruce FOWLER, a guy named CHARLIE BROWN, Johnny Laape, and J. C. Conklin . . . We stayed at the trailer until about 0330 when Bruce and I returned to the apartment on Clark St. When we got back, Diane HEDDEN and Don HARRIS were there painting the apartment. About ½ hour later Helena and Greg MITCHELL arrived. They had been out in either Greg's yellow Plymouth or HARRIS' light blue 1969 Fairlane GT . . .

On the stand, Mahon is also asked if Helena Stoeckley was polygraphed.

RICHARD MAHON: Yes, sir, she was administered a polygraph examination on the 24th of April, 1971 . . . The polygraph examination was administered at Nashville, Tennessee, by Mr. Brisentine.
VICTOR WOERHEIDE: What were his conclusions?
RICHARD MAHON: He concluded that due to Miss Stoeckley's confused state of mind and excessive drug use during the period of the homicides, that a conclusion could not be reached as to whether or not Miss Stoeckley actually knew who had committed the homicides, or even whether or not she was present at the scene of the homicides.

And so Brisentine's polygraph exam was admitted into evidence. But Mahon omitted Brisentine's conclusion. Brisentine had stated that Stoeckley believed that she was at the crime scene and that she believed she was telling the truth. Mahon changed that. And he made it seem cut-and-dry. No conclusion could be reached.

20

MUTE WITNESS

The criminologist re-creates the criminal
from traces the latter leaves behind.
—Edmond Locard

Dr. Edmond Locard, the French detective and scientist who established scientific procedures for criminal investigation, is principally remembered for his transfer theory (or exchange principle), often known as the transfer theory of Locard. As the American forensic scientist Paul Kirk put it:

> Wherever he steps, wherever he touches, whatever he leaves—even unconsciously—will serve as a silent witness against him. Not only his fingerprints and his footprints, but his hair, the fibers from his clothes, the glass he breaks, the tool mark he leaves, the paint he scratches, the blood or semen he deposits or collects. All of these and more bear mute witness against him. This is evidence that does not forget. It is not confused by the excitement of the moment. It is not absent because human witnesses are. *It is factual evidence.* Physical evidence cannot be wrong; it cannot perjure itself; it cannot be wholly absent. Only in its interpretation can there be error. Only human failure to find, study, and understand it can diminish its value.[1]

Imagine a white cat on a black cashmere sweater. Fibers and fur are transferred from one location to another. Black cashmere to the cat. White fur to the sweater. According to Locard's theory, it is impossible for someone to enter a room without leaving some sort of calling card, a residue of himself. Or in turn, picking up some element of that environment. Hair follicles, exfoliated skin, fingernail clippings—or blood.

Locard's original theory was designed for intruders, interlopers, outsiders. Someone who breaks into a house and leaves evidence. But what kind of traces are we looking for here? Jeffrey MacDonald was not an intruder. He *lived* at 544 Castle Drive, and so we would expect to find hairs from his body and fibers from his clothes throughout the house. And we would expect to find blood. His blood and blood from the three members of his family. Locard's exchange principle, which makes perfect sense in theory, becomes problematic in practice. When there is a glut of evidence, how do you separate meaningful evidence from background noise? 544 Castle Drive was military housing, transient housing. It's fine to imagine a white cat on a black sweater, but what about a house filled with "unsourced" fibers? Not just unsourced fibers, unsourceable ones?

The crimes were committed just before the dawn of the modern era of forensic investigation. DNA analysis was still unknown. Tests that can be done today were not available then. But government investigators seized on a remarkable fact. They must have thought they hit the jackpot. The four members of the MacDonald family each had a different blood type. Statistically, this was unusual.

Colette MacDonald: A
Jeffrey MacDonald: B
Kimberley MacDonald: AB
Kristen MacDonald: O

Paul Stombaugh, a special agent and chief of the Chemistry Lab for the FBI, had the idea that each blood type could be identified, linked with each family member, and as a result the pattern of the crimes could be reconstructed. He described his theory to the grand jury.

VICTOR WOERHEIDE: Now, Mr. Stombaugh, on the basis of your analysis of the physical evidence that you have referred to here today, the blood marks on the sheets, the source of blood . . . on the bedspread, the location of the place where Colette MacDonald bled directly and very profusely in Kristen's room, have you developed any theory of how all these things fit together? What happened that night? . . .

PAUL STOMBAUGH: I believe Dr. MacDonald probably struck his wife in the face with a fist, knocked her down. This would cause the blood to start flowing. She probably had a bloody nose, and through a struggle there, is where the blood got onto his pajama top, on the side up here before it was torn. This group A blood . . . Kimberley, I believe is the child who was found in this bedroom [*indicating Kimberley's bedroom*]. She might have come up, due to the screaming, awakened, and tried to help her mother.

He might have pushed her aside, and this is just supposition on my part. I feel probably that this club which is the type of thing used for painting, I imagine it could have been kept in this utility room which is a very short place from this bedroom.

I sort of suspect possibly Colette might have picked this club up and socked Jeffrey with it which could account for the bump on his head. He was a bruiser, so he took the club away from her and went to swing at her and probably accidentally or on purpose, struck Kimberley on the side of the head with it, who was standing here, causing her to bleed, and this would account for the AB blood found in this area. And in the doorway here, in the rug, it has soaked through pretty much through, indicating someone had laid here bleeding a good bit.

When he did that, I think our little bent knife comes into play, because this is the type of knife that's very dull, and the type a lot of people, including myself, keep around for painting because it makes a good thing to scrape paint with when you drop some on the floor. I think this was in the proximity of this club in the utility room, and I think she grabbed this and attacked Jeff with this thing, possibly causing the little cut. The report said he had a cut in his left abdomen, wasn't it?

VICTOR WOERHEIDE: Yeah, in this area, that approximate area . . .

PAUL STOMBAUGH: It was slight and was made with a tearing action. A knife such as this would do that. And when she did that, he leveled her with this club. Then things, I think, sort of quieted down, because I believe Colette undoubtedly had to have been unconscious at that time.

Then I think he picked Kim up, carried her into her bed here. Due to the AB blood splatters on the wall, I believe he hit her again with the club and killed her. While this was going on, or possibly before that, I think Colette came to, came into this room [*indicating Kristen's bedroom*], to protect the only child that is not dead, and he caught up with her in there and really let her have it with the club again. This possibly could be where both her arms were broken, because they're defense wounds, and she has nothing—and she was knocked across to the wall here, and then he—she was here at sometime to have bled this much.

I guess he kind of got himself oriented, picked these up, the bedspread here, and the blue sheet and carried them back into this bedroom, reached over and picked up Colette. Now, at this time his pajama top had been torn, but it probably isn't too bloody, and I believe all the blood on the pajama top, the bulk of it, got on there when he reached across the bed and picked her up and put her down on this bedspread.

Then, he covered her with this sheet, and having blood on him, fresh blood, wet blood, and also on his hands, he reached down, picked her up, carried her back into this room where she eventually was found.

After that, he probably went to the kitchen and he could have been bleeding by this time from the cut here [indicating]. He picked up the Old Hickory knife, went back in and did the job on the rest of them, ended up with the ice pick on Colette.

I think when he put her body down here, that is when he took this pajama top off and threw it across her body, and after he cleaned things up, I believe that the bath mat could have been in the bathroom in here, because of the sink here and the fact of finding all this blood in here. That's where I believe he put the weapons down on this bath mat in there, and then as he left, he threw it down, went out the back door, threw the knife and the ice pick out.

That would be somewhat of a sequence of events.[2]

There is a lot of detail here, but Stombaugh doesn't claim to be giving an exact account of what happened. "I sort of suspect possibly Colette might have picked this club up." "He probably went to the kitchen." "Probably accidentally or on purpose." Stombaugh is absolutely certain Jeffrey MacDonald is the culprit, but it is not clear—at least to me—that the evidence supports that conclusion.

Any blood in the house was assumed to have come from the family member with the matching blood type. But ABO blood typing does not connect a blood stain with a specific individual.

This became an issue with the speck of O-type blood found on MacDonald's glasses. Since Kristen had O-type blood, the prosecution took this as proof that MacDonald had attacked his daughter and her blood splattered on his glasses. Janice Glisson, a CID chemist at Fort Gordon, discussed it briefly at the grand jury:

JANICE GLISSON: There was a small speck of type O on the right lens of the eye glass[es], found right here . . . It was one other smaller speck on the floorboard, is that right?

VICTOR WOERHEIDE: There was a small speck that was so minute it could not be typed. All they could say was that it was blood. Actually, it could have gotten

BLOOD TYPES

COLETTE MacDONALD A JEFFREY MacDONALD B KIMBERLEY MacDONALD AB KRISTEN MacDONALD O

* indicates the blood finding omitted from prosecution blood diagram. / indicates that the sample contained multiple blood types.

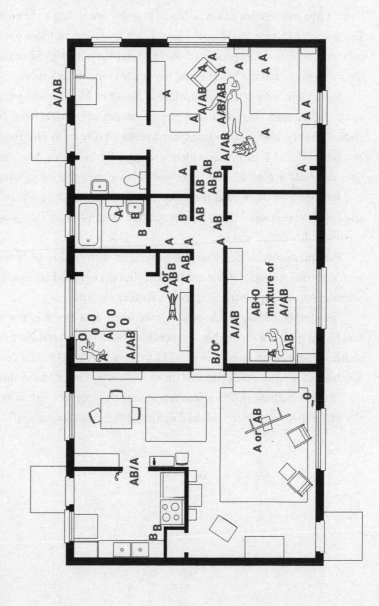

on the floor from contact of the eye glasses. In other words, a little bit came off the eye glasses onto the floor, but not enough to type it.[3]

The FBI had investigated this claim. They sent an agent to Hamlet Hospital where MacDonald had worked as an emergency room physician on February 15. He had treated five patients with O-type blood that day, including a man with a cut foot. The speck of O-type blood could have come from any of these patients. But this information was never presented at the grand jury. And so jurors were left with the impression that the blood could have only come from Kristen.

Then there were bloody footprints in Colette's blood leading out of Kristen's room. Stombaugh claimed that they were produced by MacDonald's stepping on a sheet that he had used to transport Colette's body from one room to another. But he produced little or no evidence to support his claim. The sheet was much later carefully examined, and there was no evidence that MacDonald or anyone else had stepped on it. And the footprints were gone. Craig Chamberlin, a CID chemist, had destroyed them in a misguided attempt to literally saw them out of the floor.[4] It went on and on.

The questions remain: Was the pattern of distribution of blood compatible with only one scenario? What did the distribution of blood types tell us? Could an intruder (or multiple intruders) leave a similar record?

The simple mistake made by the government was that it is not enough to say that blood evidence shows that it is *possible* MacDonald could have committed the murders. Something more is needed. Proof that *only* MacDonald could have done it. If intruders could have produced the same distribution of blood, there is no proof.

There is nothing in Stombaugh's account that prevents us from crossing out the name "Jeffrey MacDonald" and writing in "unknown assailant."

FINGERPRINT COLLECTION

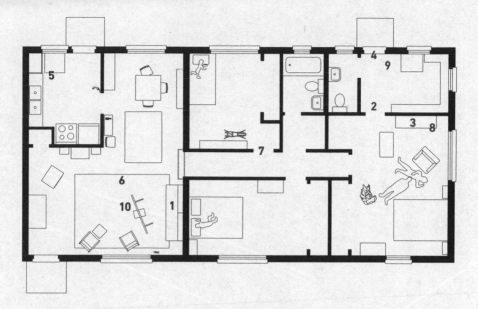

In a letter to the director of the FBI, forensic expert Dr. John Thornton called the Castle Drive crime scene "bungled beyond all measure" by the CID fingerprint expert, Hilyard Medlin. The errors in fingerprint collection include:

1 The wall behind the couch where MacDonald was attacked was not dusted completely for prints.

2 Large areas on both sides of the swinging door from the utility room into the master bedroom and the light switch in the utility room were not dusted.

3 An unidentified finger and palm print were found on Colette MacDonald's jewelry boxes on top of a dresser, and MacDonald claimed that jewelry was missing. Still, the dresser was not completely processed for prints.

4 Two prints were lost from the back screen door of the house leading into the utility room. The inside of that door was not dusted at all.

5 Two walls of the kitchen and the back door in the kitchen were not dusted.

6 The flowerpot in the living room was not dusted immediately, even though it could have indicated who had interfered with the crime scene.

7 A bloody footprint was cut out of the floor, and the boards it was on came apart.

8 MP Richard Tevere used the phone in the master bedroom, and yet no prints—his or anyone else's—were found on that phone.

9 Medlin twice tripped over a vacuum cleaner inside the utility room door before deciding to move it. On the washing machine next to it, he found a palm print that proved to be an investigator's.

10 The fingerprints of William Ivory, an FBI agent, and unidentified prints were found on the *Esquire* magazine.

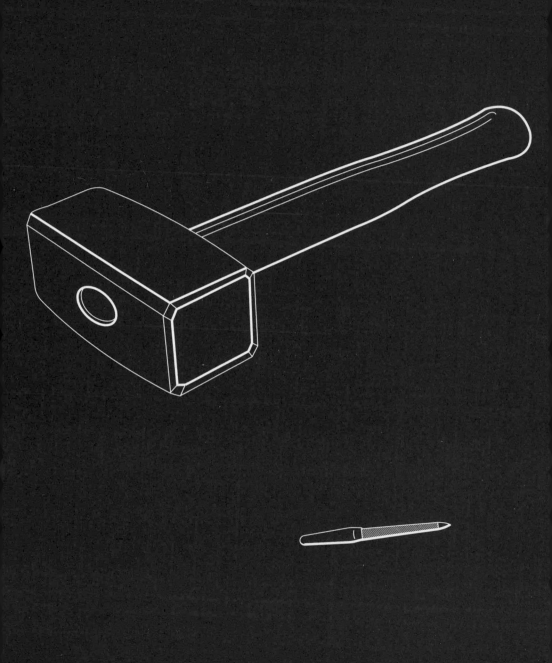

I'M NOT A CSI GUY

Between the Article 32 hearing in 1970 and when the grand jury was convened on August 12, 1974, the government had worked overtime to construct a comprehensive account of what had happened that night. And when Dr. Sadoff was interviewed by the prosecutor, it was as if the physical evidence had been assembled not only against MacDonald but also against *him* and *his* diagnosis of MacDonald.

Sadoff started to present the results of his examination of MacDonald. Woerheide cut him off and launched into a minute description of the prosecution's case prepared at the FBI crime laboratory:

VICTOR WOERHEIDE: Well, before we get into your immediate conclusions, may we jump to this? This is a photograph taken of Colette's chest. It shows twenty-one ice pick wounds, penetration, stabbings. The pathologist says that these stabbings were straight in and the body was motionless at the time. You have seen the pictures showing the—Dr. MacDonald's pajama top as it was lying on her chest. The FBI made a detailed study of those photographs [and] was able to reconstruct the manner in which the pajama top [was] folded with the right sleeve inside out and with the torn left side trailing down in this direction. Having reconstructed those folds, the pajama top had in it forty-eight ice pick holes. Some of which were made with the ice pick going in one direction and some of them going into it in the other direction. The ice pick was—penetrated the pajama top while it was stationary. There was no movement involved, except from straight in stabbings. Having refolded it they came up—the holes matched together. And the forty-eight holes matched together. And in such a way as to correspond to the twenty-one holes on her chest. He had no injuries in his back and you will notice the penetration marks in his pajama top.

Now there is one other item of evidence that is of great significance . . . These photographs are the photographs made of the sheet that was found together with a bedspread in the bedroom where Colette's body was lying in a heap on the floor. In Kris's room, the top sheet of Kris's bed had a large pool of Colette's blood over a portion near the top of the bed and against the wall. There is none of her blood on the floor. There are two bloody footprints of Captain MacDonald, the blood being Colette's blood exiting from the door of that room. Now, this as I say, these photographs are made of the sheet that was found in the east bedroom and some of Colette's garments or Captain MacDonald's pajama top. The FBI studied this sheet and determined from the pattern of the blood that had been trans-ferred to the sheet, that the sheet had been laid over the body of Colette while she was laying face downward—that it was folded partially—that someone wearing Captain MacDonald's blood-stained pajama top picked it up, which at that time was torn. And the marks of his bare left shoulder—it was torn on the left side—his collarbones and his chin, all of which have blood on them, are found on this sheet. And the bedspread that was found in conjunction with the sheet had a large amount of blood, type A blood [Colette's blood type], caused by direct bleeding.

The [inference] from the bedspread, the sheet, the pool of blood on the top sheet in Kris's bed and the two bloody footprints is that Colette, being on top of Kris's bed, bled severely. She was laid on the floor on top of the bedspread, the sheet placed over her and then she was picked up by whoever was wearing Captain MacDonald's pajamas. The marks of the design—of the design of her pajamas, the seams, the lace on her cuffs, the tear on his pajama top, the bead-ing here in the sleeve area, the pattern of blood that was on the sleeve and on the front part of the right of his pajamas were transferred directly to the sheet. So, you can see it. Here's a photograph indicating the marks where—you know—his chin, the bare left shoulder and sleeve marks there, the hand marks were—[1]

I can only imagine the effect of this tirade. Woerheide was telling Dr. Sadoff that MacDonald was the killer, by going into enormous detail about how the killings were "done." How could Sadoff reconcile his psychiatric diagnosis with these forensic facts?

ROBERT SADOFF: [*Interposing.*] How do you know all this?

VICTOR WOERHEIDE: It's like fingerprint analysis. The same principle. My question is, had you known the facts that we are presenting to you at this time which have been developed during the course of this grand jury investigation, had this information been furnished to you, would you possibly have arrived at a different determination than you did . . . ?

Dr. Sadoff is being told (incorrectly) that the government's methods are *foolproof* and its findings are incontrovertible. That therefore he is *wrong*.

ROBERT SADOFF: And I am not sure how to judge the scientific excellence that you are going with. I am terribly impressed with what you have done. But I don't know how—how to—

Dr. Sadoff, when pressed, explains, "You're talking to a psychiatrist who is dealing in a fairly broad arc, not so scientific." But he repeated that he had "found no serious psychiatric illness." But Woerheide once again asked if it was "possible" that MacDonald could have committed the crime.

ROBERT SADOFF: Well, I would say that he could, which is true for most anybody . . . I would say, yes, it is possible. But I have to find it very unlikely from a psychological standpoint.

VICTOR WOERHEIDE. On the basis of the information that was available to you at that time?

ROBERT SADOFF: Yes, that's right.

VICTOR WOERHEIDE: Now, is it possible that, having further information made available to you, you might revise that?

ROBERT SADOFF: If I had a chance to discuss this with him, and know his reactions to it and see how he has fared over the last five years, how he may have handled it or, let's say, adjusted to it . . . there are a lot of things I'd have to go through . . . would have to discuss this with him. However, as I indicated, what you were talking about is the sledgehammer to my nail file . . . I am not so sure that a psychiatrist right now is the proper person to be talking to.

I called Robert Sadoff.

ERROL MORRIS: There's a powerful moment in your testimony for the grand jury. Victor Woerheide confronts you with this physical evidence—representing it as incontrovertible. He says, "It's like fingerprint evidence." You're being told that your view of Jeffrey MacDonald is absolutely incompatible with the physical evidence. And you say, "You have a sledgehammer to my nail file."

ROBERT SADOFF: [*Laughs.*] Yeah, I remember that. You see, he presented this sledgehammer of evidence, and I only had a nail file. I had *nothing*. Except I had my own psychiatric examination. Look, I wasn't there. I didn't see what he did or didn't do. But I had what he said, and how he said it, and the consistency of his statement with his personality—

ERROL MORRIS: Here's what troubles me about this. Regardless of what Victor Woerheide said to you in the grand jury hearing, the physical evidence is not incontrovertible.

ROBERT SADOFF: No, no, it isn't. If you're talking about the pajamas and the stab wounds in the pajamas, I think that's really reaching, frankly. But I'm not a CSI guy!

ERROL MORRIS: But what happens when you don't have physical evidence that's incontrovertible? What happens is that people fall back on questions of charac-ter, so ultimately it becomes a question, the questions that *you* concern yourself with—is this the kind of person who *could have* committed this murder? The psychologists and psychiatrists were unanimous more or less at the Article 32 hearing. Both the prosecution's expert witnesses and the defense's expert wit-nesses agreed.

ROBERT SADOFF: Yeah. And the judge dismissed the case. When they indicted him five years later, Bernie Segal asked me to go out to California and reevaluate him, talk to people who knew him and worked with him. And all I can tell you is that the police and the firefighters and the emergency room doctors, they loved him. He was responsible, reliable, and a very good surgeon, and I spoke to two of his girlfriends, not a negative word. He was never a violent person. If anything, he was very constructive and productive. There were things about him that came out at the trial, about an affair that he may have had, or something like that, and of course the whole theory was that he got into an argument with his wife and lost control. If you're a surgeon, and a Green Beret, you don't lose control. It's just not part of your makeup. You just can't be a surgeon if you lose it. I couldn't be a surgeon; I probably don't have enough of that kind of calmness. It's nice for me to be a psychiatrist because I can exude emotion if I want, if I feel it's appropriate, but you can't do that if you're a surgeon, you've got to maintain a control and a coolness all the time, someone's life will depend on it.

ERROL MORRIS: Do you remember your initial impressions of MacDonald when you met him?

ROBERT SADOFF: Oh yeah, they were very positive. Here's a guy who was a physician, he was charming, he was good-looking, he was pleasant, and even after the tragedy, that he lost his wife and his kids—as I recall, he showed appropriate emotion, and he wouldn't do that in front of the prosecution, because that was the kind of guy he was, and they held that against him, that he wouldn't even cry or show emotion. Well, he did with me, so again, it depends on who's doing it, and how you present it, because there are people who will never get a person to open up, they don't have the skill or the emotions to do it.

ERROL MORRIS: Also, it seems less likely that you are going to open up if you know that the people you're talking to are trying to convict you of murder. But what do *you* think? Do you think that he's innocent?

ROBERT SADOFF: I have always thought that. And the fact that he has never accepted the offer to show remorse for something that he did not do. He may be stubborn, but he's got a certain integrity that says, "Look, I am not going to show remorse." He said, "I'm sad, I've lost my whole family, but I didn't do it, I didn't kill them, and I'm not going to admit to something I didn't do just to get my freedom."

ERROL MORRIS: I find it very hard to believe that a person could consistently profess his innocence over forty years. If he's a deranged killer, he certainly has hidden it extraordinarily well.

ROBERT SADOFF: Well, he's not deranged, and I don't think he's a killer. I don't think he stabbed himself. His chief of surgery at Columbia testified that it was so close to the heart that not even a cardiac surgeon would know exactly where to place the ice pick in the chest to collapse the lung without hitting the pericardium.[2] And if it hits the pericardium, he's dead. They said he stabbed himself, and they called it a minor wound. A collapsed lung is not a minor wound.

ERROL MORRIS: They may not have had the evidence to convict him, but they were able to present the evidence in such a way as to make a case.

Sadoff's complaints, in keeping with his role as an expert psychiatric witness, were directed toward his perception that there was something *inconsistent* in the prosecution's description of MacDonald's state of mind. The idea that MacDonald—

in the middle of a rage—could suddenly become *a different* person, a person solely concerned with covering his tracks.

> **ROBERT SADOFF:** I felt this was so far from what he was capable of doing. Anybody is capable of losing control in an argument and lashing out. That's what they [the prosecutors] argued he did with Colette. And then with his older daughter [Kimberley], who they say came to the doorway and saw it. But then, because the younger daughter [Kristen] was sleeping, he had to go in there and, in cold blood, take this ice pick. And that's where they got the first degree. The rest of them were second-degree murders. To me that is not in keeping with the kind of person that he is.

22

A COMB AND A TOOTHBRUSH

The grand jury handed down an indictment on three counts of murder on January 24, 1975. Within an hour, MacDonald had been arrested in California.

Bernie Segal asked MacDonald to provide a running account of what was happening to him. MacDonald wrote it all down at his destination, the federal prison in Bastrop, Texas.

The account has the quality of a dream:

I was sitting at my home at Huntington Beach in my underwear. Present were my mother, Mrs. Dorothy MacDonald and my girlfriend, Antoinette Day, who is a nurse at the hospital. I was on the phone to Bob Keeler, a reporter from *Newsday*. I was on the phone with him discussing my appearance during the prior week in North Carolina and I was sitting in my office, like I said, in my underwear, and I noticed three men in business suits, who looked like police, knocking on the front door. I mentioned to Bob Keeler on the phone, which he later published, Gee, I hope that isn't the FBI . . . My mother had opened the door at this time and had come into my office and said, The FBI is here to see you.

`. . . I walked into the living room and I was confronted by three men. I was completely unclothed except for shorts, boxer-type underwear shorts, and I was confronted by three men, one of whom identified himself as an FBI agent. I believe it was an Atherton who showed me his badge and his credentials. He said, I have some bad news for you, can we talk? And I said, Sure, let's go into my office. So I walked into my office and the three men came in behind me and sort of surrounded me and I said, What is it about? And Mr. Atherton said, The grand jury in North Carolina has returned an indictment against you and we are picking you up for murder. And I apparently appeared a little stunned and just stood there for a moment and said, You're kidding? And they said, No we are not and we have to take you to jail. So I started to sit down on the couch and the other FBI agent, a guy by the name of either Cornett or Colnett, I don't know at this point but I will find out later, sort of grabbed me by the arm and said, Don't sit down, and the other FBI agent said, That is okay. Let him sit down. They let me sit down on the couch and one of the three agents, I believe it was Atherton, read me my rights at that point. I am sorry—correction. He asked me, Is there anything that you want to say about the case? And I said, You mean like a confession—you want me to confess now five years later . . .

I said, Should I bring a comb and a toothbrush and stuff?, and they said, The jail won't let you keep them anyway, so there is no sense bringing it. So I left without anything except the shirt, slacks, underwear, socks, shoes and a watch. They then handcuffed me by handcuffing both hands in front of me with the handcuffs going under the belt. So one hand was below my belt and one hand was above my belt and the belt sort of ran through the handcuffs. They then walked me out to their car, got me in the right side of the car and then put the seat belt around me also, weaving it through the belt, that was weaved through the handcuffs and we took off. Colnett was in the back seat with me to my left and Atherton was in the front seat driving. The third man, whose name I never found out, was apparently in another car and he was parked on the other side of the brick wall separating my condominium from the Pacific Coast Highway. We went out the Pacific Coast Highway and turned into a Pacific Divers Shop parking lot which is opposite my house on Pacific Coast Highway, and had a rendezvous in the parking lot with the other FBI agent in his car. He was by himself. They talked briefly and he mentioned that he had radioed ahead to Orange County that the subject was in custody and that we were on the way. So we took off. We went back down Pacific Coast Highway towards Long Beach and took a right on Seal Beach Blvd. and went out to the 405 Freeway and took a right on the Freeway so we were heading south towards San Diego . . .

I asked, Where are we going? And they said, You have to appear before the magistrate. You have to appear before the magistrate and he is waiting for us. So we eventually arrived in Santa Ana, which is about 10 miles from my house or maybe 15 miles from my house, and parked about two blocks away from the magistrate's office and they walked me through downtown Santa Ana in hand-cuffs with everyone turning and stopping and staring.[1]

––––––––

The legal wrangling continued. MacDonald's defense argued that too much time had elapsed between the Article 32 and the grand jury hearing. The government replied that the delays had been caused by the defense. The defense argued that the Article 32 hearing had provided an exoneration, and that MacDonald should not be subjected to double jeopardy. The government replied that the Article 32 hearing was not a trial, and since he could not have been convicted at the Article 32 hearing, there was no double jeopardy.

Never has an Article 32 proceeding been found to be more than a preliminary hearing or pretrial discovery proceeding . . . Hence petitioner [MacDonald] could not have been convicted at the Article 32 proceeding. Without risk of a determination of guilt, jeopardy does not attach. Since an accused must suffer jeopardy before he can suffer double jeopardy, petitioner's indictment does not violate the double jeopardy clause.[2]

BOOK THREE

1963 ■ **May 13**
In *Brady v. Maryland*, the Supreme Court rules that withholding exculpatory evidence violates due process "where the evidence is material either to guilt or to punishment."

1979 ■ **Pretrial**
Jeffrey Puretz, a prosecution law clerk, sends Brian Murtagh a memo regarding the prosecution's duty to disclose exculpatory material according to the *Brady* ruling.

July 19
The trial of Jeffrey MacDonald begins.

August 1
Mildred Kassab testifies about Colette's relationship with Jeffrey MacDonald and their last Christmas.

August 7–9
Paul Stombaugh, former chief of the chemistry lab for the FBI, testifies.

August 9–10
Shirley Green, the technician in the microscopic analysis unit of the FBI who performed the pajama-top experiment, testifies.

August 10
The issue of *Esquire* magazine from March 1970 is read into the record.

August 13
The defense moves to strike the entire *Esquire* transcript from the record. Judge Franklin Dupree rules that MacDonald will submit to psychiatric and psychological testing by the government's experts later that afternoon. The defense makes a motion of acquittal for lack of evidence brought by the prosecution.

MacDonald is examined by Drs. James Brussel and Hirsch L. Silverman.

August 14–15
Dr. John Thornton, forensic expert for the defense, testifies.

August 15
Judge Dupree announces that Helena Stoeckley is in custody in Greenville, South Carolina.

August 17
Helena Stoeckley testifies. Outside the hearing of the jury, six witnesses testify to Helena Stoeckley's confessions.

August 20
Judge Dupree rules to exclude the testimony by the witnesses to Stoeckley's confessions.

1979
cont.

August 22

Judge Dupree rules that psychiatric testimony will not be admitted.

August 22

Helen Fell, a friend of both the MacDonald and Kassab families, testifies.

August 28

Closing arguments.

August 29

Jeffrey MacDonald is found guilty of one count of first-degree murder and two counts of second-degree murder.

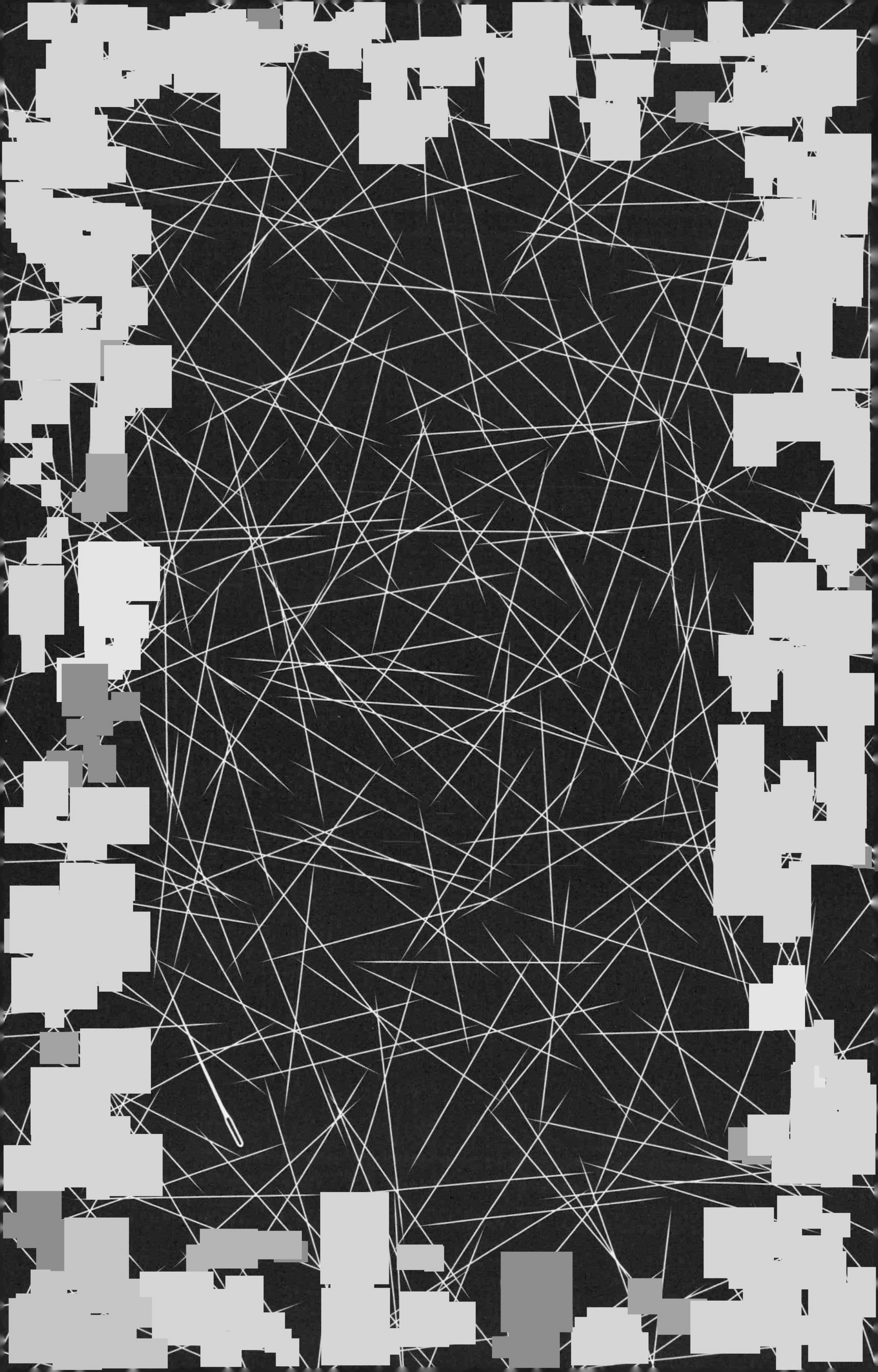

23

THE JAIL CELL

About three months prior to the start of MacDonald's trial, after years of haggling about access to the physical evidence, Dr. John Thornton, the forensic expert hired by Segal, was finally invited to inspect it. It had been crammed into a small jail cell in Raleigh. The federal prosecutor Brian Murtagh was present, as was Donald Murray, a special agent for the FBI.

At the time of the trial, Thornton was an associate professor of forensic science at the University of California at Berkeley. He went on to become one of the most prominent forensic experts in the United States, chairman of the criminalistics section of the American Academy of Forensic Sciences. He processed about eight hundred homicide cases over a forty-seven-year career. He is now, in his words, "retired for the third time."

JOHN THORNTON: Okay. You know, I really don't know whether he was innocent. I feel very strongly that he did not get a fair trial. And that's been essentially my focus for the last—well, since 1979. I don't know, Mr. Morris. I don't know. Everything that I'm capable of thinking, I probably have thought. Everything that I'm capable of saying to anyone, I've already said. I'm pretty much depleted. So I don't really know how I could help you.

ERROL MORRIS: Well, how about the beginning? Can you describe that scene to me?

JOHN THORNTON: The evidence was in a jail cell, which measured probably eight feet by ten feet. And there was box after box after box of evidence. I had asked for the evidence to be released to me for examination out here [in California]. I have the laboratory facilities to do that. The prosecution resisted that, and the court did not compel the production of the evidence—until the eve of trial. It might have been a month, maybe two, prior to the trial.

Then they said, "Okay, here it is. What do you want to see?" And I wasn't in a position to say, "I want to see everything," because there simply wasn't time. And there were no real facilities. This is in the U.S. marshal's office, in Raleigh, in a jail cell. But I was allowed to ask for certain items that were examined in the state crime laboratory. At least I could open up the boxes and bags and look at the material. And I asked for samples, and I didn't get them. Then there was all the courtroom litigation over what was going to be—

ERROL MORRIS: You asked for samples prior to being shown the samples in the jail cell?

JOHN THORNTON: Yes, I had asked for evidence through the defense attorney, Mr. Segal. But the prosecution was resistant to any of the evidence being sent to California. At the same time, they were sending evidence to the FBI laboratory in Washington, D.C. So they were playing their games. Both sides were posturing. There's another aspect of this which really I think colors the issue of accessibility to the evidence. And that is that the defense—Bernie Segal—was absolutely convinced that there would be an acquittal, that he would be handily acquitted. And the physical evidence wasn't really on a front burner.

Now, he could have said, "We're not going to go to trial. You can throw me in jail if you want, but we're not going to go to trial until the defense has an opportunity for an examination of the evidence." Now, he could have done that, and it was a tactical decision on his part not to do so, because he felt that the sooner the case went to trial, the sooner Jeffrey MacDonald would be acquitted and be out on—well, he would be acquitted. So rather than prolong the fight over accessibility to the evidence, the defense just accepted what the prosecution was offering, which was the right of visitation, but not the right of examination.

ERROL MORRIS: But of course it was prolonged—I mean, it was years before this thing went to trial.

JOHN THORNTON: Yes, it went up to the Supreme Court several times. But never on physical evidence issues. And then, when it was clear that there was going to be a trial, then the defense said, "Okay, let's get it over with." There were some ritual pleas for evidence accessibility. They really weren't fought out tooth and nail. Brian Murtagh, the prosecutor, during the trial gave me some envelopes of clippings for blood typing. This is when the trial had already commenced. And he knew of course that there wasn't enough time. But that was part of the tactics.

ERROL MORRIS: And Bernie Segal just felt he didn't want to push it?

JOHN THORNTON: Well, he was pushing a lot of things. And this was just one of the irons in the fire. But it wasn't his principal one. I don't think he was insincere; it's just that he was very much trying to track down the Helena Stoeckley issues and other things.

ERROL MORRIS: And so when you finally got into the cell, how was this set up? I mean, what was the immediate history behind that visit to the cell?

JOHN THORNTON: Well, there was a point at which the prosecution said, "Okay, Thornton can look at the evidence. It's secured in the federal marshal's office, actually in the jail cell." And at some point I went there. And the cell was pretty much filled with boxes.

ERROL MORRIS: Labeled boxes?

JOHN THORNTON: Boxes, bags. I don't have any specific recollection. Bags inside the boxes. That would be typical of evidence packaging.

ERROL MORRIS: Carefully labeled, or just higgledy-piggledy?

JOHN THORNTON: I would say that they were fairly carefully labeled, yes.

ERROL MORRIS: Were you given some kind of inventory?

JOHN THORNTON: Well, I had reports. I could ask for a particular thing. And at no point was I denied access. I had to ask for something in particular, and then it would be produced. But not necessarily made available for any examination. Out here in California, there's pretty much free discovery. And the defense is accustomed to being able to reexamine anything. And federal law says that the defense has an opportunity to confront the evidence, to look at it. But the federal law doesn't really say that the prosecution is compelled to turn it over for any examination, particularly if there is any destructive aspect to it. And in a blood typing, there is going to be some destructive aspect. And that, of course, is what the prosecution is thumping. They say, "Well, we can't release any of the evidence that's going to be consumed in the analysis." The judge had been around quite a while. And he knew just how much he could get away with, without making a reversible error. So, in short, the defense went to trial without an adequate examination of the evidence.

ERROL MORRIS: And what could you have found if you had had better information going into that cell?

JOHN THORNTON: Well, the prosecution had this reenactment which was based largely on bloodstain evidence. But if there was one error in the bloodstain, type A mistaken for B, or AB mistaken for O, or whatever, it would have altered the reconstruction totally. So I was very much interested in the bloodstain evidence, and urine-stain evidence as well. That is, blood type secreted in urine, in the case of the children.

ERROL MORRIS: You never really had an opportunity to examine the blood typing?

JOHN THORNTON: No.

ERROL MORRIS: Is it easy to make confusions of that sort between one blood type and another?

JOHN THORNTON: Yes. And my understanding was that there was some discrepancies in the blood typing between Janice Glisson in the army crime laboratory at Fort Gordon and the FBI laboratory in D.C. People in the FBI laboratory have conceded that there were some differences, and they just didn't bring them to the attention of the defense.

ERROL MORRIS: They suppressed them?

JOHN THORNTON: There came a point where—I'm going to use an indelicate expression—where I just saw the whole case as a colossal clusterfuck.

———

By the end of a seven-year reexamination of the evidence, the lawyers for the government had an intimate familiarity with all of the evidence against Jeffrey MacDonald. They were comfortable with the structure of their case—its strengths and its weaknesses. The lawyers for the defense, at the end of their protests, got to look over evidentiary reports for a matter of days and guess which pieces of evidence would be most important. And once John Thornton had the evidence, the rule was "look, but don't touch."

Was this fair? Were those reports reliable? Or is it possible that the Article 32 hearing had repeated itself? That, while the case had changed hands, evidence was *still* being withheld?

The possibility was dramatized by the discovery of the so-called Puretz memo. Prepared at the behest of Brian Murtagh and written by his law clerk Jeffrey Puretz, the memo tells us that the prosecution was interested in what evidence could be *legally* withheld. It was written weeks prior to the 1979 federal trial. To MacDonald's appellate attorneys, who saw it years after the fact, it looked like a strategem for suppression.

TO: Brian Murtagh
FROM: Jeffrey S. Puretz, Law Clerk
RE: The Prosecutor's Duty to Disclose Exculpatory Materials in the Fourth Circuit

and Other Criminal Discovery Issues relating to United States v. MacDonald, CR-75-1870

> 1. What are the Constitutional Due Process Requirements for Disclosure of Exculpatory Materials by the Prosecutor pursuant to Brady v. Maryland, in the Fourth Circuit?
>   a. Basic Principles
>   b. Need the detailed data of a lab report, as distinguished from the conclusions of the report, be disclosed, where such conclusions have been disclosed and are non-exculpatory?
> 2. What are the ramifications of an open file policy of disclosure by the prosecutor?
> 3. At what point in time must exculpatory materials be disclosed to the defense in a criminal proceeding?

The memo could be routine. A series of questions a prosecutor asks about disclosure. And yet there is that one word that appears in the slug line—"exculpatory." It's not "materials"; it's "exculpatory materials." But the finding in *Brady v. Maryland* had been that exculpatory material must *always* be available to the defense. To do otherwise is to violate due process, "where the evidence is material either to guilt or to punishment, irrespective of the good faith or bad faith of the prosecution."

Puretz was being asked to find the outer limits of that requirement. He surveyed the recent rulings on *Brady* and furnished an answer, written in legalese:

> These timing cases again indicate the difficult showing required for a Brady violation under circumstances where a partial open file policy has been followed, with non-disclosure items submitted for in-camera review and with government witnesses subject to cross-examination at trial.

"A partial open file policy." The plan worked. The road map provided by Puretz gave the prosecution what it needed. Bernie Segal had been filing repeated requests to be given access to the physical evidence since April 1975. But his requests were not being heard. By letting John Thornton into the jail cell, by giving Segal a chance to question the experts who had pored over the evidence for years, the prosecutors had given the defense attorneys *just* enough access to the evidence, in *just* enough time—and as a result made it difficult to argue that they had been given little or nothing.

24

THINGS DO NOT LIE

The trial began on July 19, 1979, roughly nine years after the start of the Article 32 hearing. Meanwhile, MacDonald had established a successful career in Long Beach, California, as the director of emergency medical services at St. Mary Medical Center.

What had changed by 1979? The FBI crime laboratory had finally conducted analysis of the few key pieces of physical evidence. James Blackburn, the assistant U.S. attorney appointed to the prosecution along with Murtagh, began his opening argument with a brief introduction and description of the charges.

> **JAMES BLACKBURN:** The government has the responsibility of proving to you beyond a reasonable doubt that the defendant—the man sitting right there [*pointing to MacDonald*]—is the man that killed Colette, Kimberley and Kristen MacDonald. That is the burden of proof that the government of the United States has, and that is what we intend to show you at this trial.[1]

Blackburn then turned to circumstantial evidence. He defined it as evidence "where there is a chain or a web of circumstances that point unerringly to the fact that a certain individual may have done a certain thing."

> **JAMES BLACKBURN:** . . . What is a good example of circumstantial evidence? What am I talking about when I speak of circumstantial evidence? Suppose during the nighttime, you are asleep in your own bed, and everything is quiet; and all of a

sudden, you are awakened in the middle of the night by a loud crashing sound. You don't pay any attention to it. You go back to sleep; but you have heard it.

The next morning when you awaken and you get up, you look outside and you see that it has snowed during the nighttime; and so, you go to your back door and you see your two garbage cans—those metal things that clank so loud—both knocked over. You see a set of dog tracks coming to the garbage can from your neighbor's yard; and you see a set of dog tracks going back to your neighbor's yard and the dog tracks stop where your neighbor's dog is sitting. You can probably assume that that dog had something to do with knocking over those garbage cans. That is circumstantial evidence, ladies and gentlemen.

Blackburn went on to say that his circumstantial case relied on a familiar set of physical objects: the four murder weapons—the ice pick, the two knives, and the wooden club—MacDonald's pajama top, the *Esquire* magazine.

JAMES BLACKBURN: The circumstantial evidence is real. Physical evidence is real.

It's equally true that the Defendant, Jeffrey MacDonald, was there that night as he is today. It is equally true that physical evidence was there that night. Let me assure you—it is also equally true that things do not lie. This is not a complicated case—it is straightforward.

I think we are going to make it easy for you to understand—or we are going to try—that the circumstantial physical evidence in this case points swiftly and unerringly to the fact that one person killed his family. Every purpose that the government has at this trial—every question that we ask—every witness that we examine—every argument that we make—is for only one purpose and that purpose is to bring out the truth.

Wade Smith—a well-regarded North Carolina defense attorney who had been hired to work alongside Segal on the defense—told the jury they were going to see a human-interest story. Rather than the physical evidence, the defense argument focused on MacDonald himself.

WADE SMITH: The focal point in the case is this: the government must prove to you that Jeffrey MacDonald raised his hand to his wife and stabbed her forty times, if I counted correctly in Mr. Blackburn's opening statement; that he raised his hand to his wife and struck her with a club on the same evening at the same time, or close to the same time, at least five times; that he used an ice pick; that he used a knife; that he used three weapons—three separate weapons—to slay his wife. And they must prove to you that he did basically the same thing with his children. And that is the focal point. They cannot prove to you that it might have happened. They cannot prove to you that maybe it happened—that maybe a knife was used— they cannot use [the] words "maybe," "possibly," because, ladies and gentlemen of the Jury, they are saddled with the heaviest burden of proof that you will find in any system in the civilized world—they must prove beyond a reasonable doubt and to a moral certainty. The Judge will tell you, as members of the Jury, that you must be fully satisfied, entirely convinced . . . that Jeffrey MacDonald did the things that they alleged that he did. And if they fail in the slightest, he is entitled to his acquittal.

If they are using circumstantial evidence they cannot make it as simple as a dog walking over to a garbage can. This is not a case that is that simple. Circumstantial evidence must point unerringly to the guilt of Jeffrey MacDonald . . .

We will go back to the beginning.

We will show you a young boy growing up who is just like hundreds of young boys you have known. Just like them, Jeffrey MacDonald. Athlete, good student, leader, always excelling. Always doing well. Always motivated to do his best. Not a lot of money. Going to school at Princeton on a scholarship. Doing well. Going to medical school at Northwestern. Doing well.

We will bring into the picture then, Colette. C-o-l-e-t-t-e. A fine woman. A fine person.

We will show you how he got a choice residency because of his work at Northwestern.

We will show you how he volunteered for the Military. How he volunteered for the Green Beret. How he was proud.

We will bring to their home the two children, Kim and Kristen.

We will bring them to Fayetteville, to Fort Bragg.

We will produce testimony that Dr. MacDonald—he was a doctor then—was working two extra jobs; "moonlighting" to make enough money so that his family could live, not die.

We will show you how they had bought a pony for the children. We will show you how they had bought a few other things for the home because they were now getting on their feet, ready to live, not die.

We will show you how they eagerly anticipated the arrival of a new little one. Colette was five months pregnant. And then, we will show you how it ended. How the whole thing In a matter of minutes ended—ashes.[2]

25

PIGS ON ICE

On August 1, 1979, Mildred Kassab was called to the stand. Blackburn had asked her to tell the story of her daughter's last Christmas.

> **JAMES BLACKBURN:** [D]irecting your attention to December of 1969, did you and your husband have an occasion to visit Jeff and Colette at Christmas?
>
> **MILDRED KASSAB:** Yes, we went down at Christmastime. Colette wasn't herself. I thought it was because of her pregnancy. She was very subdued and quiet. As a matter of fact, little by little Colette ceased to be the bouncy, happy person she had been at the beginning; but with all of the money problems—one can only help to a certain extent—I thought it was that—but she wasn't herself.
>
> Then Christmas morning when the gifts were opened, Jeff said with his mother's gifts, "Didn't she send money? I told her not to buy gifts; why didn't she send money?" So, I thought perhaps there was a new emergency.
>
> I went inside and wrote a check and put it on the Christmas tree, thinking that if something is wrong—it wasn't for much. It was for $100, but I had already bought the gifts and things and that is what I could spare at the moment. There [was] also an incident in the afternoon.
>
> **JAMES BLACKBURN:** Go ahead.
>
> **MILDRED KASSAB:** Jeff wanted to call guests down from upstairs. There were these people who lived upstairs; we didn't know them. We rode several hundred miles to come see Colette and Jeff and the children, and he wanted to call the people from upstairs down; and Colette said no.

We already had the dinner in progress. It was around 4:00 o'clock. She was making a special dinner then and the dinner would be ruined, but Jeff had to have it done as he wanted, so he called them down.

We took turns. I made eggnog and drinks in the kitchen and run in and sit for a moment, and run to the kitchen again, do a few things. Colette would take her turn, and they finally left about 8:00 o'clock.

We had a dried-up dinner. We didn't say anything about it, made the best of it—put it on the table. It wasn't until I realized there was a heavy, heavy silence [that] I saw a couple of tears going down Colette's face.

She wasn't saying anything, but just two big tears. I said, "What is wrong?" Her children were saying nothing. Jeff got up—his chair flew over—and said, "She's always that way," and so forth; and I said, "What way?" "Well, with guests, the way she acts and so forth." I said, "You're being very childish, Jeff. You were told we didn't want guests." We reseated ourselves at the table and proceeded with our Christmas dinner the best way we could.[1]

———

Let's jump back nine years. At the Article 32 hearing Freddy Kassab was the ideal character witness. MacDonald had always been a good boyfriend, a good husband, a good father, a good son-in-law.

Colette and Jeffrey met when they were only twelve. And they became on-and-off-again boyfriend-girlfriend a couple of years after. Segal asked about their last Christmas. It was in Fort Bragg, 1969.

ALFRED KASSAB: Christmas morning, at about six o'clock—I'm an early riser—I was up walking around and Jeff said to me, "I've got a surprise," he said, "for the kids for Christmas, and I want you to come down and take a look." So he and I got dressed and left the house before my wife and daughter and grandchildren got up and we drove down the road three or four miles and he showed me a pony that he had bought for the children . . .

BERNARD SEGAL: And what happened when you went down to visit the horse?

ALFRED KASSAB: Well, we went down to where the horse was being kept and when I saw the horse I thought it was terrific for the children—pony, I should say. And then we went back to the house and Jeff proceeded to tell Colette that he had ordered a gift for the children for Christmas and that since Sears & Roebuck fouled it up, that there was one in the window and if we'd all get in the car we'd go down to see this thing so at least they could see what they were getting for Christmas. And we drove down the road and then we turned off and Colette didn't understand why we were turning off the road and not going straight down to Sears & Roebuck and he said, "Well I got to stop here and pick something up." And we drove down to the corral and we all got out of the car and he said, "I want you to see something over here." And we took them over there and showed them the pony.

BERNARD SEGAL: What was Colette's view of the gift for the children?

ALFRED KASSAB: To the best of my recollection, she cried for half an hour.

BERNARD SEGAL: Now when did you leave your stepdaughter and son-in-law in December?

ALFRED KASSAB: It was the day after Christmas.

BERNARD SEGAL: . . . What was her attitude as far as family relationship at the time you left her?

ALFRED KASSAB: . . . As I said, they were the happiest I've ever seen them.

BERNARD SEGAL: When you indicated that Colette cried on seeing the horse, was that—as far as you could tell—was that because she was sad or disappointed?

ALFRED KASSAB: No, Colette being, always was a sensitive child, and anything that made her very happy, she cried.[2]

Freddy Kassab was describing a happy marriage.

ALFRED KASSAB: Well, they were like a couple of pigs on ice . . .

Somers, the Article 32 prosecutor, had never heard the expression before. "Pigs on ice?"

CLIFFORD SOMERS: . . . You've used the phrase which I don't really understand, and the phrase was "like pigs on ice," . . . I think what you mean to say is that, in describing the relationship between Colette and Jeff that they were very happy together and devoted to one another. Is that what you are saying?

ALFRED KASSAB: Yes, sir.

———

Back to the trial. And it had all changed. No more tears of joy. A family besieged with financial troubles. A burned dinner. An inconsiderate husband and a wife on the edge of a nervous breakdown. Blackburn asked about the ice pick—a subject never very far from his mind. Both of the Kassabs had previously denied seeing the ice pick, or at least that ice pick in the MacDonald home. Now Mildred had a clear memory of it.[3]

> JAMES BLACKBURN: During the time that you were in the kitchen area this Christmas occasion, did you ever have occasion to go in the refrigerator or the ice part?
>
> MILDRED KASSAB: Definitely; I made some puff pastry, hors d'oeuvres and I brought them down and, finding no place that was cold enough, I had to use an ice pick to jimmy some ice trays out.
>
> JAMES BLACKBURN: Now, where did you get the ice pick?
>
> MILDRED KASSAB: Out of the kitchen drawer.
>
> JAMES BLACKBURN: Now, during this time, did you ever have occasion to see the pony that was bought for the children for Christmas?
>
> MILDRED KASSAB: Yes, the following morning—Christmas morning—there was a big surprise. We waited anxiously to see what it was. We went down a few miles from the house. It was a little Shetland pony that Jeff had bought from one of his officers who was transferred. There was a little shack to keep it in. I remarked to Colette, "This is the first part of your dream of the big old house with the dogs, cats, ponies, and so forth." She burst into tears. I thought it was tears of joy, but mothers always look for the best.[4]

———

The shifting sands of the MacDonald case. People who believed in MacDonald later turned against him. If at first MacDonald could do no wrong, suddenly he could do no right. Mildred Kassab, who had been operated on for cancer, had told him that he would be sorry if he moved to California.

Helen Fell, an acquaintance of the Kassabs and MacDonalds, testified at the trial about the last meetings between MacDonald and the Kassabs, just before he left for California.

> HELEN FELL: He talked to them, and he was very nice to them—very solicitous—and just kind of explained that he felt that he had to get away from the New York area, that it was just imperative to his own sanity and that he wanted to take this position at Saint Mary's in Los Angeles . . .
>
> WADE SMITH: Now, did Mrs. Kassab make any response to him?

HELEN FELL: Yes . . . Mildred had been quite ill and she first kind of talked to Jeff, tried to talk him out of going, telling him things [like], "Jeff, you can't go. I need you. I don't trust the doctors here and, if you leave"—you know—"I don't trust them and"—you know—"I need you." He said, "Mildred, they are very good doctors," et cetera, et cetera—you know—"You don't have to be concerned with that. I will stay in touch with your doctors even from California if that will make you feel better."

She said no; that would not do. She wanted Jeff to stay and she also told him, "I want you to stay and mourn with me." He said, "I can't do that, Mildred." He said, "I just can't." And she ended up by saying, "If you leave, I will make you live to regret it."[5]

On the stand, Fell stopped at "regret." When I interviewed her, she provided several additional details.

HELEN FELL: Jeff said, "I have to get out of here. I can't go on like this. I need to keep my sanity." She finally said, "If you leave, you're going to live to regret it." She said, "I will never stop until you go to the gallows."
ERROL MORRIS: And Freddy?
HELEN FELL: Freddy Kassab was a nebbish. Do you know what a nebbish is?
ERROL MORRIS: Yes. I believe I do.
HELEN FELL: Well, that describes Freddy to a tee. Everything was, "Yes, Mildred. No, Mildred. Well, Mildred, I don't think that's right." And she said, "Shut up, Freddy! I didn't ask you." And he'd just sit there and take it. I even said to my husband, "If I ever talked to you like that, what would you do?" He said, "I don't know what I'd do, but I wouldn't sit there with my finger up my ass. That I can tell you."

It just gets me so upset. It's a travesty. It's a wasted life, of a guy who was absolutely brilliant. And he was better to Mildred than anyone had ever been in her entire life. The kids wanted a horse. Mildred went out and bought them a rocking horse. They didn't want a rocking horse, they wanted a *horse* horse. So Jeff went out and bought them a pony.

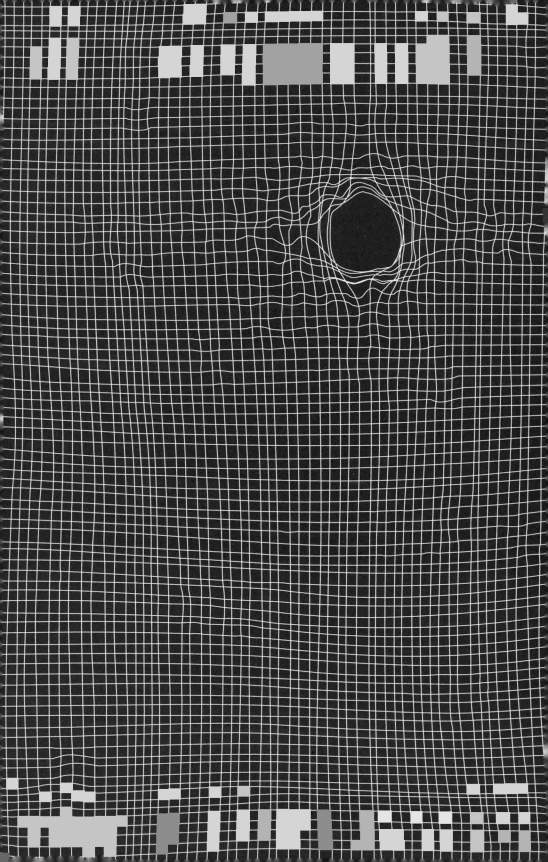

FORTY-EIGHT HOLES

They have fallen into the gross but common error of confounding the unusual with the abstruse. But it is by these deviations from the plane of the ordinary, that reason feels its way, if at all, in its search for the true.
—Edgar Allan Poe, "The Murders in the Rue Morgue"

It is the Shroud of Turin of the MacDonald case. Jeffrey MacDonald's torn pajama top. At the crime scene, it was found draped over Colette's body—blood-soaked, torn, and full of punctures. In one government brief the pajama top was called "the single most inculpatory piece of evidence"[1] in the trial. The government brief continued, "[MacDonald] claimed it was torn in the living room during his efforts to ward off the attackers and that he later placed it over his wife's body to keep her warm."

During the April 6, 1970, interview by the CID, MacDonald explained how his pajama top came to be on top of his wife:

ROBERT SHAW: Captain MacDonald, you told one of the other investigators earlier that you were wearing a pajama top that was pulled over your head or something like that.

JEFFREY MACDONALD: . . . [A]fter I had been hit the first time, I was struggling with these guys; and my—somehow, my pajama top—I don't know if it was ripped forward or pulled over my head . . . It was around my hands and it was in my way . . .

My hands were kind of wrapped up in the thing. And they were punching me . . . So, in effect, I was blunting everything by, you know, holding this up, and I couldn't get my hands free out of the thing.

MacDonald described how he was knocked out. When he regained consciousness, he stumbled into the master bedroom and found Colette lying on the floor, a knife sticking out of her chest. He removed the knife, and then covered her at some point with his pajama top.

JEFFREY MACDONALD: And I remember I ended up, when I was laying on the floor— I forgot to say that—when I woke up on—it was still around my hands and every- thing, and I took it off as I was going in the bedroom. And after I took this knife out of my wife's chest, I—you know, keeping her warm. You know, to treat shock that would be [inaudible] and keep them warm.

ROBERT SHAW: Was Colette alive then?

JEFFREY MACDONALD: I . . . I didn't think so, sir, because medically, I don't think she could have been because when I gave her mouth-to-mouth, I remember distinctly the bubbles were coming out of her chest . . .

I don't think she was alive because she was just lying there, very still, and made no response at all; and I didn't check her pulse initially. All I did was see her and take the knife out of her chest and breathe into her mouth.

In MacDonald's account, he was wearing the pajama top when Colette was stabbed.

The government's version of events is a bit more complicated, and it's the version told in *Fatal Vision,* the TV miniseries. The pajama top is introduced by Victor Woerheide, the federal prosecutor, and Paul Stombaugh, the FBI forensic expert. The scene is the imagined fateful meeting between Freddy Kassab, the father-in-law, now sworn to avenge the murders of his stepdaughter and his grandchildren, and the forensic scientist who will see that MacDonald is brought to justice.[2] Stombaugh explains to Kassab that if they could prove that Colette had been stabbed through the pajama top, the only explanation would be that Mac-Donald stabbed her through it.

This is the dialogue from the TV miniseries.

"VICTOR WOERHEIDE": . . . This is Paul Stombaugh, he's chief of the FBI's chemistry and physics branch. Freddy Kassab.

"FREDDY KASSAB": How do you do?

"BRIAN MURTAGH": Paul, I told them I felt the most damning evidence would have to be MacDonald's pajama top.

"PAUL STOMBAUGH": Yes, somewhat difficult to explain, but damning nonetheless.

"VICTOR WOERHEIDE": Suppose you make it less difficult for us?

"PAUL STOMBAUGH": I'll try. [*Stombaugh holds up the pajama top.*] This is a blue pajama top, similar to the one that he wore. [*He wraps it around his hands and holds it up to his chest.*] Now, I hold it up in front of me to keep off the blows of my attackers, but they come at me with an ice pick! [*He moves as if struggling.*] The pajama top is punctured, over and over. We carefully examined those puncture holes in the actual pajama. Every one of them. Under the microscope.

"VICTOR WOERHEIDE": And?

"PAUL STOMBAUGH": Not one single puncture showed the kind of ragged tearing that would've occurred if the pajama top had been in motion. Each and every hole was a small, clean puncture.

"FREDDY KASSAB": The pajama top had to be stationary at the time?

"PAUL STOMBAUGH": In my opinion.

"FREDDY KASSAB": Where?

"PAUL STOMBAUGH": Well, it was found on top of Colette's body.

"VICTOR WOERHEIDE": You think he stabbed her there? Through the pajama?

"PAUL STOMBAUGH": She had twenty-one ice pick wounds. We discovered that if you fold the actual pajama the way it was found on top of her body [*holding it up to his chest and folding it over itself*], the clean-cut holes match the pattern [*poking at his chest as if he's pointing at the puncture holes*] of the twenty-one ice pick stabbings on her body. Oh, I'm sorry, Mr. Kassab.

"FREDDY KASSAB": No, it's all right.[3]

The TV version simplified things. In 1973, Stombaugh had not performed the experiment himself. He had given the task of matching up the holes to Shirley Green, a physical science technician in the Microscopic Analysis Unit of the FBI Laboratory. Color-coded probes, graph paper, and pushpins were used to arrange the pajama top so that forty-eight punctures could be aligned with the twenty-one holes.

But one moment. What was Shirley Green reconstructing?

There were two separate sets of photographs taken of the crime scene. The pajama top is seen in two different positions, folded in different ways. And there is disputed testimony about where it was actually found.[4]

SHIRLEY GREEN: . . . We weren't concerned about having them angled and having the photographs match up. All we were concerned about was matching the holes in the same position in the same number.[5]

Shirley Green was just trying to find a way (in some hypothetical universe) to match up forty-eight punctures with twenty-one holes. Can you do this? Of course you can. There are multiple ways the pajama top could have been folded to match up forty-eight punctures with twenty-one holes. But where was the proof that this folding was anything like the actual, original position of the pajama top on Colette's body? Could you also find a way to match up the holes if the pajama top was bunched up, as MacDonald said it was, around his hands? Yes. Call it the origami problem.

Stombaugh and Green had also completely ignored the fact that Colette was covered with another piece of fabric—her own pajama top. There was no effort to correlate the holes made in MacDonald's pajama top with the holes in Colette's pajama top. The government did not connect the two pieces of evidence.

BERNARD SEGAL: When you looked at the pictures of Mrs. MacDonald's body, did you notice whether she had anything on the upper part of her body besides the blue pajama top? I will give you a picture if it will help. For the moment let me give you two of the three, which are C-1139 and G-1137.

SHIRLEY GREEN: Her own pajama top.

BERNARD SEGAL: That is the pink pajama top, is that right?

SHIRLEY GREEN: Yes. . . .

BERNARD SEGAL: Did you ever attempt to do this little experiment: first putting on the pink pajama top across the dummy, then putting on the blue pajama top, and then trying to put through—these skewers through it all?

SHIRLEY GREEN: No.

The underlying premise of the experiment was meaningless; it didn't relate to the crime scene and proved nothing. We could leave it at that, but there are other details that show just how ridiculous the whole exercise was.

Each stab could create multiple holes as it passed through different layers of folded or bunched fabric. If a tapered ice pick was used, it meant the top punctures would be wider in diameter than the ones below. Shirley Green conceded that the varying size of the holes had never been considered. Another omission. The

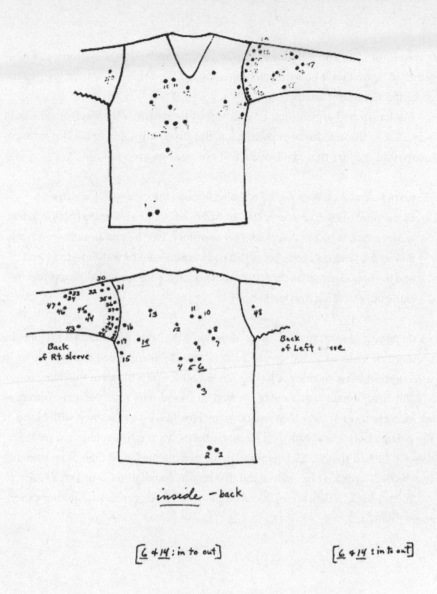

inside − back

[6 + 14 : in to out]   [6 + 14 : in to out]

"experiment" only had the veneer of scientific method. The evidence was distorted to reach a foregone conclusion.

Under cross-examination, Stombaugh admitted the limitations of the experiment:

PAUL STOMBAUGH: All I am saying is that we used up all forty-eight holes with twenty-one thrusts, and we're just saying it can be done. We are not saying this actually took place.[6]

It is one thing to correlate holes to puncture wounds. It is something else altogether to prove that is how the stabbing occurred. And this was something that the government never proved.

Blackburn had argued that he didn't need to explain why MacDonald would stab his wife through his own pajama top. But Brian Murtagh, in his closing arguments, told the jury that MacDonald had not one but *two* reasons:

BRIAN MURTAGH: . . . We have the stabbing through the pajama top which we contend serves two functions. One, he had to have some puncture holes in it, we would argue, to be consistent with his own story. Two, he had already, we submit, placed it on Colette's body because it had become soaked with Colette's blood and the only explanation consistent with his innocence would be the one that he came up with, "I put it on top of her."[7]

So there you have it. According to Murtagh, MacDonald needed to explain the presence of Colette's blood on the pajama top. He also needed to make holes in it, to support his own story of having fended off ice pick blows in the living room.

But MacDonald was already covered in blood. His torn pajama bottoms—which were thrown away at Womack Army Hospital—were stained with blood. If the pajama bottoms already had blood on them, Murtagh's explanation makes no sense. If he had stabbed Colette through his pajama top—and there is no evidence that he did—wouldn't he understand that he was leaving incriminating evidence?

It goes back to the coffee table. Another really bad argument. Another experiment that failed.

TARGET IN MOTION

Having failed to prove that MacDonald had stabbed his wife in the master bedroom, the prosecution decided to attack MacDonald's version of what happened. The basic premise set up by Stombaugh at the grand jury was that the shape of the punctures could tell us where they were made—in the master bedroom or in the living room:

PAUL STOMBAUGH: In examining these holes, I determined they could have been made by an ice pick . . . And further, that these holes were put in this pajama top when it was stationary. My conclusion as to the holes being put in here when it was stationary is the fact that none of the holes had tearing.

If someone is fighting off an assailant, and they go after you with an ice pick, and you dodge, this material is going to tear where that ice pick goes through.

None of these forty-eight holes had any of this tearing. So therefore, it is my opinion that they were put in there when it was stationary.[1]

Stombaugh had set up a series of equations:

Circular holes = stationary fabric = the holes were produced in the bedroom.

Tearing = moving fabric = the holes were produced in the living room.

When Stombaugh was questioned by Blackburn on August 7, 1979, his first day of testimony, he presented this theory as fact. John Thornton, the defense expert and a professor of criminology at the University of California at Berkeley, begged to differ:

> **BERNARD SEGAL:** Do you agree or disagree with the opinion expressed by Mr. Stombaugh that the puncture holes in the blue pajama top were made while the garment itself was in a stationary position?
> **JOHN THORNTON:** I disagree that that is the only possible conclusion . . .
> **BERNARD SEGAL:** What is the basis, if any, for your [disagreement] with the statement made by Mr. Stombaugh as I have read it to you?
> **JOHN THORNTON:** I conducted a series of experiments in which I put a target in motion and stabbed at it with an ice pick. I then examined the holes resulting from those punctures and found that the holes were circular in appearance despite the fact that the target was in motion.[2]

The discussion turned to fussy details of the experiment. It was designed to disprove Stombaugh's claim that it was impossible to produce a circular puncture in a moving target. Did Thornton use a pajama top? He did. Was it the same kind of fabric? It was—65 percent polyester, 35 percent cotton. It was blue—not dark blue, but pale blue. Close enough. And it was brand-new, not washed many times over the course of years. Any good Hollywood costume designer would have distressed the fabric through repeated washings and rinse cycles, but here it was offered in pristine condition.

Murtagh objected, but Dupree allowed the experiment to be introduced. Dupree was in a jocular mood and was playing the role of hanging judge:

> **THE COURT:** I am inclined to let them go on through. Everything that you told me so far is just something that you can show up by cross-examination, if you are able to do it—that the age of the fabric and the way it was moving, all that stuff . . . Somebody asked me with a completely straight face within the last 24 hours if it was possible for a federal judge to direct a verdict of guilty.
> **JAMES BLACKBURN:** We would go along with that.
> **THE COURT:** So, I said I don't know, but if the motion is made, I will rule on it.

Thornton had prepared a slide show to introduce the terms of his experiment, which involved plywood, screws, and clothesline. A Rube Goldberg device par

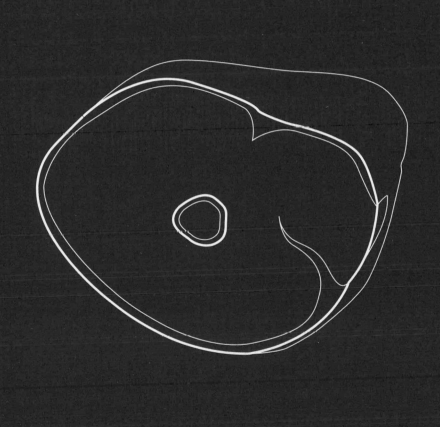

excellence. Essentially, Thornton wrapped the fabric around a ham to create a target, and then attached the target to a moving sled that he stabbed repeatedly with an ice pick. Here is the testimony from the trial:

> **BERNARD SEGAL:** All right, now, will you describe the slide, please, and the portion of the experiment that you say you conducted that you say this slide depicts? . . .
>
> **JOHN THORNTON:** This slide illustrates the basic arrangement of the experiment I conducted. I took a piece of ¾-inch plywood, put a screw eye on either end, and affixed a piece of clothesline to the screw eye on either end.
>
> By whipping the loose end of the cord, where you see the hand in the upper left-hand corner of the slide, the sled can be placed into motion to and fro. On the sled is affixed a target. Over the target is placed a piece of cloth which is 65 percent polyester and 35 percent cotton . . .
>
> There was a particular reason for designing the experiment in this manner, and that is that the motion that I can produce by this is a close approximation of a harmonic oscillation. The significance of that is that it facilitates any computations that I might want to do concerning the velocity of the sled and the target. When the sled was in motion, approximating the maximum motion of a human, the thrashing around, say, on the floor or some other hard surface, I made a number of tests of punctures into the target material.
>
> Then I removed the fabric and examined it under the microscope, looking for the configuration of the margins of the puncture.
>
> The second slide illustrates essentially a circular puncture mark in the fabric . . .
>
> **BERNARD SEGAL:** When this particular hole was made, what was happening to the target in which this piece of cloth was fashioned?
>
> **JOHN THORNTON:** This sled was in motion.

Thornton had repeated his experiment fifty times. Microscopic examination showed that the holes were circular. No tearing. (The experiment was similar to Colonel Rock's demonstration that the coffee table could land on its side.)

> **BERNARD SEGAL:** Were there any significant differences in the type of hole that you made when you were doing these punctures of the fabric and as the fabric was being moved back and forth on the sled?
>
> **JOHN THORNTON:** No.

BERNARD SEGAL: [How] did the holes appear to you, as you examined them micro-scopically?

JOHN THORNTON: They were all circular.

A trial is not a science fair, but rather a magic show. A show based on appearances and logical fallacies and sleight of hand. It isn't about proof. It is about convincing the jury.

Murtagh asked to approach the bench: "Your Honor, it seems to me that Dr. Thornton has testified to half of an experiment. He has got the better but not the bitter. I think we are entitled to test the validity of the entire process . . . I want to do an experiment of my own." The defense had no objections, and so the show went on.

BRIAN MURTAGH: Dr. Thornton, if I could, I am going to stand in front of you, placing great trust in Mr. Blackburn. I am going to ask him to flail away at me with an ice pick.

[*Experiment is performed.*][3]

BRIAN MURTAGH: That was a certain amount of realism. That wasn't part of the act, Judge.

THE COURT: Okay, anybody got a Band-Aid?

BRIAN MURTAGH: That's okay. Dr. Thornton, I'll ask you to take a look at this pajama top and tell us what you see?

JOHN THORNTON: I see a number of tears, and they do appear to be, in fact, tears.

BRIAN MURTAGH: Yes, sir. Are they straight puncture-type holes?

JOHN THORNTON: . . . [W]ell, yes, several of them are, but not all of them. I can count—you understand this is an approximation.

BRIAN MURTAGH: Yes, sir.

JOHN THORNTON: This is not an atmosphere conducive to good work; but there are three areas here that are circular in their appearance. There is one here that's slightly elongated, and the remainder appear to be tears.

BRIAN MURTAGH: Okay, thank you. Your Honor, may I publish this to the jury?

THE COURT: Yes, if they haven't already seen it.

[*Exhibit passed among the jury.*]

BERNARD SEGAL: Do you need a doctor, Mr. Murtagh?

BRIAN MURTAGH: Thank you, no.

Murtagh had been slightly "wounded" during the demonstration.

> **BRIAN MURTAGH:** I take it, Dr. Thornton, that you have conducted no experiments such as the one we have just done in court . . . ?
>
> **JOHN THORNTON:** No, I considered it and rejected it. I think it would be a little bit silly from a number of standpoints—scientifically silly being something other than—
>
> **THE COURT:** [*Interposing.*] Than silly-silly.
>
> **JOHN THORNTON:** Yes, Your Honor . . . It is questions such as this that make me shy away from devising some sort of ricky-tick experiment, if I can use that terminology—

In Thornton's opinion the ice pick fight was not science. It was not even an experiment. What exactly had been proved? That you could tear a pajama top by flailing at someone with an ice pick? It seemed silly. Possibly even silly-silly. Blackburn and Murtagh's demonstration didn't prove that MacDonald's story was false, but Thornton's experiment did falsify Stombaugh's theory.

The next day, Murtagh asked just what was on Thornton's sled. He knew the answer already, as did the jury and all present—because he'd asked the exact same question the previous day and gotten the same answer.

> **BRIAN MURTAGH:** Could you tell us what that was on your experiment?
>
> **JOHN THORNTON:** Ham.
>
> **BRIAN MURTAGH:** You mean, you took a piece of ham?
>
> **JOHN THORNTON:** Yes.
>
> **BRIAN MURTAGH:** You mean, like in a ham sandwich?
>
> **JOHN THORNTON:** Yes.[4]

————

In *Fatal Vision*, the book and TV miniseries, Thornton became the nerd, the effete college professor with his "harmonic oscillations"; Murtagh, the prosecutor, the man of the people injured in the line of duty. A ridiculous image of ham on a sled set against "the stark, expansive landscape" of Stombaugh's testimony.

> "Ham!" Murtagh repeated, walking away from the witness, toward the prosecution table, shaking his head. Some of the jurors began to smile and even titter.

It had not been sliced ham, of course, but a whole ham. Still, ham is ham, and no matter how earnest and erudite John Thornton appeared from that point forward—and his credentials were impeccable, his intelligence above question, his reputation in his field above reproach—the image that lingered was of this bearded Californian, with utmost seriousness, wrapping a piece of cloth around a ham and calling that a scientific experiment. It was an image that cast a very slight shadow indeed upon the stark, expansive landscape of Paul Stombaugh's earlier testimony.[5]

28

CALIFORNIA EVIL

August 10. The midpoint of the trial.

The government was about to rest its case, but Blackburn asked to move the March 1970 issue of *Esquire* magazine into evidence, Exhibit 139.

Clearly, Blackburn and the rest of the prosecution had not given up on the staged crime scene theory. Just as the CID reinvestigation team was determined to keep flipping the living room coffee table end over end or reenacting the stabbing of the pajama top, they were happy to return to one more absurd demonstration. The cover story was "California Evil," and there was a Whitman's Sampler of satanism tucked inside—"Charlie Manson's Home on the Range," "The Banality of the New Evil," "Kicks Just Keep Getting Harder to Find," "The Style of Evil: Paraphernalia for the Newest Freakout."

Over the defense's objections, Jack Crawley, an assistant U.S. attorney, started this odd exercise, reading verbatim articles from the magazine into the court record. It would be a couple of hours of mindless recitation. Six pages into the reading, the jury heard about Princess Leda, Lord Satan, and how "the devil looks groovier."

JACK CRAWLEY: [*quoting*] "I've been around that scene, man, cats who have given themselves up to the Lord Satan. If you sense an evil here, you are right, and I'll tell you what it is: too many people turned on to acid. If you make a habit of tripping—well, acid is so spiritual, so, uh, metaphysical, that you are going to be forced into making a choice, between opting for good, staying on a goodness or Christian trip, and tripping with the Lord Satan. That's the whole heavy thing about too many people turned on to acid: to most of them, the devil just looks groovier. Acid is incredible—I've been on one hundred and seventy-two trips now—but it shouldn't be available to everybody and anybody . . ."[1]

One hundred and seventy-two acid trips, but Crawley barely pauses to catch his breath. Twenty pages of trial transcript later. Reading the magazine itself seems designed to imitate a heavy acid trip. And what was the effect on the jurors?

> **JACK CRAWLEY:** "'You have the time, man?' asks the blond girl, grabbing one's wrist to see if there is a watch. 'You must be a Capricorn, because your eyebrows fluff out at the ends,' the dark girl says suddenly. 'You a native of Chicago, man?' says the colored boy loudly, grinning. 'Well, whether you are or you ain't, we are going to do a number on you.'"

Eventually, Wade Smith objected—for the second time—to the evidence on the grounds of relevancy.

> **WADE SMITH:** I mean, it just—it never connects up in any way to the case. It is just way out—the most out-of-left-field stuff I have ever heard in my life.
> **THE COURT:** Well, I think you are too far into it to raise it again. The thing came in without objection and you are down this far. I am just going to let him go on. If it is not relevant, I will instruct the jury on it, but I am not going to do anything about it at this stage.
> **WADE SMITH:** Well, Judge, let me remind you that we objected to it originally, and we thought it was going to be relevant because they said it was. We kept listening to see if it would be, and it never was.
> **BRIAN MURTAGH:** Well, let me say for the record—I think the relevance is apparent. It is the imagery, the "acid," "ring," "groovy," "hippies," doing a number, a "black," a "blond," "two males." I think it speaks for itself.

Murtagh and Blackburn were looking for specific words and phrases that matched MacDonald's account of the intruders. Not surprising that they found the words "groovy," "hippies," and "blond" among the ten-thousand-plus words in over a dozen articles. Could you have combed through another randomly selected magazine from March 1970 and found these words? Probably.

The *Esquire* word search was not unlike the search for other kinds of evidence. Search until you find the details that corroborate the theory you already have in hand, and then claim that you have proved your theory.

On August 13, Segal moved to strike the entire transcript from the record. What was the purpose of introducing the magazine? And what harmful effect—intended or accidental—might it have on the jury? Perhaps none of them had even heard of *Esquire*.

BERNARD SEGAL: . . . It does have the substantial tendency, though, of planting in the mind of one or more jurors that it must be connected to the case; otherwise, why would we have been subjected to an hour and a half of reading about witch-craft, Satanism, and cultism? . . .

The word "acid" was not newly revealed by *Esquire* magazine. We had known about and read about the effects of LSD at that point for more than ten or twelve years. The whole generation of Woodstock had taken place. *Life* magazine and every television station, every radio station had made Woodstock and drugs and acid and all those terminology commonplace and well-known . . . It just seems to me on balance that the court has to say, "I know the words the government wanted, but the total effect of what they read to the jury tends to convey some larger, different image," and that to leave that to lie in this case—to leave it in at all—is to present considerable danger of prejudice . . .

THE COURT: . . . Let me say that I was of the impression that the jury was bored and to the point that they were getting impatient. That was my own feeling. It was hard for me to follow this thing, and I seem to recall—having said, "Well, wonder why doesn't somebody cut this short or make an objection?"

You say now that one was made,[2] and I do not recall it, but I don't say that you did not because in four weeks I give myself credit with being able to forget one or two things.

But that was my impression of the jury's reaction. Of course it was just a silent thing, but you can see them fidget occasionally . . .[3]

Dupree not only had allowed the testimony to be read to the jury, he had casti-gated Segal for not objecting more strenuously.

The *Esquire* magazine, the entire staged crime scene scenario, was a magic trick. It shifted the burden of proof onto MacDonald. Guilty until proven inno-cent. It deflected the jury's attention from the elephant in the room—the very real

Rosemary's Baby transmogrified.

black boy

Clark Gable emerges from the Garden.

Negro

The King in repose.

Princess Leda's Castle in the Air

by Tom Burke

In subterranean Hollywood there lives a witch, an acid goddess. Don't go there without a cross.

"Christ" perceives a distant vision.

groovier.

Charlie Manson's Home on the Range

by Gay Talese

No deer and no antelope. But strange sounds for a blind man's ear

The horse wrangler, tall and ruggedly handsome, placed his hands on the girl wearing white buckskin...

Greathouse on the Manson family.

blonde hair

PIG on the wall

Four people

Most automatic automatic.

Kodak Instamatic 814 camera.

Banality of the New Evil

by William Eastlake

Games the survivors play

Entrance: the needle goes here.

candle burning

kitchen knife

(Continued on page 182)

Andrew Cohen

possibility that there were intruders, that the crime had actually happened the way MacDonald said it did. The reading of *Esquire* assumes that MacDonald is lying, and then shifts the jury's attention to the question "Where did the lie come from?" It changes the mystery from "Who did it?" to "How did he do it?"

It shouldn't have been allowed, but like so many questionable things in Judge Dupree's courtroom, it was.

29

TROUBLESOME PSYCHOPATHY

On August 13, 1979, Dupree turned to the question of psychiatric testimony—ultimately, the question of MacDonald's motivation (or lack of motivation) for the crimes. The prosecution had been left with a substantial pile of favorable psychiatric evaluations and reports. MacDonald had been evaluated during the Article 32 by a three-man team from Walter Reed Army Hospital picked by the prosecution. Several of these psychiatrists also testified before the grand jury in 1974 and 1975. All of the exams were essentially positive, including two recent ones—by Seymour Halleck, a professor of psychiatry and an adjunct professor of law at the University of North Carolina at Chapel Hill, and a reevaluation by James Mack, a former colleague of Robert Sadoff, who had examined MacDonald in 1970.[1] None of the psychiatrists found any evidence of pathology, despite some minor differences of opinion.

BRIAN MURTAGH: Your Honor, at this time we would also renew our motion on the psychiatric testimony.

THE COURT: Now, listen, you fellows have opened a can of worms on that . . .

I worked all weekend but I did not get to read it or do any research on that until last night beginning about 8:00 o'clock. I worked about four hours on it and read all the cases that they cited and so forth, and have done a little this morning; and of course the clerks did not even have it, so they were not able to do anything on it.

But it looks like we are doing business with a can of worms here on that proposition, and this is not something that I want to handle at a side bar conference. I want to hear you gentlemen on that score. As much as I dislike to have the jury running in and out I think this is important. It ought to be given a full airing in open court.

BRIAN MURTAGH: Yes, Your Honor. Something else I would bring to the Court's attention is we have the forensic psychiatrists and psychologists here. As you can imagine, they are antsy witnesses to have on tap.

THE COURT: Well, what I am going to do on that—I think maybe we had better stop this morning. We are going to have to send them out anyway for arguments on the motion for Judgment of Acquittal, but I can say this—I will tell all of you this now— if the evidence is to come in, then of course because it has been so delayed in bringing it to a head and getting the Defendant's side of it, then I am going to give you an ample opportunity to have the man examined and get your own evidence.[2]

Murtagh won the day. Judge Dupree declared that if the defense hoped to have its psychiatrists testify at trial, MacDonald would have to submit to an additional evaluation by experts picked by the prosecution.

It was a setup.

The prosecution had two experts—a psychiatrist and a psychologist—in its back pocket. Arrangements were made, and the meeting took place in Wade Smith's office later that evening, August 13, 1979.

The examiner was Dr. James Brussel, the same psychiatrist who had been consulted by Kearns and Ivory in 1971. MacDonald's defense attorneys did not know that the man they had welcomed into their building had decided eight years ago that their client was a liar, who probably had killed his family. And that he had offered these opinions long before he had ever had an opportunity to interview the defendant.

Dr. Brussel was accompanied by a New Jersey psychologist, Hirsch Lazaar Silverman. Brussel and Silverman had worked together on a number of cases, including Albert DeSalvo, the Boston Strangler,[3] and took enormous pride in their ability to tell whether someone was telling the truth or lying. (I myself have always been amazed by the belief among many psychiatric experts that they have solved the Cartesian riddle, that in their hands epistemology has become a dead science. If you want to know what's true or false, ask a shrink.)

Dr. Silverman eventually prepared their report. It was not just unfavorable to MacDonald. It was the exact opposite of every psychiatric and psychological report that had preceded it. If Dr. Sadoff's report was white, Dr. Silverman's report was black. Very, very black:

Summarily, in the view of this therapist predicated on scientific psychodiagnostics and psychological evaluation, Dr. MacDonald may well be viewed as a psychopath subject to violence under pressure, rather effeminate as an individual, and given to overt behavior when faced with emotional stress. He is no less subject to blotting out that past of what to him is convenient and truly essential—to block out for his own emotional preservation. As a sociopathic individual with troublesome psychopathy, with an overlay of submerged and confused sexuality, Dr. MacDonald despite his hedonism seems self-destructive, naive, superficial, and even illogical at times, a man who seeks freedom and emancipation only for personal removal from constraint, controls, and restrictions. To suit his whim, he has the faculty to manufacture and convolute circumstances. He seeks attention and approval, and is given to denial of truth. He can be critically sarcastic. As a seriously emotional man, he gives evidence of secretiveness, with questionable moral standards. He is detailistic and lacks insight in seeing the gestalt, the whole quality of things and events and persons, as well as circumstances. (As a physician, he probably is given to treating the symptom rather than the illness and the disease.) In essence, then, Dr. MacDonald in personal and social adjustment is in need of continuous, consistent psychotherapeutic intervention, coupled with psychiatric attention.[4]

It was an elaborately disguised version of "I think you're a maniac" or "I think you're guilty" dressed up like a Thanksgiving turkey with all the trimmings.

Most of Silverman's analysis is really an accusation. The rest is just nasty. That Dr. MacDonald can be "critically sarcastic" brings out, I have to admit, a level of critical sarcasm in me. For example, just what is a "sociopathic individual with troublesome psychopathy"? Is it like a narcissistic individual with troublesome self-infatuation? Or "a man who seeks freedom and emancipation only for personal removal from constraint, controls, and restrictions"? Like Dred Scott? And in the parenthetical aside, Silverman, presumably unaware of the inherent ironies in what he is saying, argues that MacDonald as a physician "probably is given to treating the symptom rather than the illness and the disease"? But what does this *mean*? He's an emergency room doctor. (If you were an emergency room patient, wouldn't you want the attending physician to be "detailistic"?) Who is Silverman describing? MacDonald? Brussel? Himself?

MacDonald was shell-shocked. What had happened? Following the exam, he talked with Bernie Segal and Wade Smith, and then that night produced his own hurried account of the meeting. He calls Dr. Brussel "Dr. Brussels" and Dr. Silverman "Dr. Silverstein." Given what transpired, I too would have trouble getting the names right.

[Brussel] read from three major documents during this time. The first document that he read from was a typewritten three-page document and it was simply a series of questions in typewritten form. I asked him what the document was and he replied to me that it was a document of questions that had been compiled and typed by the government attorney. I asked him was this Brian Murtagh and he replied in the affirmative . . .

He did not inquire about my family, my feelings toward my family, my relationships with my parents or my siblings, the quality of my relationship between my wife and myself, the quality of my relationship between my children and myself, my relationship with my friends, my relationship with the Kassabs, my feelings towards the prosecution, my feelings regarding the loss of my family . . .

At the close of the interview at 8:55, Dr. Brussels informed that he felt that I was "a homicidal maniac, with psychopathic tendencies, and was a chronic liar." I sat there absolutely stunned and repeated back to him "did I hear what I just thought I heard?" He repeated to me that he felt that I showed psychopathic tendencies and tendencies of a "homicidal nature," at which time I asked him how did he come to those conclusions. He stated to me in front of Dr. Silverstein that he had reached those conclusions from "Dr. Silverstein's tests." I asked him how he had reached those conclusions since the tests were not graded yet, and he stated to me "they will be graded soon" . . .

As we were getting ready to leave the room and as we were leaving the room, his disorientation became more apparent. He asked me if I had taken his hat, I replied I arrived in the room after he did and that I did not see him with a hat. He then asked me if I had his coat. I replied I didn't know anything about a coat. He asked me what motel he was staying at. I asked Dr. Silverstein what motel he was staying at and he replied the Royal Villa, so I told this to Dr. Brussels. I then asked Dr. Brussels if he knew where he was. He said somewhere in the south . . . He then went to Wade Smith's waiting room and began trying on a hat from the hat rack and he asked me if it was his hat. I told him I didn't know but it didn't appear to fit his head. He then asked how he was to get back to the airport and Dr. Silverstein said he wasn't going to the airport he was going to the motel.[5]

Did Dr. Brussel ever find his hat? No one seems to know. It may be one more unanswerable question about the case.

———————

The haggling over the admissibility of psychiatric evidence at the MacDonald trial continued. The defense attorneys waited another eight days for an answer from Judge Dupree. Segal had made a deal with the prosecution: if Dupree refused to admit psychiatric evidence, the Brussel-Silverman report would be destroyed, unseen. And the various favorable reports—all of the reports from the Article 32, the grand jury, and the new ones, prepared by Seymour Halleck and James Mack—would also remain off the record. It would be a Mexican standoff.

But for MacDonald it was a lose-lose proposition. Admit the Brussel-Silverman report and make the defendant look like a monster. Throw all the psychiatric testimony out and remove one of the pillars of the defense—namely that the defendant was not the kind of man to have committed these crimes.

On August 22, Dupree ruled that psychiatric testimony would not be admitted. He argued that the prosecution "was prepared to call a parade of experts who would give opinions antipodal to Dr. Sadoff's." He decided that "an expansion of the inquiry into this uncertain area would more likely confuse, rather than assist, the jury." Of course, he neglected to mention that he had called for the antipodal testimony.

Drs. Brussel and Silverman were hired, in the middle of the trial, for one reason and one reason alone—to say what the prosecution wanted them to say. That had been evident since 1971, eight years earlier. Their report created the enduring illusion that the psychiatric findings on MacDonald were totally inconclusive— that for every witness who suggested MacDonald could not have committed the murders, there would be another witness waiting in the wings, looking for his hat, happy to incriminate him.

———————

Brussel died in 1982. I wondered, where is Hirsch Lazaar Silverman? Is he still alive? He would be in his late nineties. His last address was somewhere in West Orange, New Jersey, but his phone was disconnected, and he did not respond to letters.

According to one Web site, he is the author of twenty-one books, including ten volumes of poetry. Among them: *Vignettes of the Intellect: An Odyssey in Experience,*

Moments of Eternity: A Sheaf of Poetry, and *Alpha/Omega: A Sheaf of Psychopoetry.* He is described on the site as "one of the greatest literary figures of the age, and an active sharer in the stirring life of his times."[6] Here is one of his poems:

> Life is a twisting road
> With unpredictable fork,
> And unexpected tomorrow.

ROUND IN CIRCLES

July 31, 1979. Twelve days into the trial, before the name Helena Stoeckley appears in the transcript. Her name had surfaced at the end of the Article 32 hearing and then more or less disappeared for eight years. Or so it seemed. (Her lie-detector test in 1971 was mentioned in the grand jury hearings, but she herself did not testify.) And then in a bench conference, an argument on motions, she finally came up:

> THE COURT: Thank you. How about this girl with the floppy hat on who was in that house that night, named Helena Stoeckley alias something else . . . ?
>
> BRIAN MURTAGH: We feel that there are two issues with the Helena Stoeckley thing: one, we anticipate that the Defense is going to say that because she is apparently unavailable to them, or they haven't found her, that [secondhand] statement[s about Stoeckley] should come in.
>
> Well, without regard to her availability or lack thereof, we think that the statements themselves, because of their inherent lack of credibility and because . . . they are hearsay statements that are being sought to be introduced by the Defense as to the truth of the matter stated. You know, she thinks she did it; therefore, the Defendant couldn't have done it . . . We don't think they are admissible, Your Honor . . .
>
> THE COURT: Well, that is still a live motion, then.

BRIAN MURTAGH: Yes, sir.

THE COURT: All right, I will put that one over there in something to do after court.

BRIAN MURTAGH: Your Honor, I might add that those statements were first made, as I understand it, by Helena to Mr. Ivory. I would represent to the court that I have spoken to Helena Stoeckley in years past and—you know—you say, "Well, why do you think you were there?" And she says, "Because I think I was there."[1] You know, you go round in circles on that one.[2]

August 13, 1979. Helena Stoeckley had not yet been located. Now Segal had brought Stoeckley's parents up to Raleigh under subpoena in the hope that they could help find her. What makes the following exchange utterly surreal is that Murtagh informs the court that he had been talking to Stoeckley. No dates are given, but it's said matter-of-factly, as if it must have been common knowledge.

BERNARD SEGAL: I might say, by the way, the only reason they [Stoeckley's parents] are here is because that is the address that the Government gave us with their list three days before trial . . .

BRIAN MURTAGH: That is the last place I saw her, Judge—was her parents' address.

THE COURT: Well, is this woman under subpoena?

BRIAN MURTAGH: Not by us.

THE COURT: Why not?

BRIAN MURTAGH: Judge, she can't testify to anything. She thinks she was involved and that's it.

THE COURT: But you have been aware for five years that the Defendant was going to try to get her testimony in if she was not available.

JAMES BLACKBURN: We have been trying to locate her. Because of that very reason, we are not going to stand up and argue we cannot locate her and not have her in the trial.[3]

What is going on here? Here's my attempt to make sense of it. Segal points out that Stoeckley was on the prosecution's list of potential witnesses. Dupree wants to know if she is under subpoena. Murtagh tells him of course not. They don't consider her testimony important. And why is her testimony unimportant? Why is it that "she can't testify to anything"? Murtagh explains it all for us: "She thinks she was involved and that's it." Good Lord. The prosecution had been talking to Stoeckley in the recent past; now they don't have a clue where she was?

There was a continuing refrain. Where is Stoeckley? How can we find her? Who knows where she is? Are we ready to put her parents on the stand and start grilling them for pertinent information?

Another bench conference a couple of days later, outside the hearing of the jury. Dupree took some time off from the pajama-top folding experiment testimony to once again address the Stoeckley question, but in the meantime, Stoeckley had been located and taken into custody.

> THE COURT: Gentlemen, first off, and this is not why I got you up here but it is something that is on my mind so I am going to tell you: all these experiments and all this examining and cross-examining and so forth—it is interesting and it is technical and it may be going somewhere. But, for whatever it is worth, I think this case is going to rise or fall on one thing and one thing alone, and that is whether or not this jury buys the Defendant's story as to what happened . . .
>
> What I really got you up here for is to talk about this Stoeckley problem. I understand she is in custody. I understand that she can be kept like that for 72 hours without being let out.
>
> Now, as far as finding her and making her available is concerned, I think the Court has done about all it can do. I suggest to you that you ought to get your evidence so scheduled as to accommodate this particular thing rather than run the risk the next time she goes that she can't be found by anybody.
>
> So, now that she is available, I think that moots the question of whether or not we can take up secondary evidence of what she would have said, and I don't think in this kind of case—if she is available—it ought to be done. My feeling about that is that, having made her available, that you must now avail yourself of her availability.[4]

But why is it secondary evidence? Somewhat hidden in Dupree's remarks is a trade-off. Okay, you've got Stoeckley, but you're not getting any of the six witnesses who heard Stoeckley's confessions to testify in front of the jury.

> BERNARD SEGAL: Is she in custody here in Raleigh or is she in Greenville?
> LAW CLERK: She is in custody in Greenville—
> THE COURT: [Interposing] Greenville, South Carolina.
> LAW CLERK: And they are ready to transport her here.
> JAMES BLACKBURN: Pickens County Jail is what I have been told.

Helena Stoeckley was at Pickens County Jail, twenty miles west of Greenville. Why is it that Blackburn always seems to know a little more than everybody else?

> **BERNARD SEGAL:** Well, Greenville is about three hours—two and a half hours.
> **THE COURT:** More than that. It is three hours comfortably to Charlotte, and Green-ville is almost that same distance the other side.
> **BRIAN MURTAGH:** Do you know who runs the police department in Greenville? Paul Stombaugh.

Paul Stombaugh?! The pajama-folding guy?! After leaving the FBI in 1976, he had become director of the Greenville Police Service Bureau. Bernie Segal doesn't seem overjoyed to hear the name:

> **BERNARD SEGAL:** Maybe he will drive her down for us. Your Honor, I understand she has been taken into custody pursuant to a warrant as a material witness in this case. I would request that she be brought here forthwith to Raleigh and, as soon as she is here and we have a chance to interview her, we intend to call her as a witness. That is my request and if I can be notified—
> **THE COURT:** That is all we needed to know. Just tell the magistrate that there is no bond and just bring her here and make her available to the Defense counsel.

August 17, 1979. Stoeckley was finally called as a witness. She had spent the last three nights in custody. She had been interviewed by both the prosecution and the defense. And she wasn't represented by an attorney.

> **JAMES BLACKBURN:** This is the [witness], of course, we all talked to yesterday. I remember you talking about a *voir dire*.[5] I know that Wade mentioned this morning that she had commented on the necessity of wanting an attorney. I just wanted to be sure, before we got started, how we are going to go.
> **WADE SMITH:** I think our position, Judge—of course, we will do whatever Your Honor wishes to do—but I feel that we will just go ahead with her, if we can, and see what happens.
> **JAMES BLACKBURN:** I think that is fine.
> **THE COURT:** Well, let's go.[6]

Helena spoke very quietly through it all. Her testimony was so hard to hear that Judge Dupree had to ask the gallery, which was full to capacity, to quiet down.[7] She was wearing a cast on her broken left arm, from an injury she claimed to have sustained in an argument over drugs.

Segal began with questions that established a context for her activities in 1970—the apartment on Haymount Hill, the daily use of heroin and LSD, the fascination with witchcraft. He needed to make clear that what was powerfully unusual or frightening to the jury might, in Stoeckley's world, be commonplace. It was strange territory to be exploring before a courtroom, and the government repeatedly objected to Segal's questions. But the questions continued—about priestesses, candles, sacrificed cats.[8]

The questioning turned to the events of February 17. She recalled taking a tablet of mescaline at midnight with her then-boyfriend, Greg Mitchell. Her next recollection? "Returning to the house . . . about 4:30 or 5:00."

She had a blond wig, too, but she burned it on February 19 or 20. (She remembered that well.) And why? "Because it connected me with the murder." (This is testimony from someone who supposedly remembered nothing. Stoeckley's day in court was far stranger than that.) She stopped wearing the floppy hat that she wore all the time, because "people were coming up to me and assuming that, since I wore the floppy hat, I was the girl in question."

And then Segal confronted Helena Stoeckley with a group of photographs from inside the MacDonald house. He had shown her the same photographs the day before.

BERNARD SEGAL: All right, now, did each of those people I have mentioned to you—Jane and Red and Bill Posey—each tell you what they remembered of their conversation of the various dates that I have been talking about this morning?
HELENA STOECKLEY: Yes, sir.
BERNARD SEGAL: And, after they told you what they remembered, did it in any way revive or bring back a memory of what you have said?
HELENA STOECKLEY: Only pieces of the conversation.
BERNARD SEGAL: Did it revive your memory fully as to what you said to those persons about the MacDonald murders?
HELENA STOECKLEY: No, sir.
BERNARD SEGAL: Do you recall me showing you a group of photographs, of which the four I am about to show you now were part of them? Please take a look at those, if you will, Ms. Stoeckley?

Segal showed her pictures of Colette, Kimberley and Kristen. She could remember nothing. He then showed her pictures of Kristen's bedroom.

> **BERNARD SEGAL:** Let me just ask you about an item in the photos that are marked G-59 and G-145. I want to hold them up, please, if I may, and ask you if you see first of all an item in the foreground here, in the left corner of both of these photographs? Can you see that, Ms. Stoeckley?
>
> **HELENA STOECKLEY:** A hobbyhorse.
>
> **BERNARD SEGAL:** Beg your pardon?
>
> **HELENA STOECKLEY:** A hobbyhorse.
>
> **BERNARD SEGAL:** Does that item seem familiar to you in any way?
>
> **HELENA STOECKLEY:** No.
>
> **BERNARD SEGAL:** It does not?
>
> **HELENA STOECKLEY:** [*Witness nods negatively.*]

Segal wasn't about to give up.

> **BERNARD SEGAL:** I ask you to give particular attention, if you will, please, to the photograph which is marked G-75, which shows the sofa, coffee table, and part of the hallway and some clothing in the MacDonald house. Would you look at that, please? Do you have any reason to believe that you have seen that scene before, prior to being shown the photographs yesterday and today?
>
> **HELENA STOECKLEY:** No, sir.
>
> **BERNARD SEGAL:** Do you have any reason to believe that you were ever standing in that place?
>
> **HELENA STOECKLEY:** No, sir.
>
> **BERNARD SEGAL:** May we approach the bench, Your Honor?

You can almost hear the walls crumble around him.

When the lawyers for the defense had met with Stoeckley the day before, presumably she had been their witness. Just moments before, she clearly remembered having destroyed evidence that could have incriminated her. Now, she remembered nothing. Why?

> **BERNARD SEGAL:** At this time, Your Honor, I ask for leave of Court to take this witness as on cross, because she is a surprise and hostile witness.

I represent to the Court that during the interviews with me and with other persons present she stated that when she looked at the picture she had a recollection of standing over a body holding a candle, seeing a man's body on the floor.

I also may say, Your Honor, we are now down to the bottom five or six critical things that she revealed yesterday. I have a feeling, based upon her answer to this one now, that when and if I ask her in direct fashion, that I may get negative answers.

I had no anticipation of that, because yesterday throughout the time that she made these statements, we accepted them, did not expect contrary.

Segal returned to the hobbyhorse.

BERNARD SEGAL: Please, Ms. Stoeckley, what did you say about the rocking horse?

HELENA STOECKLEY: That was the first thing I muttered, is that it was broken, and when you asked me what I said, I just said nothing.

BERNARD SEGAL: Beg your pardon?

HELENA STOECKLEY: You asked me what I said, and I said nothing and shrugged it off.

BERNARD SEGAL: Did you say anything at all about your having touched or used that rocking horse at the time?

GEORGE ANDERSON [A U.S. ATTORNEY]: Objection.

THE COURT: Overruled.

HELENA STOECKLEY: Not at that time, no.

BERNARD SEGAL: At what time?

HELENA STOECKLEY: I don't even remember saying that yesterday at all.

BERNARD SEGAL: At what time did you ever say anything about touching the broken rocking horse?

JAMES BLACKBURN: Your Honor, we object.

THE COURT: I sustain that.

BERNARD SEGAL: I thought the witness said "Not at that time." What did you mean, Ms. Stoeckley, when you said "Not at that time?"

HELENA STOECKLEY: Just that I didn't say it yesterday, no.

BERNARD SEGAL: Did you ever say it?

HELENA STOECKLEY: Not that I recall.

BERNARD SEGAL: Ms. Stoeckley, do you have a recollection of standing or of ever being outside of 544 Castle Drive late at night?

JAMES BLACKBURN: Your Honor, we object.

'Mystery Woman' Tells of Blanking Out

Can't Recall Fatal Night, She Testifies in MacDonald Trial

RALEIGH, N.C. (UPI)—A "mystery woman" who dabbles in witchcraft testified Friday she blanked out on drugs the night Dr. Jeffrey MacDonald's wife and two young daughters were slain, but denied she was responsible for the killings.

Helena Stoeckley, who was picked up by the FBI at the request of the defense and taken to court as a material witness, testified at the trial of MacDonald, who is accused of the killings that took place nine years ago while he was stationed at Ft. Bragg with the Green Berets.

MacDonald, 35, now a Long Beach, Calif., emergency room surgeon, claims four hippies, one a blonde woman carrying a candle and chanting "Acid is groovy, kill the pigs," broke into his home, knocked him out, and fatally stabbed his pregnant wife, Colette, 26, and daughters, Kimberly, 6, and Kristen, 2.

Miss Stoeckley, plump and dark-haired, became known as the "mystery woman" when it was rumored that an unnamed witness could vouch for much of the defense's case.

She bears little resemblance to the blonde MacDonald described as one of the attackers, but conceded from the stand Friday that she had owned a blonde wig at the time of the slayings in 1970.

She said she was interested in witchcraft, owned books on the subject and had a friend who claimed to be a witch. She said she had studied many rituals of witchcraft, including incantations that involved the killing of animals.

"A lot of the rituals involved killing animals and using their blood," Miss Stoeckley told the court. She said the animals most commonly used were cats.

The slayings of MacDonald's family have been frequently compared to the ritualistic killing of Sharon Tate by the Charles Manson family. The word "pig" was scrawled in blood across the headboard of the MacDonald's bed.

Miss Stoeckley also testified that at the time of the killings in the pre-dawn hours of Feb. 17, 1970, she had blanked out after taking heroin, opium and mescaline and smoking marijuana.

While she admitted she did not know where she was at the time of the killings, Miss Stoeckley testified she was sure she did kill the MacDonalds, has never been in the former Green Beret's Ft. Bragg apartment and does not know who committed the slayings.

"The last thing I remember doing was talking to a friend of mine in my driveway," she said. "That was about midnight."

She said the friend gave her a tablet of hallucinogen mescaline. She said she went back into the house and the next thing she remembered was when she was riding back to her apartment in the early morning in a small blue car with two or three people whom she could not identify.

When chief defense lawyer Bernard Segal asked Miss Stoeckley about her whereabouts at the time of the killings, she said she could not remember what happened between midnight, Feb. 16, and 4:30 a.m., or 5 a.m. Feb. 17. Investigators have placed the time of the killings at about 4 a.m. Feb. 17.

When she admitted that at the time of the killings, Miss Stoeckley testified she had blanked out after taking heroin, opium and mescaline and smoking marijuana.

acquaintances she might have been involved in the slaying. Those acquaintances are also expected to testify.

Edison Asks Hike in Rates, Wants 16% Rise for Homes

The Southern California Edison Co. asked the California Public Utilities Commission Friday to let it raise electricity rates an average of about 20% to offset the higher cost of imported oil.

The utility asked permission to raise residential rates 16%, commercial rates 20% and industrial rates 23.6% to generate $463 million.

The increase would add $2.61 to the typical monthly residential electricity

THE COURT: Overruled.

BERNARD SEGAL: Do you have such a recollection?

HELENA STOECKLEY: No, sir.

Segal was stunned. Is it possible that he hadn't seen this coming?

Blackburn piped up, claiming that Stoeckley, who had spoken to the prosecution immediately following her meeting with the defense, had "not indicated anything" to them. He provided a running commentary of the questions he asked her and the answers he received. "'Did you recognize any of the scenes in those photographs?' The answer was no. I asked her, 'Have you ever been in that house?' She said no. I said, 'Do you know anything about that?' 'No.'"

"Who do you think did it?" "Dr. MacDonald." Indeed. She even told them MacDonald was guilty, something she never said on the stand. In cross-examination, Blackburn did finally get Stoeckley to deny all involvement, all knowledge of the crime:

JAMES BLACKBURN: To your knowledge, did you participate in the killings of the MacDonald family?

HELENA STOECKLEY: No, sir.

JAMES BLACKBURN: How do you feel towards children?

HELENA STOECKLEY: I love children.

JAMES BLACKBURN: Of your own personal knowledge, did you kill Colette MacDonald?

HELENA STOECKLEY: No, sir.

JAMES BLACKBURN: How about Kristen?

HELENA STOECKLEY: No, sir.

JAMES BLACKBURN: How about Kimberley?

HELENA STOECKLEY: No, sir.

JAMES BLACKBURN: Did you try to kill Dr. MacDonald?

HELENA STOECKLEY: No, sir.

JAMES BLACKBURN: Do you know who did?

HELENA STOECKLEY: No, sir.

Segal tried to make the best out of a bad situation. He again questioned her. The answers to his questions were clear prevarication and lies. A perverse reenactment of "he said, she said." She denied remembering even simple things that had happened the previous day.

31

ACE IN THE HOLE

Stoeckley had turned out to be a bust, but Bernie Segal had an ace in the hole. The six witnesses who came to Raleigh, called by the defense, to corroborate Stoeckley's confessions: Jane Zillioux; Charles Underhill; James Gaddis; Robert Brisentine; Prince Beasley, the narcotics cop who used Stoeckley as an informant; and William Posey, her neighbor in Fayetteville. Because of Stoeckley's performance, Judge Dupree had ruled that the witness testimony would be given "outside the hearing and the presence of the jury." After hearing the testimony, he would decide whether it should be repeated in front of the jury.

Jane Zillioux was one of Stoeckley's neighbors after she moved to Nashville in late 1970. On August 17, 1979, she took the stand.

BERNARD SEGAL: All right, go ahead and tell us about that evening.

JANE ZILLIOUX: I went to her house to see if she was all right, because I was worried about her. I hadn't seen her for a few days and I didn't know if those hippies were feeding her or not or how she was getting her food.

So, I went over and I knocked on the door and I called and I said, "Helena, are you there?" And she said, "Yes." She came to the door. It took her a few minutes, and, as she opened the door, she turned around, and I followed her into the house.

I went into her room. It was the front room right on the street. And she went over. She was weak and she was shaky and she sat down on the bed, and I sat down beside her, and I said . . . "I haven't seen you for a few days and I was worried about you—you know—are you all right?"

She said, "I've been sick," and I said, "Well, Helena, why don't you go home. You know, why don't you go home to your family and let them take care of you?"

And she said, "I can't. I can't ever go home again."

I said, "Well, why?" She said, "Because I was involved in some murders," and she said, "My family don't want me around." . . .

I didn't say anything. I was just too shocked. You know, I expected a teenage confession like "I hate my mother," you know, or "I'm a runaway." I didn't expect *that*. I was horrified.[1]

Helena had shared some specific details about the night of the murders:

BERNARD SEGAL: You were describing where Helena was crying, that she was talking about standing in the rain, and she hugged herself?

JANE ZILLIOUX: Yes.

BERNARD SEGAL: Did she at any time look at her hands or say anything about her hands?

JANE ZILLIOUX: . . . [W]hen she leaned over and she hugged herself like this, and she was telling me about standing out in front of the rain when she came to herself—she was speaking with her hands.

So she flipped her hands like this, and she said, "So much blood. I couldn't see or think of anything except blood," and she said, "I asked the boys to take me home. I had to get home."

I did ask her at that time, "What did you do with your clothes?" She said, "I got rid of them." I didn't ask her how she got rid of them. She just got rid of them. I didn't ask her any questions, you know.

BERNARD SEGAL: Did she say anything about not wanting any more connection with those clothes?

JANE ZILLIOUX: Yes, she did.

BERNARD SEGAL: What were her words, if you can remember?

JANE ZILLIOUX: I said, "Well . . . why did you get rid of them?" She said, "Because they were the same clothes that the woman in the case was supposed to have been wearing."

BERNARD SEGAL: Now, did she say who were the persons murdered either not by name or—

JANE ZILLIOUX: [*Interrupting*] She said a woman and two small children.

BERNARD SEGAL: Did she ever mention something about her wig?

JANE ZILLIOUX: Yes, she told me she had on her blonde wig and her white boots. I know that they were white plastic-leather boots because before that when we had been working in Bonnie's Shoetique, she pointed the boots out to me— a pair that was in the store—and she said, "I had a pair of boots like these, and I loved them, but I had to get rid of them."

I caught up with Jane Zillioux, now Jane Graham-Bailey. It was no easy matter finding her. Zillioux is a relatively uncommon name. But there were multiple marriages and name changes subsequent to her testimony in 1979. Calls to many of her ex-husbands, endless phone conversations with people who *could* be Jane Zillioux, but weren't. The usual thankless detective work. One ex-husband was absolutely convinced she was dead. (She is not.) Often the new wives were not as cooperative as one might hope. I finally found a Jane Bailey who was on the board of a condominium association in Jensen Beach, Florida. But it wasn't her. She just happened to live in the same town where the *real* Jane Graham-Bailey lives. We live in a universe of false leads.

Then I found her son. False leads, but also interlocking skeins. The more than thirty years since the trial had not diminished her feelings about what happened in the courtroom. Jane Graham-Bailey had forgotten some of the details of the crime, but she remained incensed by the trial and by the TV miniseries.

JANE GRAHAM-BAILEY: It was such an injustice. And the way they portrayed Mr. Kassab, Karl Malden, it's all wrong, it's just wrong.

ERROL MORRIS: What's wrong about it?

JANE GRAHAM-BAILEY: The movie that they made. To me, when I saw Mr. Kassab, he was a tall, fat, mean-looking man, and then for them to portray him as Karl Malden, who has always been a hero for my generation. They didn't bring out any of Mr. Kassab's real qualities. And what was that actress's name, that pretty actress that played Mrs. Kassab?

ERROL MORRIS: Eva Marie Saint.

JANE GRAHAM-BAILEY: Yes. She's so pretty. I would have felt better if they had made them look like more of what they really were, their real appearance. Mrs. Kassab was *not* Eva Marie Saint, who is a beautiful blonde. I saw the real people, and the people who saw the movie didn't see the real people. What they saw was Karl Malden and Eva Marie Saint, the perfect people. So that biased them right away.

ERROL MORRIS: Perfect people and perfectly likable people.

JANE GRAHAM-BAILEY: Yes, absolutely. No warts, so to speak.

ERROL MORRIS: When you say it was such an injustice, what are the specific details that bother you?

JANE GRAHAM-BAILEY: The judge would just overrule anything that Dr. MacDonald's defense was trying to put over. It was obvious. I wasn't in the courtroom the whole time, but from what I saw, he just didn't give Dr. MacDonald's defense any credence. He was just so biased.

I asked Jane Graham-Bailey to return to her experiences with Stoeckley in Nashville in 1970.

JANE GRAHAM-BAILEY: She was just one of hundreds of hippies hanging around the Vanderbilt University area. I had a little efficiency apartment. And I would see Helena in front of her house, which was directly across the street. And at Bonnie's Shoe Store. She called it a "shoetique," but it was a shoe store. My little apartment complex was a neat place, and it was a good era. People seemed content, satisfied with themselves. They weren't running around complaining all day long, even though they had good cause to be.

ERROL MORRIS: When you say they had good cause to be?

JANE GRAHAM-BAILEY: Well, they were poor, desperately poor. They would come to me wanting to borrow a bar of soap, and then they would bring me cans of peas or corn to trade for the soap, because they were all on welfare. I didn't know at the time why they couldn't have their own soap, and then one of them told me. They were on welfare, and welfare didn't supply soap.

ERROL MORRIS: No soap?

JANE GRAHAM-BAILEY: I couldn't understand that. Cleanliness is next to godliness, right? You can feed the physical body, but the body still needs to be clean. And that's probably why I say everybody deserves the right to soap. I thought it was sad that they had so little that they couldn't buy soap, because back then soap was really cheap. I could buy ten bars for a dollar. And I really didn't need the peas.

ERROL MORRIS: So how did you meet Helena?

JANE GRAHAM-BAILEY: Well, sometimes Bonnie would get in a fix. She would have so many customers when she would have sales and things, so she would call me, and I would go over and help her out, working the shop on a Saturday or Sunday to help her. And she did Helena the same way.

One day she came over, and she wanted to know if she could use my shower, my bathtub, because they had no water over there at her little house. They hadn't paid the bill or whatever. And I told her, "Sure." So she would come over from time to time, not often. And that's the way it was. I certainly wouldn't have included her in any of my social activities, few as they were, because I didn't like her that much. I was polite to her and I was kind to her, like I am to most people. But I was afraid to be her friend. I didn't trust her.

ERROL MORRIS: Why not?

JANE GRAHAM-BAILEY: It's just my gut instinct. And I knew she was doing drugs—marijuana and stuff. That's probably why. I was quite prejudiced toward that sort of thing back then. So, I suppose, I don't know. I wasn't at such a lofty place in my life at that time, but I guess I looked down on her. I shouldn't have, but I did, because of her lifestyle. She's living in that place, and there were all those young men—hippies, mostly guys, not many girls.

ERROL MORRIS: Was she sick at that time?

JANE GRAHAM-BAILEY: She was, but I didn't know that she was. I learned that later on. To me she just looked like a washed-out hippie. It looked like she needed some sun and some correct food, instead of the junk that they seemed to be snacking on all the time. I remember one of the hippie boys she lived with. His name was—I can't remember whether it was Buckle or Rumple, but he wore a hat like Rumpelstiltskin does, and it was a beaver-type top hat. He was cute, a little redheaded skinny guy, about five three. And I warned him about her, because I didn't want him to get caught the next time that she ratted everybody out. She would bring all these kids into the house. Sometimes there would be twenty kids. They stayed for a week or so, and then they would all be gone and a new batch would be coming in. And she had ratted them out.

ERROL MORRIS: Was that how she made money, just simply by ratting people out?

JANE GRAHAM-BAILEY: I don't know. I guess she made money by selling drugs. I have no idea how she made money. I never asked her. Southern women don't generally ask a whole lot of questions. We're brought up to consider it rude. You're a reporter, so I forgive you.

ERROL MORRIS: Thank you.

JANE GRAHAM-BAILEY: I'm teasing you.

ERROL MORRIS: So when did you first hear about her possible connection to the murders in Fayetteville?

JANE GRAHAM-BAILEY: Well, I asked her what she was doing there: "Why are you living like this? Why don't you go home?" Or words to that effect. And she said, "I can't ever go home again." And she started crying. And I said, "Why?" She said, "I got involved in something—in some murders." And she was very, very upset. I mean, she was crying and her nose was running, and she was heaving. Looking back on it, it could have been drug withdrawal. But I was just stunned, and so I left. What could I say? What could I do?

ERROL MORRIS: Is that the closest that she ever came to telling you that she was involved in the MacDonald murders?

JANE GRAHAM-BAILEY: That was it. She didn't name any names, she didn't say how many, just that she was involved in some—I can't remember if it was *a* murder or *some* murders.

I asked Jane about her trip to Raleigh for the trial.

JANE GRAHAM-BAILEY: Well, it was a boring trip, really. You get on the airplane. That was something for me because I have a deathly fear of airplanes, and I've turned down lots of plane rides because of the fear. But I went, because I knew that she was guilty, and if she was guilty, then Dr. MacDonald was innocent. And I believe in right and wrong.

ERROL MORRIS: So you get up to Raleigh. Did you stay in a motel?

JANE GRAHAM-BAILEY: Yes, it was upstairs on the second floor. And I stayed in my room, mostly. Red [Underhill, another witness] and I had a hamburger or something one day. We talked about the years that had gone by since I had seen him—what he had been doing, what I had been doing. We didn't talk about Helena, because that had all been talked out.

ERROL MORRIS: Red and you had been boyfriend/girlfriend when you knew Helena, correct?

JANE GRAHAM-BAILEY: At the time, yes.

ERROL MORRIS: Where was Helena at that time?

JANE GRAHAM-BAILEY: She was in Raleigh, too. She was in one of the motels. It might have even been the same one that I was at, I don't know. Joe McGinniss [author of *Fatal Vision*] wanted me to be there. I guess he wanted to see if I really knew Helena. I walked into the room, and I saw Helena. I said, "Hello, Helena, how are you?" And she said, "Hi, Jane." She recognized me right away. And she was looking at those pictures of the children and Mrs. MacDonald and the apartment, or the little duplex or whatever it was that they lived in.

ERROL MORRIS: These are pictures of them dead or alive?

JANE GRAHAM-BAILEY: The dead pictures. The pictures of the children's room and living room and of Mrs. MacDonald. They're pretty horrendous. And she just sat there and just kept turning the pages and looking, said, "There's the rocking chair," or "There's the rocking horse."

ERROL MORRIS: Who was in this room? Helena's in the room, you're in the room—

JANE GRAHAM-BAILEY: Helena and Joe McGinniss.

ERROL MORRIS: Were any of the lawyers, like Bernie Segal?

JANE GRAHAM-BAILEY: No.

ERROL MORRIS: Just the three of you?

JANE GRAHAM-BAILEY: Yes.

ERROL MORRIS: So tell me what happens.

JANE GRAHAM-BAILEY: Well, there was a couple of those big books, perhaps three. Joe was sitting across the table taking notes, I don't know what about. Of course I couldn't see. And Helena was just looking at the pictures, and I was sitting beside her, and I was glancing over at them, too, but she didn't seem to have any kind of a reaction to what she was looking at. I think that's what Joe was looking for, some kind of reaction from Helena. That was all there was to it. We were there maybe twenty, twenty-five minutes—that's all.

ERROL MORRIS: This is before you testify, right? Tell me about when you were on the stand.

JANE GRAHAM-BAILEY: When I would try to say something, the prosecution would object, and the judge would allow it. Before I talked, the judge sent the jury out so they couldn't hear what I had to say.

ERROL MORRIS: But Red Underhill was also convinced that Helena knew something, right?

JANE GRAHAM-BAILEY: Oh yeah, absolutely, absolutely.

ERROL MORRIS: And I guess that Helena must have said things to Red on a number of occasions.

JANE GRAHAM-BAILEY: Oh yeah, she did, because he came in back in Nashville one day, and he was visibly upset. And he told me, he said, "She just told me about—" I can't remember his words exactly. But the murders. And he was upset.

ERROL MORRIS: Why do you think she told people this?

JANE GRAHAM-BAILEY: I think she was trying to get it off her conscience. They say that the more you confess, the easier it gets. I find that true In talking about pain-ful times of my life, that when I used to hold it inside, and then as I got older and I learned to confide and get that out. Probably that's what she was trying to do.

ERROL MORRIS: But no one really did anything about her confessions.

JANE GRAHAM-BAILEY: Well, I thought it was over. How can somebody mixed up in a murder be walking around on the streets unless somebody had proclaimed her innocent? See, you forget how naive we were back then. I didn't even have a television set. I figured, she's here now. She's living, she's breathing, she's walking around. True, her lifestyle wasn't what I would call good, but she was alive.

ERROL MORRIS: Do you think it's possible that she could have made all of this up?

JANE GRAHAM-BAILEY: No. I always felt that Dr. MacDonald was innocent. I can't imagine anybody killing his wife—for the reasons they gave. Even then, divorce was easy. He didn't have to kill anybody. To me murder is just . . . It's unthinkable. Okay. I felt like murdering one of my husbands a couple of times. And even had the opportunity to do it. We were on a boat. We were fishing in the middle of Lake Darling in North Dakota. And there wasn't a soul in sight. I was really angry with him.

And he didn't know that I could start that engine up and he was diving. You know, I thought about it. But I didn't.

ERROL MORRIS: Buy why did you believe Helena?

JANE GRAHAM-BAILEY: She couldn't suffer that much over a made-up thing, because, believe me, she was suffering.

ERROL MORRIS: She was tortured by this stuff?

JANE GRAHAM-BAILEY: Absolutely. And maybe every time she told someone, she was just hoping that something would happen so that she would be punished for it. That's just in retrospect. Well, it's like a giant cover-up. She was an informant, I don't know how high her father's connections went.

ERROL MORRIS: Well, he was a lieutenant colonel.

JANE GRAHAM-BAILEY: That's not a lot, then. I was married to an officer in the air force—one of my many husbands.

ERROL MORRIS: How many husbands have you had?

JANE GRAHAM-BAILEY: Six.

ERROL MORRIS: Wow.

JANE GRAHAM-BAILEY: I could have had a hundred.

ERROL MORRIS: Really? Why do you say that?

JANE GRAHAM-BAILEY: Well, I didn't marry everybody who proposed to me. I married a concert pianist. I married an officer in the air force. I married—oh my goodness, let me see. I married a man from one of the oldest families in Tennessee. I married a scientist, a doctor. I married a gigolo, and I married an old man. And I divorced them all. I don't like being married. But when you're alone for eight or nine years, you start thinking, "Well, marriage isn't so bad. I'm lonely." And then you marry again and you remember.

ERROL MORRIS: What's so bad about marriage?

JANE GRAHAM-BAILEY: It's me; it's not marriage. I would get very bored with marriage. After four or five years I knew everything they were going to say and do.

When you're getting ready to go to bed with your husband, and he takes a full glass of water to bed, and he drinks the whole glass. Now, if he drinks half a glass, you know he's going to make love to you. You see what I'm saying? It's just boring.

ERROL MORRIS: It does sound boring. Do you think Red will be willing to talk?

JANE GRAHAM-BAILEY: Oh, he's able to talk, and he will talk and talk and talk. But you have to separate the flotsam from the jetsam. When it comes down to the nitty-gritty, he will tell you what you want to know.

Charles "Red" Underhill, a Nashville music promoter, also knew Stoeckley in 1970. On the stand, he told how Helena was near hysterical when she confessed to him.

BERNARD SEGAL: Do you recall what month that was?

CHARLES "RED" UNDERHILL: It was in the month of December [1970].

BERNARD SEGAL: What happened when you got to the door of her apartment?

CHARLES "RED" UNDERHILL: Well, I just walked up and knocked on the door. After I had knocked—of course, this was like in the same second, really, or two seconds, and I heard someone crying—more or less, just into a hysterical sob instead of a normal cry. I asked, "Helena?" The voice that came back was, "Get away."

I asked again—I said, "Helena, is that you in there crying?" She said, "Get away. I don't want to see you or nobody," so I said, "Well, I will go down and get Bonnie and she can come down here and maybe straighten you out."

She said, "Who is it?" I said, "It is Underhill." She said, "Red?" I said, "That is right. I am going to get Bonnie," which is the lady who had been working with her and helping her along and so forth. Then, she said, "Wait a minute. Don't go get Bonnie. I will let you in," and she came to the door and unlocked the door and I walked in—the first and only time I have ever been in her apartment.

I asked her—I said, "What in the world is wrong with you carrying on like this—something happen to you? What is wrong? Tell me." She just started sobbing worse and just terrible.

The next thing that came from her mouth was, "They killed her and the two children." I said, "What is wrong with you, you goofy fool, are you on dope or something?"

BERNARD SEGAL: What did she say?

CHARLES "RED" UNDERHILL: And then, at that minute, she reversed it for some reason—why, I don't know—and said, "They killed," and sobbing just hysterically at the same time getting these words out, "they killed the two children and her," so it was stated one way and then reversed . . . [2]

I called Underhill, who, like Jane Graham-Bailey, is now living in Florida, but farther north.

ERROL MORRIS: Hi. I was on the phone with Jane Graham-Bailey yesterday. I'm one of these people writing about the Jeffrey MacDonald case. And she told me, "Give Red a call."

RED UNDERHILL: Jane called me last night. First time I talked to her in a number of years.

ERROL MORRIS: Yeah. She's a character.

RED UNDERHILL: Yeah, she's quite a person. She sure is. But anyway, what did you really have in mind that you wanted to ask me this morning?

ERROL MORRIS: I'll cut to the chase here. Can you tell me about what Helena told you?

RED UNDERHILL: That night I was at Jane's apartment and I had parked my van across the street, right in front of the place where Helena Stoeckley was living, and I heard her in there just crying and hollering and carrying on. And I beat on the door, but she wouldn't answer the door. So I went back to my van, a little extra compartment, and got one of them reliable .357 Colts. I said to myself, "Maybe someone in there is killing her. They come to kill her to shut her up."

So I took the butt of that gun and beat on her door and kept hollering. I said, "Helena, it's me." I said, "If you're by yourself, open the door. If you're not, I'll shoot the son of a bitch who is going to come open the door." Well, she come and open the door. And she said, "I don't know what I'm going to do, Red. I'm going crazy. I can't take it no longer." And she is just hysterically crying. I said, "Take what, Helena? What in the hell is it? Someone scaring you or harming you or threatening to kill you or what?"

Well, she had come to a breaking point on this murder situation of Colette and those two little precious babies. And sitting on the side of her bed next to her, she described that whole room where those children were to me, and she said, "Every time I lay down at night, Red, it gets clearer and clearer. And I'm going crazy. I can't take it no more." I said, "What room are you talking about?" She said, "The babies' rooms."

And let me tell you something, my friend, she described that damn room right to a tee, I never had been there, never had seen it, and then in the lawyer's room in Raleigh, North Carolina, they brought them eight-by-ten pictures out to me, and I told them ahead of time, I said, "Make sure her ass is sitting here at this table whenever you bring in them pictures."

ERROL MORRIS: And when the pictures were brought in?

RED UNDERHILL: I looked at them one by one very slowly, glancing up periodically at Helena, and she had her head down.

And I looked at all of them. I said, "Helena Stoeckley, that night, sitting on the side of your bed, you described everything that's in these photographs to me. Let me tell you something. You need to have the damn decency and the fortitude and the backbone and everything it takes. You need to go in there later today in front of Judge Dupree, say, 'Yes, I was there. Yes, I took part. And here's the other three. They know they're guilty too.'" I said, "Let me tell you, no one could never, never just describe the furniture alone and how it was placed in that room and those children's toys identically to this picture. The person that took them took them right after these babies were murdered, slaughtered. They didn't know I'd ever see you; they didn't ever know where you would wind up or nothing. So they knew nothing. But see, you know everything."

I asked Bernard Segal, I said, "Can everybody be excused except me and her?" That's when I had a little private conversation with her. I said, "You're guilty as sin. You're guilty as sin. You and the rest of them damn fucking worthless-ass thugs." I said, "You need to step forward, Helena." And she looked at me, crying. She said, "No, I'll never step forward. Why should I go to prison when all I got to do is make off that I'm a drug addict and they won't take my word for nothing?"

So there you go, Mr. Morris.

ERROL MORRIS: So you were alone in the room with her?

RED UNDERHILL: Oh yeah. Yeah, that's what I just told you.

ERROL MORRIS: Did she say anything incriminating in front of the lawyers that day that you remember?

RED UNDERHILL: Not a word. The only thing she said was, "I don't know what you're talking about. I've been on drugs."

ERROL MORRIS: Did you believe Helena from the first time she told you this stuff down in Nashville?

RED UNDERHILL: Well, at first she said something to me about it, that she had moved there to get away from a horrible thing in her life. I said, "What was that? You go out with a Mexican or something?" She said, "Oh no." She said, "You've heard of Jeffrey MacDonald's wife and children?" I said, "Well, sure I have, very familiar with it." She said, "They're being part of that, and I just wanted to get away from it."

ERROL MORRIS: Why do you believe that she was there? Why are you convinced that she wasn't making it up?

RED UNDERHILL: Well, let's go back to one thing. Let's go back to the eight-by-ten color photographs of those children's room. That's the best proof in the world, other than God coming from heaven and saying, "I was watching you. You was there. You're guilty." Pictures tell the truth. And it all boils down to one thing, back to her, those two children, and that room.

ERROL MORRIS: Could she have read about those details in the paper or heard about them from people?

RED UNDERHILL: Oh no, these pictures was never published. These pictures was never discussed. These pictures was sealed. And they never let the press in that room.

ERROL MORRIS: What were some of the details that she mentioned to you, do you remember?

RED UNDERHILL: Well, the way the crib was placed in the room and the little pig stuffed animal. She said, "I looked down at this stuffed animal by the door," which they had an eight-by-ten of it, and said, "And its big button eyes looked like they were crying whenever I left the room with them." I said, "Well, damn, you took the babies with you?" She said, "No, I'm talking about my friends."

ERROL MORRIS: There's something also about the hobbyhorse, no?

RED UNDERHILL: Yeah. I'm trying to remember all the toys I remember.

ERROL MORRIS: So you're convinced Helena was telling the truth?

RED UNDERHILL: There's no doubt in my mind.

ERROL MORRIS: When you looked her in the eye in that room with those photographs, why do you think—is it that she got scared? Or what made her change her story?

RED UNDERHILL: Very simple, I told you. She looked at me, she said, "Do you think I'm going to go in there and tell the truth, tell them I knew who was there and I was with them or anything of that nature? Hell no, I ain't. All I've got to do is play crazy and I'm a druggie, and I'll walk free." I said, "Yeah, but by you not doing this, you're sending an innocent person to the damn federal institution the rest of his life probably." She said, "Well, that's too bad."

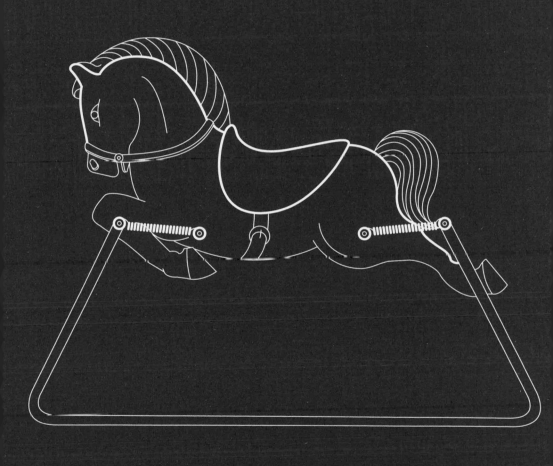

32

WANTED

Many of the witnesses who had heard Stoeckley's confessions were current or ex-cops. Can this be surprising? She was a drug informant. James Gaddis, an undercover police detective in Nashville, testified next.

> **WADE SMITH:** Did she ever make statements to you about any murders which took place in Fayetteville, North Carolina, in February 1970?
>
> **JAMES GADDIS:** Yes, sir. She did . . . I talked with her on several occasions about the murders. She said that she thought she had been there when the murders took place. The night that the murders took place, she had tripped out on some mescaline and some LSD and she remembered being there. On other occasions, she would say that she knew who had done it, but that she wasn't there. She would get very depressed when she talked about it. In fact, on several occasions, she would become so depressed that we could not even talk with her . . . It led me to believe that she was there . . .
>
> **WADE SMITH:** Did she ever make any further description to you about what occurred . . . ?
>
> **JAMES GADDIS:** The only information that she related to me was that she had been at the scene. She felt she had been there, and that the clothes she wore while she was in Nashville fit the exact description of the clothes of the female that was involved in the murders themselves.[1]

And then Robert Brisentine, the CID polygraph expert who had examined Stoeckley April 23 and 24, 1971, took the stand. It was a recitation of what Stoeckley had told him on that first day, which was detailed in his report. But the testimony concluded with a discussion of Stoeckley's sincerity.

WADE SMITH: As a matter of fact, Mr. Brisentine, you were very impressed with the sincerity of Helena Stoeckley with you; weren't you?

ROBERT BRISENTINE: I was impressed with the fact that she made such admissions; yes.

WADE SMITH: And based on everything that you could observe about it, you had to figure that she was making those statements to you with some conviction; didn't you?

ROBERT BRISENTINE: That's true, sir.

WADE SMITH: All right. No further questions.

THE COURT: That is that she honestly believed that these things were true.

ROBERT BRISENTINE: I would have to say, Your Honor, that she honestly believed in her mind that what she was telling me was true.

BRIAN MURTAGH: One question. Would that be all of it? I mean, "I did it; I didn't do it."

ROBERT BRISENTINE: No; I would have to say, based on my investigation, that when she said she was physically present that she thought in her mind that she was.[2]

————

Robert Brisentine, now in his mid-eighties, remembers many of the polygraph exams he gave in the early 1970s, including the April 24, 1970, examination of Helena Stoeckley.

ROBERT BRISENTINE: Did I tell you how Stoeckley's house was decorated? The interior of her house, in Nashville?

ERROL MORRIS: No.

ROBERT BRISENTINE: Solid black. Everything. The sink, the bathtub. The detective asked me if I wanted to see the inside of her house. I said, "Not really." He said, "I think you'd like to see this." So I went with him to her house. We were still looking for her. They had her, and somehow she'd gone someplace. She hadn't tried to evade him. She liked him.

ERROL MORRIS: This was who, now?

ROBERT BRISENTINE: What was his name? Started with a "G."

ERROL MORRIS: Gaddis?

ROBERT BRISENTINE: Yup. Gaddis! Gaddis was the detective who was using her as an informant. In addition to the black house, her living room had condoms all pasted on the ceiling, just like you'd look at the tombstones at the National Cemetery. Perfect. They were lined up perfect. They weren't just thrown up there. So this is the kind of person I was dealing with. They just appeared to be condoms that she'd rolled out and pasted on the ceiling. But I didn't examine them.

ERROL MORRIS: I can understand why.

ROBERT BRISENTINE: Helena Stoeckley had been on drugs so long that it was hard— The first time I saw her in Nashville, she was so strung out that I couldn't even think about polygraphing her. So I told the detective that she was—

ERROL MORRIS: Gaddis?

ROBERT BRISENTINE: Yes, Gaddis, right. Gaddis knew she was a druggie, but he was using her to apprehend other drug users. But in any event, she was an addict. I couldn't examine her the first day because she was in bad shape.

And so they brought her back [the next day] and I examined her. Helena would tell you that she didn't have anything to do with it, she wasn't there. Then she would say, "I kind of believe I might have been there. I dreamed that I was." And then she would tell you, "I was there."

ERROL MORRIS: You write in your report that she was convinced in her mind—

ROBERT BRISENTINE: How familiar are you with polygraphs?

ERROL MORRIS: A little familiar with them.

ROBERT BRISENTINE: Well, as you know, the polygraph is not based on fact. It's based on the feeling of the individual undergoing the exam. If the individual is color-blind and he thinks green is red, that's the way he'll respond. That's not fact, but that's what he's thinking. That's what we're dealing with. With Helena, I'm satisfied that she's not lying, but it's based on her thinking, her dreams, and so forth. That's why I had to put a caveat on it. It was due to Stoeckley's admitted state of mind and excessive drug use during and immediately following the homicides. That's the best I could do because of her drug use.

ERROL MORRIS: The exam was done in Nashville?

ROBERT BRISENTINE: It was in an actual police department in Nashville, Tennessee, and there was a polygraph room. And it had a two-way mirror. My command had a lot of agents working on that case, because the case had bothered us considerably. We felt—I shouldn't say "we"—our commander was satisfied in his mind that MacDonald had committed the homicide.

ERROL MORRIS: Who was your commander?

ROBERT BRISENTINE: Henry Tufts—at that time. T-u-f-t-s. Henry Tufts. Henry was satisfied in his mind that the only way that those people could have met their death was from MacDonald. Anyway, that was his feelings and that was his opinion.

ERROL MORRIS: What convinced him, do you think?

ROBERT BRISENTINE: I don't think it was any one specific thing that convinced him. I just think it was all of the evidence. The fact of how that coffee table had been turned over. The blood work. I think that's what really convinced him. And that coffee table incident was very impressive.

When I went down to examine MacDonald, I went to Fort Bragg to examine him, when he wouldn't take the test I went over to the crime scene and looked at it. And went through the house—I don't know if it's still sealed or not. But it was sealed at that time.

And that coffee table could not have turned over the way MacDonald described it. We tried it several times and it wouldn't do it. But anyway, this evidence caused my boss to say, "I want the investigation to continue."

ERROL MORRIS: If Stoeckley wasn't there, why was she confessing? Do you think she was suggestible?

ROBERT BRISENTINE: If you are an interrogator and you're talking to a person with a double-digit IQ versus a person with a triple-digit IQ, you would be different. If you didn't, it would be easy—not easy, but— If you didn't watch yourself you could cause a person with a double-digit IQ to be convinced of what you're telling him or her.

ERROL MORRIS: Do you think that Stoeckley was stupid?

ROBERT BRISENTINE: No, but she was a druggie. She wasn't the brightest bulb in the pack, but she was not really stupid. I wouldn't say she's stupid. But she was so strung out on drugs that she could be easily persuaded. You may not know it about drugs, but you know it from interrogating. You have to be careful when you're talking to somebody that can be influenced easily. When we train interrogators and polygraph examiners, a large part of the interrogation is to know the IQ of your examinee, or the person you're interrogating. Because if a person is strong enough, and they're overbearing over the person who is not as strong mentally, then you can convince that person to tell you something that's not the truth. And they actually come to believe it.

Helena would hallucinate and have delusions when she was on drugs. But part of her mental faculties had not been totally contaminated. And so she was getting some truth—or what she thinks is truth, or which may have been truth—confused with the results of the drug use. Am I making myself clear?

ERROL MORRIS: I think so.

ROBERT BRISENTINE: I think that's why I had to put the paragraph in, or the statement in, that you can't come to the conclusion that she did or did not witness it. I really don't know. I personally think she didn't. I don't know, but I personally think she did not.

ERROL MORRIS: Because you think MacDonald did it, right?

ROBERT BRISENTINE: Oh yes. I do.

33

IN MY MIND, IT SEEMS THAT I SAW THIS THING HAPPEN

On one weekend in Raleigh in 1979, the Stoeckley witnesses could be found within a block of one another. Now they are scattered. Some are in Florida, some in Alabama, and some are dead. Prince Beasley, a retired Fayetteville police officer who had used Helena Stoeckley as an informant, testified as to his first meeting with Stoeckley after the murders. He died in 1996, but we still have his trial testimony. Beasley is different from the other witnesses. Helena didn't confess to him years after the fact. He sought her out the morning after the murders because she matched the description of the female intruder.

PRINCE BEASLEY: Then, after I received descriptions of the suspects, I went to this trailer I knew she had been living at, and there was no one there. So I proceeded to look for her that day, and I couldn't find her or anyone else—the ones I was looking for.

So I went back home and went to bed. During the time I was at home, some other officers got my warrant and went back to the trailer, but we had searched this trailer prior to this—and recovered a large amount of drugs that she had told us was there, and they were there. We confiscated these drugs and we returned to the police station. I signed a warrant—I believe I signed it, and they went back later that afternoon and arrested one man.

And when I went to work, I found out that this had been done, so I went back to the apartment house where Helena was supposed to have been living. There was no one there, so I staked the place out, I guess, until 2:30 or 3:00 that morning.

She drove into the driveway with a group of people in—I believe it was an old convertible, Plymouth-looking car.

WADE SMITH: All right; Mr. Beasley, at this time it would be the 18th of February?

PRINCE BEASLEY: Yes, sir; I believe it would.

WADE SMITH: All right; go ahead. What happened?

PRINCE BEASLEY: I was driving an unmarked car and I was dressed in dungarees and leather jacket. I walked up behind the car and I called her to me, and as I called her she came towards me and the other subjects in the car also came toward me.

She turned around and told them it would be all right to sit down. So I took her to my car and asked her had she heard about this incident at Fort Bragg. She said she had, and I said, "Well, Helena, according to the information we've got, you and these people you are with fit the description that was given out." I said, "Now, I am going to ask you straight out, I know you and you know me. I want to ask you to tell me the truth." She backed off and hung her head. She says, "In my mind, it seems that I saw this thing happen"; but she says, "I was heavy on mescaline." And she would not commit herself any further.

WADE SMITH: All right; what happened next?

PRINCE BEASLEY: I got names of the other people that were in the car with her. I called CID at Fort Bragg and told them that I had some suspects in custody that fit the description—would the police come down?

I believe that was about 2:30 and at 4:30, or almost daylight, nobody had ever come or either returned my call. I released these people and let them go.

WADE SMITH: Did you ever see any of them again, other than Helena Stoeckley?

PRINCE BEASLEY: Never.

WADE SMITH: Did you ever see Helena Stoeckley again?

PRINCE BEASLEY: Yes; I did.

WADE SMITH: When did you next see her?

PRINCE BEASLEY: I can't recall the time, but it wasn't long after that. Later, I went up to her apartment, tried to locate her again, and I believe the last time I saw her there was a bunch of wreaths out in the front yard, and I believe there was also one hanging on the front door.

WADE SMITH: Did you ever talk with Helena about that?

PRINCE BEASLEY: Yes; I did.

WADE SMITH: What did she say?

PRINCE BEASLEY: She said that she was in mourning.

WADE SMITH: In mourning?

PRINCE BEASLEY: Yes, sir.

WADE SMITH: What was she in mourning about?

PRINCE BEASLEY: In reference to the MacDonald murders.

WADE SMITH: Did she tell you she was in mourning about the MacDonald murders?

PRINCE BEASLEY: Yes; she did, and she was wearing black, and I might add that she would not—I was really wanting some information really—and she would not even talk to me about it.[1]

The final witness was William Posey, a laundry deliveryman and one of Stoeckley's neighbors who had approached Segal during the Article 32. At the 1979 trial, he essentially reprised his surprise testimony.

BERNARD SEGAL: Were you aware of the time when the MacDonald funerals took place over at Fort Bragg?

WILLIAM POSEY: Well, I didn't know exactly what day, you know, that it happened; but my wife and I—we were going somewhere one day, and Helena was dressed in a solid black dress, you know, a long one. And she had a black thing over her face.

BERNARD SEGAL: You mean a veil?

WILLIAM POSEY: Yeah, and she went and got some wreaths like you see at a graveyard, and placed them along by her door and stuff; and she was setting there like she was crying all day, you know.

BERNARD SEGAL: Sitting where?

WILLIAM POSEY: By her door; by her front door. And that evening on the news it showed Dr. MacDonald in his uniform and it said that he had just come from the funeral thing. You know, they had had services that day.

BERNARD SEGAL: Did you talk to Helena about why she was sitting there in black?

WILLIAM POSEY: No, she wouldn't talk to nobody. Her boyfriend come up in the afternoon, and was trying to get her to go off; and, you know, they got in a big argument because she wouldn't leave. She just sat there real quiet like all day.

BERNARD SEGAL: At some point thereafter, did you talk to her about whether she was involved in the murders at the MacDonald house?

WILLIAM POSEY: Yeah, I talked to her—well, she left shortly after that, and I didn't see her no more for a while; and then about two days before I testified I went to Haymount.

I had already talked to you, and you wanted to know what her name was—her full name—and I didn't know what her full name was, so I went to Haymount to try to find out.

You know, I knew that people up there knew her and I could find out her name. Well, when I went up there she was there. Haymount's a section of town that everybody hung out in; and I talked to her then . . . I'd asked her where she had been and everything, and she said, "Just around . . ."

We started talking about the murder and everything, and we got into that.

BERNARD SEGAL: And what did she say about the MacDonald murders?

WILLIAM POSEY: Well, when you talked to her—it is like—one, I don't know how to say it enough. One minute she's with you like in a normal conversation, then the next minute she's, you know, she was referring back to the murder . . .

Like she said that all she did was like hold the light, that she didn't—she wouldn't kill anybody because she wasn't a hostile person, you know.

BERNARD SEGAL: What about this light she was talking about?

WILLIAM POSEY: Holding the light would be the only thing she would do, you know . . . I said something to reference that some policemen had seen them that morning, and she named the street, Honeycutt— said that, yes, she remembered, you know.

But it was like one minute she was there at the thing; then the next minute she was drifting back.[2]

On cross-examination, Blackburn learned that Stoeckley had told Posey "about trying to ride the toy."

JAMES BLACKBURN: Has Helena ever told you that she was in the MacDonald apartment?

WILLIAM POSEY: She never point-blank said that she was in the apartment . . . One minute she would be in a normal conversation and then the next minute she would be like she was right there. But like she told me about trying to ride the toy and like she said about holding the light and things like that.

At the end of Posey's testimony, the defense and the prosecution argued about the six witnesses waiting in the wings. The arguments have an *Alice in Wonderland* quality. Segal argued that Posey, Beasley, Brisentine, Gaddis, Underhill, and Zillioux's testimony should be heard by the jury.

BERNARD SEGAL: . . . If we were to say in this case, because maybe somebody thinks that Helena was using some drugs that her statements are inadmissible, what are we saying about statements we take all the time in connection with the criminal process. . . ? In my view, it is not in any way improper under the rules.

THE COURT: All right, what says the Government?

BRIAN MURTAGH: Your Honor, I would again reiterate—and I think Mr. Segal is missing the point—that we are talking about whether a reasonable person making this statement at the time would so appreciate the gravity of the statement that they wouldn't make it unless they meant it.

I don't think we have that in this case. What we are talking about is somebody who is hysterical, perhaps hallucinating, certainly at times I think going through withdrawal, has hepatitis, is completely in a drug-oriented state and suffering continually from the effects of drugs.

At this time, she makes various statements. Now, those statements are never of an unequivocal nature. It can all be drawn back to her lack of an alibi and the fact that she is constantly being interviewed, picked up, hassled by the police, and having to account for her whereabouts . . .

I still think, Judge, that the issue here is that these statements are being offered not by the government but by the defendant to exculpate the defendant, and then I think the rule mandates that the statements should not be admitted unless there are corroborative circumstances which clearly indicate the trustworthiness of the statement. I just don't see how Mr. Segal can argue that these various statements which are all over the lot are trustworthy or unequivocal or, for that matter, are really statements against interest.

THE COURT: What do you say about Rule 403? Does that have any pertinency here?[3]

Rule 403 is remarkable in its vagueness. It allows evidence to be excluded if its probative value is outweighed by the danger of, among other things, misleading the jury or wasting time. Segal tried to take up the various subclauses of Rule 403, each in turn, including "wasting time." To which Dupree replied:

THE COURT: Well, we have suspended the operation of the time-wasting factor for this particular trial, so you need not address that issue.

But what if it is evidence that the prosecution doesn't like? Can it be excluded on those grounds as well? Segal had come well prepared to argue that Rule 403 did not apply, but his arguments fell on deaf ears.

BERNARD SEGAL: We are talking about the denial of the right of the Defendant to show that there is evidence that could raise a reasonable doubt on his behalf, because it tends to show the involvement of someone else . . . I think that the Constitution would say to us . . . that the 403 rule cannot be used as a basis of denying a defendant his right to be heard.

Judge Dupree took the matter under advisement and adjourned court for the weekend. He would rule on the issue of the corroborating witnesses Monday morning.

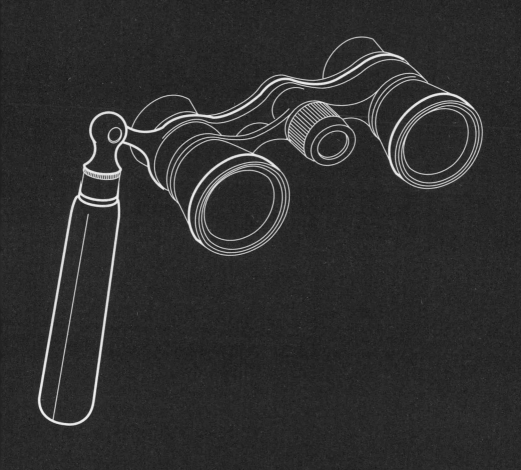

34

THE JOURNEY'S END

There was one more odd wrinkle in the story. Wendy Rouder, a law clerk for Segal, had been asked to check in on Stoeckley. It was the weekend when Dupree deliberated about putting the Stoeckley witnesses before the jury. I talked to Wendy Rouder, now a lawyer in Northern California, about her bizarre weekend with Helena Stoeckley, hoping for a few salient details that might help put Stoeckley in perspective.

WENDY ROUDER: I was just out of law school. I started working on the case in March of '79. And I was waiting for my bar results, which I passed in May of '79. And then, by June, I was off to Raleigh and wound up living in the dormitory with the defense team. And it was a Saturday morning.

ERROL MORRIS: You were in a dormitory?

WENDY ROUDER: At North Carolina State. It was a Saturday morning, the very next day after she testified. I remember little things that stand out that don't have any legal significance—being told the judge had ordered MacDonald to pay for Stoeckley's hotel room.

ERROL MORRIS: Wasn't she brought in as a witness?

WENDY ROUDER: She was brought in as a witness by the FBI, on the judge's orders. I don't know whether she was under arrest or not. She wasn't free to leave. They didn't keep her in custody, at least that weekend. And it was a Saturday morning, and I was the only one in the office. I had gone in early. I answered the phone. And I spoke directly to the motel woman who was yelling, "Get them out of here. Get them out of here." I called Bernie, and he said, "You better go down there and see what's going on." He told me something about the motel woman saying that Helena was being beaten up in the swimming pool. He said, "Take Underhill with you." And I remember that when we got to the motel, the Journey's End, the motel lady showed me the room. I walked in and Helena's holding her hand to her nose, and there's blood all over the place. And the motel woman is still screaming, "Get them out of here. Get them out of here." And I don't know what's going on. I had not had any prior contact with her. And Helena is screaming at the boyfriend, who's there only in his underwear—no shoes, no socks, no shirt. And there's blood on the bed. And I said, "What happened to you?" She says, "I walked into the doorway." Unlikely, but that's what she said to me.

ERROL MORRIS: Who is the boyfriend?

WENDY ROUDER: Ernie Davis. So the motel woman is screaming, and Helena is screaming at Ernie, and Ernie is screaming at Helena. It was an incredible scene. And finally I was able to get her attention to focus on me long enough to say, "Do you want him out of here?"—meaning the boyfriend. She said yes. So Red started, and I started saying, "Come on, she wants you out of here. Pack up." And his suitcase was opened up, but she's still with her hands, still with the blood coming out of her hands to her nose. And she's throwing everything in the motel room that she can think of into the suitcase—the ashtrays, the towels. And Underhill agrees to take him to the Greyhound bus station. And he agrees to go. And I agree to get the landlady to—

ERROL MORRIS: He was not a witness, right? He was just along for the ride?

WENDY ROUDER: Yeah, he was along for the ride, right, right. He was with her when the FBI picked her up. And we got the motel lady to back off about kicking her out right then and there. Now I'm alone with her. My heart is pumping because here I am alone with a woman who was in the house with the killers. And also so important to the case. Meanwhile, I was busy calling Bernie every fifteen minutes. And he's saying, "Just talk to her. Just talk to her naturally." And I asked her if she wanted me to go? And she said no. So I stayed with her, and we started a conversation talking about—well, I have a background in theater, and I shared that with her. And then we got into her love of opera. We talked about opera and theater.

ERROL MORRIS: She loved opera?

WENDY ROUDER: Yes.

ERROL MORRIS: Any operas in particular?

WENDY ROUDER: I can't remember. I just remember my efforts to keep the conversation going.

ERROL MORRIS: I have this picture of Helena Stoeckley listening to *La Traviata*.

WENDY ROUDER: Who knows. But when I became a public defender, I worked with a lot of mentally disturbed persons. And she was not mentally disturbed. She may have had all kinds of neurotic kind of problems. But she was not what we call in California "5150." She was not in that league at all.

ERROL MORRIS: Fifty-one fifty is—

WENDY ROUDER: It's the code for involuntarily committing somebody. I expected somebody zombie-ish, because I heard about all the drug use. And she wasn't. She came from a fairly middle-class background too. Her father was a big shot in the military. And so we made small talk. And suddenly she interrupted whatever it was to say, "You know, I still remember being in that room." I said, "What room?" She said, "That room in the MacDonald house." She had the memory of holding the candle, only it wasn't dripping wax, it was dripping blood. At some point she started talking about feeling guilty. And I said to her, "Why don't you just get on the stand and just say it like it happened." And that's when she made a comment about, I can't do that. The prosecutors will—I don't remember if she said "fry me," "burn me," or "hang me." It was one of those three. But I didn't know that she had been interviewed by Blackburn.

Indeed, after her interview with the defense and its witnesses, Stoeckley had been interviewed by James Blackburn.

WENDY ROUDER: And at one point I said to her, "Well, what do you expect me to do with this information?" I said to her, "Don't tell me all of this, because it's useless. You've got to come clean with somebody that's in a position to clear Jeff." And she kept saying, "I can't do that." That was the extent of it. Bernie wanted me to hang out with her as long as possible, but the judge interrupted that. He got on the phone—

ERROL MORRIS: The judge called you?

WENDY ROUDER: Yeah, he called me. And he called me—she had by that time moved to another hotel.

ERROL MORRIS: I guess she did get thrown out eventually.

WENDY ROUDER: Right. We agreed to have her go. I rode in the car with her to the Hilton. She asked me to spend the night with her. She said, "Couldn't you just stay with me? I don't want you to leave me alone." I don't know what would have happened had the judge not called.

ERROL MORRIS: But how did the judge know where to find you?

WENDY ROUDER: That was the weirdest thing. It was in the lobby of the Hilton. Somebody says, "Are you Wendy Rouder?" I say, "Yeah." They say, "Judge Dupree wants to talk to you." And he gets on the phone and says, "Rouder?" That's what he called me, Rouder. [Rouder is doing her best impression of Dupree's southern drawl.] "Yes, Your Honor." He said, "Are you with Ms. Stoeckley?" And I said, "Yes, Your Honor." He said, "Well, I don't think that's a very good idea for a defense lawyer to be with a witness." He said, "I think you just better go and leave Ms. Stoeckley to herself." "Yes, Your Honor." How he knew—who was watching? The motel lady may have called the police, the police may have called him. I don't know. I have no idea how he knew. It was so weird to get a call in a hotel from the judge. And that was my Helena experience.

ERROL MORRIS: During the weekend that Dupree was deciding on whether or not to allow the testimony?

WENDY ROUDER: Yes. But I assumed that MacDonald was going to be acquitted and I'd be out of a job. I didn't know—

ERROL MORRIS: Really? You thought that this was going to be an acquittal?

WENDY ROUDER: Yes.

ERROL MORRIS: Why?

WENDY ROUDER: I didn't think that they had the evidence. I thought their evidence was all speculation. If this happened, then there would have been this piece of evidence. I just didn't think the evidence added up.

ERROL MORRIS: Did you believe Helena Stoeckley?

WENDY ROUDER: I truly expected somebody who seemed a little bonkers. And she seemed totally level to me. First of all, when Jeff described the person, besides the officer who saw somebody fitting the description, Mica's testimony—when Jeff describes to the police artist and then that particular drawing is shown to people and they recognize it—how lucky can Jeff get to pick somebody at random who then is going to confess? To make up a description of a person who happens to falsely confess? That gave me a mind-set to believe her. Because I just couldn't imagine Jeff being that lucky. That didn't fly with me. She carried on a conversation with me about stuff totally unrelated . . . I believed her. Yeah, I believed her.

ERROL MORRIS: Do you believe that she was hidden by the prosecution?

WENDY ROUDER: Yes. Don't forget it was a shock when the government found her.

Segal had been asking them for years, "How can I find her? How can I locate her? I want to interview her." It had been going on for nine years. And the answer was, "We don't know." Then within hours they bring her in. Segal announces, "I want to call all these witnesses," and she's found in hours. What do you think? How was she found in hours? I believe they knew where she was all along.

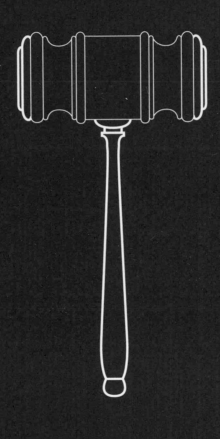

UNCLEARLY TRUSTWORTHY

I could imagine Stoeckley's eight-year-old confessions could be seen as inadmissible evidence, but her statements to Rouder over that weekend changed all that. Except for one thing. Dupree ruled on the inadmissibility of the evidence before Rouder could testify.

> **THE COURT:** Since court adjourned on Friday afternoon, I have spent a substantial portion of my waking hours researching and deciding the rather interesting evidentiary question which was posed, the question being whether statements tending to be against the penal interests of the witness Stoeckley should be admissible through other witnesses—statements made outside of court in far distant times . . . I will rule that these proposed statements do not comply with the trustworthy requisites of [Rule] 804(b)(3)[1]; that far from being clearly corroborated and trustworthy, that they are about as unclearly trustworthy—or clearly untrustworthy, let me say—as any statements that I have ever seen or heard.[2]

Which is it? Unclearly trustworthy or clearly untrustworthy?

> **THE COURT:** This witness, in her examination here in court—and cross-examination—has been, to use the Government Counsel's terminology, "all over the lot." The statements which she has made out of court were "all over the lot," so it can't

really be said that the hearing of those statements would lead to any different conclusion than what the jurors got while she was here in open court . . .

As I stated, this testimony, I think, has no trustworthiness at all. Here you have a girl who, when she made the statements, was in most instances heavily drugged, if not hallucinating.[3] And she has told us all that herself. She has stated that in person.

. . . [O]n the question of trustworthiness, I just can't see it.

Now, on the question of impeachment, as I stated, I don't think it is admissible on that theory for the reason that I don't think it is impeaching. There are other reasons which I won't elaborate on right now.

Finally, I think that this evidence ought to be excluded as a matter of discretion by the Court under Rule 403, because its probative value is substantially outweighed by the danger of unfair prejudice. It would tend to confuse the issues, mislead the jury. It would cause undue delay and a waste of time.

So I think in the interest of time—having devoted two days to this subject—that that is enough; and for the additional reason that it ought to be excluded under 403, I will hold that it is not admissible.

The rug has just been pulled out from under him, but Segal soldiers on. He will be allowed to put the six witnesses in front of the jury, but he will not be allowed to ask them about Stoeckley's confessions. Yes, you can call John Wilkes Booth to the stand, but please don't ask him about the Lincoln assassination.

Jane Zillioux is on the stand. Segal has returned to the meeting on August 16. Stoeckley was in an office with the various witnesses.

BERNARD SEGAL: Did Ms. Stoeckley continue to look at those photographs more than once?

JANE ZILLIOUX: At least four times she kept going back to the photograph of the smallest MacDonald child—the one that the baby was laying in bed in a pool of blood and had its little bottle.

BERNARD SEGAL: Now, let me show you some photographs that have previously been marked in evidence and see perhaps if you can tell us which one of the photographs Ms. Stoeckley returned to . . .

JANE ZILLIOUX: It was this one.

BERNARD SEGAL: The witness has indicated the photo that has been marked for identification as Government Exhibit G-60, Your Honor, which has previously been identified here in court as a photograph of Kristen MacDonald in her pajamas on the bed . . . [D]id she say anything the first time she looked at the picture?

JAMES BLACKBURN: Your Honor, we would object.

THE COURT: Sustained.

BERNARD SEGAL: Did Helena Stoeckley ever indicate to you that she had ever seen the scene or the person depicted in that picture previous to the time that she looked at that book?

JAMES BLACKBURN: Objection.

THE COURT: Sustained.[4]

It continues in this vein. Objection. Sustained. Objection. Sustained. The discussion turned to the photograph of the rocking horse.

BERNARD SEGAL: Now, in regard to this particular photo, what, if anything, did Ms. Stoeckley say to you about that photo?

GEORGE ANDERSON: Objection.

BRIAN MURTAGH: Objection.

THE COURT: Sustained.

BERNARD SEGAL: Did in any way Ms. Stoeckley indicate that she recognized seeing that scene herself?

GEORGE ANDERSON: Objection.

JAMES BLACKBURN: Objection.

THE COURT: Sustained . . .

BERNARD SEGAL: Did Ms. Stoeckley say anything at that time about the totality of the scenes depicted in there; that is, did she say anything indicating recognition and prior knowledge of the places and events depicted in those photographs?

GEORGE ANDERSON: Objection.

JAMES BLACKBURN: Objection.

THE COURT: Sustained.

BERNARD SEGAL: Did Ms. Stoeckley say anything to you within the time that you were in the room—witness room with her—about having carried a lighted candle in February of 1970?

JAMES BLACKBURN: Objection.

THE COURT: Sustained.

BERNARD SEGAL: I have no further questions of Ms. Zillioux at this time, Your Honor.

The goal of the lawyers for the prosecution was to discredit Stoeckley as well as the supporting witnesses, and it was entirely successful. No narrative emerged. For the jury, a hopeless jumble of story fragments conjoined with equivocations and evasions. Not inherently untrustworthy. Untrustworthy because of the way it was presented to the jury. But that's the way the court wanted it.

Later that day, Wendy Rouder took the stand. Her testimony showed that Stoeckley had not only confessed in the past, but was still confessing.

WENDY ROUDER: After a pause, she said to me, "I still think I could have been there that night." I then asked, "What makes you think so?" She said, "I don't know." There was a pause, and then she said, "That rocking horse." There was another pause, and she added, "You know, Kristen, Kristen Jean. Those pictures, when I looked at those pictures, I knew I had seen her somewhere before." Another pause, and she added, "And that driveway, I remember being in that driveway."

BERNARD SEGAL: Was that the end of her remarks about the MacDonald case at that juncture?

WENDY ROUDER: Specifically, placing herself on something concrete, yes. There were more allusions to her involvement, though, in that particular conversation.

BERNARD SEGAL: Later on in the conversation, did she have occasion to be specific about some connection or involvement with the MacDonald case?

WENDY ROUDER: The specificity was I had said to her, "Helena"—well, let me read. I am sure I could say it.

At one point I asked her if the guilt over all these years has ever left her, and she said, "No, what do you think I have taken all these damn drugs for?" I later asked her if drugs help relieve this memory, and she said, "No, because you always have to come down." I volunteered that the guilt must be awful trying to live with, and she said, "Yes."

BERNARD SEGAL: All right, now, did this conversation continue until some point when she made some further statements about the MacDonald case or relative to the killing of the MacDonald family?

WENDY ROUDER: There was another conversation about guilt. I asked her, "If MacDonald were convicted, could you live with that guilt too?" She said, "I don't think so . . ." She repeatedly asked me if I would stay with her at the hotel, and I said I didn't think that that would be such a good idea but Red would stay with her if that was okay. "Would you feel comfortable with Red?" She said, "Oh, yeah. I would trust him any day."

BERNARD SEGAL: All right, now, at some later time then at the Hilton Inn, did she make some statement to you in regard to her knowledge of the MacDonald case or the killings that took place in February of 1970?

WENDY ROUDER: The first statements she made were not at the Hilton. They were down at the Downtowner Motel.

BERNARD SEGAL: How did that take place?

WENDY ROUDER: Mr. Underhill had gone upstairs to get his clothes. Again, our conversation was predominantly small talk. There was a pause. She said, "I still think I was there in that house that night." And I said, "Helena, is it a feeling you are having or a memory?" She said, "It's a memory. I remember standing at the couch, holding a candle, only—you know—it wasn't dripping wax. It was dripping blood."

BERNARD SEGAL: Is that the last conversation you had with her yesterday that related to this case?

WENDY ROUDER: My follow-up to that was, "Helena, why don't you just go and say that in court," and she said, "I can't with those damn prosecutors sitting there."[5]

THE FOUR-LEGGED TABLE

August 28, 1979. The start of closing arguments. Blackburn had said in his opening arguments, "Physical evidence doesn't lie."[1] To which Segal replied in his closing arguments:

> **BERNARD SEGAL:** The government says, "Physical evidence doesn't lie." They said that in the beginning. They say it now. I want to tell you something. Physical evidence doesn't say a darn thing.
>
> Physical evidence lies there. The fibers lie there. Everything lies there. The only thing that is speaking is not the physical evidence, but it is the interpreter speaking. Who is the interpreter of the evidence for you? The non-partisan, the fellow on the white horse [in the] shining armor? Not at all. It is my adversary— my opponent on the other side.[2]

On May 18, 2011, I spoke to Bernie Segal for the first time. He had become a professor of law at Golden Gate University in San Francisco. But I had heard that he had been deeply wounded by this case.

> **BERNARD SEGAL:** Let me tell you an anecdote, which is a favorite piece of pain of mine in this case. Starting in 1970, I was begging for the forensic evidence, and we were not getting it. For almost ten years, we begged and pleaded to get the CID and the FBI lab reports, and we never got them. So the forensic evidence

was something of a mystery in the case up until the moment it was going to be tried. When it was clear that the case was to be retried, I made the motion to have discovery of the forensic evidence given to the defense. And Judge Dupree denied that motion for discovery.

I wrote twenty-nine letters to the government saying, "Let us see the evidence." It was always, "Not now. Not now." Finally, about six months before we were going to go to trial, I made a second motion. The first motion was in 1975, and this one is in 1979. "Give us the forensic evidence." The government said, "Defense is not entitled to this forensic evidence because they didn't ask for it in a timely fashion." What are you talking about? For the last two and a half years I'm begging and pleading with you guys. I was absolutely livid. Absolutely livid. So I said, "I want a hearing on this motion, Judge, and the government to answer me."

I fly out to North Carolina, and the judge calls the case. I walk up to the bar of the court, and I say, "Your Honor, the government's answer that we never asked before is an outrage. It's an absolute outrage." And all of a sudden—*bang*. The gavel is smacked. "I won't have it. I won't have it. I won't have you talking about the government that way. You apologize." And we then had a staring contest. The judge was waiting for me to apologize. And I'm not apologizing. In the end, his answer was their answer: that we were not entitled to get the timely access to the forensic evidence because we hadn't asked it in time.

ERROL MORRIS: Under normal circumstances, might this even be grounds for dismissing the case or reversing the case, no?

BERNARD SEGAL: Well, the courts are not quick to dismiss cases for what may be considered a procedural gap such as not giving us the evidence there that we needed. But this was a terrible, terrible miscarriage. In a case entirely built upon forensic evidence, to not allow the defense to examine it? Now, we did look at a few pieces of it. We got to go into a jail cell, and there's a table with a lot of junk piled upon it. And an FBI agent's standing there with his arms folded over his chest giving me the evil eye. And two of my associates—we walked around the table and we looked at it. We couldn't touch anything of course, lest we contaminate the evidence. Thereafter it was pointed out, "The defense has been given the opportunity to examine the evidence." You have to be without scruples, without moral backbone, to have said that to us.

ERROL MORRIS: Now, you had already hired Thornton, right?

BERNARD SEGAL: Yes. And John was going to bring aboard other forensic scientists. We would have had a team. Although we were so far behind. The government had four and a half years to put this together. And we had only four and a half months, and we still didn't get the chance to really examine everything.

ERROL MORRIS: Let me ask you something. You say Judge Dupree's decisions were so outrageous. Why do you think Dupree did this? Did he hate you? Did he hate MacDonald? Is there some reason that you can think of why he conducted himself in this way?

BERNARD SEGAL: Maybe he didn't like me because I was Jewish. And I went to MacDonald at some point and said, "Jeff, everything about this judge is wrong. It may be that he will take it out on you that he doesn't care for me as a Jewish lawyer. And I'm going to withdraw immediately, and you can get somebody else." And Jeff said no, he didn't want to do that.

ERROL MORRIS: So that was your first meeting with Dupree. And then what happened?

BERNARD SEGAL: The next four and a half or five months we spent racing around, trying to get the little bit of evidence that we got from the government, and trying to get our case together. I put together a case, it was, we said, "Four legs of a table." Leg No. 1 was the psychiatric testimony. It was an absolutely critical and an amazing facet of the testimony. If you want to see what kind of man Jeffrey MacDonald was in 1978, '79, I can show you. Because I have the videotapes of the hypnotic session, where I had him examined by a psychologist from Los Angeles. He did a hypnotic interview of MacDonald, and I have those tapes around.

In fact, I have seen the tapes of MacDonald's hypnosis session, and they have a powerful effect on the viewer—suggesting a deep reservoir of painful, vivid memory inside MacDonald, one that he does not show in television interviews. But I can't consider them evidence on their own.

BERNARD SEGAL: Leg No. 2 was Helena Stoeckley's confessions. My God, I had seven different people from seven different sources all say that over a period of two years or so, Helena Stoeckley made a confession to being at the crime scene. Now, she never said that she murdered anybody. She said she was there and she said she was along with them for the ride, but she herself didn't use a knife or weapon on anybody. And the other side of it was that the judge said, "No, I'm not going to let it in. It is unreliable testimony. It's prejudicial." How the hell is it prejudicial? It's a confession made to third parties. So, two up and two down.

Then, Leg No. 3. We wanted to introduce the findings of the military court. There was actually a Federal Rule of Evidence which said that we could introduce the ruling of the military court. And I said, "Well, that's pretty good. Now we've got three things going for MacDonald."

Leg No. 4. The forensic evidence. We were prepared to show how it was really fraudulently put together. That it was the weakest part, not the strongest, of the case. Okay. So, we had four legs of our table here, and the judge chopped off each one of them. It was the great four-legged defense that never got off the ground. It was a nightmare. An absolute nightmare.

ERROL MORRIS: And the allegation that the judge's son-in-law was one of the original prosecutors?

BERNARD SEGAL: I wouldn't say that was the reason. Dupree was a typical right-wing judicial appointment. When the vacancy in the federal bench came up, they made him a judge. He was a lawyer of no distinction, of no federal experience. And so in his view, whatever the government tells him, the government is always right. So there was a bias that we felt all the time. Also he was a moron.

ERROL MORRIS: A moron?

BERNARD SEGAL: An absolute moron. And a racist. A very nice young woman, about twenty-two, twenty-three years of age, was one of the speculative jurors. She was African American. She walked up to the witness stand to be questioned, and before anybody had asked a question, Dupree said, "You're from over in Johnston County, aren't you, young lady?" And her answer was yes. "Well, then, of course you would like to be excused so you can go on home and help your daddy pick tobacco." She said, "No, I made preparations as soon as I got notice to serve on a jury. I made preparations. I'm available." He said, "No, no, young lady, your daddy needs you on the farm. I will excuse you." Not "the government excuses you"; not "Segal excuses you." Dupree just kicked her out. And there went one-third of the black jury pool that we needed. The government didn't even have to use up a challenge. For God's sakes, what's going on in American justice?

———

Just before the beginning of the trial, MacDonald had hired—with the blessing of Segal—Joe McGinniss, a successful young journalist who had published a number of bestsellers, including *The Selling of the President 1968*. It had been on the *New York Times* bestseller list when he was twenty-six years old. McGinniss had defended MacDonald in a short column for the *Los Angeles Herald-Examiner* on June 14, 1979, entitled "Jeffrey MacDonald: Living a Nightmare." Its last paragraph read:

He finished his coffee, picked up the check. He had left half of his ham and eggs on his plate. In two weeks, he would fly to North Carolina accused of the slaughter of his family. For now, he would work the four-to-midnight shift as director of the emergency room at St. Mary's Hospital in Long Beach, where, if it were a typical shift, he would quite likely save a life or two.[3]

McGinniss was invited to join the defense team, and lived with them at the Kappa Alpha fraternity house on the North Carolina State campus where they had assembled during the summer months of 1979. I asked Segal about McGinniss.

ERROL MORRIS: And how does Joe McGinniss figure into all of this?

BERNARD SEGAL: This case was tried on a zero budget. There was no way of raising funds. That's why we did the book routine. The book routine was intended to give MacDonald access to some funds that could be used for his defense. After the conviction, McGinniss started worrying about the story line. At first he said, "My God, how unbelievable. What a catastrophe." And then later McGinniss said—it could have been a month or two later, but it's clear in my mind that he said it—"I don't think that the publisher will be interested in this story. Only guilty men get convicted."

Segal died on August 12, 2011. He was eighty-one years old. There were many questions I had hoped to ask him. And didn't get a chance.

Segal was a Philadelphia Jew with a skullet—bald on top, long on the sides—in a North Carolina courtroom. He was contending with a deck heavily stacked against him. Dupree rejected motion after motion after motion. Some were provocations issued by Segal; others were entirely reasonable but rejected nevertheless. How about bail? Denied. What about giving Thornton access to the handwritten lab notes? Denied. Segal was forbidden to introduce psychiatric testimony beneficial to his client, forbidden to present Stoeckley's extraordinary history of confessions, forbidden to introduce Colonel Rock's report or any of the findings from the Article 32. The government was allowed to grandstand and peddle junk science in court. Was it really necessary to read into the trial record much of an issue of *Esquire* devoted to satanism? Dupree allowed it. And much more.

Segal met Dupree in 1975, at the beginning of the grand jury hearing. They hated each other instantly. But every indication shows that Segal did little to mitigate it, and much to exacerbate it. By 1979, there was open hostility in the courtroom.

THE SLAUGHTERHOUSE

For truth is but justice in our knowledge,
and justice is but truth in our practice.
—John Milton, *Eikonoklastes*

The closing arguments continued. Although the physical evidence was discussed in detail, the defense never effectively dealt with any of it. Instead, the arguments devolved along predictable lines. For the government, the proof through physical evidence that MacDonald was the killer; for the defense, the almost total absence of motive.

Murtagh began:

BRIAN MURTAGH: Our duty was to take you through a tour of a slaughterhouse—not a slaughterhouse for the defendant, certainly, but a slaughterhouse for Colette, Kimberley, and Kristen. It was our duty to show you many pieces of physical evidence—much of it grotesque—and to put these bits and pieces of the jigsaw puzzle together . . .

Just as the defendant is not entitled to a perfect trial—only a fair trial—he isn't entitled to a perfect crime scene either. The government's case does not rise or fall on whether the crime scene was perfect. The government's case rises and falls on whether the physical evidence connects the defendant beyond a reasonable doubt to the commission of this crime . . .

Now, since the defendant had been trained by his own admission in Special Forces to withstand interrogations such as a prisoner-of-war doctor might be subjected to, he knew that if he was going to tell a story, he would have to tell as much of the truth as possible. He would have to tell the sequence as nearly as possible, but the reason why he touched something would, we contend, be fabricated. This, we would argue, is really a cover story within a cover story. Now, since he would have to repeat this time and time again, as I have said he would have to, there is a grain of truth in the sequence of his movements throughout the house . . .

. . . [W]e believe that we have proven by physical evidence which is indisputable and which is cold and which is logical that the defendant and no one else committed this crime. Now, if we have convinced you of that beyond a reasonable doubt, but you are still uncomfortable because we haven't answered the question as to whether the defendant is the type of person who could have done this, I submit to you that that is an emotional doubt and not a reasonable doubt. I would again ask you to recall the Court's instructions that you decide the case on the basis of the evidence and not on the basis of emotion or prejudice.[1]

Blackburn continues where Brian Murtagh left off. His summation is concise and moving:

JAMES BLACKBURN: . . . I am not trying to suggest by and in of itself that because the defendant was not killed, he is, therefore, guilty of the slaughter of his family. I don't think that is sufficient evidence. I am not saying that. I am saying that when you compare and contrast his injuries to their injuries with the other physical evidence that we have, it certainly should raise in your mind the question as to why he was not hurt worse . . .

Ladies and gentlemen, the defendant's theory of defense in this case has sort of been like this. "I tell a story and you are to trust me. I am telling the truth. I loved my family. I loved Colette. I loved Kimberley and Kristen. Trust me. I couldn't have done this. I could not have done this. There has been a lot of character testimony. They say I can't do this; and therefore, because I am not the type of person, I couldn't do that."

Ladies and gentlemen, as Brian Murtagh told you this morning, if we convince you by the evidence that he did it, we don't have to show you that he is the sort of person that could have done it . . .

Ladies and gentlemen, if in the future after this case is over, if in your jury deliberations, you should think again of this case, I ask you to think and remember

Colette, Kimberley, and Kristen. They would have liked to have been here. They have been dead for almost ten years. That is right now around 3,400 or 3,500 days and nights that you have had and I have had and the defendant has had that they haven't. They would have liked to have had that. If in the future, you should cry a tear, cry one for them. If in the future, you should say a prayer, say one for them. If in the future, you should light a candle, light one for them . . .

We ask for everything in the name of truth. We ask you, ladies and gentlemen, that this horribly tragic and horribly sad as it is because you know that you have seen Mrs. Kassab and you have seen Mrs. MacDonald and it is sad for both of them—both of them were grandmothers, not just one—it is sad for the defendant—but it is sad most of all for those who paid the highest price of all, with their lives. And we ask you, ladies and gentlemen, to return a verdict of guilty as to clubbing and stabbing Colette, guilty of clubbing and stabbing Kimberley, and guilty perhaps most of all for stabbing little Kristen . . .

I am sure you have heard it many times—part of the 13th chapter of Ecclesiastes—"There is a time for everything under the heavens—a time to be born and a time to die." Surely, God did not intend on the 17th of February, 1970, for Colette, Kimberley, and Kristen MacDonald to die. It is time, ladies and gentlemen, it is so late in the day, it is time that someone speak for justice and truth and return a verdict of guilty against this man. I ask this jury to make what I know to be a very courageous decision that he did it and we are sorry, but he did it. Thank you.[2]

———

Segal starts the summation for the defense. It goes on for two and a half hours. A desultory mess.

BERNARD SEGAL: Now, what kind of proof and how are you to weigh the kind of proof the Government has offered, which must be beyond a reasonable doubt in this case? It is circumstantial evidence. It is the indirect kind. Circumstantial evidence should not be less clear than direct evidence. It should not be more obscure and more difficult to follow. It ought to point correctly and clearly to the conclusions as argued by the side that offers it. It ought to point in a way in which when you would hear it, you would say to yourself, "I do not hesitate. This is a matter of importance right now. I do not hesitate on these facts or on the conclusions that they want me to draw from it. These facts don't allow any hesitation and doubt. I do not have a reasonable doubt. I must convict." That is what circumstantial evidence is.

It says that it has got to be clear enough for you to figure out that it really does stand for proof beyond a reasonable doubt on that subject. It is the indirect evidence and you have heard all about that, but do not for a moment consider the idea that because someone has called it circumstantial evidence, that therefore, you are allowed to be confused by it, and therefore say, "Well, I will accept some lesser amount—some lesser quality of this proof because they have called it circumstantial evidence." That is not the law . . .

We all too frequently take the system that we cherish and fight for and that we hope to preserve, we sometimes take it rather for granted and do not consider why the elements exist. The presumption of innocence is something that exists only in a criminal case. It does not exist in a civil case. The reason for that is that there is an inherent fundamental imbalance in a criminal case which no defendant can ever correct. That imbalance is this: On one side of the criminal case are the prosecutors. They are not the government. They are the prosecutors who use the power of the government on their behalf of their clients—their interest in this case. I dare say that it is obvious to comment that there is no individual defendant, let alone Jeffrey MacDonald, there is no individual defendant that you or I could conceive of whose power ever would equal that of the government . . .

Take the worst CID agent you saw, the most inexperienced MP investigator, the newest FBI agent and you send him knocking on a door. He says, "I would like to talk to you about the MacDonald case." "I don't want to talk to you." "I am an agent of the FBI, CID, MP."

What is going to happen when you tell somebody, "I am the representative of the government's criminal prosecution process"? What happens is that you will think, "Gee, if I don't cooperate, what are they going to do? Take me downtown? Is someone going to call my employer and tell him that this is the government and your man will not cooperate? Are they going to look at my tax returns, perhaps?" I don't know if that is real, but they are the suspicions that we all have.

JAMES BLACKBURN: Your Honor, we would object to this.

BRIAN MURTAGH: Your Honor, we would object to this.

THE COURT: Well, I will just instruct counsel for both sides to confine your argument to the evidence that has been offered and received in open court. Go ahead.[3]

Has Segal forgotten where he is? This is not San Francisco nor Philadelphia. This is Raleigh, North Carolina. Is he going to lecture a jury of white tobacco farmers and ex-military men on the dangers of a police state? Tax audits, the specter of the jackboot? Has he hopelessly misjudged his audience? What does he think he's doing? In my view, if the case had not been lost already, it was lost here.

Segal had used up more than his allotted time, leaving no time for Wade Smith to address the jury. Blackburn and Murtagh graciously forfeited part of their time to allow Smith to make a closing argument.

JAMES BLACKBURN: Your Honor, the government has, as I understand it, forty minutes left, and the defendant is out of time.

THE COURT: That is right.

JAMES BLACKBURN: We have agreed, since Mr. Smith has not had an opportunity to speak, to give him ten minutes of our time.

THE COURT: All right, Mr. Smith.

WADE SMITH: I am grateful for the ten minutes and I would ask Your Honor to tap the Bench, please, when ten minutes are concluded.

Wade Smith addressed the jury:

WADE SMITH: Don't you wonder why when you think about this—why did it happen? Don't you wonder when you are thinking about whether Jeff did it, why would he have done it? Can you think of a reason why he would have done it? There isn't any . . .

The prosecution is not under any obligation to furnish a motive. The law does not place that burden on them. Nevertheless, that is natural law. That is law that we feel inside of us. Every one of us. We feel that we can say to the prosecution in any case, "Tell us why. Tell us why this man would have destroyed his family?" Think about the photographs that you saw of Jeff with the family, Jeff with the children, Colette with the children, the children playing. Think about Major Moore arriving at an unscheduled lunch stop.[4] Think about the children running out and grabbing Jeff and climbing all over him a few weeks before this happened. Think about how Colette came to him and announced with joy that she was expecting a child. Think about how they embraced, according to Major Moore, and how they walked into the house with Jeff with his arm around her and Major Moore walking with the children, talking and enjoying themselves at lunchtime. Everything was going well. There was not anything going on in their home that you have seen in this evidence that would indicate that this man would do a thing like this . . .

If you look at the autopsy photographs of those little children and think about what it would take to cause someone to raise a knife and destroy them— to destroy Kristen—not just destroy her but absolutely mutilate her—just beat her to death, thrust after thrust after thrust. It can't be true. He needs peace. He hasn't had it in a long time. You, as a jury, are immensely powerful because you can give him peace for the first time in years and years.

Thank you for hearing me.[5]

———

The next day, August 29, the case went to the jury. They deliberated for only six hours and found MacDonald guilty on two counts of second-degree murder, for the murders of Colette and Kimberley, and one count of first-degree murder, for the murder of Kristen. The verdict was announced on the same day. Dupree sentenced him to three consecutive life sentences.

MacDonald, facing Dupree in the courtroom, said, "Sir, I'm not guilty. I don't think the court heard all the evidence. That's all I have to say."

Freddy Kassab described that moment. According to Kassab, MacDonald had requested twenty-four-hour U.S. marshal protection. And when the jury returned with their verdict, there were six U.S. marshals between Kassab and MacDonald.

FREDDY KASSAB: It seems that MacDonald was afraid I might kill him because in January 1976, when the Circuit Court dismissed the case on speedy trial grounds, I had publicly made the statement and it was printed in the press, "If the courts of this country won't administer justice. I most assuredly will."

BOOK FOUR

1980 ◾ **August 22**
Jeffrey MacDonald is released from prison after the Fourth Circuit Court of Appeals rules that his right to a speedy trial had been violated.

October 24–25
Helena Stoeckley and Prince Beasley leave for Los Angeles. Stoeckley takes a polygraph examination and makes a detailed statement about her involvement in the murders to Ted Gunderson.

November 1
MacDonald returns to work at St. Mary Medical Center in Long Beach, California.

December 4
Beasley and Stoeckley make a second trip to Los Angeles.

December 7
Stoeckley's second polygraph examination. Stoeckley is examined by Dr. Rex Beaber, a forensic psychologist.

1982 ◾ **March 31**
The Supreme Court reverses the lower court's ruling on MacDonald's "speedy trial" claim. MacDonald is returned to prison the same day.

May 21
Helena Stoeckley is interviewed for a segment on *60 Minutes*.

June 2
Stoeckley gives birth to a son, David.

June 3
Gregory Mitchell dies from heart failure.

June 4
Gunderson writes to the director of the FBI requesting legal immunity for Stoeckley.

June 9
MacDonald's second appeal comes before the Fourth Circuit Court.

August 16
All of MacDonald's remaining evidentiary claims are rejected by the Fourth Circuit.

1983 ◾ **January 14**
Stoeckley is found dead in Walhalla, South Carolina.

1984 ◾ **April 5**
The defense files a motion to have the conviction set aside or to have a new trial on the charges based on new evidence of Stoeckley's involvement.

1984
cont.

June 7

The contents of 544 Castle Drive are destroyed.

1985

March 1

Judge Franklin Dupree denies MacDonald's motion for a new trial on new evidence.

THE USE AND ABUSE OF PHYSICAL EVIDENCE

We need history, but not as a spoiled loafer
in the garden of knowledge needs it.
—Nietzsche, "The Use and Abuse of History"

Too little, too late. Almost immediately after his testimony, Thornton learned that essential laboratory notes had been withheld.

I asked Thornton about the prosecution's role in restricting the defense's access to evidence.

JOHN THORNTON: I was powerless to do anything. Now, after the trial, I got a visit from someone in the attorney general's office, and an FBI agent out here came to my house and said, "Do you really think he's guilty?" How the heck would I know? It isn't my business, really, to determine guilt. Any notions that I have about guilt or innocence are really irrelevant. And a little bit dangerous, too, for somebody that does the kind of work that I do, or did.

ERROL MORRIS: Dangerous?

JOHN THORNTON: I need to consider evidence as *evidence*. Not from a position of advocacy. But I thought that it was kind of telling that the prosecution would send somebody out from D.C., a couple of people out from D.C., to sound me out. And right after the trial—

ERROL MORRIS: Why would they do that?

JOHN THORNTON: Well, I don't know. But right after the trial, within a few days, I spoke to Brian Murtagh on the phone. And he asked me the same question: "Do you really think he was guilty?"

ERROL MORRIS: Does that mean that they *themselves* had doubts?

JOHN THORNTON: That was how I construed it, yes.

ERROL MORRIS: Here's a question. Do you have an opinion about MacDonald's guilt or innocence but prefer not to say? Or do you think that the evidence has been so screwed up that one is really deprived of an ability to form any rational conclusion?

JOHN THORNTON: The latter. No, I'm being candid with you. I'm not totally convinced of Jeffrey MacDonald's innocence. If he is in fact guilty, then it's an incredible thing. Somehow he's managed to convince himself that he didn't do it, and in the process convince other people as well. But I don't know. I think there's a residue of possibility that he did.

But in terms of proving that he did, I don't think the prosecution did that at all. And they played dirty. See, my feeling is that physical evidence has to be held in trust for both sides. That's pretty much California law. It's not federal law. In this case, the federal prosecutors viewed the evidence as chattel. It was their *property*. And they were going to use it in a manner that they alone would determine.

ERROL MORRIS: Did they frame MacDonald?

JOHN THORNTON: No, it's more complex than that. It's like some Kurosawa drama or something.

ERROL MORRIS: Like *Rashomon*?

JOHN THORNTON: Exactly. Here's my take. Right from the outset, the case was really mismanaged. MacDonald went to the Article 32 proceedings and he was cut loose. And if he had kept his mouth shut, that probably would have been the end of it. But no. He went on *Dick Cavett*. And he would complain about his treatment to anyone who would listen. And that pissed off his father-in-law and the attorney general's office, because they were outraged at Jeffrey MacDonald's hubris in going public. And then, *that* pulled the trigger and set in motion all these irreversible activities, the grand jury, the trial.

ERROL MORRIS: Yes.

JOHN THORNTON: I don't think it was an intentional thing to frame an innocent man. Here was the prosecution's thinking: we have a really marginal case, screwed up to begin with. But just because it was screwed up, that shouldn't mean that he should escape justice. Let's go back and see what we can come up with.

ERROL MORRIS: But it was your feeling that Dupree was biased?

JOHN THORNTON: Yes. Dupree was affable with the prosecution and would scowl at Segal. But that isn't going to be reflected in the records. No appellate court is going to say, "Well, the judge did something improper." But when I asked for samples at the start of the trial, that went back to court. Judge Dupree, of course, ruled against those motions. Prior to that, Dupree had said to both sides, "You people work it out." That's like expecting red ants and black ants to work it out.

ERROL MORRIS: But was it unbiased?

JOHN THORNTON: It was corrupt. Particularly the reconstruction of the ice pick holes through the pajama top. It was specious. But it really wasn't just Stombaugh, it was Shirley Green that did it. And Stombaugh signed the report.

ERROL MORRIS: Why do you call it specious?

JOHN THORNTON: MacDonald is saying that the pajamas were pulled over his head, like in a hockey fight. That the stabs were not when his hands were in the sleeves, but rather when the garment was stretched out between the assailant and himself. And so the stabs were through unoccupied fabric. I don't think that's implausible. But the way they *presented* their reconstruction—my God, the color photographs with the pins sticking out. And the pajamas on the mannequin at the trial. Yes, they were effective. I'd use the word "seductive," but they were effective. But Stombaugh said, "Well, you know, it could be other ways. There could be some other interpretation. Hole 17 might be correlated really with number three instead of number seven." But he passed over *that* very quickly. And his fingers were never held to the fire.

On May 7, 1982, a month after MacDonald's final return to prison, Thornton wrote to William H. Webster, the director of the FBI.

Dear Judge Webster:
    . . . I have exceedingly grave reservations concerning the physical evidence aspects of the MacDonald case. As I perceive them, the defects are not all of the same sort and have arisen from different circumstances. Taken in concert, however, the defects have had the same effect—that of distorting the physical evidence and in some instances representing clearly erroneous interpretations of the evidence. I have no particular interest in embarrassing the Bureau, and indeed with one exception my criticism of the handling of the physical evidence is directed at other agencies. The one exception, however, is in my mind an example of the abuse, rather than the use, of physical evidence . . .

What follows is a recapitulation of Shirley Green's testimony about the folded pajama top, but there is something new here. And disturbing. Thornton had only been given the *typewritten* reports from the FBI. The bench notes, and other records, had been withheld.

> The defense did not have an opportunity to examine Mr. Stombaugh's bench notes until after he had finished his testimony. At that time it was apparent that a number of discrepancies existed between Ms. Green's reconstruction and Mr. Stombaugh's original determination of the directionality of the punctures . . . Of the 13 holes designated, there are six discrepancies with the Shirley Green reconstruction. Changing the directionality of even a single hole contravenes the Shirley Green reconstruction . . . The reconstruction therefore is not valid.[1]

Thornton had argued something like this during the trial, but here was proof that the FBI lab knew that the reconstruction was bogus, but presented it as evidence nonetheless.

It's not clear whether Webster ever wrote back to Thornton. In all likelihood, he did not. But Thornton's views were discussed in an October 27, 1982, letter to Webster from D. Lowell Jensen, an assistant attorney general. It was made perfectly clear that the government was going to close down this line of inquiry. "It is our view that any reprocessing of the crime scene for alleged undetected evidence should occur only as a result of an order from the district court, and that in that event no processing should be done by defense experts . . ."[2]

There would be, of course, no order from the district court. Dupree had no intention of processing or reprocessing anything. Nor did the government. From the end of the trial there were petitions from the defense to be given access to the crime scene. Murtagh refused. He argued in a 1983 response to the request that, "the quarters, in their present condition, have no evidentiary integrity as a crime scene . . . In the absence of any factually accurate, legally sufficient, scientifically valid, or other compelling grounds for a second re-examination of the scene, the motion should be denied and the quarters returned directly to military control."[3]

On June 4, 1984, the CID removed the medical supplies—ear plugs, Cepacol, syringes, and tongue depressors—seven candles, and two decorative wine bottles covered with wax. On June 7, 1984, in the middle of an appeal, whatever was left in 544 Castle Drive was burned.[4]

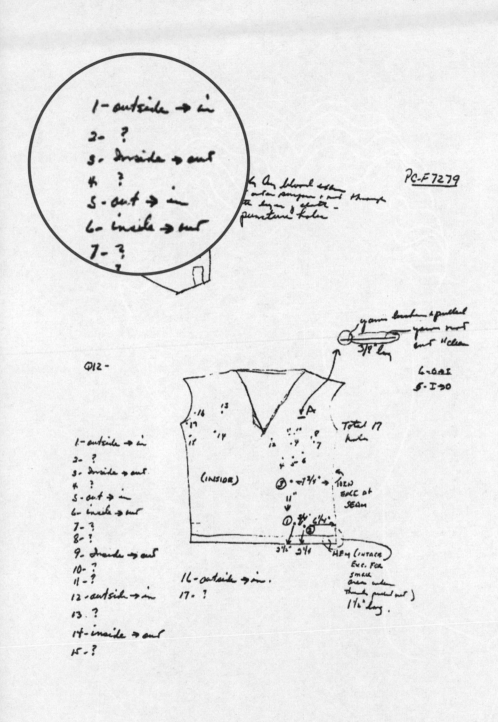

1 - outside → in
2 - ?
3 - inside → out
4 - ?
5 - out → in
6 - inside → out
7 - ?

PC-F 7279

Q12 -

1 - outside → in
2 - ?
3 - inside → out
4 - ?
5 - out → in
6 - inside → out
7 - ?
8 - ?
9 - inside → out
10 - ?
11 - ?
12 - outside → in
13 - ?
14 - inside → out
15 - ?

16 - outside → in
17 - ?

(INSIDE)

Total 17 holes

6 - O → I
5 - I → O

TURN
EDGE of
SEAM

HEM (INTACT)
EXC. FOR
SMALL
AREA WHEN
THREAD PULLED OUT)
1½" long.

A ROUNDED PICTURE

Following his conviction, MacDonald was sent through a revolving door of legal review: the federal prison on Terminal Island immediately following his conviction, released by the Fourth Circuit on a speedy-trial claim on July 29, 1980, returned to work at St. Mary Medical Center in November 1980, then back to prison—by a 6–3 decision of the Supreme Court—on March 31, 1982, with Chief Justice Warren Burger writing for the majority:

> However, once the charges instituted by the army were dismissed, MacDonald was legally and constitutionally in the same posture as though no charges had been made. He was free to go about his affairs, to practice his profession, and to continue with his life. The Court of Appeals acknowledged, and MacDonald concedes, that the delay between the civil indictment and the trial was caused primarily by MacDonald's own legal maneuvers.[1]

Ah, shades of Kafka. If MacDonald had cooperated, rolled over and merely admitted guilt, then these unfortunate delays could have been avoided. But the issue of Stoeckley's unheard testimony stubbornly remained a part of the case. Justice Thurgood Marshall in his dissent wrote:

> It is possible that Stoeckley's trial testimony would have been less confused and more helpful to MacDonald at an earlier date. This testimony was critical to MacDonald, whose principal defense was that she was one of a group of intruders

who committed the murders. Although Stoeckley was hardly a reliable witness, she did testify at trial that she had no memory of the events that night, in contradiction to some of her earlier out-of-court statements . . . The majority's opinion in this case is a disappointing exercise in strained logic and judicial illusion.[2]

Six months after the Supreme Court decision, MacDonald's lawyers were back in front of the Fourth Circuit. This time the appeal challenged Dupree's exclusion of the testimony of the six corroborative witnesses from the MacDonald jury.

What were his reasons? According to an exception in the hearsay rule—Federal Rule of Evidence 804(b)(3)—you can present secondhand testimony (1) if it is "against interest," and (2) if it has been corroborated. Stoeckley's statements to those witnesses were clearly against her interests. She was claiming to be present at a triple homicide. And there were six witnesses to her statements—*seven* if you include Wendy Rouder. What more corroboration do you need? Don't these statements corroborate each other? Essentially, Dupree argued that 804(b)(3) didn't apply, because if Stoeckley's mind was a potato, there was nothing to corroborate, and nothing could be against her interest.

The Fourth Circuit agreed:

While MacDonald is able to point to a number of corroborating circumstances, he does not demonstrate, finally, that they make Stoeckley's alleged declaration trustworthy. Her apparent longstanding drug habits made her an inherently unreliable witness. Moreover, her vacillation about whether or not she remembered anything at all about the night of the crime lends force to the view that everything she has said and done in this regard was a product of her drug addiction.[3]

She was a drug addict. What more needed to be said?

The decision of the three-judge panel on August 16, 1982, was unanimous and against MacDonald—except for one odd wrinkle. One of the judges, Francis D. Murnaghan Jr., felt compelled to write a concurrence— simultaneously agreeing and disagreeing with the majority opinion. Murnaghan wrote, "The case provokes a strong uneasiness in me."

It was an uneasiness precipitated specifically by the Stoeckley evidence or, more specifically, its partial exclusion from the MacDonald trial.

The defense of a marauding, drug-crazed purposeless group of homicidal maniacs is one which, absent the events surrounding the behavior of Charles Manson and the excruciating horror of the indescribably base murder of Sharon Tate, would have been dismissed as so incredible as to merit no serious attention. All that changed with the advent of Manson. Thereafter the possibility of such an occurrence, while still macabre, was considerably enhanced. The evidence, in my humble judgment, tended to show an environment in the vicinity of the military base where MacDonald was stationed in which persons might indeed emulate Manson or independently behave in such a fashion. Helena Stoeckley was shown to be a person of no fixed regularity of life, roaming the streets nocturnally at or about the time of the crimes, dressing in a bizarre fashion, and capable of so short-circuiting her mental processes through an indiscriminate taking of drugs that (a) she could well accept her presence and, to some extent, her involvement in the MacDonald murders and (b) she could become so separated from reality that, on the fatal evening, she was ripe for persuasion to participate . . .

I conclude with the observation that the case provokes a strong uneasiness in me. The crimes were base and horrid, and whoever committed them richly deserves severe punishment. As Judge Bryan [the senior judge on the Fourth Circuit Court] has pointed out, the evidence was sufficient to sustain the findings of guilt beyond a reasonable doubt. Still, the way in which a finding of guilt is reached is, in our enduring system of law, at least as important as the finding of guilt itself. I believe MacDonald would have had a fairer trial if the Stoeckley related testimony had been admitted. In the end, however, I am not prepared to find an abuse of discretion by the district court, and so concur.[4]

But how could Murnaghan concur with the majority opinion, if he truly believed that MacDonald "would have had a fairer trial if the Stoeckley testimony had been admitted"? A *fairer* trial? Where does fairness shade off into unfairness? Should the phrase be changed—*some* justice for all?

Murnaghan called attention to one of the central problems with the case, namely, the problem of context—how the world had changed between 1970 and 1979. Justice Marshall had said essentially the same thing. In 1970, it was *easy* to conjure in the mind "a marauding, drug-crazed purposeless group of homicidal maniacs." It didn't take much conjuring at all, since it was only months after Charles Manson and his "family" were arrested and splashed across the national news. But in 1979, *nine years later,* Manson had already receded into the crepuscular memory palace of history. In this different setting, MacDonald's claim that his family had been killed by drug-crazed hippies seemed far-fetched. Unbelievable. Even laughable.

Murnaghan remembered that in 1970 it was neither far-fetched nor unbelievable. Certainly not laughable.

The concurrence contains one more counterfactual. One more what-if:

[I]n view of the issues involved, and the virtually unique aspects of the surrounding circumstances, had I been the trial judge, I would have exercised the wide discretion conferred on him to allow the testimony to come in. My preference derives from my belief that, if the jury may be trusted with ultimate resolution of the factual issues, it should not be denied the opportunity of obtaining a rounded picture, necessary for resolution of the large questions, by the withholding of collateral testimony consistent with and basic to the defendant's principal exculpatory contention. If such evidence was not persuasive, which is what the government essentially contends in saying that it was untrustworthy, the jury, with very great probability, would not have been misled by it.

If Murnaghan had presided over the 1979 trial, he would have allowed the Stoeckley testimony. But Dupree took a different tack. When it came to the *Esquire* magazine, the pajama top, the blood evidence—Dupree let the jury decide whether the evidence was meaningful. But in the case of Stoeckley and the corroborative witnesses, he said, in effect, leave it to me.

But what does Murnaghan mean by the "large questions"? Isn't the largest question the question of guilt or innocence? Did he do it? Did he commit these terrible crimes? The Murnaghan concurrence reminds us—or should remind us—that legal procedure should be in the service of justice, not the other way around.[5] But it is the last sentence of the concurrence that is backward reasoning. "The jury, with very great probability, would not have been misled" by the Stoeckley testimony; that is, they would have convicted MacDonald anyway. Since he's guilty, he would still be guilty with or without the Stoeckley evidence. Then why bother with evidence at all? In *Through the Looking-Glass,* Lewis Carroll takes this argument a step further. Not just sentence first, verdict afterward—better yet, punishment without crime.

"It's a poor sort of memory that only works backwards," the Queen remarked.

"What sort of things do *you* remember best?" Alice ventured to ask.

"Oh, things that happened the week after next," the Queen replied in a careless tone. "For instance, now," she went on, sticking a large piece of plaster on her finger as she spoke, "there's the King's Messenger. He's in prison now, being punished: and the trial doesn't even begin till next Wednesday: and of course the crime comes last of all."

"Suppose he never commits the crime?" said Alice.

"That would be all the better, wouldn't it?" the Queen said, as she bound the plaster round her finger with a bit of ribbon.[6]

ABSOLUTELY BATSHIT CRAZY

There is a tendency to separate people into the good and the bad. Ted Gunderson defies such easy categorization. Crazy, self-serving, lost in a funhouse of his own contrivance, he is responsible for further blurring the line between fact and fiction (given that that line is blurry to begin with) rather than adding any clarity to the case. He had been the special agent in charge of the Los Angeles office of the FBI. The scuttlebutt is that he was being considered for the post of FBI director, but it was given to Judge William H. Webster. Gunderson took early retirement from the FBI in March 1979 and started Ted L. Gunderson & Associates, a private detective agency. Jeffrey MacDonald was one of his first clients.

I tried to talk to Gunderson in 2011, just before he died. A string of nonworking numbers, and then I finally reached him—after a fashion. In an era of bad telephone connections, this was among the very worst I've experienced. I could barely hear Gunderson, but he somehow conveyed through the static that he was dying and that he was trapped in various conspiracies too terrible to describe. He kept saying over and over and over again, "Terrible. It's terrible. Terrible, terrible, terrible." I had planned to meet him in L.A., but by my next trip out there, he was already dead. It was almost as if he had disappeared.[1]

———

After the decision by the Supreme Court that sent MacDonald back to prison, Segal finally quit. He had been replaced by Brian O'Neill, who inherited the investigative duo of Gunderson and Prince Beasley.

I asked O'Neill about Gunderson.

ERROL MORRIS: You inherited Gunderson from Segal?

BRIAN O'NEILL: Oh yes. He was a good guy. But he was nuts, really nuts. I went to a Catholic law school, so I can say this. Guys with Irish names who go to Catholic law schools, half of them become FBI agents. One of my classmates told me the following is the FBI culture. If you're ambitious, you become a supervisor. If you're a supervisor, you never investigate anymore. And if you don't investigate anymore, you really don't know what you're looking for or what you're doing when you're investigating. Gunderson was one of those guys. A decent guy. A well-intended guy who really loved Jeff and really thought that Jeff got screwed, but he was a loose cannon. Ted had come to believe, somehow, that Helena and the gang she ran with were part of a satanic cult.

ERROL MORRIS: Satanic cult?

BRIAN O'NEILL: Yes, he was jumping up and down about it. I told him that I believed that she was involved with the murders, but I also told him it *doesn't matter* whether they are part of a satanic cult or not. There is no way we can prove this frickin' thing. It doesn't advance our case. And he went absolutely batshit crazy. He was screaming there was a conspiracy against Jeff at the highest levels of government, and I, Brian O'Neill, was part of it, or assisting it, because I refused to accept this claim.

ERROL MORRIS: And Beasley went along with this?

BRIAN O'NEILL: He was dying. He wasn't in-bed dying, but he was really on his last legs. He was a good guy, too. Ted had found him, and Beasley was a very nice kind of a country guy who was in love with Ted. Ted looked like an FBI agent in the movies; in fact, I think he had worked as a consultant to the movies. Wore great suits, had a nice head of white hair, spoke very authoritatively on damn near everything— sometimes with accurate information, sometimes not. And he quite impressed Beasley. Prince Beasley was a very good guy. I think he did something good in the case. He was the first guy to get to Helena on behalf of Jeff, back before the trial.

ERROL MORRIS: And Beasley and Gunderson were trying to prove a conspiracy from early on?

BRIAN O'NEILL: Yes. They wanted to prove that there was a conspiracy between the military and these druggies. And once we proved that, which would have taken a lifetime, we would thereby have come upon information which would aid Jeff's defense. Gunderson was a big believer that the government had mobilized to get MacDonald.

ERROL MORRIS: He's Oliver Stone.

BRIAN O'NEILL: Yes! But Ted was not a bad guy. He was just so difficult. If you weren't with Ted, you were part of something else. He was always kind of accusatory. And then he'd back off and be nice, and then he'd lose it again. But he really had Jeff's best interest at heart, I have no doubt of that. That was why he was unreliable. He was just so willing to accept any possible explanation. I was confident we would never prove anything, if we had to prove a conspiracy, prove the DEA or the FBI was in league with somebody. I hope he was wrong. I hope our failure to chase that wasn't—well, who knows? I hope there was nothing there, and I didn't think we could prove it, even if it was there.

ERROL MORRIS: Satanic cults or conspiracy?

BRIAN O'NEILL: Both. That was what Gunderson tried to prove. I think he got it from Helena. Helena was nutty enough that she could have told him that, and nutty enough to be involved.

———

I try to imagine what happened. It is so many years after the fact. Beasley and Gunderson are dead. But they left a paper trail, as well as a video, as a record of their efforts. Gunderson was hired by Segal shortly after MacDonald's conviction and turned his attention to Helena Stoeckley. He hired Prince Beasley to find (and manage) Stoeckley for him.

It's a road-trip movie. Prince Beasley summarized some of this early history in a report entitled "My first encounter with Ted Gunderson." It could be an elementary school essay, like "Why I Like Firemen" or "My First Trip to the Bank." It is typed on what looks like an old portable and filled with x-ings out, misspellings, dyslexic letter-reversals, and the like. The letter resembles the investigation as a whole. An admixture of the obscure, the lucid, the probative, the manipulative, and the insane. And it is a prelude to the several trips to California, described by Beasley in this and several subsequent documents.

Several scenes stay in the mind. Gunderson and Beasley prowling "the Drug Jungle" (in Beasley's words) of Greenville, South Carolina, trying to find either Stoeckley or Ernie Davis or both. At first, they fail. Beasley and Gunderson, crammed into a phone booth, speak to Stoeckley at an undisclosed location, but she won't meet them. Gunderson returns to Los Angeles. Gunderson engaged two psychics (spelled "phychics"). Beasley provides few details. (Did the psychics employ articles of clothing? Were they like bloodhounds?) The psychics go to the shoe store where Stoeckley works. They go to her home. (She is living with

Clarence, her older brother.) And then by serendipity or pure chance they finally find Stoeckley shopping for a nurse's uniform in a J.C. Penney.

A phone call with Gunderson in Los Angeles is arranged. Offers of money. (Stoeckley was adamant that she had never accepted payment in exchange for her cooperation.) Various subterfuges designed by Gunderson to get her to cooperate. Already, I feel that there is tension between Gunderson and Beasley. Beasley truly likes Helena. There are limits to what he will say to her, particularly to what he will promise. Gunderson, on the other hand, was willing to say or do anything. "During one of our conversations, I mentioned the amount of money that Ted told me to tell her. Helena just laughed, and said, 'Let's drop this.' She said the reason she was going to talk was that she knew Jeff was not guilty." Gunderson seems conniving.

> Gunderson told me that it was very important that I got Helena to talk. I asked him if he thought she was a fool, that she was not going to talk her way into prison. He stated to me that if he made it worth while she might. I asked him what he meant and he told me to offer her any amount. That money was no object.
> I asked him how much was no object, and he stated $25,000 to $50,000 or even higher, that Jeff's life was at stake and we had to clear this case up, to offer her anything as long as we got what we wanted.[2]

If the machinations of the prosecutors during the 1979 trial were terrible, this was arguably worse. And had its own sad outcome.

Gunderson summoned the two of them to California. Before they left, Beasley interviewed Stoeckley at the Bordeaux Motor Inn in Fayetteville, the one next to the miniature Eiffel Tower.

> Helena stated that Dr. MacDonald was indirectly involved with the deaths of his family. She stated that he had cut several people off and refused to give them treatment for Drug addiction and that he would turn them into their Commanding Officers and this would cause them problems . . .
> She stated that she was into Black Witch Craft and at that time the Black Cult was very active in Fayetteville. And they would stop at nothing. She stated that she was still a Witch and that some people could see stars in her eyes and that Black Cats shied away from her . . .
> Helena stated that she was in the MacDonald home on the night of the killings and further stated that the little rocking horse had a broken spring on

it. That until this day every time she sees a rocking horse or an ice pick she just about flips out.

––––––––

On October 24, 1980, Beasley and Stoeckley flew to California. While in the air, Stoeckley once again "admitted that she was in the MacDonald house on the night of the murders."

> She periodically dozed off during the flight and would wake up with a scared look in her eyes. Each time Beasley asked what was the matter and she stated that she could not get the MacDonald murders off her mind.[3]

And more details were offered up voluntarily. It is hard know what to make of any of it. Stoeckley had spent a day looking at photographs with Segal, Zillioux, Underhill et al. Was it possible, now, to distinguish her genuine memories from what had been enhanced or changed by repeated conversations with attorneys, prosecutors, FBI agents, detectives, acquaintances?

> She began to cry and Beasley told her if it would make her feel any better to go ahead and talk about it. She then started repeating the words "rocking horse, rocking horse." She said she was in one of the children's rooms, but she didn't know which one and there was a rocking horse there. Beasley asked her if she tried to ride it and she stated she didn't try to ride it but that she sort of squatted down on it but it didn't work because a spring was broken on it. She repeated over and over again about the rocking horse and hid her face saying that she just couldn't talk about it. She also told Beasley that she was at the couch where MacDonald was sleeping and she did have a candle and the candle was lit. Beasley asked her who was with her and she was reluctant to say, although she did mention Greg Mitchell and a person known as Wizard.

In Los Angeles, she was given a lie-detector test by Scott Mero. Mero had provided two sets of questions. The first set—he called it Phase One—concerned her possible involvement in the murder of the MacDonald family.

> Were you in the house when the murders were committed? YES. Did you see any of the cult members hitting or stabbing Dr. MacDonald or his family. YES. On

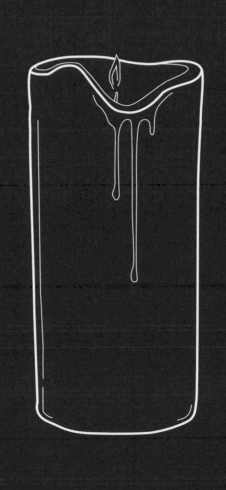

February 17, 1970, were you holding a candle in the MacDonald house while Dr. Jeffrey McDonald was being beaten? On February 17, 1970, did you back into the MacDonald toy rocking horse? YES.[4]

Mero concluded that there was no deception in Stoeckley's responses. Stoeckley specifically was asked and denied that she saw the picture of the hobbyhorse in the newspaper. (She could have heard about it from someone who had seen the picture in the newspaper. Or she could have been shown a photograph, but still, it suggested something rather than nothing.) Like Brisentine nearly a decade earlier, Mero concluded that she believed in her mind that she was there.

> After a careful evaluation of all test questions, including relevant, irrelevant, and control questions, it was the examiner's opinion that Ms. Foster [Stoeckley's alias] answered all the preceding relevant questions truthfully during this first phase of the polygraph examination.

And then Phase Two. Mero continued with a *new* line of questioning. Did Stoeckley know that the MacDonald family was going to be murdered that night? NO. Was there a preexisting plan to kill the family? NO. Were cult members present during the murders? NO. Was "Wizard" with you in the MacDonald house during the February 17, 1970, murders? NO.

Stoeckley didn't perform as well on the Phase Two questions. The test showed deception. But what did that mean? It is part of the perplexing nature of lie-detector examinations that a deceptive answer can mean anything. When she answered no to the question of whether there was a preexisting plot to kill the MacDonald family, does that mean that there *was* one?

THE SOUND
OF MUSIC

Around December 4, 1980, Beasley and Stoeckley flew back to Los Angeles. Gunderson asked for another series of statements. He didn't know where to stop. He saw conspiracies everywhere. And he wanted Stoeckley to support his various cockamamie theories. Oddly, it is Gunderson who convinced me that Stoeckley might have been in that house that evening. Why? Because she resisted his attempts to influence and ultimately subvert her story. Robert Brisentine, the polygraph expert, had told me that he believed she was highly suggestible. This made me believe the opposite. Stoeckley's story might have been hopelessly confused, but it was *her* story—and her confusion.

Gunderson offered her immunity, but it was pretty clear that he didn't have the authority to make such an offer, and once more, both Stoeckley and Beasley knew this. Beasley wrote, "Ted told her that he would give her immunity if she would tell all that she knew about the case. I asked him if this was legal for him to promise this. He stated that he would not add it into the statement."[1] Gunderson tried to get her to name high-ranking army officials, but she was adamant in insisting there was no coverup "other than the possibility that the CID did a sloppy investigation." Stoeckley was not interested in conspiracies; Gunderson was.

After two days of this, Stoeckley insisted that she had to go home. She had had enough. And this is where it starts to get really crazy. You can feel the underlying tone. Gunderson's relentless pressure, Stoeckley's annoyance, and Beasley's reluctant acquiescence. Beasley was the good cop; Gunderson, the bad cop. Except here it seems more than a strategy.

Stoeckley was sent in by Gunderson for yet one more lie-detector test with Mero. And just before the test began, Gunderson started pressuring her again about a possible conspiracy involving the army. Again she told him that there was no such conspiracy. There is something both horrible and comical about this lunatic ex-FBI agent trying to decide whether Stoeckley herself was a lunatic. Beasley writes:

> About fifteen minutes before the test was administered Ted told Helena that she would only get about 30 or 40 years in prison for the part she played in the MacDonald case. Helena looked as though she went into a trance of some sort. She muttered to herself that she just could not go to prison. She stated that she was trying to clear things up and submitted to all that was required of her and that was the thanks she was getting . . .
>
> About thirty minutes later, Mr. Mero returned to the room where me and Ted was. He made the statement "what in the hell did you say to Helena prior to the test." I told him what Ted had told her about her going to prison. At the time Mr. Mero stated that from the report that he had just gotten and from the questions that he had asked her it was his opinion that she was nowhere near the MacDonald home on the night of the murders nor did she know anyone that was involved.
>
> At the time Ted went to where Helena was at and tried to calm her down but to no avail. Mr. Mero stated that he would not give her another test at this time. But that he would rule the test just given as being inconclusive. However, he did say that the first test given Helena on the first trip to California was conclusive.

Afterward, Gunderson dragged Stoeckley off for one more evaluation—to Rex Beaber, a lawyer, clinical psychologist, and an assistant professor of medicine at UCLA. Beaber gave her the usual battery of psychological tests—the Minnesota Multiphasic Personality Inventory (MMPI), the Thematic Apperception Test (TAT)—and then interviewed her about the events of February 16–17, 1970. It was a five-hour examination.

Beaber's notes are extensive: ten single-spaced typewritten pages filled with Stoeckley's vivid memories. It was a convincing list of details—an off-air television left on in the MacDonald living room, an open book resting on MacDonald's chest, his glasses on the floor, a child covered in blood.

Beaber (referring to himself in the third person) writes:

> [Stoeckley tells Beaber] From car to house I remember, and fumbling at the door, someone saying to be quiet or you'll make the dog bark, going through kitchen,

finding Dr. Mac, television on but off the air, seeing his glasses lying on the floor. Just then all I can remember is that I was peaking on mescaline. Somewhere after this I was seeing blood, in one room I panicked and screamed, thought I headed outside through utility room, went back in, everything was out of control. All I knew was we had to get out of there.

Went out utility room, around house to the car, I don't know who was with me, overwhelmed, made a U-turn, passed the Information Center, then don't remember the ride, apparently stopped at Dunkin' Donuts, washed up, was seen there. Pulling into driveway in blue mustang, guy was holding a Dunkin' Donuts box ([Stoeckley] knows who this was), got out of car, light rain . . .

Beaber asks, Can you remember the murders themselves?

[Stoeckley responds] No, I didn't see any, I saw Dr. Mac struck with fists, and it drew blood. When I saw child in bedroom she was already covered in blood from what I could see from a dimly lit hallway; there was no rise and fall of her chest and judging by the amount of blood she was dead, I wouldn't go in, there was a small doll on the floor that I wanted to go in and pick up, you know how children sleep, she was in a position that looked like she was sleeping but you knew she wasn't so I wouldn't go in the room . . .

MacDonald supposedly pulled a paring knife out of her throat, when I left, there wasn't a paring knife in her throat, yet one time when I heard her in there when she was calling out to him "Jeff why are you letting them do this to me?" her voice was in a gurgle as if she had been stabbed in the throat already, like someone that had something in their throat and were trying to talk . . .

Dr. Mac was in the living room, he had fallen asleep watching television or reading a book, he had a book on his chest turned upside down, he was on the couch, she was in the back bedroom, one child with her (not sure which one) . . .

Beaber asks, Anything significant that I haven't asked about?

[Stoeckley responds] I don't think so. I don't blame anyone for what's happened to me. I used to. But not now.[2]

Beaber concluded that while details had changed in Stoeckley's retellings of her story, the crux—that she was present during the murders—had *not*:

It is my opinion that, notwithstanding the internal inconsistencies in Helena Stoeckley's various statements regarding the MacDonald murders, she has been relatively constant in her contention that she was present during the offense and that the offense was carried out by persons other than the defendant, Dr. Jeffrey

R. MacDonald . . . It is possible, and consistent with psychological-scientific thinking, that this profound event and its memory could remain intact, while [other]
factors would blur the accuracy of various details and event sequences.[3]

———————

I called Beaber.

ERROL MORRIS: I assume she told you that she had been a witness to the murders
in Fayetteville in 1970.

REX BEABER: My recollection is that she said she was there.

ERROL MORRIS: Did you have a feeling about whether she had actually been there
or that she believed that she was there?

REX BEABER: I certainly had the sense that she believed that she was there. I did
not feel like this was a bad-faith report, or a false report made for ulterior motives.

There are some kinds of mental disorders that simply are disabling to
someone in the sense of being able to tell the truth. And I had a strong sense that
she was capable of telling the truth and she certainly was capable of some recall,
however rudimentary. The one thing that made her story have an element
of believability to it to me was the story that she provided made sense to me.

I've never been able to understand the prosecution's theory of why MacDonald perpetrated these homicides. It's a very unusual crime, unlike any crime I've
ever been involved with. And I've been involved with some of the strangest of
crimes. It doesn't mean it's not possible. He could be the rare case. But having
said that, it just didn't make a lot of sense.

ERROL MORRIS: Why?

REX BEABER: People who have severe mental illnesses commit bizarre crimes
because they have some bizarre delusion. I'm going to give you an example.
I once examined a suspect who suffered from a relatively rare subspecies of
schizophrenia, who had never committed a crime in his life. He noticed that in
his street address—5154—if you added up the 5 and 1, you got 6, and if you
added up the 5 and the 4, you got 9. So, that meant that his address, from his
point of view, was secretly 69; and 69, he thought, was a sign of the devil. He
knew that *he* wasn't the devil, because he was a very religious and observant
person. So, if the house had the sign of the devil on it, and he was not the devil,
therefore, his wife and children were the devil, at which point he proceeded
to kill them all.

Jeffrey MacDonald, by any measure I know, does not suffer from any severe mental illness, and certainly not the kinds of mental illnesses that would produce delusions consistent with a bizarre crime. That knocked him out of one whole series of explanations of his involvement. So, now we're left with people who aren't mentally ill and why they commit crimes. A large cluster of those—especially family homicides—are people who commit the crime in the heat of passion, in response to some specific dispute or argument and of some momentous quality. I've seen no evidence of that here. And more importantly, even in those instances the person that's killed is the wife, not the wife and the children.

ERROL MORRIS: Does that make you think he's innocent?

REX BEABER: I'll put on my other hat now. You know I'm also an attorney. What's frightening about cases like this—and I say this as somebody who doesn't have a strong sense about whether he's guilty or innocent—is that it ignores the principle of law that we'll not convict a person of a crime if there is any reasonable doubt. It's inconceivable to me that someone doesn't have a reasonable doubt when the evidence is as thin as this and so completely lacking in some kind of explanation and motive. To me, this case represents a failure of the system. It happens more often in the most horrible cases: in a jury's passion that somebody be punished, they often ignore the reasonable-doubt standard to ensure that somebody is punished, rather than live with the feeling that such a horror went unpunished.

ERROL MORRIS: People like closure.

REX BEABER: There is a concept in social psychology called the just-world hypothesis. People want to believe it's a just world. So horrible, horrible crimes must be punished. The way the jury sees it is, "Either I convict this man or woman, or this horrible crime goes unpunished."

A jury is not given the choice of saying, "I want you to go out and for one year, forget about Jeffrey MacDonald and work harder at finding somebody else, and then come back to me after that year." They're only permitted to say he's guilty or to set him free. That's a very painful choice for ordinary, good people who see the evidence of a tragedy beyond measure in the most inflammatory presentation.

ERROL MORRIS: But there was somebody else—Helena Stoeckley. The prosecutors argued that she was lying or confabulating or was in such an addled state that it was meaningless even to talk about what she knew or didn't know.

REX BEABER: There's something humorous about that argument. Because a day doesn't go by in the United States where a prosecution does not rest its case on the statements of a cooperating co-conspirator who has an Indisputable history of felonies, lies, and perjuries. Their standard for credibility, for integrity and honesty, could not be lower.

And yet all of a sudden these prosecutors require that a defense witness be held up to a high standard of psychological health. I know why they did it. They did it because they decided MacDonald's guilty. Having decided he is guilty, the end of having a guilty person in prison justifies the means.

ERROL MORRIS: Do you think it was ever possible to figure out whether she was telling the truth?

REX BEABER: The best way to know if someone is telling the truth is to have a description of the crime so complete, so detailed that there is no way the accuracy could have been achieved without personal knowledge. She gave us an extraordinary amount of detail. She described the doll on the floor, the location of MacDonald's glasses, the book on his chest turned over. These are not trivial details. These would be details that would only be known, if accurate, to somebody in the house.

ERROL MORRIS: That's the $64,000 question. She gave details about this rocking horse, which was in one of the children's bedrooms. Then it was pointed out that the picture of the rocking horse was published in the *Fayetteville Observer* the day after the murders, so that may mean nothing. And it goes on and on and on. Claim and counterclaim. Did she see something? Did she hear about it from the newspapers? You don't know what's real, what's confabulated. And then often there are contradictions and holes in her memory . . .

REX BEABER: That's often the case. Let me give an example. Have you seen *The Sound of Music*?

ERROL MORRIS: Yes, of course.

REX BEABER: Just tell me, in a few sentences, what the story is?

ERROL MORRIS: Do I even remember the story? I remember Julie Andrews. I remember the Trapp Family Singers. I have a very bad memory for plot. I remember the Nazis—the Nazis figured into it. Okay, have I failed this one?

REX BEABER: No. Go on, say what you can remember.

ERROL MORRIS: I remember Christopher Plummer. He referred to it as *The Sound of Mucus*, because he hated it, even though he starred in it.

REX BEABER: I want to hear your memory of the movie, not your memory of—

ERROL MORRIS: I remember the nun singing "Climb Every Mountain." I remember Julie Andrews running in the field.

REX BEABER: Are you sure you saw it?

ERROL MORRIS: I can even remember where I saw it.

REX BEABER: Come on, now. You can't even remember what the story is about.

ERROL MORRIS: No, but I can remember where I saw it.

REX BEABER: I don't believe that you've seen the film.

ERROL MORRIS: Really?

REX BEABER: If you saw the film, you would know what the story is about. How could you see one of the most famous films made in the twentieth century and not know the story line? Is there something wrong with you?

ERROL MORRIS: There is something wrong with me. You have no idea.

REX BEABER: The point I want to suggest to you is this film, which you saw in Technicolor, under optimal viewing circumstances, probably without any stress, without bad lighting conditions or any other problems—that your memory of it is just a bunch of fragments.

ERROL MORRIS: It is indeed.

REX BEABER: And that's exactly what her memory was of this homicide. The little snapshots are not the same snapshots, but it was a snapshot here and a snap-shot there, and if I would have asked you, when Julie Andrews is on the mountain and she is singing "The Sound of Music," the big theme song, "What color is her skirt? What's growing in the field?" you might give me an answer that would be your best recollection. And you probably would be wrong, half the time or more. But if I said to you that because you were wrong, because you couldn't remember this or you misremembered that, that you didn't see the film, you'd say that's ridiculous. There is a big difference between the ability to remember whether you saw a film and to remember the content of that film with any level of detail.

That's exactly what crimes are like. It's very easy to remember that you were at the scene of a homicide. A person could be an extremely impaired human being and can have all kinds of problems with the circumstances of viewing that event, and that basic fact would remain.

ERROL MORRIS: In your experience, given the kinds of details that she provided, you have to really know what that crime scene looked like. Why would there be the book on Jeffrey MacDonald's chest? I mean, he talked about, for example, the fact he was reading a Mickey Spillane mystery novel, *Kiss Me Deadly*.

REX BEABER: It's another oddity of memory that what people remember is often not correlated with the significance of the thing. People will be involved in an incident and will remember with very good detail something that you think is a trifling detail and not remember something else that's very important; and no one knows why that's true. But if when the police enter the house, there is a book on his chest or a book on the floor nearby, that's not a trivial concurrence of memory.

The simple fact is that with all of this information, in the end, no one is going to know whether she was there or not. Certainly nothing you're going find out at this late date. The system always makes its decisions in the face of informational uncertainty. So the master question is, how much uncertainty is too much?

ERROL MORRIS: On the way to the crime scene, one of the MPs saw a woman wearing, as he described it, a wide-brimmed hat. There was a light rain. She was standing in a deserted part of the base but a couple of blocks from the MacDonald residence. The MP was answering an emergency call. He was going to the scene of the crime and didn't stop. But when MacDonald provided a description of these four assailants, one of the people he described was a woman with a floppy hat.

REX BEABER: What to make of it? What to make of it requires that you know what to make of it. But it certainly is the stuff on which reasonable doubt is built. Is she the only woman in the world who wears a floppy hat? Of course not. Whoever made that floppy hat sold them by the millions, probably.

But it contributes to how much fog is in the room when the jury has to decide on guilt or innocence. If you think of each piece of exculpatory evidence as a bit of fog, at some point there's enough fog in the room that twelve good people say, "I really can't make out who's in here anymore."

————

After her evaluation, Stoeckley once again asked Gunderson if she could leave. This time she was more successful. Beasley writes:

Helena stated over and over that she wanted to return home but Ted did not let her come. He was still trying to pry information out of her. We did not have return tickets to North Carolina so the both of us was at his mercy . . . Helena told him that if he did not send her back she was going to hitch hike back to North Carolina. I then told Ted that the best thing for him to do was to send her back because he may be violating her rights.

At this Ted took the both of us to the Los Angeles Airport and purchased tickets for the return flight, the next day. He left us there alone to find our way the best we could saying that he had to meet someone. And also the remark was made that now that he had everything he needed, he couldn't care less if she was run over by a truck.[4]

A SATANIC CULT

You would think that would be the end of it. Beasley and Stoeckley at LAX on their way back east. But there is one more trip to Los Angeles. On May 21, 1982, Gunderson persuaded Helena Stoeckley to tell her story, on camera, in an interview for *60 Minutes*.[1]

The interview footage looks like it was shot on 16mm film, then transferred to video and copied hundreds of times. The image has a nacreous quality. Who knows what it looked like then? The screen goes to white. And then an image pops up. A wide shot of a hotel room. The production slate is sitting on the cushion of a floral-patterned wingbacked chair, as if the slate is to be interviewed. The screen goes to white again, and up pops Helena Stoeckley—eight months pregnant in a purple plaid frock. The interview begins with a voice-over, the voice of Ted Gunderson, and there is Stoeckley, shaking her head back and forth, for reasons we will never know.

Gunderson interrupts constantly, but when Stoeckley is allowed to talk, a powerful story emerges filled with endless detail.

TED GUNDERSON: Helena, these murders—the MacDonald murders—occurred the early morning hours of February [17], 1970. Since that time a number of people have said that you talked to them and advised, in some instances, you were there, others said that you said you were there, but you're not sure, in other instances, you advised that you were not there. And then in October and December of 1980, you gave Mr. Beasley and me a statement wherein you advised that you were definitely there . . . Can you tell us why you've changed your mind through these last twelve years so many times?

HELENA STOECKLEY: Yes, sir. Because at the time of the murders, I was involved with a satanic cult. Since then, I have been contacted. I'm now pregnant. Anyone who knows anything about witchcraft knows the firstborn child can be sacrificed. And will be. I have been threatened; threats have been made on me, my family and everyone else.

TED GUNDERSON: So you've changed your story.

HELENA STOECKLEY: I haven't changed my story. I'm only dropping names.[2]

Stoeckley goes on to describe how she became a member of a cult. Although she was a practicing Roman Catholic, she became interested in white witchcraft. Gunderson asks her about the difference between white and black witchcraft. Stoeckley's answer? One is for "benevolent purposes," the other is for "curses and things such as that."

He asks about a motivation for the crimes. Stoeckley told him that they were trying to punish MacDonald for his treatment of drug addicts. That they were going to teach him a lesson.

Gunderson then asks Stoeckley to describe how she was dressed and the details of what she saw in the house on the night of the murders.

TED GUNDERSON: Where did the group meet immediately prior to going to the MacDonald house the night of the murders?

HELENA STOECKLEY: Early in the evening we met at Rowan Street Park, and then at 1108 Clark Street . . . I had a floppy hat that I used to wear all the time. I had on boots that night. And before we left—before I dropped the mescaline, I was already smoking marijuana and everything. And as a joke, I put on the blond wig that belonged to my roommate. I was wearing a black vest and it was a combination of pants and skirt . . .

TED GUNDERSON: Helena, tell us what happened from the time you entered the house that night.

Up to this point, Gunderson asked a question, and Stoeckley briefly answered. Here she provides an uninterrupted narrative.

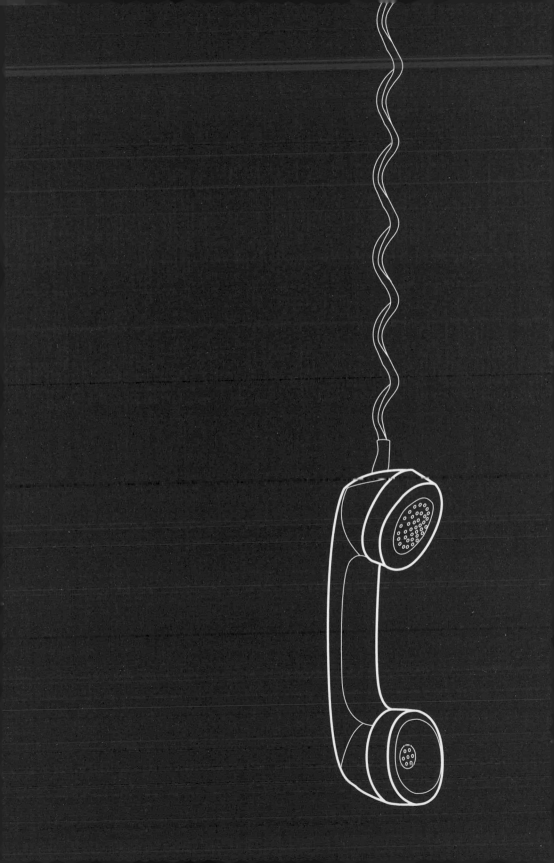

HELENA STOECKLEY: I entered the house with another member of the cult. We had to struggle with the door, which is the reason I lit the candle to begin with. We went in. There were three members in there already, talking to Dr. MacDonald. I thought they were simply asking for drugs or something like that. As it turns out, it turned into violence. I said, "Leave him alone," and they asked him to go to the telephone and call someone and see if he could get a prescription or to get the drugs themselves. He said he would, he tried to, and we realized he was calling the MPs. That's when—they forced him back to the couch, someone knocked him unconscious. After that, I went into the back bedroom—that's when I saw two other members in there. Colette was struggling with them. There was a child laying on the bed next to her that I presumed was asleep. She had already been beaten several times, and was calling out to her husband to help her. I presume he was still unconscious or something like that. But she was bleeding profusely by that time. It was all over the bed, it was on the child, so I don't know if the child was dead or not. I said, "Let's leave her alone," that this was unnecessary and someone called me a do-gooder or something. I'd already been called a goodie-goodie two shoes in the front living room, and I left the room. [There was] a hobbyhorse, like a rocking horse. I backed up against it but the spring was broken, so I moved away from it. In the room, there was a child's toys, there were children's books, things like that. I don't know whose bedroom it was but there was another child in there asleep. There was no blood in there or anything at that time. I went back out front and by that time, Dr. MacDonald had regained consciousness and someone was in there beating him. I know who it was but, like I said, I'm not going to give names or anything because of my own safety and the safety of my family and the threat of personal danger.

TED GUNDERSON: Where did you go after you went into the living room?

HELENA STOECKLEY: At that time, the phone rang. Everyone was standing around and said who should answer it, and I was designated as the person to go answer the phone. I picked it up, and someone asked for Dr. MacDonald, well, by that time, I was pretty high on mescaline, and I just giggled and said he wasn't there, or something like that. They accepted that, and that was it, so I hung up the phone.

The phone rang?

On August 17, 1979, the day that Helena Stoeckley was on the stand in Raleigh, a man named Jimmy Friar provided the FBI with an affidavit about his call to the

MacDonald house on the night of the murders. (He had contacted Wade Smith shortly before going to the FBI.) According to Friar, he was trying to call someone else. A *different* Dr. MacDonald. Did he make the phone call? We'll never know.

The affidavit goes into considerable detail. A Greyhound bus station in Fayetteville, the Green Lantern Bar, an old hotel in the Haymount area, about "one half to one mile from the Green Lantern Bar." Friar was an AWOL soldier who had been treated by a psychiatrist, Dr. Richard MacDonald, at Walter Reed Hospital.

> Friar then hung up, waited a few minutes and then called Womack Army Hospital again. During the second call, he represented himself as being a doctor and stated an emergency existed and that he needed to get in touch with Dr. MACDONALD. Womack Army Hospital then gave him the residence number of Dr. MACDONALD.
>
> Friar then called the operator at the same pay telephone and told her that he had just lost 10 cents in the telephone, and requested her to dial the telephone number which Womack Army Hospital had given him. The operator dialed the number and a female answered the telephone. FRIAR asked for Dr. MACDONALD and the female broke into hysterical laughter. FRIAR asked again to speak to MACDONALD and this same female continued to laugh . . . The only words which FRIAR could recall being said were, "Hang up the goddamn phone."[3]

––––––––

Who knows what the Friar story means? Who knows what Segal told Stoeckley? Or Murtagh or Blackburn? Or Gunderson or Beasley? Who knows what she would have said, if properly deposed in early 1970? Could Stoeckley's stories all be imagined—constructed out of the bits and pieces that Stoeckley was told by investigators, prosecutors, defense attorneys? Or was there something here? To be sure, there were internal inconsistencies in Stoeckley's account. And inconsistencies between her account and MacDonald's. However, Rex Beaber would say that the richness of detail supplied by Stoeckley was more than "a trivial concurrence of memory." Perhaps not proof that she was there. But something more than a recitation of information she had heard from others. And what about that other phone call, the one that MacDonald was forced to make? Did that ever happen? MacDonald certainly never mentioned it.

HELENA STOECKLEY: I went back into the bedroom again and this one person—by that time, for some reason, the one child had been moved to the other bedroom, that was laying with Colette at the time. When I went back, Colette appeared to be either asleep or unconscious and I suggested we leave, and that was it.

TED GUNDERSON: Tell us about when you left the house?

HELENA STOECKLEY: Well, previously, when we entered the house, there was a dog in the yard, and I was raised in an army environment around guard dogs and things like that. It was a German Shepherd. I told them to be quiet when we went in, because I went over there and I tried to pet the dog. It didn't try to bite or anything. Going out, I told them again to be quiet. So when we went out, I still had the candle in my hand . . .

TED GUNDERSON: Didn't everyone get out of the house then, at the same time?

HELENA STOECKLEY: I'm not sure, I didn't check. I just wanted to get out.

TED GUNDERSON: Where did you park the car? How many buildings down from the MacDonald residence did you park the getaway car?

HELENA STOECKLEY: One car was parked on the road, the other one was parked in a parking lot. They had parking lots with about five spaces each to them. And we were in one of them.

Joe Wershba, the *60 Minutes* producer, took over the questioning:

JOE WERSHBA: When you left where did you go?

HELENA STOECKLEY: We stopped at Dunkin' Donuts, and picked up several other people there, who were not involved in the murders. I went inside to the restroom, washed my hands, and came back out and we left.

JOE WERSHBA: Did you have blood on you?

HELENA STOECKLEY: I don't know.

JOE WERSHBA: When you left where did you go?

HELENA STOECKLEY: Back to 1108 Clark Street.

JOE WERSHBA: Which is?

HELENA STOECKLEY: My residence at the time.

JOE WERSHBA: Who were you living with at the time?

HELENA STOECKLEY: I was living with two other females, Kathy Smith and Diane— her married name is Cazares.

JOE WERSHBA: What time did you arrive back at your house?

HELENA STOECKLEY: About four-thirty, five o'clock.

JOE WERSHBA: How did you get there?

HELENA STOECKLEY: In the blue Mustang.

JOE WERSHBA: Did somebody drop you off?

HELENA STOECKLEY: The blue Mustang pulled in; we were listening to the radio. I took the box of donuts out and walked in the house. And my two roommates were in there, painting on the wall.

———

Stoeckley's description was very close to Posey's account given at the Article 32 and in his various depositions during the reinvestigation. On March 19 and 22, 1971, Posey had given a statement to Richard Mahon of the CID:

I heard a car skid into HELEN's [*sic*] driveway and I also heard some giggling and laughing. I went to my front door to see what was going on, and I saw Stoeckley get out of a blue Mach I Mustang and enter her apartment between 3 and 4:30 AM . . . I had seen the Mustang at HELEN'S house several times before 17 February 1970, but I don't think I saw that car again after that day.

I also saw one of the girls that HELEN lived with painting the bathroom walls . . . I woke my wife up to see because I thought it was unusual, kind of weird, to be painting at that time of the morning.[4]

Painting at 4:00 a.m.? Gunderson asked Stoeckley what happened to the group after the murders.

HELENA STOECKLEY: Well, most of the people in the group decided it was in our best interest to disband, temporarily.

TED GUNDERSON: And?

HELENA STOECKLEY: Some of us went to other states, others feigned innocence.

JOE WERSHBA: How about the day after the murders? Were you stopped?

HELENA STOECKLEY: Very early the next morning [the eighteenth], Detective Beasley stopped me and several other people in the band.

JOE WERSHBA: In the cult, that were involved in the murders?

HELENA STOECKLEY: Yes, sir.

JOE WERSHBA: And what happened then?

HELENA STOECKLEY: At the time I was an informant for Mr. Beasley. He started to get out of the car, and the people in the car had weapons and such. They started to approach him, as if to assault him in some way. And I turned around to them and said, "It's all right. I can talk to him for a minute." And they got back in the car.

Gunderson turned his attention to Colette's jewelry box. MacDonald had long claimed that two rings were missing.

> TED GUNDERSON: And you knew the location of the jewelry box, where the jewelry box was located?
>
> HELENA STOECKLEY: It was in the master bedroom.
>
> TED GUNDERSON: And where in the master bedroom?
>
> HELENA STOECKLEY: On the high dresser.
>
> TED GUNDERSON: You told us on the low dresser.
>
> HELENA STOECKLEY: No. There was one dresser that was just a chest of drawers, but as far as the dressers go, there was one nightstand, too. So, you know, if you want to be particular, it was the low dresser . . .
>
> TED GUNDERSON: A big issue in the case is the fact that you said that the hobby-horse was broken, the prosecution claims that you saw a picture in the newspaper several days after and therefore you knew it from looking at the newspaper. But actually, the only people that knew that [the hobbyhorse was broken] were the MacDonalds themselves. Did you see this picture in the newspaper?
>
> HELENA STOECKLEY: I never knew anything about the hobbyhorse again until 1979.
>
> TED GUNDERSON: You knew that night that the spring was broken?
>
> HELENA STOECKLEY: The night of the murders, yes. But it was never mentioned again until 1979, at the trial in Raleigh.

Indeed. It was the one detail that Stoeckley mentioned on the stand.

More questions by Joe Wershba:

> JOE WERSHBA: The night of the murders, were all the members of the cult high on drugs?
>
> HELENA STOECKLEY: Very much so.
>
> JOE WERSHBA: Aren't you concerned about being on television with this interview?
>
> HELENA STOECKLEY: Not at this time anymore. Since I've been off of drugs for over three years now, I feel that what needs to be done is to have the truth brought out once and for all and to have people who had been prosecuted in this case and indicted and all that, freed once and for all.
>
> JOE WERSHBA: So your motivation is out of conscience for both MacDonald and for your personal safety and the safety of your future child?
>
> HELENA STOECKLEY: Yes, it is.

After their third trip back from Los Angeles, Beasley visited Helena on December 30, 1982, at her room in the Seneca Gardens Apartments, in Walhalla, South Carolina. It was their last meeting.

> She stated that the only thing she had to live for now was her son. That she intended to live in the Walhalla area until her husband was near parole, and then she was leaving the area for parts unknown, so he could not find her. I told her to continue to think along this line, and I thought she would come out O.K. I have been to S.C. many times and I never found Helena to be on drugs or anything else.
>
> The day that I took her home from the hospital with her son she seemed to be in good health and spirits, and made no complaints about being sick. (In fact she was in a joyful mood that she had her son back home).[5]

Two weeks later, on January 14, 1983, Helena Stoeckley was found dead in her apartment; her baby was found at her side, severely dehydrated but alive. Beasley suspected foul play. He went back and spoke to Ersley Fitzgerald, a neighbor who lived in number 26, and who had come to know Helena well when she lived there. Fitzgerald told Beasley that Helena was "a very scared person most all the time, always seemed to be looking over her shoulder . . . She would not trust many people."

Since she was "the only possible witness" (as described in the police report) in the MacDonald trial, the South Carolina authorities performed an autopsy.[6] It determined that there had been no foul play. Stoeckley had died from a combination of pneumonia and liver disease. Various swabs and tissue samples were forwarded to the FBI labs in Washington. She was still a possible witness in the MacDonald case—albeit a silent one.

Beasley returned to Fayetteville, eventually terminating his involvement in the investigation of MacDonald's case altogether. He was still protective of Helena years after her death, and her treatment at the hands of his former hero and partner, Ted Gunderson, caused him to undergo a conversion. He decided that Jeffrey MacDonald was guilty, as if any investigation involving Gunderson would surely be on the wrong side.

"I can't prove it. I didn't see him kill them. But all the evidence and all the circumstances around the investigations by both the government and the defense points that way," said Prince Beasley, a retired narcotics officer.

He said he changed his mind about Dr. MacDonald when he became convinced that the defense's key witness, Helena Stoeckley, was manipulated by investigators working for the convicted physician . . .

Mr. Beasley's reversal was a "complete surprise" to Mr. Gunderson, who said in a telephone conversation from his Los Angeles office that he believes Mr. Beasley or his family "must have been threatened."

Mr. Beasley said he was not threatened.[7]

I agree with Prince Beasley that Helena Stoeckley was manipulated. Manipulated by the defense, manipulated by the prosecution. Manipulated by lawyers and investigators on both sides of the fence. That fact is unfortunate. It has thrown more than one monkey wrench into this case.

But I do not agree that it proves MacDonald's guilt, or that Helena was not somehow speaking the truth.

In February 1970, a group of inexperienced military policemen and investigators failed to protect the crime scene at 544 Castle Drive. As a result, the integrity of the physical evidence was compromised. And then, from 1980 to 1982, Ted Gunderson, with the help of Prince Beasley, essentially compromised the value of Stoeckley's and other witnesses' testimony. Gunderson coerced, bribed, and threatened Stoeckley—contaminating her as a witness. Although he was trying to help, his errors worked against Jeffrey MacDonald. Michael Malley told me that he was appalled by Gunderson's "techniques."

Gunderson was fired and replaced. But it might have been too late.

———

I had wanted to talk to Gunderson, but I had also been afraid of talking to him. How crazy was he?

Stoeckley died in 1983; Beasley died in 1996. Gunderson outlived them both and went on to be a fixture in the online world of conspiracy theorists and skeptics. His Web site became a compendium of loony-tune concerns: "9/11 was an inside job," the healing power of colloidal silver. For Gunderson the entire world, as we experience it, was a lie, waiting to be unmasked.

For years, Gunderson appeared on radio and TV talk shows and on DVDs, often arguing—among many other things—that Jeffrey MacDonald was innocent of all charges, a victim of corrupt and cunning government agents and a powerful cabal of satanists. One of his last appearances is still on YouTube: a video shot on the evening of January 12, 2011. Gunderson is standing in the middle of a field in Los Angeles. Compared to the Ted Gunderson of the 1980s, this version looks gaunt and tired. (He died of cancer seven months later.) It looks like a nice night. The camera tilts up over his right shoulder, into the sky. Condensation trails from jet engines over a hill, against an orange sky.

But they aren't ordinary condensation trails, Gunderson tells us. They're "death dumps," poisonous chemicals being released into the atmosphere daily by the United Nations. He goes on:

> Birds are dying around the world. Fish are dying by the hundreds of thousands around the world. This is genocide. This is poison. This is murder by the United Nations . . . I personally have observed the planes that were standing still in Nebraska—Lincoln, Nebraska—at the Air National Guard. They have no markings on them. They are huge, bomber-like airplanes with no markings . . . Somebody has to do something about it.

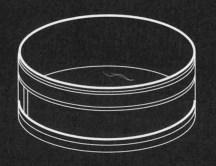

E-323 AND Q-89

A Freedom of Information Act (FOIA) request had been filed, but it wasn't until 1983—the same year *Fatal Vision* was published—that suddenly hundreds of documents previously unknown to the defense were released. Many of them concerned the physical evidence collected by the CID and FBI—hundreds of samples and thousands of hours of laboratory work involved in analyzing them. O'Neill hired Raymond Shedlick, a twenty-year veteran of the New York City and Nassau County police, who had retired to Durham, North Carolina.

There were so many people who were caught up in the case—on both sides. But one of the most moving of the stories involves Ray Shedlick and his daughter, Ellen Dannelly, who joined her father as an investigator in the case.

I asked Ellen Dannelly how they came to be involved.

ELLEN DANNELLY: I was living in North Carolina. And then my parents decided to move down around 1982. My father was a New York City detective, and he worked for the district attorney of Nassau County. When he moved down here, he retired, and he got a call from one of his people he worked with, John O'Connell, in New York. He said he had a case down in North Carolina and was wondering if my father wanted to take a look at it part-time. So my father started to look at the case, and it was the Jeffrey MacDonald case. And he told John, "There is no way this is a part-time kind of a case." The reading material alone was overwhelming. So he eventually went onto the case full-time, and he needed somebody that could work for him, trust, do the filing, because this was obviously going to be a very big issue. And that's when he hired me. And when he got hired, he told the attorneys, he told everyone, "Whatever I find, that's what it is. It's only the facts."

ERROL MORRIS: So how old were you when you became your father's assistant in this case?

ELLEN DANNELLY: I would've been about twenty-three. And he got licensed as a private investigator in North Carolina so he could interview people. Later on, when he got sick and died, I got my license so I could carry on his work. The case became so big, my father started to get all this material that included Ted Gunderson's material, which was about three black notebooks. And my father started to put together a time line. We went back over and interviewed people and found new people. He read the CID reports. As many reports as we had, every piece he read, and notes were made on it and we would type up everything. Everything was kept in files, cross-referenced, so it was a really good system we had going on. He put together a time line. It was depressing to read about Colette and these kids and what happened to them over and over and over. But to my father, this was a job. It was just something he was going to do. I was probably a little bit more emotionally upset by this whole scenario than he was. To him, it was business as usual, I guess. And then my father got sick. He got cancer.

ERROL MORRIS: What kind of cancer did he have?

ELLEN DANNELLY: He had lung cancer. He smoked. He knew it was a death sentence, you know? That was it. We wanted to get every piece of FOIA paperwork we could get our hands on. So the lawyers sent away for every scrap of paper they could get, particularly the CID and FBI lab notes. The lab work was always of interest to me, and that was one area where we could just cross-reference it, go through it, put it together, and that's when I found the fibers. And that was absolutely the bombshell.

ERROL MORRIS: Your father was still alive at this point?

ELLEN DANNELLY: He was still alive. The government's whole case was that Jeffrey MacDonald could not explain the purple fibers on the club [threads from the seams of his pajama top]. Bernie Segal, his first lawyer, had built his whole case on Helena Stoeckley. He had never done anything with the forensics, never questioned the government. Nothing. So of course when Judge Dupree threw out Helena Stoeckley, their whole case went out the window. But once we were given the technician's paperwork, the lab notes—for every exhibit recorded on that paper, if there were 100 exhibits on that paper, if it said D-6, D-7, E-5, whatever it was, I would Xerox it that many times. Across the house I'd have 120 piles. Down the hall, through the bedrooms.

ERROL MORRIS: But you had no access to the actual exhibits themselves, correct?

ELLEN DANNELLY: No, no access to the exhibits. The only thing I had was the lab work from the FBI, their notes, the handwritten notes from the little scientist in the room. Everything that they had. And everything the CID had, anything in this case that had to do with any exhibit was put in a pile for that particular exhibit. Say it was Q-10, everything that had to do with Q-10 in this case was in this pile called Q-10. Then we put it all into date order. And now you start flipping the pages and seeing what was found in '72 or what was found in '90, or whenever this work was done. And, of course, all the blood work was very suspicious. We knew something was wrong with it, but somebody else would have to handle that. But when we went through the paperwork—

ERROL MORRIS: Whoa, whoa, whoa. When you said you knew something was wrong with it, independent of the question of whether you have a degree in hematology or whatever, why did you think there was something wrong with it?

ELLEN DANNELLY: I could see discrepancies, I could see where they would say it was B In one handwritten note and then later on they would say that it was A.

ERROL MORRIS: So go on, I'm sorry.

ELLEN DANNELLY: When we started to go through the exhibits and we got to the crucial ones, lo and behold, in addition to purple fibers, they're describing black wool fibers. Black wool fibers—in Colette's mouth, on the club, on her pajama top. In court, the government kept emphasizing the fibers that came from Jeffrey MacDonald's pajamas, but there were additional fibers that were not revealed to the defense. The night that MacDonald was—his family and he were attacked—he describes seeing Helena Stoeckley with the long blond hair and wearing some black outfit—black wool skirt or whatever she said she wore. And of course, Mica, the MP that night, going to the scene, sees a woman on the corner, who they never picked up. What a shame. He told his superior, "There was a woman on the corner with long blond hair and a floppy hat." So all of it fell into place. Bottom line is they lied. And then there was the blond hair, going through the next exhibit—I can't remember the numbers [E-323]—but then they find these three blond, synthetic fibers—twenty-two to twenty-four inches long—in a hairbrush. The government said it came from a doll.

ERROL MORRIS: You found the blond wig fiber?

ELLEN DANNELLY: Yes. Yes, I did. And the black fibers. I was in my kitchen when I found them, and I called my dad and told him, "Dad, you've got to come here. You

won't believe what I'm seeing. I think I'm crazy. Am I seeing what I'm seeing?"
And when he came over and he looked at the paperwork, he said, "That's it. That's
it. That's the case."

ERROL MORRIS: And what year would this have been that you discovered—

ELLEN DANNELLY: My father died in '89, so this would have been '88, 1988. And then
from there, of course, we put together reports, submitted them to Alan Dershow-
itz and Harvey Silverglate, and they took the case, and that was it. That was the
stuff they needed. Those two pieces right there, those two major findings.

These two "pieces" of evidence were black wool fibers (unsourced to anything
in the home) taken from Q-89, a vial of material from the club; and the strands
of saran (a synthetic fiber developed by the Dow Chemical Company) found in
E-323, Colette's hairbrush. Q-89 and E-323 reveal how two seemingly innocuous
details can change our perception of a crime.

———

First, from Q-89, the wool fibers.[1]

Back on August 28, 1979, Blackburn was summing up to the jury: "You could
throw the whole shooting match away except for these two pieces of evidence." He
brandished the club and the pajama top. The club had been found outside the back
door of 544 Castle Drive with "two little purple threads" (stitching threads) on it,
matching MacDonald's torn pajama top. Blackburn was asking a seemingly simple
but misleading question.

If MacDonald had entered the bedroom and found Colette after the assailants
had left the house, how was it that fibers from his torn pajama top were found
outside on the club? As Blackburn described it for the jury, "This sounds sort of
minor, really, until you think about something. How did they get there? . . . If the
pajama top was not taken off of his body in the hall or the living room until this
club was out the door, how in the name of all that is reasonable did they walk out
the door and get on the club and stick to it?"[2] Indeed.

In the name of all that is reasonable, Blackburn proposed to the jury that the
only way the pajama top fibers could have gotten on the club was in the master bedroom. Not so. They could have gotten on the club when MacDonald was
attacked in the living room. Blue pajama-top fibers had been found in the hallway
in the place where MacDonald had been knocked unconscious.[3]

WAS MACDONALD ATTACKED IN THE LIVING ROOM?

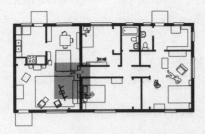

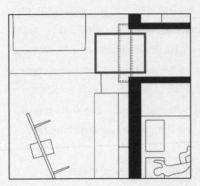

THE ARGUMENTS

The government argued that there was *no* evidence—no blood and no fibers—that suggested that MacDonald was attacked in the living room.

The defense argued that that area of the scene had been badly preserved, and that investigators had *still* found evidence that MacDonald had struggled and bled at the end of the hallway.

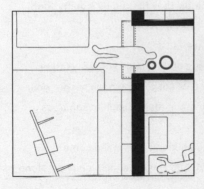

THE EVIDENCE

CID Agent ROBERT SHAW admitted under oath to finding "a pile" of fibers or threads at the south wall of the hallway, the same area where MacDonald claimed to have collapsed.
July 5, 1970

CID Lab Report Number FA-D-P-C-FP-82-70 lists Exhibit D-144, a "portion of the hall floor at west entrance bearing red-brown stains" that possibly matched MacDonald's blood type
March 29, 1972

But Dannelly's discovery wasn't about cotton fibers. There were two kinds of threads on the club—purple cotton and black wool—the black wool unsourced to anything in the house. Dannelly had discovered a crucial piece of evidence that had never been presented to the jury. And, unlike the purple cotton, its presence on the club could not easily be explained.

Plus, other black woolen fibers had been found at the crime scene that were similar to the black woolen fibers on the club. They were found inside Colette MacDonald's mouth.[4]

ERROL MORRIS: So your father believed he was innocent?

ELLEN DANNELLY: In the beginning, my father's feeling was, "I'm law enforcement, so I tend to lean a little bit towards thinking that they're in the right." But I remember him reading this stuff and shaking his head. He couldn't believe it. "It was sloppy, sloppy work," that's what he always said. MPs tramping through a crime scene and all the other stuff, he became convinced that this guy was innocent. Certainly deserved a new trial. I don t know if he'll ever get out, but at least give the man a fair trial. Bring all of this stuff out, and then wherever the chips fall, they fall.

ERROL MORRIS: Do you feel the government went out of its way to make—

ELLEN DANNELLY: They knew darn well that the threads weren't all purple. They had the notes, the same notes that I was looking at. So they picked and chose what they wanted to use, because, in their minds, they figured he's guilty. Right or wrong.

ERROL MORRIS: So they select the evidence that—?

ELLEN DANNELLY: Oh yes, I'm definitely convinced of that, and I know my father was convinced of that. How could you not? You've got your own lab people, your people are telling you this is black wool. Who made the decision to suppress that evidence?

ERROL MORRIS: And were they ever matched to anything else in the home?

ELLEN DANNELLY: No, they were never matched. And you have the blond hair along with everything else.

ERROL MORRIS: Do you remember when you became convinced he was innocent?

ELLEN DANNELLY: It was really an accumulation. It took a long time. I've never been a big Jeff fan, I'll tell you that right up front. I've butted heads with him a lot of times.

ERROL MORRIS: How so? Explain this to me.

ELLEN DANNELLY: Well, you know, I was very sensitive about the evidence that we did find and my father's work. Well, Jeff is in jail and Jeff will crawl over your back to get out. If you're not moving fast enough for him, he would send somebody else over to knock on your door to get you to. He wanted out of there. He wanted to be vindicated. I don't blame him for that. But I was very sensitive at the time, so I would get very nervous. As you will see through this case, a lot of people have claimed credit for my work or my father's work. Gunderson was going to make a movie. I think he was given a $50,000 check based on what we found on these black wool fibers and blond hair. I called out to California and spoke to the lawyer, Brian O'Neill, about it. And then I finally had somebody call the TV station that he was working with, and, of course, he had to give back the check and the whole thing ended. He never found anything. I was very, very sensitive to a lot of things. They went over our witnesses, they reinterviewed them, and the next thing you know they're getting better and better. You ruin the credibility of your witnesses when you do that, you know?

ERROL MORRIS: This must have been terribly frustrating, the fact that your father was dying, and he still couldn't crack this case?

ELLEN DANNELLY: It was sad. I would say he was saddened by it. He'd say, "No matter if I brought Colette before the court, the door is shut. It won't open. They won't concede." Yes. I guess it was frustrating. And this was the last-ditch effort. But at the end of the day, my father was the kind of person that he shut the door and he had his own family to concern himself about. He couldn't save the world. He wrote a very nice letter for when Jeff went before the parole board. He knew it would be after he was dead. He said, "These are not killing hands. These are the hands of a healer."

IT WASN'T A DOLL

Ellen Dannelly's second piece of new evidence was found in handwritten lab notes prepared by the CID chemist Janice Glisson on April 20, 1971. It was a record of a "blond, synthetic wig hair, 22 inches in length" found in a clear-handled hairbrush—CID Exhibit E-323—that belonged to Colette MacDonald.[1] The appearance of this evidence raised all sorts of questions. If the CID investigators had known about E-323, wouldn't they have linked it to MacDonald's description of the blond-haired intruder? Was it overlooked? Or was it a deliberate suppression of evidence? Wouldn't the jurors at MacDonald's trial eight years later see the blond fiber as relevant to MacDonald's claim that a blond-haired intruder was present at the crime scene? Wouldn't the presence of the blond fiber (which was unmatched to anything else at the crime scene) have contradicted the claim made by the prosecution that there was *no* physical evidence at the crime scene in support of MacDonald's account of what had happened?

———

Christmas 1993. My wife and I had again flown from Boston to Raleigh-Durham to spend another holiday with my mother-in-law and aunt. By this time I had been bitten by the MacDonald bug and had become friends with Harvey Silverglate, MacDonald's appellate attorney.

Silverglate had asked us to look for wigs in the Fayetteville area. I-95 joins St. Pauls and Fayetteville, but dotted along the old federal highway U.S. 301 there is a series of pawn and resale shops. There is also a wig emporium called the Wig Outlet. I found that shopping for wigs over the holidays can be depressing, but we were determined to help with the investigation. Our goal: find wigs made from saran fibers, circa 1970. Since the FBI had claimed that the saran fibers were from one of the MacDonald children's dolls and that wigs had never been manufactured from saran, it would be a significant piece of evidence—the proverbial black swan. It would be even more significant to find a black swan in the Fayetteville area.

Ultimately, we were not successful.

There was too little to go on. Helena Stoeckley had destroyed her hat, boots, and wig in 1970, and so there was no hope of matching the fiber found in Colette's hairbrush with Stoeckley's wig. All that we could hope for was to prove the FBI wrong—to prove that saran had been used in the manufacture of wigs. And to prove that the *length* of the saran fiber (twenty-two inches) suggested that it had *not* been used in the manufacture of a doll.

In 1993, Brian Murtagh, the lead prosecutor, summed up his position on the E-323 fibers in a survey of the collection of fibers and hairs in the possession of the FBI crime lab.[2] His argument was straightforward. There were several fibers found. One was a gray modacrylic wig fiber that matched one of Colette's wigs. The other, the saran fiber, was unmatched to anything in the house but was presumed to have come from one of the children's dolls.

The unidentified "wig" fibers were crucial to MacDonald's defense because of where they were found and because they supposedly "linked" Helena Stoeckley, now deceased, to the crime scene. Two hairbrushes, a clear-handled hairbrush found on a sideboard near the kitchen phone and a blue-handled hairbrush found under Colette's body, became important . . . The defense scenario alleged that at some point during the crimes, Helena Stoeckley, wearing a blond wig, had answered the kitchen telephone in the MacDonald residence. If actual unidentified human "wig" fibers, which did not originate from the MacDonald household, were found in these hairbrushes, this would tend to corroborate Stoeckley's presence and would be "exculpatory" to the government's case . . .

The presence of these blond synthetic fibers was noted in the CID examiner's bench notes; however, they were never mentioned in the final CID laboratory reports. They had never been disclosed to the defense prior to the 1979 trial.

This fact that the presence of the wig fiber was never disclosed to the defense is mentioned in passing, as if it had little or no significance.

> The "wig" fibers found in this hairbrush were analyzed with the following results. The blond synthetic hair was found to be a Saran fiber often used for doll hair; [*above*] at far left is a blond Saran doll hair from the FBI reference collection for purposes of comparison. The grey modacrylic wig fiber found in the hairbrush (far right) was found to match grey modacrylic fibers from the blond fall Colette was known to wear.
>
> The source of the "blond synthetic hair" from the clear handled hairbrush posed more of a problem. Again, the same microscopic, optical and instrumental techniques were used, ultimately determining that the "blond synthetic hairs" were composed of Saran fibers. Due to problems in manufacturing and the physical properties of Saran fibers, they are not suitable for human wigs. They do not look like or "lay" like human hair, therefore, they are not used to make human hair goods.
>
> One of the main uses of Saran fibers during the same time of the murders was for doll hair. These "blond synthetic hairs" were very similar to the blond doll hair in the FBI reference collection. In fact the early "Barbie" dolls made by Mattel had hair made of Saran fibers.
>
> Since the MacDonald girls were known to have owned dolls with blond hair, and since little girls are known to brush the hair of their dolls, it can be inferred that the "blond synthetic hair" found in the hairbrush probably came from a doll belonging to the MacDonald girls or one of their friends. Unfortunately, none of the dolls originally belonging to Kimberley or Kristen are available today for testing purposes.

This article provides Murtagh and FBI forensic analyst Michael Malone's argument in a nutshell. The fibers came from one of Kristen's or Kimberley's dolls, not from a wig. Since saran fibers were not used for wigs, including Stoeckley's wig, the fiber had to have come from a doll. Murtagh's analysis, however, omitted a central problem. The blond synthetic hairs were long—up to twenty-four inches—probably too long to have been used for a doll's hair.

Enter the doll experts.

On December 5, 1990, a couple of agents from the FBI (Malone and Raymond "Butch" Madden) and an assistant U.S. attorney (Eric Evenson) interviewed two doll experts, employees of the Mattel toy company, Judith Schizas and Mellie Phillips.[3] *Both* Schizas and Phillips told the government that Mattel had never made a doll with saran hair fibers as long as twenty-four inches, and Phillips told them that she was not aware that any other manufacturer was using saran in the making of dolls in the late 1960s and early 1970s.

Schizas, according to a statement made later to MacDonald's defense attorneys, recalled her initial meeting with Malone. They went to her home in Hawthorne, California, and viewed her collection of four thousand dolls.

We discussed generally the different types of synthetic fibers used to make doll hair, including Saran, nylon and Kanekalon. The agents told me that they were interested in any doll or dolls, made by Mattel or any other manufacturer, which might have had hair 22 or 24 inches long. I replied that, to my knowledge, no Mattel doll had ever been made with synthetic fibers that long, and that one might possibly find a doll hair fiber that long if the fiber were doubled over in the hair rooting process to produce two 11–12 inch hairs, but that I did not know of such a doll.[4]

Schizas then gave them several doll collectors' books to look at. Finally, the investigators revealed that they were looking for a blond-haired ballerina doll, approximately twenty-four inches in height. Schizas knew what they were talking about. It was a doll called "Dancerina," sold by Mattel in 1969, and was in her collection. "During the course of the interview, the agents told me that the defense was contending that the 22- or 24-inch saran fibers had come from a wig, and the agents told me that they simply wanted to show that it was 'possible' for such a long fiber to come from a doll. I told the agents that while it was 'possible,' it was 'not probable,' because even if fibers of that length were used in a doll, it would be very difficult to pull out an entirely intact fiber because of the way that the fibers are rooted, and they had witnessed how I had to use tweezers to carefully extract the intact fibers from the Pollyanna and Dancerina dolls."

Schizas told the FBI that the Pollyanna and Dancerina dolls both had hair made from nylon fibers, and that none of the fibers were longer than eighteen inches in total length. She then surveyed her own doll collection to determine whether any of her dolls had synthetic fibers as long as twenty-four inches. There were none. The fibers weren't from a doll. As Schizas had told the FBI, there was no Dancerina doll with saran fibers longer than eighteen inches.

The Fourth Circuit disposed of all this in 1998:

> The evidence at issue is not truly exculpatory. It does not directly bear on the question of innocence but rather provides some evidence to support the theory that the hairs found in the hairbrush came from a wig.[5]

Well, the Fourth Circuit, technically speaking, was correct. The evidence was "not truly exculpatory." Without Stoeckley's actual wig, where was the basis for a comparison? Of course the absence of the wig was a result of a failure by law enforcement to collect the evidence in a timely fashion. Before it could be collected, Stoeckley had burned it. The opinion continues:

> The overall weight of the evidence still suggests that the fibers most likely did not come from a human wig. Even if it is accepted that the fibers came from a human wig, however, this fact does little more to prove MacDonald's claim of innocence because it merely provides some support for yet another theoretical possibility; that the wig fibers found in the hairbrush came from an intruder. In our most recent decision in this case, we stated: The most that can be said about the evidence is that it raises speculation concerning its origins. Furthermore, the origins of the hair and fiber evidence have several likely explanations other than intruders. The evidence simply does not escalate the unease one feels with this case into a reasonable doubt.[6]

This story might seem quite ordinary except for an additional wrinkle discovered once again long after the fact. It was based on half-truths about the use of saran. Information that saran had been used in human wigs was in the FBI files but was not disclosed to the court. That evidence had been withheld. Laurie Cohen in the *Wall Street Journal* provided an effective summary of these shenanigans:

Was Mr. Malone accurately describing what FBI texts said about Saran? To find out, the lawyers requested all materials in the FBI's possession about the possible uses of the fiber. In April 1993, the Freedom of Information Act search turned up two books belonging to the Justice Department that said Saran was indeed used for wigs. One of the books was clearly marked as belonging to the FBI crime lab's own collections. Mr. Malone had made no mention of these in his affidavit—and the court had relied on the absence of any such materials in reaching its decision not to reopen the case.

Was it actually impossible to make Saran in the "tow" form required for wig-making? The MacDonald lawyers obtained from National Plastics Products Co., in Odenton, Md., a "tow" of blond Saran fibers that the company had once made, contradicting Mr. Malone's statement that Saran couldn't be manufactured in this form. The MacDonald defense team also located wig manufacturers and whole-salers who asserted that Saran fibers were used in wigs in the 1960s and 1970s.[7]

Here is an important piece of evidence rejected by the courts that reveals the mind-set of the police and prosecutors. The government investigators may have believed that the saran was not used to make wigs *and* that the twenty-four-inch fibers came from a doll, but if so, why did they mischaracterize the evidence they had obtained from the doll experts? Indeed, the wig-fiber evidence might *never* speak to Stoeckley's presence at the crime scene, but it *did* speak to the government's willingness to ignore information favorable to the defense.

Laurie Cohen continues:

Mr. Silverglate also learned that Mr. Malone had sought, but failed to get, a state-ment from a Mattel Inc. doll specialist, Judith Schizas, that a 24-inch Saran fiber might have come from a Mattel doll. Though Ms. Schizas says she told Mr. Malone and two of his colleagues that neither Mattel nor other manufacturers she knew used such long fibers, the government agents continued to press her, she says. "You aren't trying to railroad this guy, are you?" Ms. Schizas says she asked. She says Mr. Malone laughed and then responded, "No, we know he's guilty, and there's a ton of other evidence to prove it."

"No, we know he's guilty . . ." And hence the evidence has to be interpreted and selected to accommodate that "fact." But what about all the other evidence that tends to disprove it?

A couple of weeks after the visit, Ms. Schizas says, she received a draft affidavit from federal prosecutors. It stated that Saran was "the major fiber used for doll hair by Mattel" and others until the 1980s. The affidavit also said that doll hairs could be doubled during the weaving process to reduce a 24-inch fiber into a foot-long hair. Disagreeing with both assertions, Ms. Schizas refused to sign.

———

There was another problem with the FBI wig fiber analysis by Michael Malone. Nicknamed "Agent Death," for years Malone was a go-to guy at the crime lab, one of the "supersleuths."[8]

Malone's specialty was hair and fiber. Time and again in cases with no eyewitness, no confession and no motive, Malone would peer into his twin-eyepiece microscope and come up with the evidence that helped send somebody to prison or death row . . .

Malone quickly became a star. He grabbed headlines for his work in the "Fatal Vision" appeals of Jeffrey MacDonald, the Green Beret Army surgeon convicted of murdering his wife and children at Fort Bragg, N.C. He won praise for helping with the case against John Hinckley, who shot President Ronald Reagan. And Hillsborough County sheriff's deputies credited him with finding the key evidence—tiny strands of fiber—that put away Bobby Joe Long, a Tampa Bay area serial killer who tied up his victims before raping and strangling them.

The more famous Malone got, the more eager police and prosecutors around the country became for his testimony . . .

And in time, with all the glory Malone achieved came whispers, whispers that turned to murmurs and then a steady buzz: Mike Malone was sloppy. He was a government shill. He stretched the truth, maybe even made things up.[9]

On May 21, 1991, Malone testified at the murder trial of Jay William Buckley the same day he prepared a second affidavit for the MacDonald case.[10] Buckley and an accomplice had been accused of murdering thirty-three-year-old Kathy Wilson in a van. The only physical evidence was hair. It was sent to the New York State Police crime lab, but came back inconclusive. The prosecutor then asked Malone at the FBI to take a look it.

Malone testified that not only was there the "very, very strong possibility" that the hair was the defendant's, he also found one of the victim's hairs on a white blanket in the van that belonged to the accomplice.

The only problem was, the New York lab had shipped the wrong blanket to the FBI. Even after he was confronted with this fact, Malone stood by his results. William Buckley was acquitted.[11]

But Malone's questionable cases kept piling up. Finally, in 1997, he and twelve other agents became the subjects of a Justice Department probe. It found three thousand suspected cases of misconduct. Malone continued to work in the lab after his malfeasance was first reported. He retired in 1999, but that was after the Fourth Circuit had disposed of the blond saran fiber issue once and for all.

Mellie Phillips died over a decade ago, but Judith Schizas, now retired from Mattel, still has her collection of over four thousand dolls.

ERROL MORRIS: I wanted to know if you could tell me about the people that initially contacted you with respect to the MacDonald case.

JUDITH SCHIZAS: Are you trying to prove his innocence or that he's really guilty?

ERROL MORRIS: There's little point in trying to prove he's guilty at this point, since he's spent thirty years in prison.

JUDITH SCHIZAS: I know. It's so sad. And the only reason is because he won't admit to doing something that he says he didn't do.

ERROL MORRIS: Do you think that's the only reason?

JUDITH SCHIZAS: In the long run, it comes to that. Because they've said if he would admit to it, he could get out. And he said he wouldn't admit to it.

ERROL MORRIS: And your own feeling? Do you believe he's innocent?

JUDITH SCHIZAS: I have no idea. I only know from reading the book and watching the movie. There are times you think, yes, he could have done it. And then there's other times you think no.

ERROL MORRIS: Well, you had suggested at one point that they were trying to railroad him.

JUDITH SCHIZAS: They were trying to prove it [the fiber] came from a doll. And the longest one that would have been for a doll at that time was twelve inches long.

ERROL MORRIS: Well, there was a Dancerina doll, I remember.

JUDITH SCHIZAS: Dancerina. Okay. It was a Dancerina. And they said, could it be longer? And I said no. I said, when you're sewing, you go in the skull and then out. So up and down. So twelve and twelve is twenty-four. And that's when they said, "All right, we got him."

ERROL MORRIS: I'm not sure I understand.

JUDITH SCHIZAS: When you're brushing a doll's hair, you're not going to get the roots, because inside the scalp it's knotted so many times. You cannot pull out *one* strand. You'd have to loosen a whole section. And that's never going to happen. I showed them how it couldn't be done. I said, "So you can see it's illogical."

ERROL MORRIS: So if I understand this correctly, they claimed the hair could have been doubled over? Or something like that?

JUDITH SCHIZAS: The claim they were trying to make was that it was not from a wig, it was from the daughter's doll. Because they had hair on a brush, right?

ERROL MORRIS: Yes.

JUDITH SCHIZAS: Okay, the daughter had used the hairbrush and brushed her doll's hair, and the hair came out on the brush. And the hair was twenty inches—

ERROL MORRIS: I believe twenty-two inches long.

JUDITH SCHIZAS: Twenty-two. But they weren't concerned about the logic of it. When it's folded over, you can't pull out one strand. It can't be done. Unless it has been totally rooted wrong, and if they had the doll, the doll would have bald spots where they pulled that whole section out. The material that they used for the doll's hair was the same material that was on the wig. The wig hair was something that was logical. Because they did make wigs out of that particular kind of hair. But they didn't make doll hair. They were just trying to prove that there could have been a piece of hair that could have been that long. And yes, it could have.

ERROL MORRIS: But you think it's very unlikely?

JUDITH SCHIZAS: Have you ever tried to pull a doll's hair out and get one strand?

ERROL MORRIS: My experience with doll's hair is limited. You're saying it doesn't work like that?

JUDITH SCHIZAS: No, it's going to snap off at the scalp. You're not going to pull one hair and get it to come all the way out.

ERROL MORRIS: And you told the FBI this?

JUDITH SCHIZAS: Yes. They were very, very nice. But I said, "I don't believe that it's a possibility." I said, "I hate to tell you this because I don't believe it." I said, "But I don't want to tell you this because I think that would be railroading him."

WAS STOECKLEY IN THE HOUSE?

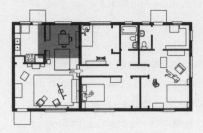

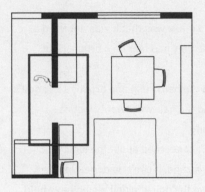

THE ARGUMENTS

The government argued that there was no physical proof that Stoeckley was present in the MacDonald house, other than her confessions. (Judge Dupree agreed.)

The defense argued at trial that there was some evidence Stoeckley was present—candle wax and Stoeckley's memories of the house. But that was only part of the story.

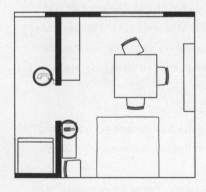

THE EVIDENCE

JANICE GLISSON of the CID lab found long blond synthetic fibers in a clear-handled hairbrush by the kitchen doorway. But the CID reports given to MacDonald's defense do not mention these fibers. *March 1970*

JANE ZILLIOUX remembered that Stoeckley told her in 1971 that she wore a wig to the crime scene, and that she had worried about getting it wet. *August 17, 1979*

JIMMY FRIAR told the FBI on the day Helena Stoeckley testified at the trial that he had called the MacDonald home by mistake during the murders and a girl had answered: "The female broke into hysterical laughter . . . then proceeded to hang up the telephone. " *August 17, 1979*

HELENA STOECKLEY told Ted Gunderson after the trial that the kitchen phone rang during the murders, and she picked up: "I just giggled and said he wasn't there, or something like that . . . I hung up the phone." *May 21, 1982*

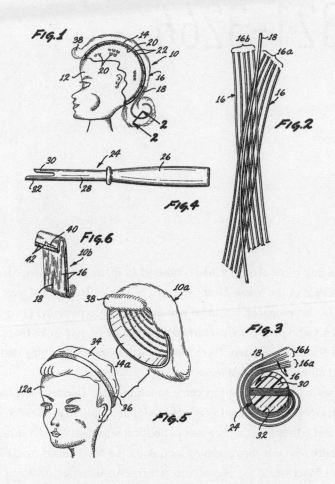

And that's when they told me he definitely did it. And I said, "Are you positive?" And they said yes.

ERROL MORRIS: They said they were positive?

JUDITH SCHIZAS: Yes. They said that they were positive and that they had all this new information and this would just be another piece of evidence that they had against him to prove that he was guilty. And that his father-in-law definitely knows he did it. The three of them told me exactly what they thought. They were quite positive he did do it. But like I said, it was tough because I would have to say I knew it wasn't a doll.

1-821-3266

Nineteen eighty-three. Stoeckley had confessed so many, many times. MacDonald saw *four* people in the house. Over the years, Stoeckley had named over a dozen people as her accomplices, but three names came up repeatedly: Greg Mitchell, her boyfriend who had recently returned from a tour of duty in Vietnam, Dwight Smith, and Shelby Don Harris. There was also Allen Mazerolle, Cathy Perry, Bruce Fowler, and others. What about *them*?[1]

The question of other suspects came to haunt Ellen Dannelly and her father, Ray Shedlick. She sent me a videotape of a question-and-answer session between her father and Jeffrey Elliot, a professor of political science at North Carolina Central University who was then planning a book on the MacDonald case. Elliot later interviewed MacDonald for *Playboy* magazine. (An interview that was brutally direct, perhaps because Elliot believed in his innocence.) Elliot died in 2009, and his manuscript for the book, the unabridged interview, and thousands of pages of his notes can no longer be found. Some of his papers are in a storage unit or in a bookcase in his father's house. All that remains is the videotape and the *Playboy* interview with Jeffrey MacDonald.

More ghosts from the past.

The tape is nearly five hours long. Elliot—off camera—feeds Shedlick name after name, topic after topic, and waits for a reply. Meanwhile, Shedlick, in a white shirt and tie—in close-up, in front of a wood-paneled wall—smokes, drinks water, and stares resolutely into the lens of the camera. The scene is flatly lit. This is a movie with limited production values. Shedlick presents his revision of the story that failed to convince the jury in 1979—Jeffrey MacDonald's story. If it weren't for a few minutes of jokes at the end, it would look like a hostage tape. Shedlick looks exhausted. (He's a big malapropism guy. My favorite? "Confibulation." That unmistakable combination of fibbing and confabulation.)

The tape begins with Shedlick's recollection of joining the case. And, as if to prove his own bona fides, a summary of his own encyclopedic investigations recited without notes of any kind.

RAYMOND SHEDLICK: I believed, almost intently, that Dr. MacDonald was guilty of these homicides. I live in a section of Long Island which is probably two towns away from where Dr. MacDonald grew up. So naturally the local newspapers had a great deal of publicity about the homicides, and I read avidly of the case. At a certain time, from reading these stories, it finally [added up] in my mind, that he was guilty . . . I knew also that in this type of investigation you have to be very, very independent, and I was concerned that I perhaps couldn't be independent because I had a predisposition to his guilt . . .

I told Brian O'Neill and I told Dr. MacDonald, ultimately, that I would conduct his investigation independently. No matter where the chips fell, I would tell him exactly what I had found. So it was from that point, Dr. Elliot, that I commenced my investigation into the MacDonald homicides.

JEFFREY ELLIOT: How did you launch the investigation? How did it take shape? How did you go about cultivating witnesses, questioning them, and generating information which would either prove or disprove—

RAYMOND SHEDLICK: [Interrupting.] The first thing I had to do was to gain legal status here in North Carolina, and that meant that I had to become a licensed private investigator. So I applied for my private investigator's license and secured that in March of 1983. I then proceeded to read every single document I could get pertaining to the MacDonald case. The documents were interesting, but I needed witnesses to come forward. So I ran an ad in the Fayetteville paper, advertising the fact that we were conducting an independent investigation of the homicide of the MacDonald family, and it wasn't very long after that I began to receive telephone calls. Some of them, of course, were crazy calls, and some of them were meaty calls. I had to screen out which ones were apparently from people who were obviously deranged from those that might have had decent information.

JEFFREY MACDONALD

a candid conversation with the imprisoned "fatal vision" doctor convicted of murdering his wife and two children—who still maintains his innocence

At approximately four A.M. on February 17, 1970, Military Police were summoned to the Fort Bragg, North Carolina, residence of Dr. Jeffrey R. MacDonald, a physician and captain in the Army Medical Corps, where they discovered Dr. MacDonald's pregnant wife, Colette, and two children, Kimberly, five, and Kristen, two, clubbed and stabbed to death. MacDonald was lying partially across his wife's body in the master bedroom. The bodies of Kimberly and Kristen were found in their bedrooms. MacDonald, who apparently sustained a number of stab wounds—one of which resulted in a partially collapsed lung—was rushed to Womack Army Community Hospital, where he was treated and released. So began one of the most bizarre and celebrated murder cases in recent history—best known through Joe McGinniss' best-selling book "Fatal Vision" and NBC's two-part docudrama based on the book, but endlessly debated by virtually everyone who has heard of it.

What occurred next depends upon whose version of the crime you choose to believe: MacDonald's or the Government's. MacDonald's version is as follows: Upon retiring for the night—at approximately 2:30 A.M.—he discovered that his younger daughter, Kristen, had crawled into bed with his wife

and had wet his side of the bed. He picked Kristen up, returned her to her bedroom and went into the living room, where he lay down on the sofa and fell asleep. Shortly thereafter, he was awakened by the screams of his wife and elder daughter, Kimberly. He saw a woman—who he later alleged was a local resident named Helena Stoeckley—with blonde hair, a floppy hat, boots, a short skirt, carrying a flickering light or candle and chanting, "Acid is groovy, kill the pigs." He saw three other people, two white men and a black man, and described the black man as stocky and wearing an Army jacket with sergeant's stripes; one of the white men, he said, wore a cross on a chain around his neck.

According to MacDonald, the three men—who were standing near the couch—proceeded to attack him, pulling or tearing off his pajama top, which he then used to ward off their blows. The three assailants continued to club and stab him until he lost consciousness. When he awoke, he walked to the master bedroom, where he found his wife dead. He pulled a knife out of her body, attempted to give her mouth-to-mouth resuscitation and covered her with his pajama top and a bath mat. He then went to his children's rooms, where he unsuccessfully attempted to revive them. Finally, he went to the bathroom, where

he washed; then he telephoned the Military Police. At that point, he lost consciousness.

The Government's version—and that of McGinniss—is that MacDonald himself murdered his wife and two children and then staged the crime scene to cover up the murders.

After the murders, the Army's Criminal Investigation Division (CID), the Federal Bureau of Investigation and the Fayetteville, North Carolina, Police Department immediately began searching for the four assailants whom MacDonald had described. But examining the crime scene, the investigators discovered evidence that caused them to question MacDonald's story. The Government contends that, although MacDonald stated that his pajama top had been torn during his struggle with the assailants in the living room, no fibers from its fabric were discovered in that room. However, fibers were found both inside and outside the body outline of Colette in the master bedroom, as well as in the bedrooms of Kimberly and Kristen. In addition, a small particle from a rubber surgeon's glove—which was stained with Colette's blood—was discovered inside a sheet in a pile of bedding near the doorway that led to the hall. Ultimately, without forensic evidence to support MacDonald's explanation of

"Fifteen years is a long time. I experienced the mass tragedy of losing my family; then I was charged with the murders; then I was victimized by 'Fatal Vision.' It seems as if I've been fighting for my freedom forever."

"When I entered the master bedroom, I saw Colette. There was blood everywhere. I remember kneeling down on my hands and knees and attempting to give her mouth-to-mouth resuscitation. Air was bubbling out of her chest."

PHOTOGRAPHY BY DAVID CHAN

"Yes, I did find it difficult to express emotion in my 20s. I'm one of those men who created the need for an Alan Alda. But that doesn't mean I'm pathological. It simply means that I'm fairly typical of many men."

61

The phone calls started coming in. The "meaty" with the "crazy." The "obviously deranged" mixed in with significant leads. As part of his arsenal of techniques, Shedlick had assembled twenty-five photographs.

RAYMOND SHEDLICK: There were twenty-five [photographs]. Among the photographs were pictures of Shelby Don Harris, Helena Stoeckley, and the rest of the group that we identified . . . Aside from that there were lookalike pictures. There were only five alleged perpetrators, and there were twenty lookalikes.

Shedlick recalled giving the photo group to Edith Boushey, a professor of English at North Carolina State University's Extension Program, who told him that she had seen a group of people matching the description of the killers approach Colette MacDonald after her class on February 16.

The names go on and on, like a prison roll call: Sherriedale Morgan, Rev. Kenneth Edwards, Frankie Bushey, Joan Green Sonderson, Marion Campbell. Carlos Torres, a retired army sergeant who was working as a bouncer at the NCO club the night of the murders. You can hear Elliot's offscreen prompt:

JEFFREY ELLIOT: Let's turn to Carlos Torres.
RAYMOND SHEDLICK: Carlos Torres was a retired army sergeant. On February the seventeenth, 1970, between the hours of two and three o'clock in the morning, he was on his way home to Spring Lake. In order to get to Spring Lake, he had to go along Honeycutt Boulevard [sic]. And Honeycutt would bisect with Bragg Boulevard. He made a left turn at Bragg Boulevard. Dr. MacDonald's house—we calculated by footage—is probably about 150 to 250 yards from the intersection of Honeycutt and Bragg Boulevard . . . So Mr. Torres said that he came to the traffic light at Honeycutt and Bragg Boulevard, and he stopped. And as he stopped, his attention was drawn to the left of him. When the light changed and he made the left turn, he saw three people run from what is considered the grassy knoll of that area. Two of the people he saw were military types and one was a hippie type. They came into vivid sight, by the light inside the van.

The grassy knoll? Which unsolved mystery is this?

Once again Elliot's offscreen voice and the name "Dorothy Averitt."

Dorothy Averitt was delivering the *Fayetteville Observer* early the morning of February 17. She had seen Stoeckley days before the murders, and then a second time early in the morning after the homicide. The second time, the girl who she identified as Stoeckley was covered in blood.

> **RAYMOND SHEDLICK:** She had been given a lead for a person who wanted to sub-
> scribe to the paper. It was in a trailer camp—the identical trailer camp that we
> have identified as the one Helena Stoeckley used to hang around in . . . When she
> arrived, she saw people [that were] drugged out. Men and women. Some people
> were vomiting. And she saw Helena Stoeckley. Because that was the name on
> the lead card: Helena Stoeckley. She went up, and she talked to her for a few
> moments, and she got back in the car, and she thought to herself that she would
> never deliver a newspaper here, because she'd never get paid.

Then, on the morning of February 17, around 6:00 a.m., Averitt had driven to a convenience store. Mrs. Johnson's Grocery Store, a few miles from where, and a couple of hours after, Mica had seen the woman with the wide-brimmed hat standing in the light rain.

> **RAYMOND SHEDLICK:** As she came close to the convenience store, she noticed a car
> parked. Two white men were sitting in the backseat slumped. She parked the
> car and she went into the convenience store. She noticed the girl whom she had
> talked to the week before [Helena Stoeckley] inside the convenience store. She
> said she looked like she was covered with blood . . . As she stopped to talk to her,
> and asked her what happened, there was a black male who was getting a soda
> out of the soda case. He saw Ms. Averitt talking to this girl, whom we identified
> as Helena Stoeckley. He hurriedly put the soda back into the case and grabbed
> this girl by the arm, and said, "Let's go," and went outside. Shown the photo-
> graphs, she identified her as Helena Stoeckley. And in fact, she said she knew it
> was Helena Stoeckley because she had had business with her the week before.

Shedlick takes a cigarette and inhales deeply.

And then, a sudden cut. The time stamp jumps an hour or so. The greenish cast in the video is gone; it's replaced with a bluish cast. Shedlick is back, smoking a cigarette and waiting. The video carries on: Elliot provides a name, Shedlick tells the story, and finally confirms whether the person named picked any of the suspects out of a group of photographs.

Stoeckley herself was already dead by the time Shedlick got involved in the case, but he spoke to her former husband, Ernest Davis.

Helena said she believed she was at the MacDonald house the night of the killings. "She wanted to speak to other people involved. Helena began to drink a lot. She became upset and angry and would get very violent at times. It seemed like at night she would actually relive that night because she would lie in bed and say 'It's my baby.' She would get up and she would wash her hands, and be half-asleep getting her hands clean. She told me she went to Dunkin' Donuts and washed her hands. They had blood on them . . ."

At times, Ernest recalls, Helena would come up with things that made you believe she was at the MacDonald house. "One day we were walking and there was a rocking horse sitting on the side of the road. She grabbed my hand and started crying. 'Look at the spring.' She said that the spring on the kids' rocking horse was broken in the MacDonald house. Another time she said there was supposed to be a fence around the back of one of the houses and a dog was inside. She told me she hated jewelry boxes because someone went into the MacDonald jewelry box and got some stuff out . . .

Ernest said Helena told him she went into the bedroom to keep the kids quiet. She came out and MacDonald was already stabbed and his wife was screaming and then she began to trip out. She said the next thing she remembered was standing there with a candle. She said everybody was scared. They dropped the weapons and left with the exception of a pair of scissors.[2]

In his video interview with Elliot, Shedlick described his conversation with Earnest Davis:

RAYMOND SHEDLICK: I asked him, finally, why do you believe that Dr. MacDonald is innocent, and why do you believe that your wife—your former wife, she was dead by then—was there. And his parting words were, to me, "I never pressed her. I never asked her for anything. Whenever she wanted to talk or tell me something, I listened." That's Ernie Davis.

Then Shedlick stops abruptly, on tape, and waits for Dr. Elliot to feed him the next name.

One by one. A legion of people, their statements committed (mostly) to memory. Addie Willis Johnstone, an older woman, who saw a group matching MacDonald's description wandering around Fayetteville soon after the murders. Marion Campbell and Frankie Bushey—who had seen Helena Stoeckley, Greg Mitchell, and a black man at Dunkin' Donuts early the morning after the murders. Campbell watched until the group took off in the direction of Fort Bragg.

IN BRIGHT RED

One more confession—this time, not Stoeckley. Her ex-boyfriend Greg Mitchell.

In 1971, Ann Cannady had been a volunteer at the Manor House, a Christian halfway house in the Haymount neighborhood of Fayetteville. She reported meeting a young man who went by the name Dave—a blond man, about five feet eight. The story was corroborated by two other volunteers: Juanita Sisneros and the Reverend Randy Phillips. Shedlick had all three statements read to a court stenographer and prepared a transcript. He told Jeffrey Elliot that story:

> **RAYMOND SHEDLICK:** I interviewed first of all Ann Sutton Cannady . . . In 1971, she was involved with what she called the Manor House. Now, the Manor House was sort of a halfway house in Fayetteville, in the downtown district, where if you were a drug addict, and you didn't have a house to go to, they would take you in. If you drank too much and you were homeless, the Manor House would take you in. Ann Sutton Cannady was involved in that ministry, and very interested in it; she's a born-again Christian.[1]

The story can be variously described, from Shedlick's tape and from a number of depositions.

She told me of an incident that occurred sometime in August of 1971. She stated that one day, a young man came into the Manor House . . . They washed his clothes, and they had him share a room that night with a licensed minister which was the Reverend—?

Elliot doesn't wait for Shedlick to come up with a name. He's on top of it.

JEFFREY ELLIOT: Randy Phillips.

RAYMOND SHEDLICK: Randy Phillips. Now on the Wednesday of that week, the whole group at the Manor House went out to the suburbs of Fayetteville in Cumberland County, to an old farm that they were refurbishing—for the Manor House—for the purpose of having a country retreat, so to speak. This young man went out there with them, and helped them work on the house. That Saturday night, they had a revival, a prayer meeting, where people were confessing to various crimes.

Shedlick provides an account, but Cannady had provided her own account of "Dave's story."

ANN CANNADY: And he was there. And when it came time that he asked for prayer— he asked us to pray for him—there were several men gathered around him, and they were praying for him. And he began to confess. He began to confess that he had murdered. He began to confess using drugs. He began to confess all these things that were inside him, and he became very emotional, asking God to forgive him for the things that he had done . . . It was as though he was just absolutely torn apart from everything right then. Because, I guess, you can just get so guilty, then you've got to do something about it.[2]

The next morning, "Dave" was gone, along with the clothes of the minister who shared his room. That evening, Ann Cannady, Reverend Randy Phillips, and another woman—Juanita Sisneros—went to check on the farmhouse. They told similar stories.

ANN CANNADY: There's a little road that wound down through the pines to get to the old house, and as we drove through the woods and got to the house, we had to turn our lights on because it was dark enough in the woods that we needed the lights from the car—you know, to see to get in there. And as we got there and drove into the circle where the big tree was, this young man ran out the back door and there was someone with him.

JUANITA SISNEROS: We took a ride out there, and as we got close to the farmhouse, I remember somebody running out of the house, and it was like dusk—it wasn't quite dark, but it wasn't light enough—and the police were called, and when they came in, we went in to see what was in there. I didn't see his face, but his figure, his form, the form of his body—he looked like a young boy that had been at the Manor earlier.[3]

ANN CANNADY: We had the key, unlocked the door, went into the house, and everything seemed okay—the living room—and I walked through the door into the bedroom beside the living room, and there on the wall, written across—the walls were painted an off-white, we had just finished that room on Saturday—were the words—and it was written in red and I don't know what he had used, what the person had used to write on the wall—but it was in bright red and it said, "I KILLED MACDONALD'S WIFE AND CHILDREN."

It was in four rows, but it wasn't written smoothly and evenly. It was written erratically across the wall, just slashed against the wall. And the red was sort of dripping down, and it just sent cold chills through my body.

JUANITA SISNEROS: And there, on one of the bedroom walls, was written in— it looked like blood, but it could have been paint. Anyway, when you write with a brush—there were the words, "I KILLED MACDONALD'S WIFE AND CHILDREN." To me, at the time, it didn't mean anything, because I didn't know who MacDonald was.

Shedlick asked each of the witnesses why he or she didn't come forward earlier. Juanita Sisneros said it wasn't that important to her. Ann Cannady expected that asking a sheriff's deputy to make note of the painted words was enough. The deputy told her he intended to photograph it the following day.

By the time Cannady and others returned to the farm days later, the wall had been painted over. The farm stayed open for a year and a half, until the Manor House—which had been struggling financially—was forced to sell it. The building did not last long.[4]

ANN CANNADY: It was a very fine house. It was a very sad thing that it was destroyed. And had it not been destroyed, we could go there and scrape that paint away now, and those words would be written on that wall.

I killed
Macdonald's
Wife and
children

Back to the video. Shedlick linked together the various statements. Each of the witnesses from the Manor House was shown the twenty-five photos and identified "Dave" as Greg Mitchell, Stoeckley's boyfriend.

RAYMOND SHEDLICK: Mrs. Cannady picked out Greg Mitchell as being the person who ran away from the Manor House, who confessed to the killing, and the one she saw running from behind the house in the country. I went and saw the Rev. Randy Phillips in Tennessee . . . He picked out Gregory Mitchell. I had Mrs. Sisneros come from Colorado to Raleigh. She remembered the full story as told to me by Mrs. Sutton Cannady . . . When I showed her some photographs, she picked out Gregory Mitchell.

So here we have a case of three independent witnesses, testifying on a sworn affidavit, that a subject who came into that house was in fact Gregory Mitchell, and the fellow who ran from the back of the house out in the country was Gregory Mitchell. And the writing on the wall was written by Gregory Mitchell.

I interviewed Gregory Mitchell's wife—she gave me a sworn statement. She stated that to her knowledge, Greg Mitchell was in rehabilitation in Fayetteville in 1971.

I tried to follow up on a couple of Shedlick's leads. When do you stop?

Cathy Perry had been investigated by the CID in 1970. According to a statement, later prepared by Peter Kearns:

[Betty Garcia, her landlady] described PERRY as Caucasian, brown hair, about 20 years old, a hippie and mentally unbalanced. GARCIA claimed that PERRY had been picked up by Fayetteville Police for an alleged stabbing of a male in the Spring of 70; that on 29 Dec 70, PERRY was again involved in a stabbing incident wherein she allegedly stabbed another male. On about 30 Dec 70, PERRY allegedly attempted to stab GARCIA's son and for this action she made PERRY leave her residence. GARCIA claimed that PERRY's relatives allegedly had her placed in a mental institution in Raleigh, NC, on that date.[5]

One male was stabbed some time in the spring of 1970. Another male on December 29, 1970. And then a third, Mrs. Garcia's son, on December 30. She had also stabbed her pet dog to death some time in the winter of 1970 while under the influence of drugs. With the dog, that makes four. According to a police report, the dog was stabbed "until it was flat."

When Mrs. Garcia threw her out, she turned over a "a pair of woman's knee-high white boots, personal papers, and photographs" to a lawyer, who in turn gave them to the CID. Kearns writes:

> A review of the items . . . revealed that the white boots did not meet the description as furnished by Jeffrey MacDonald. No blood or debris of interest to this investigation was located on the boots. Hair from the brush was removed and it was sent to the USACID Laboratory for comparison with those hairs found in the hands of Colette MACDONALD and this examination proved the hairs to be dissimilar.

And then Jackie Don Wolverton contacted the defense during the 1979 trial. A July 21 defense memo tells one more strange story:

> This morning a Mr. Jackie Don Wolverton called the Fraternity House. He said he wanted to talk to someone about the girl who allegedly was one of the intruders on 2/17/70 involved in the MacDonald murders.
>
> He told me there was a woman who had been living in a commune type lifestyle in Fayetteville. For some reason she asked Wolverton if she could live with him. He said it was okay. One night the woman, whose name is Cathy Perry, attempted to kill him. (All of these events are subsequent to the 2/17/70 crime.) When this happened, he said he went and got himself sewed up at the military hospital, that he had the girl admitted for mental evaluations and that when he went through her belongings he found the following: a blond wig, a pair of white go-go boots (dirty) and an address book with Jeff MacDonald's name and address in it.[6]

The statement included Wolverton's conjecture that "the group of people that did this probably were out to get people in the Special Forces."

Perry had denied any involvement in the murders to the CID when she was questioned in 1972. But the day before the airing of the *Fatal Vision* TV miniseries—November 17, 1984—she called the FBI and gave a detailed confession. She recalled that she had been picked up by a crowd of strangers on the night of the murders and that they had forced her to go with them to 544 Castle Drive, and that there they had entered into the MacDonald house. Mayhem ensued.

> [PERRY] advised that during all of this commotion the mother woke up once but then went back to sleep. [PERRY] said that she woke her up again and tried to get the woman to jump out the window with her. She said she also asked the woman for a gun because she said that the other people were going to kill them. She described the woman as being skinny and possibly being pregnant. A little while later, the dark-skinned, dark-complected male ordered CATHY to tie the woman up and to kill her. She said that she stabbed the woman several times in the leg and several times in the abdomen. After murdering the woman she wrote in blood on the wall, "Fuck you pigs from all of us to you."

Her details were confused, often wrong. Murdered sons, not daughters. (Not so surprising given her history of male stabbings.) She claimed to have written a sentence in the MacDonald bedroom, but there was only one word on the headboard. All reported fourteen years after the fact.

And in 2006, she died.

There was also Dwight Smith.

At first, I couldn't understand why Dwight Smith hadn't been discussed on Shedlick's tape—since he was one of the people mentioned repeatedly by Stoeckley. But when I called Smith, it was clear he didn't want to be interviewed. He told me "I'm not giving any statements. That's history, and I'll leave it alone." Stoeckley had implicated a good number of people but claimed that she wouldn't say who was *really* involved until after she was given immunity.

There is an important fact about detective work—often unacknowledged: the need for triage. You can't investigate everything. You make an assessment about what will pan out and what won't. Here, my call to Dwight Smith ended up as due diligence, not much more.

Unlike Dwight Smith, Shelby Don Harris *was* mentioned on the tape. Shedlick contacted the Harris family—Don, Jeanette, and two young children—and brought them to Raleigh from their home in Tennessee to discuss the case in the 1980s. Back to the video:

RAYMOND SHEDLICK: I had two sessions with Shelby Don Harris, one lasting maybe six hours. When he first came into my office, he denied any knowledge of Helena Stoeckley, Greg Mitchell, or anybody. As we progressed in questioning, he admitted he knew Helena Stoeckley. He eventually said he knew Greg Mitchell. Little by little he began to tell me things . . . He was very nervous. He excused himself no more than about 100 times to go to the men's room. When I asked him what was wrong, he said he was quite nervous. And so I put it straight to him—I told him what I had read about him, and what I thought about him. He denied it . . .

He told me at the time of the MacDonald homicides he was AWOL, and he was hiding out because he was involved in drugs. After he had told me that, he became extremely excited. I tried to allay his fears so we could continue talking, but he wouldn't go any further . . . At the conclusion of the interview, he said to me, "If I had a million dollars, I would tell you the whole story." Harris ran off, flew out of Raleigh, and went back to Tennessee.

Harris died in 2008. I contacted his widow, Jeanette Harris, through Facebook.

I would gladly tell you about the conversation between Mr. Shedlick and Don, but I was not "in" the meeting. I can tell you what I know from what he shared with me. He made it a point not to know anything [more] about the MacDonald murders than he had already heard. He was given a copy of the *Fatal Vision* book by someone, I'm not sure who, but they suggested he read it. He refused, insisting the less he knew, the better. (He did eventually read the book and felt nothing pointed to him. Not even Helena's "fabrications.")

Don Harris was a man of honor. He was a Special Forces combat soldier—a soldier's soldier. He was not a man that would ever harm a woman or a child. As for Capt. MacDonald, my understanding from Don was that he never met the man.

Best Regards,

Jeanette Harris

One more inconclusive lead.

The tape goes on and on. Five hours. Shedlick was obsessive, determined, and decent. A detective not motivated by pecuniary interest, but rather by a desire to find things out. To determine the answers to the most difficult question: what is true and what is false? What really happened? The sadness of it, the futility of it, is that at the time of these investigations, the courts had already lost interest. The judges were looking for reasons to ignore the Stoeckley material, not to revisit it.

Shedlick continued his investigations until he died of lung cancer in 1989.

It is a quixotic story, and a moving one. Ellen Dannelly kindly sent a copy of her father's letter for the parole board on MacDonald's behalf. The letter is dated December 29, 1988. It was delivered to the parole board after he died. This is the concluding paragraph:

I respectfully ask that you show compassion and mercy in reviewing this case when Dr. MacDonald comes before you for parole consideration in 1991. I strongly urge his release at the earliest possible time. My investigation clearly points to his innocence and confirms his basic integrity as a caring, compassionate human being. He is not a threat to society; to the contrary, his entire career has been one of extraordinary compassion in his chosen field of emergency medicine. Anyone who has evaluated his past has concluded he is a positive force in our society, not a negative one.

Respectfully,

Raymond R. Shedlick, Sr.

THE ALMOST INESCAPABLE CONCLUSION

And that would be the end of it. Or the beginning.

The writing on the wall might have been gone. But Greg Mitchell felt the need to carry on confessing. In 1984, as MacDonald's defense attorneys were preparing yet another appeal, Norma Lane—a friend of Mitchell—called the FBI. They didn't return the call. Then she called Brian O'Neill, and he called Ray Shedlick. Lane's husband, Bryant, told Shedlick the story:

> In 1982, before Greg Mitchell entered the hospital where he died in June 1982, Greg called me by telephone and told me he wanted to speak with me about something. He said he did not want to talk on the telephone, however, as he believed his phone might be tapped. I agreed to meet with Greg and we did meet, and when we met he was very pale and visibly upset . . .
>
> I began the meeting by asking Greg what the trouble was, and he told me, "It's something that happened back when I was in the service. If they find out about it I'm going to have to leave the country and live in Haiti or something." Greg did not tell me anything specific about what happened . . . He told my wife that he was guilty of a crime that happened a long time ago at Ft. Bragg and that he was concerned about being prosecuted.[1]

Norma added:

When I read the news story in the *Charlotte Observer* about the Ft. Bragg
murders, in which Greg Mitchell's name was mentioned, I realized that what Greg
had told my husband and me was that he had taken part in the murders.
I contacted Dr. Jeffrey MacDonald's lawyers at that time.[2]

Lane's story supported the story Mitchell's widow had told Shedlick on March 28,
1983:

Two weeks before Greg died he was visited by the FBI agent George Battles [*sic*].
He became very worried and started to sleep with a gun by him.[3]

When it became clear that the Lanes' statements were going to be used by the
defense, then the FBI got involved. On May 23, special agents Brendan Battle
(from the Charlotte office) and Raymond "Butch" Madden (from Raleigh) came to
Charlotte to take a statement.

MacDonald's attorneys made a motion for a new trial in 1984, based on all
the new evidence substantiating the Stoeckley claim and introducing the parallel
claims of Greg Mitchell and Cathy Perry Williams. Again it fell to Judge Dupree to
determine MacDonald's fate. He reviewed the statements taken by the FBI. None
of them changed his mind.

Dupree wrote in closing:

Helena Stoeckley, Cathy Perry Williams and, to a more limited extent, Greg
Mitchell were drawn to the case and have contributed to a factual charade which
has allowed it to continue for more than a decade and a half. Their "confessions"
have been shown to be unbelievable and, even with the affidavits offered to corroborate the statements, if the government were again called upon to present its
evidence at a new trial and MacDonald was able to put all, or even selected parts
of his new evidence before a second jury, the jury would again reach the almost
inescapable conclusion that he was responsible for these horrible crimes.

I am not so sure.

Five years passed. In 1989, Norma Lane saw her statement for the first time.
(The FBI had taken her statement, but apparently Mrs. Lane was not asked to verify or sign it.) She felt compelled to correct it.

... I find the following inaccuracies and misrepresentations in Mr. Madden's affidavit regarding Greg Mitchell's admissions to me:

In section 30 of Mr. Madden's affidavit he writes: "... she concluded that Mitchell had been involved in the murders and noted that this was purely an assumption on her part." This is not true. I did not say this. I read about the murders, learned that Greg Mitchell had been implicated, and I remembered that he told me that he had done something horrible at Fort Bragg for which the FBI was after him. Mr. Madden's word "assumption" is his word, not mine.

The general content and tone of Mr. Madden's affidavit ... seems designed to discount and discredit what I actually told him.[4]

In Shedlick's statement from April 1984, Bryant and Norma Lane come across as concerned friends of a guilty man. In the FBI statements—made less than a month later—Norma Lane is a confused attention-seeker with nothing to say. And so, once again the intruders disappear.

———

One really bad ruling deserves another. MacDonald's attorney, Brian O'Neill, filed a motion insisting that Dupree should have recused himself, because James Proctor, his former son-in-law, had been heavily involved in pursuing MacDonald after the Article 32. The request was denied. Dupree gave his reasons.

The indictment was not returned until almost four years after Jimmie Proctor left the United States Attorney's Office and over two and one half years after he had ceased to be my son-in-law. Moreover, the reinvestigation of the case had nothing to do with Proctor's activities. Proctor personally believed that MacDonald had committed the crimes, but any statement he may have made expressing this personal conviction appears to have fallen upon deaf ears . . .[5]

Proctor, so secure in his rectitude, felt that it was time to give an interview to his hometown newspaper, *The Fuquay-Varina Independent*. The article appeared on November 28, 1984. Here's an excerpt from the article:

Proctor was deeply involved in the investigation of the MacDonald case from the beginning. As assistant attorney in the eastern division of North Carolina and chief of the criminal division, he personally supervised the Fayetteville division. . . .

Proctor talked to Helena Stoeckley, once considered a possible suspect. He had her take a polygraph test, which she passed successfully.[6]

Stoeckley was given a "polygraph test, which she passed successfully." But it was a polygraph test in which she admitted to being in the MacDonald house that night. In Brisentine's phrase, Stoeckley was "convinced in her mind" that she was there.

The article continues:

He said the investigators were also satisfied that she had a credible alibi. They talked to people who knew where she was that night. (MacDonald had said the murders were committed by a band of hippies and Ms. Stoeckley was questioned because of her hippy lifestyle.)

Stoeckley was questioned because she answered to the description given by Mac-Donald and Ken Mica, and she subsequently confessed to being in the house that night. Many times. She had no alibi for that night. But the best part of the article is Proctor's claim: that MacDonald not only staged the crime but the Article 32 hearing, as well.

Proctor said the defense attorneys did a superb job of public relations, of staging scenes, as one intended to indicate MacDonald was being mistreated by MPs, and then calling the press. "They were saying the tall, short, skinny, fat guy did it," Proctor said. And they apparently had the public taking it all in for a long time . . .

O'Neill filed another motion for recusal. Hadn't Proctor just publicly claimed that he had been involved in the case from the very beginning? It, too, was denied.

BOOK FIVE

1979 ◾️ **July 13**
Joe McGinniss is retained as a member of the defense team.

August 3
Jeffrey MacDonald gives away the rights to his story to Joe McGinniss and agrees not to claim defamation "provided that the essential integrity of my life is maintained."

August 30
Jeffrey MacDonald sends his first letter to Joe McGinniss from prison: "I've got to write you so I won't go crazy."

September 11
McGinniss writes to MacDonald: "Total strangers can recognize within five minutes that you did not receive a fair trial."

September 28
McGinniss to MacDonald: "What the fuck were those people thinking of? How could twelve people not only agree to believe such a horrendous proposition, but to agree, with a man's life at stake, that they believed it beyond a reasonable doubt?"

December 18
McGinniss to MacDonald: "Someone, without a specialty in any particular criminological area, but with major-league scientific qualifications might be able to review the physical evidence and come up with so many flaws in methodology and deduction as to invalidate any conviction based upon such material."

1980 ◾️ **January 16**
MacDonald begins recording tapes about his life for McGinniss's book.

February 15
McGinniss writes to the Kassabs: "I have been told, Mr. Kassab, that you have said you will not speak to me because you will do nothing that would help put one more dime in the pocket of the man who murdered your wife's daughter, your stepdaughter, and your grandchildren. . . . It is impossible for me to project myself into your place, but I do sense that my own feelings in that regard might be extremely similar to yours."

July 29
The Fourth Circuit Court of Appeals overturns MacDonald's conviction on speedy-trial grounds.

August 22
MacDonald is released from prison.

October 12
McGinniss gives an interview to the *San Francisco Chronicle*. Asked if MacDonald is guilty: "I can't talk about what I think. At the end of the book, the reader can draw a reasonable conclusion. . . . This is so sad and horrible, and I'll be so glad when it's over. . . . I didn't realize I would become so emotionally involved."

1981 ■ March 3
McGinniss writes his agent, Sterling Lord: "The irony of all this is that so far MacDonald has not even seen the book and still has no idea how mad he's really going to be. But the more he hears ahead of time about how mad he should be, the more time he has to work on his strategy to discredit me and my findings."

1982 ■ March 31
The Supreme Court rules 6–3 that MacDonald's right to a speedy trial was not violated. He is returned to prison.

August 6
McGinniss to MacDonald: "By all means, hype the book and (advice from Putnam's) be sure, in any conversations about it, to get across that while you have cooperated fully, this is not an 'authorized' (hence, less believable) version of events. . . ."

1983 ■ June 1
Mike Wallace and the *60 Minutes* crew interview Jeffrey MacDonald at FCI Bastrop.

September 16
Fatal Vision is published by Putnam.

September 18
The *60 Minutes* story on *Fatal Vision* airs.

1984 ■ August 31
MacDonald sues McGinniss for fraud and breach of contract.

November 18–19
The TV movie adaptation of *Fatal Vision* airs.

1987 ■ July 7
MacDonald v. McGinniss begins in Los Angeles under Judge William Rea.

August 21
MacDonald v. McGinniss results in a mistrial.

November 23
MacDonald and McGinniss settle out of court. MacDonald receives $325,000, much of which goes to pay legal fees.

December 1
Alfred and Mildred Kassab file a civil suit against MacDonald.

COPS WHO CAME IN FROM THE COLD

On August 30, 1979, the day after being sentenced to serve three consecutive life sentences in prison, MacDonald began a four-year correspondence with Joe McGinniss. It culminated in the book *Fatal Vision* (published on September 16, 1983), the adapted miniseries (which was broadcast on November 18 and 19, 1984), in a civil suit MacDonald filed against McGinniss for fraud on August 31, 1984, and ultimately in a second civil suit filed by Freddy and Mildred Kassab against MacDonald to recover any of the money that had been paid to MacDonald by McGinniss.[1]

This correspondence is famous. Or infamous, depending on how you look at it. It ended up serving as the centerpiece of a two-part article by Janet Malcolm that appeared in the *New Yorker* in 1989 and was later published in a book of the same title: *The Journalist and the Murderer*. It was used by her as proof of the depravity of all journalism. Malcolm wrote, "Every journalist who is not too stupid or too full of himself to notice what is going on knows that what he does is morally indefensible."[2]

Malcolm writes that the early letters between the two men, "like the overture to an opera, announce all the themes of the coming correspondence":[3]

[McGinniss] wrote letters assuring MacDonald of his friendship, commiserating with him about his situation, offering him advice about his appeal, requesting information for the book, and fretting about competing writers. The passages dealing with this last concern—a very common one among writers (every writer thinks someone else is working on his subject; it is part of the paranoid state of mind necessary for the completion of the infinitely postponable task of writing)— make especially painful reading.

The letters—excerpts of which are provided below—provide a mystery of their own. Assuming that McGinniss believed that MacDonald was innocent when he first became involved, at what point did he come to believe MacDonald was guilty? Was it during the trial? Was it after MacDonald was freed in August 1980 following his successful appeal to the Fourth Circuit? Or was it after MacDonald was returned to prison on March 31, 1982, when the Supreme Court reversed that decision? And what provoked this change of heart? A new appraisal of the evidence? Or the exigencies of delivering a manuscript?

———

MacDonald's first letter to McGinniss following his conviction:

Zero hour + 18

I've got to write to you so I won't go crazy. I am standing in my cell only because they don't allow chairs in solitary. I'm trying to fathom—trying to figure out what the fuck happened? Those words from [the foreman] Mr. Hardison's mouth crashed into my brain & I can't think straight.[4] I heard "not guilty" to 1st degree and instantly felt "Finally—justice and maybe some peace down the road"—in the next instant he said "guilty" of 2nd degree murder. The room was spinning and I couldn't hear the rest. I remember the tears on many jurors' faces, and I remember the look of "Please forgive me" on the face of the black juror & the lady who cried so much—but I really can't remember the jury polling except how forceful the guy with the pinched face in the front row (3 in from the left, I think) said "guilty" 3 times. He *really* believed it. I can't understand how it happened— twelve normal people heard a good portion of the "evidence" (not all of course) and bought the gov't line of bullshit? Was it just? Because the gov't said so? Were our jury selection people wrong?? I guess so—they were so right wing, middle class they couldn't believe the gov't would falsify evidence, or fake it, or redo it, or build an imaginary web of circumstances based on vicious Mildred Kassab now remembering "something was going wrong in that house" . . .

I want to see Bernie [MacDonald's attorney] because I love him + he is
probably hurting beyond belief + want to know he is not to blame. I want to see
my mom because no matter how I look, by seeing me she will be better (and
I probably will be too). I would also love to see my best friends like Dudley +
Steve and now (I hope) you. But in all honesty I'm crying too much today and do
cry whenever I think of my close friends. I feel dirty + soiled by the decision +
can't tell you why and am ashamed. I somehow don't feel that way with Bernie
+ Mom but think today it would be difficult to look at you or shake your hand—I
know I'll cry and want to hug you and yet the verdict stands there, screaming,
"You are guilty of the murder of your family!!" And I don't know what to say to
you except it is not true, and I hope you know that, and feel it, and that you are
my friend.[5]

———————

In McGinniss's first letter to MacDonald in prison McGinniss is MacDonald's
somewhat unctuous champion. "Total strangers can recognize within five minutes
that you did not receive a fair trial."

September 11, 1979

Every morning for a week now, I've been waking up wondering where you
are. A bus! Christ! It seems that the only function a ride across country in a prison
bus might serve is to make your final destination seem not quite as awful as it
otherwise would have. On the other hand, I'm sure your destination seems awful.
Is awful. Terminal Island. Pretty terrible name, on top of everything else . . .

Did not see any point in writing back until now because I suspected they did not
deliver mail to the bus. I am awfully glad you have written so much though. Both for
personal and professional reasons—and it's getting pretty hard to tell the two apart.
I am glad to see that you are able to write—to describe and analyze both what happened to you and your own feelings about it. I have plenty of my own thoughts, which
I'll be getting to sooner or later, but honestly I am relieved to see that you are apparently able to function constructively despite the extreme limitations. Also, I'm glad
you didn't kill yourself because that sure would have been a bummer for the book.

. . . There could not be a worse nightmare than the one you are living through
now—but it is only a phase. Total strangers can recognize within five minutes that
you did not receive a fair trial.

. . . It's a hell of a thing—spend the summer making a new friend and then the bastards come along and lock him up. But not for long, Jeffrey—not for long.

More soon—

Joe[6]

In his next letter to MacDonald, McGinnis reiterates his belief in MacDonald's innocence—criticizing the jury and suggesting that their book will vindicate MacDonald in the end:

September 28, 1979

What the fuck were those people thinking of? How could 12 people not only agree to believe such a horrendous proposition, but agree, with a man's life at stake, that they believed it beyond a reasonable doubt? In six and a half hours?!!

. . . It's a damned good thing I'm writing a book: otherwise I don't know how I would cope with all these reactions . . .[7]

Many of the letters that follow reiterate McGinniss's belief in MacDonald's innocence—but there is something new. There is talk that Freddy Kassab will write a book. If McGinniss's book is the pro-MacDonald book, Kassab's book will be the anti-MacDonald book. And, indeed, as it turns out, there are multiple books in the works.

What to do with his own book? McGinniss could write a piece of advocacy and defend MacDonald against the depredations of the justice system. Or accept the results of the trial and tell the story of the killer who nearly got away. Two possible approaches: investigation into an open case or the history of a closed one. "He shouldn't be in jail" versus "why he's in jail."

A long letter from December 18, 1979. (I call it the Boyd Norton letter because of the reference to the scientist friend of McGinniss's.) A laundry list of points—from the threat posed by a possible Freddy Kassab book to the nature of the pajama top demonstration. But what is going on here? Is McGinniss showing MacDonald that he still believes in his innocence, that he is truly appalled by the junk science presented in the courtroom? Or has he descended into a world of calculation and manipulation? There are two points. "The government's case is bogus" and "I need your help in preventing other books from appearing before ours":

December 18, 1979

Freddie Kassab has made it official. *The New York Times* book division—called *New York Times Books*—has given him a contract for a book about you and the murders and how he eventually brought you to trial.

I wonder whether, from your end, it might not be a good idea to have Bernie send some sort of letter to *New York Times Books*, and/or to the writer, reminding them of the extent to which libel and invasion of privacy laws might apply in this situation . . .

Boyd Norton, wilderness photographer and former nuclear physicist, was staying with us last week. Boyd points out that if one's wrists are entangled in a garment and one is being attacked, the only natural defensive motion would be not lateral, but directly <u>toward</u> the attacker. In other words, your forearms would be vertical, not horizontal, and you would be pushing toward the ice pick, thus causing contact to be perpendicular, and permitting the holes to be cylindrical, as they were, rather than elongated tears. At the very least, Boyd is astonished that the defense did not perform such a demonstration to counter the government's, but even more astonished that such hocus pocus could be admitted as evidence in court . . .

In general, Norton makes the point that most criminologists are phony scientists. Cops who got tired of standing in the rain. Or: cops who came in from the cold. Why would a person with any genuine scientific gift work in police or Army labs at those wages, doing that drudge work, when there are so many options available . . . ?

Boyd himself says he would fly to San Francisco and go over all that is available—not the actual pajama top, etc., but all reports on procedures, and conclusions—and he would do it simply for expenses, no fee involved, because he thinks you got screwed by lousy, lazy pseudo-science and, as a true scientist, he is angered and offended by that.[8]

McGinniss concludes with a reference to Gunderson's investigations:

Of course, by now maybe Gunderson has signed confessions and all of this [namely, the consideration of physical evidence] is academic, but somehow I doubt it. And possibly with the brief already written, it is too late . . .

Joe,

I've got to write to you so I won't go crazy. I am standing in my cell only because they don't allow chairs in Solitary. I'm trying to fathom — trying to figure out what the fuck happened? Those words from Mr. Hardison's mouth crashed into my brain & I can't think straight. I heard "not guilty" to 1st degree & instantly felt "Finally — justice & maybe some peace down the road" — in the next instant he said "guilty" of 2nd degree murder. The room was spinning and I couldn't hear the rest. I remember the tears on many jurors faces, and I remember the look of "please, forgive me" on the faces of the black juror & the lady who cried so much — but I really can't remember the jury polling except how forceful the guy with the pinched face in the front row (3 in from the left I think) said "guilty" 3 times. He really believed it. I can't understand how it happened — 12 "normal" people heard a good portion of the "evidence" (not all of course) and bought

And then in a letter to MacDonald dated January 10, 1980, McGinniss asked for more help. The "take-the-lid-off" letter.

It is your life—your book, in that sense, at least—and I need you to take the lid off and climb down in there and accomplish the distasteful task of telling me about your life in minute detail and with as honest an attempt to communicate the emotional content as you can manage. We just can't keep putting it off.[9]

JUST BE JEFF

Somewhere around the start of 1980, a tape recorder had been smuggled into Jeffrey MacDonald's prison cell. In response to McGinniss's goading, MacDonald started speaking into it. It recorded an excursion into his own interior—days' and days' worth of recollections and thoughts.

By January 5, MacDonald began to speak into the recorder:

> I have sent 4 tapes so far. The first 2 stink, the 2nd 2 start to get more info. out, and I now feel I'll eventually get you good tapes. I hope to tape at least a tape every other day—more if you *need* it, but it is difficult. The process itself is difficult, the memories are either vague, or stark, or uncomfortable . . , although it *does* occasionally seem to be cathartic. I felt silly at first + still really haven't told you inside feelings in the tapes, but realize you saw the raw wounds, so I have to suck it up + plow ahead + get some info to you.[1]

The first tapes are, if anything, unexceptional—nothing jumps off the page and says, "I am a killer." An account of a routine childhood, acceptance at Princeton, marriage to Colette, birth of Kimberley, car trip to Chicago, and medical school at Northwestern. There are hundreds upon hundreds of pages of transcript.[2] But if the goal is to ferret out evidence of psychopathology, one would be disappointed. The themes include dreaming of a farm near the water, working around the clock at medical school, his father's death, and a what-if: What if he had been sent to

Vietnam right away, before February 17?

TAPE THREE: I was in Princeton and having a great time, and got married to Colette and we had Kim, and we were just living, we thought, a gravy life, but we watched the chaos beginning around us with a little bit of alarm. I was reasonably right-wing, not from the viewpoint of racial intolerance or anything like that, but I sort of believed what the President said and felt that if there was an undeclared war it was only because of some left-wing liberals in Congress that didn't have the sense to see what my father had seen and what other fathers saw and what all of us could see, that Vietnam needed defense and we were the ones who should be helping to defend it. It was a lot of turmoil, and it seemed like, you know, death and destruction around us. I might add that Colette and I never felt to be part of it, really. We were deeply in love and were having a good time, you know, trip-ping through life. When I say "tripping" I mean having a blast as far as life was concerned, working very hard but not really complaining, both of us thinking that down the road there are rewards. We envisioned and planned a good life together. The ultimate goal was a farm near the water, a great combination.

TAPE THREE: The freshman year of medical school, from nineteen—from September of 1964 until June of 1965, was a tough year. There's really no other way to describe it. In my usual optimistic fashion I look back on it as a good year, but I think if pressed on details, it was a tough year. Scholastically it was very hard; I had worked hard in Princeton, so I was prepared, I was not as ill-prepared as some of the other students coming in. But by the same token I wasn't quite as ready as some of the other students coming in, some of whom had only had two years of college, they were in special six-year programs from Northwestern; and some of the students thought nothing of studying around the clock. I started out studying extremely hard and learned that if I wanted to do as well in medi-cal school, or better in medical school, than I did in college I had to work even harder. And by the end of the year I also was working around the clock almost non-stop. It was definitely a year of trials.[3]

TAPE FOUR: I'm getting down near the end of this tape and I want to talk about two things: one was my father's death . . . I was a medical student and I myself recog-nized how sick he was when I was home just a few weeks earlier, and had been steeling myself for it. And Colette and I had talked at length about it. I remember sort of the world fell away, couldn't believe that my father actually could die. And tears started coming down my face and I went into the bedroom and sat down on the bed for a while, and Colette came in and tried to comfort me. Wasn't easy to do, I didn't give up those feelings very gracefully or easily. But we got things together, threw a suitcase together that afternoon; I called the school and told them what happened and we flew out, flew to New York right away.[4]

TAPE SEVEN: I met her in the eighth grade. We were in junior high school, on South Ocean Avenue in Patchogue. And I can still remember when I first met her—she was walking down the hallway with her best friend, June Besser . . . They were kind of inseparable. They had gone to Bay Avenue Elementary School together and were very inseparable all through elementary school and junior high school . . . I can still remember them—it was on the fifth floor, the highest floor of the Patchogue Junior High School, which I think was the fifth floor, and my homeroom was up there, and they had walked past my homeroom. And I remember seeing Colette and June, and Colette had turned around and looked at me and I looked back, and they just kept going. And I remember then for about a week I kept trying to find out who was the good-looking blonde who was always with the other blonde. Some people told me they were sisters and some people told me they weren't sisters. But they had their reputation of being kind of aloof . . .

I met her later, like, it was two or three weeks after I'd initially seen her in the hall and tried to figure out who she was. I can still remember as they walked past my homeroom, I was standing in the doorway, and she had this sort of very lovely appearance, quiet beauty, and a sort of vulnerable look . . . I met [her] later on again, like two weeks later, in passing, and eventually I found out what her full name was and where her homeroom was, and we met on and off in the hallways and I believe in one class. I finally had her in either a history or an English class. And we started talking and eventually I found out where she lived and I drove my bicycle over to her house one day and we met that way. Those were seemingly—in retrospect now—painful times: driving past her house on a bicycle until she noticed you and then she'd call you over and you'd go over and stand outside and talk in kind of a confused fashion, not trying to be forward or aggressive but trying to talk to her and get to meet her and know her better.[5]

TAPE ELEVEN: I was staying with my mom at that time; we went back out to the island, to her apartment. That was a very painful time; I wasn't talking about what had happened at Fort Bragg, and yet that was my only thought. It was totally obsessive, and little bits and pieces, and Kimmy's face would come into view and

Kristy running across the lawn would come into view, and Colette's incredible loving face; and little bits and pieces. The song that we always fell in love over each time was "The Summer Place" from the movie with, incredibly enough, Troy Donahue. It was either in the last part of eighth grade or the first part of ninth grade that we went to the Rialto Theatre and sat in the balcony and held hands and watched that movie; and I think we sat through it twice because we were so stunned by its beauty, and it was sort of always our movie—although it was an outrageously bad movie, I think—it was a beautiful thing to us in the ninth grade at that time, and we fell in love to that song. And that was always our song, and whenever we heard it, it was, you know, it was a tremendous reminiscence . . . I still to this day when I hear that song, get this big flood of sadness and nostalgia: and Colette and warm eyes and her blond hair and her warmth and me holding her in the theatre as a ninth-grader, and us making love for the first time, and me going up to Skidmore and seeing her on "Happy Pappy Weekend," and her coming down to Princeton and being a little frightened by it all.[6]

TAPE THIRTEEN: Goddamn, Joe, it's hard to talk to a stupid machine. There's no feedback, you know—there's no sense of the other person, there's no questions that take you off on a tangent: there's no interest. It's really hard to sit here and try to relate your love for a woman to a stupid box. And I'm now on tape thirteen—that's a lousy thirteen hours. And I think that I could have told you all that I've told you on these thirteen hours in a couple of hours: maybe not, but it would have been a hell of a lot more interesting and more anecdotal had we been together. But not in the visiting room at Terminal Island. That's the problem.[7]

TAPE SIXTEEN: But I remember when I got the discharge papers and went over to have my last physical, like on December 3rd or December 4th or the morning of December 5th, and finally got those papers in my hand, I thought to myself, Why would I stay here one more night? There's no reason to stay one more night, and I left. And I drove up north . . . I felt almost a feeling, not of exuberance, but there was a real relief to get off Fort Bragg. I had strange thoughts as I drove away from Fort Bragg . . . like, if the Army had sent me to Vietnam when I first got to the Green Beret status, after my first couple of training trips and when I came back from Puerto Rico and had my true Green Beret on . . . if they had sent me, that would have meant that Colette and the kids would have moved off-post and back up north, probably to the house next to my mom, and therefore they would be alive and I would have been unwounded and I would be in Vietnam or I would have come back home after a year with this year of experience under my belt and would have felt, you know, good about myself for having done that. So that was going through my mind.[8]

TAPE EIGHTEEN: Nothing could happen, by the way, Joe, you know, for months and months and months, as a matter of fact probably up to a year and a half later, nothing happened ever that did not somehow tie back into Colette, Kimberley, and Kristy; there's just nothing that happened. You couldn't hear the music on the radio, you couldn't hear a song; if it was an old song it's because I heard it with them; if it was a new song it's because they would have loved to have heard it; if it was a bad movie, Colette and I could have laughed over how bad it was, and we could have remembered back to the one movie we walked out of, and that was *Taras Bulba* with Yul Brynner.[9]

I find it hard not to like MacDonald in these accounts. Who among us has not enjoyed talking about movies we hate with someone we love?

More from tape eighteen:

TAPE EIGHTEEN: A lot of recriminations, self-recriminations about not having told Colette I loved her enough; Colette would have flourished and flowered even more than she did with, I think, a little more obvious love from me. She had plenty of love from me, but she didn't get a lot of verbal reassurances; I wasn't capable of it then. I'm not making excuses, I'm just saying I didn't give it.[10]

But what does all of this tell us about Jeffrey MacDonald? When reading great blocks of material—here, a binder of more than six hundred pages—one has a tendency to skim. To look for the juicy parts—the parts that suggest conflict, even an intimation of violence. But they're just not there.

If McGinniss was looking to find a monster lurking in the wings, he'd be keenly disappointed.

I CAN'T TALK ABOUT WHAT I THINK

A month after McGinniss asked MacDonald to "take the lid off," he wrote to Freddy Kassab. This letter, which was never part of Malcolm's book, is for me at the dark center of this story. McGinniss wants to assure Kassab that they share common goals. Rough translation: there is no reason for Kassab to be involved in a separate book. Their interests are no longer incompatible. Their interests might be the same.

> February 15, 1980
> Dear Mr. and Mrs. Kassab,
>   We have not met, but I believe you may have been aware of my presence . . .
> . . . I feel a deep and growing need to talk to you about the case, and would like to
> persuade you that seeing me would not be, for you and from your point of view,
> the distasteful experience it might seem . . .

McGinniss goes on to outline the two conditions that he had given to MacDonald, but in essence, he is providing a series of reassurances for Kassab.

> One was, for the duration of the trial and beyond, I would want guaranteed and
> total access to him, his lawyers, his files, his family, his friends, etc. I would,
> in other words, insist on being able to live with him throughout the trial . . .
>   My second major condition was that there be an agreement in writing
> whereby it was acknowledged that I was totally independent, and free to write

whatever sort of book I saw fit to, even if, and this would have to be specifically spelled out, the eventual conclusions I reached in regard to the case were not those which Jeffrey MacDonald would have wished me to reach. In other words— and the agreement was very precise in this regard—even if the jury were to find him innocent, and I were then to write a book suggesting, or stating, he was guilty, he would be unable to do anything about it . . .

I have been told, Mr. Kassab, that you have said you will not speak to me because you will do nothing that would help to put one more dime in the pocket of the man who murdered your wife's daughter, your stepdaughter, and your grandchildren. I would not attempt to persuade you that there is anything unreasonable about that position. It is impossible for me to project myself into your place, but I do sense that my own feelings in that regard might be extremely similar to yours.

McGinniss writes he is aware of Kassab's own plans for a book on the case. He tells Kassab that he has access to transcripts and "thousands of pages of other materials, ranging from personal letters to diaries to things that I probably should not even mention, because my awareness of their very existence may be privileged information."

And then McGinniss compares himself to Kassab. He, too, has visited 544 Castle Drive. He, too, has a little girl, called Christine, who "is the age Kristen would be now."

I have been at 544 Castle Drive, and the horror of what occurred there will remain with me, in some capacity, as long as I live. I have two daughters of my own, as well as two sons. My older daughter, whose name is Christine, is the age Kristen would be now. I am trying to say that this is no longer just a piece of work I have to do. It has already affected me more deeply than anything else I've ever been involved in, including Vietnam, and I feel a passionate commitment—to myself— to write the best, fullest, fairest, most accurate and truthful book possible.

In that regard, as I say, two main points: 1) I am uncomfortable having the major architect of the portrait of Colette be the man who has been convicted of murdering her. In writing a book in which her death is the central fact, I want the portrait of her in life to be drawn from those whose love for her, and knowledge of her, can never be called into question—yourselves. Secondly, I am well aware of the significance of the role you played, Mr. Kassab, in bringing about the prosecution and eventual conviction. Clearly, you are a central figure in the book—in any book—about this matter. Again, I'm uncomfortable having my major source of information about you and Mrs. Kassab be Jeffrey MacDonald. And I would deeply regret having to minimize your contribution simply because I was unable to gain sufficient information and detail about it.

I would like you to understand here that I am not attempting in any way to double-cross or betray Jeffrey MacDonald. I have told him from the beginning that it would be my intention, someday, to try to talk to you. I am, at present, drafting a movie treatment for the eventual screenplay for the film that will be made from the book I write.[1]

"I am not attempting in any way to double-cross or betray Jeffrey MacDonald." It's the kind of sentence written by someone who intends to do just that.

––––––––

It is the beginning of the end. MacDonald, having won an appeal on speedy-trial issues, is living in California and working as an emergency-room surgeon. McGinniss is already beginning to publicize his book on the case. And in October 1980, eight months after McGinniss's letter to the Kassabs, MacDonald, for the first time, tentatively expresses some concern that McGinniss might not believe in his innocence.

October 14, 1980
Sheree took me to our favorite restaurant (The Mandarin) for Sunday dinner + gave me a handsome watch. She's tired of my black runner's watch day + night—(I tried to explain it's not important, but you know). Anyway, we had a great time + had too much champagne. We even toasted you. Then, I read the Sunday paper while she slept + noted the interview of you—needless to say, in my usual unexpected brand of naiveté, I hadn't expected comments like that from you + don't really know what to make of them. It's a little confusing because I had just finished a strange conversation with Bernie in which he was telling me how he sort of confronted you with some sort of request as to how you view my guilt or innocence—I pooh-poohed (sp?) it/him, thinking he was exaggerating his state-ments + your lack of response. Reading your quotes gave his version of your meeting a new weight + sobered me significantly. Sheree, interestingly enough, tells me to go with my original + recent gut feeling about you as a human being

The lessons learned in Alaska's grip

By Mickey Friedman

Joe McGinniss' new book is 'Going to Extremes'

JOE McGINNISS went to Alaska because "It was an opportunity to have a totally existential experience on America's last frontier." He found, in his time there, raw violence and unimaginable beauty, drunkenness and determination, greed for of money and commitment to preservation of the wilderness, pathetic losers and "some of the deepest friendships I've ever had."

McGinniss found extremes, and he wrote a book about them. "Going to Extremes" chronicles his discovery of this vast northern state, which is one-fifth the size of the rest of the country, contains fewer miles of road than Vermont, stretches over four time zones and has a population smaller than Columbus, Ohio. The experience changed him because, McGinniss discovered, "The land doesn't let go of you once it gets hold of you."

Back in the mid-70s, when the idea of going to Alaska and writing a book about it had "gotten a grip on my imagination," McGinniss found that publishers were not as enthusiastic as he was that Alaska could capture the public's attention. This was before the appearance of John McPhee's bestselling "Coming into the Country" which McGinniss calls "a wonderful book"; and five or six publishers turned down the idea. The 37-year-old former journalist, whose best-known previous work is "The Selling of the President 1968," finally sold the project to NAL, a paperback house, which in turn sold it to a hardcover publisher, Alfred A. Knopf. Convinced that "I couldn't help but write an interesting book about it," McGinniss headed for the Far Northwest.

When McGinniss left, he had just finished a book called "Heroes" that had, he says, "become such an introspective kind of book. I'd gotten real tired just of thinking about myself, and I wanted something that would take me outside myself." Alaska did that. He experienced the withering cold and darkness of the Alaskan winter; stayed with a family of Eskimos in a remote village; visited the state legislature, where an afternoon break gives the lawmakers an opportunity to snort cocaine; survived a blizzard in a makeshift cabin; and, hiking in the Brooks Range, saw an overwhelmingly beautiful valley where, it is possible, no human had ever been before.

After nine months in Alaska, McGinniss came home to New Jersey and tried to write the book. "I did the first two chapters. Then I began to feel I had to go back, even though this was unfeasible economically as well as every other way. My advance had been for two years, and at the end of the second year I was out of time and money and I still had to go back." He sold his house, took out bank loans, and returned.

about the Alaskan experience of those who'd gone up there for — you might say — more legitimate reasons.

"Two types of people, McGinniss found, go to Alaska. "Those who are totally self-reliant and those who are totally unable to cope. Somebody said to me soon after I arrived that there were those who couldn't make it anywhere else and those who didn't want to make it anywhere else." The non-copers grow in to alcoholism, violence and depression. "Most people don't go to Alaska. Those who do are making a break. You're confronted once you get there with long winters where the dark affects you emotionally, and it's very primitive. When people who have a tendency to psychological instability arrive in a land with such extremes, they're going to be broken or bent."

McGinniss' frankness in portraying this aspect along with the more positive side has caused him some problems in Alaska. His book, he says, is "a wildly controversial thing" there. "One Anchorage paper loved it, the other was very hostile and said I was a typical outsider. There is a sense among most people who live there that Alaska is a member of the family, and you can't criticize. One woman told me: 'We know these things exist, but we don't want to have to read about them.'"

Going back to Alaska to live is something he thinks about. McGinniss says "I'd like it, and my wife would like to. But I have three children from my first marriage who live in the Philadelphia area, and I don't want to leave them. My wife had a baby last year, and we have connections in the East that would be hard to sever, but we'd love to go for a year or so."

His current project is a far cry from the freewheeling spaciousness of Alaska. McGinniss says. He is working on a book about Jeffrey McDonald, the Green Beret accused of murdering his wife and children in a notorious case a decade ago. This book is changing him, too, McGinniss says, and "it's for the better right now." During McDonald's trial, years after the murder, McGinniss lived with McDonald, and when McDonald went to prison for a time he smuggled tapes out to McGinniss.

Was McDonald guilty? "I can't talk about what I think," McGinniss says. "At the end of the book, the reader can draw a reasonable conclusion. I spent a great deal of time with both sides, and got full cooperation. But this is so sad and horrible, and I'll be so glad when it's over. It has affected my dream life, and not for the better. I didn't realize I would become so emotionally involved."

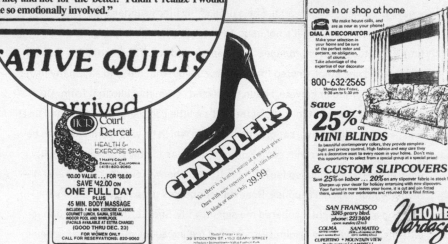

and/or friend (hopefully both) and to ignore quotes in papers etc. She feels the real story will be told effectively by you and "truth will out . . ."[2]

Doubts, but MacDonald continues to make tapes.

P.S. I've half-finished a tape to you. Hopefully, will finish it shortly + get it + some letters to you + anything I can find from Colette. I'm avoiding that, in case you haven't caught on.

———

I looked for the telltale newspaper article and finally found it. It is from the *San Francisco Examiner & Chronicle,* October 12, 1980. It is mostly about McGinniss's Alaska book, *Going to Extremes,* but contains a cryptic paragraph about MacDonald. "Was MacDonald guilty? 'I can't talk about what I think,' McGinniss says. 'At the end of the book, the reader can draw a reasonable conclusion. I spent a great deal of time with both sides, and got full cooperation. But this is so sad and horrible, and I'll be so glad when it's over. It has affected my dream life, and not for the better. I didn't realize I would become so emotionally involved.'"[3]

About a year later, on October 28, 1981, another article appeared in a paper. This time in *The Hollywood Reporter.* Dan Wigutow, a producer who had bought the rights to McGinniss's forthcoming book, was quoted, "Dr. Jeffrey MacDonald, convicted of having murdered his wife and children . . ." Days later, MacDonald found out about the *The Hollywood Reporter* article and complained in a phone conversation to McGinniss.

McGinniss had already written to MacDonald, discussing sundry sums of money, urging him to sign a release for Wigutow giving permission to turn the book into a movie, and informing him that Robert Mulligan, the director of *To Kill A Mockingbird* and *The Summer of '42,* was interested in directing. Days later, McGinniss was writing his editor about the whole espisode.

On November 3, 1981, McGinniss wrote to his editor, Morgan Entrekin at Delacorte:

[MacDonald] was astounded that Taylor-Wigutow [the production company] could have given a story to the *Hollywood Reporter* to the effect that they were planning a film on Dr. Jeffrey MacDonald, convicted of having murdered his wife and children, when the whole point of the film and book obviously was that he was falsely [McGinniss's underlining] convicted, as he had been falsely suspected for 10 years, et cetera, et cetera. He's letting this one pass, writing it off to the sloppiness of a trade paper, but the ice is getting thinner, and I'm still a long way from shore.[4]

Clearly, McGinniss was misleading, if not outright lying, to MacDonald in early November 1981—as he had a year earlier when the *San Francisco Examiner & Chronicle* article appeared. And back on February 15, 1980 when McGinniss started his "negotiations" with Freddy Kassab. When did McGinniss become "certain" of MacDonald's guilt? There may be *no* specific date. Just a slippery slope of tergiversation, opportunism, and self-interest. But at some point McGinniss's mind was made up. MacDonald was guilty. All that remained was the literary task of changing the narrative.

In the letter that follows, it becomes clear that MacDonald has fewer and fewer people to confide in, and less and less of a reason to confide in McGinniss.

October 19, 1982
. . . I have no idea why I'm even writing you this note. I'm sure at this point you could care less for another letter from prison. But I can't write it to mom, and Brian I want to concentrate on the case + not my prison conditions, so I'm saving his 3 sheets of paper for other type of discussions . . .
. . . I must be very dumb at times. I guess we all make mistakes, and I certainly do, but my judgment vis-à-vis Bernie since trial, Sheree, and Randi has seriously caused me to evaluate myself during these past 3 yrs.[5]

The book was moved from Delacorte to Putnam, and Phyllis Grann, Putnam's editor in chief, became McGinniss's editor. She sent notes:

October 14, 1982
In going back and rewriting from the beginning I think that your conviction that Jeff is guilty creeps into this version of the script too early in the story.[6]

In another letter to McGinniss, Grann writes:

November 4, 1982
Is Mildred [Kassab] trying to railroad Jeff? Should reader get that impression? Would you want to add some explanation for the change in testimony? Reader is certainly left with the impression that Mildred will lie to get Jeff convicted. Wouldn't it be better to close this chapter with some comment of your own? . . .

All of this does make the reader wonder if Jeff might be innocent. Would you want to add a few paragraphs of your own to lessen the impact?

. . . Please make sure that it is clear that Jeff is convicted because he is truly guilty and not just because he has a bad lawyer. You may wish, from time to time, to add a paragraph underscoring the fact that the judge is impressed with the evidence and not just disgusted with Bernie. You might even insert a sentence or two pointing out to the reader the irrefutable nature of certain pieces of evidence against Jeff.

Did McGinniss alter his manuscript to make MacDonald look more guilty? It seems inarguable. So much so that his editor had to pull him back, like the good student who, in an effort to please the teacher, overdoes it. Make him a little less guilty at first to ratchet up the drama. Alter the story here and there for a more effective presentation.

But it is Grann, McGinniss's editor, not him, who raises the issue of truth. "All of this makes the reader wonder if Jeff might be innocent . . . Please make sure that it is clear that Jeff is convicted because he is truly guilty."

Guilty in the story? Guilty in real life?

McGinniss had an additional problem. He needed a new protagonist. If MacDonald was going to be the hero in the first version of the book, who would become the hero in subsequent versions? Peter Kearns, the crusading CID detective? (Not likely. McGinniss called Kearns a "piggy Irish type" in a letter to MacDonald.) James Blackburn and Brian Murtagh, the prosecutors? (Maybe, but they appear too late in the story to be central characters.) The simple choice was the in-laws, Mildred and Freddy Kassab. In particular, Freddy, the author of the competing book project.

There is a sense that anything goes throughout McGinniss's correspondence and book. First, McGinniss ridicules the pajama-top demonstration in the Boyd Norton letter to MacDonald, then praises the experiment in *Fatal Vision*. The crucial passage in *Fatal Vision* concerns the Unnamed Criminologist:

> "This is very convincing evidence," the paid expert said, referring to Stombaugh's pajama-top reconstruction. "Now I see why they got the indictment." Segal attempted to be dismissive, discoursing at some length about how even the government's own theory of the crime offered no plausible explanation for why MacDonald would have placed his pajama top on his wife's chest before stabbing her with the ice pick. The criminologist simply shook his head. "You can raise all that, Bernie, but this is like a fingerprint. Holy Christmas! That's very convincing stuff. Bernie, I'm not an attorney, but after seeing this, my advice to you"—and here he leaned forward and gave Segal an avuncular pat on a pin-striped knee—"is to get as much as you can into the record for appeal."[7]

This passage is damning—but to McGinniss, not MacDonald. It suggests a score of unnamed characters to be brought into the narrative—the Unnamed-Expert-Waiting-to-Be-Pulled-Out-of-the-Hat. In the Boyd Norton letter the pajama-top demonstration is "hocus pocus," in the book, it is "very convincing evidence," and in the movie, "difficult to explain, but damning nonetheless."

On December 14, 1982, McGinniss delivered the manuscript of *Fatal Vision* to the publisher. McGinniss changed the title of his forthcoming book. No longer *Acid and Rain*, it became *Fatal Vision*—a title based on Macbeth's dagger soliloquy, delivered just before the murder of Duncan, the king:

> Is this a dagger which I see before me,
> The handle toward my hand? Come, let me clutch thee.
> I have thee not, and yet I see thee still.
> Art thou not, fatal vision, sensible
> To feeling as to sight?[8]

The old title alluded to the "discredited" Stoeckley story, the new title to Macbeth's guilt-ridden conscience, his blood-and-gore-spattered hallucinations, as if Jeffrey MacDonald might share them.

Eventually, distress creeps into MacDonald's writing:

February 9, 1983

. . . I need to see a copy of the book as soon as humanly possible. I can't for the life of me understand the arrogance (and, in fact, hypocrisy) in the stance that I'm like the general public in this case. It was one thing not to have <u>control</u> over the book/ contents/you—I granted you that [and] have lived with it except I asked you to treat Sheree well + Jay well (for very different reasons). But to coyly play games, suggesting things to book reviewers + trade journals while I hear different versions, is not right. Putnam's (and you) shouldn't deny me the right to read a copy of the book—if not today, certainly in March when your revisions are complete and a manuscript is definitely available . . . I would appreciate hearing back from you on this as soon as you can do it—I need to see the book.[9]

But McGinniss is adamant. MacDonald won't be given a copy of the book.

February 16, 1983

At no time was there ever any understanding that you would be given an advance look at the book six months prior to publication. As Joe Wambaugh told you in 1975, with him you would not even see a copy before it was published. Same with me.[10]

McGinniss had finished work. The publishers had secured coverage on *60 Minutes*, by Mike Wallace, to run just after the book's release. On May 15, 1983, MacDonald wrote McGinniss. He was still in prison in Bastrop, Texas, but he had heard back about the first interviews the *60 Minutes* crew had conducted with his friends and colleagues in Long Beach:

May 15, 1983

The 60 <u>Mins</u> crew + Mike W. were in LB Fri + Sat + it seemed to go exceptionally well. They really know the case well + M.W. seems to be able to discard chafe (sp?) from wheat, or whatever the expression is. Everyone was unusually nervous, but it went well by all reports. They'll be here in 2 weeks.[11]

A BOOK STORY

Histories are more full of examples
of the fidelity of dogs than of friends.
—Alexander Pope

June 1, 1983. When Mike Wallace showed up at the federal prison in Bastrop, Texas, MacDonald was expecting to be interviewed about the new evidence uncovered by his appellate attorneys. Helena Stoeckley had been interviewed by *60 Minutes* two years earlier. It was all coming to some kind of conclusion, possibly a new trial. But MacDonald soon learned on camera, in his interview with Mike Wallace, that his worst fears were confirmed. He was being reindicted and reconvicted in a book that would ultimately sell millions of copies; on a news show that would be seen by tens of millions of people; and eventually in a TV miniseries that would be seen by over sixty million people. He also learned that he had been betrayed by Joe McGinniss.

It didn't matter whether MacDonald was guilty or innocent or whether he had been treated unfairly by the courts. Now everyone—virtually everyone—*believed* he was guilty. The Count of Monte Cristo never had such odds against him.

Mike Wallace's opening comment set the stage. "Why did Green Beret captain Jeffrey MacDonald kill his wife and children? He says he didn't." It signaled that the show would be about MacDonald's motivation for the murders, not about his guilt or innocence—*that* was a given. Hand in hand with Joe McGinniss, Mike Wallace introduced America to a new theory of the murders. One of the problems with the 1979 trial had been the lack of a reasonable motivation. Hadn't the U.S. attorney written in his 1973 memo that the weakest aspect of the case was the absence of a motive?[1] McGinniss had realized that *his* story had the same weakness. And so he supplied an explanation, a mechanism for how the murders happened: diet pills. MacDonald was taking diet pills.

Late in the program, Mike Wallace started in on the diet pills. As if MacDonald's claim of guilt or innocence should rest on the question, did he or didn't he take a lot of diet pills prior to the murder? The question might seem absurd save for the weight placed on it by Wallace and McGinniss:

MIKE WALLACE: One has to say, look, why would he be taking off twelve to fifteen pounds in a period of three to four weeks . . . ?

JEFFREY MACDONALD: But if I did take off those twelve to fifteen pounds over three to four weeks, using three to four tablets of Eskatrol, that's not abnormal. That's a normal thing . . .

MIKE WALLACE: MacDonald first learned of McGinniss's conclusions when I talked with him in prison, and he was devastated. "Why hasn't Joe McGinniss asked me," he says, "about drugs and listened to my answer?"

JOE MCGINNISS: Well, if there's one thing that the past thirteen years have demonstrated conclusively and repeatedly, it is that Jeffrey MacDonald's answers to pointed questions are not truthful. He would have said he was not taking the drug in any quantity. He would have said if he had taken one that night, it would not have had any effect on his behavior. He would have said that since he didn't commit the murders in the first place, any kind of speculation as to why he might have would be off-base and irrelevant.[2]

An odd and perverse argument. According to McGinniss, there was little or no reason to ask MacDonald questions about the diet pills because MacDonald's answers were "not truthful." But it is easy to turn this around. McGinniss thought that MacDonald's answers were untruthful because they were not what he wanted to hear. McGinniss saw no reason to ask MacDonald questions about the diet pills because he had already decided that MacDonald was guilty, and the diet pills were an essential part of his "proof" of MacDonald's guilt.[3]

Think of *60 Minutes* (and the *Fatal Vision* miniseries that followed the publication of the book) as another round in the battle between MacDonald and his adversaries. Not only *United States v. MacDonald,* but *MacDonald v. McGinniss* and *Kassab v. MacDonald*—and anyone else who felt like piling on. (Both *Kassab v. MacDonald* and *MacDonald v. McGinniss* became actual court cases.)

You can ask the same question of the television coverage and the 1979 trial: How can a reader (or a viewer, or a juror) know if pieces of the narrative are missing? Yes, McGinniss provided a narrative: the sociopathic MacDonald flew into an amphetamine-fueled rage and killed his family. But neither the *60 Minutes* credits nor the on-air commentary mention that another interview had been conducted but never used: the interview with Helena Stoeckley, in which she confessed in front of a *60 Minutes* producer and camera crew. At the very end of her interview, Stoeckley is asked by Joe Wershba (the *60 Minutes* producer) whether she is willing to go back into court.

> **JOE WERSHBA:** Do you realize, of course, that if you went into court, that the questioning would be a million times tougher than it was tonight . . . ?
>
> **HELENA STOECKLEY:** I realize that.
>
> **JOE WERSHBA:** Yes. They will try to rip you to shreds, right? Do you think you could withstand that?
>
> **HELENA STOECKLEY.** I think that—well, this baby is due any day now. I think, once the pregnancy's over—I'm a pretty tough person . . . I'm not afraid of what they could ask me . . .[4]

I would have liked to interview Joe Wershba and Mike Wallace about the story. But Wershba died in 2011; Mike Wallace was infirm and couldn't be interviewed, and then he died in 2012. So I discussed the Stoeckley interview with Ted Landreth, a former CBS News producer who made a film in the late 1980s titled *False Witness,* which made a case for MacDonald's innocence.

> **ERROL MORRIS:** I never talked to Joe Wershba, the *60 Minutes* producer.
>
> **TED LANDRETH:** It's such a shame you didn't, because he died about four or five months ago. But it was he who taped the interview, which was supposed to be on

6o Minutes, with Helena. The only existing interview, but it was never aired . . . Joe Wershba was one of the great heroes of the early days of CBS News. He worked with Murrow; he was Murrow's star reporter. He worked with Don Hewitt back in those days—*See It Now.* And Joe and I knew each other from my CBS days. The point I'm making is that Joe wanted to do the story of Jeffrey MacDonald and set about to do it for *6o Minutes.* And he discovered Gunderson, and interviewed Helena Stoeckley, and did a few other things. Mainly the interview with Helena Stoeckley. And then Don Hewitt said to him, "That's not the story. The story is McGinniss's book." Nobody even so much as looked at the interview that they had with Stoeckley, much less did they use it.

Mike Wallace, who did the piece, later on said to MacDonald that it was a book story. He hated—*hated*—doing book stories, because it wasn't journalism. It was just the book and McGinniss. And Wershba wrote a note to MacDonald in which he said he thought Stoeckley should have been cross-examined under oath. He believed she was telling the truth. Imagine: *6o Minutes* paid no attention to any of that, and the piece that they put on the air pretty much sealed MacDonald's fate. It aired just about the time of the big appeal, and it made McGinniss's book a bestseller. CBS paid absolutely no attention to the journalism that they might have done. They just paid attention to McGinniss.

Mike Wallace unintentionally outlined the underlying problem. The *6o Minutes* story had become disconnected from reality—from what really happened. All that was left was a story about a book that *also* might be disconnected from reality. The investigative element was gone, and in its place was a sorry kind of journalistic pugilism—*McGinniss v. MacDonald.* Did you or didn't you use Eskatrol? How much did you really use? How often? The assumption is that MacDonald killed his family, and the only issue to be resolved is whether Eskatrol was involved. It is like the question: when did you stop beating your wife? The question posed with an arched eyebrow. All possible answers are incriminating. As if the question of who did it could be answered simply by watching the convicted man fidget on television.

On November 17, 1982, Joe Wershba wrote MacDonald a letter.

I am sorry for your troubles. Rumor had it wrong. I thought Miss Stoeckley made a competent witness and would have wanted to see her tested in court under cross-examination. I have a continuing interest in the case and I regret that I can-

not give you a firm word as to whether we will do anything on it on *60 Minutes* . . .
You are fortunate in your many friends who have never ceased to believe in you.

Yours,

Joseph Wershba[5]

––––––

Bernie Segal wrote to MacDonald after watching the show:

September 19, 1983
Re: "Sixty Minutes." I sat there holding my breath for the entire segment on The
Case. When it ended I was wondering why I felt gaspy. Then I realized I was still
holding my breath. I let out the air, started normal breathing, checked my pulse
and concluded that you and the case *will* survive . . .

Joe McGinniss had a couple of desultory conversations with me during the
trial and then we had only one meeting after that. The latter meeting was
the one at the Mark Hopkins Hotel. His only interest was how I came into the
case. That was the meeting I was asking him "where" he [stood] in regard to
you and his conclusion about the case. He categorically stated that he had no
conclusion—contrary to his present assertions. If he had ever talked to me
about whether I pursued the question of the Eskatrol, he would have found his
phony theory deflated [6]

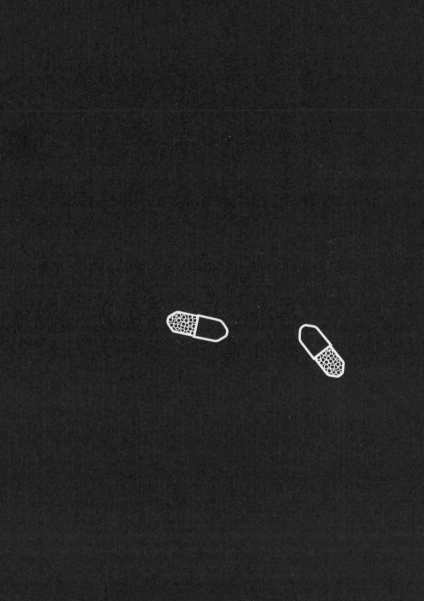

ESKATROL

While he was still preparing his manuscript, McGinniss had asked MacDonald for access to his condo in Huntington Beach, where his files were stored, and MacDonald had given him the key. In *Fatal Vision*, McGinniss writes, "On my last day at the condominium, I found more pages of notes in Jeffrey MacDonald's handwriting. The heading said, 'Activities—Monday, 16 Feb. 5:30 PM—Tues. in Hospital, 17 Feb.'" McGinniss continues:

> This, too, was part of the detailed account which MacDonald had prepared at the request of his military attorney immediately after the April 6 announcement that he was being held as a suspect . . . This, he had told Woerheide, was the most accurate, most complete, most coherent account of the murders which he had ever compiled. He had not, however, made it available to Woerheide or to the grand jurors. He had not made it available to any investigator.[1]

McGinniss sets the stage: ". . . This 'most accurate' account had lain at the bottom of a cardboard box, covered by dozens of other files. With the warm Southern California sun of late November shining brightly through the sliding glass doors, I started to read."

He makes it sound as though MacDonald was hiding something. According to McGinniss, MacDonald hadn't shown the notes to Victor Woerheide, the prosecutor at the grand jury. But why should MacDonald share the notes written for his defense attorneys with those determined to put him behind bars? He did share them with his own investigators, lawyers, and McGinniss himself. McGinniss's claim that he learned about the diet pills only from the material in MacDonald's condominium is deeply disingenuous. McGinniss knew about the diet pills during the trial, and had discussed them with Michael Malley and Bernie Segal long before he "discovered" the document at the bottom of the cardboard box. Diet pills had been discussed and dismissed as early as the Article 32. In Malley's account from 1971, he wrote, "Jeff worried that he might have taken an amphetamine the day of the crime—he was running a weight-control program for the 6th Special Forces group, and he himself was participating, including using diet pills. But one pill, even if he did take it, hardly could be worth worrying about too much . . ."

Here is the diary entry. (It is reprinted at greater length in *Fatal Vision*, but this is the essence of it.)

We ate dinner together at 5:45 PM (all 4). It is possible I had one diet pill at this time. I do not remember, but it is possible. I had been running a weight control program for my unit and I put my name at the top of the program to encourage participation. I had lost 12–15 lbs. in the prior 3–4 weeks, in the process using 3–5 capsules of Eskatrol Spansule (15 mg. Dextroamphetamine) ("Speed") and 7.5 mg. Prochlorperazine (Compazine) to counteract the excitability of the speed. I was working out with the boxing team and the coach told me to lose weight. In any case, the reason I could have taken the pill was two-fold—1) to eat less in the evening when I "snacked" the most and 2) to try to stay awake after dinner since I was baby-sitting. It didn't work if I did take a pill, because I think I had a 1/2 hr. nap on the floor from 7:30–8 PM after I put Kristy to bed.[2]

For McGinniss it is the smoking gun.

How did he transform an innocuous diary entry into something incredibly sinister? How did he transform two phrases—"it is possible I had one diet pill at this time" and "3–5 capsules of Eskatrol Spansule"—into a raging amphetamine habit?

How much he might be consuming will forever be, to employ a phrase used by Freddy Kassab before the grand jury, "a dark area," but if the "three to five" were a daily dose it would have been enough—taken over a period of three to four weeks—to have caused chronic amphetamine psychosis, many of the symptoms of which MacDonald did, in fact, display. (In the hospital after the murders he also displayed symptoms associated with abrupt cessation of high dosages of the drug, such as [as cited in the *Physicians' Desk Reference*] "extreme fatigue and mental depression.")[3]

McGinniss implied that the drug was taken off the market because of severe problems connected with its use. According to an article in the *New York Times*, "U.S. Sets Diet Drug Recall in Drive on Amphetamines" (April 2, 1973, front page), the decision was made by the FDA for two reasons—the fear that the products were being taken recreationally and the contention that they were not effective in controlling obesity. At the time of the recall, the usage was 480 million dosage units. If diet pills really had the potential to trigger homicidal rages, wouldn't there have been other murders? That is a lot of pills to be floating around. It is interesting to note that a few drugs—Obetrol, Eskatrol, Dexamyl, Bamadex, and Delcobese—were exempted from the initial recall. Eskatrol was not initially recalled and wasn't removed from the market until 1981, when the manufacturer, Smith, Kline & French, failed to prove its effectiveness for weight loss.

Something more was needed. Diet pills plus something else. McGinniss suggested a two-part mechanism. If an amphetamine was the trigger—to continue the metaphor—what was triggered? For McGinniss, it had to be MacDonald's underlying psychopathology. And it is here that Hervey Cleckley comes to the rescue. Take Cleckley's idea of the psychopath (who is indistinguishable from a normal person, except that he is evil) and mix it up with some additional pop psychology—in this case, Christopher Lasch's *The Culture of Narcissism*. Set up a simple equation: misogyny + narcissism + diet pills = a triple homicide.

The quote from Lasch occurs in a chapter entitled, "The Castrating Women of Male Fantasy." McGinniss writes:

The narcissist's "ideal concept of himself," Kernberg [a psychoanalyst who further developed the concept of the "borderline personality disorder"] writes, "is a fantasy construction, which protects him from such dreaded relationships with all other people . . . and also contains a helpless yearning and love for an ideal mother who would come to his rescue."

Should such a "dreaded relationship" (such as marriage) materialize, the complex defense mechanism which has been constructed within the psyche of the pathological narcissist would come under severe stress, because, as Christopher Lasch notes, such a person perceives the female, "child or woman, wife or mother," as a monster who "cuts men to ribbons or swallows them whole."

Thus, in Lasch's view, "fear of the devouring mother of the pre-Oedipal fantasy gives rise to a generalized fear of women," and this fear, "closely associated with a fear of the consuming desires within, reveals itself . . . as a boundless rage against the female sex."[4]

McGinniss builds to his ultimate conclusion. It is near the end of *Fatal Vision*. And even though it is a bluff, he plunks it down with ultimate bravura—as if he is the proud owner of a royal flush.

> Might it be too much to surmise that since early childhood he had been suffering from the strain required to repress the "boundless rage" which psychological adjustment had caused him to feel toward "child or woman, wife or mother . . . the female sex"?
>
> And that on this night—this raw and somber military-base February Monday night—finally with the amphetamines swelling the rage to flood tide, and with Colette, pregnant Colette, perhaps seeking to communicate to him some of her new insights into personality structure and behavioral patterns [Colette was taking a course in psychology.]—indeed, possibly even attempting to *explain* him to himself . . . his defense mechanism, for the first and last time, proved insufficient.
>
> Would it be too much to suggest that in that one instant . . . the ensuing explosion of rage had destroyed not only Jeffrey MacDonald's wife and daughters, but all that he had sought to make of his life?
>
> Perhaps.[5]

McGinniss disappears into a sea of conjecture. "Might it be too much to surmise . . ." "Would it be too much to suggest . . ."

In *Dr. Jekyll and Mr. Hyde,* Robert Louis Stevenson imagined two characters— one good, one evil—bound together in what he called "the agonized womb of consciousness":

> If each, I told myself, could be housed in separate identities, life would be relieved of all that was unbearable; the unjust might go his way, delivered from the aspi-

rations and remorse of his more upright twin; and the just could walk steadfastly and securely on his upward path, doing the good things in which he found his pleasure, and no longer exposed to disgrace and penitence by the hands of this extraneous evil. It was the curse of mankind that these incongruous faggots were thus bound together—that in the agonized womb of consciousness, these polar twins should be continuously struggling.[6]

What if these "polar twins" could be separated?

And so, Dr. Jekyll "drank off the potion" and is transformed into the satanic Mr. Hyde before our eyes. Just substitute Eskatrol for the "large quantity of a particular salt," and you have uncovered the essence of McGinniss's argument. As in Stevenson, it just happens.

> I had long since prepared my tincture; I purchased at once, from a firm of wholesale chemists, a large quantity of a particular salt which I knew, from my experiments, to be the last ingredient required; and late one accursed night, I compounded the elements, watched them boil and smoke together in the glass, and when the ebullition had subsided, with a strong glow of courage, drank off the potion . . . I knew myself, at the first breath of this new life, to be more wicked, tenfold more wicked, sold a slave to my original evil; and the thought, in that moment, braced and delighted me like wine.[7]

Stevenson's *Dr. Jekyll and Mr. Hyde* is a work of fiction. People, real people, do not become "tenfold more wicked." People, suddenly and without warning, are not transformed into monsters.[8]

I asked Rex Beaber about this. He was the UCLA lawyer/psychologist who interviewed Stoeckley in 1982 and has decades of experience both as a criminal defense attorney and as a forensic psychologist.

ERROL MORRIS: When Joe McGinniss wrote his bestselling book, *Fatal Vision*, he claimed—actually contrary to most of the psychiatric opinion that had been offered—that MacDonald was psychopathic, and he argued that MacDonald was taking diet pills, Eskatrol, and that the combination of the two were the cause of the murders.

REX BEABER: That's a non-explanation. First of all, stimulants on their own don't cause homicidal impulses. I'm not saying that people on stimulants haven't committed homicides, but there's always an adequate explanation of the homicide without the stimulant. All the stimulant added was the loss of impulse control to allow you to act out an impulse that was already there. That's number one.

Secondly, the diagnosis of psychopathy is a diagnosis that you always have to be very careful of, because it often begs the question. By that I mean, if you say to the person who gives a diagnosis, "If you knew to a certainty that he did not commit the crime, would you give him the diagnosis of psychopath?" And almost always in these kinds of cases the answer is no. I mean, a psychopath has a very specific kind of history: engaging in illegal conduct, poor performance in school, conduct disorders as a child, disrespect for authority, failure to learn from experience, frequent long-term affairs, drug and substance abuse. MacDonald doesn't have any of these characteristics to my knowledge. This is a guy who was an ideal student, who was a physician, who not only acquiesced to authority but lived within a universe where respect for authority and obedience is absolutely required.

The diagnosis of psychopathy under these circumstances is simply made retroactively, because one believes that the person committed the crime, and you can't do that. That's not logically appropriate to assume the conclusion to prove the conclusion. You have to be able to prove the diagnosis independently from the allegations. Otherwise it all becomes a sham and a game.

ERROL MORRIS: A sham and a game?

REX BEABER: Yes. By the way, abuse of stimulant medication amongst physicians, especially physicians who do emergency work—which he did, as I remember—is extremely common. When I taught in the residency program at UCLA, I don't think I knew anybody in an internship that didn't use Dexedrine or methamphetamine to stay awake during the long shifts. Nothing about that explains a homicide. Did he take those drugs?

ERROL MORRIS: Yes, he said he may have taken one on the day of the murders.

REX BEABER: Stimulants don't cause homicide, period. It's a non sequitur. No more than heroin causes burglaries. Do heroin addicts often burglarize houses? Yes. But that's because heroin costs a lot of money and the only way to buy it for some people is to commit burglaries. That he took some amount of stimulants doesn't explain anything.

———

The issue of MacDonald's possible amphetamine usage and the diary he had prepared for Bernie Segal had come up in Michael Malley's journal. I spoke to him again.

MICHAEL MALLEY: Yes. That was an issue that came up and went away. It was an issue that the defense clearly thought about and talked about a lot, that Jeff brought up himself. He said that he was running a weight-loss program for, what was it, the Sixth Special Forces Group, and that included amphetamines, because, at the time, that was the weight-loss drug. And he had taken some, too. I'm not even sure the government ever brought this up, but I certainly remember the defense brought it up with Jeff and his friends, his escort officers and the other people in the Special Forces Group, you know, "Have you ever seen Jeff out of control for any reason after he's taken these kinds of drugs?" And the answer was always no. We kind of put it away.

And the docs in the hospital, at Womack, they all said he was agitated when he was brought in, but he didn't exhibit any signs of drug abuse or anything else. So, it kind of just went away before it ever became an issue. Now, McGinniss—I have no idea where he came up with all that stuff, but he did.

ERROL MORRIS: He came up with it because Jeffrey allowed him into his condo in Huntington Beach.

MICHAEL MALLEY: That's exactly right. I have to say, we all trusted McGinniss. I didn't distrust him, but I never felt good about it. My view was, you really don't want outsiders being inside the defense offices. But Bernie wanted him there, and Jeff wanted him there. He was making some money out of the thing. And to be honest about it, I never thought of Joe as an enemy. I never thought of him as a friend, either. He was just there. And when I finally read the book, I was kind of astounded, to be honest. But it was way too late by then.

ERROL MORRIS: Yes. Now, I don't think that book started out as an attack on Mac-Donald. I think it started off as a defense of MacDonald.

MICHAEL MALLEY: That's true. Here's what I know. I know that up until the day of the verdict, Joe was always around. I liked him being around, particularly because he and Jeff would go out running around the North Carolina State running track, and they played pool. They were best buddies. And I had stuff to do. I was trying to round up witnesses, I was trying to keep people showing up on time. And I had to take a leave of absence from my own law firm, and I had a couple of big cases going on, so every once in a while I'd have to take a couple of days and fly to San Francisco for something or other.

Joe filled the role of Jeff's best friend. So I didn't have to fill the role of Jeff's best friend. And that was good. I mean, I liked that. And Joe was—he's very likable. He always has kind of a hangdog look, and you always are wondering whether somebody kicked Joe yesterday, and he's unhappy, and you always kind of pet him a little bit to make him feel better. And that's how he works. And I'm sure that's how he really is. But I never got the feeling, you know, we were living in that stupid fraternity house—which, that really did drive me nuts, but that was Bernie's idea, too. It was cheap and we all got to live together. And Joe was always kind of hanging around and talking and stuff.

So I never, never, never got the feeling that Joe was hostile. But the day the verdict came back, we had had to move out of the fraternity house because school was starting, and we were in a motel of some kind, and I remember, I think my room was next to Joe's, right next door to Joe, and so when they led Jeff out in handcuffs and we went back to the hotel, and I remember we were standing on the balcony, looking over a parking lot, a very scenic parking lot, and Joe was there, and I was kind of, he said, "What do you think?"

And I said, "It's just awful." I said, "It can't be." I said, you know, "An injustice has been done," or something like that. I said, you know, "Whether you think he's innocent or not, they simply did not prove he's guilty, so he is not guilty, and the jury just got it all wrong." And I started to light into Judge Dupree about that. And I looked at Joe, and he said, "Well, this changes everything." And I said, "What does it change?" And he said, "Everything." And I said, "What does that mean?" And he said, "Everything." And that's as far as he would go.

ESSENTIAL INTEGRITY

On August 31, 1984, MacDonald filed a lawsuit against Joe McGinniss in federal court. It claimed "fraud, breach of contract, breach of the covenant of good faith and fair dealing."

During the 1979 trial, MacDonald had signed a contract with McGinniss granting McGinniss exclusive rights to his life story and releasing him "from any and all claims, demands or causes of action that I may hereafter have against you—whether from libel, violation of right of privacy, or anything else." It went on:

> I realize, of course, that you do not propose to libel me. Nevertheless, in order that you may feel free to write the book in any manner that you may deem best, I agree that I will not make or assert against you, the publisher, or its licensees or anyone else involved in the production or distribution of the book, any claim or demand whatsoever based on the ground that anything contained in the book defames me.[1]

But Bernie Segal had added a clause to the contract: "provided that the essential integrity of my life story is maintained."

What makes this additional clause unusual is the reference to the "essential integrity" of the story. Integrity is defined as wholeness, completeness, and purity, but in the litigation that followed, "essential integrity" became identified with the truth.

Janet Malcolm, in her book about the case, *The Journalist and the Murderer*, recalls the receipt of a letter, dated September 1, 1987, from Daniel Kornstein, McGinniss's lawyer, which warned of a grave threat to the First Amendment posed by the lawsuit: "The MacDonald claim suggests that newspaper and magazine reporters, as well as authors, can and will be sued for writing truthful but unflattering articles should they ever have acted in a fashion that indicated a sympathetic attitude toward their interview subject."[2] It was the beginning of her interest in the case.

Sifting through the thousands of pages of transcript of the *civil* case, several themes emerge—the issue of MacDonald's guilt or innocence (which, technically speaking, wasn't supposed to be discussed); MacDonald's claim that McGinniss had lied to him or at best misrepresented his intentions; and MacDonald's claim that McGinniss had misrepresented the facts of the case. I asked Gary Bostwick, MacDonald's attorney, about this. And about Kornstein's claim that these were First Amendment issues.

ERROL MORRIS: What about McGinniss and Kornstein's claim?

GARY BOSTWICK: I don't buy it. It just isn't a disguised First Amendment case or a First Amendment issue. If a writer *promises* to do something, they can actually contract away their First Amendment rights. And I thought that he did just that when he was given this unusual access throughout the trial. He was part of the defense team; he was right in the middle of it. If he hadn't promised, well then, we wouldn't have any argument, but he promised to maintain the essential integrity of MacDonald's life story. He signed a contract.

ERROL MORRIS: But was the fraud that McGinniss had lied to Jeff or was it that he had lied about the evidence?

GARY BOSTWICK: There was an element of both. We sued because Segal had an agreement in writing to maintain the essential integrity of Jeff's life's story. Add to that, fraud, that McGinniss lied to Jeff in order to get Jeff to cooperate and to get Jeff's friends to cooperate. So it was really two parts. Part of it was lying in the book and part of it was lying to Jeff about what he was doing.

ERROL MORRIS: Lying about the Eskatrol?

GARY BOSTWICK: Yes. He made up part of a quote from the *Physicians' Desk Reference*. McGinniss was on the stand. "I've got the *Physicians' Desk Reference* in front of you there. You quote the parts that talk about the really bad side effects of the drug that you know he was taking." And I said, "But look, you don't have in there all these other mitigating comments about the fact that it rarely happens." He's smart. He flips to the front and says, "This is not the one I was using. You can take a look at the bibliography. I was using year so-and-so, edition so-and-so, and this isn't it."

The judge says, "Maybe we should break for lunch now." And I was standing back there, not knowing what to do, and thinking, "Well, I tried. It didn't work." And suddenly Jerry Potter [who co-wrote *Fatal Justice*, a reexamination of the MacDonald case and an extended brief arguing for MacDonald's innocence] is standing there and he says, "You've never asked me what I do." And I said, "No, I never have." And so I thought, "Why is he asking me at this moment about what it is that he does?" And he says, "I'm a medical book salesman." And he said, "One of my good friends is the librarian at the USC Medical School, and I was going to have lunch with her. Do you want me to ask her if she has got the right edition?" He comes back at the end of lunch with two shopping bags, and there's four *PDR*s in there for different years, including the one precisely that's in the back of *Fatal Vision*.

And so I go up to the stand and I replace the one that is up there. And I say as we start the afternoon, "Okay, I'd like you to look at this again." And he looks at me: "What the heck is this? We already did this. I already answered you before lunch, Mr. Bostwick. I didn't use this one, I used the 1977 version." And I said, "Oh yes, well, I believe the 1977 version is in front of you right now. It's the same color and everything."

The blood just drained out of his face. And he flips to the front. He looks and he says, "Yes, yes, okay, well, yes, I see that." And then he says, "Well, I didn't think all the rest of that was important."

MacDonald was at Womack Army Hospital the day after the murders. McGinniss had written that MacDonald's "extreme fatigue and mental depression," observed by one of the doctors who treated him, had been caused by a withdrawal from amphetamine. It produced a memorable exchange between Bostwick and McGinniss.

GARY BOSTWICK: What did the three investigators tell you about the way Dr. Mac-Donald was acting on that night that led you to believe that he had been taking three to five Eskatrol Spansules on that day or any other day?

JOE McGINNISS: I don't think those three investigators saw him on that night. I believe that Dr. Bronstein, who saw him at the hospital to which he was taken, described symptoms which were not inconsistent with possible ingestion of amphetamines.

GARY BOSTWICK: . . . The bottom of the first paragraph there . . . It's a parenthesis, "In the hospital after the murders he also displayed symptoms associated with abrupt cessation of high doses of the drug such as [as cited in the *PDR*] 'extreme fatigue and mental depression.'" Are those the symptoms they told you he manifested?

JOE McGINNISS: [That] in conjunction with Dr. Bronstein's testimony, which I believe is quoted more extensively earlier in the book . . . I, as you know, Mr. Bostwick, stopped well short of stating flatly that I know it to be a fact that MacDonald took three to five Spansules a day.

GARY BOSTWICK: I'm not sure if that was a question to me or not, but if it was a question, I don't know that. And what I'm asking then is, did it ever occur to you that someone who had just watched his family being murdered would manifest symptoms such as extreme fatigue and mental depression?

JOE McGINNISS: Well, he didn't watch them being murdered.

GARY BOSTWICK: You know that?

JOE McGINNISS: Well, he watched them being murdered as he murdered them.[3]

But in this cavalcade of whys without answers, if Jeffrey MacDonald suddenly snapped and destroyed his family and "all that he sought to make of his life," what motivated Joe McGinniss to betray MacDonald? A love of truth? A sudden epiphany—Oh, my God, he's guilty!—triggered by reading the Eskatrol diary entry? Opportunism?

Theories abound. Following MacDonald's conviction, McGinniss was presented with a different narrative and with a different set of choices. He could argue *against* the verdict in Raleigh and declare MacDonald's conviction a terrible miscarriage of justice. (Which he did in a letter to MacDonald.) But where was the bestseller in that? MacDonald as an innocent man is not a terribly compelling figure. Tinged with hubris, an unerring instinct for making bad choices and creating trouble for himself, and a self-righteous temerity, he is a complex, often annoying person. Furthermore, he doesn't play the part of the innocent man the way he should. He elides certain details. His story has inconsistencies. He overreacts. He doesn't keep his cool. He is smug, sarcastic, supercilious.[4] But MacDonald as a guilty man offers incredible possibilities—the possibility of presenting to the world a character so ruthless, so depraved, that he would in a rage kill his wife and daughter and then cover it up with a *third* murder, the murder of a little girl, his daughter. Indeed, if MacDonald did kill his family, as argued by the prosecution, he would be a truly demonic figure. He would have to be, and since it was assumed by the jury, by the prosecutors, and eventually by McGinniss that he *did* do it, an explanation had to be found to account for this level of depravity.

The civil trial bounced along, a Rosencrantz and Guildenstern sequel to the criminal trial. Characters who never appeared in previous proceedings, such as Joseph Barbato, the Fort Gordon chemist who analyzed MacDonald's blood and urine on the day after the murders. Characters who could have been called in the criminal trial, but weren't. There were also several people called who were involved in the publication of the book and the making of the miniseries—Dan Wigutow, the television producer, and John Gay, the screenwriter credited with the teleplay. (Gay went on to write the teleplays for two more McGinniss books, *Cruel Doubt* and *Blind Faith*.)

On day eighteen, August 5, 1987, Dan Wigutow took the stand. He described how the rights were acquired for the miniseries. It is clear that McGinniss was hedging his bets. To some people it looked like he believed in MacDonald's guilt, to others that MacDonald was innocent. This could be interpreted in different ways: indecision on McGinniss's part or an attempt to curry favor. It came out in the questioning.

GARY BOSTWICK: You talked about ideas that Mr. McGinniss had to help sell the story. What ideas did he tell you to try to help sell the story?

DAN WIGUTOW: About a fascinating character who had been through an unusual background, having gone to Princeton, having become an Army doctor, Green Beret, and then was involved in the killings of his wife and kids.

GARY BOSTWICK: Those are the ideas he had to help sell the story?

DAN WIGUTOW: Well, the idea was basically to tell the story first and that was part of [the] telling of the story, is who the character was, the uniqueness, the unusualness of it, the all-American boy aspects of it, if you will.

GARY BOSTWICK: An all-American boy who had gone bad, right? That was the idea to sell the story, right?

DAN WIGUTOW: No, that was not the idea to sell the story at that point.

GARY BOSTWICK: It was the all-American boy who had been prosecuted unfairly; is that the idea that was going to help sell the story?

DAN WIGUTOW: No, it wasn't that either.

GARY BOSTWICK: Well, what was the idea that he had that was going to help sell the story?

DAN WIGUTOW: Say the idea was that there was an all-American boy, who had gotten caught up in these circumstances, and there was ample evidence on both sides to see that he could be guilty, or he could be innocent.[5]

Smith Kline & French—Cont.

are relatively stable. Total reliance must not be placed on serum levels alone. Accurate patient evaluation requires both clinical and laboratory analysis.

Overdosage: The toxic levels for lithium are close to the therapeutic levels. It is therefore important that patients and their families be cautioned to watch for early toxic symptoms and to discontinue the drug and inform the physician should they occur. Toxic symptoms are listed in detail under ADVERSE REACTIONS.

Treatment: No specific antidote for lithium poisoning is known. Early symptoms of lithium toxicity can usually be treated by reduction or cessation of dosage of the drug and resumption of the treatment at a lower dose after 24 to 48 hours. In severe cases of lithium poisoning, the first and foremost goal of treatment consists of elimination of this ion from the patient. Treatment is essentially the same as that used in barbiturate poisoning: 1) gastric lavage, 2) correction of fluid and electrolyte imbalance, and 3) regulation of kidney function. Urea, mannitol, and aminophylline all produce significant increases in lithium excretion. Infection prophylaxis, regular chest X-rays and preservation of adequate respiration are essential.

How Supplied: 300 mg. capsules in bottles of 100 and 500.

[Shown in Product Identification Section]

ESKATROL® SPANSULE® CAPSULES ℞

Amphetamines have a significant potential for abuse. In view of their short-term anorectic effect and rapid development of tolerance, they should be used with extreme caution and only for limited periods of time in weight-reduction programs.

Description: 'Eskatrol' contains dextroamphetamine sulfate and prochlorperazine. Dextroamphetamine sulfate is the dextro isomer of the compound d,l-amphetamine sulfate, a sympathomimetic amine of the amphetamine group. Chemically, dextroamphetamine sulfate is d-alpha-methylphenethylamine, and is present in 'Eskatrol' as the neutral sulfate. Prochlorperazine is 2-chloro-10 [3-[4-methyl -1- piperazinyl)-propyl]-phenothiazine, and is present in 'Eskatrol' as the maleate.

Each 'Eskatrol' *Spansule* capsule contains dextroamphetamine sulfate, 15 mg., and prochlorperazine, 7.5 mg., as the maleate, so prepared that an initial dose is released promptly and the remaining medication is released gradually over a prolonged period.

Actions: Dextroamphetamine sulfate is a sympathomimetic amine with CNS stimulant activity. Peripheral actions include elevation of systolic and diastolic blood pressures and weak bronchodilator and respiratory stimulant action. The anorectic effect diminishes after a few weeks. Prochlorperazine, a nonsedative tranquilizer, minimizes the stimulation which may occur in some patients on dextroamphetamine sulfate alone. The 'Spansule' capsule dosage form provides the convenience of once-a-day dosage.

Indications

Based on a review of this drug by the National Academy of Sciences—National Research Council and/or other information, FDA has classified the indications as follows:

Possibly effective: In exogenous obesity, as a short-term (a few weeks) adjunct in a regimen of weight reduction based on caloric restriction.

Final classification of the less-than-effective indications requires further investigation.

Contraindications: Advanced arteriosclerosis, symptomatic cardiovascular disease, moderate to severe hypertension, hyperthyroidism, known hypersensitivity or idiosyncrasy to the sympathomimetic amines.

Agitated states.

Patients with a history of drug abuse, phenothiazine-induced jaundice or blood dyscrasias, or in the presence of bone marrow depression. During or within 14 days following the administration of monoamine oxidase inhibitors; hypertensive crises may result.

Lactating (nursing) mothers.

Because of the antiemetic action of the prochlorperazine component, 'Eskatrol' *Spansule* capsules should not be used where nausea and vomiting are believed to be a manifestation of intestinal obstruction or brain tumor.

Warnings: Tolerance to the anorectic effect usually develops within a few weeks. When this occurs, the recommended dose should not be exceeded in an attempt to increase the effect; rather, the drug should be discontinued.

Amphetamines may mask extreme fatigue which can impair the ability to perform potentially hazardous activities such as operating machinery or driving motor vehicles; patient should be cautioned accordingly.

Drug Dependence: Amphetamines have significant potential for abuse. There are reports of patients with dosage to many times the recommended dose. For these reasons, care should be exercised in the selection of candidates for 'Eskatrol' therapy. Should psychological dependence occur, discontinue medication. Abrupt cessation following prolonged high dosage of amphetamines results in extreme fatigue and mental depression; changes have also been noted on the sleep EEG.

Manifestations of chronic intoxication with amphetamines include severe dermatoses, marked insomnia, irritability, hyperactivity, and personality changes. The most severe manifestation of chronic intoxication is psychosis, often clinically indistinguishable from schizophrenia.

Usage in Pregnancy: Safe use in pregnancy has not been established. Reproductive studies in animals at high multiples of the human dose of amphetamines have suggested a teratogenic potential.

Although prochlorperazine has no clinically significant potential, phenothiazines may intensify and prolong the action of central nervous system depressants including alcohol. If hypotension should occur, epinephrine should not be used, since there may be a reversal of its usual hypertensive effect.

Adverse Reactions: Dextroamphetamine sulfate: *Cardiovascular:* Palpitation, tachycardia, elevation of blood pressure. *Central Nervous System:* Overstimulation, restlessness, dizziness, insomnia, euphoria, dyskinesia, dysphoria, tremor, headache; rarely, psychotic episodes at recommended doses. *Gastrointestinal:* Dryness of the mouth, unpleasant taste, diarrhea, other gastrointestinal disturbances. *Allergic:* Urticaria. *Endocrine:* Impotence, changes in libido.

Prochlorperazine: Sedation, dizziness, hypotension, tachycardia, dry mouth, skin rash, tinnitus, vertigo, nasal congestion, miosis, lethargy, cholestatic jaundice, leukopenia, agranulocytosis, extrapyramidal or parkinsonism-like symptoms (spasticity, painful constriction of skeletal muscles, or myotonia dystonica, chiefly those of the head, neck, and shoulders, sometimes resulting in dislocations and fractures, opisthotonos, oculogyric crises, carpopedal spasms, dystonias and persistent tardive dyskinesia), convulsions, catatonic-like reactions, and reversal of epinephrine effects.

Adverse Reactions Reported with Prochlorperazine or Other Phenothiazine Derivatives: Adverse reactions with different phenothiazines vary in type, frequency, and mechanism of occurrence, i.e., some are dose-related, while others involve individual patient sensitivity. Some adverse reactions may be more likely to occur, or occur with greater intensity, in patients with special medical problems, e.g., there have been reports of sudden death in patients receiving phenothiazines. In some cases, the cause appeared to be asphyxia due to failure of the cough reflex. In others, the cause could not be determined. There is not sufficient evidence to establish a relationship between such deaths and the administration of phenothiazines.

Dosage and Administration: One capsule daily, taken in the morning. If appetite control is desired through evening hours, shift dose to had declined to do; the notes which had lain in the bottom of a file drawer since 1970 when MacDonald had learned that CID testing had failed to discover the presence of amphetamines in his blood—MacDonald had lost twelve to fifteen pounds in the three to four weeks preceding the murders.

That was a lot of weight to lose for an already fit, twenty-six-year-old Green Beret officer, fresh from paratroop training at Fort Benning. And boxing would not account for it: his last workout with the boxing team had come more than three weeks before the killings. Neither would an odd hour of basketball late on a rainy afternoon produce that sort of weight loss. And the notes suggest that MacDonald had eaten steak for breakfast, he'd been eating cookies pansules over a three-to Valentine's Day and drinking nights later, and—he had accounted for the weeks of Hamlet Hospital breakfast.)

however, could have had a marked three-to-four-week the weight loss. ion could also have had a number of a marked effect. such as, according to the *Physicians'* and irritability, nd insomnia, tenseness and irritability, nations, panic n, assaultiveness, hallucinations, states, "may hree of which severe . . . psychosis. mediate after-

tions," the reference book states ent which can *Desk Reference*, or . . . headache," all three f the Spansule— vation of psychotic ld exhibited in the immediates that the drug was eased promptly and the ily. gradually over a prolonged as one capsule per day, to be taken amine compo

"If appetite control is desired through evening hours," the *PDR* states, "shift dose to midmorning. Late afternoon or evening medication should be avoided because of the resulting insomnia."

Yet Jeffrey MacDonald—outstanding medical student though

Next up, John Gay, the screenwriter. Bostwick questions Gay about his outline for the teleplay. He was working closely with McGinniss, and some of their first conversations concern MacDonald's motivation. How should it be handled in the teleplay?

> **JOHN GAY:** . . . I called [McGinniss] and asked him what the motives are?
> **GARY BOSTWICK:** Did he ever tell you . . . ?
> **JOHN GAY:** No . . . I don't think he was specific about the motives.
> **GARY BOSTWICK:** You didn't put anything about the motives in the script?
> **JOHN GAY:** The motives to me are inexplicable.[6]

And then Bostwick turns to the teleplay itself, Exhibit #409. The revised shooting script from May 24, 1984. Specifically, the green revised pages. (Pages are color-coded according to the date of the revisions.) I feel that I am in the front row of the theater. I can actually see reality being revised. Not because of bad intentions on John Gay's part—he wrote an excellent teleplay for *Fatal Vision*—but because the story being told diverged from the truth and helped cement in the mind of the audience the presumption of MacDonald's guilt. Bostwick asks Gay to describe several scenes. In one scene, Ivory and Paulk are walking down the hallway at 544 Castle Drive, the morning of the murders. Ivory, in the teleplay, is saying, "I want all access to the house restricted. Keep your men posted outside until further notice. I'm going to check with the people upstairs. Don't let anyone touch a thing."[7] Fabulous. It leaves the impression of a preserved crime scene, but don't we all know better? It just didn't happen that way. Before Ivory demands that access be restricted, we see an MP pick up a tipped-over flowerpot and put it upright. Lip service to reality, but in the context of the miniseries, it means nothing.

And then there are the scenes with Helena Stoeckley—set pieces on how to portray an unreliable witness. (If all else fails, just cast an unreliable actress.) Few actresses pass the portrayal-of-insanity test. Notable exceptions are Joanne Woodward in *The Three Faces of Eve* (an adaptation from Cleckley's book) and Olivia de Havilland in *The Snake Pit*. But in those films, the crazy person is the protagonist and hence *must* be sympathetic. Here, Stoeckley is the exact opposite. She is strung out, stupid, mean-spirited, and, yes—last but not least—unreliable.

Here is the dialogue from a scene set in a hippie apartment, somewhere in Fayetteville.

> **"WILLIAM IVORY":** Were you in the MacDonald house the night of the murders?
> **"HELENA STOECKLEY":** I don't even know where he lives!

"WILLIAM IVORY": But you said you don't remember what happened, exactly.

"HELENA STOECKLEY": [*indignant.*] We just went out riding. I don't know. How the hell do I know?

"WILLIAM IVORY": That's what I'm trying to find out.

"HELENA STOECKLEY": I wasn't there, OK? I wasn't there.

And then a second scene. This time in a diner.

"HELENA STOECKLEY": I get this dream, like I'm on the couch there, and he's standing over me.

"A CID AGENT": Who?

"HELENA STOECKLEY": He's got an icepick, drippin' blood.

"A CID AGENT": Go on.

"HELENA STOECKLEY": I don't know. I was on LSD, and mescaline, and grass, too. I don't know, but I get this dream.

"A CID AGENT": What dream, Helena?

"HELENA STOECKLEY": Like I told you. I told you, didn't I? I mean, the guy did it himself!

"A CID AGENT": Who?

"HELENA STOECKLEY": MacDonald! He killed 'em! I'm sick. I'm gettin' out of here! [*Stoeckley runs out of the diner.*]

"A CID AGENT": [*Still in his seat.*] Wait!

It's the '60s and all that. "Sunshine of Your Love" is playing on the stereo in the hippie district when Ivory shows up for his meeting with Stoeckley—her first scene. She says, "I wasn't there, OK? I wasn't there." In the second scene, she says, "MacDonald! He killed 'em . . ." In the artificial universe of the miniseries, Stoeckley's presence only serves to reinforce the claim that MacDonald is solely responsible for the crimes. No one else. "I mean, the guy did it himself."

The scenes essentially replicate Stoeckley's testimony on the stand. Her equivocations, her vacillations. But the scenes purport to show the *investigation* of Stoeckley. And we know full well that during the investigation, a more detailed and less equivocal picture emerged.

John Gay told the jury that he wanted his teleplay to be faithful to the book and the truth.

GARY BOSTWICK: You said you wanted the script to be faithful to the book; isn't that right?

JOHN GAY: Right.

GARY BOSTWICK: You didn't necessarily want the script to be faithful to the truth; you wanted it to be faithful to the book, right? . . .

JOHN GAY: I wanted the script to be faithful to the truth and the book.[8]

But Gay never addressed the possibility that the book and the script might be incompatible with the truth.

———

Kornstein, in his closing remarks, once again claimed that McGinniss was protected by the First Amendment. He said at the very close, in a somewhat hyperbolic mode:

> A verdict for MacDonald would be a verdict for censorship. Make no mistake about it. It's a type of book-burning, really . . . We'll be going back to the Dark Ages, where people were burned because they wrote things that other people didn't like. The lights will go out one by one so that the only light that will remain will be the light from a bonfire of burning books.[9]

Well, the First Amendment does protect speech. And writers should be able to write things contrary to fact. But as Bostwick forcefully argued, McGinniss had signed a contract that invoked "essential integrity." And, truth became the central issue.

The correspondence between McGinniss and MacDonald shows a writer misleading his subject. But the book shows a writer misleading the public about the facts of the case.

GARY BOSTWICK: Someone asked Mr. McGinniss at a book signing about when he became certain that Jeffrey MacDonald was guilty of the murders, and he said, "When the woman in the floppy hat testified at trial, that's when I knew." Well, I had already gone through boxes and boxes of letters between him and MacDonald that showed McGinniss saying to MacDonald, "You'll be out in no time. This is a big travesty. This is nothing." And, "Now, can I stay in your condo? Because it's more convenient to read all of your private papers there." And, "Can you call so-and-so and tell them it's okay to talk to me?" And, "I am now sending you another tape that you can give me your recollections on and send them back."

And I said to myself, "That's just dishonest."

He's pinned down. He said this in public. That's when I thought he was guilty. If you are obtaining cooperation, if you are obtaining something of value from someone, that's fraud.

So, that was the genesis, but at the same time I realized that we wanted to attack the truth of what he had written. But I was never able to get anybody, from Sterling Lord or anybody else, on cross-examination that showed that he had changed the ending. But I believe it happened. I believe he showed it to the publisher and they said, "This is nothing. This is just like you're standing there with the camera. Everybody has read about this. You're going to have to come up with something more." And that's when he came up with the diet pills.

The trial ended with a hung jury. MacDonald agreed to accept a $325,000 settlement from McGinniss. The Kassabs then sued MacDonald for part of the settlement. This time the court proceedings were held at Terminal Island. The lawyers, the Kassabs, and MacDonald assembled at a room in the prison. As Bostwick described it, "Every day we would go in there, and the warden would let us in and talk to us. It was a courtroom inside of the prison. But I'm glad we decided to do it that way. It was easier than having Jeff go to court every day."

It produced another settlement. MacDonald ultimately received about $48,000 toward his defense. Bostwick summed up:

GARY BOSTWICK: I'm the one with the best outcome. I mean, basically I got a lot of my fees. Jeff got some, the Kassabs got some. I understood that they were trying to say that it was a Son of Sam type situation. [The "Son of Sam Law" was designed to keep criminals from profiting from their crimes.] But even then MacDonald didn't make money from writing about it. Somebody else made money from writing about it, and then he made money for suing for something that somebody had done to him that was wrong.

_____

McGinniss had claimed that MacDonald was "the kind of guy who could do it." But who was McGinniss? Who was the guy who betrayed not only Jeffrey Mac-Donald, but the entire defense team? Not only did he live with them, eat with them, exercise with them—he worked with them, investigated with them, and worried with them. Or so it seemed.

There is a curious passage in Joe McGinniss's book *Heroes*, which was published in 1976, long before he met Jeffrey MacDonald and began work on *Fatal Vision*. The passage was part of a diary kept by McGinniss and dated 1970. It starts in January of that year—just before the triple homicide in the MacDonald home—and chronicles McGinniss's increasing fame, the end of his first marriage, and his affair with Nancy Doherty, who was to become his second wife.

Here are two brief quotes from the diary:

JANUARY

My book was number one. Great to be young and a Yankee. I came to town
to do the Cavett show and I threw a party in my suite at the Warwick. Six months
earlier, I had lain in front of a television set with my wife, watching the Cavett
show, and it had seemed another world, light-years away. She had said maybe
someday you'll be on it, and I had said oh, don't be silly, and I'd meant it. Now
I had done Cavett, Carson, Griffin, and all the rest. I had debated the House
minority leader, Gerald Ford, on the David Frost show, and, quite clearly, he had
come out second best.

MAY

And warm mellow weekends. Nancy's two teen-age sisters came to visit. And
brought another girl along. The five of us swam naked in the river. We traveled
a lot: to the Caribbean, to the Kentucky Derby, to speeches I was making around
the country. Then we came back and gave a party. We opened up the whole
house and gave a party for sixty people on the weekend of the Preakness. It was
marvelous. I was Gatsby. And the rest of my life would be a party. Except that
my wife called often on the phone. She pleaded with me to return. There were
long, stuttering silences filled with sorrow. And my mother called, and my father,
and pleaded, too. And my dreams were bad. I dreamed of going back to my wife
and finding her old and horribly wrinkled. And I dreamed terrible dreams about
the maiming and destruction of my daughters.[10]

McGinniss wrote these diary entries nine years before the beginning of his partnership with Jeffrey MacDonald. The parallels between the biographies of Joe McGinniss and Jeffrey MacDonald are endlessly suggestive. McGinniss is writing about himself in these entries—not about Jeffrey MacDonald. And yet the outline of what McGinniss was to write about Jeffrey MacDonald nine years later was (in some nascent but clearly identifiable form) already there.

They were roughly the same age. McGinniss was born on December 9, 1942, MacDonald on October 12, 1943—less than a year apart. Both came from lower-middle-class families. Both were on the fast track. McGinniss in 1969 had published a bestseller, *The Selling of the President 1968*. MacDonald had gone to Princeton, received early admission to medical school at Northwestern, and became a Green Beret doctor with a promising career ahead of him. Both had married early and had been unfaithful to their wives. Both had two young daughters, and (at the time these diary pages were written) both of their wives were pregnant with a third child—a son.

But here's a terrible irony. There is no evidence—despite McGinniss's desperate efforts to find it—to suggest that Jeffrey MacDonald had "terrible dreams of the maiming and destruction of my daughters." And there is evidence that Joe McGinniss did. He wrote about them in his diaries, and published them in 1976.

DELIGHTFULLY BLUE

*Reality is that which, when you stop
believing in it, doesn't go away.*
—Philip K. Dick

Janet Malcolm's *The Journalist and the Murderer* was published two years after the conclusion of the lawsuit. There is no mention in her book of the passages from *Heroes* involving the mutilation of McGinniss's children, even though *Heroes* provides the cornerstone of Malcolm's analysis of journalism. Instead, she quotes the episode in which McGinniss stole William Styron's treasured crabmeat in the middle of the night, baked it into a pie, then wrote about it. (Styron was upset.)

> What the incident is about, what lies below its light surface, is the dire theme of Promethean theft, of transgression in the service of creativity, of stealing as the foundation of making . . . The rare, succulent crabmeat, picked out of the shell, packed, sealed, refrigerated, jealously hoarded, is like the fragile essence of a person's being, which the journalist makes away with and turns into some horrid mess of his own while the subject sleeps.[1]

Janet Malcolm turned McGinniss's betrayal of MacDonald into a generic problem of journalism—"a grotesquely magnified version of the normal journalistic encounter." This is absurd. It's like creating a general theory of human relationships based on Iago's relationship with Othello.[2] In short, Malcolm misses the point, by missing the element of the aberrant in what McGinniss did. But it gets worse.

MacDonald and Malcolm corresponded for a year as she was preparing her manuscript first for *The New Yorker* and then for Knopf. A letter from MacDonald to Malcolm starts with five iterated "No's" followed by an exclamation point.

January 24, 1988

No, no, no, no, no! Not every work "that imposes some form on the flux and disorder of actuality" is a fiction masquerading as nonfiction. I think narratives do have, as you put it, an element of choice, but that is not the same as "fiction." Putting one fact first and another second can be an act of imagination, yet not deceitful—for instance, relative importance of 2 aspects of a case can be juggled with some discretion, yet still be truthful—you would call, I suppose, the juggling "the act of fiction," yet it really isn't. It is judgment based on your knowledge of the facts and your perceptions of reality. Author and subject can certainly disagree on that. That is <u>not</u> the same as the author <u>changing</u> facts; hiding truths; not exploring any alternative other than, in this case, the government's view; or (constructing) imagining alternatives that not only are not proven, but are distinctly disproven by all the known facts by all other observers.

Hippocrates said, "To know is science; merely to believe one knows is ignorance." McGinniss goes much further than that—by altering the known facts, he has constructed an evil thing—his book—which unfortunately impacts many, many people as well as myself—all negatively—with the end result that a climate has been created that prevents any neutral airing of real facts. By lying for money, by selling an artificial view of reality, McGinniss has stolen from me, (or anyone) the ability to ever get the full truth out. Even assuming more truthful accounts of these eighteen years eventually are in the public domain, his work will always linger there, to poison the minds of many. How do you fight it . . . ?

In short, no—not every narrative is a kind of fiction. Every narrative requires judgment and probably some choices by the author—but the narrative doesn't require artful lying, crucial deletions to force the reader only one way, and fictional creations by the author damaging to the truth-seeking process of nonfiction writing. McGinniss can choose between "deep blue" and "delightful blue" when describing a blue sky—he cannot make it into [a] "towering, black, cumulonimbus cloud obscured the sky" in nonfiction. And <u>that</u> is what he did in *Fatal Vision* . . .[3]

Janet Malcolm wrote back a week later, on February 4, 1988:

> I like your figure of the blue sky very much; it nicely describes the situation of journalism as one of freedom within constraint—sort of like the sonnet form. As the poet can't change the rhyme pattern, so the journalist cannot alter facts. Where McGinniss gets the facts wrong, you are right to charge him with falling down on the job. But in the area of interpretation, as you concede, things get less tidy and more murky. In objecting to McGinniss's characterization of you as a superficial hedonist, are you not meddling with his right to describe the blue sky as, say, "insipidly blue" or "menacingly blue," even if others see it as "delightfully blue"? The whole question of what a person is "really" like is so complicated, since we are different things to different people. Our self-presentation is always influenced by our idea of what the other person is like. Accordingly, I imagine that you presented yourself differently to Joe McGinniss than you present yourself to Jeffrey Elliot [the professor who interviewed MacDonald for *Playboy*], based on your perception (or, as the case may be, misperception) of what each man is like. It is in this sense that writers of nonfiction create the characters in their texts—through the two-way force of the author/subject encounter.[4]

I agree with Malcolm. "As the poet can't change the rhyme pattern, so the journalist cannot alter facts. Where McGinniss gets the facts wrong, you are right to charge him with falling down on the job." But in *The Journalist and the Murderer*, a year later, Malcolm decided that facts don't really matter.

> I asked MacDonald about his life in prison, and he spoke for twenty minutes on the subject. You ask this man a question and he *answers* it. After my return to New York, and for the next eight months, I experienced—as McGinniss had experienced—MacDonald's exhaustive and relentless responsiveness. The briefest and slightest of inquiries on my part would bring twenty-page replies from MacDonald, and huge packages of corroborating documents. MacDonald does nothing by halves, and, just as McGinniss had felt oppressed by the quantity of extraneous details in MacDonald's tapes, so was I oppressed by the mountain of documents that formed in my office. I have read little of the material he has sent—trial transcripts, motions, declarations, affidavits, reports. A document arrives, I glance at it, see words like "bloody syringe," "blue threads," "left chest puncture," "unidentified fingerprints," "Kimberley's urine," and add it to

the pile. I know I cannot learn anything about MacDonald's guilt or innocence from this material. It is like looking for proof or disproof of the existence of God in a flower—it all depends on how you read the evidence. If you start out with a presumption of his guilt, you read the documents one way, and another way if you presume his innocence. The material does not "speak for itself."[5]

I find this passage to be disturbing and problematic. Also wrong. The *only* way you can learn anything about MacDonald's guilt or innocence is from this mountain of documents. The material—read, evidence—does not speak for itself. But evidence *never* speaks for itself. It exists as part of a theory or story or narrative. And stories can be tested against reality. Janet Malcolm may not have wanted to look at the evidence in the folders in front of her, but the real story is in those folders—the evidence that remains—as well as the evidence that has been lost or left uncollected.

Note the comparison between "the quantity of extraneous details in Mac-Donald's tapes" and Malcolm's feeling that she was "oppressed by the mountain of documents," as if the evidence had committed an act of aggression against her. If anything, it shows once again how poorly MacDonald had gauged his audience. Malcolm was not focused on MacDonald's guilt or innocence. But isn't this, among other things, the story of the man who has steadfastly proclaimed his innocence? Surely that claim cannot be ignored. Did he do it? Or is someone else responsible? For me, truth and falsity, guilt and innocence, are not incidental to the story; they are the story. "The whole question of what a person is 'really' like is so complicated, since we are different things to different people." Yes, people are different things to different people, but this is not the real issue. It is not that MacDonald is one person to his defense attorneys, and someone quite different to his prosecutors, or to, say, Joe McGinniss. It is that our understanding of his character is based on an assumption of his innocence or his guilt. Not that our assumption of his innocence or his guilt is based on our understanding of his character.

Is this what it all comes down to? Two journalists—one who betrays MacDonald by twisting the facts and another who tells him facts don't make a difference?

———

Dumas created a story about a fictional man who escapes from a fortress, the Château d'If. MacDonald is a real man in a federal prison of concrete and steel. *Fatal Vision* locked him in a far more sinister prison. And Malcolm suggested that it might be a prison from which there is no escape. A prison where truth is drowned out by narrative. There is no escape because there is nowhere to escape *to*.

In a chilling passage in *The Journalist and the Murderer*, Malcolm writes:

> Once I began writing this chronicle, I lost my desire to correspond with MacDonald. He had (once again) become a character in a text, and his existence as a real person grew dim for me (as it had grown dim for McGinniss, until MacDonald's lawsuit brought it back into glaring incandescence). A long letter from him lies unanswered on my desk. It tells me about the developments in his criminal case—"extraordinarily powerful new evidence," which he is "not yet free to make public," but which he will send me if I want it. I do not want it. If MacDonald has nothing to lose anymore from his encounters with writers, a writer has little to gain from him. The story of the murders has been told—by Joe McGinniss—and it has acquired the aura of a definitive narrative. Should MacDonald actually get a new trial, and even turn out to be innocent, he will be able to rebuild his life, but he will not be able to efface McGinniss's story—any more than "powerful new evidence" of Raskolnikov's innocence would efface Dostoevsky's fable.[6]

When Malcolm compares a real person with a character in a novel—it could be Daniel Deronda or Miss Havisham or Lord Jim—is she telling us that we need look no further than the story? But this tragedy—and it is a tragedy—is a tragedy because people did *not* look further than the story, because they did not look further than McGinniss's book.[7]

Malcolm goes on to tells us that "what gives journalism its authenticity and vitality is the tension between the subject's blind self-absorption and the journalist's skepticism." I would put it differently. What gives journalism its authenticity and vitality is the pursuit of truth. This applies to the law, as well. The *real* story is our attempt to separate fact from fiction—to find out what really happened, no matter how difficult that might be.

———

I called Malcolm and asked her about MacDonald's guilt. Does she think he is guilty? (Many readers of *The Journalist and the Murderer* infer from the book that she believed that MacDonald is innocent, but I did not have that impression. Why call it *The Journalist and the Murderer*?) I was left with the feeling that the question made her uncomfortable and that she preferred not to answer it. She threw it back at me. "Why do you think people think he's guilty?" There are many answers, but here is one I gave Janet Malcolm. "Because the alternative is too horrible to contemplate."[8]

The alternative? That an innocent man's life has been destroyed, and that he remains in jail, still claiming his innocence after forty-two years.

BOOK SIX

BEFORE THE LAW

It is possible to cherry-pick evidence to support any conclusion. And it is possible to interpret evidence to support a conclusion. But evidence can also be made to disappear.

After twenty-five years of silence, Jimmy Britt, a retired federal marshal, came forward with a surprising confession. Helena Stoeckley had been silenced by the prosecution, and he had watched it happen.

Britt was suffering from a guilty conscience. He told several of his fellow marshals that he "had been carrying this moral burden," and then in 2005 he contacted Wade Smith. An affidavit was taken. Britt explained that he had not come forward earlier "out of respect for the late Judge Franklin Dupree, who presided over the trial, and others who were with the courts at the time of the MacDonald trial."

Here is his account from the affidavit:

I was assigned to travel to Greenville, South Carolina, to assume custody of a witness by the name of Helena Stoeckley. I picked Ms. Stoeckley up at the County Jail . . . and drove her back to Raleigh . . . During the course of the travel from Greenville, South Carolina, to Raleigh, without any prompting from me whatsoever, Ms. Stoeckley brought up the matter of the trial of MacDonald. She told me . . . about a hobbyhorse in the MacDonald home, and that she, in fact, along with the others, was in Jeffrey MacDonald's home on the night of the MacDonald murders. I knew at the time that what Ms. Stoeckley had said was very important, and it was something I was not about to forget. I remember her words clearly, and they are among the most important words I've ever heard in my life in connection with any case or any of my official work.[1]

If this was all of Britt's affidavit, it could probably be explained away or discarded. No one doubts that Stoeckley had confessed to being in the house. That Stoeckley "remembered" a hobbyhorse in the MacDonald home seems to be a meaningless detail. The picture of the hobbyhorse had been in the Fayetteville newspapers. Stoeckley could easily have seen it there and imagined that she had seen it in the house. And even if she didn't read the *Fayetteville Observer,* she could have heard about the hobbyhorse from people who did. Her recollection provides no proof that she was at the crime scene that night. (It may have impressed Britt, who heard her describe it on their ride to Raleigh, but presumably that's because he didn't know about the photograph in the Fayetteville newspaper.) But it *does* tell us that Stoeckley was still claiming to have been at the crime scene. Yet one more confession in a week filled with confessions.

But Britt's affidavit continues. The following day he brought Stoeckley to the courthouse, first to an office that was being used by MacDonald's attorneys, and then to the eighth floor of the U.S. attorney's office, where she was interviewed by James Blackburn. According to Britt, he remained in the room. I have excerpted the most relevant sections from the affidavit:

Ms. Stoeckley told Mr. Blackburn the same things she had stated to me on the trip from Greenville to Raleigh. She specifically mentioned the hobbyhorse and various other things, and specifically told Mr. Blackburn that she, along with others, had been inside Jeffrey MacDonald's home on the night of the murders. She also said that she had gone to the MacDonald house to acquire drugs . . .

After Helena Stoeckley had given the history of her visit to Jeffrey MacDonald's home, Mr. Blackburn stated: "If you testify before the jury as to what you have told me or said to me in the office, I will indict you for murder."

. . . Upon conclusion of the interview, I took Helena Stoeckley from the eighth floor by stairway down to the seventh floor, and took her into the courtroom.

When Judge Dupree asked Stoeckley in court what had happened in her meetings with the defense and the prosecution, she claimed she had told "both sides the same story," and yet her story had changed from right to left, from top to bottom.

We now have—thanks to the affidavit from Jimmy Britt—an explanation for Stoeckley's testimony. Taken at face value, the fix was in. Blackburn, Britt said, had effectively eliminated Stoeckley as a witness, and as a result had effectively eliminated the other seven witnesses who corroborated her story. (After she forgot her story, there was no story to corroborate.) If she, herself, couldn't remember her confessions, what good was she to MacDonald's defense? Ah. But she *could* remember. She had confessed to Murtagh even before the trial started. And then she had confessed to Blackburn and had been silenced.

Blackburn and Murtagh could truly have believed that Stoeckley's testimony was unreliable. They could have been right. But it was *not* their job to exclude that information from the jury. If Blackburn did threaten Stoeckley and lied about doing it, that alone would be grounds to have MacDonald's conviction overturned.

In a December 16, 2005, article in the *Fayetteville Observer,* defense lawyers were quoted as saying that Britt had passed a polygraph examination. Blackburn was also interviewed.

Blackburn said Wednesday that Britt's account is untrue. He said he only met once with Stoeckley—in the presence of three Justice Department lawyers and never alone with Britt. He said Britt's description of the furniture in the office was incorrect. "I don't recall him ever being in a meeting with me or anybody," Blackburn said. "That is not standard procedure."[2]

The significance of Stoeckley's testimony depends on whom you believe: Blackburn or Britt.[3]

I believe that if the jury in the 1979 trial had heard Stoeckley's confessions, either directly or through the various witnesses called by the defense, they would have voted to acquit. But the various appellate court judges and Judge Dupree thought otherwise. Repeatedly, in court decisions and in briefs by the prosecutors, reference is made to a moment when Wade Smith seemed to imply that Stoeckley did not remember being present in MacDonald's house that night. His actual comments, made in court, hint that there was more to the story.

WADE SMITH: Judge, here, I think, is where we are. Generally, she said to us the same thing and that is, "I don't remember." But in two or three or four instances . . . she says something that would give an interesting insight into her mind. I would submit that we have the right to cross her on those [two or three or four instances]; if she denies them, then they have a right to impeach her on the statements or show she didn't say anything like that.[4]

I KNOW. I KNOW. I KNOW.

I wanted to know when James Blackburn met with Helena Stoeckley, what did he say? What happened in the room? I started by tracking people who were with Stoeckley the week of the trial.

I first saw his name in a brief filed on September 20, 2011, by Hart Miles, one of MacDonald's attorneys:

> Mr. Leonard is a licensed attorney in Raleigh, North Carolina, who was appointed to represent Helena Stoeckley shortly after she testified in the 1979 trial. His communications with Helena Stoeckley shortly after her testimony could be additional evidence of innocence if Mr. Leonard is ordered by the court to reveal those communications in the interest of justice.[1]

Well, until then I had been unaware that Helena Stoeckley *had* an attorney. (It is hard to read through the documents on this case without finding a new name from the inexhaustible cast of characters.)

I called Leonard. He was surprisingly forthcoming, although *not* about what Stoeckley had or had not said to him, more specifically about whether Stoeckley had once again confessed to being in the MacDonald house on February 17.

> **JERRY LEONARD:** There are some things I can talk about; other things I can't talk about. What I'm speaking about is stuff that might be client/attorney privilege.

There's a special rule [in North Carolina] that before I can talk about what Helena told me that might be incriminating, the judge has to order me to respond to the questions. So as to what Helena told me that might relate to the actual commission of the crime, I'm not at liberty to talk about.

ERROL MORRIS: Fair enough.

JERRY LEONARD: If you want me to talk to you about Helena Stoeckley as a person, then I certainly can.

ERROL MORRIS: That's terrific. There are so many recorded interviews with Helena linking her to the crime scene. So I would welcome talking about those aspects of Helena that we *don't* know about.

JERRY LEONARD: I knew she had a military brat background. Her father was a high-ranking officer. I was thinking he was a colonel.

ERROL MORRIS: Yes, I believe he was a lieutenant colonel when he retired. I may be wrong.

JERRY LEONARD: And when I met her, she had boyfriend problems. She had a broken forearm—she had a cast on it—because her boyfriend had beaten her up. And one of my jobs was to keep her away from her boyfriend. [*Chuckling.*] As well as to make sure that she was around the courthouse every day.

ERROL MORRIS: Did you meet the boyfriend?

JERRY LEONARD: No, I didn't. I don't think I did. You know, it's been thirty-two years.

ERROL MORRIS: Yes.

JERRY LEONARD: I enjoyed talking to her. She was smart, and she would ask questions about you. She was in one heck of a predicament, but yet she would say, "Where are you from originally? Da-da-da. What do you like to do? Da-da-da." Stuff like that. She was a pretty pleasant person to be around. I'm sure she was a pleasant person to everybody.

At the beginning of our discussion, I had talked about how Stoeckley was pulled in opposite directions like a piece of taffy—by the defense and the prosecution.

JERRY LEONARD: Yes, MacDonald was pulling her one way, the government's pulling her another way. Part of my job was to keep her from being pulled apart.

ERROL MORRIS: A hard job.

JERRY LEONARD: I just kept her isolated. I found a room at the courthouse for us, and we just sat in the room all day long for a number of days until the trial was over. Until it was determined she was not gonna be used as a witness and then she was released. I've got somewhere—I don't know where I put it—she wrote a poem, and she said, "I am onstage, people laugh at me and make fun of me and then they eat their popcorn." But it rhymed. And she drew a picture, which I do have somewhere. That's how she was feeling at that particular time when she was involved in these court proceedings.

ERROL MORRIS: If you could find any of the writing or the picture, I would—

JERRY LEONARD: I'll try.[2] I can say this. I got a call from the FBI or whoever was working for the government to keep this case from being overturned at one point. The question was, "Did anybody try to influence her testimony?" And the answer was, "Not to my knowledge, because I kept her sequestered." We might walk down the hall, but everybody would purposely totally ignore her. They were concerned at that time as to whether or not the prosecutors had told her that if she testified that she was in the house that night, she was going to be prosecuted for first-degree murder. Ah, but you know, I didn't know anything about that. There was no contact between the attorneys or anybody on either side. Not that I knew of.

ERROL MORRIS: And how did you get this job—

JERRY LEONARD: Of representing Helena?

ERROL MORRIS: Yes.

JERRY LEONARD: I was the judge's first law clerk, in 1971. He didn't have any sons, and so he and I stayed real close. He had two daughters, and he stayed real close to all of his clerks. There were annual parties, birthday parties, given by the clerks, for Judge Dupree. I had been head of Legal Aid here after I left Judge Dupree, so he thought I could understand Helena, because probably I had a drug background or something. I'm kind of kiddin' about that. But he told me he thought I could communicate with her better. He didn't have a great opinion of her mental stability. [*Chuckling.*] So that wasn't much of a compliment. The reason why I say that is because he basically discredited her testimony. He would not let her testify before the jury because of her alleged past drug use—I mean, that was my job to keep her from testifying. Whatever she might have said on the witness stand, whether or not it was true, could have gotten her charged with a crime. Could have, depending on what she said. [*Pause.*] Are you writing? What are you doing?

ERROL MORRIS: No, I'm thinking.

JERRY LEONARD: [*Chuckling.*] Okay.

ERROL MORRIS: But you said something that I am curious about. You said that your job was to keep her from testifying.

JERRY LEONARD: Well, my job was to protect her. I was her lawyer. She was there in custody. She was picked up on a warrant for her arrest. And my job was to keep—protect her legally as best I could. And you never want somebody to take a witness stand knowing that if they said something wrong, they might be charged with it. And I knew her history.

ERROL MORRIS: So as her lawyer, is the job to prevent her from saying anything that can be incriminating to herself?

JERRY LEONARD: Right. The job is to keep her from being charged with any crime.

ERROL MORRIS: But what if she has information helpful to MacDonald?

JERRY LEONARD: I would have lunch with the judge every day in the court chamber, but I wasn't really party to what was going on as far as who wanted her and who didn't. I just had her there every day in her little room. I actually think that MacDonald's [lawyers] were the ones who tried to get her arrested, as I remember.

ERROL MORRIS: I believe that's true, yes.

JERRY LEONARD: And he was the one who probably wanted to put her on the witness stand. Even if she said, "I was there. No, I wasn't there. Yes, I was there. No, I wasn't there." You see what I mean? Somebody was gonna say, "Well, maybe she was there." And maybe that might be reasonable doubt for some of the jurors. But you want me to comment on the trial?

ERROL MORRIS: Well, whatever you would be willing to comment on.

JERRY LEONARD: Here's the scene. You got a federal judge in a monstrous courtroom who graduated from law school at age nineteen and has a photographic memory. That was Judge Dupree. The court in Raleigh draws its jurors from eastern North Carolina, and you're talking about 1979, so you're talking about farmers, you're talking about rednecks, you're talking about—I believe there was a guy there that was in the military as an enlisted man. You got a judge who was raised on a farm and who would say, "Ladies and gentlemen of the jury, we're expecting thunderstorms this afternoon to begin around four thirty or five o'clock, so I'm gonna adjourn court at three o'clock so you can go home and protect your crops." You see what I mean?

ERROL MORRIS: Yes.

JERRY LEONARD: So they loved this judge. So the judge has control over the courtroom, and usually the jury has utmost respect for that judge because the judge was looking after the jury. And you had Bernie Segal, coming in from San Francisco. And I knew who he was, and I knew he was smart. As a matter of fact, he wrote one of my law books. And he came in with his long gray ponytail and brought with him some law students that were working on the case with him. They were all girls, and they were all—no bras, good-looking, long hair—hippie girls from San Francisco. He had with him as local counsel a guy named Wade Smith, who's from eastern North Carolina and then captain of the North Carolina football team. Was a Morehead Scholar. And could really talk to a jury in eastern North Carolina. And you had MacDonald dressed up like a Chicago model—perfectly coiffed hair and very, very tailored suits. So that was the scene. Segal acted like he was above everybody and smarter than everybody, and he was particularly disrespectful to the judge.

ERROL MORRIS: Uh-huh.

JERRY LEONARD: And the judge just handled him wonderfully. But would not give way, and that kind of frustrated Segal. He wouldn't let Wade Smith handle anything, hardly anything in the case. At the closing argument, Segal took the whole time the judge allots—like an hour for each side to do their closing arguments. And Segal used the whole hour.

ERROL MORRIS: If it had been a different lawyer, do you imagine a radically different outcome to the trial?

JERRY LEONARD: I think so, yes. I really think so. Well, let's put it this way, if you could identify more with Jeffrey MacDonald—if he looked more like an emergency room doctor from Huntington Beach than some model from Chicago—they might be able to identify him as a doctor, you see what I mean?

ERROL MORRIS: Yes.

JERRY LEONARD: If he'd come in with these doctor shoes that—I mean, every time I see a new doctor, they have shoes that are comfortable, you see what I mean? Maybe rubber-soled shoes or even tennis shoes. He just didn't stand a chance with Segal. The jury just didn't like him as MacDonald's representative. If he had a different lawyer and he had a different—if he postured himself in a different manner, I think he would have been a whole lot better off.

ERROL MORRIS: Would Wade Smith have won the case for him?

JERRY LEONARD: Yes. Uh-huh.

Could the question of MacDonald's fate have come down to Bernie Segal and inappropriate footwear?

ERROL MORRIS: Here's a question for you. Do you have an opinion about MacDonald's guilt or innocence? Maybe you can't answer that.

JERRY LEONARD: I can't answer that. You're right, I can't answer that, okay?

ERROL MORRIS: Had to ask it anyway.

JERRY LEONARD: I know. I know. I know. I know. I know.

ERROL MORRIS: I didn't ask you about Judge Dupree—

JERRY LEONARD: He's passed away. He would be a hundred years old, I guess.

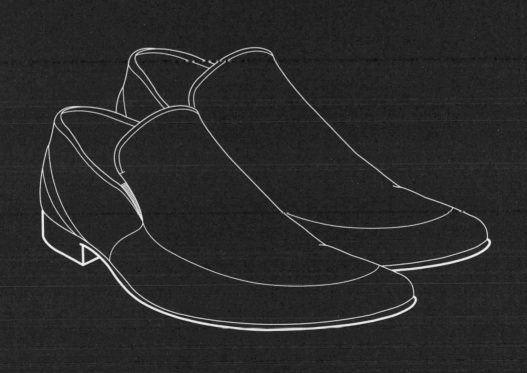

ERROL MORRIS: Judge Dupree wouldn't allow Helena Stoeckley to testify because of her previous drug use. The presumption was that she was a disorganized, confused, addled person.

JERRY LEONARD: Uh-huh.

ERROL MORRIS: From Judge Dupree's decision, I never got the feeling that she was intelligent. That she was a credible person. That you could carry on a conversation with her. That she was likable. That she related to other people—

JERRY LEONARD: I just didn't see a lack of focus or any effect of overuse of drugs or what have you. She was fine, as far as I was concerned.

————

Jerry Leonard had arranged a chaperone, Kay Reibold, to sit with Stoeckley during the remainder of the trial. Reibold had effectively replaced Wendy Rouder.

I called Kay Reibold. She didn't recall much about her time with Helena Stoeckley, but fortunately, there is a detailed statement she gave to Ted Gunderson in Wade Smith's office about five months after the trial. Here is the statement.

During the trial of Dr. Jeffrey MacDonald in August of 1979, I was asked by Jerry Leonard, the attorney who represented Helena Stoeckley, if I would spend time with her acting as a companion and friend to her. It was understood that I spend time with her to and from her hotel room, in her hotel room and in the witness room at the courthouse. Mr. Leonard requested I not discuss Dr. MacDonald's case with her. I agreed. I also explained to Mr. Leonard at this time that I felt he should know that I believed in Dr. MacDonald's innocence. He stated that it was permissible for me to listen to Helena's comments and feelings regarding the case as she volunteered them, but not to request information from her or ask her questions regarding the case.

My experience with Helena Stoeckley took place over a three-day period of time. [Most likely, from Monday, August 20, to Thursday, August 23.] During this time, we established a rapport and in our conversations, she made some statements that I felt were significant . . . At one point when we were discussing her involvement with children at the Tammy Lynn Center [a center for children with disabilities in Raleigh], she hung her head and said quietly, "I still remember Kristen's face. Her face seems familiar to me." This statement was repeated at least one other time when we were discussing her love for children and in particular, an epileptic child she had cared for. Other significant remarks were made in a similar context; that is, a feeling or an image seemed to push to the front of Helena's mind and into her conversation with me. She stated to me that she "still felt" she "was there" at least three times during our experience together. She recalled at one time she "remembered Dr. MacDonald on the couch." She recalled at least two times that she remembered the hobbyhorse being broken.[3]

Stoeckley and Reibold are sitting in a witness room while the trial continues— waiting for a call from the courtroom in the same building. A call that never comes. Stoeckley pipes up once again. But only Reibold is listening, as the trial moves inexorably to a conclusion.

The last day that I spent with Helena as we were sitting in the witness room, she stated to me that she had not indicated on the witness stand the extent to which she was involved in witchcraft. She told me that she was "into it" "much heavier" than she had testified. She also noted that she intended to return to it (her involvement with it). [Here, she is presumably referring to witchcraft.] It was at this same time that she confided that when "everything was over" she was going to disappear and no one would ever find her.

Other than the statements made above, I do not recall any other statements Helena made, pertaining to the trial, that were significant.

During the time I spent with Helena, she seemed depressed and in ill health, but I felt that her state of mind was lucid. I had the impression she had undergone some horrendous experiences considering the extent of her involvement with drugs; however I felt that her feelings and her remarks were reliable.

Lucid and reliable. Reibold had been told by Leonard that it was "permissible for [her] to listen to Helena's comments but not to request information from her." Reibold didn't have to request information. Stoeckley wasn't waiting to be asked.

And so, here we have another series of 1979 confessions from Stoeckley. Three. Reibold, Britt, and Rouder. Well, four. There was also Lynne Markstein, a patient in the emergency room in Raleigh where Helena was taken by Rouder and Red Underhill after her "fight" with Ernie Davis at the motel. Markstein was in the emergency room waiting for an X-ray. Stoeckley started talking to her and told Markstein that she was in the MacDonald house during the murders and that she remembered seeing a bloody child.

She said she was at the MacDonald house during the murders and she remembers looking down and seeing the small child in the crib. She said she was
standing over the crib looking at the child who was covered in blood. I believe she
said the child's throat was cut but I'm not sure. However, she did say something
about a lot of blood and how horrible it was. She also said something to the effect,
"Can you imagine someone like me doing that to those babies?" The reason I
remember this statement is because it stood out above the others. I remember
it because of her hand motions and it was weird . . . According to her there was
no doubt in her mind about being at the crime scene. Not once did she say she
"thought" she was there . . .[4]

I prepared a time line of all of the confessions that Stoeckley had made during the
course of her stay in Raleigh. It raised even more questions.

I called Jerry Leonard a second time.

ERROL MORRIS: I'm confused.

JERRY LEONARD: You told me that last time!

ERROL MORRIS: Well, it's probably true! Stoeckley arrives on a Wednesday—
I believe she was put up in jail. And subsequently moved to a hotel. She was
interviewed by the defense and the prosecution on Thursday. And she testified
on Friday, outside of the presence of the jury.

JERRY LEONARD: Yes, and the judge was of the opinion that she'd taken too many
drugs in the past to offer reliable testimony. Those were the issues that I was
dealing with as far as trying to keep her from testifying.

ERROL MORRIS: Keep her from testifying?

JERRY LEONARD: Lawyers don't like for their clients to talk to juries, anyway. The
bottom line is anything they say can be taken out of context and used against
them. Are you still confused?

ERROL MORRIS: Yes. How come she didn't get a lawyer until after she had testified?

JERRY LEONARD: She was arrested as a material witness, put in jail. She should
have been allowed a lawyer at all stages, but she wasn't assigned one.

ERROL MORRIS: But why not?

JERRY LEONARD: I can't remember. I think there was no one there. Somebody
needed to step up and say, "Hey, she's entitled to a lawyer at this stage." And no
one did. I was appointed as an afterthought. You know, court systems are not
perfect. She was arrested, and I bet until Friday she didn't even have any—
"Ma'am, you're entitled to have a lawyer, da-da-da-da. If you cannot pay, we will

appoint one for you." When she was subjected to whatever she was subjected to prior to my being appointed.

ERROL MORRIS: She wasn't read her rights?

JERRY LEONARD: Not until I was appointed.

Doesn't every schoolboy know that you're supposed to be read your rights? Okay, she wasn't read her rights because she wasn't a suspect. But why wasn't she a suspect? What do you have to do to be a suspect?

But of course the government wasn't particularly interested in listening to what Stoeckley had to say.

JERRY LEONARD: The government called me about two years ago—some FBI agents, I assume. So I said, "I'm not gonna talk to you about what she told me, but I'll hear your questions and make a decision as to whether or not I can answer them." But the questions were, "Has anybody made any threats to her on either side to make her testify one way or the other?"

ERROL MORRIS: Right.

JERRY LEONARD: They didn't ask me anything about what Stoeckley had to say. And then a marshal submitted an affidavit that said that she told him that she was there. Are you familiar with that?

ERROL MORRIS: I am, actually. James Britt.

JERRY LEONARD: And of course Britt didn't have a [legal] privilege in relation to Helena. I can tell you that Britt was very well respected. He certainly wasn't defense oriented. He was one of these hard-nosed marshals that you couldn't get to smile. He wasn't really about being for any defendants.

ERROL MORRIS: And so this story is not something he would just make up?

JERRY LEONARD: No, no, no, no, no. It certainly wasn't in his best interest to be sitting there and saying something that could be used against the government.

———

What was going on? Stoeckley told people she was at the crime scene at least six times during that week. Before her appearance with the defense attorneys and with the prosecutors on Thursday. And after her appearance on the stand on Friday. How do you explain it? Her story was remarkably consistent—except for those two days. The obvious explanation is that she was threatened. Britt tells us

STOECKLEY AT TRIAL, AUGUST 1979

Mon 13	Franklin Dupree issues a bench warrant for Stoeckley.
Tue 14	Stoeckley is arrested by the FBI in Walhalla, South Carolina, and is committed to Pickens County Jail.
Wed 15	Stoeckley is turned over to U.S. marshals, who bring her to Raleigh. She spends the night in Wake County jail.
Thu 16	Stoeckley is brought to the courthouse. She confesses to U.S. Marshal Jimmy Britt. **9:30 am–1:00 pm** Stoeckley is interviewed by the defense. According to Segal, she claims "that she has a recollection of standing outside the house looking at her hands and saying, 'My God, the blood; oh my God, the blood.'" **2:00 pm** Stoeckley is interviewed by the prosecution. According to Jimmy Britt, Blackburn threatened Stoeckley.
Fri 17	Stoeckley is brought to the courthouse. **9:00 am** Defense and prosecution agree that Stoeckley does not need an attorney. **~10:00 am** Stoeckley takes the stand. Segal claims Stoeckley is a hostile witness. Dupree replies: "I have detected nothing in the demeanor or answers . . . to indicate any hostility whatever to your questioning. She has answered the questions forthrightly and intelligently . . ." **1:59 pm to 3:58 pm** The six Stoeckley witnesses testify outside the presence of the jury.
Sat 18	Stoeckley is brought to the Journey's End motel. **1:00 pm** Red Underhill meets her there. She has a black eye.
Sun 19	**11:30 am** Stoeckley and Ernest Davis are ejected from the Journey's End motel. Red Underhill and Wendy Rouder pick up Stoeckley. They go from one hotel to another, ending up at the Hilton. Rouder receives a call from Judge Dupree. **LATER** Stoeckley is taken to the emergency room. Stoeckley tells Lynne Markstein that she remembers standing over a child covered in blood. Red Underhill keeps watch on Stoeckley at the Hilton overnight; she tells him she knows the names of the murderers.

Mon 20	Jerry Leonard is appointed as Stoeckley's lawyer. Kay Reibold becomes her chaperone.
	10:00 am
	Judge Dupree rules on the Stoeckley confessions: they "are about as unclearly trustworthy—or clearly untrustworthy, let me say—as any statements that I have ever seen."
	2:32 pm
	Rouder and Underhill testify that Stoeckley made inculpatory statements over the weekend.
	Dupree rules them inadmissible.
Tue 21	**~3:00 pm**
	Dupree lashes out at Segal over Stoeckley:
	"I think that I have gone just as far as I could to give you every consideration . . . [You] took all day to interview this Stoeckley . . . with your people going with her all over motel rooms and all over the lot . . ."
Wed 22	Dorothy MacDonald, Jeffrey MacDonald's mother, testifies.
	Helen Fell, a friend of the family, testifies.
	Stoeckley confesses.
Thu 23	**2:30 pm**
	Stoeckley is released from custody, despite the protestations of the defense.
	JAMES BLACKBURN: Her lawyer, Jerry, is still around.
	JUDGE DUPREE: I asked Mr. Segal—I said, "What is he still doing here?"
	WADE SMITH: I talked to Jerry Leonard at great length, Your Honor, this morning—talked to him for a long time, and this woman continues to say things that tie her to this case . . .
Wed 29	MacDonald is convicted of the three murders and sentenced to three consecutive life sentences in prison.

that indeed is what happened. One reason we should believe Jimmy Britt is that, without his affidavit, what happened in the courtroom doesn't make sense.

But there is still something deeply puzzling. Leonard was not appointed by Dupree as Stoeckley's attorney until Monday, August 20. She had arrived in Raleigh the previous Wednesday, August 15. She was a material witness—possibly an accessory to the murders. Shouldn't she have been given an attorney promptly on arrival in Raleigh—maybe even before? But she wasn't given an attorney. An oversight? I find that hard to believe.

It could have gone down differently. Imagine the following hypothetical situation. Stoeckley arrives in Raleigh and the court appoints an attorney for her. She appears on the witness stand on Friday, takes the Fifth—refusing to answer any questions. Segal moves to put the six Stoeckley witnesses on the stand. And that is what the prosecution feared—as much as the possibility of Stoeckley testifying under oath that she had been in the house.

In retrospect that is probably what the defense should have done. They *should* have insisted that she have an attorney. But Segal was so convinced that Stoeckley would confess that he seemed utterly surprised—indeed, dumbfounded—when she turned out to be a hostile witness.

Here's my theory. On the stand Stoeckley performed as the prosecution expected. Having been threatened, she remembered nothing. Or so she claimed. And as a result, the corroborating witnesses were eliminated because they supposedly no longer had anything to corroborate. Once Dupree had decided to throw out the six witnesses—saying the Hearsay Rule didn't apply—the prosecution (and perhaps Dupree as well) was worried that Stoeckley would change her mind and agree to appear as a friendly defense witness. To prevent this from happening, Stoeckley was appointed an attorney to keep her from offering any further testimony.

I found an additional document, a statement given by Jerry Leonard on January 23, 1980, to John Dolan Myers, a defense investigator.

Jerry Leonard is the attorney appointed to "represent-protect-etc." Helena Stoeckley while she was in Raleigh for the MacDonald trial. He was appointed to represent Ms. Stoeckley by the court.

Mr. Leonard stated, "They called me from the courthouse and told me that Helena had asked for a lawyer and asked would I be interested in representing her."

Leonard stated that he never received any suggestions or instructions from the court regarding Ms. Stoeckley after he was appointed to represent her.

Mr. Leonard stated that he received permission from Ms. Stoeckley to discuss the things she told him with attorney Wade Smith. Mr. Leonard stated that he had a conference with Mr. Smith and told him what Helena had told him. He stated that he also gave Mr. Smith some insight as to his impressions of Ms. Stoeckley . . .

Mr. Leonard stated that he had several private conversations with Judge Dupree about Helena Stoeckley. Mr. Leonard stated that he was not sure if, as an officer of the court, these conversations were privileged information. He did state that anything Judge Dupree might or might not have told him concerning the Judge's feelings about the guilt or innocence of Jeff MacDonald seemed to have been expressed by his mood and actions in the courtroom during the trial . . .

NOTE: Mr. Leonard stated that he did not know if MacDonald was guilty or innocent; however, he stated that he did feel that the prosecution did not prove their case. He stated that he thought MacDonald had been screwed.[5]

I called Leonard again.

ERROL MORRIS: I have so many questions about this document. Let me see how I can start off simply. Why did you contact Wade?

JERRY LEONARD: I don't know. I don't remember doing it.

ERROL MORRIS: You don't have any memory of it at all?

JERRY LEONARD: No, I sure don't. It would be very interesting to know what I told Wade. I just do not know, and I don't remember the circumstances at all. Honestly, my memory is not one hundred percent, and for anything that I say to be reliable even as I'm trying to fill in the facts for you, it's fairly dangerous, I think, because honestly I'm wrong on some key facts.

ERROL MORRIS: There are things about the trial that just seem wrong. The feeling that I get is that you were used. I can just lay it out on the table. You were used by the court in a way that seems to me unsavory.

JERRY LEONARD: Okay. I think I was used, but unsavory because of what?

ERROL MORRIS: Because the judge was watching Stoeckley like a hawk, because he maneuvered this deal to keep her testimony away from the jury. It seems to me deeply wrong and unethical.

JERRY LEONARD: Okay. Well, I can't dispute that one way or the other.

ERROL MORRIS: Let me give you my interpretation, and you can tell me if you think I'm completely off base. Stoeckley said things to you and implicated her in these murders. What she said, how she implicated herself, I don't know. But you went to Wade Smith because you believed the defense should know about it.

JERRY LEONARD: Okay. Well, that is a logical interpretation. But you have to ask Wade. I'd like to be a little shining light, but I just don't know that I can. What happened was I got this call from the clerk—it wasn't Judge Dupree—asking if I would represent a hippie girl. My job, I had been thinking all of these years, was just to fade away, keep her out of the courtroom. I didn't even know that she had testified.

ERROL MORRIS: Well, you were appointed the week after she took the stand. Perhaps with the intention of keeping her off the stand in the future.

JERRY LEONARD: I can't imagine that I was not told that she testified. I would have thought I would have ordered a transcript of her testimony right away. Obviously, I didn't. I just remember sitting there, and it seemed pretty boring to me. The pay at that time was thirty-five dollars an hour, and you were losing money running an office on thirty-five dollars an hour. I take it back; back then it was thirty-five dollars an hour for out of court and forty-five dollars for in court, so I guess that was in court.

ERROL MORRIS: Here is another issue. In Myers's deposition, you indicate to Myers that you had had several conversations with Dupree about Stoeckley. It seems to me—and you know this stuff better than I do—isn't it improper for Dupree to do that?

JERRY LEONARD: Well, it may have been. In hindsight, it certainly would have been better not to do that.

ERROL MORRIS: Had Dupree already made up his mind?

JERRY LEONARD: I don't remember any exact words, okay, but my impression was that Dupree thought that MacDonald was guilty; and I focus on the word "thought."

ERROL MORRIS: If Stoeckley spoke with you about her involvement, would you have said something also to the judge about that?

JERRY LEONARD: I don't know. My thoughts are that I was trying my best to keep her from being a witness.

ERROL MORRIS: But she would have pled the Fifth if she had been called, would she not?

JERRY LEONARD: Do you know when the murders occurred?

ERROL MORRIS: On February 17, 1970.

JERRY LEONARD: Okay. And the jury trial was August of 1979?

ERROL MORRIS: Right.

JERRY LEONARD: There was a ten-year statute of limitations on murder in the federal system. And that was my concern. If I could get her past that ten-year period, she was clear. They couldn't indict her.[6]

ERROL MORRIS: It was not very far off. It would have been February 1980. Six months.

JERRY LEONARD: Yes. That was key in my mind.

CRUMBS

Wade Smith's comments at trial, taken in tandem with Bernie Segal's, have troubled me. They are incompatible. During the 1979 trial, Segal had argued to Judge Dupree that Stoeckley had remembered a lot.

BERNARD SEGAL: The photograph that I showed her of the bedroom of Kristen MacDonald: during the interview yesterday, she stated that she remembered riding the rocking horse when she looked at that picture.

She also stated yesterday she remembered standing at the end of the sofa holding a candle. She also said when she saw the body of Kristen MacDonald—the one when she was clothed, with the baby bottle—that that picture looked familiar to her.

That scene looked familiar. She also said when she was shown the photograph of Colette MacDonald—the same one I showed her today—that she said that the face in that picture looked familiar, except that the chin was broken and made it a little hard.

She also stated—and I'm going to get to it—she's gotten to the point where she does not sound like she is going to cooperate further—that she was standing on the corner of Honeycutt across from Melonee Village.

She has a recollection of standing there during the early morning hours of February 17, 1970. She further stated yesterday, and I intend to ask her now, that she has a recollection of standing outside the house looking at her hands and saying, "My God, the blood; oh my God, the blood."

She said that took place February 17, 1970. There are witnesses to each of these things. I must say, Your Honor, there were persons present the entire time this took place.

I intend to now ask her directly each of these questions. If she refuses or denies her statements, I ask for leave to confront her: "Did you not say that yesterday when you were confronted with these photos?"[1]

I called Wade Smith hoping to get the bottom of it. What had Stoeckley said?

ERROL MORRIS: Here is what puzzles me. Helena testifies on Friday, but she was interviewed by you and Segal the previous day. Can you tell me about it?

WADE SMITH: We sat down in a room, at a little table, a little wood table. There were four of us sitting around the table. Joe McGinniss was there. Helena was there. Bernie was there. And I was there. Helena looked nothing like I would have thought she would look. I imagined her as a lady with a blond wig and a floppy hat. I imagined her as she would have looked ten years earlier. I imagined her as being a very attractive woman, hippie-like and so on. But she was a terribly wasted, terrible-looking woman. Much, much overweight. She looked like Mrs. Khrushchev. Do you want me to go on?

ERROL MORRIS: Absolutely, yes.

WADE SMITH: So, I'm thinking, how would I do this? She came in, and she sat down in her chair. And Bernie was sort of steepling his hands, you know, doing push-ups with his fingers in his hands, and looking into the distance.

And he said to her, "Helena, it is rare in one human life when a person has an opportunity to make something wonderful happen in an instant. And you have the power to do that. You have the power to make something wonderful happen. And you have the power to end this agony for this man, to put it all to rest for him, and to let it be ended. And I hope you will do that today. I hope you will do it."

And there was this moment.

And she said, "I don't know anything about it. I certainly wasn't there. And I think he did it. And you promised me some food. And no one has given me any food. And you promised me I'd get something to eat." It had gone from sublime hope to deepest of ridiculous statements. And she sat there, as she ate her sandwich, and leafed through the bloody photographs that were exhibits in the case and seemed completely and totally unmoved by them.

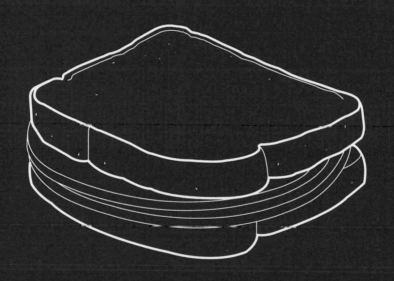

ERROL MORRIS: Quite a turn of events.

WADE SMITH: And we hoped that after she had some food, we would be able to persuade her. But we never were. We never were. She stuck to that story. And she certainly stuck to it when she testified.

ERROL MORRIS: You were all shocked?

WADE SMITH: Yes, we were. We had our hopes so built on the idea that this was the way to finally put the case to rest.

ERROL MORRIS: So, here's the problem that I have. Bernie Segal is now dead. I can't ask him. But I can't reconcile it with—

WADE SMITH: With what Bernie was asking, what Bernie was saying?

ERROL MORRIS: That's correct. And here's a quote from you. "Judge, here, I think, is where we are. Generally, she said to us the same thing and that is, 'I don't remember.' But in two or three or four instances—whatever the list would reveal—she says something, which would give an interesting insight into her mind. I would submit that we have a right to cross her on those. If she denies them, they have a right to impeach her on those statements or show that she did not say anything like that."

How do I reconcile this with what Segal says in court?

WADE SMITH: Well, let's see if there's anything to reconcile. For example, remember what I said: that, from my perspective, we didn't get what we wanted, but what we wanted was a flat-out admission that she was there. But I mean, and I confess to you that I do not have the detailed recollection of her looking down and saying, "I do seem to remember," though I mean and I confess to you that I believe that is true. I mean and I know that there must have been a number of little things she said that would cause us, as lawyers, to pick up a few little crumbs, you see what I'm saying?

ERROL MORRIS: Yes.

WADE SMITH: We didn't get the whole cake, but we did see a few crumbs fall down on the floor and we're gathering those up. And that's what we're asking the court to give us an opportunity to go into.

ERROL MORRIS: Here's Segal again: "She has a recollection of standing there during the early morning hours of February 17, 1970. She further stated yesterday, and I intend to ask her now, that she has a recollection of standing outside the house, looking at her hands, and saying, 'My God, the blood; oh my God, the blood.'"

WADE SMITH: Yes, I remember that. I remember that.

ERROL MORRIS: You remember her saying that?

WADE SMITH: Yeah. Wait, let's back up. Because it is, I mean, history will not tolerate my misstating this one iota. I remember her saying, "My God, the blood, the blood." But I honestly can't tell you, as I sit here right now, if she said it in that meeting. But I know that she said it. She had said it before. I will never be able to remember, I know, whether she said that to us in our meeting with her the day before. But I know that she had said that. Now, it could be that she said it to Jane Zillioux and Red Underhill, and it may be that that's where we got it.

ERROL MORRIS: Or do you think that Bernie just imagined this?

WADE SMITH: No. I would say this: there is one principle that I believe I could go to my grave on, and that is that Bernie would not have told the judge an untruth. Nor would I.

ERROL MORRIS: Let me go back over this for a second. It's so peculiar. Here's Segal again: "She also stated yesterday she remembered standing at the end of the sofa holding a candle. She also said when she saw the body of Kristen MacDonald—the one when she was clothed, with the baby bottle—that that picture looked familiar to her. That scene looked familiar. She also said when she was shown the photograph of Colette MacDonald—the same one I showed her today—that she said that the face in that picture looked familiar, except that the chin was broken and made it a little hard."

WADE SMITH: All of that may absolutely have been things that she said in that meeting with us. I don't doubt it one bit. I mean, I don't doubt it. It could be, but it's been so long, I don't know whether she said those things right then. I just don't know.

ERROL MORRIS: Memory is so weird. Here is something else that bothers me. And if you think it's completely off base, I'd love being corrected. I asked myself, "How come the prosecutors didn't give her an attorney?" Jerry Leonard was not appointed, by his own account, until the following Monday. I think they didn't appoint an attorney because the attorney would have told her to plead the Fifth. And then the jury would have had to have been aware of that fact. I know this may seem far-fetched.

WADE SMITH: Well, I don't think what you're saying is far-fetched. Judge Dupree believed that Jeff was guilty. I thought the world of Judge Dupree. He was, in so many ways, a father figure to me. But I don't think Judge Dupree gave him a fair trial. I think Judge Dupree had his mind made up. And there were many instances in the trial, when maybe unwittingly, he telegraphed to the jury how he felt.

What you say may be a possibility, but it's always made a little bit more sense to me that they started thinking, "Wait a minute. Wait a minute. We've brought this woman in here in the custody of the FBI. We have turned her over to people to examine her. She's been on the witness stand. Whoa. We better at least let her have counsel to help her to feel that she's been treated properly." And I've always thought they appointed her a lawyer to protect themselves.

ERROL MORRIS: Another thing that puzzles me is if prosecutors had any access to Stoeckley before you interviewed her?

WADE SMITH: Not that we know of, not that they have ever said.

ERROL MORRIS: When Stoeckley blurts out this stuff, and then demands the sandwich, you don't remember what kind of sandwich, by the way, do you?

WADE SMITH: It was a bologna sandwich.

ERROL MORRIS: Oh good grief.

WADE SMITH: That's true. I'm so sorry to tell you. That's my memory. That's my recollection. I may be wrong. That's a pretty tiny fact for me to store away for thirty-one or thirty-two years.

ERROL MORRIS: Do you believe that she was there in the house?

WADE SMITH: Well, yes I do. I mean, the fact that she told her own mother that she was there, and the fact that she said it over and over. Now, I know that people get fixations and things like that. But it's so strange that this woman who was described by MacDonald in his earliest statements to the police, would, in effect, say, "Yeah. You know, he's right. I was there." We should have won. There was a reasonable doubt. The government did not prove their case beyond a reasonable doubt. It is still an enduring mystery. And if he's found guilty, it should not be a mystery.

———————

Following my last conversation with Leonard, I called Smith again. He once again tried to recall what Stoeckley had said that day in Segal's office. This time, he rummaged around for a copy of *Fatal Vision* and started reading from the book. It included the detail about the bologna sandwich.[2] Here was one of MacDonald's principal defense attorneys, and it was as if his memories were gone, and all that remained was McGinniss's account.

As for what Leonard had said to Wade Smith, neither of them remembered the conversation.

WADE SMITH: Well, I can't say that I never had that conversation with Jerry. If he says I had it, I would trust him.

Although, I can't remember what Jerry would have told me, this woman [Stoeckley] had the ability to dance around and dance around this tantalizing, unbelievably delectable morsel as to was she in the house. She would say things like "I still remember all the blood, all the blood"; and just when you would think,

"Okay, she has said once and for all that she didn't do it," she would say, "But somehow I still can't help but remember," and it would be like some tantalizing series of words that caused you to come back. You had flown away and you'd come back; and that may be what Jerry told me.

Over the years I've had at least one conversation with Jerry, maybe ten years ago, where I said, "Jerry, isn't there something dramatic that you need to tell me?" And I always was left believing there may be, but that he wouldn't just tell me.

ERROL MORRIS: Although she gave him permission to talk you, clearly.

WADE SMITH: Yes. But I never have believed that Jerry has felt comfortable telling me everything he knows.

It was a conversation mentioned in a transcript and a statement, but otherwise forgotten.[3] Has Leonard waited so long to reveal what Stoeckley told him that now, his memories have faded and there's nothing to reveal?

———

Britt's affidavit was filed on November 3, 2005. Britt died of congestive heart failure on October 19, 2008. He had been ill for several years.[4] Judge James C. Fox, Judge Dupree's friend and successor—he gave the eulogy at Dupree's funeral—finally ruled on November 4, 2008. It was fifteen days after Britt's death. Even if Britt was telling the truth, Fox wrote, it would not have mattered: "MacDonald has not demonstrated that the Britt affidavit, taken as true and accurate on its face and viewed in light of the evidence as a whole, could establish by clear and convincing evidence that, but for constitutional error, no reasonable fact finder would have found MacDonald guilty of the murder of his wife and daughters."[5]

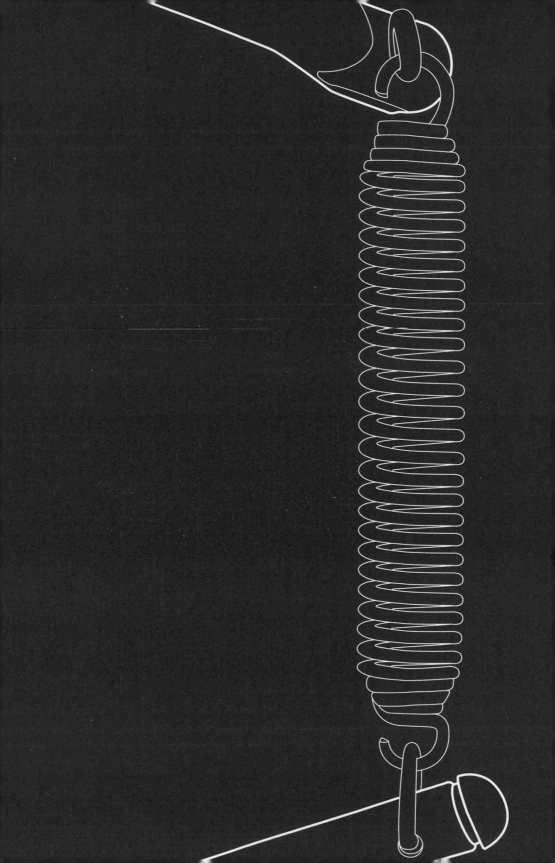

THE MORNING NEWSPAPER

Shall he suffer not thinking on, with the hobby-horse,
whose epitaph is "For, oh, for, oh, the hobby-horse is forgot."
—Shakespeare, *Hamlet*

In 2005, MacDonald had appealed on the basis of Britt's claim that Stoeckley's testimony was coerced. That if Stoeckley had not been pressured and had been allowed to testify, there would have been a different outcome to the trial. (The same argument had been put before the Fourth Circuit over twenty years earlier.) The government in turn argued that Stoeckley's memory had been refreshed by Segal. Hadn't he shown her pictures of the hobbyhorse the day before she testified?

On August 17, 1979, Stoeckley was on the stand. Segal was questioning her about their meeting the day before.

> **BERNARD SEGAL:** Let me hand the group of photos back to you again. Ms. Stoeckley, do you recall, just as you are now, sitting on the stand, looking at those photos, do you recall staring at those photos at some length when Jane Zillioux was sitting just about next to you in that room in this building?
>
> **HELENA STOECKLEY:** I mentioned something about the rocking horse.
>
> **BERNARD SEGAL:** Yes; all right, will you tell us about the rocking horse—what you recall saying about it?

HELENA STOECKLEY: I made some comment about it being broken or something.

BERNARD SEGAL: Does the picture show anything about a broken rocking horse?

HELENA STOECKLEY: I can't tell if it is broken or not. It looks like it is.

BERNARD SEGAL: Beg your pardon?

HELENA STOECKLEY: It looks like it is broken.[1]

But it doesn't look like it is broken. I looked through the various CID photographs of Kristen's bedroom. You can see part of the hobbyhorse from two different angles. And in the picture of the horse that had appeared in the *Fayetteville Observer*, the springs seem to be intact.

On the stand, Stoeckley was insisting that she had no memory of anything that night, and at the same time offering a very specific memory about that night. There was the very real possibility that Stoeckley's memory had been refreshed by Segal the day before she testified, or that she had seen the photograph of the hobbyhorse in the *Fayetteville Observer* days after the murders. Blackburn made a point of it during his summation to the jury. He brandished the newspaper page:

> They made a big deal about the hobbyhorse—that the hobbyhorse looked familiar. Ladies and gentlemen, we showed you yesterday—the one thing we did on rebuttal evidence—the only thing we did—we showed you the fact that the newspaper on the day after the murders had a photograph of that hobbyhorse in that room in the paper. I suggest to you that you can infer from the evidence that's where Helena Stoeckley, if she saw that hobbyhorse at all, saw it, like everybody else in Fayetteville, in the morning newspaper.[2]

But the paper never mentioned a *broken* hobbyhorse.

Had Stoeckley made any mention of the broken hobbyhorse before 1979?

I asked Max Larkin—my researcher with an encyclopedic knowledge of the case—about anything that Stoeckley had said about the broken hobbyhorse. Anything that *anybody* had said. And he came back with a surprising document. Maybe not a slam-dunk proof of anything, but something tangible. Some small reason to believe that Stoeckley was telling the truth.

On March 27, 1971, Richard Mahon—the detective assigned to Stoeckley on the CID reinvestigation team—interviewed William Posey, Stoeckley's next-door neighbor. Posey was describing a conversation from August 1970. He remembers the date because it was just before he testified at the Article 32 hearing.

[Stoeckley] was alone and I walked up to her outside of the Village Shoppe and started a conversation with her. I asked her during the conversation if she was really involved in the MacDonald murders. HELEN said that she didn't know she was involved or not because she had been on drugs that night. She said she didn't think she could kill anybody but she was capable of "holding a candle." She mentioned something about CPT MacDONALD being a masochist and that she had the same tendencies.

She said somebody, some guy, but I don't recall if she mentioned a name or not, had ridden a child's hobbyhorse in the hallway at CPT MacDONALD's house. She said that some part of the hobbyhorse had gotten broken. She sometimes talked like she had really been at CPT MacDONALD's house.[3]

I called William Posey. What did he remember about all this? It was over forty years ago. And about four years ago, he suffered a massive stroke that left him unable to talk except with great difficulty. Rock Posey, his younger brother, served as our interpreter. Rock had lived with his brother in 1970 and had known Stoeckley himself.

ERROL MORRIS: Tell me about Stoeckley and the hobbyhorse, what she told you.

WILLIAM POSEY: Broke. Bolt.

ROCK POSEY: She described the hobbyhorse as being broken, and at that point none of that had been released to anyone.

WILLIAM POSEY: Beforehand.

ROCK POSEY: What he's saying is Helena Stoeckley had knowledge of things before they became public knowledge. Right after the incident she was aware of the hobbyhorse. So my brother went to the cops—

WILLIAM POSEY: No, no. MPs . . .

ROCK POSEY: MPs.

ERROL MORRIS: Does your brother believe Stoeckley was there the night the murders occurred?

ROCK POSEY: Do you believe she was there that night?

WILLIAM POSEY: Oh, yes.

It was a seemingly irrelevant detail. But its seeming irrelevance makes it important. Who cared about a broken toy? Presumably, no one. The CID was focused on coffee tables and flowerpots. It was at the crime scene but was not related to the crime. Was Stoeckley trying to tell us something? Could it be like Poe's "Purloined Letter"—a crucial piece of evidence, left in plain sight, that everyone ignored?

I had originally called Helen Fell—the friend of the MacDonalds' who testified at trial—because I wanted additional details about MacDonald's relationship with his in-laws. I called her again.

> **HELEN FELL:** Mildred—you can ask anybody who ever knew Mildred how she perceived or engaged in a conversation with Jeff. She was all bright and chirpy. "Oh, he's so wonderful, I wish he was my son." Mention Colette, and she'd say—"She's just a lazy bitch. She can't even get her ass out of bed." And that was about her daughter. And as far as the kids went, Mildred used them as the bludgeon.
>
> **ERROL MORRIS:** Did Jeffrey's mother like Colette?
>
> **HELEN FELL:** Oh, yeah. Colette had a much better relationship with Mac [Jeffrey's mother] than she did with her mother, by far. In fact, Mac would say to her behind the scenes, "Colette, nothing terrible is going to happen to you because you talked to your mother. Whether you like her, you don't like her, you hate her, she's still your mother." And tried to encourage her to at least be civil.

And then out of nowhere, she brought the hobbyhorse up.

> **HELEN FELL:** And the story of the rocking horse. Nobody but nobody knew that rocking horse was broken. And I ended up knowing about it because, inadvertently, I was talking to Jeff the day that it happened. And he said, "Oh, God, I'm gonna have to listen to Mildred. She got the kids a rocking horse. And she got it at probably a yard sale." Things for herself she bought at Nordstrom's and Lord and Taylor; things for everybody else she bought them catch as catch can. And that was the day that the thing was broken. And no one ever knew it; no one ever went around advertising that the kids had a broken hobbyhorse, or whatever you want to call it. But Helena Stoeckley knew it. And there's only one way she knew it—she was there.

SLAYING SCENE—Ft. Bragg Provost Marshal Col. Robert J. Kriwanek goes over a floor plan to the home of Army Capt. Jeffrey MacDonald. No suspects have yet been apprehended in the slayings of Capt. MacDonald's wife and two children. The children's bedroom is shown at right with some toys overturned. The bed, shown partially at the right, had blood stains on it. Photograph was made through the window.

Massive Search On For Killers

(Continued from Page 1A)

treatment. We're looking into every patient he had."

The provost marshal revealed that a four-inch paring knife, an ice pick and an 18-inch wooden stick, all bloodied, were found by investigators.

The knife was located in the master bedroom and the stick and ice pick were located outside the rear door. Capt. MacDonald has been "moonlighting" at Cape Fear Valley Hospital and also at a Hamlet hospital, primarily in the emergency room.

FBI agents this morning were checking records of all persons who might have been treated by the doctor at those two hospitals.

Narcotics agents joined the investigation Tuesday and had questioned several dozen persons who are part of the Fayetteville - Cumberland County hippie community.

As a member of the Preventive Medicine section of Sixth Special Forces, Dr. MacDonald had patients who were involved in drug abuse.

However, early reports that most of his work at Ft. Bragg dealt with narcotics users was not true. There is a special drug education program in Sixth Special Forces

but MacDonald was not part of that program.

His fellow officers in the Sixth Special Forces were shocked when news of the deaths reached the headquarters in the JFK Center Tuesday morning.

One officer said that Mrs. MacDonald had called his wife the previous day, urging her to visit the MacDonald home Tuesday to see her new maternity clothing.

Mrs. MacDonald was approximately four months pregnant, according to her friends.

MacDonald entered the Army as a captain on June

20, 1969. All of his duty, of course, has been with the Medical Corps.

He won his parachute wings as a military parachutist on Aug. 27.

All of the officers who discussed the murders Tuesday described MacDonald as "an excellent officer."

Col. Francis Kane, commanding officer of the Sixth, said he had talked with MacDonald a day or so before and that they had discussed his becoming a career officer.

"He hadn't made up his mind, yet," Col. Kane said, "but he was leaning that way."

Officers Reconstruct Nightmare

(Continued from Page 1A)

was taken from the MacDonald's kitchen.

It is not known at this time whether MacDonald was attacked before the children were killed. The youngsters were stabbed repeatedly about the chest and neck, once again apparently with both the ice pick and knife.

MacDonald has told the investigators that he believes he was awakened by his wife screaming.

There have been confusing reports at this point from Ft. Bragg. The initial release stated that the doctor awoke to see a young white girl, wearing a large-brim, floppy hat and muddy boots, standing at the foot of the couch. The initial report stated that the doctor said the girl was holding a candle.

Later, however, ranking officers stated that the story about the candle may not have been accurate. It wasn't clear if the doctor's story had varied or if the persons involved in the initial investigation had erred.

MacDonald said he saw a Negro man, age unknown, wearing an Army fatigue jacket with sergeant's stripes on the sleeve. He said he also saw two white men, ages unknown. There was no clear description of the latter two assailants.

One of the men struck MacDonald on the head with a stick or club. Another stabbed him in the chest and stomach and upper arm.

MacDonald reportedly has told investigators that he struck out blindly with his fist and that he believes he hit one of the men in the face.

At this point, MacDonald apparently became unconscious. There is a lapse of time in the picture puzzle that could have been only a matter of a few minutes. At this time, it has been impossible to pin down the exact time.

MacDonald apparently awoke and crawled or staggered to a telephone. There are two telephones in the house and both receivers were off the hook.

Once again, it hasn't been made clear whether MacDonald can his wife and children before he dialed "O" for the Fayetteville operator.

Miss Carolyn Landen, assistant chief operator, answered the call. He told he he needed military police and an ambulance, that he had been stabbed. He did not mention his wife and children.

At that point, MacDonald either dropped the phone or hung up. Miss Landen called Ft. Bragg and relayed the message.

Five or downminted in Inku, she called MacDonald's number. She said he answered the phone but that he said nothing further than repeat his address.

MORE MORE EMORE

Military police arrived at the home minutes later and knocked on the front door. There was no answer. One of the MP's went to the back door and found it open.

There was a light burning in the master bedroom and also in the kitchen. The MP saw the body of Mrs.

MacDonald. He also saw the captain lying near her.

He said there were signs of a struggle. He turned and ran outside to notify the duty officer who in turn entered the home to examine the bodies of the couple. He discovered MacDonald was still alive and the MP's gave him first aid.

The bodies of the two children were found in their rooms, lying in pools of blood. They had been stabbed over and over again in their chests and necks.

MacDonald was revived and gave a few details to the police before the ambulance arrived.

A military policeman ran next door to the home of Warrant Officer D. L. Kalin. He awoke the neighbor by pounding on the door. The MP had not wanted to use the phone in MacDonald's apartment because of the possibility of fingerprints on the receiver.

Kalin told investigators the first indication he had of the tragedy was when the MP knocked on his door. He said he had heard no noises.

Other neighbors said they did not hear any outcry. Persons questioned throughout Corrigidor Courts said they had not seen any suspicious persons in the area.

Col. Robert Kriwanek, post provost marshal, said a press conference Tuesday that it was "quite apparent" that whoever entered the home and committed the crimes "was quite knowledgeable of Army quarters."

He did not elaborate, only to say that his reasoning was based on the fact that "this thing happened so fast."

Kriwanek said that the word "pig" was scrawled on the wooden headboard of the bed in the master bedroom. This was the only word found by investigators to have been written by the intruders.

There were bloody footprints in the house but it was quickly pointed out that they could have been made by military policemen who first entered the home.

There was no light in the hallway or living room where MacDonald was sleeping. Kriwanek said in his press conference Tuesday that this was the reason that MacDonald could not give a more detailed description of his assailants.

The assumption that all four of the persons who were in the house were young, is nothing more than an assumption at this point. It was clear from MacDonald's statements that the girl was young but the age of the other three had not been established Tuesday.

It is also an assumption that there were only four people involved in the murder. MacDonald said he saw only four persons but the investigators have admitted there could have been more.
— By PAT REESE

President Asserts Soviet Increasing Nuclear Threat

(Continued from Page 1A)

had new planned at the State Department and replaced such documents issued in former years by the Defense Department, was built around his own speeches of the past year and quoted at length from his own previous

It officially labeled as the "Nixon doctrine" the policy line he laid down at Guam last year during a Pacific trip that the U.S. wanted no more Vietnams and was cutting its involvement in Asia while promoting Asian self-help.

Nixon tried the paper "United States Foreign Policy for the 1970's—A new Strategy for Peace" and keyed it to the idea that the cold war days of conflict with Russia are fading and that the negotiations are opening up.

"This," the President told reporters in a meeting at the White House Monday, "is the

most comprehensive statement on foreign and defense policy ever made in this country."

He also called it a "policy for a decade" and said it marked a watershed in the life of the nation because it

shows a shift from the politics of the past—of the cold war—to the politics of negotiation which Nixon proclaimed on taking office in January 1969.

Yet in those sections dealing with the Soviet Union Nixon repeatedly raised questions about whether the leaders in Moscow were playing a different diplomatic game—seeking ends other than those of accommodation, at times he professed puzzlement.

The United States has made some progress in negotiations with Russia since he took over, he said, but "our overall relationship with the USSR remains far from satisfactory."

He named three specific complaints.

"To the detriment of the cause of peace, the Soviet Union has failed to exert a helpful influence on the North Vietnamese in Paris."

Three Arrested For Possession Of Three Drugs

Narcotics agents early today arrested three men on charges of possessing marijuana, hashish and LSD. Bail was set at $15,000.

Robert M. Sanders, 26, Hickory Trailer Park, is accused of possessing marijuana, hashish and LSD. Bail was set at $15,000.

Lewis Norman Grenier, 22, and Larry Scott Thurberg, 20, 219 Brentwood Ave., were arrested at their home on charges of possessing marijuana. Bail for each man was set at $500.

The Fayetteville Observer
North Carolina's Oldest Newspaper
ESTABLISHED IN 1817
Published Every Week Day Afternoon
and Sunday Morning by
THE FAYETTEVILLE PUBLISHING
COMPANY
Fayetteville, North Carolina 28302
PHONE 483-2111
...
SUBSCRIPTION RATES BY CARRIER

I wish I could say that this is proof that Stoeckley was there. It is not. Helen Fell hated the Kassabs. I did my level best to confirm her claims, but none of MacDonald's friends from Fort Bragg remembered it. And Pamela Kalin, the babysitter, never replied to my phone calls or letters. Ultimately, her husband told me not to contact them again.

There is a temptation in any investigation to look for *one* detail that cracks the case. But in the end, it is a net of interlocking pieces, an accumulation of evidence, that does it—not one thing.

A search through the *Fayetteville Observer* every day from February 17 through early 1971 produced no mention of a broken hobbyhorse. And if Stoeckley didn't see it in the paper, where did this odd detail come from? It is only suggestive, one more unresolved piece of the puzzle.[4]

THE FIVE PERCENT

This is the Wandering Wood, this Error's Den,
A Monster vile, whom God and Man does hate.
—Edmund Spenser, *The Faerie Queene*

Many of the MPs who first arrived at the crime scene have been interviewed and reinterviewed. Principal among them was Ken Mica, who had seen the woman with "a wide-brimmed hat" on Honeycutt Road on the way to the crime scene. He was also the first to hear MacDonald's description of one of the assailants as "a woman with a floppy hat" and the first to make a *connection* between the two. Mica never identified the woman—nothing more than the descriptions he had provided to the CID, to the FBI, and eventually to MacDonald's defense attorneys.

Mica was twice called as a witness in the Article 32, and then again at the 1979 trial. He has given affidavits over the years. But he has also appeared in a number of television documentaries and specials on the MacDonald case: *False Witness* on the BBC in 1989, *20/20* in 1990. He appeared as recently as 2007 on *48 Hours*, in a segment titled "Jeffrey MacDonald: Time for Truth."

He spoke to me in the wake of Hurricane Irene, while he was helping his son-in-law clean up his damaged pizzeria in Aquebogue, New York.

KENNETH MICA: I'll be right up front with you. I've done interviews for NBC, CBS, BBC, a bunch of *Unsolved Mysteries*, and other things. I was so misquoted. That is why I'm just very hesitant to talk to people about the case.

ERROL MORRIS: I'm sorry.

KENNETH MICA: I did one for Stone Phillips. It was *20/20* and taped for about eight hours, ten hours maybe. When the thing came out, the answers I was giving weren't to the questions I was asked. They edited the whole thing, made it look like we [the army] framed MacDonald. It was so far from the truth that it was a real turnoff. And I did the BBC. They did a three-hour special. I figured, "Well, BBC. Everything I've seen, they have always been unbiased and straightforward with their stories." And this one was a hatchet job.

ERROL MORRIS: You felt Stone Phillips put words in your mouth?

KENNETH MICA: Absolutely. They asked me about this girl that I saw. It's the big sticking point—this mystery woman who was standing on the corner. They make a big deal out of it, and I've told them a hundred times—they try to intimate that it was Helena Stoeckley. And I knew it wasn't her. I knew just by seeing her that it wasn't her.

ERROL MORRIS: Have you said this clearly before? That the woman was not Helena Stoeckley?

KENNETH MICA: Yes. Yes. I told them right out.

It was an odd moment. I thought, "Oh no." If that were so, if the woman on the corner—the woman he had seen—was definitely not Stoeckley, then what? This was a *critical* piece of information. Could there have been *another* woman in a floppy hat? Another woman on Honeycutt Road who never came forward? MacDonald's arguments for his innocence took substance from the interlocking pieces: Mica's observation of the woman with the wide-brimmed hat; MacDonald's account of the woman with the floppy hat; and the belief, at least of many of the drug enforcement police in Fayetteville, that Stoeckley answered to both descriptions.

The question became, if Mica *knew* that Stoeckley wasn't the woman, why didn't he communicate that fact to the various authorities involved in investigating the crime? When was he certain? Or had he reinvented the story in recent years? Needless to say, there were pressures to believe that it wasn't Stoeckley. Mica had been criticized by his colleagues for the role he had played at the Article 32 and the trial. If MacDonald was guilty, then it didn't matter whether Stoeckley was on the roadway that night. And so, maybe it was easier to mentally remove her from the story.

It dated all the way back to the very beginning.

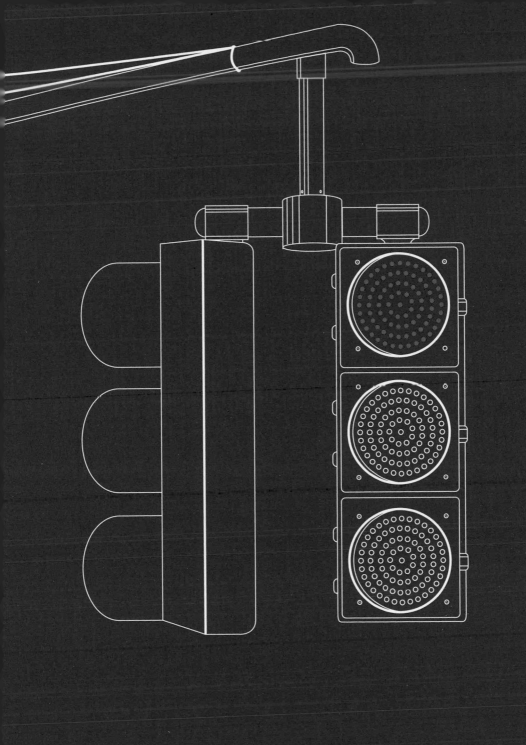

KENNETH MICA: During the initial investigation, when this mysterious woman appeared, Bernie Segal kept saying, "We've got statements from Helena Stoeckley," which were presented at the hearing in 1970. Come on. I knew Helena Stoeckley. She wasn't the woman that I saw. And I was told other things about the woman that I supposedly saw there. First, they told me it wasn't a woman; it was a man. Then I was told it was an officer's wife who was fooling around with an enlisted man. That's why she never came forward. Because that road, Honeycutt Road, separates enlisted men's barracks from the officers' housing. Then I was told by CID that they knew who it was. But I don't know. I've been told so many things that I don't know what the truth is.

ERROL MORRIS: Well, there's been a lot of pressure to believe one thing versus another. Did you know Helena Stoeckley before the murders?

KENNETH MICA: I knew what she looked like. I didn't know her personally.

ERROL MORRIS: But did you meet her prior to the murders?

KENNETH MICA: No, I never met her. I knew about her. But I never had any conversation or contact with her.

ERROL MORRIS: What did you know about her?

KENNETH MICA: That she was one of the druggies from downtown Fayetteville. At the time, back in the late sixties, there was a load of them. But I knew her just by reputation.

ERROL MORRIS: If you didn't know her or knew her only by reputation, how can you be positive—forgive me for asking—that this was not her?

KENNETH MICA: Well, I knew what she looked like, and I knew what the woman that I saw that night looked like. And they were just not even close.

ERROL MORRIS: What was the difference?

KENNETH MICA: I only got a quick glimpse of the woman on the corner, but it wasn't Helena Stoeckley.

ERROL MORRIS: Okay. Can you take me back to that night—to seeing the woman on the road? Is that possible?

KENNETH MICA: We were responding. We were coming up to an intersection. It was raining. It had been raining earlier. I think it had stopped. We had a red light. And off to the right-hand side, Honeycutt Road has a little PX gas station, convenience-store-type place. And I wasn't the driver. The junior man [Dennis Morris] was the driver. And as we came up to the red light, I looked to the right to see if anything was coming, and the woman was standing back off the corner. And I commented to my partner. I said, "What the hell is she doing here at three thirty in the morning?" I don't think he ever looked. But he remembers me saying it.

But we responded to the scene, got to the house, and there—I think there was another car or two cars there. And banging on the front door. And then we went around the back, and the back door was open. There's a utility room off the back of the master bedroom. And we went in and found MacDonald and his wife on the floor. I thought he was dead. He started moaning about, "Check my kids. I heard my kids." I went down the hallway, checked the kids. They were both dead. Checked the rest of the house, came back to him, and he is telling us he can't breathe and he needs a chest tube and everything else. I started doing mouth-to-mouth. And from then on it just went downhill.

ERROL MORRIS: When you say it "went downhill"—?

KENNETH MICA: Well, I'm on the floor working on MacDonald. The duty officer is there, and a couple of other MPs come in. The driver comes in. I asked MacDonald, "What happened? Who did this?" And he starts describing people—a black guy with E-6 stripes on his field jacket and a woman. And as soon as he said "a woman," I said, "What did the woman look like?" And he starts describing her. I turned around to the lieutenant [Joseph Paulk] who was standing behind me ready to pass out, and I said to him, "Lieutenant, I saw a woman two blocks away on a corner." But he never sent a car down, never checked to see if he could locate her.

ERROL MORRIS: And nobody wanted you talking about it.

KENNETH MICA: It was the internal affairs division of the CID. This was after the Article 32. And they had me in there all day from nine o'clock in the morning until almost ten o'clock, eleven o'clock, at night, trying to get me to admit that I made the whole thing up about seeing this woman. And I told them. I said, "You know, you can keep me here for twenty-four hours. This is what I saw." I said, "Hey! I told you what I saw. I told the lieutenant what I saw. My partner heard me say I saw this woman on the corner when we were responding to the call." Nobody wanted to listen. And then when the shit hit the fan, everybody was pointing fingers at everybody else. They were trying to get me to say this whole thing was made up, that I never saw this woman.

ERROL MORRIS: Were there other things that they wanted you to retract?

KENNETH MICA: The big thing was seeing the woman. That was really their big thing. And what happened—well, the FBI got involved. And the colonel [Kriwanek], they told him, "Don't make any statements. Don't this and that." And I get up the next morning, and on the front page of the Fayetteville Observer they've got a picture of the colonel holding a floor plan of the house, pointing out where the bodies were and how they came in and everything. The FBI pulled out of the case that same night, I believe. There's a memo from J. Edgar Hoover to the local office in Raleigh, saying, "Under no circumstances will the FBI be involved in this case." Because Hoover apparently saw where it was going.

There was a big pissing contest between the CID, the FBI, and then the local sheriff's office and the police department. They all thought they could have jurisdiction over this. And it got ugly real quick.

ERROL MORRIS: So, everybody heard you talk about this woman. And of course at the time you thought MacDonald is describing this woman that could have been the woman on the roadway.

KENNETH MICA: Right.

ERROL MORRIS: And then, when you reported this—tell me if I'm mischaracterizing this—you were told not to talk about this. You were told to shut up?

KENNETH MICA: It came out during the Article 32. We had a meeting with the JAG [judge advocate general] officers in the last week of June. They are going over things, and I said, "Well, the woman that I saw on the corner." And they were shocked, "What woman?" I said, "The woman that I saw when I was responding to the call." They said, "We don't know anything about that." And they said, "If they don't ask you about it, you don't tell them about it." He said, "Because it is something we can't explain right now." I was never told not to bring it up. But I was told not to volunteer it. It just wasn't the right thing to do.

ERROL MORRIS: How was it that the defense attorneys heard that you had seen this? How did that—I guess the term would be—how did that leak out?

KENNETH MICA: Oh, it didn't leak out. I saw Bernie Segal. I told him. He was around post. I ran into MacDonald's mother, and I said, "Just have Bernie Segal give me a call." And he called me. And I said, "Look. I don't know if they told you about this, but I saw a woman." And he was like, "Whoa!" That's why I think the army was not real happy with me because I was testifying for the army, but I was also going to testify for Bernie Segal.

ERROL MORRIS: So, he was not aware of the woman on Honeycutt Road when you first testified at the Article 32.

KENNETH MICA: No. I made him aware during the Article 32. Because he brought me back in on the stand as a witness for him.

ERROL MORRIS: Why did you do that? Why did you make him aware of that during the trial?

KENNETH MICA: I thought it was very important. I had my own opinions as to whether he did it or he didn't do it. It was important whether Stoeckley was involved in the case, or it was just something that they couldn't explain, a coincidence or whatever.

ERROL MORRIS: And if not for you, the defense would never have known about this.

KENNETH MICA: Probably not. Probably not, unless they found it later on in discovery going through—I don't know if it was written in any of the reports or anything. It was a long time ago.

ERROL MORRIS: So when did you first see Helena Stoeckley?

KENNETH MICA: Oh, I don't remember. I don't know if I saw her downtown or I saw her on post or whatever. Probably downtown. We had to patrol downtown a lot. Probably was pointed out to me by a Fayetteville cop or something. I don't remember exactly where I saw her, but I knew what she looked like.

ERROL MORRIS: This was before the murders?

KENNETH MICA: Probably before.

ERROL MORRIS: Here's what bothers me about this case. Years ago, I was involved in a murder case in Dallas that I was able to resolve. This case, often I don't know what to make of it.

KENNETH MICA: I know. It's a tough case. We don't get many cut-and-dried stories where they take it to their grave. I don't think he is ever going to fess up to it. I don't think he is ever going to tell us he did it.

ERROL MORRIS: That's assuming that he did do it—

KENNETH MICA: Yeah. I don't know. You read all the psychological reports about him. He's a pathological liar. He's a sociopath. I tell you, it's an interesting case. You know, it's fascinated me. I mean, I don't even talk about it much anymore. It's one of those. I just happened to be at the wrong place the wrong time. Actually, when I was testifying, they asked something like, "What were you thinking that night when you responded?" And I said, "I was thinking I wished I had joined the navy." And Bernie Segal and Colonel Rock, the hearing officer, cracked up. It's just one of those things. It just keeps coming up. It never dies.

ERROL MORRIS: How old were you when this happened?

KENNETH MICA: At the time, that was 1970. I would have been twenty-three.

ERROL MORRIS: Twenty-three years old.

KENNETH MICA: I was twenty-three years old, almost twenty-four. Actually, they started the Article 32 on my twenty-fourth birthday.

ERROL MORRIS: But since you went to MacDonald's mom—I know this is a long, long time ago—and then to Bernie Segal, you must have had doubts that he was guilty.

KENNETH MICA: Well, at that time I had no idea. After being in the house initially, we were never interviewed again by CID or anything else. We were kept out of it. I'd run into CID guys in the Provost Marshal's office and say, "Hey! What's going on?" They'd say, "Oh, we're still working on it." But they would never tell you anything. So I really had no idea what was happening until they charged him. I didn't want someone to say six months down the road, "Oh, you knew about it all along, and you didn't tell anyone." And I wasn't comfortable being told not to bring it up.

ERROL MORRIS: At the time of the Article 32 hearing, they were already looking at Stoeckley as a possible suspect, correct?

KENNETH MICA: I don't know. I really don't know, because I wasn't privy to any information. We were kept in the dark the whole time. I know she came up during the trial. I don't know about the Article 32 hearing.

ERROL MORRIS: So you might not have heard her name in connection with this case until much later.

KENNETH MICA: Probably much later. But I knew, when they said, "Oh, this is the mysterious woman," I knew it wasn't her because that is not the woman I saw.

ERROL MORRIS: How were they different?

KENNETH MICA: Just a total different appearance. There was no resemblance. It just wasn't her.

ERROL MORRIS: Here is another question. Wouldn't it have just been laid to rest if you had said to the FBI or Murtagh, "Well, it wasn't Helena Stoeckley," and they had had you testify to that at trial?

KENNETH MICA: I don't even remember if her name came up during the reinvestigation. But—

ERROL MORRIS: But you knew, certainly, that she was the object—

KENNETH MICA: Well, during the trial, during the actual trial. But the trial was 1979.

ERROL MORRIS: Right.

KENNETH MICA: I don't know if her name actually came up in '75, or '74. [During the grand jury.]

ERROL MORRIS: But you never told Murtagh that the woman you saw that night was *not* Helena Stoeckley.

KENNETH MICA: No. During the actual trial, I don't think I was asked about that. But they had Helena Stoeckley there, and the judge ruled that she wasn't a reliable witness. They didn't let her testify. Stoeckley was pathetic. She would have confessed to the assassination of Abraham Lincoln. You asked her anything, and she just agreed with you.

ERROL MORRIS: Are you absolutely convinced he's guilty?

KENNETH MICA: I'm about ninety-five percent convinced. His story doesn't make sense. It's just too many coincidences. And just looking at the physical injuries on the kids and the wife and then at his. I mean, I wish he would just get up and say, "Hey! Look! I did it. I screwed up. I've been in here for twenty-five years. Let me out of here." But I don't think his personality will allow him—even if he knows he did it—I don't think he would ever admit it.

ERROL MORRIS: Why?

KENNETH MICA: I just don't think he is that type of personality. He is always right. He has always been number one, and I don't think he will ever admit it.

ERROL MORRIS: But of course if he didn't do it—

KENNETH MICA: If he didn't do it, that's a whole other thing. That's the five percent. I wish I could say one hundred percent. Ninety-five percent, I think he did it.

ERROL MORRIS: So let's go to the five percent. Where do your doubts lie?

KENNETH MICA: My doubts are in that woman. But I don't think—I really don't think she was involved in it. I think that was a total coincidence. But it is a fly in the ointment that they can't explain.

————

Mica's insistence that the woman wasn't Stoeckley was shocking. But it didn't quite make sense. Why hadn't he said *anything* about it in the Article 32, in the reinvestigation of the case in the early 1970s, or in the 1979 trial?

ERROL MORRIS: But you never told Murtagh that the woman you saw that night was *not* Helena Stoeckley.

KENNETH MICA: No.

His reason for not telling anyone? He hadn't been asked. He didn't know whether Stoeckley's name had come up in 1974 or 1975—that is, during the grand jury hearings—but Stoeckley's name had been published in the *Fayetteville Observer* for the first time on October 19, 1970. "Helena A. Stokely [*sic*] was one of a number of individuals picked up and questioned by authorities but not charged after Captain MacDonald said a 'hippie' type band of intruders, including a blonde woman wearing a floppy hat . . . wiped out his family." Colonel Rock's report asking for Stoeckley to be investigated had been turned over to Major General Edward Flanagan, the commander of Fort Bragg, two days earlier.

Mica gave an interview for the BBC documentary *False Witness* in 1989. I asked Ted Landreth, the producer, whether Mica had told him that it wasn't Stoeckley on Honeycutt Road.

TED LANDRETH: No, he did not. You saw the interview we did with him?

ERROL MORRIS: Yes, but I didn't see the whole interview. I just saw the material included in the program.

TED LANDRETH: I can tell you that never—in the run-up to the interview, during the interview, or after the interview—did he say any such thing that the woman on the roadway was someone other than Stoeckley.[1]

ERROL MORRIS: If he didn't say anything to that effect in your interview, twenty years ago, but is saying it now, it makes the claim suspect, doesn't it?

TED LANDRETH: It's just beyond the realm of rational possibility. If he *always* knew something, he would have known it then. And he would have said something. He certainly never said it during any of the hearings. Yes, I think that's latter-day thinking.

Mica appears about twenty minutes into the ninety-minute documentary. There's ominous synthesizer music, archival footage of a telephone switchboard. A card—white text on black—that reads: "3:40 am, February 17, 1970." The narrator begins to speak:

NARRATOR: At 3:40, the Fayetteville operator connected a call to military police at Fort Bragg . . . On the way to Castle Drive, one of the MPs saw a woman standing in the rain, alone.

KENNETH MICA: She was wearing a floppy hat—a wide-brimmed hat—and a raincoat. And what appeared to be boots.

NARRATOR: How unusual was it to see somebody standing there at 3:40 in the morning?

KENNETH MICA: Very unusual.

NARRATOR: Ordinarily, if you hadn't been responding to an emergency call, what would you have done?

KENNETH MICA: We'd have stopped. We would have asked who she was, where she was going, what she was doing there at that time of the morning.[2]

───────

We are constantly struggling to make our beliefs fit together. Imagine Ken Mica on his way to 544 Castle Drive. He sees a woman standing in the light rain, but he and his partner keep on driving to the house. He wonders: Who was she? At first he was pressured to deny he had seen anything. But conscience got the better of him, and he told MacDonald's mother and his attorneys what he had seen and testified to that fact at the Article 32 hearing. It is only in the decades since that that impression has been replaced.

Fortunately, Mica's various accounts of what happened that night and in the aftermath were written down. His memory of the events may change, but the testimony under oath, the official statements, remain the same. As the case lapses out of the world of journalism and into history, as the people involved die off, one by one, the written record reminds us that Mica *did* see someone and was pressured to say he saw nothing.

I returned to the Article 32 transcript, to Mica's description of that strange moment. It was almost as if I could be transported back through time to that street corner in 1970. The light rain that had just stopped. The jeep. The gas station. The traffic light.

> **BERNARD SEGAL:** Were there lights on at the gas station at that time?
>
> **KENNETH MICA:** Yes, sir.
>
> **BERNARD SEGAL:** Was the traffic light operating at that time?
>
> **KENNETH MICA:** Yes, sir.
>
> **BERNARD SEGAL:** Was she standing in some proximity to the traffic signal that you can identify for us?
>
> **KENNETH MICA:** Yes, sir, she would have been standing in some light that was cast by the signal.[3]

SIGHTINGS

CORREGIDOR COURTS, FORT BRAGG
February 17, 1970

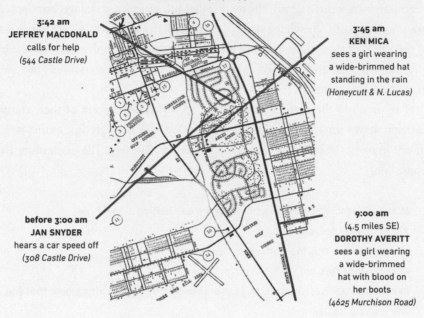

3:42 am
JEFFREY MACDONALD
calls for help
(544 Castle Drive)

3:45 am
KEN MICA
sees a girl wearing
a wide-brimmed hat
standing in the rain
(Honeycutt & N. Lucas)

before 3:00 am
JAN SNYDER
hears a car speed off
(308 Castle Drive)

9:00 am
(4.5 miles SE)
DOROTHY AVERITT
sees a girl wearing
a wide-brimmed
hat with blood on
her boots
(4625 Murchison Road)

HAYMOUNT, FAYETTEVILLE
February 16–17, 1970

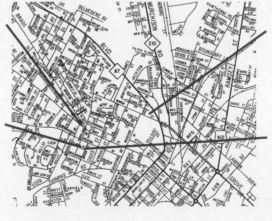

February 16, 11:00 pm
PRINCE BEASLEY
sees Stoeckley get
into a blue Mustang
with three men
(The Village Shoppe)

February 17, 4:30 am
WILLIAM POSEY
sees Stoeckley leave
a blue Mustang and
enter her apartment

KATHY SMITH
sees Stoeckley
come home with
Greg Mitchell
(1106-8 Clark Street)

Later in 1970
DEBRA HARMON
and RICHARD COMISKEY
hear Stoeckley
and male friends
make incriminating
statements
(Rowan Street Park)

February 18, 2:30 am
PRINCE BEASLEY
sees Stoeckley return
home with Greg Mitchell
and others; she jokes
about showing him her
ice pick
(1108 Clark Street)

FEBRUARY 16–17, 1970

February 16

around 11:00 pm
1211 Hay Street, Fayetteville, NC

PRINCE BEASLEY sees Stoeckley exit the Apple House, a head shop in the district of Fayetteville:
"He recalls seeing Helena Stoeckley and three male individuals, two white males and one black male, outside the Village Shoppe, a local drug hangout in Fayetteville, N.C."

February 17

12:45–2:00 am
Dunkin' Donuts, Bragg Boulevard, Fort Bragg, NC

Two women—**FRANKIE BUSHEY** and **MARIAN CAMPBELL**—recall seeing a group like the one MacDonald described, including a girl in a floppy hat who appeared to be high on drugs. Campbell recalled that they left around 2:00 am, some of them in a blue van.

before 3:00 am
308 Castle Drive, Fort Bragg, NC

JAN SNYDER, a neighbor of MacDonald's, was awoken by a car roaring away:
"The car was going down the road when I glanced at the back of the tail lights and they were— well, like round Ford lights, because I distinctly remember that they were large."

3:42 am
Honeycutt Boulevard and Lucas Drive, Fort Bragg, NC

WILLIAM BOULWARE answers **JEFFREY MacDONALD**'s distress call at MP headquarters.

3:45 am
Honeycutt Boulevard and Lucas Drive, Fort Bragg, NC

KEN MICA observed a lone young woman standing outside in the rain:
"From what I remember she had on a wide-brimmed hat . . . and she appeared to have long hair."

around 4:30 am
1106 Clark Street, Fayetteville, NC

WILLIAM POSEY sees Helena Stoeckley return to her apartment:
"It was a Mustang, and the one girl got out . . . She had something in her hand, but I did not take note of what it was, but she walked kind of fast into her house . . . faster than she usually walks."

1108 Clark Street

KATHY SMITH, Helena Stoeckley's roommate, recalls Stoeckley coming home with Gregory Mitchell:
"The next day, Helena said to me that the police were looking for her to question her about the murders . . . She didn't have an alibi and she didn't want to get Greg MITCHELL in trouble."

around 9:00 am
Mrs. Johnson's Grocery, 4625 Murchison Road, Fayetteville, NC

DOROTHY AVERITT recognizes Stoeckley, whom she knew from her paper route, at a grocery store. She is wearing a floppy hat and is covered in blood:
"I looked down there at her boots . . . It smelled like it might have been in a hog killing . . ."

60

COINCIDENCES

*Among events which are within the bounds of possibility, some are very
probable and other highly improbable, and still others are in between the two . . .
If we do not give judgment even on the basis of a very strong presumption,
the worst that can happen is that the sinner will be acquitted; but if we punish
on the strength of presumptions and suppositions, it may be that one day we
shall put to death an innocent person; and it is better and more satisfactory to
acquit a thousand guilty persons than to put a single innocent man to death.*
—Maimonides

Mica told me that MacDonald's story didn't make sense. "It's just too many coincidences. And just looking at the physical injuries on the kids and the wife and then
at his. I mean, I wish he would just get up and say, 'Hey! Look! I did it. I screwed
up. I've been in here for twenty-five years. Let me out of here.'"

But just what are these coincidences? That MacDonald was alive and his family was dead? Is that what he's talking about?

Mica also used the expression when talking about Stoeckley. "It was important
whether Stoeckley was involved in the case, or [whether] it was just something
that they couldn't explain, a coincidence or whatever."

Think about it this way. If Jeffrey MacDonald was the killer, then it was a coincidence that his description of the woman with a floppy hat was similar to Ken Mica's
description of the woman with a wide-brimmed hat on Honeycutt Road.

It could be.

And it was a coincidence that Prince Beasley had seen a group of hippies answering to the description of the intruders, including Helena Stoeckley, hours before the murders in Fayetteville?

A coincidence? Why not?

That Helena Stoeckley, according to Beasley, was wearing a blond wig and white boots?

Okay.

That multiple witnesses recall seeing a group like the one MacDonald described, high on drugs, at a Dunkin' Donuts between Fayetteville and Fort Bragg? That they left around two in the morning?

A coincidence?

That William Posey, who lived nearby, saw Stoeckley arrive home early that morning?

That Helena Stoeckley, Beasley's drug informant, started confessing to the murders and continued confessing to the murders over the next thirteen years?

A coincidence?

That Greg Mitchell, Stoeckley's boyfriend, also confessed to the murders?

A coincidence?

At what point does a coincidence become something more than a coincidence? At what point does a coincidence become *evidence*?

61

GENE STOECKLEY

*The true picture of the past flits by. The past can be seized
only as an image which flashes up at the instant when it can
be recognized and is never seen again.*
—Walter Benjamin, "Theses on the Philosophy of History"

A room in a nursing home. Helena Stoeckley's mother, a lifelong smoker and a onetime heart attack victim, had less than two years to live.

Her son Eugene, the youngest of the four children, had heard his mother talk about Helena's confessions and decided that he should say something to someone. But to whom? He called Hart Miles, one of MacDonald's North Carolina attorneys. Miles and Kathy MacDonald, MacDonald's wife since 2002, journeyed down to Fayetteville.

The affidavit that resulted was signed on March 21, 2007.

In her affidavit, Mrs. Stoeckley (also Helena) described two confessions. The first was after the 1979 trial; the second, just before Stoeckley's death in 1983. "My daughter knew she was dying. She wanted to set the record straight with her mother about the MacDonald murders, and that she wished she had not been present in the house and knew that Dr. MacDonald was innocent."[1]

There is something stark and simple about this document. The affidavit with a notary public seal affixed at the end. No videotape. Gunderson is gone. Stoeckley with her infant son is quietly telling her mother that MacDonald is innocent and that she was there. What am I to make of this? It is shorn of all the drama of the 1979 trial. "She told me she was afraid to tell the truth because she was afraid of the prosecutor." But this time, no threatening prosecutor. Just her mother and her infant son. It's much easier to dismiss the previous confessions of a drug-addled Stoeckley. But this is clearly different. She is talking to her mother just before she herself died. What did she have to gain? Notoriety? Publicity?

I called Gene and left a message on an answering machine. He was one of the witnesses to his mother's affidavit. I wasn't optimistic about his willingness to talk to me. But he called back.

> **ERROL MORRIS:** Helena is such a central figure in the story, and what bothers me is that we really don't know much about her.
>
> **GENE STOECKLEY:** First of all, you'll have to excuse me, because I don't trust anyone when it comes to this case. This case has corruption; it has pain; and the consequences are far-reaching. The damage done to individuals goes way beyond the central core of the case. Everybody that gets touched has been affected in a negative way. As far as my sister, so much that was written was just pure speculation, rumor. People wanted to create this persona for her. But in reality, she was a whole lot different. People just didn't know.

Gene did not feel comfortable talking about his sister on the phone but clearly wanted to talk further. Had no one ever bothered to ask—that is, apart from the insane wrangling about her confessions—who was this person? Who was she beyond Dupree's condemnation that she was "clearly untrustworthy"?

We met in a suite on the top floor of the Raleigh-Durham Airport Hilton. I liked him immediately.

> **GENE STOECKLEY:** My sister was pretty, well, I wouldn't say "maligned"—but maybe "traduced" might be a better word?—by the media. She had aspirations and dreams. She wanted to be a nurse. When she was in high school, she was a candy striper at the local hospital there in Fayetteville, at the Highsmith Rainey Hospital. She wore a little candy-striping outfit and the hat and stuff. And she just gave it her all. She was so caring for the patients. She was just a natural. Even though I'm her brother, I don't quite understand the forces that ultimately led to her downfall. Her friends were all from very respected families around Fayetteville. I

used to say she had all the talent. And she was definitely an open, outgoing person. Once you met her, she was disarming. You just immediately felt warm to her. And she was so approachable and well liked by everyone. She didn't have any boyfriends. She had her group of girlfriends. But she also knew people that used to hang out at some of the local places where people would gather on weekends.

ERROL MORRIS: Hippies?

GENE STOECKLEY: I guess that's what they called them. There was a little trendy head shop up there in Haymount. I remember Helena talking about it. We walked in there. And some of these so-called hippies, they were just sweet people doing their thing. Peace, love, drugs, all of that. I don't know how she found herself entrenched in that culture, because it was so opposite from how she was in high school.

ERROL MORRIS: She studied languages, too—is that correct?

GENE STOECKLEY: She was fluent in French. While my father was still in the military, his duty station overseas was in France. And over there, they didn't have a school for the children of servicemen to go to, like they have here. Instead, the children went to a French school. And Helena became so fluent in French that when she began school here, her French teacher, Mrs. Rulnick, would have her get up in class and actually give little talks about the French culture and stuff, to give herself a break.

She was also musically talented beyond belief. She was professionally trained for voice lessons from the conductor of the Fayetteville Symphony. And the sad part is, all that was just so wasted. That's the really tragic part of Helena's life. She had so many things she could have done, so many choices she could have made. And she would have excelled in any of it. And she would have been such an asset, in the later years, for the family, as my parents aged and had health issues and things. I just think of what might have been.

ERROL MORRIS: Sounds like you were very close.

GENE STOECKLEY: I know she loved me. I was her little brother, and I remember walks to Rowan Park to ride the swings. I just remember us walking. She would have my hand, walking me down the street. She was my protector, and all.

ERROL MORRIS: Your sister would take you around town?

GENE STOECKLEY: Yes. She worked at the Village Pizza Shoppe. My brother, when he was still in high school, would take me up there after the football games. But that's also where the head shop was. I think it was called the Apple Shop. I think it was just kind of a rip-off of the Beatles record label. It was just black-light posters, beads, incense, lava lamps, that kind of thing. It all was pretty innocent.

But apparently, that area started drawing in some of the hard-core drug dealers. Somehow, along the way, these two narcotics detectives engaged my sister since she seemed to know everybody. She worked up there, and she knew everybody who was coming and going.

ERROL MORRIS: Was she still in high school?

GENE STOECKLEY: She was probably a senior in high school at that time. And I think it was just a matter of the fact she knew who everyone was. She was just that person who watched. I think she liked to study people. I think that was one of her favorite pastimes.

ERROL MORRIS: What were the detectives' names again?

GENE STOECKLEY: Detective Studer and Detective Beasley. They were getting her to provide information because they wanted to get to these dealers who were dealing hard-core drugs, not just pot or stuff.

ERROL MORRIS: What kinds of drugs are we talking about here?

GENE STOECKLEY: There was talk about heroin and opium being brought back from Southeast Asia through the base. So Studer and Beasley are wanting information to help pin down some of these big-time dealers.

ERROL MORRIS: Were there a lot of drugs around at that time?

GENE STOECKLEY: Oh yes. And Helena knew who to go to. If you wanted something, she knew who to see. I was at home, of course, the night she set up a drug bust right there at my folks' house. She was to bring this guy over to the house as a date. And the police were waiting at the end of the road. She actually told my mother that once they left to go out on their date, she was to turn on the porch light as a signal. And I was there for all of this.

ERROL MORRIS: This may show my naiveté, but isn't the usual deal that you get into trouble with the police and then the police use you as an informant? Usually, you don't go to the police and say, "Hey! I would like to inform on a lot of people."

GENE STOECKLEY: Hell, you would think it would be a conflict of interest, in a way.

ERROL MORRIS: Of sorts.

GENE STOECKLEY: But she felt like she could be good at this. There was a certain part of her personality that was interested in being the star. And that may have played into things later on during the trial. Now, my parents really had cautioned her about even getting involved with the police. They didn't like it.

ERROL MORRIS: So they knew about it.

GENE STOECKLEY: Oh yes. They were acutely aware of that. And Mother told me that she was telling Helena, "I don't like this. This can't be good." And she wanted her to quit being an informant. And I don't know if Helena had told these detectives that she couldn't help them anymore. But Mother said she got a call from the narc police and they threatened her. They said, "You let her help us." And she didn't go into specifics about the threat. But Mom wasn't some exaggerator. She told things as they were. If anything else, she would portray it from a more conservative light. But I distinctly remember her telling me several times when we got to talking about it, they threatened them. We had to change phone numbers, un-list phone numbers, all of that. And I was growing up there, so I could see the concerns. The whole feeling at home had changed from just a great place to grow up—a great family life—to just constant tension. By the time February of 1970 came around, Helena was definitely in deep.

ERROL MORRIS: So, do you remember the night in question? The night of the MacDonald murders?

GENE STOECKLEY: Well, my birthday was February the sixteenth, and she had been over to the house. She never missed my birthday. She doted on me, so she had to bring me a gift and have birthday cake and ice cream. Helena came by with somebody, I think a girl. Maybe there was a fellow with them. And they just stopped by because she wanted to come by and wish me happy birthday and give me a birthday present; I don't even remember what it was.

ERROL MORRIS: But she wasn't high, as far as you remember?

GENE STOECKLEY: No. They seemed perfectly normal. They weren't acting unusual in any way. I'm certain that Mom would have headed that off at the pass if they had come over to the house jacked up on crazy drugs. And Helena knew better. She wasn't going to come over to that house messed up like that.

ERROL MORRIS: What happened on the next day?

GENE STOECKLEY: What I remember most is a lot of talk, my parents watching the news. And the days following it I remember them being contacted by reporters. Let's see, the MacDonald murders happened in February. And that summer, when school was out, they sent me to live with my sister Dollie and her husband down in Florida. And Mom attributed that, later on in our talks when I was an adult, to the threats coming back on the family.

ERROL MORRIS: But where were those threats coming from?

GENE STOECKLEY: I wish I had that answer. I don't know. Dad wouldn't talk about these things. His old-school thinking was, you keep your family laundry in the laundry basket. You don't air it out for the public. Really, Mom was the only one that would discuss the MacDonald situation with me. And that was years later.

ERROL MORRIS: You mentioned that Helena left town after the murders. Did you see her at all during this period?

GENE STOECKLEY: She had gone to Nashville and was going to try to resume her nursing studies at the Thomas Aquinas school up there. And then, I think, she decided to go into law enforcement. My parents did everything they could to try to help her get a new start, so to speak. And I remember taking a couple of trips with Dad up there to visit her, probably no more than twice that I remember. The MacDonald case was never really on the radar screen during that time.

ERROL MORRIS: So, what would have been Helena's motivation for confessing years later?

GENE STOECKLEY: She had a conscience. She was—aside from her addictions, if you could have taken that out of the equation—she was a loving and caring person. And I'm sure the only thing that would have motivated her is her conscience, just gnawing away. Mom had formed her own opinion, that Dr. MacDonald was guilty. I guess because she had been there at the trial and listened to the evidence. But after I discussed it with her when she was at the assisted living, she had changed her mind. We were just having some heart-to-heart talks. I knew her time was short. And there were just things I wanted to talk about.

ERROL MORRIS: It must have been a difficult time.

GENE STOECKLEY: I basically was trying to leave the door open for Mother to talk to me if she felt like there were things she wanted to talk about, anything that was bothering her, whether between us or anything else. And it was the same thing with Helena. And Helena must have been pretty persuasive in convincing my mom that she was there because my mom had changed her belief. Now she was convinced MacDonald was innocent because of what my sister told her. And to me, that is pretty significant. My sister had health issues: the cirrhosis, the hepatitis. But my sister was smart. She was a very intelligent person. Through to the end. And I believe with all my heart what she told my mother was the truth. She was trying to make things right. She had no reason to make it up. The end was near for her, and Mom said she was acutely aware that she was dying.

ERROL MORRIS: Why didn't she go back to the police?

GENE STOECKLEY: Helena always said that she wanted immunity. She said, "Not unless they promise I will have immunity." And here is what I don't understand. If you're a prosecutor, you have a material witness, and they say, "I've got information that could break this case open without a doubt." If you weren't afraid of that information coming out, if you didn't think there was some truth to it, why wouldn't you just give her immunity? If you thought she was just some drug-crazed witness, a person whose testimony had no merit, why not throw her a bone and say, "Sweetheart. We will give you immunity. Now you tell us. Here is a piece of paper. You tell us."

ERROL MORRIS: But what if the prosecutors were afraid of that information? They would never give her immunity. It would be admitting that she knew something.

GENE STOECKLEY: It's possible. I have never understood it. For the longest time I felt like there were only two people who knew the truth. Now it's only Dr. Mac-Donald and the good Lord.

ERROL MORRIS: Could it be—the devil's advocate view—that she just felt guilty that MacDonald was in jail and that she was dying anyway and this was a way to help somebody?

GENE STOECKLEY: Why would she feel that it would benefit Dr. MacDonald when nothing had helped him so far? What would make her believe that telling Mother these things was going to make a difference? That kind of takes the wind out of that sail. I think it was purely her conscience, her heart.

ERROL MORRIS: I have to ask these questions. Statistically, when a family is killed, the killer is most likely the husband. And then MacDonald gives an account of hippies breaking into the house. And people say, "Well, that's a really preposterous story. He's just trying to trade off the Manson killings." Okay. But then what about the woman on the roadway? What about that? Who somehow matches the description that MacDonald gives. That changes things because it is a deserted area of Fort Bragg. It's bad weather, really early in the morning. What's that about? If this woman had been involved in the killings, why is she hanging around? That's another puzzling thing. Why would she be alone on that street? But we can't answer any of that, because the cops didn't stop. The woman was never identified. Beasley then decides, on the basis of MacDonald's description, that your sister was involved. He finds her. Then later on, he gets mixed up with this ex-FBI guy, Gunderson. And they became convinced that witchcraft was involved.

GENE STOECKLEY: She did have this fascination with—not so much the occult and witchcraft—but just being mysterious, a mysterious woman. She had a black cat. I don't like cats. I'm sorry. I'm a dog person. And she named it Satan. Because he was just coal black.

ERROL MORRIS: "Satan"?

GENE STOECKLEY: Yes. And she just liked to create this alter ego of herself, that she was kind of a witch or whatever, nothing to do with satanic stuff. I think, whether it was Gunderson and Beasley concocted that part of it or what, but it was more like just the occult, astrology, things like that.

ERROL MORRIS: Standard head-shop-type stuff.

GENE STOECKLEY: Yes. There was some things circulating in the media about how they found animals sacrificed and crazy stuff like that over at the Davis Street apartment. But my sister, she is too tenderhearted. She couldn't. She wouldn't squash a spider. She would more likely invite it to tea than to step on it.

We returned to the issue of drugs.

GENE STOECKLEY: I listened to my mom talk about how she and my dad were trying their best to save my sister from this destructive path. They felt like they had a foothold on it, and then my mother, more than once, blamed Beasley and Studer for getting her mixed up in it. My mom always said it centered around drugs. I know MacDonald did some work over at Cape Fear Valley Hospital at times, not just at Womack [the military hospital on the base], in the emergency room there. And somewhere their paths crossed. The way Helena told it to my mother and the way my mother relayed it to me in our discussions was that Helena went with these guys to MacDonald's place to intimidate him. That's the part I wish I knew—intimidate him over what? But in Helena's words, this was my mom quoting what Helena said, "It got out of hand, and it just went crazy." And so she left.
ERROL MORRIS: So, she left the others.
GENE STOECKLEY: That's what she said. That's what she told my mom.
ERROL MORRIS: So, she could have ended up—
GENE STOECKLEY: Left behind. Left standing out there on that road, alone.

BOOK SEVEN

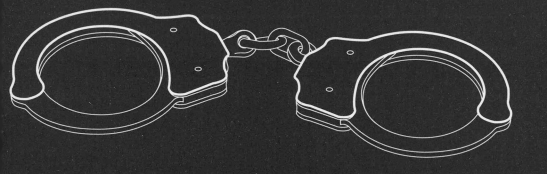

62

TWO PRISONERS

In the years that I have been fascinated with this case, I have wondered about how Harvey Silverglate, for many years MacDonald's appellate attorney, has maintained his equanimity about all of this. And how the case has affected the many, many other lawyers who have been involved with it over the last forty years. And, so, recently I asked Harvey to talk about the lawyers.

HARVEY SILVERGLATE: The case has been disastrous for almost everybody who touched it. It's like a third rail. It undermined Bernie Segal's career as a trial lawyer. He never stopped licking his wounds. He went and became faculty at a law school in California. I could see that he had been devastated by this experience.

ERROL MORRIS: Just Segal?

HARVEY SILVERGLATE: Not just Segal. As I went down the line of all of the lawyers who had handled the case, almost every one had come to a bad end. There was one guy killed. It was like a third rail for everyone. The only survivor of the whole dramatis personae of the whole MacDonald case, at the time I became involved [1988], was Wade Smith. Wade has this ability to extract himself, take a few steps back, not get himself quite so emotionally wrapped up in the tragedy of the case. He will tell you in no uncertain terms why he thinks that Jeff is innocent, but it's not ripping him up inside.

ERROL MORRIS: But what about the prosecution side?

HARVEY SILVERGLATE: Murtagh and Jeffrey have been condemned to prison: Jeffrey's is the Federal Correctional Institution in Cumberland, Maryland, and Murtagh's is the Department of Justice. Murtagh can never leave the DOJ. They have a system in the department that if you try a case, and years later if you're still in the department, and there's a new trial motion, a new habeas petition filed, no matter where you may have been assigned in the department, you get to handle the defense of the habeas! No one else is going through the file—it's your file, your notes. You're burrowing through it. If you leave, and a habeas is filed in one of your cases, someone else starts burrowing through the file. And my theory is that Murtagh decided to became a lifer because he needed to be there. He knew that Jeffrey was going to keep filing petitions as long as he could get lawyers to do it. They're both prisoners, only at different ends of the Department of Justice: one's a prisoner of the department, and one's a prisoner of the Bureau of Prisons. Two prisoners.

ERROL MORRIS: Is the presumption that Murtagh's hiding something?

HARVEY SILVERGLATE: In going through the materials that we've dug up over the years, we've found a lot of material sitting in the government's MacDonald files that MacDonald's defense team was never given. I mean, we found the Puretz memo and all of the lab notes. God knows what we haven't found because every time we file a habeas, it's Murtagh again. And then, of course, there's Blackburn. He was at the U.S. attorney's office. Remember, Murtagh was from the Department of Justice in Washington. They had to have somebody from the local U.S. attorney's office, and so Blackburn got the job, figuring it was a career maker. But it was a career breaker. And when I decided to take it, I said, "You know, I want to be careful, the lawyers who have touched this case got wrecked." And the year after that even more of them got wrecked.

ERROL MORRIS: Who else got wrecked?

HARVEY SILVERGLATE: Blackburn, the local North Carolina prosecutor, got disbarred.

ERROL MORRIS: Do you think that it's driven you crazy?

HARVEY SILVERGLATE: No, no, it hasn't! I haven't let it. At a certain point, I decided that I didn't want to share the fate of the people who forty years later were totally exhausted from the MacDonald case and couldn't even look at it with any kind of objective eyes, and that's when I backed out for Jeffrey's sake and for my own. I felt very badly for Jeffrey, and I saw what was going on, and I thought the whole thing was a giant illusion of a justice system without the justice. With Dupree and his son-in-law, the whole "too cozy" system down in North Carolina, it grabbed me on an emotional level that initially made me very effective. I did get a front-page story in the *Wall Street Journal* about the case [written by Laurie Cohen] that opened their eyes down there, but never enough to get a court to look at the case fairly and objectively. After about twenty years I was starting to feel that my judgment was threatened because I was so angry at the prosecution, so angry at the FBI, felt so sorry for Jeffrey, was so angry at the judge. I just felt that I had to get out.

ERROL MORRIS: The judges were trapped too. No? Dupree had to sit on this thing, didn't he? He never gave it to another judge.

HARVEY SILVERGLATE: That's right, until he finally died [on December 17, 1995]. And then it was inherited by his friend Judge Fox, who carried the legacy, is still carrying the legacy. Do you know that I've never met Jeffrey? And that was intentional. You always have to meet the client that you're representing in a trial, but on appeal you're entitled to more distance because it's done on the basis of the record, the transcript of the proceedings. And I decided not to meet him so that I wouldn't have this extra burden of an emotional tie with the client. I was trying to be objective. One lawyer I know says, "It's so much easier representing somebody that I know is guilty." And it's true. The strain of representing somebody who's getting screwed all along the way. You have very strong feelings that he is innocent. It's the defense attorney's worst nightmare.

In June 2011, Brian Murtagh retired from the Department of Justice. McGinniss mentioned it on his blog. He described how, in accepting the "True Thriller" award at ThrillerFest, sponsored by the International Thriller Writers, he paid tribute to Murtagh,

> . . . the just-retired U.S. Department of Justice attorney who for forty-one years stayed on the case of Jeffrey MacDonald. If it weren't for Brian, MacDonald never would have been brought to trial, much less convicted, and since that 1979 conviction Brian has been the man who's thrown up the roadblocks every time new lawyers tried to find a way to help MacDonald weasel out of paying the life-sentence price for having murdered his pregnant wife and two daughters at Fort Bragg in 1970.[1]

63

FLAME-OUT

The Blackburn story doesn't end with the 1979 trial. One could easily imagine the following scenario. Successful prosecutor goes into private practice and becomes a legendary defense attorney. But Blackburn's story has a few more salient details. Blackburn becomes U.S. attorney for the Eastern District of North Carolina, becomes a partner at a prominent law firm (Smith, Helms, Mulliss & Moore), is disbarred, and goes to prison.

I spoke with James Blackburn by phone.

ERROL MORRIS: I know it's asking you to go back so many years, but what initially convinced you of MacDonald's guilt?

JAMES BLACKBURN: I don't know if it's any one thing. It's a compilation, just a mass of information. I don't think there's any one piece of evidence, I just think there was a tremendous amount of evidence against him. Which I still believe is there. I still believe he's guilty. I know with all the technology that has come about today, it still doesn't take away so much of what he said. The main thing that convinced me, essentially, is that he told a story of what took place that night, and that story just was inconsistent completely with the evidence. I think that's what hurt him so much. I think that if he had not talked so much, you know, initially, he might have been better off.

ERROL MORRIS: I have often wondered why people are still arguing about this case—

JAMES BLACKBURN: This is like the Hatfields and the McCoys in West Virginia. You've got the bride and the groom, you've got two entirely different sides in this case. You've got his side, and you've got Colette MacDonald's family's side. You've got the defense attorneys and then you've got the government. They are never going to agree. There is no resolution beyond what the jury did that you're going to get. I really don't think so. This is not like a rape case, where you say, "Aha, DNA proved this person did not do this." You don't have that kind of thing that brings some finality to it. I think that there's just so much evidence that the government believes is true that the government will never concede or agree to MacDonald. MacDonald, on the other hand, has the totally opposite point of view. He's had so many defense lawyers over the years, and he has defense lawyers now and people who believe in him. It's sort of a cottage industry, almost.

ERROL MORRIS: Many people have trouble understanding how MacDonald could have done such a terrible thing.

JAMES BLACKBURN: Well, somebody did. That's the bottom line.

ERROL MORRIS: Yes, someone had to have done it. But did he seem like the kind of person who could do it?

JAMES BLACKBURN: You have to remember, I wasn't focused on that. I understand why you would be interested in that, and why a lot of people would be interested in that, but the government was not really interested in that. The government was interested in whether or not he did it, not whether or not he was the kind or person who could have done it. If we could prove that he did it, we didn't have to prove that he was the sort of person who could have done it. I think that's one of the strengths of the government's case. The government did not fall into a psychological study of him. You can't talk about this case and talk about it independent of the physical evidence because that is the case.

It's like a football field. You got the fifty-yard line, and there are two separate sides, side A and side B. Well, MacDonald wants to talk about his side of the turf. And he doesn't want to talk about the other side of the turf. Well, the government did not want to talk so much about his side, the government wanted to talk about its side, which was the physical evidence side. To the government, the physical evidence is the case. You can't separate it out. We don't get into the psychological study of Jeffrey MacDonald. We got into whether or not he did it from a strictly prosecutorial point of view.

ERROL MORRIS: Is it fair to ask you what your thoughts are about his character?

JAMES BLACKBURN: I don't know that I would get into any of that, simply because I think he committed these crimes. That's what I believe. I never thought too much about his character. What I tried to do was prove he was guilty. I got involved in it because I became an assistant United States attorney and the case was assigned to me while it was still in appeal to the United States Supreme Court. I started to do research and read about the case. I went to the crime scene, looked at the grand jury testimony, looked at lab reports—

ERROL MORRIS: And you went to the crime scene, what effect did that have?

JAMES BLACKBURN: Well, I think it had a strong effect on me. The jury went there, and it had a strong effect on the jury. It would have a strong effect on anyone.

———

I felt compelled to ask Blackburn about his experiences following the 1979 trial: his own trial and conviction for embezzlement and fraud and his subsequent incarceration. (It may seem unfair to bring up these issues, but they are part of the story, at least the story of the effect the trial had on the people who were involved with it.)

ERROL MORRIS: I don't know if you want to talk about it—but what happened to you in the aftermath of the case? Was it related to the strain of the case in any way?

JAMES BLACKBURN: I don't really think so. I really don't think it was. I think it was just two separate incidents. My career obviously crashed a number of years ago, almost a generation ago, seventeen or eighteen years ago, and I have just sort of built a new career since then. I wrote a book about it called *Flame-out*.[1] But I don't really think the incidents are all that related. I really don't.

ERROL MORRIS: *Flame-out*?

JAMES BLACKBURN: Well, my career just sort of flamed out. My life sort of flamed out at one point. But I don't really think the two go together. I know that MacDonald tries to put the two together to some degree, but I really don't think they are.

ERROL MORRIS: You mean MacDonald has written about this or has commented on it?

JAMES BLACKBURN: No, no. The motions that they filed—if you were a scumbag on one, you're a scumbag on the other kind of thing—to try to tie the two together. I don't think it holds a great deal of water, but, you know, that's my own personal opinion.

ERROL MORRIS: Right. It would be nice to have you explain why these appeals have no merit. For example, the Jimmy Britt claim. Does that have any merit?

JAMES BLACKBURN: No. I will answer that one. That has zero merit. It never happened. I can tell you that.

ERROL MORRIS: So, how was it that Britt imagined that it did happen?

JAMES BLACKBURN: He has passed away. I don't know. But I can tell you, I was there. I know. Nobody else who writes about this *knows*. But I was there. And so, I can tell you that that is not so.

Blackburn had cheated his clients and his law firm—and in the process created fake documents and forged the signatures of several federal judges. According to a November 30, 1993, AP story:

> Mr. Blackburn was scheduled to enter his plea in October. That hearing was delayed after the psychiatrist, Dr. Jean Spaulding of Duke University, said Mr. Blackburn had stopped taking his medication and was difficult to deal with. Mr. Blackburn underwent psychiatric examination before entering his plea.
>
> He is taking the prescription drugs Prozac and lithium, according to testimony during the hearing.
>
> Mr. Blackburn prepared seventeen phony court orders and forged the signatures of state and federal judges, an SBI [State Bureau of Investigation] agent said during the sentencing hearing. He also made up an entire lawsuit that never existed in the process of diverting $234,054 from his Raleigh law firm.
>
> Mr. Blackburn is scheduled to be sentenced next month. He faces a maximum 110-year sentence.
>
> He testified that he can't remember events that occurred in 1990 or 1991.[2]

On November 29, the day before, Blackburn pled guilty to twelve counts of forgery, fraud, and the embezzlement of hundreds of thousands of dollars. He was represented by Wade Smith, the same Wade Smith who had represented Jeffrey MacDonald. At the sentencing hearing, Dr. Spaulding argued that Blackburn was suffering from "psychotic delusional depression." A suggestive phrase.

Wade Smith had the 110-year sentence reduced to three years. Blackburn did most of his time on work release at former U.S. senator Robert Morgan's law office. Law office during the day; prison at night. He was paroled after three months. Who says there isn't a North Carolina old-boy network? He became a greeter, and then a waiter, at the 42nd Street Oyster Bar. (Not the Oyster Bar in Grand Central Station; this one is in Raleigh.) Today he is a motivational speaker with a Web site. Those interested can choose between a multiplicity of lectures: *Landmines on the Way to the Top . . . and How to Avoid Them, The Unforgiving Minute,* and *Ethics in Life, the Marketplace, and Business.*[3]

––––––––

In *Flame-out*, Blackburn describes that crucial moment in the MacDonald trial when everything went south for the defense. The passage was written approximately five years before Jimmy Britt provided his affidavit for MacDonald's lawyers. According to Blackburn, "We kept waiting for MacDonald to come up with some new evidence and blow us out of the water. He had only two chances— Helena Stoeckley and his own testimony."

The FBI found her hiding under a bed in her boyfriend's apartment in South Carolina. She was brought to Raleigh as a court witness, and both the defense and the prosecution were given a half day each to interview her in private while the trial recessed for one day.

The defense took her first on a Thursday morning. I was not happy. I was concerned that Helena would get under the spell and direction of the defense team and testify that she was indeed present at the MacDonald apartment the night of the killings, and that Jeffrey MacDonald was a victim and not the killer we had portrayed.

One of the judge's law clerks told me late that morning that it looked bad for us, that it looked as if Helena was "delivering for the defense." My heart sank.

Shortly after lunch, it was our turn. We met with her in the office of the U.S. Attorney to discuss her testimony, which would take place the next day. We did not know what she would say.

Helena sat in a dark blue chair and looked right at me. I took a deep breath and asked, "Helena, were you there that night? Did you kill anyone, or do you know anyone who did?"

"No, Mr. Blackburn, I don't. I didn't kill anyone. I have never killed anyone. I have never been to that apartment. I don't know who killed Dr. MacDonald's family."

Now, everyone in the room took a deep breath and relaxed.[4]

Blackburn goes on to describe how it happened—his fall from grace, the obloquy, the shame. But how do you pick a passage from *Flame-out*? Okay, here's my favorite. James Blackburn's warning to his mother that her obituary had just appeared in the Raleigh newspapers.

"Mother, I need to tell you something."

"What's that?"

"Well, it's been in the *Raleigh News and Observer*, I understand, though I haven't actually read it myself. But you're going to find out, and you might as well know from me."

"Know what? I don't understand."

"Well, let me tell you, I had to kill you."

There was a long silence as we drove down the road. Finally, "You had to do what?"

"I had to kill you. It was for a good cause though, I suppose. At least, it seemed like it at the time."

Another long silence. "What was the cause?"

"There was this case. I needed a continuance. I couldn't think of a reason, so I used you. You had a heart attack and died. Sort of sudden, though you had been sick for some time."

"How did you come up with that?"

"I don't know. I remembered you did have that slight heart attack back in 1978. Seemed normal to me, so that's how and why you died. It was in the paper."[5]

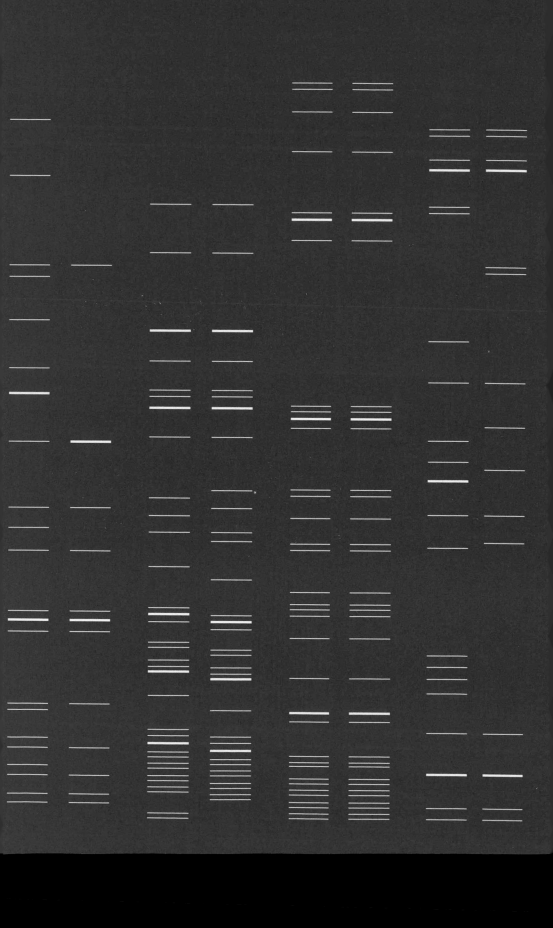

SPECIMEN 91A

In theory, theory and practice are the same.
In practice, they aren't.
—Attributed to Yogi Berra

It was a Hail Mary pass. A request for mitochondrial DNA testing of hairs and bloodstains, added to the end of a 1997 brief on Michael Malone (the discredited FBI analyst) and the saran wig fiber.[1] None of the defense lawyers believed the request would be accepted, but it was.[2]

Simple enough, but endless arguments ensued. What are we looking for? How many samples? At long last, twenty-eight hair samples (out of thousands of specimens) were submitted in 1998 to the Armed Forces DNA Identification Laboratory (AFDIL). The results finally came back on March 10, 2006, *eight years* later:

Nine were inconclusive
Thirteen were from Kristen, Kimberley, and Colette MacDonald
Three were from Jeffrey MacDonald
Three could not be matched to any known samples, including Helena
    Stoeckley and Greg Mitchell[3]

I called Kim Murga, the former assistant technical leader of the Nuclear DNA section at the AFDIL, the lab responsible for the testing of the samples. She was reluctant to talk, because the case is still being litigated. But she gave me an overview.

KIM MURGA: I spent seven years of my life involved with this case. It's one of the most difficult, one of the most challenging and lengthy cases that I've ever dealt with in my career, and I probably will ever deal with.

ERROL MORRIS: Why seven years?

KIM MURGA: The science is very complicated. We were in the process of validating a lot of new technology to accommodate the case and accommodate the sample types that we were being asked to evaluate. But then there were other challenges. The lawyers were telling the scientists what to do. And that's really not appropriate. You have to look at the mission of the lab, which is to identify deceased U.S. military service members from current and previous military conflicts. The lab was court-ordered [to do the DNA analysis] in 1999, and it wasn't completed until May 10, 2006. But during that seven-year period, there was the USS *Cole* bombing, and then the September 11 attacks. There were a lot of mass disasters that the lab has to deal with first and foremost. There's a lot of complicating factors, which led to the length of that case. Still, I don't think it should have taken that long, honestly.

ERROL MORRIS: How do you evaluate a crime scene like this? You can't say, "Well, there's no evidence of intruders," and at the same time tell us that there were literally dozens of people traipsing through the crime scene that morning.

KIM MURGA: Right.

ERROL MORRIS: That's one thing that puzzles me.

KIM MURGA: And then on the flip side of that, you have to look at the fact that it was transient housing. It's not like you had the same set of people living there for an indefinite period of time. It was military housing. So you have a lot of different genetic information already present in the home. It really just depends on the placement. And this applies to any crime scene. If you're talking about hairs, I'm sure if you look around your desk, you can probably find a number of different hair fibers in your vicinity that probably don't belong to you. So it just depends on where the item is found. If we're talking about hairs, then the most probative hairs are found in the orifices of somebody—in their mouth, in their vagina, in their anus, what have you. Because generally, you're not going to have transient type of hairs found in those areas unless it was most likely during the commission of a crime.

ERROL MORRIS: Right.

KIM MURGA: So it can vary. It can vary from scene to scene and crime to crime. I'm constantly working with detectives in trying to really figure out what it is that you want answered. And then, apply that to the value of the evidence that you're asking to be tested.

ERROL MORRIS: Does the MacDonald case seem to be more difficult than any other case?

KIM MURGA: Yes. It is. There are special challenges. You have to remember that it's our job to do the science and to report the science as we find the results. It's the investigating agent's responsibility to determine what it means.

ERROL MORRIS: Would you have liked to have tested more?

KIM MURGA: There were hundreds and hundreds and hundreds of items of evidence that were collected. And it's challenging from the fact that it's very old. It's challenging from the fact that when the crimes were committed DNA was not on the horizon. Therefore, people did not exercise the same caution and care that they might today at a crime scene, with frequent changing of gloves, with limitation of people who were traipsing around. And so that's a challenge.

ERROL MORRIS: How odd that a case that's gone on for forty years still manages to create perplexity.

KIM MURGA: The one thing about DNA is it's not just for the suspects, it'll get all genetic information that's present. It could be just about as probative, honestly, as swabbing the door handles of a 7-Eleven. The more genetic information you have, the less probative it becomes. DNA can't tell you when something occurred. It can't tell you the order that something happened. DNA can point the finger, DNA can solve cases. But it's really up to the investigators to figure out what does it mean. We can explain the science, but we can't explain *how* it got there, or if it was consensual, or when it got there.

ERROL MORRIS: Right. But if investigators found Stoeckley or Greg Mitchell's DNA there, that would be a different matter altogether.

KIM MURGA: But even if they didn't, that doesn't mean they weren't there. That just means that we haven't found anything scientifically to implicate them. Or maybe they were there, but there was so much other DNA already there, that their DNA was overwhelmed. I mean, it's just a matter of happenstance when it comes to some of the evidence. That's all. I am hopeful it'll be resolved.

On March 10, 2006, when the test results came back, the Department of Justice issued a press release.

> DNA testing, conducted by an independent laboratory selected by Jeffrey Mac-Donald, has determined that neither the DNA of Helena Stoeckley nor Gregory Mitchell was present in any of the questioned hair or blood samples tested, and thus has produced no evidence exculpatory of MacDonald.[4]

The press release also pointed to a limb hair, found in Colette's hand; MacDonald had argued that it surely belonged to one of the intruders, but testing showed that the hair was in fact MacDonald's. But there were three unsourced hairs mentioned only in passing. One of them—Specimen 91A—was found under Kristen's fingernail. MacDonald's lawyers argued that it might exonerate him. Specimen 91A was "in a location that shows that during Kristen's attempts to defend herself, a hair from her attacker was lodged under her fingernail. The DNA results establish that this hair is <u>not</u> the hair of Jeffrey MacDonald."[5]

One hair, one fifth of an inch in length.

The government's theory? Speciment 91A had not in fact been found at the crime scene, but rather ended up in a laboratory test tube as a result of contamination. Murtagh and his Department of Justice colleagues had never objected to the testing of 91A before, but once it became a piece of evidence in MacDonald's favor, it suddenly became nonevidence.

———

The story of 91A is complex. Captain William F. Hancock performed the autopsy of Kristen MacDonald on February 17, 1970. And Dr. George Gammel took scrapings from under her fingernails and put them in an unmarked vial. From there the vial went to the U.S. Army Criminal Investigation Laboratory (USACIL) at Fort Gordon, Georgia. There the vial was labeled Vial #7 by Dillard Browning. (He did not label the vial directly, but a piece of paper attached to it.) But the hair—what was eventually labeled 91A—was not *noted* until July 27, 1970. The notation appears in the lab notes of Janice Glisson, the same USACIL chemist who discovered the synthetic blond fiber. As forty years of calendar pages flipped by, its moniker changed. Vial #7 became D-237 became Q-137, then GX-285, and ultimately, 91A. From the CID to the FBI and eventually to AFDIL.

Part of the uncertainty about what was originally in the vials came from the fact that they had not been labeled properly. I looked at Janice Glisson's handwritten notes, dated July 27, 1970. She was performing an inventory of the evidence. After almost every entry, she has added the phrase "not labeled by Browning" or "not noted by Browning." If Browning had overlooked 91A, it was not a unique or even unusual error. It certainly doesn't mean that it wasn't originally in the vial. We don't know for sure whether the hair was there or not. That is, before July. But do hairs just pop up on slides or jump into vials?

When the government argued that the samples were contaminated, there was a certain attendant irony. With 91A we're not talking about the crime scene. We *know* the crime scene was not protected. But here we're talking about a crime laboratory. It's one thing to imagine that there were unidentified MPs and onlookers in the MacDonald living room on the morning of February 17; it's another thing altogether to contend that there were all kinds of particulate matter floating around in the Fort Gordon laboratory.

What *would* count as evidence of intruders? A saran wig fiber? Not really. (Deny that it's from a wig.) Dark wool? (Leave it off the lab report.) A woman who confesses repeatedly to being present during the murders? (Suggest that it happened only in her mind.)

How do you win an argument like this—when you are on constantly shifting grounds?[6]

When the defense filed its first request for DNA profiling in 1997, it was a nascent science. An alphabet soup of new techniques—Touch DNA, Y-STR, Y-Filing—have been developed that the defense hopes will provide a new interpretation of the evidence. There are now ways of conducting DNA testing based on contact with a doorknob, a drinking glass, or a club.

MacDonald appealed once again based on Britt's affidavit and the DNA evidence. In 2008, Judge Fox denied the appeal.

On April 2, 2009, Barry Scheck of the Innocence Project submitted a brief on the DNA evidence to the Fourth Circuit. I spoke with Scheck about the MacDonald case.

BARRY SCHECK: It's part of the mission. If DNA testing can shed light on guilt or innocence, then the Innocence Project just takes on the case. That's our criteria. So, I could easily imagine—it wasn't that hard—that there could be a number of DNA testing results that could, with luck, prove MacDonald's innocence and identify the people that really committed the crime.

ERROL MORRIS: So it *all* rests on the DNA testing?

BARRY SCHECK: Well, I'm very clinical about all of this. I act on evidence, because I learned a long time ago that there were a lot of people who would call us from prisons and they would say, "I'm innocent, I'm innocent, I'm innocent," and they were a real pain in the ass, and the evidence against them looked pretty strong, DNA could prove them innocent, but if I had to wager on it and given how disagreeable they were, I'd say, "Well, the test is not going to exonerate this person." And it did. And then there were plenty of people that looked like the perfect picture of innocence. They seem valiant; they are very sympathetic, and they say all the right things to engage your sympathies. You look at the case and say, "Oh, this looks like a terrible eyewitness identification or a false confession," and then you do the DNA test and they turn out to be totally guilty. Once you've gone through that experience, you learn some humility.

ERROL MORRIS: I read that you were troubled by McGinniss. But McGinniss could be a bad guy and still be right about MacDonald's guilt.

BARRY SCHECK: Absolutely! But it wasn't so much that he betrayed MacDonald's trust—it was that evidence wasn't involved. McGinniss had come to dislike Mac-Donald. MacDonald offended him. And he clearly offended other people as well. He offended his father-in-law with that *Dick Cavett* appearance; he offended people that he went to Malibu and was running around in sports cars, that he wasn't grieving appropriately. And I have seen a lot of people that were convicted because they're jerks, not because the evidence merited it. And so that was troubling to me. That's what I took away from the Joe McGinniss stuff—that MacDonald got convicted in no small measure because people decided they just didn't like the guy.

ERROL MORRIS: And in not liking the guy, they may have failed to explore certain leads.

BARRY SCHECK: That's the big problem we have in these non-DNA cases—that most crimes are solved, if they're solved at all, within the first few days. And it's very, very hard decades later to start reconstructing what wasn't done, and the clues, and the trail of evidence. If you fail to pursue exculpatory leads, they disap-pear. That's what's so troubling.

ERROL MORRIS: Let me ask the question directly: are you absolutely convinced of his innocence?

BARRY SCHECK: I'm convinced that he was wrongly convicted, and I have a deep intuition that he's innocent. My role was to get him the DNA testing, and I must

UNEXPLAINED EVIDENCE

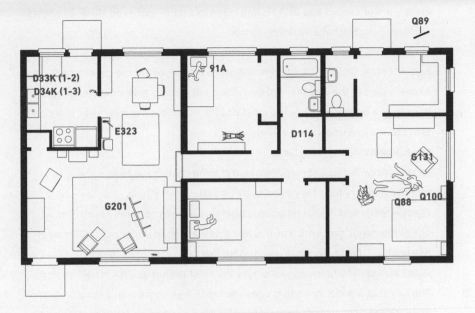

From the CID's first processing of the crime scene, the government kept a record of the findings made there. Included in that record are odd details, many suggesting evidence of intruders or related to the re-creation of MacDonald's path through the home that the government presented at trial.

CID Exhibits D33K (1-2) & D34K (1-3)
Five bloody gloves—two rubber and three cloth—were found in the kitchen.

CID Exhibit E323
The blond fibers up to 24" in length were found in a clear-handled hairbrush by the kitchen doorway.

CID Exhibit G201
Wax was found on the coffee table tipped on its side in the living room. It was never matched to any of the candles in the MacDonald home.

AFDIL Exhibit 91A
A short hair not matching any of the MacDonalds' DNA was found under the fingernail of Kristen MacDonald's left hand.

CID Exhibit D114
A bloodstain was found at the edge of the hallway closet door—the same closet in which Hilyard Medlin claimed on February 21, 1970 to have found a half-filled bloody syringe. Medlin's claim was never disclosed to the defense.

CID Exhibit G131
More wax was found on the chair and bedspread in the master bedroom that did not match any of the candles in the MacDonald home. (A burnt match was also found on the floor of Kristen's bedroom.)

FBI Exhibits Q88, Q89 & Q100
Dark wool fibers were found on the club that was apparently used in the murders, as well as on Colette MacDonald's left arm and around her mouth. The fibers could not be sourced to anything in the MacDonald home. FBI notes that mentioned these fibers were not available to the defense.

apologize, because I got him the only form of testing that we could arrange, and it turned out to be outrageously dragged out. It was disgusting. Never in the history of our project has DNA testing taken this long—not even close, by orders of magnitude. So that's upsetting to me.

ERROL MORRIS: Can you tell why it took this long?

BARRY SCHECK: Oh, it's just total intransigence on the part of the government. At every step of the way they did everything possible to slow down the process to not just a grinding halt, to the most viscous molasses I've ever seen in a court process. It's just unbelievable. Eight years.

ERROL MORRIS: A long, long time.

BARRY SCHECK: It's just absurd. This kind of thing could have been done in two months. At every turn, they needlessly contested everything.

ERROL MORRIS: And in the last amicus brief that you wrote to the Fourth Circuit, one of the major concerns was this hair that was found under the fingernail of Kristen MacDonald. So, what was it about that one piece of evidence?

BARRY SCHECK: The hair was just simply the most probative DNA result we had. The hair that's under her nail is consistent with a struggle with a third party. So that's the best evidence we got out of it. We were hoping for a lot more redundancy in results, although I always knew it was a long shot.

ERROL MORRIS: And then, of course, the government comes back and says, "Well, so what? You found this hair because the evidence was contaminated."

BARRY SCHECK: Of course, if this evidence is contaminated, why not all of the state evidence? Why not just say that your entire case is bogus to begin with? Where do you draw the line?

A BLACK SKY

On August 14, 2003, I spoke to Jeffrey MacDonald from the Boston offices of his then appellate attorneys, Harvey Silverglate, Phil Cormier, and Andy Good. They had scheduled a Thursday conference call with him, and they were kind enough to give the time over to me. I was particularly interested in the role of the media in the case.

ERROL MORRIS: Your case has been on my mind for many, many years. It never goes away. I'm sure that's true for many people. It is not just a story about a miscarriage of justice, but a miscarriage of justice story that's been hidden by the media.

JEFFREY MACDONALD: Amen to that.

ERROL MORRIS: People who are fifty, or thereabouts, all remember your case. And if they don't remember the name Jeffrey MacDonald, they remember the Green Beret doctor who killed his family. And blamed it on hippies. They remember the book, and they remember the miniseries. It becomes very, very difficult to discuss the case with anyone—if not impossible—because they think they know it already.

JEFFREY MACDONALD: This is our problem with judges. Getting them to look at the case through new eyes. It has proven to be an insurmountable problem.

ERROL MORRIS: They think they know all they need to know about it. They have read the book and seen the TV miniseries and have been convinced that you are guilty. And if anything, the situation was exacerbated by Janet Malcolm. The book generated an enormous amount of press itself.

JEFFREY MACDONALD: That's because it was about the press.

ERROL MORRIS: Indeed. I called her, because there was a passage in *The Journalist and the Murderer* that I did not like. And I never heard anyone else complain about it. So, I thought, I'll complain about it because it bothers me. It's a passage in the book where she is seated in front of a pile of folders that contain evidence of the MacDonald case.

JEFFREY MACDONALD: And she wouldn't read them.

ERROL MORRIS: And she wouldn't read them, because, in her words, "Can't one interpret this evidence any way one chooses?"

JEFFREY MACDONALD: Yes. She and I had several letters over that exact topic. And my point to her was that there is a truth at some point. And she said, "There isn't." And I said, "There is." She said, "Give me an example." And I said, "Let's say that Joe McGinniss says the sky is black and, in fact, it was a blue sky. Is there a truth there?" And she said, "No one ever knows," or something like that. And I said, "That's false." I said, "If the sky is blue, then it has to be some shade of blue. Now, he can use his artistic craft to say they were studying clouds in the light blue sky, or it was a deep blue sky, or it was azure. But he can't write that it was a black sky."

ERROL MORRIS: It comes down to an issue of truth. Is there such a thing? And yes, there is such a thing. There is a fact of the matter of whether you killed your family or you didn't. It's not just somehow thinking makes it so.

JEFFREY MACDONALD: Exactly.

ERROL MORRIS: Evidence is our way of trying to find out about the world. What's true? What's false? When police arrive at a crime scene, like any of us, they try to formulate an idea about what happened. They take the seeming chaos of a crime scene and interpret it. They provide a model for it, an explanation for it. Often, the explanation is based on convenience. Is it easier to believe one narrative about a crime than another. The *Thin Blue Line* case is a perfect example. It became convenient, easy for people to believe that the Dallas police officer was killed by a drifter from out of state. The only problem is that the narrative they picked was wrong.

JEFFREY MACDONALD: Exactly.

ERROL MORRIS: It was wrong. But once having picked a narrative, they could never be torn from it, no matter what evidence was uncovered. Part of telling your story is a story about how that narrative came into being. How it became entrenched, and why, if you like, the other narrative—forgive me for talking about it in such abstract terms—why the other narrative was rejected and eventually ridiculed. We know that part of it was prosecutorial misconduct. Part of it was the incompe-

tence of the military police at the crime scene. But part of it goes deep into how we try to explain the world to ourselves and how the media can exacerbate error.

JEFFREY MACDONALD: As I said to my lawyers recently, there's been a lot of things in the last thirty-three years where I have gone against my gut feeling. And almost every time, one, two, seven, or ten years later, my gut feeling turns out to have been the right one. For instance, we never fought with Judge Dupree. I was told by my lawyers in North Carolina, if you can't kill the king, you can't fight with him. Because we couldn't defeat Dupree, we shouldn't fight with him. So he ran over us for seven weeks, and I lost the case. Now in retrospect, nothing anyone could have done would have won the case for me in Judge Dupree's courtroom. But we should have fought Dupree tooth and nail at every single turn, on every issue, on every piece of evidence, and put everything in the record. And I was screaming that daily for seven weeks. I lost that fight. Okay?

Then I had a big fight with John Thornton, our forensic guy. I said, "John, I'm a doctor. That doesn't make me any more special than anyone else. But I can think a little scientifically. And what you're telling me about your upcoming testimony is not good enough. I'm saying you've got to state things a little clearer. You're playing this neutral scientist bullshit role, and they're going to run over you." "Oh no, no, no. Science speaks for itself." Well, they ran over John Thornton, and they made his experiments look silly. Okay? And then, during trial, my lawyers, highly paid and well respected, had me undergo a psychiatric exam during trial, at night, at the judge's insistence. And I told them that this was imbecilic. And if they didn't see a blooming disaster, I certainly did. Well, needless to say, my objections were overridden, and I was led kicking and screaming into my lawyer's office where I was promptly disemboweled by the fake psychiatric exam by a guy [Dr. James Brussel] who had just had a stroke. Then there's Joe McGinniss. I sort of made a promise to myself about five or six or seven years ago that I'm going to have to stand up for myself a little better. I'm going to have to do what I think is right, not just what other people think is right.

Since then I've gotten married. That's probably strange to you, someone in prison getting married. And I would have thought it was strange, too, until Kathy and I decided to take this gigantic step. So I'm sort of trying to think for two. I'm trying to do what's best for Jeff MacDonald because I need to come home. I've been fighting this case for thirty-three years. And I've been in prison twenty-three years. And I've been waiting for DNA for six goddamn years, not six months. Honest to God, it seems no closer. And no matter what we hear from the AFIP [Armed Forces Institute of Pathology], every single answer [to the question when will testing be done] is vague—some indeterminate time in the future, if we can get to it, if we agree with you that we should test that exhibit. I'm sitting here doing triple life for something I didn't do. I've done twenty-three years. I've waited six years for DNA tests that should, by all rights, have taken two to four months. He told us that. And a month later he was gone, mysteriously disappeared out of the bowels of AFIP, to be replaced by a new bureaucrat. There is all this false bullshit that's out there about me. I'm not a narcissist. I'm not crazy. I don't have problems. I didn't murder my wife and family. You know, my great sin in life is I had a couple of one-night stands. Who didn't in the sixties? That doesn't make me innocent of adultery. Okay. But it certainly doesn't make me guilty of murder.

I'm tired of being in goddamn prison. I shouldn't be here. I spend every hour of every day trying not to say, "Why me?" And I'm getting pretty damn good at it, you know.

And yet I'm getting tired. I'm fighting all these battles all the time on every front. Somehow, I need a break. And I'm praying that it's a DNA break, and that it gets me into a hearing, and that hearing will eventually get me home.

My interview with Jeffrey MacDonald took place in 2003. He is still hoping for a break with DNA testing. In April 2011, the Fourth Circuit Court of Appeals sent the case back to Judge Fox, ordering that further consideration be given to the results of the DNA testing and to Britt's affidavit.

By its decision of November 4, 2008, the district court denied the DNA motion, on the ground that the court lacked jurisdiction as a result of MacDonald's failure to secure additional prefiling authorization from this Court . . . The district court also refused to consider the DNA test results and other evidence proffered by MacDonald as part of the "evidence as a whole" relevant to the Britt claim. And finally, after performing its more searching assessment of the Britt claim than we had conducted for purposes of prefiling authorization, the district court denied MacDonald leave to file the §2255 motion [another habeas petition].

As explained below, the district court erred in assessing the Britt claim by taking an overly restrictive view of what constitutes the "evidence as a whole," and further erred in renouncing jurisdiction over the DNA claim. Accordingly, without expressing any view on the proper ultimate disposition of either claim, we vacate the Opinion and remand for further consideration of both the Britt claim and the DNA claim.[1]

The Fourth Circuit is clear that "the evidence as a whole should be considered." The court further made it clear that an "innocence claim should be evaluated in light of all the available evidence, including that considered unavailable or excluded at trial and any evidence that became available only after trial."

Nevertheless, it seems that "a federal constitutional right to be released upon proof of 'actual innocence'" remains an open question.

> Finally, without expressing any view on the proper disposition of the DNA claim, we acknowledge that MacDonald has a daunting burden ahead in seeking to establish that he is eligible for *habeas corpus* relief solely because of his "actual innocence." The Supreme Court has only "assume[d], for the sake of argument . . . , that in a capital case a truly persuasive demonstration of 'actual innocence' made after trial would render the execution of a defendant unconstitutional . . ." In any event, MacDonald is entitled at least to the prefiling authorization for his DNA claim that we grant herein, as well as the more searching evaluation of such claim that the district court must conduct on remand.

A new hearing has been set for August 20, 2012, in Wilmington, North Carolina.

———

MacDonald became eligible for parole in 1991, but since parole depended on an admission of guilt, he refused to apply.

Meanwhile, Dupree and the Fourth Circuit rejected petition after petition. What did MacDonald's lawyers expect? That Dupree would reverse his own opinions?

One new appeal, based on new evidence produced by Ray Shedlick, Ellen Dannelly, and Ted Gunderson, made it all the way to the Supreme Court in 1992. This, too, was rejected. In *McCleskey v. Zant,* decided a year earlier, the Supreme Court had tightened the rules for appeals due to constitutional error—the exact procedure MacDonald was trying to use to secure his freedom. Once a prisoner submitted an initial habeas corpus appeal, the justices ruled, any further constitutional claims would automatically be dismissed, regardless of their merit, if there was any chance they could have been raised in the *first* appeal. This was a radical departure from the previous standard, which essentially required prisoners to make a good-faith effort to raise habeas corpus claims as early as possible. Justice Marshall, writing in dissent, accused the majority of creating a "near-irrebuttable presumption" against new claims. And indeed, in MacDonald's case, the Supreme Court decreed that the constitutional issues in his petition should have been raised by O'Neill in the 1981 appeal, even though O'Neill wasn't aware of them until years later.[2]

The Kassabs died in 1994, and then Judge Dupree in 1995. Dupree was replaced by Judge Fox, his close friend.

MacDonald, although still refusing to admit guilt, applied for parole in 2005. It was at his wife's insistence. The Kassabs were dead, but the ghosts of the Kassabs remained. They had written a letter to any future MacDonald parole board. It contained a series of accusations that would be repeated again and again: "MacDonald has shown no remorse whatsoever. As a true psychopath, he feels no guilt, no remorse and most assuredly given the right provocation, he would lose all control and kill again."

Bob Stevenson, Colette's brother, also sent a tape recording to the Parole Commission made by James Blackburn and Freddy Kassab in 1989.

Here is an excerpt from the Kassab-Blackburn tape.

FREDDY KASSAB: It has been shown by psychiatrists and psychologists that the man is what they refer to as a true psychopath. He is exceedingly believable when he talks to you. And he puts on an air of complete innocence. And he's convincing. He's very articulate. He doesn't shake very easily, as you know from having him on the witness stand. He comes across very well.

JAMES BLACKBURN: Is there any doubt in Mildred's mind today about his guilt in these crimes?

FREDDY KASSAB: Not one iota.

JAMES BLACKBURN: Is there any doubt in your mind that he's guilty of these crimes?

FREDDY KASSAB: None whatsoever. Beyond a reasonable doubt. Beyond a shadow of a doubt.

JAMES BLACKBURN: Freddy, a number of people have asked me over the years, and I suspect have asked you as well, that you and Mildred have seemed to be obsessed about this case, that you have let it destroy or ruin both your lives, that you have spent time on it that perhaps better would have been spent somewhere else. I think what I want you to do is just tell the Parole Commission: do you think you have been obsessed about this case? And is that something that you think you should have done?

FREDDY KASSAB: Yes, I think we have been obsessed. People have accused me of running a vendetta. But one must remember that everything that I did and that my wife did, our aim was to get the man tried and convicted. And everything we did was within the system, within the legal framework if you will. It could have been very easy to seek vengeance outside of the system. But what I wanted was within the system to get him convicted. And it was done . . .

I had been trying to find Bob Stevenson's number, and then he called me. He must have heard that I was trying to reach him. It's hard to capture the nastiness of the conversation. He explained that he lived "in peace" knowing that MacDonald was in jail. But then he imagined himself locked in a room with Jeffrey MacDonald, so he could hurt him, the way MacDonald had hurt his family.

Many of the true MacDonald haters hate him even more because he won't confess. But if MacDonald could get parole by admitting guilt, then why does he refuse to do so? Stevenson told me, "Even if I thought through my psychosis that I was not guilty, I would confess to having killed Jesus Christ himself, all by myself, if I could then get out and walk on the face of the earth again without bars." The thought that MacDonald might be innocent is not an option for him. Stevenson offered to come to my office to talk to me further, but when I called him back, he hung up on me.

It is *Breaking the Sound Barrier* all over again. The controls of the airplane are reversed. Up is down. Pull back is push forward. Evidence of innocence is evidence of guilt. He shows no remorse, therefore he's guilty. He shows no remorse because he's guilty. Stevenson concluded his tirade, "I'm happy he doesn't want to confess. And I will never try to make him confess. I like the fact that he's there."

Bob Stevenson had written a letter to the parole board in 2005.

MacDonald as a free man on parole without remorse and repentance would be an act that would serve to bring disrespect and disrepute to the legal system of justice in the United States. This is no mere white collar criminal . . . no repeat offender in DWI cases . . . but a man now legendary enough as a guilty killer that his name was used recently in the game called *Jeopardy* . . . the lead being, "The man who killed his family on an army base and tried to blame it on hippies," and the question, of course, being—"Who is Jeffrey MacDonald?"

We may never be able to prove with absolute certainty that Jeffrey MacDonald is innocent. But there are things we *do* know. We know that the trial was rigged in favor of the prosecution; that the CID, the FBI, and the Department of Justice pursued an unethical vendetta against Jeffrey MacDonald; that evidence was lost, misinterpreted, and willfully ignored. We know that Jeffrey MacDonald was railroaded.

I have asked myself: What does this case *mean*? What is it *about*? Is it about the failure of our institutions? Of our courts, prosecutors, and investigators? Is it about how we trick ourselves into believing that we *know* something? That we have *proved* something when we have proved nothing? Is it about how we muddy the waters rather than seek the truth? About how we fail to examine evidence (or even look for evidence) that could lead us to the truth? About how we pick one narrative rather than another—for whatever reason—and the rest becomes a self-fulfilling prophecy?

When detective stories—both fiction and nonfiction—emerged in the nineteenth century, there were no untidy ends. No leftover pieces. For the three great masters of the detective novel—Edgar Allan Poe, Emile Gaboriau, and, perhaps most famous of all, Arthur Conan Doyle—there were always answers. It's an unstated guarantee—every mystery comes with a solution. Gaboriau's detective, Monsieur Lecoq, surveys a crime scene and with supreme confidence says, "Now I know everything." (*"Maintenant je sais tout!"*) His colleague is skeptical. LeCoq reassures him, "This expanse of earth covered with snow is a white page upon which the people we are in search of have written, not only their movements, their goings, and comings, but also their secret thoughts, their alternate hopes and anxieties." There can be no limit to the powers of ratiocination. No limits to knowledge. A trail of evidence leads inevitably to a solution of the mystery. Arthur Conan Doyle proclaims in *A Study in Scarlet*, "All life is a great chain, the nature of which is known whenever we are shown a single link of it."

But unlike detective stories, our world is a lockbox that only reluctantly gives up its secrets. Vincent Bugliosi, the Manson prosecutor, writes in *Helter Skelter* about the untidiness of any real investigation.

> In literature, a murder scene is often likened to a picture puzzle. If one is patient and keeps trying, eventually all the pieces will fit into place. Veteran policemen know otherwise. A much better analogy would be two picture puzzles, or three, or more, no one of which is complete. Even after the solution emerges—if one does—there will be leftover pieces, evidence that just doesn't fit. And some pieces will always be missing.

Here are his words of caution. Even after the solution emerges, there will be leftover pieces. But what if no clear solution emerges?

Every detective tries to crack a case. I was lucky. I got an innocent man out of prison. And got the real murderer to confess. The MacDonald story has stubbornly resisted resolution. But I do know—like Michael Malley—that MacDonald should never have been convicted of these crimes. And that much of the evidence points to his factual innocence. I am repulsed by the fabrication of a case from incomplete knowledge, faulty analysis, and the suppression of evidence. Repulsed and disgusted. Whether MacDonald is innocent or guilty, the case is a terrible miscarriage of justice.

The die was cast within a few days of the murders—once it was decided by the CID that MacDonald was guilty and had tried to cover up the crime. They are not unlike the Prefect in "The Murders in the Rue Morgue," who has been charged with the analysis of the crime: "Our friend the Prefect is somewhat too cunning to be profound." His only great ability is—and here, Poe quotes Rousseau—"to deny that which is and to explain that which is not" (*"de nier ce qui est, et d'expliquer ce qui n'est pas"*).

The CID could have done things differently. The crime scene could have been protected. The base could have been closed, and someone could have been sent out to Honeycutt Road to see if the woman with the wide-brimmed hat was still

standing there. Stoeckley could have been more thoroughly investigated. Her clothing could have been seized. The boots, the blond wig, the floppy hat. There would have been a basis for a comparison—the fibers from her wig and the saran fiber from Colette's hairbrush (E-323); the black woolen fibers from her coat and the black woolen fibers on the club (Q-89). Not a hypothetical comparison, but a *real* one.

Questions could have been asked early on to determine whether she knew details about the crime scene that could not have come from the newspapers or from Fayetteville gossip. Knowledge that could only have come from her being there. There is Stoeckley's statement to Posey about the broken hobbyhorse. And Helen Fell's statement to me that the hobbyhorse was broken *before* the murders. But it is *one* piece of evidence. The broken hobbyhorse is a piece of the puzzle, but it is one piece among many. The saran wig fiber, Mica's description of the woman on Honeycutt Road, Stoeckley's repeated confessions from 1970 through to her death in 1983. MacDonald's lack of motivation. It is the totality of the evidence. Look at the totality of the evidence.

A perfect storm. As MacDonald describes it, "a towering, black, cumulonimbus cloud obscured the sky." A botched investigation that corrupted and destroyed evidence; a nine-year delay that stripped the crimes from their context; a vendetta carried out by law enforcement officials and prosecutors intent on "winning" no matter what; a judge who eliminated exculpatory evidence from the trial; appellate judges who passed the buck rather than reexamining the issues; a craven and sloppy journalist who confabulated, lied, and betrayed while ostensibly telling a story about a man who confabulated, lied, and betrayed; and a *New Yorker* writer who instead of pursuing the truth lost herself in a misguided discussion of journalism. Bad luck. Sure. But it goes beyond bad luck. It suggests an endlessly perverse universe where guilt is assumed and issues of truth are left dangling in favor of procedural haggling. We may never know all the details of the night of February 17, 1970, at 544 Castle Drive. Perhaps it was once but it is no longer possible to know. Forty years of wandering in a wilderness of error. Not a wilderness created by some metaphysical obstacle to knowledge, but a wilderness created by ourselves.

"WHAT WOULD YOU SAY IF I TOLD YOU I WAS THERE?"

I wrote *A Wilderness of Error* because I felt that there was something deeply wrong with the MacDonald case. I still do. It has very little to do with my liking or disliking MacDonald, who has treated me with indifference over the years. My interest—even obsession—with the case is for me a matter of principle. I believe many of the facts of the case were excluded from the trial.

The 2012 federal hearing in Wilmington was supposed to be different. The Fourth Circuit, the last step before the Supreme Court, had ordered James C. Fox, the senior circuit court judge, to give Jeffrey MacDonald an opportunity to present "the evidence as a whole"—a much broader mandate than the defense attorneys had been given during the previous thirty years of litigation.[1] Now, all the confessions, all the physical evidence, all the suggestions of government misconduct could be considered.

It didn't happen that way. Instead, the hearing in Wilmington in 2012 was a reprise of the entire MacDonald spectacle, compressed into a few days. But something *did* happen in that courtroom that strongly argues for overturning MacDonald's 1979 conviction. Even the presiding judge, who has hardly been sympathetic to MacDonald over the years, turning away appeal after appeal, called it "somewhat exculpatory." But it happened very near the end of the hearing. Few people heard it. Few people wrote about it. It was almost as if it had never happened. But it did.

What follows is a chronicle of the seven days in court—from September 17 to September 25, 2012, and the climactic conclusion to that hearing.

———

Day One, Monday, September 17, 2012. I had arrived the night before. The street outside the courthouse that morning was choked with reporters with microphones and cameras. Remote news vans with microwave dishes. Joe McGinniss was giving an interview to *Inside Edition* around the corner.[2]

The court was gaveled into session by Judge Fox—eighty-four years old, in a crisp yellow bow tie. He was dwarfed by his own courtroom—twenty-foot-high ceilings, tall windows shuttered with wooden blinds, marble trimmings, and a huge eagle hovering over the mahogany bench. In one corner stood a black box with blinking lights, presumably housing recording equipment—one of the few indications that this was the twenty-first century. The witnesses, who were not allowed to listen to the hearing before testifying, waited in a room down the hall. But the visitors' gallery was nearly filled. There were journalists—from *60 Minutes*, *Fox News*, *Dateline*, and AP. The *Fayetteville Observer* was there and the *Washington Post*. There were also those devoted to getting Jeffrey MacDonald out of prison and those dedicated to keeping him there. And a few locals.

In his opening statement, Gordon Widenhouse, MacDonald's new appellate attorney, briefly touched on the DNA evidence. In the popular imagination, DNA is supposed to prove everything. Here, it ultimately proved nothing—neither for the prosecution nor for the defense. The MacDonald home at 544 Castle Drive was military housing for many families over the years. There was traffic in and out of the house. Unsourced hairs in such an environment tell us very little. One unsourced hair fragment, 91A, found under Kristen's fingernail, was debated, but ultimately it proved inconclusive. MacDonald's hairs could be expected to be found anywhere in the house. He lived there. If Helena Stoeckley's or Greg Mitchell's DNA had been found in the house, that would have changed everything. But it was not.[3]

Later in his opening statement, Widenhouse asked the judge to allow Jerry Leonard, Helena Stoeckley's court-appointed attorney, to testify. He said, "We believe he'll invoke the attorney-client privilege, but we're going to ask the court to lift the privilege and hear his testimony at least *in camera*, to hear what he has to say about what Ms. Stoeckley told him about this incident."[4] It would become an ongoing plea.

The defense first called Wade Smith, one of MacDonald's defense attorneys in 1979, who also served as his North Carolina counsel on and off for more than thirty years.[5] Smith is considered to be the premier criminal defense attorney in North Carolina and has been a practicing lawyer for more than fifty years.

> **GORDON WIDENHOUSE:** Can you tell us what the basic theory of the defense was for the trial?
>
> **WADE SMITH:** I think the basic theory of the defense was that MacDonald was in the home sleeping on the couch in February of 1970. Intruders came into the house and killed his family and wounded him.
>
> **GORDON WIDENHOUSE:** And what was the importance of the crime scene with regard to the defense theory?
>
> **WADE SMITH:** Well, it was our theory that intruders came into the house, and in order to show that intruders came into the house, we needed the crime scene to be as pristine as possible. We needed the walls and the floor to tell the story that intruders had come.[6]

Everything comes down to this issue. Take the endless arguments about the puncture wound that collapsed MacDonald's lung. If there were no intruders, it was self-inflicted. But first, ask yourself the question: Can I prove that the injury was self-inflicted *independent* of the assumption that there were no intruders? Is there something about the wound itself that tells me it was self-inflicted? Expert witnesses didn't think so.[7] Perhaps if the wound had been carefully examined or photographed immediately after the murders, the question could be answered. But it was not. If you assume that MacDonald is guilty, then the wounds were self-inflicted. If you assume there were intruders, the picture looks quite different. The horrible circularity of these arguments has characterized much of this case.

Widenhouse's questioning soon turned to Jimmy Britt, the deceased U.S. marshal who claimed he had heard Helena Stoeckley confess. Britt also claimed he was present when prosecutor Jim Blackburn threatened Stoeckley, a claim that, if true, could cause the 1979 conviction to be overturned.

Smith had heard Britt's first statement under oath in his offices on February 24, 2005. Widenhouse asked him to read from it: "At the conclusion . . . Mr. Blackburn stated to Helena Stoeckley, 'If you go downstairs and testify before the jury as to what you have told me or said to me here in this office I will indict you for murder.'"

Smith continued, stressing how he "wanted to try to measure those words and to be sure that this man was real and was telling the truth."[8] A polygraph test was administered. Britt passed. But there was a serious problem. Britt's initial statements and his two subsequent affidavits were inconsistent. In one affidavit, Britt claimed that he had picked Stoeckley up in Charleston before transporting her to Raleigh; in the other, he claimed that he picked her up in Greenville.[9]

Then it was the government's turn to cross-examine. John Bruce, the lead government lawyer, questioned Smith about his memory of the defense meeting with Stoeckley on August 16, 1979. When I interviewed Smith about that meeting, he couldn't remember many details. He rummaged around his office and returned with a copy of *Fatal Vision* to refresh his memory. Now, Bruce was paraphrasing those same passages from *Fatal Vision* in federal court. And for the most part Smith went along—except for one passage where McGinniss uses Stoeckley to set up his theory that MacDonald had taken substantial amounts of amphetamine in the weeks prior to the murders. It's a novelistic device, a foreshadowing, but is it fact?

> **JOHN BRUCE:** And do you recall Ms. Stoeckley responding, "Someone on drugs could do something like that, not acid, maybe speed?"
> **WADE SMITH:** I don't remember that. . . .[10]

Bruce questioned Smith about comments he had made in 1979 about the defense meeting with Stoeckley.

> **JOHN BRUCE:** I would like for you to read lines 24 and 25 and over to the next page.
> **WADE SMITH:** Okay. "**MR. SMITH:** Judge, here I think is where we generally are. Generally, she [Stoeckley] said to us the same thing and that is, I don't remember. But in two or three or four instances, whatever the list would reveal, she says something which would give an interesting insight into her mind."
> **JOHN BRUCE:** All right. Stop right there. You're responding to what Mr. Blackburn has told the judge about his understanding having talked to you about the two interviews, is that right?
> **WADE SMITH:** Yes.
> **JOHN BRUCE:** Now, Mr. Smith, you have a well-deserved reputation as a gentleman, do you not?
> **WADE SMITH:** I don't know the answer to that.
> **THE COURT:** I do.
> **WADE SMITH:** Thank you.

JOHN BRUCE: Isn't it true when you made this statement to Judge Dupree—weren't you just too much of a gentleman to say it outright that Bernie Segal was exaggerating what had gone on in the defense interview?

WADE SMITH: I have not read much of the transcript. I have read this. And I have puzzled and puzzled and puzzled. I puzzled into the night last night about what I could have meant. And as you can see, my words are very vague. I said it "would give an interesting insight into her mind."

JOHN BRUCE: An "interesting insight into her mind" is not a confession, is it, Mr. Smith?

WADE SMITH: It was, it was certainly—let me just put it this way, I was absolutely devoted to this case and upheld my role as counsel. And I'm still devoted to this case. But I did not hear Helena Stoeckley say useful things for us. It is certainly possible, as I mentioned a while ago, maybe I was out of the room. I do not know the answer. But I can only speak for myself and that is that when I was present she did not say things that helped us."

When I interviewed Smith in 2012, he told me "there must have been a number of little things she said that would cause us, as lawyers, to pick up a few little crumbs. . . . We didn't get the whole cake, but we did see a few crumbs fall down on the floor and we're gathering those up."

Now, months later in Wilmington, his story had changed. He testified, "I did not hear Stoeckley say useful things for us. . . ." What *had* Stoeckley said? Would we ever find out?

Finally, Bruce questioned Smith about a conversation he had had with Jerry Leonard during the 1979 trial, and that Smith had mentioned in court.

JOHN BRUCE: . . . I want to ask you about [your] comment about Jerry Leonard. It states that Jerry Leonard talked to you that morning [Thursday, August 23, 1979] and then you make the statement that "this woman continues to say things that tie her to this case." This woman refers to Helena Stoeckley, is that right?

WADE SMITH: Yes.

JOHN BRUCE: All right. Do you recall talking to Jerry Leonard?

WADE SMITH: Yes, but I doubt that Jerry Leonard told me things that Helena Stoeckley had said. I think it could very well be that I was referring to Wendy Rouder and what Wendy had said. But Jerry is very professional and I don't think he would quote his client to me.

JOHN BRUCE: All right. So, the two parts of that first sentence are not necessarily connected in that you weren't saying to the judge that Jerry Leonard had told you that Helena Stoeckley was saying things to tie her to the case?

WADE SMITH: No, I didn't mean to be saying that. No. . . .

JOHN BRUCE: So, it's your testimony that Jerry Leonard has never disclosed to you what his client told him in confidence, his client Helena Stoeckley?

WADE SMITH: He has never—he has never told me anything that she said, that I recall.[12]

————

Day One, Monday afternoon. Mary Britt, Jimmy Britt's first wife, took the stand. She was in her seventies, a kindly grandmotherly type with rust-colored hair. She had been divorced from Britt in 1989. By all accounts, the divorce had not been amicable. He had been cheating on her with the woman who became his second wife.

Her testimony started with Britt's commitment to his work. His love of the U.S. Marshals Service. And his involvement with Helena Stoeckley.

After the hearing, I interviewed Mary Britt.

MARY BRITT: I know that he was telling the truth—because I lived it. I know he went to South Carolina and picked up Helena Stoeckley.

ERROL MORRIS: How do you know this?

MARY BRITT: When he came in that evening, I was in the den, and he came in the side door—I remember it clearly. He was excited, because he thought the person riding in the car back from South Carolina with him that day described what had happened at the Jeffrey MacDonald house. He said, "Mary, she described the inside of that apartment to a T. She has been there." And he said, "She even described the hobbyhorse—a broken hobbyhorse." He thought that it was a major breakthrough. And the next morning he got up and went to take Helena Stoeckley to meet with the defense attorney and with the assistant district attorney. I just couldn't wait for him to get home that day. And when he came in that evening, I asked him, "Well, what did they say?" And he told me, "[The prosecutors] say they can't use her testimony, because her brain's fried from using drugs for so many years." And back then, here in eastern North Carolina, drugs were just not something we heard about, or talked about, or knew anything about.

ERROL MORRIS: Did your husband say anything about James Blackburn?

MARY BRITT: No. He never said to me what happened in that room.

ERROL MORRIS: And he was very upset?

MARY BRITT: Yes.

ERROL MORRIS: Did your husband believe that MacDonald was innocent?

MARY BRITT: No, I didn't say that. Jim never knew. I heard him say more than one time that he wished somehow or other he could know if MacDonald was guilty or innocent. But if he ever thought he was guilty or innocent, he never said that to me.

Mary Britt included one additional detail in her testimony at the hearing. After MacDonald was found guilty, her husband had been asked by Hugh Salter, a U.S. marshal, to "lock him up." Britt refused. According to Mary Britt, he said, "I was not doing any more of the dirty work. I was going home."

————

Day Two, Tuesday, September 18, 2012. Gene Stoeckley, whom I interviewed for the book, repeated on the stand many of the things he had told me—that he believed his sister, he believed his mother, and that they had no reason to lie. The prosecution tried to imply that Stoeckley's mother was unreliable, and argued that she had changed her views on whether Helena was involved.[13]

Late in the day, Widenhouse raised the issue of Jerry Leonard. Edwin West, Leonard's lawyer, approached the bench:

GORDON WIDENHOUSE: We're under the impression that he's going to assert the attorney-client privilege, and we've simply come to the bench to ask you if you want us to do that in open court to start with or if you'd rather hear us in chambers. I'm just trying to get some guidance from the court is all. And Mr. West obviously is here to represent him.

THE COURT: Mr. Leonard's former client was—

GORDON WIDENHOUSE: Helena Stoeckley.

THE COURT: And she's deceased.

GORDON WIDENHOUSE: Correct.

THE COURT: I don't think I've ever had the privilege asserted in this situation before, but I'm sure you can enlighten me on it.

GORDON WIDENHOUSE: Well, he's told me he's going to assert the privilege.

THE COURT: Well, I've never had the occasion where it was asserted where somebody was departed and not subject to prosecution. It seems to be somewhat moot.

EDWIN WEST: And, Your Honor, we will obviously comply with whatever Your Honor orders, but out of a sense of caution under the rules of professional conduct the way I read them, I think we have a duty to assert it. And then if you order Mr. Leonard to answer, then he has to, and that takes care of the concern.[14]

———

Day Three, Wednesday, September 19, 2012. The government began to present its case. Bruce questioned several former marshals, Eddie Sigmon, Dennis Meehan, and Bill Berryhill. They claimed that Britt was argumentative, self-aggrandizing, a drinker, a philanderer, and so on. And that he lied. Evidence was presented that Mary Britt was wrong—that Jimmy Britt did *not* pick up Stoeckley in Charleston, Greenville, or anywhere else in South Carolina.[15]

Bruce seized on all of this. He highlighted and then pounded away at the inconsistencies in Britt's story.

Jerry Leonard still lingered near the door of the courtroom, like a diver waiting his turn at the high board. And then Judge Fox announced that he would not be allowed to testify.

THE COURT: Counsel, I've looked into the question of privileged communication. As you know, the Supreme Court has dealt with this issue to some extent, and I think the attorney-client privilege survives the death of the client, and I so rule. And in doing so, I am following *Swidler vs. Berlin* [sic], a Supreme Court case to which you are both aware. Thank you, counsel.

GORDON WIDENHOUSE: Your Honor, I just want to make sure the record reflects that we were asking you to breach or waive the privilege based on our client's Fifth and Sixth Amendment due process and compulsory process rights to present a defense. . . .

THE COURT: Well, I understand. And, of course, I think it's—the question of privilege has been debated many, many times, but I think for the most part in common law it survives, and the Supreme Court so held in *Swidler*, and I think that their reasoning is correct. Thank you.[16]

The discussion turned back to Britt. MacDonald's defense attorneys introduced convincing evidence that Britt brought Stoeckley from the jail to the courthouse the day after she arrived in Raleigh. There are dated photographs (from AP, UPI, and the *Raleigh News & Observer*) of the two of them walking into and out of the federal building. No one disputes that he escorted her to the defense interview and then picked her up and took her to the prosecution interview on the eighth floor.

Still, the government attorneys claimed that he was not in the room when Stoeckley was interviewed by the prosecution. James Blackburn took the stand.

> **JOHN BRUCE:** In your experience as an assistant United States attorney, did you make it a practice to include deputy United States marshals in witness interviews?
>
> **JAMES BLACKBURN:** To the best of my recollection, I have never interviewed a witness with a deputy U.S. marshal in the room.[17]

But why should Blackburn be trusted? Hadn't he been indicted for embezzlement, obstruction of justice, and fraud? Hadn't he pled guilty?

Day Four, Thursday, September 20, 2012. Jack Crawley, one of the government attorneys from the 1979 trial, testified. Like Blackburn, Crawley had a tarnished history. And like Blackburn, he claimed that a mental condition was the source of his problems. In 1995, the North Carolina State Bar cited Crawley for failure to act "with reasonable diligence" in two cases. The next year he was cited again, this time because $4,500 owed to a client went missing from his trust account. In the spring of 1997, the bar finally determined that Crawley was "disabled from the practice of law." He has not practiced since March 18, 1996.

The prosecutors called Crawley to the stand.

> **JOHN BRUCE:** All right. Who was present in Room 839 [the office of the U.S. attorney, George Anderson] for the interview of Helena Stoeckley by the prosecution?
>
> **JACK CRAWLEY:** I do not have a recollection of all the specifics of that interview, but

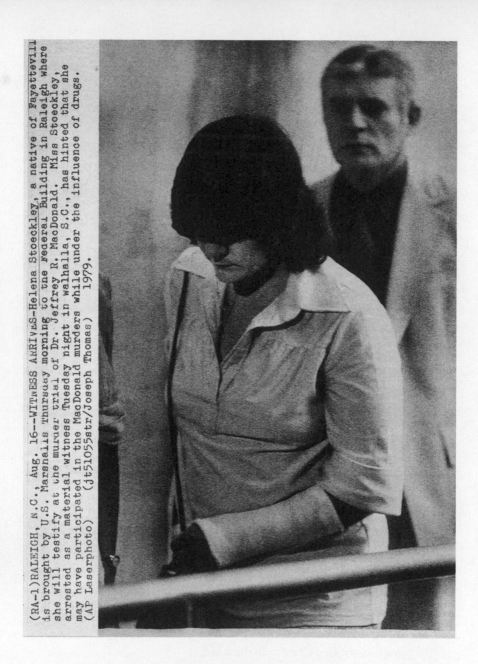

I'm sure that I was there, Mr. Anderson was there, Mr. Blackburn was there, Mr. Murtagh was there and, of course, Ms. Stoeckley was there.

JOHN BRUCE: Do you remember anybody else being there?

JACK CRAWLEY: No.

JOHN BRUCE: To your recollection, was there a deputy United States marshal there?

JACK CRAWLEY: No. No.

JOHN BRUCE: In your experience as assistant United States attorney in the '70s, would it have been typical for an AUSA to ask a deputy marshal to sit in on an interview with a witness?

JACK CRAWLEY: No.

JOHN BRUCE: Do you know Jim Britt?

JACK CRAWLEY: Yes, sir.

JOHN BRUCE: Was Jim Britt in that interview?

JACK CRAWLEY: To my recollection, no. I believe it was—it was just those five people and no deputy marshal.[18]

I called an official at the U.S. Marshals Service and asked if it was standard procedure for marshals to accompany witnesses during interviews. He told me that it was. He added, "It would be logical because they may be a reluctant witness, so they might try to make a break for it. We have to literally guard the proceedings. Generally, I don't see why the marshal would not have been around. It just doesn't make a great deal of sense to me." He gave me permission to print his opinion. But the following day, he called me back and told me it was all off the record. He had been instructed not to talk by officials in both Raleigh and Washington.

Thursday afternoon. Widenhouse was still trying to convince the judge to lift the confidentiality requirement and allow Leonard to testify.[19]

Lawyers approached the bench. *Swidler & Berlin v. United States*, a Supreme Court case on attorney-client privilege, took center stage.[20] (Who would have imagined that Bill and Hillary Clinton would suddenly appear in these proceedings?) Vince Foster, the deputy White House counsel in the early years of the Clinton administration, had committed suicide. Kenneth Starr, the independent prosecutor, tried to subpoena notes taken by Foster's attorney. The request had been rejected, and a lawsuit ensued that ended up before the Supreme Court. In the 6–3 decision, the Supreme Court extended the attorney-client privilege past the death of a client. There would be no exceptions. That is, except as provided for in an easy-to-overlook footnote, footnote #3: "Petitioners, while opposing wholesale abrogation of the privilege in criminal cases, concede that exceptional circumstances implicating a criminal defendant's constitutional rights might warrant breaching the privilege."

––––––

Joe McGinniss took the stand. I have no doubt that McGinniss truly believes that MacDonald is guilty. But I do not think that he proven that is true.

McGinniss was set up by the prosecution as "The Reader," the witness of historical reality, the arbiter of what is true and false. First, Bruce asked McGinniss to read Blackburn's statements from the 1979 trial, then Wade Smith's statements. Finally, Bruce asked McGinniss to read straight from his own book, including the theory of the case he presents at the end of *Fatal Justice*—the diet pills, the psychopathy, the bedwetting. As if all the years of uncertainty and mendacity could melt away through the sheer repetition of his narrative.

McGinniss seemed to have forgotten that many of his claims had been introduced in the 1987 civil trial—MacDonald's lawsuit against him—and had been successfully and repeatedly impeached by Gary Bostwick, MacDonald's lawyer.[21] By 2012, the civil trial had faded into the past. All that remained were Xerox transcripts in cardboard boxes and excerpts from Janet Malcolm's *The Journalist and the Murderer*.[22]

Fatal Vision, for the purposes of the hearing, was called exhibit 2201—evidence, evidently, but evidence of what? McGinniss was cross-examined by Keith Williams, another of MacDonald's attorneys. McGinniss had been sequestered during the hearing but had been busily sending tweets from the witness room down the hall.

> **KEITH WILLIAMS:** . . . Directing your attention again to the screen. Again, on your Twitter account—this was Wednesday—you said, "It looks like 'Back to the Future,' but good to reconnect with old pals." Is Mr. Murtagh one of your old pals?
> **JOE McGINNISS:** I'd say I consider him a friend now, yeah. And with Mr. Smith, too. It was great to see Wade again. And Jim Blackburn, it was great to see him, too.[23]

––––––

Day Six, Monday, September 24, 2012. On Monday morning, the discussions about Leonard's testimony continued. Should it be heard in open court or sealed and forgotten? A bevy of lawyers approached the bench. Finally, Judge Fox ended the discussion. The Fourth Circuit had demanded a full presentation of the evidence in the case. And an opening had been provided by footnote #3 in *Swidler*.

Preventing Leonard's testimony and affidavit from being introduced as evidence and heard in open court would raise a red flag with the Fourth Circuit. Better to get it over with. Judge Fox explained his reasoning from the bench.

> **THE COURT:** When I made that decision, my decision was that Ms. Stoeckley was dead, her parents were dead. Her brother joined in the request that the privilege be waived. . . . This happened some 40 years [ago]. I never saw any of these people involved, but I feel that the Fourth Circuit's directive was that everything be heard. Everything.[24]

The judge continued.

> **THE COURT:** To me, as I read her material, the sworn statement—it was somewhat exculpatory.
>
> **GORDON WIDENHOUSE:** Yes.
>
> **THE COURT:** And my feeling was that if a man is innocent then that testimony that favors his innocence trumps the attorney-client privilege. Although . . . I reached that conclusion reluctantly. . . . Let me look at the Fourth Circuit mandate again. It says, and I recall it distinctly—It says, everything means everything.[25]

"Everything means everything."

The courtroom in Wilmington was virtually empty. I had returned to Massachusetts. The national press corps and television crews were gone. Most of the press had come to Wilmington to see a confrontation between McGinniss and MacDonald—MacDonald in leg chains at the witness table; McGinniss reading from *Fatal Vision* on the stand. And that was over by Monday morning.

On Monday afternoon, Leonard took the stand.

> **JERRY LEONARD:** I received a telephone call from Judge Dupree's office asking me if I would represent Helena Stoeckley. . . . I understood she was a material witness involved in this case, the MacDonald case.
>
> **GORDON WIDENHOUSE:** Were you following the MacDonald case at the time?
>
> **JERRY LEONARD:** Not particularly.
>
> **GORDON WIDENHOUSE:** Okay. Can you tell us how you began interacting with Ms. Stoeckley once you were appointed?

JERRY LEONARD: I picked her up, and I can't remember where I picked her up. I was thinking it was from the federal building, but I'm not sure. . . . I didn't know what to do. I didn't know anything about her. She didn't know anything about me. And it was obvious that, to her, I was part of the establishment, and I felt that I had to build trust. I was worried about where she was going to stay, and I had to get lodging for her, and I had to make sure that she was there in court, and so I took her to my house, and we sat around and talked and talked very generally. And I got to know her a little bit, and I hoped that—my job—I was trying to establish trust so I could represent her.[26]

They discussed a number of things: the statute of limitations on capital cases, the attorney-client privilege (that what she told Leonard would remain private), whether she could be tried and given the death penalty, and her Fifth Amendment right against self-incrimination.

JERRY LEONARD: She said, "What would you do if I told you that I was there?" And I said, "I'd still represent you. I need to know the truth." She said, well, she was there, and then she told the story about what happened that evening. I thereafter told her that I could not—that she should not take the witness stand again and testify, that she could plead her Fifth Amendment right not to incriminate herself and that I would help her with that.
GORDON WIDENHOUSE: And what did you do toward that end of helping her with that Fifth Amendment right?
JERRY LEONARD: We wrote out—I wrote out what I thought was the proper way to invoke the Fifth Amendment for her to read and she had that thereafter. . . . Well, I think she had it thereafter. I told her to keep it when she was in the courtroom.
GORDON WIDENHOUSE: And did she ever get called as a witness?
JERRY LEONARD: No, she didn't.[27]

Leonard had been asked by Judge Fox to prepare an affidavit that detailed what Helena Stoeckley had told him on Monday, August 29, 1970. It was a confession that Judge Fox described as "somewhat exculpatory."

Here is an excerpt from Leonard's affidavit.

Sometime on Monday afternoon, Ms. Stoeckley asked me what I would do if she actually had been "there." I recall telling her that I would still help her, but that she had to tell me the truth. She then told me she had been scared to tell me the truth, but that the truth was "not as bad as everybody thought." Shortly thereafter she began telling me that she was, in fact, at the MacDonald residence at the time of the murders. . . .

She stated she belonged to a cult. This cult had a core group of followers and a larger group of people that came to some of the cult's larger meetings. . . .

According to what Ms. Stoeckley told me, the idea to go to the MacDonald residence came up one night when she was doing drugs with some of her friends. These friends were part of this cult's core group. At least one man in the group had an issue against Dr. MacDonald because the man felt MacDonald discriminated against hard drug users in his work at a drug treatment program—something to the effect that heroin users would be recommended for court-martial or discharge and would not receive treatment, while others got more favorable treatment. Ms. Stoeckley said this man talked them into going to Dr. MacDonald's house to confront MacDonald about this unfair treatment and, therefore, they went to his house on the night of the murders. Ms. Stoeckley said the end result was that things got out of hand and the people she was with committed the murders.

Ms. Stoeckley also said that, during the violence, the MacDonalds' home phone rang and she answered the phone. She hung up quickly after one of her friends yelled at her to hang up the phone. She also said she noticed a toy rocking horse at the MacDonald home, and that the horse was broken. Ms. Stoeckley said one of the springs was not attached to the horse and she took that fact as a sign that Dr MacDonald did not care for his children.

Our plan thereafter was for Ms. Stoeckley to refuse to answer any questions if re-called as a witness. We had the script written down for her to read from the stand in order to properly invoke her Fifth Amendment rights.[28]

The mystery of why Stoeckley never testified is only heightened by a statement made by John Dolan Myers, a private investigator that Smith himself hired. Smith can repudiate what he said in federal court in 1979 and in his interviews with me, but the Myers statement casts doubts about his credibility.

Mr. Leonard stated that he received permission from Ms. Stoeckley to discuss the things she told him with attorney Wade Smith. Mr. Leonard stated that he had a conference with Mr. Smith and told him what Helena had told him.

He stated that he also gave Mr. Smith some insight as to his impressions of Ms. Stoeckley. . . .

Mr. Leonard stated that he had several private conversations with Judge Dupree about Helena Stoeckley. Mr. Leonard stated that he was not sure if, as an officer of the court, these conversations were privileged information. He did state that anything Judge Dupree might or might not have told him concerning the judge's feelings about the guilt or innocence of Jeff MacDonald seemed to have been expressed by his mood and actions in the courtroom during the trial. . . .

NOTE: Mr. Leonard stated that he did not know if MacDonald was guilty or innocent; however, he stated that he did feel that the prosecution did not prove their case. He stated that he thought MacDonald had been screwed[29] (emphasis mine).

Admittedly, Myers does not tell us explicitly what Leonard told Smith, but we know enough: (1) Leonard discussed the case with Judge Dupree; (2) he got permission from Stoeckley to discuss the case with Smith; and (3) he thought that MacDonald had been screwed.

On Thursday, August 23, 1979, in court, in front of the judge, Smith had said:

WADE SMITH: I talked to Jerry Leonard at great length, Your Honor, this morning—talked to him for a long time, and this woman continues to say things that tie her to this case. I will be frank with Your Honor, we have no plans to use her at this moment, but we have got too much at stake. It is too important a case, and she has said too much for us to just, you know, out of hand say, "Oh, sure, go on. Go away. We will never see you again. Go back in hiding and let the years roll by." She is here. The defendant is on the stand, and we feel that we need to be able to talk with Jerry and have her available at least for this afternoon.[30]

How could Smith have forgotten this? After all, he was MacDonald's defense attorney. Is it that easy to forget about such a thing? To forget about Stoeckley's confessions is to forget the facts, and in effect to support the prosecution. In 1979, Smith's great hope was that Stoeckley would tie herself to the case. According to his own statements in court, she did.

The confessions were not limited to Leonard. On August 24, 1979, with MacDonald on the stand, another bench conference:

THE COURT: Well, now, listen, enough of the thing is enough, Wade. If you are going to ever call her, you call her right now or I am going to release her from her subpoena.

WADE SMITH: Judge, I understand what you are saying. Let me just say this: that woman made the most outrageous statements to a lady at the hospital when she got her nose fixed that you have ever heard.

THE COURT: They could not be any more outrageous than the ones she has [already] made.

WADE SMITH: They are. They are more outrageous. They are more incriminating, and, Judge, we don't know what she is going to do. We don't know what she is going to say.[31]

I believe that Smith knew from Leonard that Stoeckley had said something incriminating. But he also had reason to believe that Dupree would never let Stoeckley take the stand again—nor any of the witnesses to her confessions. According to Dupree, Stoeckley was "heavily drugged, if not hallucinating," and the witnesses to her confessions were simply repeating testimony that was "clearly untrustworthy." All Smith could do was preserve what was happening for the record. One final bench conference from August 24:

WADE SMITH: We don't want to do that and waste the Court's time, but we have a feeling that the chapter on Helena Stoeckley may not be over. We don't want to call her unless there is something for her to say. There may ultimately be something.

BRIAN MURTAGH: That doesn't change the Court's previous finding as to her mental state. I think we should not go to the wire or to the jury for that matter with Helena Stoeckley still lurking in the wings. I think they have had ample opportunity to put her on. I think this is about the third time that it has come up, "Are you going to put her on or not," and, I think, Judge, that we are entitled—everybody is entitled—the Court, the jury, and all concerned—that we don't have to sit on the edge of the chair and wonder whether Ms. Stoeckley is going to have another hallucination.

THE COURT: Why would you—if you are so confident about Helena, why would you be sitting on the edge of your chair?[32]

Now, neither Leonard nor Smith can remember discussing the case with each other. Once more, from the first day of the hearing in Wilmington:

JOHN BRUCE: So, it's your testimony that Jerry Leonard has never disclosed to you what his client told him in confidence, his client Helena Stoeckley?

WADE SMITH: He has never—he has never told me anything that she said, *that I recall* (emphasis mine).

I don't buy it. They may not remember, but the written documents do remember.

––––––

There is a buddy-buddy photograph from James Blackburn's autobiography (*Flame-out: From Prosecuting Jeffrey MacDonald to Serving Time to Serving Tables*) of McGinniss, Smith, and Blackburn on a hiking trip in 1993, shortly before Blackburn was indicted for embezzlement, fraud, forgery, and obstruction of justice. It suggests that Wade Smith had divided loyalties.

Blackburn also reproduced a buddy-buddy conversation, in which he and Smith are at an International House of Pancakes discussing the "upcoming indictment and how we would handle it."

> . . . I leaned across to Wade and whispered to him, "Wade, you know, being convicted of a felony is a bad thing, but I've always been told it's not bad as an aphrodisiac. What do you think?" He looked at me and didn't miss a beat. "Jim, there is no doubt. Being indicted and convicted of a felony is one of the great aphrodisiacs in the world. I've been thinking of doing it myself."[33]

They pay the bill and walk out into the night.

> Wade looked pensively at me and asked, "Jim, what do you think you have learned from all of this? What is the greatest lesson in life you can take from here . . . ?" I thought of a response and didn't hesitate. "I have learned that the next time I forge somebody's signature, I'm going to do it with my left hand. That's what I think about all of this."[34]

––––––

On cross-examination, John Bruce asked Leonard about a poem that Helena Stoeckley had written while waiting in the conference room.

Three good friends on a hike, *left to right*, Wade Smith, me, and Joe McGinness

whom I'd gotten to know well during the time Joe researched his book, *Fatal Vision*. Joe had flown that day from his home in Massachusetts to Raleigh just to go walking with Wade and me. The three of us walked like what seemed forever, and at the end of the afternoon, with muddy boots and wet clothes, we went to 42nd Street Oyster Bar for a prearranged dinner. It was my first social event out of the house since I entered Duke University Medical Center.

I talked to few people, outside my family, on the specific advice of Jean Spaulding. Perhaps I owed friends and others an explanation of what I had done and what was happening to me, but I was in no condition to do that. Slowly, however, friends

OFF THE CHARTS 87

JOHN BRUCE: Is that a handwritten poem that Helena Stoeckley wrote and gave to you?

JERRY LEONARD: Yes.

JOHN BRUCE: And do you have it displayed on your wall or something?

JERRY LEONARD: Well, I did and I can explain—I can tell you about this—

JOHN BRUCE: Did she write it and date it while you were representing her?

JERRY LEONARD: She wrote it on the stationery that was in the conference room we were in.

JOHN BRUCE: Actually, it looks like the court reporting paper, doesn't it? If you—

JERRY LEONARD: Yes.

JOHN BRUCE: Okay. And did you give a copy of this to Jim Blackburn at some point?

JERRY LEONARD: I don't remember doing it, but obviously I did. I told you about this, and I told other people about it. I remember her giving it to me, and I told

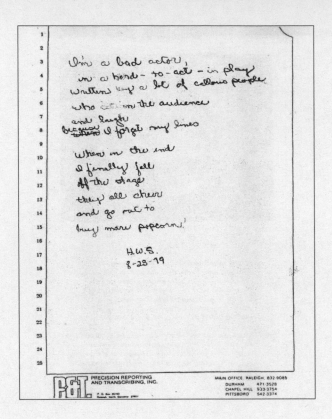

her I thought it was really kind of . . . beautiful writing. And she said, "It's
yours," and I said, "Well, do you mind if I frame it and put it on my office wall?"
And I did.[35]

I had to get permission from Stoeckley's next of kin to use the poem, so I asked
Gene Stoeckley. He had never seen the poem before.

He wrote me back: "There's no question this was written by my sister, Helena.
She peeled away the layers of the onion quite nicely. Helena was able to simplify in
two paragraphs what is to this day a labyrinth. And sadly she was portrayed as a
drug addict incapable of distinguishing ghosts from reality."

Here is the poem:

I'm a bad actor,
in a hard-to-act-in play
written by a lot of callous people
who sit in the audience

and laugh
because I forget my lines.

When in the end
I finally fall off the stage
they all cheer
and go out to
buy more popcorn!

———

Day Seven, Tuesday, September 25, 2012. The last day of the hearing. As part of his closing arguments, Brian Murtagh said: "We know that Blackburn did not threaten Stoeckley with prosecution because she hadn't admitted to anything that would have provoked such a threat, even if he was inclined to make it."[36] I disagree. Stoeckley admitted to many people—including Brian Murtagh—on many occasions that she was present during the murders. For Murtagh to argue otherwise in 2012 is ridiculous.

In the same closing argument, Murtagh also said, "The great thing about the court record, when we can find things in the trial record, is it was put down on paper in 1979 by a court reporter. It doesn't rely on anyone's memory of a 33-year-old event."[37] Indeed. And what the trial record shows is a persistent fear among the prosecutors that this woman would confess on the stand, in the presence of the jury, and destroy their entire case. Murtagh was "on the edge of his chair"; Jack Crawley, his associate, was "on pins and needles." The prosecutors would not allow that to happen. And it didn't happen. But the record of their fear cannot be erased.

I had a theory of what happened in Raleigh in 1979. Very little in Wilmington changed that. Dupree didn't want Stoeckley to testify—that is, after her first "performance" in court. But he knew that Stoeckley was continuing to confess—that's why he appointed Leonard to represent her. Dupree knew, Smith knew, Blackburn knew, Murtagh knew. I am convinced more than ever that—as Jerry Leonard put it to John Dolan Myers—MacDonald got screwed.

Despite their inconsistencies, Jimmy Britt's affidavits did accomplish one thing: they put Stoeckley and her confessions squarely back in the spotlight. And Stoeckley's confession to Leonard matters. This wasn't a passing statement made to a stranger; it was a detailed confession made to an officer of the court, under the protection of attorney-client privilege. It gives substance to the view that Stoeckley was a credible, intelligent person with a guilty conscience. Had Stoeckley's confession been heard, Jeffrey MacDonald would not have spent the last thirty-four years in prison. It is now over a year since the hearing, and MacDonald is still waiting for a decision from Judge Fox—and, ultimately, the Fourth Circuit.

The case continues.

Acknowledgments

This book could not have been written without the assistance of many, many people.

INTERVIEWS

My thanks to Jane Graham-Bailey, Rex Beaber, Hammond Beale, James Blackburn, Gary Bostwick, Robert Brisentine, Carol Butner, Richard Cahn, Ellen Dannelly, Helen Fell, Jeanette Harris, Ted Landreth, Jerry Leonard, Martin Lonky, Jeffrey MacDonald, Janet Malcolm, Michael Malley, Kenneth Mica, Kim Murga, Brian O'Neill, Ed and Rock Posey, Wendy Rouder, Robert Sadoff, Barry Scheck, Judith Schizas, Bernie Segal, Harvey Silverglate, Wade Smith, Gene Stoeckley, John Thornton, Charles "Red" Underhill.

UNPUBLISHED INTERVIEWS AND CONVERSATIONS

Dr. Robert Butner, Laurie Cohen, John Hodges, Dr. James Mack, Hart Miles, Frank Moore, Dolly Stoeckley Nobles, Chuck Probst, Kay Reibold, Leslie Reiman, Dwight Smith, Bob Stevenson, Rick Thoesen, Ralph Turbyfill, Shirley Wershba, and Colon Willoughby provided helpful background information.

Kathy MacDonald, Jeffrey MacDonald's wife since 2002, accompanied me to my one meeting with MacDonald at FCI Cumberland, a federal prison in Cumberland, Maryland. I have discussed the case with her many times over the last ten years.

EDITING AND RESEARCH

Ann Petrone. Simply, this book would not exist without her involvement in all aspects of the writing, editing, and research.

James Maxwell Larkin, my principal researcher and guide through the maze of MacDonald materials. Josh Kearney, who tirelessly fact-checked and line-edited the manuscript.

Ray Shedlick and Ellen Dannelly. Their repeated FOIA requests and analysis of government documents are essential to any understanding of this case.

Jerry Allen Potter and Fred Bost, the authors of *Fatal Justice: Reinvestigating the MacDonald Murders*. I wrote a blurb for the book when it came out in hardcover in 1995: "If you think you know the Jeffrey MacDonald case from *Fatal Vision*, think again. *Fatal Justice* is the first account of the whole story." It is a valuable book that received scant attention compared with *Fatal Vision*, a bad book that sold millions of copies.

Janet Malcolm, author of *The Journalist and the Murderer*. Despite my disagreements with some of her conclusions, her book has been essential in clarifying and understanding many of the issues involved in this case. I'm indebted to her work.

Christina Masewicz, who maintains a Web site with many documents from the case.

James Mintz and David McIntosh of the James Mintz Group.

Ted Landreth, who produced *False Witness,* a one-hour documentary on the case for the BBC. He explained to me the role that *60 Minutes* played in interviewing Stoeckley and then its decision to abandon the interview in favor of McGinniss's story and diet pills.

FORT BRAGG, FAYETTEVILLE, AND RALEIGH, NORTH CAROLINA

Michelle Luther, Mike Arnholt, and Johnny Horne from the *Fayetteville Observer;* Donna Tabor, post historian, and Jackie Thomas at Fort Bragg; Scott Sharpe and Teresa Leonard at *Raleigh News & Observer;* Cuyler Windham and Dick Washburn, former Fayetteville law enforcement officers.

THE PENGUIN PRESS AND THE WYLIE AGENCY

My fabulous publishing team: Scott Moyers, Karen Mayer, Mally Anderson, Tracy Locke, Bruce Giffords, John Sharp, and Claire Vaccaro.

And my agents: Andrew Wylie and Adam Eaglin.

DESIGN AND ILLUSTRATION

Michael Bierut and Yve Ludwig of Pentagram for the book design. Niko Skourtis, Lee Cerre, and Matt Delbridge of Pentagram for the white-on-black illustrations.

Daniel Mooney for his work on the charts, diagrams, and graphics. Steven Hathaway also contributed to these.

Alex Anmahian of Anmahian Winton Architects for the floor plans.

LEGAL

MacDonald's defense attorneys, including Harvey Silverglate, MacDonald's principal appellate attorney for fifteen years. He has helped in ways impossible to enumerate—involving everything from legal issues to understanding the various personalities involved in this case. He has seen it all and has been unwavering on the issue of MacDonald's innocence. A close friend, he is one of the reasons this book was written.

Andy Good and Phil Cormier, Harvey Silverglate's former law partners. Jason Gull, Daniel Schwarz, and Zachary Bloom, their legal researchers. Josh Good and Suzanne Hill, also from the law offices of Good & Cormier.

John Murphy, who wrote the affidavit that revealed a twenty-year history of hidden evidence in the MacDonald case.

Michael Malley, who corrected factual errors and offered insights and interpretation of the case.

READERS

Over the years, I have discussed this case endlessly with my wife, Julia Sheehan, and with my friends Charles Silver and Brad Fuller, all of whom had essential insights into the case.

Zach Arnold, Julie Fischer, Amanda Branson Gill, and Skip Skinner. Zach Arnold was particularly helpful with copyediting and clarifying many important issues. Skip Skinner read many drafts and helped simplify a complex and daunting subject.

George Kalogerakis, my editor at the *New York Times*, was one of the first readers to give me encouragement. Indeed, this book was originally conceived as a series of essays for the *Times*. Dennis Jakob, a longtime friend, read many drafts and provided helpful suggestions.

Julie Ahlberg, Maggie Causey, Elsa Dorfman, Benedict Fitzgerald, Martin Garbus, Jeanne Guillemin, Alfred Guzzetti, Ricky Jay, Martin and Terri Levin, Sarah Livermore, Dina Piscatelli, Ron Rosenbaum, Charles Rosenberg, Willie Russe, Diane Weyermann.

The MacDonald case has produced a vast quantity of source materials—the transcripts of the Article 32 hearing from 1970; the grand jury hearing in 1974–75; and the federal trial in 1979. Thousands of pages of transcripts from those proceedings alone. And then there are letters, briefs, affidavits, progress reports, and personal accounts. Some can be found in various lawyers' offices; many can be found on the Web, particularly on a Web site run by Christina Masewicz, a former MacDonald supporter who has turned against him and now operates an extensive archive of materials, www.thejeffreymacdonaldcase.com. Part Web site, part shrine to the memory of Colette and the children, ironically, it is this anti-MacDonald Web site that has provided much of the detailed information on the case that supports claims of MacDonald's innocence—the Article 32 hearing, the grand jury testimony, and the trial transcripts. It should not be confused with a Web site operated by Kathy MacDonald, www.themacdonaldcase.org.

Janet Malcolm's *The Journalist and the Murderer* has been an important book for me—equally engaging and infuriating. But it has caused me to think deeper and harder about the MacDonald case and the issues presented by it. The wealth of information, the thousands of documents and tens of thousands of pages of transcripts, reports, affidavits, notes, and so on, has worked mostly against MacDonald. It is easy to feel overwhelmed. (Malcolm expressed this sentiment in *The Journalist and the Murderer*.) There is simply too much of everything. It has been clear to me for many years that no writer can hope to include everything. Potter and Bost tried, but they produced an indispensable reference work, not a narrative. I have tried to focus on a few details that capture important themes in this case: The absurd reenactments orchestrated by Grebner and Ivory. The suppression of meaningful forensic evidence. (It is difficult to conclude anything from the evidence except that evidence useful to MacDonald was lost or suppressed.) The "mismanagement" of the crime scene—from the discarded pajama bottoms to the stolen wallet. The use of psychiatric nomenclature to provide a pseudoscientific and spurious explanation of MacDonald's motivation. The list could go on and on.

I have covered only a small part of it. It would be difficult at this late date—forty years after the murders—to prove MacDonald's innocence. Yet there is no proof of his guilt. Perhaps evidence of Stoeckley's presence that night is buried somewhere in the mountains of evidence. Perhaps it was thrown out with MacDonald's pajama bottoms. Or burned up with the contents of the house. On the other hand, it may be impossible to prove Jeffrey MacDonald's guilt. The playing field has been messed over, irrevocably messed up. One thing, however, can be proved without a shadow of doubt: Jeffrey MacDonald did not receive a fair trial either in the federal courts or in the courtroom of public opinion.

ILLUSTRATION CREDITS

Page

15   CID Case Progress File, William Ivory, 2/17/70.

16   Drawing from FBI Laboratory Report, Lab. #PC-F7279 JV, File #70-51728-66, 6/10/71.

21   "Friend Says Captain Discussed Tate Killing Before Family Died," *The New York Times*, February 20, 1970, p. 38. Copyright © 1970 The New York Times. All rights reserved. Used by permission and protected by the copyright laws of the United States. The printing, copying, redistribution, or retransmission of this content without express written permission is prohibited.

100   CID Witness Statement, William Ivory, 2/7/71.

104   Letter by Helena Stoeckley to Detective P. E. Beasley, 1971.

109   Conclusions of polygraph examination by Robert Brisentine of Helena Stoeckley, April 23–24, 1971.

115   Analysis of Crime Scene (CPT McDonald Case) by Martin Lonky, July 27, 1973.

177   Drawing from FBI Laboratory Report, Lab. #PC-F7279 JV, File #70-51728-66, 6/10/71.

190–91 "Princess Leda's Castle in the Air," "Charlie Manson's Home on the Range," and "Banality of the New Evil," *Esquire*, March 1970.

207   "'Mystery Woman' Tells of Blanking Out," *Los Angeles Times*, August 18, 1979, p. 23. Copyright © 1979 Los Angeles Times. Reprinted with permission.

265   Drawing from FBI Laboratory Report, Lab. #PC-F7279 JV, File #70-51728-66, 6/10/71.

317   U.S. Patent 3,955,587. Changeable-shape hair piece and method of styling an artificial coiffure. Ralph Dunn, J. Stephen Lewis, and Mellie M. Phillips. Mattel, Inc. May 11, 1976.

320   "Playboy Interview: Jeffrey MacDonald," *Playboy*, April 1986, p. 61.

323   Advertisement placed by Ray Shedlick.

347   Letter by Jeffrey MacDonald to Joe McGinniss, August 30, 1979.

358   "The Lessons Learned in Alaska's Grip," *San Francisco Examiner & Chronicle*, October 12, 1980, p. 5.

384   "Eskatrol." *The Physicians' Desk Reference*. Medical Economics Company, 1977.

385   Selection from *Fatal Vision* by Joe McGinniss (p. 613). Copyright © Joe McGinniss, 1983. Used by permission of G. P. Putnam's Sons, a member of Penguin Group (USA) Inc.

431   "Massive Search on for Killers." *The Fayetteville Observer*, February 18, 1970, p. 2A. Courtesy of the Fayetteville Observer Archives.

500   Stoeckley photo: Associated Press/Joseph Tomas.

510   Stoeckley poem: Used by permission of Gene Stoeckley.

Prologue: 544 Castle Drive

1. SFC Pedro Ochoa, Jr., certificate regarding property destroyed from 544 Castle Drive, June 7, 1984.

2. Ed Gein, a cannibal, grave robber, human taxidermist, and murderer, was the model for Norman Bates in *Psycho*. Ed Kemper, a mass murderer and cannibal, killed his grandparents and was put in a mental hospital as a teenager. He was released when he turned twenty-one and went on to kill eight more people, including his mother.

Chapter 1. A Convincing Story

1. Alexandre Dumas, *The Count of Monte Cristo*, translated by D. Coward (Oxford: Oxford University Press, 2008), 65–66.

2. The plot details are hopelessly arcane and convoluted. Dantès, nineteen years old, a successful merchant sailor, returns to Marseille to marry his fiancée, Mercédès. "A young and beautiful girl, with hair as black as jet, her eyes as velvety as the gazelle's . . . her arms bare to the elbow, tanned, and resembling those of the Venus at Arles." Dantès has been granted his own command by the dying captain Leclère. Leclère, a supporter of the exiled Napoleon, asks Dantès to deliver a letter to a group of Bonapartist sympathizers. Dantès is accused of being a traitor. Villefort, the prosecutor in Marseille, on discovering that the letter is to be delivered to his Bonapartist father, destroys it—choosing to save his own political career. Dantès is condemned without trial to the Château d'If. And so on and so forth.

3. *The Count of Monte Cristo* is fiction. But Dumas based his novel on the true story of Pierre Picaud, who was engaged to marry a beautiful woman and framed as an English spy by three jealous friends. It is pretty easy to see the connection between the real story and Dumas's novel. They have story elements in common: the beautiful fiancée, the thrilling escape, the retribution. Picaud could be Dantès. You could go through the novel and make a comparison side by side. But it would be beside the point. Picaud is a creature of flesh and blood; Dantès, a creature of the imagination.

4. This quote is at the end of an extended passage from Russell's *Introduction to Mathematical Philosophy* (London: George Allen & Unwin, 1920), 169–70. It starts out:

> To maintain that Hamlet, for example, exists in his own world, namely, in the world of Shakespeare's imagination, just as truly as (say) Napoleon existed in the ordinary world, is to say something deliberately confusing, or else confused to a degree which is scarcely credible. There is only one world, the "real" world: Shakespeare's imagination is part of it, and the thoughts that he had in writing *Hamlet* are real. So are the thoughts that we have in reading the play. But it is of the very essence of fiction that only the thoughts, feelings, etc., in Shakespeare and his readers are real, and that there is not, in addition to them, an objective Hamlet.

5. Kenneth Mica, Witness statement, February 17, 1970.
6. William Ivory, CID case progress file—3:50 a.m., February 17, 1970.
7. Robert Shaw, CID case progress file—4:20 a.m., February 17, 1970.
8. Ivory was thirty and had worked only one or two homicides. Investigator Robert Shaw was assigned to share work with him on account of both men's limited experience with capital crimes.

Chapter 2. Lee Marvin Is Afraid

1. This is the spelling of the phrase found at the crime scene.
2. Vincent Bugliosi with Curt Gentry, *Helter Skelter: The True Story of the Manson Murders* (New York: Norton, 1994), 62.
3. The front page also included stories about a "huge drug raid" in North Carolina, a new congressional investigation of the Vietnam War, and the burning of ROTC offices in Eugene, Oregon.
4. Martin Waldron, "Friend Says Captain Discussed Tate Killing Before Family Died," *New York Times,* February 20, 1970, p. 38.
5. Ronald Harrison, signed statement, July 13, 1970.
6. Perhaps the drug-crazed hippies weren't imitating anybody. They were just doing what hippies do. An article in *Life* expanded on the conjoined themes of hippies and crime:

> Some two years ago, says Dr. Lewis Yablonsky, a close student of the [hippie movement], criminals and psychotics began infiltrating the scene . . . But how

could children who had dropped out for the sake of kindness and sharing, love and beauty, be enjoined to kill? Yablonsky thinks that the answer may lie in the fact that so many hippies are actually "lonely, alienated people." He says, "They have had so few love models that even when they act as if they love, they can be totally devoid of true compassion. That is the reason why they can kill so matter-of-factly."

Chapter 3. Breaking the Sound Barrier

1. *Breaking the Sound Barrier*—known as *The Sound Barrier* in the U.K.—stars John Justin as Philip Peel, Nigel Patrick as Tony Garthwaite, Ralph Richardson as John Ridgefield, and Joseph Tomelty as Will Sparks. The film was released in 1952.

2. In reality the controls are *not* reversed at Mach 1. There is a phenomenon known as "control reversal," but it is not as simple as presented in the movie. It is caused not by a physical law, but by equipment malfunction or human error.

3. To be scrupulous, several different issues are involved here. There are paradoxes of induction, variations on themes from David Hume, where past patterns lead to faulty predictions. The Thanksgiving turkey is a perfect example. (I read a version of this by Bertrand Russell, but he used a chicken.) But there is a paranoid extreme to Hume. Experience is not only suspect. There are instances where everything is the opposite of what we might like to believe. The smiling man is really the frowning man with a knife hidden behind his back. All of the comforting and familiar signs of the world are masks for something deeply sinister. And then there is the Bizarro World of Superman comics where society is ruled by the Bizarro code: "Us do opposite of all Earthly things! Us hate beauty! Us love ugliness! Is big crime to make anything perfect on Bizarro World!" (In *The World of Bizarros, Action Comics,* vol. 1, no. 263 [April 1960].) It all raises the question: To what extent is our world exactly the opposite of what we imagine it to be?

4. Adams's execution had been scheduled for May 8, 1979, but the U.S. Supreme Court ordered a stay only three days before the scheduled date. Instead of conducting a new trial, the Texas governor commuted Adams's sentence to life in prison. I appeared on the scene almost ten years later.

Chapter 4. A Subtly Constructed Reflex Machine

1. Cleckley was not the first person to describe a form of psychopathy. In *A Treatise on Insanity and Other Disorders Affecting the Mind,* J. C. Prichard wrote of "moral insanity":

This form of mental derangement has been described as consisting in a morbid perversion of the feelings, affections, and active powers, without any illusion or erroneous conviction impressed upon the understanding: it sometimes co-exists with an apparently unimpaired state of the intellectual faculties. There are many individuals living at large, and not entirely separated from society, who are affected in a certain degree with this modification of insanity. ([Philadelphia: E. L. Carey & A. Hart, 1937], 20)

2. Today, textbooks are filled with references to psychopathy and to Cleckley's book (although it is difficult to find someone who has actually *read* it). Scarcely a week goes by without the appearance of a newspaper article linking brain scans on violent felons with some version of psychopathy. It has been inextricably linked with criminal behavior, and no wonder: it is classified as a personality disorder, under the general rubric of the antisocial personality. If the conclusion is that criminals exhibit antisocial behavior, I find that somewhat less than revelatory.

3. Joseph J. Michaels, "Book Review: *The Mask of Sanity,*" *Psychosomatic Medicine* 27, no. 5 (1965): 489–90.

4. *Newsweek,* May 14, 1956, p. 38. Quoted in Cleckley, *The Mask of Sanity,* 5th edition (Augusta, GA: Emily S. Cleckley, 1988), 266–67. What are we to think? Is the young man a psychopath because he expressed so little emotion while reading Cleckley's seminal book in court?

5. Cleckley, *The Mask of Sanity,* pp. 369–70.

6. Robert D. Hare and other modern experts on psychopathy would argue that there are empirical ways to identify psychopaths—through the use of various tests, in particular the Hare Psychopathy Checklist Revised (PCL-R), and more recently through various kinds of brain scans. To the reader who might feel that I have been "unfair" to Hare and Cleckley, I can offer in my defense that in the era prior to fMRIs and such, psychopathy was empirically ill defined. And yet, to my way of thinking, there are still methodological problems with the entire concept of psychopathy. I would call them cart-before-the-horse problems, problems of cause and effect. It's fine to administer a test that identifies "glibness and lack of remorse," but are these predictors of criminal violence?

7. In the preface to the fifth edition of *The Mask of Sanity,* Cleckley notes, "Revisions of the nomenclature have been made by the American Psychiatric Association. The classification of psychopathic personality was changed to that of sociopathic personality in 1958" (p. viii). For Cleckley it is a difference only of nomenclature.

8. Christopher J. Patrick, *The Handbook of Psychopathy* (New York: Guilford Press, 2007), xiii.

9. It is true that psychological evidence was not used explicitly to convict MacDonald. But phony psychology appears repeatedly in the case record. It encouraged the government to pursue MacDonald. It prevented MacDonald from getting bail in 1979. It was used to keep MacDonald from getting parole in the years since his conviction. And, most important, many of the people I spoke to for this book are convinced that MacDonald is a psychopath.

Chapter 5. The Impossible Coffee Table

1. Jeffrey MacDonald, CID interview—Part 1, April 6, 1970.

2. Jeffrey MacDonald, CID interview—Part 2, April 6, 1970.

Chapter 7. The Flowerpot

1. In the language of the Uniform Code of Military Justice, it is a "thorough and unbiased investigation" of the charges in anticipation of a general court-martial.

> The investigation shall include inquiry as to the truth of the matter set forth in the charges, consideration of the form of charges, and recommendation as to the disposition which should be made of the case in the interest of justice and discipline.

2. The details of the Article 32 hearing are summarized in a 1979 legal brief written by Segal and Malley: "The evidence presented by the prosecution had been gathered over an eight month period and was the result of the efforts of more than one hundred military and civilian law enforcement investigators. These investigators had assembled material from approximately 1500 witnesses . . . In addition to Dr. MacDonald, the defense called 29 other witnesses."

3. Alfred Kassab, telegram to President Richard Nixon, July 20, 1970.

4. Yet another photographer was called in to photograph the house after the bodies had been removed.

5. Testimony of Kenneth Mica, Article 32 hearing transcript, vol. 2, July 8, 1970.

6. From Jerry Allen Potter and Fred Bost, *Fatal Justice: Reinvestigating the MacDonald Murders* (New York: Norton, 1997), p. 50:

> Paulsen was asked by Grebner, "Can you explain why the MPs searched the ambulance and did not find the wallet?" "Yes, they searched carelessly. They

just looked under the seats and opened my medical bag. The search was not very thorough."

7. Testimony of William Ivory, Article 32 hearing transcript, vol. 8, July 21, 1970.

8. Statement of Warren V. Rock, Article 32 hearing transcript, vol. 16, September 8, 1970.

9. Ivory's failure to prove that MacDonald had placed the table on its side might be related to the general problem of induction. Alas, it really didn't matter how many times Ivory knocked over the table. All it took was the one counterexample provided by Colonel Rock and his theory crumbled.

Chapter 8. The Girl with the Floppy Hat

1. Testimony of Kenneth Mica (recalled), Article 32 hearing transcript, vol. 12, August 10, 1970.

2. Testimony of William Posey, Article 32 hearing transcript, vol. 14, August 13, 1970.

3. Testimony of William Ivory (recalled), Article 32 hearing transcript, vol. 16, September 9, 1970.

Chapter 9. No Evidence

1. Dr. Robert Sadoff, letter to Bernard Segal, April 23, 1970.

2. Testimony of Dr. Robert Sadoff, Article 32 hearing transcript, vol. 13, August 12, 1970.

Chapter 10. Not True

1. Colonel Warren V. Rock, investigative report, October 13, 1970.

2. Major General Edward Flanagan, dismissal of court-martial charges against Jeffrey MacDonald, October 23, 1970.

3. Michael Malley, account of Article 32 hearing, July 6, 1971, pp. 101–2.

4. Office of Director Hoover, telex to SAC Robert M. Murphy, October 28, 1970.

5. James C. Proctor, letter to SAC Robert M. Murphy, November 2, 1970.

6. Alfred Kassab, "How It Started," 1979.

7. Alfred Kassab, "The MacDonald Case: Prosecution or Persecution?," December 1970.

Chapter 11. Totally Wrong

1. CBS News, *48 Hours,* "Time for Truth," March 17, 2007.

2. *The Dick Cavett Show,* transcript, December 15, 1970.

3. Grand jury transcript, testimony of Alfred Kassab, September 4, 1974.

4. From Alfred Kassab, 1979 manuscript, "How It Started": "Meanwhile, I was still bombarding the Army with requests for the verbatim Article 32 transcript. They finally gave in and gave me a copy. First they were going to charge me $1.00 a page. I said I would pay it but I would publicize the fact. They changed their minds and gave me a copy."

Chapter 12. Terrible, Terrible, Terrible Idea

1. In fact, the Kassabs maintained friendly relations with MacDonald into 1971.

2. Kassab, Alfred, "How It Started," 1979.

Chapter 13. Colonel Rock

1. Colonel Henry Tufts, "Memorandum: The Kassab and Malley Allegations," January 5, 1971.

2. Colonel Warren Rock, statement to Peter Kearns, January 5, 1971.

Chapter 14. A Great Fear

1. Though Colonel Jack Pruett notes January 15, 1971, as the start date of the CID reinvestigation in a later report, an interview on February 9, 1971, by investigator Peter Kearns of Bob and Vivian Stevenson (Colette's brother and sister-in-law) makes clear this date has no actual significance. Indeed, the CID had never stopped investigating:

> **PETER KEARNS:** And as you know we are investigating the murders of Colette and the two children. We have not stopped, regardless of what anyone has told you. We have not stopped from the time the Article 32 started, which by the way is a grand-jury type of legal proceeding, as opposed to a trial. The investigation did not stop during Captain MacDonald's Article 32 hearing. It did not stop when it was closed. It hasn't stopped.
>
> **VIVIAN STEVENSON:** Is that true?
>
> **PETER KEARNS:** That is absolutely true, that it has not stopped one day since then.

2. Jack Pruett, investigative diary, February 23, 1971.

3. Vicki Kalin, CID statement, February 1, 1971.

4. John Reynolds, statement re: interview of Pamela and Violet Kalin, February 9, 1971.

5. Janice Pendlyshok, statement to the CID, March 1, 1971.

6. William Ivory, statement re: meeting with Dr. Brussel, February 7, 1971.

Chapter 15. Convinced in Her Mind

1. Affidavit of CID investigator Richard Mahon, July 12, 1984.

2. Helena Stoeckley, letter to Prince Beasley, January 20, 1971.

3. Prince Beasley, statement re: Helena Stoeckley, March 1, 1971.

4. James Gaddis, CID statement, April 29, 1971.

5. Robert Brisentine, draft report on polygraph examination of Helena Stoeckley, April 24, 1971.

6. I asked Robert Brisentine about the identities of "Linda" and "Mr. Presson":

> **ROBERT BRISENTINE:** Where in the world did you get this draft of mine? That's weird. I don't understand; it's okay. I just don't understand—Linda was my secretary. That was my secretary that I wrote that note to . . . And I had three divisions. I was the director of the Army's Crime Record Center . . . And Don Presson was the chief of my polygraph division. So now you understand that little note. I dictated this I'm sure to Linda. And I said, "Well, type it up real fast. Don't worry about the errors." And I read it over and said, "Give it to Don Presson to make sure it's right."

Chapter 16. The Impossible Coffee Table, Part II

1. Martin Lonky, "Analysis of crime scene (CPT MacDonald case)," July 27, 1973.

2. Article 32 hearing transcript, vol. 15, August 15, 1970.

Chapter 17. A Losing Proposition

1. Kearns and Pruett, "CID Case Progress File: April 27, 1971."

2. Alfred Kassab, "How It Started," 1979.

3. Letter from Alfred Kassab to Jeffrey MacDonald, November 1, 1971.

4. The military prosecutor, Clifford Somers, had requested a second round of hair samples from MacDonald, and the defense had resisted on legal grounds. The issue went to Judge Butler, who ruled against the defense, and the CID eventually took the hair samples by force after pulling over MacDonald's vehicle. (Bernie Segal and Dennis Eisman ended up—theatrically—in neck braces.)

5. Thomas McNamara, memorandum re: the Jeffrey MacDonald case, June 26, 1973.

Chapter 18. Media Freak

1. Testimony of Jeffrey MacDonald, grand jury transcript, August 12, 1974.

2. Errol Morris interview with Hammond Beale, 2012.

3. Testimony of Jeffrey MacDonald, grand jury transcript, January 21, 1975.

4. Testimony of Jeffrey MacDonald, grand jury transcript, August 13, 1974.

Chapter 19. A Conclusion Could Not Be Reached

1. Testimony of Richard J. Mahon, grand jury transcript, November 21, 1974.

Chapter 20. Mute Witness

1. This is not Locard's formulation, but Paul Kirk's, another innovator of modern forensic science. Kirk, *Crime Investigation,* 2nd edition, John Thornton, ed. (New York: Wiley & Sons, 1972, p. 2).

2. Testimony of Paul Stombaugh, grand jury transcript, January 15, 1975.

3. Testimony of Janice Glisson, grand jury transcript, January 15, 1975.

4. Testimony of Craig Chamberlain, grand jury transcript, August 2, 1979.

Chapter 21. I'm Not a CSI Guy

1. Testimony of Dr. Robert Sadoff, grand jury transcript, August 12, 1974.

2. This is a source of disagreement. Sadoff's view is supported by the testimony of several medical experts, including Dr. William Straub, one of the doctors who examined MacDonald during his hospitalization. From: Grand jury transcript, testimony of Dr. William Straub, November 13, 1974:

> WILLIAM STRAUB: I wouldn't pick the chest hardly at all. It's a bad place to get a stab wound because of the—the interior chest particular because the heart—I don't recall exactly how far laterally it was, but the heart is, you know, more on the left side than the right. And, so you are a little safer if you didn't want to hit your heart to stab yourself on the right side, but there is still a lung there and interiorly you could possibly hit your heart which is no serious problem, of course, but the chest, in general, if I was going to self-inflict a wound I wouldn't pick the chest.
>
> JUROR: But, if you did which part of the chest would you pick? I mean if you were thinking about hurting yourself—
>
> WILLIAM STRAUB: If I was going to pick the chest, which part of the chest? I'd be more inclined probably to stab myself in the back. Because the heart interior again, the right side of the liver's also here and—boy, it's not an A1 spot to pick to stab yourself. . . .

Chapter 22. A Comb and a Toothbrush

1. Jeffrey MacDonald, account for Bernard Segal, February 6, 1975.

2. *United States v. MacDonald,* 585 F. 2d 1211 (4th Cir., October 27, 1978).

Chapter 24. Things Do Not Lie

1. Opening statement of James Blackburn, trial transcript, July 19, 1979.

2. Opening statement of Wade Smith, trial transcript, July 19, 1979.

Chapter 25. Pigs On Ice

1. Testimony of Mildred Kassab, trial transcript, August 1, 1979.

2. Testimony of Alfred Kassab, Article 32 hearing transcript, August 13, 1970.

3. Testimony of Alfred and Mildred Kassab, grand jury transcript, September 4, 1974. The day after Mildred's testimony, Pamela Kalin Cochran—the MacDonald babysitter, now married—testified. Her story had changed. She now clearly remembered the MacDonalds having an ice pick she had repeatedly denied seeing. Segal asked her to explain this sudden change. Cochran said she had been terrified and intimidated by the CID. Then, at the grand jury, she remembered it.

> **PAMELA COCHRAN:** I was sitting alone waiting for them to take me upstairs or something, and I saw a chart, where Mr. MacDonald had stab wounds and just something flashed across my mind—getting the popsicles and reaching for the ice pick.

4. Testimony of Mildred Kassab, August 1, 1979.

5. Testimony of Helen Fell, August 2, 1979.

Chapter 26. Forty-eight Holes

1. Frank D. Whitney, opposition of the United States to motion for leave to file a successive habeas petition, December 21, 2005.

2. Karl Malden, who had starred in *On the Waterfront* and countless other movies, was a perfect casting choice for Freddy Kassab. He became the embodiment of probity and perseverance in this fictional universe. Malden's line in the script when told that it might take a long time to bring his son-in-law to justice: "I plan to live a long life. And I have the patience of Job."

3. *Fatal Vision* (television miniseries), November 18–19, 1984.

4. Discussed in testimony of Ken Mica, Article 32 transcript, July 8, 1970, and by Bernie Segal in an August 13, 1979 bench conference.

5. Testimony of Shirley Green, trial transcript, August 9, 1979.

6. Testimony of Paul Stombaugh, trial transcript, August 19, 1979.

7. Closing argument of Brian Murtagh, trial transcript, August 28, 1979.

Chapter 27. Target in Motion

1. Testimony of Paul Stombaugh, grand jury transcript, January 15, 1975.

2. Testimony of John Thornton, trial transcript, August 14, 1979.

3. It was the most dramatic moment in the entirety of the six-week trial, but all that remains of it are these three words:

Experiment is performed.

How can we be sure how it happened, without having been there in 1979?

4. Testimony of John Thornton, trial transcript, August 15, 1979.

5. Joe McGinniss, *Fatal Vision*, p. 516.

Chapter 28. California Evil

1. Government motions, trial transcript, August 10, 1979.

2. Two objections were, in fact, made.

3. Bench conference, trial transcript, August 13, 1979.

Chapter 29. Troublesome Psychopathy

1. Mack also recognized two MacDonalds: the confused, defensive 1970 MacDonald and the less anxious 1979 MacDonald:

> Dr. MacDonald had clearly changed in some respects from the person he was in 1970, although the basic features of his personality appeared to be essentially the same. At the time of the present examination, just as in 1970, there was no indication of an abnormal personality adjustment . . . At the time of his original examination in 1970, Dr. MacDonald was quite concerned about the fact that his feelings about the crime and his tendency to assert his innocence might make him appear overly defensive in a manner that might suggest his guilt . . . At the time of the present examination, Dr. MacDonald appeared far less defensive . . . Whereas previously, he was inclined to rigidly deny the possibility that he might have underlying emotional conflicts, at the time of the present examination he was willing to acknowledge that he was not a terribly insightful person, that he was not always aware of his inner feelings . . . He shows no signs of psychosis or

psychopathy at the present time. At times he becomes angry and oversensitive or, as he puts it, "paranoid" about the charges that have been brought against him over the years. There was no indication that such feelings have led him to lose contact with reality.

2. Bench conference, trial transcript, August 13, 1979.

3. In his *Casebook of a Crime Psychiatrist,* Brussel tells a story of Albert DeSalvo—one of the cases that made Brussel famous (along with George Meteskety, Manhattan's Mad Bomber). He described his first meeting with DeSalvo:

I flew to Boston with Dr. Hirsch L. Silverman. With rare exceptions, I use Hirsch's assistance whenever I examine alleged or known criminals prior to trial. Hirsch went in to see DeSalvo first. I had asked that the initial test he administered be the Rorschach (inkblot) . . . I always leave it to Hirsch to use as many other psychological examinations as he deems indicated and necessary to aid in the diagnostic interpretation.

In James Brussel, *Casebook of a Crime Psychiatrist* (New York: Bernard Geis Associates, 1968), 165–66.

4. MacDonald didn't get the "continuous, consistent psychotherapeutic intervention, coupled with psychiatric attention," but he has been incarcerated for almost thirty years without incident.

5. Jeffrey MacDonald, account of examination by Dr. Brussel, August 13, 1979.

6. Santosh Kumar, "Hirsch Lazaar Silverman's Post-Modern Quest for Moral Values," Bookstove.com (May 4, 2010).

Chapter 30. Round in Circles

1. Oddities. Does Murtagh know something we don't know? Ivory testified at the Article 32 hearing that Helena Stoeckley denied being there. That is, she had denied that to Ivory. Here, is Murtagh saying that she told both Ivory and him the opposite?

2. Conference on motions, trial transcript, July 31, 1979.

3. Bench conference, trial transcript, August 13, 1979.

4. Testimony of Dr. John Thornton, trial transcript, August 15, 1979.

5. *Voir dire* can refer to the examination of witnesses to assess their competency or fitness to give testimony.

6. Testimony of Helena Stoeckley, trial transcript, August 17, 1979.

7. The press had advertised the importance of the day's testimony. Among the headlines: "Woman Says She Was Present at MacDonald Murders" and "Mystery Woman Testifies." The publicity escaped the jury, who had been instructed to avoid all coverage of the trial.

8. This was a climactic moment at Jeffrey's trial. But there was always room for comedy in Judge Dupree's courtroom. For instance:

> **JAMES BLACKBURN:** You spoke of the term "pig," talked about pigs; and I assume you talked about that frequently or used that term frequently?
>
> **HELENA STOECKLEY:** [*Witness nods affirmatively.*]
>
> **JAMES BLACKBURN:** Whom did you refer to as pigs in 1970?
>
> [*Witness looks at the Court.*]
>
> **THE COURT:** Does that answer your question?
>
> **BERNARD SEGAL:** We OBJECT, Your Honor.
>
> **BRIAN MURTAGH:** We were surprised.
>
> **JAMES BLACKBURN:** Your Honor, that was a surprise answer.
>
> **HELENA STOECKLEY:** I did not mean that. That wasn't towards you.
>
> **THE COURT:** She is trying to retract it now, but it is recorded for all history.
>
> **JAMES BLACKBURN:** I think she should be given every opportunity to retract, if that is her answer.
>
> **HELENA STOECKLEY:** It is the law enforcement—
>
> **THE COURT:** [*Interposing*] All right, she is going to answer your question now. Go ahead.
>
> **HELENA STOECKLEY:** Any law enforcement agent.

Chapter 31. Ace in the Hole

1. Testimony of Jane Zillioux, trial transcript, August 17, 1979.

2. Testimony of Charles "Red" Underhill, trial transcript, August 17, 1979.

Chapter 32. Wanted

1. Testimony of James Gaddis, trial transcript, August 17, 1979.

2. Testimony of Robert Brisentine, trial transcript, August 17, 1979.

Chapter 33. In My Mind, It Seems That I Saw This Thing Happen

1. Testimony of Prince Beasley, trial transcript, August 17, 1979.

2. Testimony of William Posey, trial transcript, August 17, 1979.

3. From the *Federal Rules of Evidence*:

RULE 403. EXCLUSION OF RELEVANT EVIDENCE ON GROUNDS OF
PREJUDICE, CONFUSION, OR WASTE OF TIME.
Although relevant, evidence may be excluded if its probative value is substantially outweighed by the danger of unfair prejudice, confusion of the issues,
or misleading the jury, or by considerations of undue delay, waste of time, or
needless presentation of cumulative evidence.

Chapter 35. Unclearly Trustworthy

1. From the *Federal Rules of Evidence*:

RULE 804. HEARSAY EXCEPTIONS; DECLARANT UNAVAILABLE
(b) The Exceptions. The following are not excluded by rule against hearsay if the
declarant is unavailable as a witness ...
(3) Statement Against Interest. A statement which was at the time of its making
so far contrary to the declarant's pecuniary or proprietary interest, or so far
tended to subject the declarant to civil or criminal liability, or to render invalid
a claim by the declarant against another, that a reasonable person in this
position would not have made the statement unless the person believed it to
be true.

2. Bench conference, trial transcript, August 20, 1979.

3. This contradicts Dupree's opinion of Stoeckley's reliability just days before. On
the previous Friday, when Segal wanted to declare Stoeckley a hostile witness, telling the court, "her interest is adverse to that of the defendant," Dupree replied:
"I have detected nothing in the demeanor or answers to indicate any hostility
whatsoever to your questioning. She has answered the questions forthrightly and
intelligently." The very next time they are back in court Dupree rules Stoeckley's
statements "as unclearly trustworthy—or as clearly untrustworthy, let me say—as
any statements I have ever seen."

4. Testimony of Jane Zillioux (recalled), trial transcript, August 20, 1979.

5. Testimony of Wendy Rouder, trial transcript, August 20, 1979.

Chapter 36. The Four-Legged Table

1. From closing argument of James Blackburn, trial transcript, August 28, 1979: "I
can only tell you from the physical evidence in this case that things do not lie, but
I suggest that people can and do lie."

2. Closing argument of Bernard Segal, trial transcript, August 28, 1979.

3. Joe McGinniss, "Jeffrey MacDonald: Living a Nightmare," *Los Angeles Herald-Examiner,* June 14, 1979, A-3.

Chapter 37. The Slaughterhouse

1. Closing argument of Brian Murtagh, trial transcript, August 28, 1979.

2. Closing argument of James Blackburn, trial transcript, August 28, 1979.

3. Closing argument of Bernard Segal, trial transcript, August 28, 1979.

4. Major Moore was a defense witness who testified that his daughter, Rebecca, and Kimberley had been friends, and that he had spent time with the MacDonald family the weekend before the murders.

5. Closing argument of Wade Smith, trial transcript, August 28, 1979.

Chapter 38. The Use and Abuse of Physical Evidence

1. Dr. John Thornton, letter to FBI Director William H. Webster, May 7, 1982.

2. D. Lowell Jensen, letter to FBI Director William H. Webster, October 27, 1982.

3. Brian Murtagh, government's response to the motion for crime scene inspection, September 9, 1983.

4. CID report on medical supplies removed from Castle Drive, June 5, 1984, and CID report on evidence removed from 544 Castle Drive, June 6, 1984.

Chapter 39. A Rounded Picture

1. *United States v. MacDonald,* 456 U.S. 1 (1982).

2. Ibid. (Marshall, J., joined by Brennan and Blackmun, J. J., dissenting).

3. *United States v. MacDonald,* No. 79-5253 (4th Cir., August 16, 1982).

4. Ibid. (Murnaghan, concurring).

5. In March 1983, the University of Pennsylvania Law Review published an unsigned comment entitled "The Concurrence Requirement and *U.S. v. MacDonald:* How Things Should Not Work":

> We are left, finally, with MacDonald's conviction, which is disturbing in several respects. First and foremost, of course, is that a man is in prison for a crime that he has repeatedly denied having committed and that another has repeatedly admitted to having perpetrated with her associates. He might well be there because a rule of evidence was interpreted incorrectly and in a way that infringes the constitutional rights of criminal defendants.

6. Lewis Carroll, *Alice's Adventure in Wonderland and Through the Looking Glass* (New York: Penguin Classics, 2003), p. 172.

Chapter 40. Absolutely Batshit Crazy

1. After his involvement with the MacDonald case, Gunderson spiraled deeper and deeper into his theories: child slave labor for underground alien-controlled facilities, the Illuminati, and Satan, Satan, Satan.

2. Prince Beasley, statement—"My first encounter with Ted Gunderson," July 15, 1981, p. 2.

3. FBI SA Raymond Madden, affidavit concerning Helena Stoeckley, July 12, 1984.

4. Scott Mero, notes on polygraph examination of Helena Stoeckley, October 25–26, 1980.

Chapter 41. The Sound of Music

1. Prince Beasley, statement—"Second trip to Los Angeles," December 4, 1980.

2. Helena Stoeckley, interview with Dr. Rex Beaber, December 7, 1980.

3. Dr. Rex Beaber, declaration, undated.

4. Prince Beasley, statement, December 4, 1980.

Chapter 42. A Satanic Cult

1. I had seen the interview on YouTube, but I did not realize it was made for *60 Minutes* until I saw the clapper reading "DR MAC / 60 MINUTES / Pro. J. WERSHBA / 5-21-82." Alas, "J. WERSHBA"—the legendary CBS News producer Joe Wershba—had died months before.

2. Interview transcript, Helena Stoeckley, Ted Gunderson, Prince Beasley, and Joe Wershba, *60 Minutes,* May 21, 1982.

3. FBI report on James Earl Friar, August 20, 1979.

4. William Posey, CID statement, March 27, 1971.

5. Prince Beasley, statement on Helena Stoeckley, December 30, 1982.

6. Dr. Sandra Conradi, autopsy report on Helena Stoeckley, January 15, 1983.

7. Pat Reese, "MacDonald Loses Backer: Investigator Beasley Now Believes Doctor Killed His Family," *Fayetteville Observer,* July 7, 1991.

Chapter 43. E-323 and Q-89

1. Two kinds of pajama-top fibers were involved in this case. MacDonald's pajama top was woven with blue polyester-cotton fibers, and sewn with purple cotton thread.

2. Closing argument of James Blackburn, trial transcript, August 28, 1979.

3. On July 5, 1970, at the Article 32 hearing, Shaw—one of the original trio of CID investigators, Shaw, Grebner, and Ivory—had been asked by Michael Malley about the location of pajama-top fibers at the crime scene. He testified, "I personally found fibers and/or threads in the west entrance to the hallway on the floor, near the south wall, just a pile laying there." In other words, blue fibers had been found where MacDonald had said he had been knocked unconscious. But in 1979, when Ivory was questioned at trial, Segal asked about the area in Shaw's testimony: "[How about] the steps to the hallway? Did you find any fibers there?" Ivory out-and-out denied it.

4. Harvey Silverglate, arguing the motion for a new trial on June 26, 1991, explained to Judge Dupree the importance of the black wool fiber:

> HARVEY SILVERGLATE: What is so important about the black wool? Well, Your Honor, what's important about it is that it was found on the victim and on the club and it was not identified with anything else in the MacDonald house. Also, Stoeckley did testify, Your Honor allowed her to testify to the jury to this much, and that was that she always wore black or purple clothing . . .
>
> Maybe it came from woolen caps [as the prosecution had argued] the children got for Christmas. Maybe they did get woolen caps for Christmas but the government forgets one point . . . When [Colette] was murdered, why did she have the children's caps in her mouth? Was she eating them? It makes no sense. Clearly, the wool came from the person who assaulted her and not from the children's caps, assuming the children had woolen caps . . .
>
> . . . [What] does the government do? It comes up with a remarkable theory—a forensic theory—in its papers, called the Transfer Theory of Locard. L-o-c-a-r-d . . . This opened up my eyes. When I read that part of the government's brief I understood, I think, how this case came off track in a way that neither your honor, nor Mr. Segal, perceptive though he may have been, could not have imagined.
>
> Here's what happened. I think it's quite obvious. The Transfer Theory of Locard held in order to be forensically significant, a fiber had to be matched to some known. And so the government, early on, had this theory that MacDonald was the murderer and they went around trying to match fibers found at the crime scene . . . They found some of his pajama fibers in various places, including on the club, murder weapon, they made a big deal of that. "Oh, MacDonald's pajama fibers were on the club." Rather than assume he was clubbed with the club they assumed he was the one who wielded the club.

Chapter 44. It Wasn't a Doll

1. Janice Glisson, handwritten bench note, spring 1971.

2. B. M. Murtagh and M. P. Malone, *"Fatal Vision Revisited: The MacDonald Murder Case,"* Police Chief 60, no. 6 (June 1993): 15–23, NCJ 144394.

3. The meeting was memorialized in FBI witness statements for both Schizas and Phillips. This was the same California trip where they visited John Thornton, the forensic expert for the defense.

4. Judith Schizas, signed affidavit, April 15, 1997.

5. *United States v. MacDonald,* No. 97-7297 (4th Cir., September 8, 1998).

6. U.S. Fourth Circuit Court of Appeals decision re: saran fibers; decided September 8, 1998.

7. Laurie P. Cohen, "FBI Fiber Analysis Emerges as New Issue in Murder Case," *Wall Street Journal,* April 16, 1997.

8. "Jay C. Smith, a former Pennsylvania school principal freed from death row, dubbed Malone 'Agent Death' because, Smith says, Malone could find hair and fiber evidence where none existed." Quoted in "Good Cop, Bad Cop," *St. Petersburg* [FL] *Times,* March 4, 2001, p. 1A.

9. Ibid.

10. Supplemental Affidavit of Michael Malone, Senior Examiner of Hair, Fibers Unit, FBI. The affidavit was in response to the Reply Brief MacDonald's attorney's had filed in response to Malone's first affidavit of February 14, 1991: "I can state with certainty that no 22-inch synthetic blond wig hairs were found in Exhibit K, E-323, or in any other exhibit which I examined in this case (see my previous Affidavit)." Malone reiterates his earlier statements for five pages and then concludes that the petitioner has misinterpreted the transfer theory of Locard.

11. Laurie P. Cohen, "FBI Fiber Analysis Emerges as New Issue in Murder Case," *Wall Street Journal,* April 16, 1997.

Chapter 45. 1-821-3266

1. Mazerolle had a solid alibi: he was still serving time for a drug conviction following a bust Stoeckley had orchestrated. Bruce Fowler passed a polygraph.

2. Ray Shedlick, letter to Judge Harrison Winter, December 27, 1985.

Chapter 46. In Bright Red

1. Jeffrey Elliot and Ray Shedlick, video interview, July 1987.

2. Ann Cannady, statement to Ray Shedlick, March 29, 1983.

3. Juanita Sisneros, statement to Ray Shedlick, April 4, 1983.

4. The property was purchased by Western Publishing Company, at the time the nation's largest publisher of children's books, including the famous Golden Books. The Hope Mills Fire Department was allowed to burn down the preexisting structure for training.

5. Peter Kearns, statement re: Cathy Perry, April 5, 1972.

6. Jackie Don Wolverton, statement to John Dolan Myers, July 1979.

Chapter 47. The Almost Inescapable Conclusion

1. Noah Bryant Lane, declaration to Ray Shedlick, April 14, 1984.

2. Norma Lane, declaration to Ray Shedlick, April 14, 1984.

3. Pat Mitchell, declaration to Ray Shedlick, July 20, 1983.

4. Norma Lane, declaration, October 23, 1989.

5. Judge Franklin Dupree, ruling on motion for his recusal, October 1, 1984.

6. Shirley Hayes, "Proctor Says Movie Confirms His Memories of MacDonald Case," *Fuquay-Varina Independent,* November 28, 1984.

Chapter 48. Cops Who Came In from the Cold

1. Many additional details came out during the civil trial, and I have tried to integrate them into a chronology of the letters. Part of this correspondence is included in Janet Malcolm's account of the lawsuit between MacDonald and McGinniss, *The Journalist and the Murderer.*

2. Janet Malcolm, *The Journalist and the Murderer* (New York: Alfred A. Knopf, 1990), p. 3.

3. Ibid., p. 37.

4. David Hardison, who died in 2009, was the foreman of the MacDonald jury. A comment on Hardison's obituary that appeared in the *Fayetteville Observer* reads like the end of *King Lear*—everybody old and dying, Hardison clinging to the same theory of psychopathy.

> We spent several hours at his home, and I vaguely remember that there was an elderly relative bedridden in an adjoining room. Hardison was very candid with me, sharing his thoughts on the evidence that was presented at trial, and how the experience had affected him personally. I remember he spoke of how he would wake up at night, during the trial, hearing a child crying. It was the deaths of the two little MacDonald daughters that seemed to affect him most.

5. Jeffrey MacDonald, letter to Joe McGinniss, August 30, 1979.

6. Joe McGinniss, letter to Jeffrey MacDonald, September 11, 1979.

7. Joe McGinniss, letter to Jeffrey MacDonald, September 28, 1979.

8. Joe McGinniss, letter to Jeffrey MacDonald, December 18, 1979.

9. Joe McGinniss, letter to Jeffrey MacDonald, January 10, 1980.

Chapter 49. Just Be Jeff

1. Jeffrey MacDonald, letter to Joe McGinniss, January 15, 1980.

2. One psychiatrist, Michael Stone, whom I interviewed for my television series, *First Person,* took the extensive transcripts as *proof* of MacDonald's pathological narcissism. But wait one second. He was asked by McGinniss to give an extensive history of himself. What did Stone expect?

3. Transcript, Jeffrey MacDonald's tapes for Joe McGinniss, tape 3, side 1, pp. 41–42.

4. Transcript, Jeffrey MacDonald's tapes for Joe McGinniss, tape 4, side 2, pp. 97–98.

5. Transcript, Jeffrey MacDonald's tapes for Joe McGinniss, tape 7, side 1, pp. 165–66.

6. Transcript, Jeffrey MacDonald's tapes for Joe McGinniss, tape 11, side 1, pp. 274–75.

7. Transcript, Jeffrey MacDonald's tapes for Joe McGinniss, tape 13, side 2, p. 324.

8. Transcript, Jeffrey MacDonald's tapes for Joe McGinniss, tape 16, side 2, pp. 402–3.

9. Transcript, Jeffrey MacDonald's tapes for Joe McGinniss, tape 18, side 1, pp. 457–58.

10. Transcript, Jeffrey MacDonald's tapes for Joe McGinniss, tape 18, side 2, p. 464.

Chapter 50. I Can't Talk About What I Think

1. Joe McGinniss, letter to Freddy Kassab, February 15, 1980.

2. Jeffrey MacDonald, letter to Joe McGinniss, October 14, 1980.

3. Mickey Friedman, "The Lessons Learned in Alaska's Grip," *San Francisco Examiner & Chronicle,* Scene, p. 5.

4. *MacDonald v. McGinniss,* exhibit 70.

5. Jeffrey MacDonald, letter to Joe McGinniss, October 19, 1982.

6. Phyllis Grann, letter to Joe McGinniss, October 14, 1982, p. 1.

7. Joe McGinniss, *Fatal Vision,* p. 510.

8. Shakespeare, *Macbeth,* act 2, scene 1.

9. Jeffrey MacDonald, letter to Joe McGinniss, February 9, 1983.

10. Joe McGinniss, letter to Jeffrey MacDonald, February 16, 1983.

11. Jeffrey MacDonald, letter to Joe McGinniss, May 15, 1983.

Chapter 51. A Book Story

1. In the June 26, 1973, memorandum, Thomas McNamara, U.S. attorney, Eastern District of North Carolina, wrote, "Perhaps the overriding problem in presenting or prosecuting this case is the inability on the part of the Government to establish a solid motive on the part of Jeffrey MacDonald for having committed these murders."

2. Jeffrey MacDonald interview, transcript, *60 Minutes*, September 6, 1983.

3. At the end of *Fatal Vision*, McGinniss quotes from "the last written message" the Kassabs received from Colette. It was a card sent just before Christmas 1969. "The printed message said, 'May the Good Will and Peace of this Christmas Season be yours Throughout the coming year.' She had signed it, 'See you soon—Love, Jeff & Colette' and then had written at the bottom: 'P.S. Please get pants for Jeff in 36" instead of 34"—and he's gaining weight but doesn't like to feel like it." McGinniss provides his own acerbic rejoinder: "That, of course, was before . . . he had started taking Eskatrol." Has the issue of who committed the murder come down to pants that don't fit? What have we learned? That MacDonald was gaining weight? Okay. In MacDonald's notes to his attorney, he admits as much. But McGinniss writes about it as though he has proved his case. Aha. He was concerned about his weight, therefore he took diet pills, therefore he got strung out on them, therefore he lost control and killed his family. As McGinniss piles on circumstantial evidence, his argument remains, at its core, colossally stupid. (But then, there is no argument so stupid, so transparently manipulative, that it isn't effective.)

4. Helena Stoeckley interview, transcript, *60 Minutes,* May 21, 1982.

5. Joe Wershba, letter to Jeffrey MacDonald, November 17, 1982.

6. Bernard Segal, letter to Jeffrey MacDonald, September 19, 1983.

Chapter 52. Eskatrol

1. Joe McGinniss, *Fatal Vision* (New York: Signet, 1984), p. 604.

2. Jeffrey MacDonald, "Activities, February 16–17, 1970."

3. *Fatal Vision,* p. 607.

4. Ibid., p. 603.

5. Ibid., p. 610.

6. Robert Louis Stevenson, "The Strange Case of Dr. Jekyll and Mr. Hyde" (New York: Penguin Classics, 2003), p. 56.

7. Stevenson, p. 57.

8. McGinniss has created a new fable: Dr. Jekyll and the *two* Mr. Hydes. Mr. Hyde No. 1, the wrathful misogynist who loses his composure and strikes out viciously against his family, and Mr. Hyde No. 2, the cunning psychopath who covers his tracks through a cruel and calculated murder, the murder of Kristen, his two-year-old daughter.

Chapter 53. Essential Integrity

1. Contract between Joe McGinniss and Jeffrey R. MacDonald, August 3, 1979, p. 1.

2. Janet Malcolm, *The Journalist and the Murderer* (New York: Alfred A. Knopf, 1990), p. 7.

3. Testimony of Joe McGinniss, *MacDonald v. McGinniss* trial transcript, July 17, 1987, pp. 13–15.

4. McGinniss, in writing about MacDonald, also became smug, sarcastic, supercilious. One example among many in *Fatal Vision,* from page 518, in which McGinniss describes:

> Bernie Segal's forty-ninth birthday party—the highlight was the presentation to
> Segal of a set of darts and an enlargement of a recent photograph of Brian Mur-
> tagh. One by one each member of the defense team took a turn throwing darts
> at the picture. Jeffrey MacDonald scored a direct hit. He cheered for himself
> as his attorneys and their assistants clapped and laughed. In high spirits,
> he seemed oblivious to the possibility that, under the circumstances, it might
> not have been appropriate for him to be propelling a sharp pointed object toward
> even the photographic representation of a human being.

5. Testimony of Dan Wigutow, *MacDonald v. McGinniss* trial transcript, August 5, 1987, pp. 34–35.

6. Testimony of John Gay, *MacDonald v. McGinniss* trial transcript, August 5, 1987, p. 78.

7. *Fatal Vision,* television miniseries, 1984.

8. Testimony of John Gay, *MacDonald v. McGinniss* trial transcript, p. 72.

9. Closing argument of Daniel Kornstein, *MacDonald v. McGinniss* trial transcript, August 13, 1987, p. 78.

10. Joe McGinniss, *Heroes* (New York: Touchstone, 1976), pp. 152–55.

Chapter 54. Delightfully Blue

1. Janet Malcolm, *The Journalist and the Murderer* (New York: Alfred A. Knopf, 1990), p. 14.

2. Even McGinniss complained that this was not "a normal journalistic encounter":

> Malcolm's focus was my journalistic relationship with Jeffrey MacDonald over
> the four years before *Fatal Vision* was published. Charging that I had "deceived,"

"betrayed," and "devastated" this convicted murderer and that my letters to him during the process of research constituted a "written record of . . . bad faith," she attempted to employ this most atypical relationship between an author and his principal subject as a paradigm for the standard journalistic encounter—one which, somewhat idiosyncratically, she seems to view as the equivalent of "a love affair," doomed to end badly . . . It was not, as she wrote, a "grotesquely magnified version of the normal journalistic encounter," but something quite exceptional. I don't think she could have chosen a worse example if she'd tried—which she didn't.

3. Jeffrey MacDonald, letter to Janet Malcolm, January 24, 1988.
4. Janet Malcolm, letter to Jeffrey MacDonald, February 4, 1988.
5. Malcolm, *The Journalist and the Murderer,* pp. 126–27.
6. Ibid., pp. 143–44.
7. I had written, but never published, an essay about Malcolm's postmodernism. I have not seen any criticisms of her "God-in-a-flower" argument in *The Journalist and the Murderer,* but recently Joyce Carol Oates touched on similar themes in her review of Malcolm's recent book, *Iphigenia in Forest Hills,* "Reporter for the Defence," in *The Times Literary Supplement:*

> Journalism isn't objective, as it pretends, but is rather, in Malcolm's excoriating charge, an enterprise of (seemingly false, fraudulent) "reassurance" . . . In the gravity-free postmodernist world of Malcolm's imagination, "guilt" is just a label arbitrarily caught by someone who has had a "bad break" and whose "narrative" isn't as smoothly compelling as another's . . .

8. Following our conversation, Janet Malcolm sent me a letter. She explained what she meant by "the material doesn't speak for itself."

> No, of course, I don't believe that the question of whether MacDonald killed his wife and children has no answer in principle. What I was trying to say—and obviously didn't succeed—was that in this case the available evidence wasn't sufficient to establish the truth. ("The material doesn't 'speak for itself.'") Because of the work of the authors of *Fatal Justice,* it now seems clear that the prosecution did not prove its case and that MacDonald should get a new trial. But we still don't know what happened. That kind of evidence is still not

available. We remain in a state of doubt. (Which means he would be acquitted in a fair trial.)

A problem still remains for me. How can you know that "the available evidence wasn't sufficient to establish the truth" without looking at it? If we have no definitive answers, the task is to keep trying to find them—or, at least, to figure out why they're not forthcoming.

Chapter 55. Before the Law

1. Jimmy Britt, affidavit, November 3, 2005.
2. Julia Oliver, "Prosecutor denies threat," *Fayetteville Observer,* December 16, 2005.
3. There have been claims that Britt himself either lied or is unreliable. Some retired marshals have come forward and insisted that Britt did not bring Stoeckley to Raleigh. Memory is often unreliable, but I find it hard to believe that he would misremember the central claim of his affidavit, and I can't understand why he would lie about it. There is something else that leads me to believe Britt's claim. He provides a powerful and simple explanation of why Stoeckley changed her story on the stand in 1979. And also, by the way, there are photographs of Stoeckley and Britt walking into and out of court. He may not have escorted her on the ride up from South Carolina, but he was with her in Raleigh.
4. Testimony of Helena Stoeckley, trial transcript, August 17, 1979.

Chapter 56. I Know. I Know. I Know.

1. Hart Miles, request for hearing in *United States v. Jeffrey MacDonald,* September 20, 2011.
2. Leonard never did find the picture, or the poem.
3. Kay Reibold, statement to Ted Gunderson re: Helena Stoeckley, January 25, 1980.
4. Lynne Markstein, statement to John Myers and Ted Gunderson, January 23, 1980.
5. Jerry Leonard, statement to John Myers and Ted Gunderson, January 23, 1980.
6. The argument basically devolves to one simple question: could Stoeckley have been prosecuted in 1979? Depending on which lawyer you listen to, it was yes and no. Some argue there was a five-year statute of limitations in the federal system. Regardless of whether it's five years, ten years, doubtlessly, the North Carolina authorities could have prosecuted Stoeckley if they had wanted to. There was no statute of limitations on murder in the state stystem. Even though she was not subject to the death penalty, she could have been given life imprisonment.

Chapter 57. Crumbs

1. Testimony of Helena Stoeckley, trial transcript, August 17, 1979.

2. Joe McGinniss, *Fatal Vision*, p. 522:

> Helena Stoeckley had been given a bologna sandwich. She sat quietly, placidly, chewing her food and slowly turning the pages of the crime scene and autopsy photo albums, as if she were browsing through a movie magazine.

I didn't know if Wade Smith's memory of the bologna sandwich came from being with Stoeckley or from talking to McGinniss or from reading *Fatal Vision*.

3. It was a bench conference on Thursday, August 23, 1979, a few days before the end of the trial. MacDonald had testified for the first time that morning, and the court was back in session for the afternoon.

> MR. BLACKBURN: Your honor, may we see you for just a moment before we get started . . . ? BENCH CONFERENCE
>
> MR. BLACKBURN: Judge, we have just inquired I have just talked to Wade—we want to inquire on the situation with respect to Helena Stoeckley—whether or not she is still under subpoena here?
>
> THE COURT: I know nothing about it. I keep asking—I told them last night if they were going to use her, they had better do it first thing this morning or I was going to release her. They didn't use her, so I assume she is released, but I don't know.
>
> MR. BLACKBURN: Her lawyer, Jerry, is still around.
>
> THE COURT: I asked Mr. Segal—I said, "What is he still doing here?"
>
> MR. SMITH: I talked to Jerry Leonard at great length, Your Honor, this morning—talked to him for a long time, and this woman continues to say things that tie her to this case. I will be frank with Your Honor, we have no plans to use her at this moment, but we have got too much at stake. It is too important a case, and she has said too much for us to just, you know, out of hand say, "Oh, sure, go on. Go away. We will never see you again. Go back in hiding and let the years roll by." She is here. The defendant is on the stand, and we feel that we need to be able to talk with Jerry and have her available at least for this afternoon.

4. On September 7, 2007, the defense alerted Judge Fox that Jimmy Britt, "who had stood ready to testify in the pending *habeas* petition, is now suffering from serious heart problems and has spent an extended amount of time in the hospital."

5. Judge James C. Fox, order on motion for leave to file a successive §2255 motion, November 4, 2008.

Chapter 58. The Morning Newspaper

1. Testimony of Helena Stoeckley, trial transcript, August 17, 1979.

2. Closing argument of James Blackburn, trial transcript, August 28, 1979.

3. Richard Mahon, CID statement to Peter Kearns re: William Posey, March 27, 1971.

4. Murtagh, in his 2006 reply to a defense brief, argued that the hobbyhorse was *not* broken. That it was just something Stoeckley had made up. Just as he claimed Stoeckley made everything else up. Did he know something I didn't know? Stoeckley had testified on the stand in 1979 that the hobbyhorse was broken. She had told Posey in 1970 that the hobbyhorse was broken. (It was in a CID report.) Why hadn't the prosecution said anything until 2006 if they knew otherwise?

Chapter 59. The Five Percent

1. Mica claimed in an Amazon review of the hardcover edition of this book that he never spoke to Landreth, but only to Christopher Olgiati. I was never able to get access to the dailies from their film. Another example of the frustration of detective work done long after the fact.

2. *False Witness: Investigating the MacDonald Murders,* British Broadcasting Corporation, 1989.

3. Testimony of Ken Mica, Article 32 hearing transcript, vol. 12.

Chapter 61. Gene Stoeckley

1. Affidavit of Helena Stoeckley, March 21, 2007.

Chapter 62. Two Prisoners

1. Joe McGinniss, speech at ThrillerFest, July 13, 2011.

Chapter 63. Flame-out

1. James Blackburn, *Flame-out: From Prosecuting Jeffrey MacDonald to Serving Time to Serving Tables* (Leslie Books, 2000).

2. *Wilmington Morning Star,* Associated Press, November 30, 1993.

3. Blackburn Seminars, official Web site, http://www.blackburnseminars.com.

4. Blackburn, *Flame-out,* pp. 30–32.

5. Ibid., pp. 84–85.

Chapter 64. Specimen 91A

1. Nuclear DNA can uniquely identify an individual but is perishable. Mitochondrial DNA lasts longer—we can analyze the mtDNA of Neanderthals—but it is matrilineal, and as such not specific to any individual. That is, it can tell us whether a spot of blood came from any of the three victims in the MacDonald house, but it cannot tell us which victim or how it got there. Could it change things for the MacDonald case? Could it provide answers in a case that has stubbornly resisted resolution?

2. Memorandum in support of Jeffrey R. MacDonald's motion for an order authorizing the District Court for the Eastern District of North Carolina to consider a successive application for relief under 28 U.S.C. §2255, September 17, 1997.

3. Joseph Zeszotarski, correction of motion for appeal from February 19, 2009.

4. Department of Justice news release, "DNA results," March 10, 2006.

5. *United States v. Jeffrey MacDonald,* No. 08-8525, section IV, Supplemental Reply Brief of Appellant, August 2, 2010.

6. It goes all the way back to the very first tellings of the story, to the question of whether it was Kristen's blood on MacDonald's glasses. MacDonald claimed that he had set them down, and that they had skidded across the floor during the attack on him in the living room. He was questioned about it on April 6:

> **FRANZ GREBNER:** And your glasses, which you told originally were on the coffee table . . . you weren't wearing them, your glasses, when you went into the bedroom . . . they are lying with the outer edge of the lens down on the floor, yet on the face of the lens there's blood.
>
> **JEFFREY MACDONALD:** Maybe someone knocked them over.
>
> **FRANZ GREBNER:** But how did they get blood on them?
>
> **JEFFREY MACDONALD:** I assume from the person who knocked them over.

Later, the FBI suggested that the blood might have come from a number of patients MacDonald had treated on February 16, the day before the murders. My question: Why don't they test the speck of blood on the glasses? Mitochondrial DNA could determine whether the O-type blood came from Kristen MacDonald or from someone else.

Chapter 65. A Black Sky

1. *United States v. MacDonald,* no. 08-8525 (4th Cir., April 19, 2011).

2. "To Habe or Not to Habe: Curtailing the Writ of Habeas Corpus in *McCleskey v. Zant*" [comments], *New England Journal on Criminal and Civil Confinement,* vol. 19, issue 2 (Summer 1993), pp. 397–426, Hallisey, Martha, 19 *New Eng. J. on Crim. & Civ. Confinement* 397 (1993).

Postscript. "What would you say If I told you I was there?"

1. *United States of America v. Jeffrey R. MacDonald* (2011). http://wildernessoferror -data.s3.amazonaws.com/20110419%20-%20Fourth%20Circuit,%20opinion.pdf.

2. http://www.insideedition.com/headlines/5059-new-evidence-could-get-jeffrey -macdonald-a-new-trial. Among other things, McGinniss told *Inside Edition*: "MacDonald was first charged with these crimes forty-two years ago. Only in America could this still be going on."

3. The government collected samples containing Stoeckley and Mitchell's DNA but did not collect the DNA of any of the others that Stoeckley said might have been in the house.

4. Evidentiary hearing transcript, opening statement of Gordon Widenhouse, September 17, 2012, p. 18. http://wildernessoferror-data.s3.amazonaws.com/2012- 09-17%20-%20Evidentiary%20hearing%20for%20Jeffrey%20MacDonald%20 (Day%201).pdf.

5. In 1990, Smith prepared an affidavit about his previous involvement in the Mac-Donald case.

> Between December 1978 and December 1984 I served as North Carolina counsel to Dr. Jeffrey R. MacDonald. I represented Dr. MacDonald in (a) the 1979 trial which was held in the Federal District Court for the Eastern District of North Carolina before Judge Franklin T. Dupree, Jr., (b) the direct appeal to the Fourth Circuit Court of Appeals and the United States Supreme Court, and (c) Dr. MacDonald's 1984 court proceedings.

6. Evidentiary hearing transcript, testimony of Wade Smith, September 17, 2012, pp. 21–22.

7. See the testimony of Dr. George Podgorny at the 1979 trial and the testimony of Drs. Severt Jacobson, George Gammel, and William Straub at the Article 32 hearing.

8. Evidentiary hearing transcript, September 17, 2012, p. 37.

9. In the sworn statement from February, Britt says he picked Stoeckley up in Charleston. In an affidavit from the end of October 26, 2005, both locations are used. And in the final affidavit, from November 3, 2005, it was Greenville.

10. Evidentiary hearing transcript, September 17, 2012, p. 86.

11. Evidentiary hearing transcript, September 17, 2012, p. 114.

12. Evidentiary hearing transcript, September 17, 2012, pp. 153–54.

13. Evidentiary hearing transcript, testimony of Gene Stoeckley, September 18, 2012, p. 337. http://wildernessoferror-data.s3.amazonaws.com/2012-09-18%20-%20 Evidentiary%20hearing%20for%20Jeffrey%20MacDonald%20(Day%202).pdf.

14. Evidentiary hearing transcript, bench conference, September 18, 2012, pp. 444–45.

15. The prosecution offered some scraps of information—an FBI 302 report and a release signed by Vernon Kennedy, a marshal from South Carolina (now deceased), who supposedly transported Stoeckley from the Pickens County jail (about twenty miles west of Greenville) to the intersection of I-85 and I-77 in Charlotte, the parking lot of a Shoney's. Dennis Meehan, a retired marshal, and his wife testified that they picked Stoeckley up in Charlotte and then brought her to Raleigh but had no documentation to prove it. The paperwork? Lost or destroyed.

16. Evidentiary hearing transcript, bench conference, September 19, 2012, pp. 467–68.

17. Evidentiary hearing transcript, testimony of James Blackburn, September 19, 2012, pp. 640–41.

18. Evidentiary hearing transcript, testimony of Jack Crawley, September 20, 2012, p. 721.

19. Evidentiary hearing transcript, bench conference, September 20, 2012, pp. 844–45.

20. *Swidler & Berlin v. United States*, 524 U.S. 399 (1998), http://www.nytimes .com/1998/06/26/us/supreme-court-excerpts-opinions-ruling-extent-lawyer-client-privilege.html?pagewanted=all&src=pm.

21. Here's an abbreviated list. That he misquoted a *Physicians' Desk Reference* entry to bolster his claims about amphetamine use causing MacDonald to murder his family. That he repeatedly begged a reluctant MacDonald to supply details about his sexual life—which he then mischaracterized and used against him. That he made a big deal about MacDonald's seeming indifference to Stoeckley's presence in the courtroom in 1979 when he knew that MacDonald had been instructed not to react to Stoeckley by his attorneys. That he reprinted Dr. Brussel's examination report even though he had been outraged by Brussel's conduct during the trial, and after calling Brussel's writing "blither" in a letter to MacDonald. That he claimed MacDonald had refused to take a sodium amytal test even though he should have known that MacDonald had agreed to the test. And so on.

22. McGinniss escaped with a mistrial after a 5–1 vote *against him*, with one holdout juror. To listen to his account you would think the jurors sided with him: "After three days of deliberation, the jury expressed that they were hopelessly—not even deadlocked so much as confused—and were not going to be able to render a verdict." In Malcolm's account, however, there was no confusion—just one lone juror offended that the other jurors were not interested in her animal-rights literature. If anyone was confused, it was McGinniss.

23. Evidentiary hearing transcript, September 21, 2012, p. 1050.

24. Evidentiary hearing transcript, bench conference, September 24, 2012, p. 1095. http://wildernessoferror-data.s3.amazonaws.com/2012-09-24%20-%20Evidentiary%20hearing%20for%20Jeffrey%20MacDonald%20(Day%206).pdf.

25. Evidentiary hearing transcript, September 24, 2012, pp. 1098–99.

26. Evidentiary hearing transcript, testimony of Jerry Leonard, September 24, 2012, pp. 1108–89.

27. Evidentiary hearing transcript, September 24, 2012, p. 1114.

28. Affidavit of Jerry W. Leonard, September 20, 2012, pp. 3–4. http://wildernessoferror-data.s3.amazonaws.com/20120920%20-%20Jerry%20Leonard%20affidavit.pdf.

29. Statement of Jerry Leonard, made to John Dolan Myers, January 23, 1980. http://wildernessoferror-data.s3.amazonaws.com/19800123%20-%20Gunderson%20report%20-%20Jerry%20Leonard,%20statement%20to%20J%20D%20Myers.jpg.

30. Trial transcript, bench conference, August 23, 1979, p. 6647. http://wildernessoferror-data.s3.amazonaws.com/19790823%20-%201979%20Trial%20-%20Testimony%20of%20Jeffrey%20MacDonald%20day%201.pdf.

31. Trial transcript, bench conference, August 24, 1979.

32. Trial transcript, bench conference, August 24, 1979.

33. James Blackburn, *Flame-out: From Prosecuting Jeffrey MacDonald to Serving Time to Serving Tables* (Leslie Books: North Carolina, 2000), p. 103.

34. *Flame-out*, pp. 103–4.

35. Evidentiary hearing transcript, September 24, 2012, p. 1228.

36. Evidentiary hearing transcript, closing argument by Brian Murtagh, September 25, 2012, p. 1378. http://wildernessoferror-data.s3.amazonaws.com/2012-09-25%20-%20Evidentiary%20hearing%20for%20Jeffrey%20MacDonald%20(Day%207).pdf.

37. Evidentiary hearing transcript, September 25, 2012, p. 1365.

Index

Note: Page numbers in *italics* refer to illustrations.

Trial, The (Kafka), 35
Tufts, Henry, 89, 119, 225
20/20, 433–34

Underhill, Charles "Red," xi, 204, 209,
    214, 215, 217, 231, 236, 244–45,
    276, 411
    author's interview with, 218–20
U.S. Criminal Investigation Laboratory
    (USACIL), 474
"Use and Abuse of History, The"
    (Nietzsche), 261
U.S. Marshals Service, 501

"U.S. Sets Diet Drug Recall in Drive on
    Amphetamines" (New York Times),
    373

Vignettes of the Intellect (Silverman), 198

Wallace, Mike, 13, 363, 365–66, 367, 368
Webster, William H., 263–64, 272
Wershba, Joe, 292–94, 367–69
West, Edwin, 497–98
Widenhouse, Gordon, xiii, 492, 493,
    497–98, 501, 503–4
Wigutow, Dan, 359, 383

Williams, Cathy Perry, xi, 318, 329–31, 335
Williams, Keith, 502
witchcraft, satanism, 20, 204, 273, 288,
    290, 297, 411, 455
Woerheide, Victor, xiii, 123, 125–29, 144,
    145–46, 174–75, 371
    in grand jury hearing, 125–29, 131–33,
    136–40, 143–47
Wolverton, Jackie Don, 330
Wood, Robert, 27

Zillioux, Jane. *See* Graham-Bailey, Jane
    McCampbell Zillioux

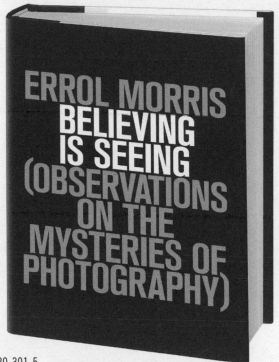